BLOOD ON THE SNOW

Also by Robert Service

The Bolshevik Party in Revolution: A Study in Organisational Change

Lenin: A Political Life
Volume One: The Strengths of Contradiction
Volume Two: Worlds in Collision
Volume Three: The Iron Ring

The Russian Revolution, 1900–1927

A History of Twentieth-Century Russia

Lenin: A Biography

Russia: Experiment with a People

Stalin: A Biography

Comrades: A History of World Communism

Trotsky: A Biography

Spies and Commissars: Bolshevik Russia and the West

The End of the Cold War: 1985–1991

Russia and its Islamic World:
From the Mongol Conquest to the Syrian Military Intervention

The Last of the Tsars: Nicholas II and the Russian Revolution

Kremlin Winter: Russia and the Second Coming of Vladimir Putin

ROBERT SERVICE

BLOOD ON THE SNOW

THE RUSSIAN REVOLUTION 1914–1924

PICADOR

First published 2023 by Picador
an imprint of Pan Macmillan
The Smithson, 6 Briset Street, London EC1M 5NR
EU representative: Macmillan Publishers Ireland Ltd, 1st Floor,
The Liffey Trust Centre, 117–126 Sheriff Street Upper,
Dublin 1, D01 YC43
Associated companies throughout the world
www.panmacmillan.com

ISBN 978-1-5290-6582-4

1 3 5 7 9 8 6 4 2

A CIP catalogue record for this book is available from the British Library.

Map artwork by ML Design
The List of Illustrations on pp. xxiii–xxiv constitutes an extension of this copyright page.

Typeset by Palimpsest Book Production Ltd, Falkirk, Stirlingshire
Printed and bound by CPI Group (UK) Ltd, Croydon, CR0 4YY

**To Oscar, Carla, Lara, Dylan,
Joely, Keira, Phoebe, Kai and Amber**

Contents

Acknowledgements

My thanks for advice on reading material and angles to be examined go to Katya Andreyev, Michael Bernstam, Vladimir Buldakov, Andrew Caldwell, Norman Davies, Simon Dixon, Sasha Dugdale, Simon Ertz, Roy Giles, Rudolf Muhs, Martyn Rady, Richard Ramage, Donald Rayfield, Christopher Read, Oliver Ready, David Shearer, Douglas Smith, Amir Weiner and Jerry White. I am also indebted to two other friends no longer with us who discussed the Russian Revolution with me over many years. Peter Frank, my doctoral supervisor, started his research activity on the Bolshevik Central Committee before switching to Soviet politics; Israel Getzler, the biographer of Yuli Martov and Nikolai Sukhanov, sustained his engagement with revolutionary history to the end of his life. I fondly recognize how much they enriched my understanding.

Certain chapters were scrutinized by Mark Cornwall, Simon Dixon, Martyn Rady and Hugo Service. Their recommendations, generously drawn from their areas of expertise, were excellent. So too were those of Vladimir Buldakov, who advised on key questions about the revolutionary period. Ian Thatcher and Daniel Orlovsky kindly agreed to look at the entire draft and their suggestions and corrections led to a lot of important improvements. Ian and Daniel are experts on the revolutionary period and I appreciate the time they expended in commenting on the draft and answering my follow-up queries. Our exchanges have been a cheerful and instructive experience for me.

My first book was about the Bolsheviks in the years of revolution, and the chapters that follow have given an opportunity to look at the documentation that is now more freely available. Back in the mid-1970s, when I was working on the newspaper holdings in the Academy of Sciences Library in Leningrad, access to party archives was forbidden. Since the late 1980s, especially after the disintegration of the USSR in 1991, a vast mound of archives and documentary publications has been opened to excavation. Not all those sources are easily accessible, and I plan to expose them to the light.

Many roots of the recent crises in Russia, Ukraine and elsewhere in the former Soviet Union were already in vigorous growth in the turbulent years between 1914 and 1924. I have held back from commenting on each and every point of continuity because the aim is to let the history of the Great War, the February and October Revolutions and the immediate post-revolutionary period breathe its own air. The events of our time, however, do not always permit this. The centenary of the Russian Revolution in 2017 was commemorated in muffled tones in Moscow because the Kremlin rulers shrank from evoking the memory of an epoch of political and social convulsion. They sought to minimize the attention paid to a period when people rose against authority and joined in a struggle for freedom. In 2022, as we shall see, the same rulers propagated a tendentious analysis of the 1920 decision on the Ukraine–Russia frontier as one of the pretexts for their war against Ukraine – a decision that has received too little discussion by commentators in Russia or abroad. One thing, at least, is clear: official Russian history under Vladimir Putin is no longer a sleeping dog but is one that snarls and bites.

The idea of going back to the revolutionary period came up in discussions with my literary agent David Godwin and Picador editor Georgina Morley. Their skill and support have made a vital contribution to the result, as indeed they have now done for a quarter of a century. I should also like to recognize the editorial help of Mike Jones in pruning the branches of the original draft.

In the first two years of the Covid-19 pandemic I benefited from the Hoover Institution Library and Archive's provision of electronic library and archival access. Simon Ertz and Sarah Patton sent me digital copies of crucial material. The files of newspapers and archives that I have been accumulating over several decades have also proved their usefulness, both those from the Hoover Institution at Stanford University and those from RGASPI and GARF in Moscow. The Hoover Archives are one of the West's pre-eminent storehouses of Russian historical documentation. My cordial thanks go to Eric Wakin, Linda Bernard and Lora Soroka for their help throughout the years when I was exploring the themes of the book. My research at the Hoover Institution, Stanford University has again been unstintingly supported by the Sarah Scaife Foundation, for which I record my warmest gratitude.

I am offering an interpretation without abundant reference to other writers except on matters where I disagree with or have particularly profited from their writings. My emphasis has fallen upon reading the original sources in archives and documentary publications. The goal was to tap those sources as directly as possible and provide a flowing narrative and analysis rooted in the 'thinginess' of the past.

A brief word on historiography may be helpful. My starting point as a researcher was the belief that nobody could make proper sense of the Russian Revolution if it was examined only through the impacts of Nicholas II, Alexander Kerensky, Vladimir Lenin and Lev Trotsky. Such a belief became known as revisionism, in contrast with the ascendant wisdom of the time. But the revisionists themselves quickly found much to disagree about, especially as to whether Lenin or even Stalin deserve some kind of political rehabilitation. Some of them avoided questions about the essential horrors of state communism. A later generation of writers has asked different questions, notably one of the continuity between tsarism and Leninism. Although this enlarged our understanding, the following chapters hold firmly to the opinion that there was a profound break in the chain of Russian history in October 1917. The years 1914 to 1924 were the object of huge discord at the time and in subsequent decades. They landmarked the twentieth century. They remain of importance in the twenty-first.

Finally I give notice of certain basic technicalities in the book. The Russian state calendar is retained that was in use at any particular time, the Julian one until 31 January 1918 and thereafter the Gregorian one. This may disconcert those who are unaccustomed to dates of international importance being rendered in this fashion, but the prime objective is to avoid confusion with Russian dates. Proper names are given in an abbreviated form of transliteration (except in the endnotes where a fuller form is employed). The exceptions are individuals such as Kerensky and Trotsky, for whom the familiar English form is used. Most place names are offered in the contemporary Russian Imperial form despite the offence that this may give to present-day sensitivities: Tiflis, Odessa and Kiev instead of Tbilisi, Odesa and Kyiv. To avoid confusion with the Western front in northern France, I have called the Eastern front what the Russians named the Western or, often as not, the North-Western, Western and South-Western fronts. I have also used Great Britain as a shorthand for Great Britain and Ireland and have not made mention of the United Kingdom, which was rarely employed in the years under consideration.

My wife Adele read all the draft chapters more than once. Our discussions have helped me to clarify the line of analysis and remove many mistakes and infelicities. The book comes back to her with all my thanks and love.

London
September 2022

Introduction

In 1913 Nicholas II celebrated the Romanov dynasty's tercentenary with no expense spared. Solemn services of praise and thanks were held. Banquets and military parades took place at which 'God Save the Tsar' was sung. The emperor and his wife Alexandra visited religious shrines deep in the provinces where they drew sustenance from the welcoming local peasantry. Industry was buoyant and the agricultural export trade flourished. There was peace on the empire's frontiers and Nicholas believed Russia could defend itself against any hostile foreign power. His diary showed no sign of concern about what might lie ahead for him and his family. His complacency was ill-founded, and within a mere four years he was to fall from the throne and the empire in its old form would be no more.

Why did the Russian Imperial monarchy collapse in the February 1917 Revolution? What explains the Provisional Government's failure to manage the volatile situation it inherited? And how did the communists storm to power in October that year and go on to enforce their dominance after years of civil war? These questions have vigorously exercised the minds of later generations because the October 1917 Revolution in Petrograd transformed the course of world history. The communist leadership imposed a form of despotism that came to be known as totalitarianism. The Soviet state spread its tentacles and antennae into every zone of public and private existence. Communism assumed governmental control over the economy. The secret police stamped out overt political opposition. The mass media became an official monopoly. The Communist International was created in Moscow to spread communism throughout the world. The USSR became an economic and military power that made the decisive contribution to the defeat of the Third Reich. The expansion of communism's influence continued. By the 1950s a third of the world's earth surface was ruled by communist administrations. The Soviet Union, armed with nuclear weaponry, waged the Cold War against the United States and its NATO allies.

This book examines the seething cauldron of developments between 1914 and 1924. The outbreak of the Great War gave rise to profound disruptions in Imperial government, administration, politics, economy and society. Nicholas II felt compelled to abdicate in February 1917. A few months later, the Bolshevik party, which at the very beginning of the year had only a few thousand members and little political following, overturned the Provisional Government of Alexander Kerensky in the Russian capital Petrograd. It was an outcome that stunned contemporaries. Questions about the events and situations that produced it continue to perplex us today, questions which prodded me into writing the chapters that follow. There are many fine works on Russia in war and revolution and civil war and there are almost as many angles of approach as there are works. But widely missing from them is one of the main things I explore, which is a sense of how 'ordinary' people coped – or failed to cope – with the shattering dislocation of Russian and global affairs that occurred from the start of the Great War through to the mid-1920s.

Misery and disappointment, of course, were far from being the whole story. The February Revolution was greeted with near universal jubilation, and the October Revolution initially brought joy to its supporters. Fresh social initiatives proliferated. Liberation was proclaimed. But the wheels of change were soon rolling mostly in the opposite direction. Dictatorship, maladministration, terror, ethnic cleansing, social persecution and famine darkened the life of society.

The traditional focus for writers has, understandably, been on the leading figures. But the result is that the experiences of the vast mass of the people – the hopes, achievements, disillusionments and sufferings – frequently fall out of the picture. Outstanding memoirs have come down to us which can fill many, but not all, of the gaps. Luckily there exist some exceptional, as yet neglected diaries such as those of NCO Alexei Shtukaturov, peasant farmer Alexander Zamaraev and accounts administrator Nikita Okunev that offer a vibrant record of their times which no memoirist has matched. They help to correct the widely held assumption that 'the masses' lacked the ability to think for themselves and simply accepted the explanation of events flung down on them by rulers or revolutionaries. Diarists of a higher social status such as Lev Tikhomirov, Shloyme Rappaport-Ansky, Rachel Khin-Goldovskaya and Alexander Blok, moreover, are an antidote to the notion that all those with money shared the self-satisfied mindset that fatally captivated the upper classes. Untouched by material hardship early in the Great War, they were hit by a deluge of troubles after 1917.

Diaries cannot automatically be believed, but they do convincingly show that the subjects of Emperor Nicholas II and the citizens of Soviet Russia were not just passive victims of history. Most of them were victims in one way or another, and millions met with a gruesome fate. Many others, both before and after 1917, were victimizers – and their commands, rifles and ideological intolerance put society through torment. In offering a multifaceted picture, I make use of all kinds of primary source to establish how people coped with and survived the troubles that besieged them.

The Russian Empire and the USSR, its successor state, covered a sixth of the globe's earth surface and a multiplicity of national and social groups. Diversity of faith, ethnicity, opinion and ambition was remarkable under both tsars and commissars. The churn of events in war and revolution sorely tested everyone's capacity to work out what was happening. Leaders themselves were often muddled in their analysis. This was just as true of Nicholas II, Alexander Kerensky or Vladimir Lenin and Lev Trotsky as it was for those who were standing on lower rungs of power or on none at all. Each in his own way made misjudgements of the circumstances that faced him. In any case, the measure of effectiveness of leadership depended on the resilience of the institutions and personnel through which the leaders governed. Emperor Nicholas had at best a patchy record over several decades. Kerensky did as well as anyone could have fairly expected. Lenin and Trotsky oversaw the construction of a state order that proved stronger than their domestic and foreign enemies had thought possible. Kerensky was the only one among them with a reluctance to use violence against those whom they ruled. Even those who favoured campaigns of suppression found themselves compelled to make accommodations to popular demands. Ruling Russia, despite appearances, has never been easy.

The book sidesteps the pitfalls of an exclusively political or military narrative and includes the whole social, economic, cultural and religious landscape in its compass. All swathes of society are considered in both the Russian Empire and the Soviet state that succeeded it. The landscape is deliberately handled as a unity and the entanglements of politics and daily life are a primary concern. The focal points alternate between society as a whole and selected individuals. An Orthodox believer could also be a trader as well as a volunteer for war service – and consequently he or she had a multiplicity of needs and wishes, and the chapters highlight the complexities of personal choice over many years. Space is given to the remarkable variety of circumstances amongst the nations, regions and religions.

Constant warfare, moreover, was the bloody backdrop to the years under consideration. The Great War and the Civil War had an impact upon everyone's daily existence even when the military fronts were hundreds of miles away. Political strife after 1917 was settled by lethal weapons. The country was also shaken by the shocks of regional and social uprisings from the Muslim rebels in central Asia in 1916 through to the Green insurgents of the Russian and Ukrainian countryside in 1920–22. Uprisings alone, however, were not the whole story. There were millions of people who stayed out of all the fighting – indeed they were the majority of the population. They tried to get through their days in safety and with enough food in their stomachs. Politics were a minority interest. This is true of most countries in most eras. In Russia it remained the case despite the resolute efforts in official propaganda under successive administrations. The longing for peace was widespread and deeply felt.

The big events stand as milestones along this historical pathway. Each of them involved turbulence and surprise: the Great War, the fall of the Romanov monarchy in the February Revolution, the Provisional Government's accession to power, the Kornilov military putsch, the communist seizure of power in the October Revolution, the initial Soviet decrees, the Brest-Litovsk peace, the plethora of civil and inter-state wars, the Polish–Soviet War, the introduction of the New Economic Policy and the consolidation of the communist one-party state.

There were sharp bends and rough potholes on the road, and I start the account by probing the Great War's importance in shaping what happened next. Quite apart from the military operations, the conditions in the vast war zone behind the front lines call for investigation. The disruption of civilian affairs by the empire's own armed forces must have massively contributed by the end of 1916 to a combustible political environment. The following year gave rise to two revolutions, in February and October according to the Julian calendar. The pivotal months of the Provisional Government's rule warrant greater notice than they have recently received and I therefore devote the second third of the book to the period when Emperor Nicholas II became citizen Nicholas Romanov and it seemed highly improbable that the Bolsheviks could emerge as realistic contenders for supreme power. As regards the early Soviet years, I emphasize the narrowness of the Reds' military victory over their enemies. The later chapters show how near the Bolsheviks came to disaster even after the Civil War. Usually the communist reforms of 1921 are depicted as Lenin's masterstroke of timely compromise. I show, I hope convincingly, that Lenin had to be dragged flailing and groaning into making the changes and that his party was infuriated by them both at that moment and later.

The book also traces why the governments in power in the decade from mid-1914 – the Imperial Council of Ministers, the Provisional Government and Sovnarkom (and the Party Politburo and Central Committee) – acted as they did even when their decisions threatened their own effectiveness or survival. What were the constraints and opportunities as they saw them? What ideas motivated the ministers and commissars? To answer these questions, I read as many of the extant official records as possible. As far as I know, it is the first time anyone has done this, and the deliberations in ministries and people's commissariats have led me down many unreconnoitred routes.

Emphasis is given, too, to the connections between high politics and the pressures that emanated from institutions at lower levels as well as from large social groups. But it is one thing to assert this and another to explain the chain of interaction. The protests by industrial workers against both Nicholas II and the 1917 Provisional Government were of decisive importance. But what has tended to fall out of the picture was the ease with which the communists suppressed the labour movement as early as 1918, and I account for how the communist leadership turned upon the very social class in whose name it took power. The peasantry put up a sterner resistance. Peasants played no direct role in bringing down the Romanov monarchy and conducted no insurrection against the Provisional Government. But they influenced events by obstructing official wartime policy on agricultural commerce and by carrying out illegal land seizures in 1917. They subsequently also withheld cooperation from the Soviet government. The questions of land ownership and peasant commercial rights were the most acute internal ones for administrations from Nicholas II to the Soviets. Peasants had the capacity to undermine everything that successive authorities sought to impose – at least until the full might of the Red Army was deployed in 1921–22. The peasantry's impact merits reassessment.

To make sense of all this, a light has to be shone on the degree of administrative, political, economic and cultural integration in the old

Russian Empire and the young Soviet state. Although the state ruled harshly when it was able to assemble the necessary armed strength against its enemies in the decade after 1914, it always depended on at least a minimum of rural consent. I investigate the paradox of Russia being in many ways under-policed while also being over-governed, in order to gauge the effectiveness of communists in founding an administrative core in town and countryside that did as it was told.

Another aim is to investigate the unlikely triumph by communists over so many formidable political and military enemies. They invented a new kind of state, one which was terrifying in its oppressiveness and extravagant in its claims of benevolence. The USSR at its birth was unique. The customary story of early Soviet statehood, as told by historians across the range of political opinion from right to left in the early decades after the Second World War, was that the Bolsheviks made their revolution in accordance with their long-held plans and practices. I shall probe the many other important factors, including both improvised reactions and sheer luck as well as the swirling geopolitical situation, which affected how everything turned out. The desire is to lay bare how much the communists advanced in a premeditated formation and how much they worked out the route as they moved along. It was a complex process, and a possibility to be tested is that even if the communists were often stumbling in the direction of the one-party dictatorship, they – especially the communist leadership – were always inspired by a set of attitudes that made them likely to choose that destination rather than the other available ones.

All this requires an appraisal of how far the party's policies were set by the central communist leadership or were conditioned by the pressure of opinion among communist veterans at lower levels of the political hierarchy. Lenin, Trotsky, Kamenev, Zinoviev and Stalin were not alone in setting the agenda of Bolshevism. Whilst they had a towering influence, it must be recognized that a broad consensus about many policies tied the Bolshevik party together in thought and practice.

After the Great War, the world was never the same again. Russia and its empire was shattered and transformed. Continuity existed, but change was the cardinal feature at the political level. Obscure revolutionary wordmongers like Lenin and Trotsky suddenly emerged as global political figures. They proved themselves able to manage chaos as well as their counterparts in the capitalist countries. In Europe and North America the communists gained a substantial following among a minority of socialist organizations. Although European fascism was not exclusively a reaction to the October Revolution, communism was certainly a weighty factor in provoking the furious emergence of the political extreme right. This brings everything back to my prime purpose, which is to tell how Russia plunged into an elemental crisis of state and society in 1914–16, succumbed to a tumult of freedom in 1917 before being overpowered by the kind of political and social order that no one had ever predicted or imagined possible. Despotic administrations had been formed in all shapes and sizes in past centuries and millennia but nothing quite like the USSR had ever existed. It was unprecedented in organizational structure and ideological ambition and introduced a formidable new piece to the chessboard of geopolitics.

Above all, this is a book of exploration. In writing it I have modified or replaced many ideas about Russia's fate in years when the shedding of blood of innocent civilians was normalized. Many communists – probably nearly all of them to some degree – were surprised by the scale of oppression that acquired permanence in their own Soviet communist order, but by the mid-1920s they had grown used to living and working within its walls. Their complacency was ill-judged. Within a few years, hardly more than a decade, most of them would pay with their lives for failing to prevent the consolidation of a totalitarian despotism. There are few episodes in modern world history that so usefully repay attention.

List of Illustrations

List of Maps

THE RUSSIAN EMPIRE, JANUARY 1914

ARCTI
GREAT BRITAIN AND IRELAND
Norwegian Sea
North Sea
NORWAY
Kristiania
NETHERLANDS
DENMARK
SWEDEN
Barents Sea
Copenhagen
Stockholm
FINLAND
Murmansk
Kara Sea
GERMAN EMPIRE
Berlin
Baltic Sea
Helsinki
Lake Lagoda
Tallin-Reval
Riga
Petrograd
Archangel
AUSTRIA-HUNGARY
Warsaw
Vilna (Vilnius)
Lake Onega
Brest-Litovsk
Minsk
Ob
Mogilëv
Smolensk
Vologda
Moscow
Ivanovo Voznesensk
RUSSIAN
Kiev
Tula
Vyatka
ROMANIA
Nizhni Novgorod
Volga
Bucharest
Dneiper
Danube
Odessa
Kharkov
Kazan
Perm
Tambov
Yekaterinoslav
Yekaterinburg
Tobolsk
Don
Irtysh
Istanbul
Sevastopol
Saratov
Samara
Ufa
Yalta
Rostov-on-Don
Tsaritsyn
Black Sea
Angora
OTTOMAN EMPIRE
Tbilisi
Erevan
Caspian Sea
Aral Sea
Syr Darya
Lake Balkash
Baku
Amu Darya
Tigris
Euphrates
Baghdad
Alma-Ata
Tashkent
Tehran
ARABIA
PERSIA
AFGHANISTAN

1000 miles
1600 kilometres
C E A N
Bering Sea
East Siberian Sea
Laptev Sea
Lena
E M P I R E
Sea of Okhotsk
Amur
Lena
Yenisei
Amur
rasnoyarsk
Lake Baikal
Chita
Harbin
Irkutsk
Verkhne-Udinsk
Vladivostok
Sea of Japan
JAPAN
MONGOLIA
KOREA
Peking
Yellow River
Yellow Sea
CHINA
Shanghai
East China Sea

RUSSIA IN THE GREAT WAR, 1914–18
International frontier
1914 Imperial War Zone
December 1917 demarcation line
Treaty of Brest-Litovsk frontier agreed by Sovnarkom, March 1918
500 kilometres
300 miles
NORWAY
Barents Sea
Murmansk
White Sea
Haparanda
Tornio
Archangel
SWEDEN
Dvina
FINLAND
Helsinki
Petrograd
Vologda
Stockholm
Tallinn (Reval)
Yaroslavl
Volga
Moscow
Riga
Mogilëv
Baltic Sea
Dvinsk
GERMANY
Don
Vistula
Brest-Litovsk
Warsaw
Oder
Kharkov
Kiev
Dnieper
Lvov
UKRAINE
Rostov-on-Don
Vienna
Dniester
Danube
Budapest
Odessa
AUSTRIA-HUNGARY
Black Sea

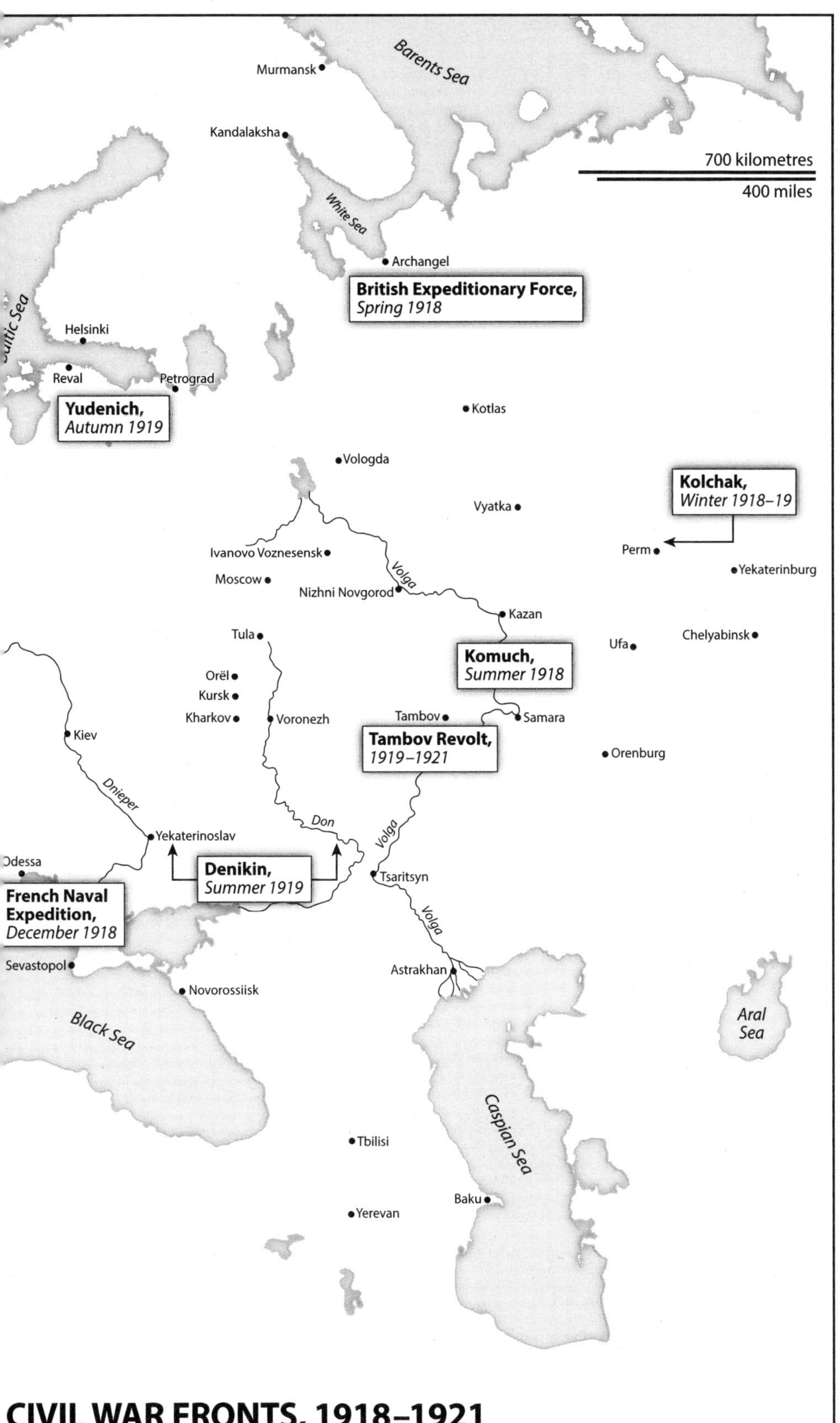

CIVIL WAR FRONTS, 1918–1921

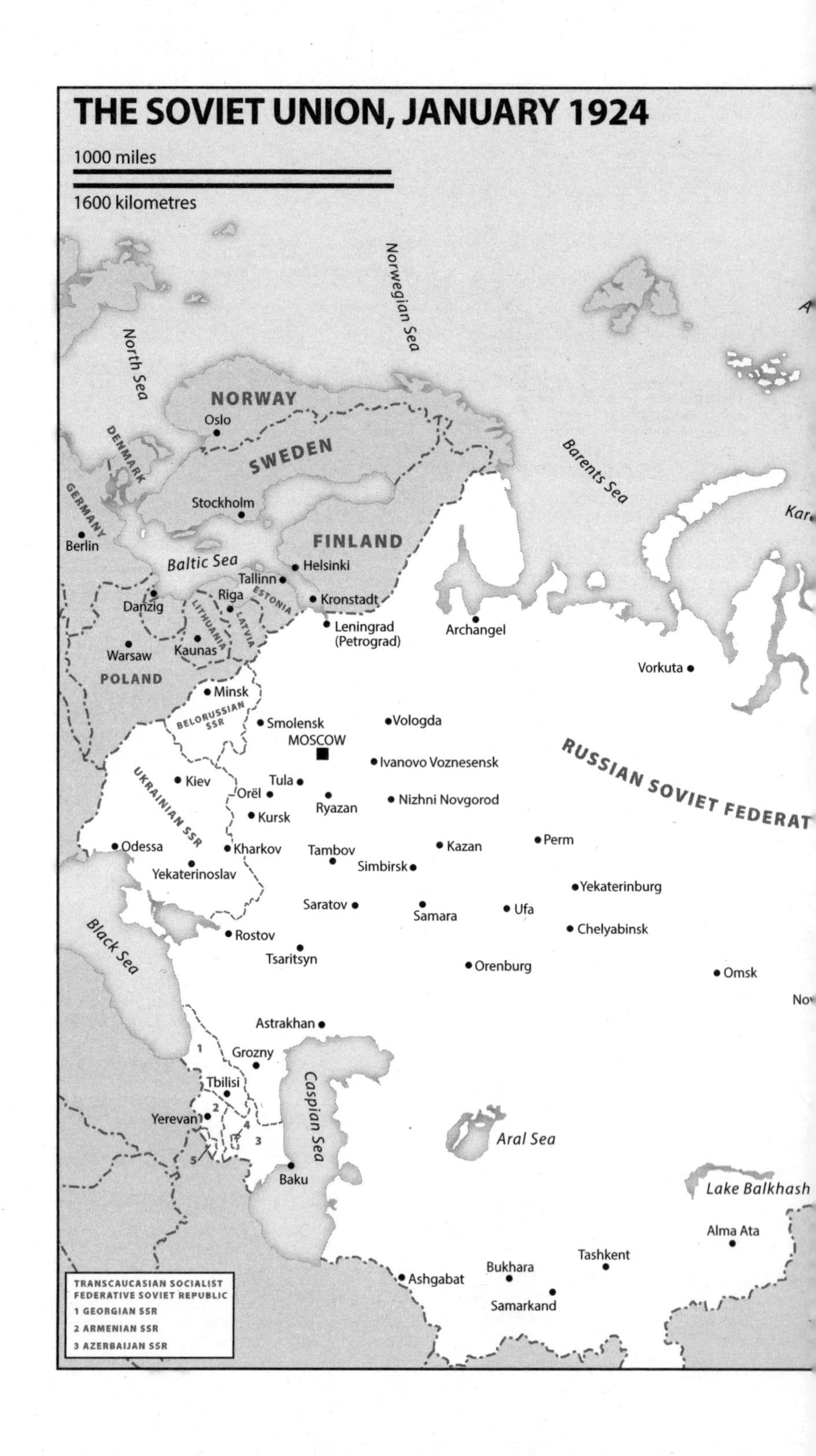
THE SOVIET UNION, JANUARY 1924
1000 miles
1600 kilometres
Norwegian Sea
North Sea
NORWAY
Oslo
DENMARK
SWEDEN
GERMANY
Stockholm
Berlin
FINLAND
Baltic Sea
Helsinki
Tallinn
ESTONIA
Riga
Kronstadt
Danzig
LITHUANIA
LATVIA
Leningrad
(Petrograd)
Archangel
Barents Sea
Warsaw
Kaunas
POLAND
Vorkuta
Minsk
BELORUSSIAN SSR
Smolensk
Vologda
MOSCOW
Ivanovo Voznesensk
RUSSIAN SOVIET FEDERAT
Kiev
Tula
Orël
Ryazan
Nizhni Novgorod
UKRAINIAN SSR
Kursk
Odessa
Kharkov
Tambov
Kazan
Perm
Simbirsk
Yekaterinoslav
Yekaterinburg
Saratov
Samara
Ufa
Black Sea
Chelyabinsk
Rostov
Tsaritsyn
Orenburg
Omsk
Astrakhan
Grozny
Tbilisi
Caspian Sea
Yerevan
Aral Sea
Baku
Lake Balkhash
Alma Ata
Tashkent
Bukhara
Ashgabat
Samarkand
TRANSCAUCASIAN SOCIALIST FEDERATIVE SOVIET REPUBLIC
1 GEORGIAN SSR
2 ARMENIAN SSR
3 AZERBAIJAN SSR

East Siberian Sea
Bering Sea
Laptev Sea
Sea of Okhotsk
Yakutsk
IALIST REPUBLIC (RSFSR)
Krasnoyarsk
Lake Baikal
Irkutsk
Vladivostok
Sea of Japan
MONGOLIAN PEOPLE'S REPUBLIC
CHINA
East China Sea

1. NO RETURN TICKET: THE RUSSIAN DECLARATION OF WAR

If ever a Russian ruler had to make an existential choice for his domains, it was Nicholas II, emperor of all Russia, in the hot summer of 1914. European diplomacy had staggered into crisis after the assassination in June of Austria's Archduke Franz Ferdinand, heir to the throne of the Habsburgs, in Sarajevo. The young Bosnian Serb Gavrilo Princip who had fired the fatal shots was quickly arrested together with his mainly Serb associates. Austria–Hungary blamed the Serbian authorities for having connived in the killing. There was discussion in St Petersburg about what to do if Serbia was attacked. To Vienna it appeared that the Serbian authorities had yet again tried to subvert the loyalties of Emperor Franz Joseph's South Slav subjects.

The murder in the Balkans tripped the electrical circuit of diplomacy in Europe. Europe has been described as a house of darkness whose owners sleepwalked to disaster. They had had years to consider the dangers of a pan-continental conflict. Russia had often been provoked, only for Nicholas to pull back at the last moment. Other rulers shared his dread of all-out warfare. The problem was that their fears were only intermittently experienced, and after so many diplomatic confrontations they assumed that any crisis could eventually be resolved. Thus the Austrians, Germans and Russians were doing things that were bound to be seen as provocative by their rivals. Rather than sleepwalkers they were like tired gamblers whose capacity for steady judgement had been eroded. Some of them trusted that if war could not be avoided, it could be confined to the Balkans. All thought that if it spilled over into a wider conflict among the great powers, the period of combat would be short. No one in power imagined the likelihood of drawn-out military confrontation. While the roulette wheels spun in Vienna, Berlin and St Petersburg those holding the chips had few worries about the chances of losing them.

Diplomats were used to dealing with limited regional conflicts. Suddenly they faced the possibility of a much bigger war than any that had happened since Napoleon's armies rampaged across the continent. The Austrians were acting recklessly but knew that behind them stood Imperial Germany. Berlin, discovering that Serbia was unlikely to yield to Vienna's terms, was concerned that the Russians would be sucked into the imbroglio. In German ruling circles there was already nervousness about the rise of Russian military and economic power. Some of Kaiser Wilhelm II's advisers pressed him to fight Russia before such power might become irresistible. Wilhelm was influenced by such thoughts, and German diplomacy encouraged the Austrian authorities to take the fateful step they had already decided upon: the invasion of Serbia. Germany's military leaders re-examined their contingency plans for a future war in Europe. Their idea had long been to crush France by a lightning campaign across neutral Belgium. The latest Balkans crisis increased the tensions among Europe's great powers. The French leadership played a delicate game, stiffening the Russian will to take a firm stand against Habsburg aggression while assuring the British that they did not want war. Great Britain, whose treaties with France and Russia entailed provisions for mutual defence, was yet to announce what it would do if the Russians chose to attack Austria–Hungary.

France's President Raymond Poincaré started a long-arranged state visit to St Petersburg on 7 July as the international crisis sharpened. Days of military parades, dinners and boat trips followed. Poincaré encouraged Nicholas to stand firm on the Serbian question.[1] On Poincaré's last day on Russian soil, the Austrians sent an ultimatum to Serbia demanding the liquidation of terrorist groups and their own participation in the criminal inquiry. If the Serbians flouted its terms, there would be war. Nicholas received a copy of the ultimatum on 12 July and immediately understood that its terms were 'unacceptable for an independent state'.[2]

Neither Nicholas nor his diplomats as yet knew about the hardening of German resolve against compromise. Nicholas was on holiday with his wife Alexandra and their four children in Peterhof on the Gulf of Finland. They were staying at the summer residence, Alexandria – or the Farm as they called it. Some twenty-five miles west of St Petersburg, it afforded them an annual respite from the daily public hubbub. The Imperial family took tea together in the afternoons and Nicholas played tennis when the sun was out. In the evenings he was fond of a game of dice or dominoes. He and Alexandra lived in the shadow of their son and heir Alexei's haemophilia. Born in 1904, Alexei was frequently severely ill. Alexandra was gnawed by guilt, knowing that he had inherited the gene from her. That the disease was incurable was a state secret, in the hope that there would be no question of Alexei's physical fitness to succeed to the throne. While they hoped and prayed for a treatment to alleviate the condition, husband and wife made the best of things. They had a lasting physical passion for each other and theirs was a happy, devoted family.[3]

But the Russian emperor could not ignore the Balkans crisis and it was his duty to decide how Russia should react. If Austria-Hungary refused to withdraw its ultimatum, was he merely to issue a rebuke and express sympathy for Serbia's plight or was he to announce a state of war between the two largest empires in Europe? Before ordering his forces into war, he had to consider the likelihood – almost the certainty – that Germany would join the conflict on the Habsburg side. And it was far from clear that Russia could count on having Great Britain or even France as allies, although the whole of Europe would almost certainly be pulled into the fighting. Who would emerge as the victors and at what terrible price would victory be achieved? Peace, though, was almost as thorny an option as war. If he avoided military action without a guarantee of Serbian independence, how would he cope with the inevitable criticism from Russian parliamentarians, the conservative and liberal press and a wide stratum of public opinion? And would the other great powers continue to treat Russia as one of their number when the next serious dispute arose in Europe or Asia?

Like his cousins Wilhelm II and George V, Nicholas was no great thinker and had made negligible efforts to escape the intellectual limits of his upbringing. Although he diligently read the reports of ministers, he lacked curiosity and was both deeply conservative and complacent. He made political concessions only under intense pressure.

A proud but inadequate dynast, Nicholas was conscious of his descent from emperors who had expanded the Russian Empire in the previous two centuries. He felt the need to prove himself a worthy successor. His father Alexander III had endlessly celebrated Russia's defeat of the all-conquering Napoleon in 1812. Nicholas had been taught to see martial success as the keystone of the dynasty's claim to legitimacy. As heir to the throne Nicholas had undergone training in a guards regiment and he always felt able to relax in the officers' mess, taking every chance he had to wear uniform. As recently as June 1914 he had gone down to the Black Sea, where he inspected 'the wonderful forces of the Odessa military district'.[4] He always liked to keep abreast of the naval vessels and artillery pieces being produced in Russian factories. Personal, dynastic and imperial honour were entwined in his calculations about foreign policy in a world that was dangerously in flux.

He knew Russia could not compete with the other great powers unless it matched them in industrial and cultural modernity. His ministers had his permission, within limits, to pursue changes in education and agrarian affairs. But his instincts tugged him in a different direction. He felt that Russia had lost some of its soul when Peter the Great forced it onto a path of Westernization. He often wore a costume similar to that worn by his seventeenth-century ancestor Tsar Alexei as a way of distinguishing himself from Peter's orientation, and he frequently visited provincial shrines held in reverence by Russian peasants.

Russia's humiliation after he ordered his armed forces into war against Japan in 1904 was a personal shame. The reckless underestimation of Japanese industrial progress had led to a crushing defeat. On 9 January 1905 a peaceful procession of the capital's workers and other residents petitioning for political and civil reforms was fired upon by troops outside the Winter Palace. Hundreds were killed or wounded and their blood stained the snow in front of the building. Nicholas had not ordered the action – he was not even in the capital at the time – but public opinion blamed him for the massacre. All the cities of the empire were enveloped by tumult and industrial workers elected their own soviets (or councils) to struggle for their interests. The Petersburg Soviet went so far as to challenge the entire basis of monarchical power before its leaders were arrested. The Moscow Soviet attempted an armed uprising and was bloodily suppressed. Disturbances spread to the villages as peasants seized the land and other property of estate holders. The gentry proved powerless to defend its possessions. Nicholas kept his throne despite mutinies in the Imperial armed forces, because he retained sufficient loyalty in key army regiments to mount a successful campaign against the rebels, and the revolutionary tide began to ebb.

Even so, the rebellions constrained him, a proud autocrat, to sanction the unprecedented election of a parliament – or State Duma – which could block the introduction of laws that earned its disapproval. Civil rights were announced. Trade unions were legalized, albeit with the provision that they should operate on a local basis. Political parties received permission to campaign in the open. Pre-publication censorship was abolished. A semi-constitutional order was in the making and optimists believed that modernity was coming to the Russian Empire.

Nicholas nevertheless resented the reformed political order that he had conceded. He had sworn an oath when succeeding his father to rule as an autocrat. He distrusted the Duma, which met in 1906 and had a troublesome radical majority, and he closed it after ten weeks. His suspicion of liberal parliamentarians peaked when the Constitutional-Democratic Party – known as the Kadets – called on his subjects to withhold their taxes to the government and refuse to deliver conscripts to the armed forces. The crisis passed but when the second Duma proved just as unmanageable he ordered a redrafting of the rules on suffrage so as to increase the number of seats available to conservative propertied strata. The electoral changes were masterminded by his prime minister, Pëtr Stolypin, who as minister of internal affairs had conducted a bloody retaliation against peasants who had risen against their landlords. Stolypin espoused dynamic conservatism. He tried to win support from the Octobrist Party, a liberal-conservative party that accepted the recent measures as a basis for collaboration with the Imperial government. The reactionary elements at court were fearful of such a partnership, but initially Nicholas was willing to let Stolypin try the experiment.

But Nicholas had inherited his father's visceral hostility to the empire's Jews, believing that if Russia was ever to reach a pinnacle of global success, it had to rid itself of such 'alien' influences. He believed in the authenticity of the *Protocols of the Elders of Zion*, a vile anti-Semitic forgery alleging that Jewish religious and business leaders were plotting to shatter civilization. He saw the Jews as primarily responsible for the revolutionary disruption in 1905–6. Nicholas even accepted a membership card from the Union of the Russian People, whose doctrines encouraged the anti-Jewish pogroms that took place before the war.[5]

Although Stolypin could not moderate his sovereign's anti-Semitic attitudes, he had approval for an innovative agrarian policy which encouraged peasants to leave their villages to set up independent home-stead farms – he believed communal collectivism was one of the causes of the near revolution in 1905–6. The peasantry, however, was hostile – and frequently violent – to those who opted for independence from the collective. Stolypin modified the reform to make it difficult for a commune to refuse applications for separation, but this did nothing to dissipate the widespread hostility. Another source of frustration for Stolypin were reports that some who applied to separate sold or rented out the land that they acquired. Stolypin's reform faltered from its very inception, and he argued that it would not only need decades for it to succeed, but that Russia required a lengthy period of peace. Ex-Minister of Internal Affairs Pëtr Durnovo put it more starkly in a memorandum he sent to Nicholas in early 1914, warning him of the fragility of international relations in Europe and the danger of going to war against Germany. If Russia suffered defeat, he argued, a socialist revolution was the likely result.[6]

But avoiding military conflict had become difficult after recent diplomatic crises. Germany and Austria–Hungary were the primary cause for Russian concern. The German authorities backed schemes to build a railway from the Turkish seaboard across the Ottoman Empire to Baghdad. The Straits of the Dardanelles was a sore spot for St Petersburg's naval planners as well as for the landowners and merchants whose grain exports depended on access to the Mediterranean. When Italy attacked Ottoman-ruled Libya in 1911, the Ottomans closed the exit from the Black Sea to Russian vessels in a vain attempt to persuade Russia to lean on the Italians to desist.[7] As a result, Nicholas and his ministers believed that there was a crucial need to seize Constantinople and the Dardanelles whenever a suitable opportunity arose. But this was an impossible objective unless there was a great European war.[8] Russia was aligned with France and Great Britain, neither of which looked fondly on St Petersburg's ambitions in the Middle East, which in the mid-nineteenth century had led to the Crimean War. Since then, though, the Russians' ambitions in the region had only grown.

Whereas Berlin befriended the Ottomans in Asia, Vienna exploited the decline of Ottoman power in Europe and in 1908 annexed Bosnia-Herzegovina, which led to increased tensions between the Habsburg Empire and neighbouring Serbia. Russia took the Serbians' side, not only to support fellow Orthodox Slavs but also to prevent the expansion of Habsburg territory and influence. The entire Balkans was a zone of incessant conflict and not one but two wars broke out in 1912–13. The first saw the Ottomans expelled from their last European possessions, while in the second the successor states – Bulgaria, Greece and Romania – fought over the spoils. This complicated foreign policy in St Petersburg, but one basic goal remained: the Habsburgs should not be allowed to benefit from the turmoil.

Nicholas retained paramount powers on questions of war or peace. He regarded his Council of Ministers as a collection of technicians conducting his business. The Council met in the Marinski Palace on the south side of St Isaac's Square in St Petersburg, which was also where the State Council held its sessions. Both advised the sovereign, but he was free to accept or reject the advice. Since 1906 Nicholas had been subject to a Basic Law stipulating that no law could come into effect without the Duma's approval – Stolypin's agrarian measures had to be introduced by Imperial decree when he failed to win a Duma majority for them. Conversely the State Council could block the passage of legislation passed by the Duma, and the emperor retained the right of ultimate veto and simply resented having to allow any of the compromises that might have made the parliamentary system workable. His relationship with his prime minister deteriorated, and by the time Stolypin was assassinated in 1911, he had already lost Nicholas's favour. Nicholas chose Finance Minister Vladimir Kokovtsov to succeed him, but by January 1914 he too had fallen from favour. The choice of the elderly Ivan Goremykin as the new premier was a surprise at a time when politics at home and abroad required energetic leadership. Nicholas, however, put his trust in Goremykin's 'kindly' personality.[9] It was a fatuous criterion for the appointment and yet another sign that Nicholas was losing the last residue of common sense.[10]

Nicholas had never been a warmonger but he felt he had made too many concessions in international relations in recent years. Vienna and Berlin were constant irritants to St Petersburg. Although Nicholas did not want a war, he now leant towards ordering military action unless Austria–Hungary stepped back from Serbia. He discussed the situation with his ministers, but it was no more than a brief consultative process. He took no counsel from the Duma leadership. Neither he nor the Foreign Affairs Ministry chose to engage at length in exploratory telegrams with potential foreign allies. Nicholas was coming to his own decision, and his judgement was that Russia could not afford to give way. Some among his advisers foresaw the huge danger of going to war, including Foreign Affairs Minister Sergei Sazonov, whose instinct was to make one final great effort to preserve European peace. Others at court felt the same, while the Imperial family's holy man, Grigori Rasputin, wrote similarly to Nicholas, predicting disaster for the dynasty and the Russian people.

But on 13 July Nicholas ordered the high command to start its pre-mobilization measures – the so-called 'period preparatory to war'.[11] Two days later Austria–Hungary declared war on Serbia. Talks continued fitfully through ambassadors and by international telegraph but Nicholas could see no alternative to ordering the mobilization of the military districts nearest to Habsburg territories – Odessa, Kiev, Kazan and Moscow. Vienna's resolve to bring the Serbians to heel was undimmed. Support was vouched from Berlin, where Wilhelm II and other German leaders were determined to prevent a Habsburg defeat and a westward expansion of Russian power. The Austrians, Germans and Russians were willing to risk the danger of war across Europe but still expected that if military conflict broke out, it would be containable in the Balkans. Diplomacy was moving more slowly than events and the rush into war was headlong.

On the morning of 16 July 1914 Nicholas received Premier Ivan Goremykin. He also spoke by phone with Foreign Affairs Minister Sergei Sazonov, War Minister Vladimir Sukhomlinov and Chief of the General Staff Nikolai Yanushkevich. The atmosphere was acrid. Sazonov felt that Nicholas talked 'with the voice of a man not obviously used to speaking on the telephone'. Nicholas still hoped to avoid war if he could. He exchanged telegrams with his cousin Wilhelm II in the hope that the personal interaction of ruler might surmount the difficulties that their ministers and diplomats reported. All to no effect. The Russian emperor, who was not given to over-statement, recorded the day as having been 'unusually troubling'.[12]

Also on 16 July 1914 Nicholas signed an ordinance designating a war zone – or 'theatre of military activities' – across hundreds of miles in the western territories of his empire. A line was drawn from St Petersburg south to Smolensk and down along the river Dnieper to Odessa. The General Staff for years had assumed that the empire's likeliest enemies in the next war would be Austria–Hungary and Germany. The plan was laid for Russia to fight an offensive campaign, carrying the campaign into their territory. The zone was to be the base from which the Russian forces would advance. Kiev, Riga, Tallinn, Vilna and Warsaw were among the great cities within the zone where martial law would prevail. The ordinance provided for the high command to exercise supreme authority, subject only to the sovereign's veto, over civilian and military affairs. Ministers and provincial governors were to obey the generals. Throughout the zone, the army leadership would set the requirements for economic, social and judicial life. Precedence on the railway network would be given to transporting troops, horses, armaments and food to the front. The General Staff was placed at the apex of state power.[13]

On 17 July Nicholas gave the command for general mobilization. Yanushkevich, Sukhomlinov and Sazonov agreed that Russia had no alternative option.[14] The plans for troops to be moved west were implemented. The impact in Berlin was immediate. Although Nicholas had not yet declared war, Russian armed forces would obviously have the potential to invade Habsburg territories. Germany reacted by announcing support for its ally and declaring war on Russia.

The Russian war plan included the need to prepare for the possibility of conflict with an Austro-German alliance. The priority on the northern sector would be to use Russia's Polish possessions as a platform from which to drive westward through East Prussia with the aim of taking Berlin. Russia's generals and diplomats felt edgy about the empire's chances, concerned about going into war without foreign assistance. Their alliances were of uncertain reliability. The Franco-Russian *entente*, signed by governments in 1894, gave no absolute surety that the French would join the Russians if Nicholas decided to enter conflict with Germany but at least their armed forces had been collaborating. The Anglo-Russian convention of 1907 had regard to Persia, Afghanistan and Tibet. Although it lessened the old tensions between St Petersburg and London and there had been growing cooperation on Balkan questions, no agreement was signed that bound the British into a military alliance in the event of war in Europe.

On 23 July 1914 Finance Minister Pëtr Bark, an ex-banker and another of Stolypin's protégés, went to Peterhof to deliver a report in person. There he came upon Mikhail Rodzyanko, the State Duma chairman, who was already waiting to have talks with the emperor. Rodzyanko expressed disquiet about Nicholas's decision to recall the State Duma from its summer recess. Bark said an active parliament was essential if Russia was to maximize its political unity in time of war. Rodzyanko, unconvinced, exclaimed: 'We'll only act upon you as an obstruction' – a prescient observation as within a few months the tensions between government and Duma would become acute. Bark and Rodzyanko were at any rate at one in wanting to unite in support of military operations. When each of them spoke to Nicholas, they found him buoyed by the news that Great Britain had announced its decision to join the war on the side of France and Russia; the emperor was now able to look calmly on the prospect of the European war.[15]

Nicholas chaired the Council of Ministers at Peterhof on 24 July 1914. He caused a surprise by announcing that he would make himself supreme commander-in-chief and stay at general headquarters near to the front line. He was always happier with generals than with politicians and deeply regretted not having gone to the Far East in 1904 during the war with Japan. He believed that a Russian emperor should be seen to share the tribulations of his armed forces. Goremykin was so appalled that he took the liberty of making an objection. Nicholas asked him to think about what he was saying. Goremykin apologized for the breach of etiquette but insisted that it would be imprudent for the emperor, in the first stage of the war, to assume direct responsibility for any setbacks that might occur. Instead, Goremykin advised, Nicholas should delay taking command until the Russian regiments marched into Berlin.[16] Other ministers stressed that Nicholas's departure would disrupt the business of government. If he stayed in the capital, they argued, he could maintain instant communication with the high command by means of the telegraph. For once, and not without rancour, he gave way while affirming that he would still make frequent visits to the front.[17]

He appointed his elder cousin Grand Duke Nikolai Nikolaevich as supreme commander-in-chief, which was welcomed by his ministers. Nikolai Nikolaevich, or Nikolasha as he was nicknamed inside the family, had spent his life in the army. At six feet six tall, he cut an imposing figure and looked the part. Although he was often harsh in his treatment of officers and men, he retained their affection. But he was a stranger to daily hard work, which he expected his subordinates to do for him. He disliked walking even the shortest distance if a car was available. Nobody could persuade him to give up taking siestas after his midday meal.[18] He was no great strategic thinker or planner either and was temperamental and impressionable – a distinct cause for concern in someone who was to direct the empire's fighting forces against the formidable German army.[19] But few of Russia's leading politicians knew much about his professional ability. They focused on the prime feature that recommended him as supreme commander-in-chief, namely that he was not Nicholas.

Bark presented his financial plans next day to the State Duma in the Tauride Palace. This stiff and ungregarious minister had never been welcomed so warmly in the vast sloped hall with its terraced seating arranged in semi-circular fashion for deputies of left, right and centre. Acceptance of Bark's arguments for heavier taxation was near universal.[20]

The mood was even more enthusiastic in the Winter Palace on 26 July when Nicholas addressed a joint session of State Duma and

State Council. He spoke of 'the enormous surge of patriotic feelings of love and devotion to the throne which has spread like a hurricane across our whole land'.[21] His audience included many who detested the monarchy and thought him among the worst of Russian emperors. But his appeal to defend Mother Russia was greeted with general acclaim. Even Premier Goremykin received a keen reception. Goremykin was no orator and most of the Duma deputies hated his arch-conservative policies, but the case that he made for war earned applause. Duma Chairman Rodzyanko was cheered for his passionate call for unity in time of mortal peril for the Russian Empire. Foreign Affairs Minister Sazonov won noisy approval when laying out the reasons why Nicholas had had no choice but to pick up the gauntlet tossed at him by Wilhelm II in Berlin. Russia's government and parliament, after years of mutual rancour, were speaking and hurrahing in unison.[22]

Only a small number of Duma deputies expressed its displeasure at the turn of events. This was the caucus of socialist deputies belonging to three political groups: the Trudoviks, the Mensheviks and the Bolsheviks. The Trudoviks were a broad grouping of political militants, including the Socialist-Revolutionaries, who focused upon the peasantry – or sometimes more generally upon the 'toiling masses' – as the best instrument to bring socialism to Russia. The Mensheviks and Bolsheviks were Marxists and the two main factions of the Russian Social-Democratic Workers Party. While seeing the urban working class as the primary instrument of fundamental change, they disagreed on strategy. Mensheviks hoped for a democratic revolutionary administration whereas Bolshevik doctrine was founded on the need for a socialist dictatorship. They were opposing factions of the same Russian Social-Democratic Labour Party, and they could barely speak to each other in peacetime. Now though, Trudovik, Menshevik and Bolshevik deputies found it possible to liaise at the Duma over abstaining from the vote on war credits.[23]

For a while it seemed that court, parliament and government were united. Nicholas set a personal wartime example by foreswearing strong drink. Moreover, the state liquor stores were closed down on 22 August 1914.[24] Extremes of drunkenness were a centuries-old scourge in Russia. Whilst their average consumption of spirits was much lower than the French or Belgian norm, many Russian drinkers, when they did sit down with a glass, supped themselves into a stupor.[25] Appeals for patriotic unity proliferated. Churches rang bells to raise enthusiasm. Empress Alexandra and their daughters trained as nurses to work in hospitals. The name of the capital was changed from St Petersburg to the more Slavic-sounding Petrograd. Official Russia rallied to the war effort.

2. RUSSIA GOES TO WAR: CONSCRIPTION, RIOTS AND DEPLOYMENT

Alexander Zamaraev, a peasant elder in a land commune near the small town of Totma in Vologda province in the Russian far north, made a note in his diary about the growing crisis in the Balkans: 'In June the Austrian heir apparent Ferdinand and his wife were killed in Sarajevo.' He paid no mind to the event again until the end of the month, and even then he gave equal space to his distress about the death of his neighbour Olga Chechulinskaya. He saw no reason to think the latest crisis in international relations would start a European war.[1]

By 18 July he was reading in the press that events had taken a cataclymic turn:

> This Friday morning the news hit everyone like a clap of thunder about the mobilization of the complete complement of forces, starting with the year 1897, which means all seventeen-year-olds without exception apart from sailors. War is expected with treacherous Austria. The Devil take that scrappy empire! In the morning, at the peak of haymaking, they took all the soldiers away from the reaping: Serov, Krutov and Makarov. The three of them were cutting hay near to us. Their wives and mothers went with them.[2]

Too old for conscription himself, Zamaraev knew scores of the young men in his commune and its surrounding district who were leaving for the armed forces and might never return home. As a patriot he prayed for victories in the battles that lay ahead but an instinct already told him that things might go wrong, and not just for the Russians: 'Seemingly all of Europe has gone mad.'[3]

Military conscription was an old tradition in Russia. Peasants for centuries had been accustomed to assume that those of their men who were taken into the armed forces would never return to their families and villages. Although the War Ministry prescribed the recruitment quotas, it was the peasant communities themselves which chose the individuals for dispatch to army service. Often they selected local miscreants. The Great War, however, required a sudden unprecedented increase of troop numbers. Stations were set up in towns to carry out the work, starting with quotas of fit young men of military age. Zamaraev observed the sobbing families on a rainy day in Totma in September 1915. The mud in the streets came up to the knees of those who trudged through it. Zamaraev felt deeply for 'the poor women' who had to say goodbye to their husbands or sons.[4]

He loved his wife Nadezhda and shared his thoughts with her at the end of the working day. They had one child, their daughter Lidia who was born in March 1910.[5] As a village elder he was one of those trusted to deliver judgements in cases of dispute. He kept up with new ideas in the *Selskaya zhizn* ('Rural Life') journal to improve his agricultural techniques. Nothing is more misleading than the idea that all Russian peasants were poor, illiterate and ill-informed. In fact the Russian Empire, while undoubtedly having tens of millions of destitute peasants, had a diverse society that included many like Zamaraev who expected to turn an annual profit, however small it might be. He took his cereal harvest for milling at the monastery, which had the necessary equipment, and he and Nadezhda tended their vegetable garden. While working the land in much the same way as generations of his family had done, Zamaraev welcomed the arrival of contemporary facilities and services in Totma. He had his photograph taken. He watched a movie on the new-fangled 'cinematograph'. He took out a fire insurance policy for his home.[6] He also brewed his own beer and drank it in moderation. When he sat down with neighbours to drink some vodka and two of them had a knife fight, he was not one of the disputants.[7]

Zamaraev was exactly the industrious kind of peasant whom Stolypin had hoped to prise away from the village commune and turn into an independent farmer. Zamaraev in fact refrained from joining the six neighbours who applied to leave the commune and have their strips of land consolidated into single holdings. Instead he acted as the commune elder who wrote out the agreed terms of departure for the peasant leavers.[8] He himself was making a good enough living by abiding by its traditions. His commune's land covered a wide area and he rode out to tend to his disparate strips. When he needed some carpentry or shepherding done, he hired a man from the locality.[9] But usually he carried out the task himself. There were few such tasks that this self-reliant man could not or would not handle.

God-fearing and diligent, Zamaraev attended church and observed all the religious festivals. He had spent New Year's Day 1914 collecting logs – he rarely took an entire day off work. Farming made tough demands in that part of the empire. The soil was poor and climatic conditions were demanding and, like his neighbours, Zamaraev kept a sharp eye on the weather. His hut was entombed by snow in the long northern winter when it was tough to ride or trudge into town. The muddy pathways in autumn and early spring were not much casier, and although the peasants welcomed the hot summer of the far north with its long hours of daylight, this season too could bring difficulties if rain ruined the harvest – and mosquitoes always caused discomfort. In spring 1914 Zamaraev sowed oats, barley and flax and decided not to sow rye until the autumn. He planted out potatoes for sale from his garden. He owned sheep, cows and a bull. He was fond of his pair of horses, which he kept for travel to town and for draught power in his fields. Zamaraev was a successful peasant who could be proud of his farming achievements.

Vologda province's economy was slowly adapting to the modern world in the decades before the outbreak of the Great War. The money economy with its banknotes and coins was spreading even while peasants continued to barter goods and labour when trading among themselves. Contact with the rest of the country increased after the completion of the Moscow–Vologda railway in 1872. Another line was added in 1908 which ran from Vyatka to Vologda.[10] Rivers had always been vital for commerce across the province. Unfortunately they froze over in wintertime, but the rail lines made transport possible without seasonal interruption. Consumer goods, newspapers and travellers arrived in Vologda and the little townships in larger numbers than they had for centuries. The province was shaking hands with the twentieth century.

Not being near any new railways, Totma continued to depend on the steamships that sailed west from Vologda and south-east from Veliki Ustyug. The town had its own hospital and high school (*gimnazia*) and was the third biggest in Vologda province, but this was not saying very much since the town's population was less than 5,000 in the census of 1897.[11] Totma district (*uezd*) was one of the most sparsely inhabited parts of European Russia: there were on average only a little over ten people per square mile even though the rural population had nearly doubled since the late 1850s.[12] The first automobile arrived in 1915 and belonged to the district administration, as Zamaraev recorded in his diary.[13]

The Russian north, and Vologda province in particular, were unusual in European Russia because they had very few gentry landowners. This was not a unique phenomenon: the same was true of parts of the Urals, another reminder of the empire's diversity. At the time of the Emancipation Edict in 1861 the Vologda provincial gentry owned more than five times more land than the peasants. By 1908 peasant ownership was nearly double the amount in the gentry's possession.[14] Not that the peasants felt content by their success. Nearly 92 per cent of the province's land under agriculture still belonged to the state, the Imperial family, the Church and other public institutions.[15]

The coming of war and mass conscription halted agricultural progress. Totma district was initially required to supply 4,000 recruits. Before being moved off elsewhere for training they were housed in school classrooms and private homes in the town. The streets teemed with recruits and families bidding them goodbye. Many parents were in tears about the sons they were losing to the Eastern front.[16] Military drafts followed each other in quick succession, and Zamaraev wondered when there would be an end to the conscriptions.[17] Half the young men and those in early middle age of Totma and the surrounding countryside were drawn into the armed forces by the end of October 1914.[18] While peace reigned, the Imperial forces had operated with 1,423,000 men under arms but by the later months of the year it had grown by 5,130,000 recruits.[19]

The Imperial authorities also requisitioned 2.1 million horses that met the standards needed in warfare. When peasants complained about losing their livestock, it was decreed that every household could hold on to two horses. The practical effect was that gentry families had to part with a greater proportion of their horses than was the case for the peasantry.[20] But both gentry landowners and peasants suffered. A quota of 800 horses was demanded from Totma district in Vologda province, where the landed gentry were few. Prices had to be agreed with their owners.[21] Murmurings of discontent were constant but the armed forces successfully obtained their equine requirements.

Allied ambassadors and journalists told the world that the Russian people universally approved of Nicholas's decision to go to war. It was a false impression given by metropolitan observers who knew little of, or chose to overlook, the situation in the provinces. The truth was that recruitment points were hit by disorder in thirty provinces of European Russia and ten of them in the Asiatic regions. Fifty landed estates were attacked in the provinces of Mogilëv, Minsk, Kiev and Volynya.[22] In the Urals, a provincial governor issued the following command to army commanders: 'Organize a peasant assembly and make this announcement: at the slightest disorder I will crush the settlement with artillery. I won't stand on ceremony. Any gathering that refuses to disperse on first demand is to be fired upon without mercy.'[23] Even in a quiet spot like Totma in Vologda province, the recruiters had to cope with a disorderly process. Men and horses jostled on embarkation. There were fears that the district might not supply the designated quota for the armed forces. The steamship's departure was delayed until 25 July 1914 when calm had been restored.[24]

The fires of defiance proved containable and mass conscription was successfully implemented. Even so, the authorities were alert to the possibility of reignition. From the targets chosen by the rioters it would seem likely that many of those who came onto the streets were taking their chance – perhaps their last chance if they were being called up for military service – to disrupt a social order that condemned them to hopeless poverty. Resentment was notably fierce among peasants who chafed against the grip that gentry landowners retained on the assets of the countryside.[25] But it was not only peasants who were resentful. Many urban workers also disobeyed the call-up. Factories in Odessa were emptied of their workforces. In Yekaterinoslav there was little mood for war and the chairman of the local branch of the Union of the Russian People, whose anti-parliamentary and anti-Semitic extremism made it a forerunner of European fascism, was beaten up by army recruits after he delivered 'patriotic speeches'.[26] The empire's social order was being tested by the experience of total war and the signs were already appearing that little would be needed to set off another revolutionary convulsion such as had happened in 1905–6.

Commanders at the highest level of the armed forces were aware that their troops would require careful indoctrination and management. Lieutenant-Colonel Alexander Verkhovski doubted that Russian peasant conscripts had the same idea of 'motherland' or 'fatherland' that had been inculcated in German troops. He wrote in August 1914: 'Many think that there is patriotism in the people at the moment!? To our great regret, this is not the case . . . Everyone must go clearly and consciously with faith in the righteousness of his cause, in whose name he accepts privations as he advances, perhaps unto death.'[27]

Anti-German feeling, though, was widespread in the cities that the conscripts left behind when leaving for the front. Few people dared speak German except in a whisper. There were angry knocks on the wall from the next-door room when a Petrograd hotel chambermaid from the Baltic provinces used the language because her Russian was too weak.[28] Moscow became an epicentre of violence in May 1915 when a mob ran amok, attacking shops and businesses and their German owners, including some of the best-known stores in the city. Alexander Adrianov, Moscow's mayor (*gradonachal'nik*), thought better of intervening with force and for a while the mayor foolishly joined what he took to be a patriotic demonstration – people were carrying images of Nicholas II. After two days of disorder and eventually recognizing his mistake in appearing to condone such anarchy, Adrianov ordered troops to fire on the crowd. Eight civilians and seven soldiers died and 300 looted enterprises were left in ruins.[29]

It was not long, though, before news began to reach cities and villages across the empire about the human cost of the war. Alexander Zamaraev talked to Totma's own sons who returned to the town after military action in Poland or Galicia. Nikolai Mishurinski, who had been called up in the first draft, came back in mid-August for a week's leave and told of the grinding difficulties facing Russian forces on the Eastern front.[30] A fortnight later Zamaraev recorded, 'It's already the case that wounded men are arriving who left here as part of the army reserve a month ago.'[31]

One of Russia's greatest writers, Alexander Blok, wrote a poem depicting the trainloads of young men going off to fight on the Eastern front. Whilst he supported the war effort, he knew that many of the conscripts were making their last rail journey:

> Petrograd's sky had been muddied by rain
> An army contingent was leaving for war.
> Platoon after platoon, bayonet after bayonet
> Endlessly fills carriage after carriage.
> A thousand lives on the train felt the bloom
> Of separation's pain, of love's anxiety,
> Of strength, youth, hope . . . in sunset distance
> There was blood in the smoky clouds.

The poem ends with a depiction of the horror at the front:

> Pity is drowned out by the gunfire,
> Thunderous armaments and clattering horses.
> Sorrow has been choked by the poisoned steam
> Rising from Galicia's blood-soaked fields . . .[32]

3. ADVANCE, DEFEAT, OBJECTIVES: FROM VICTORY TO THE GREAT RETREAT

In the event of war against Germany or Austria–Hungary, the Russian high command had long planned to take the fight into enemy territory from the first day of hostilities. Offensive preparations were updated on the basis of intelligence reports about recent German military exercises.[1] Whereas public discourse before 1914 focused on defence, the commanders gave priority to invasion. Although the Germans were projected as the more formidable enemy, there was concern that if Habsburg armies were allowed to breach the Romanov frontier they might succeed in fomenting the Ukrainians to rise against rule by Russia. Those in the high command and the War Ministry who had for years doubted Russia's military readiness and capacity were compelled to keep silent.[2]

Commanders wanted to show their fighting spirit as worthy successors of the men who had brought Napoleon low and conquered lands in the Baltic, the Caucasus and central Asia. They assumed it would be a war of short duration. The Russians believed that if they took the initiative they could snatch victory, and the alliance with France and Great Britain heightened their optimism. The objective in the north was to smash through East Prussia to Berlin, in the southern sector against Austria–Hungary to Budapest and Vienna by way of Galicia. The early results were celebrated in St Petersburg. Patriotic newspapers and the entire Duma were swept up by the euphoria. The Russian Army under Generals Samsonov and Rennenkampf burst across the northern frontier of 'Russian' Poland into East Prussia.

The shortest route from Russia's Polish lands to Berlin lay in the region parallel to the Baltic Sea coastline. Germany had concentrated its forces against France, so its eastward defences were vulnerable to attack. But the Germans already had a counter-ploy in mind, which was to let the Russians conduct an initial operation and then trap them in pincers from north and south. The Austrians could also safely predict that Russian forces would attack them in Galicia. Stout defence and a rapid invasion of the Romanov provinces in Ukraine was Vienna's approved war plan.

On 4 August 1914, the Russian high command started its campaign against the Germans by invading East Prussia. General Paul von Rennenkampf, a Baltic German in the service of the Romanovs, moved north of the Masurian Lakes in the direction of Königsberg while General Alexander Samsonov swept around the south of them. The objective was to defeat German forces under General Maximilian von Prittwitz after pinning them down along their Baltic coast. But Germany's armies regrouped after a forced retreat and caught Samsonov, whose armies were by now separated from those of Rennenkampf, in a surrounding movement. By 31 August the Germans had pulled off a stunning victory at the battle of Tannenberg. A quarter of a million Russian troops were killed, wounded or taken prisoner. The German forces under Prittwitz began a strategic offensive on 7 August. A heavy battle followed at Gumbinnen. The result was indeterminate and Prittwitz withdrew, allowing the Russians to celebrate a victory that was less of a triumph than it appeared. Dissatisfaction in Berlin with Prittwitz's performance led to a change in command with the appointment of Paul von Hindenburg and Erich Ludendorff, who brought renewed energy to the war.[3]

A second disaster befell the Russians in battle by the Masurian Lakes as the forces under Hindenburg and Ludendorff crushed the retreating enemy. Recriminations were levelled against Rennenkampf for cowardice and incompetence. Grand Duke Nikolai Nikolaevich judged this unfair but his forces had undoubtedly suffered a tremendous defeat.[4]

The Russian advance in the war's southern sector against Austro-Hungarian defences went more to plan. On 6 August Russia's forces burst across the Habsburg frontier in Galicia. Austria–Hungary was fighting a war on two fronts. In Serbia, Conrad von Hötzendorf, the Habsburg commander-in-chief, had dispatched twenty divisions for its subjugation. This left the hapless Conrad with only twenty-eight divisions to repel the Russians in the east.[5] As the diplomatic emergency over Sarajevo spiralled into a sequence of military mobilizations, he knew that he would have far fewer forces to face the Russian offensive. The Germans urged Emperor Franz Joseph, his ministers and commanders to concentrate on Russia and ignore Serbia. Conrad nevertheless insisted that a quick offensive against the Russians from Galicia was his best option. Russian armed forces were amassed to occupy Galicia before he could make his move. Russia's advance into Habsburg lands was disorderly but less so than Conrad's defence. Austria–Hungary's armies were outnumbered and out-gunned. A large-scale retreat was unavoidable and the Russians celebrated victory in late August.[6]

The struggle for Galicia was over by the end of September and Russian victories helped to limit the disappointment of public opinion about Tannenberg. Austria–Hungary had lost access to a third of its normal wheat supply in the war's opening campaign and Habsburg military disintegration was halted only by German reinforcements.[7]

In mid-September Zamaraev could already recognize it was a 'heavy' conflict.[8] There were young men in Totma who had volunteered for service in the armed forces, including twelve from the town's seminary and eight who worked as craftsmen.[9] By October Zamaraev was in still gloomier mood. He attended the wedding of his neighbour Gavriil Bulatov where the hosts could not buy a glass of wine from the state liquor store because of the 'dry law'. Zamaraev summed up the fighting on the Eastern front: 'It's a very bloody war. Our men have beaten the Austrians but cannot manage it against the Prussians. They're all being beaten in Poland. The provinces of Kalisz and Lublin are terribly devastated.'[10] He took his mind off the news by going home to tend his fields and livestock, and next day he did some late autumn ploughing.[11]

Within a few days the flags were flying and prayers were said in Totma celebrating a Russian victory to the west of Warsaw.[12] But the news got worse as the eastward impetus of German forces under Hindenburg and Ludendorff was resumed. In September the Ottoman Empire signed an alliance with the Central Powers. The Germans had made it clear that Istanbul could not stay neutral and retain their favour. One of the first Ottoman actions was to close the Bosporus and the Straits of the Dardanelles to Russian shipping. Russia got ready to open a front from the Caucasus with a view towards attacking Ottoman forces in eastern Anatolia. A scheme was prepared to supply the Ottoman Empire's Armenians with arms for a revolt.[13] Euphoria grew in Petrograd about the hammering that the Ottomans began to experience. But at the same time the Russian Imperial armies were being battered on the German anvil on the Eastern front. Through into

November 1914 Russia's forces were on the retreat, crossing back over the historic frontier of Romanov rule and yielding fifty miles before a halt was achievable. By the end of the year, the Russian Empire had lost 35,000 square miles of its lands to German military occupation.[14]

Zamaraev, who talked to the wounded servicemen returning to Totma, questioned any idea that the Allies were on the brink of triumph. He was shaken when he learned that the Allied coalition was intent on all-out victory regardless of the cost in lives. Even if the Allies beat the Central Powers, he doubted that they could ever 'dry the eyes of all those rendered destitute or made orphans by this terrible war'. It was a war like no other. The two sides – the Allies and the Central Powers – traced two great fronts, the Eastern and the Western, down the length of Europe. Zamaraev pictured all this from afar: 'In the theatre of war there aren't any big battles, but rather they are daily little ones. They've dug trenches and are living in the earth like moles. Doubtless it will all break out again in February or March'[15] When he watched the drafts of Totma's young men leave for active service, he could see that the early talk of a short war was self-deceiving. But his patriotism still burned bright. He prayed for an Allied victory in 1915 that would bring 'happiness and a peaceful life' to the entire world.[16]

The Russians suffered defeat after defeat against the Germans in 1914–15. Alexei Shtukaturov until his call-up had been a metalworker at the Putilov Works in Petrograd. He went home to Gzhatsk in Smolensk province to bid goodbye to his family. Tears were shed before he left, accompanied only by his wife, for the assembly point in town. He stopped on the way to say prayers at his father's grave.[17] Military training followed but nothing prepared him for the gruelling conditions at the front:

> Our battalion commander took a bullet in the back amidst the hail of bullets. We were moved forward into the bushes and ordered to start digging. Having dug a small trench I fell asleep. Food was brought along. I fell ill from the dirty water.[18]

Periods of immobility were interrupted by spasms of violence. Shtukaturov's unit suffered from the same problems as the rest of the Imperial Army. Logistical difficulties obstructed adequate supplies of equipment, clothing and food to the front. There was a shortage in artillery shells, as Chief of Staff Yanushkevich warned the War Ministry as early as in the third week of fighting.[19] The civilian administration acquired much of the blame but military planning agencies were not without responsibility.[20]

In January 1915, despite the snow-laden terrain, the Germans unexpectedly started an offensive against the Russian lines in central Poland. Russia's losses were enormous and necessitated a rapid retreat by the Imperial Army into Lithuanian and Belorussian territories. The cities of Kaunas-Kovno and Grodno fell to the Germans. All Poland fell under military occupation. New trenches were dug. Barbed wire was stretched along the new line of the Eastern front. Morale in the Russian high command tumbled while the harsh wintry conditions put no brake on Germany's ambition. Nikolai Nikolaevich and Yanushkevich cast around for scapegoats. They found them in the German and Jewish residents near the front line. If Russian forces had been found wanting in combat, they were surely traduced by alien elements in the war zone. Such was Yanushkevich's paranoia that he ordered the closure of the Singer Sewing and Manufacturing Company in Petrograd – he ignorantly assumed it to be a German rather than American enterprise.[21] The high command also found fault with Russian arms manufacturers whose factories failed to keep pace with the output of shells needed to confront the Central Powers. Output had risen since the start of the war but the scale of the demand took everyone by surprise, including the army commanders.

In early 1915 a British naval contingent was sent to occupy the Straits of the Dardanelles. As Sazonov made plain to the British, the Russian authorities were nervous about this – they could not forget about the Crimean War of 1853–6 when Britain's forces in alliance with France had sailed into the Black Sea and attacked the Russian Empire.[22] Even the French, moreover, were taken by surprise by the new Dardanelles initiative. The British had to work hard to persuade their allies that their goal was to shatter the defences of the Central Powers at one of their weak points and shift the balance of forces against the Austrians and the Ottomans. There was also an economic objective for the British cabinet. A downturn in the global wheat supply had occurred in 1914 and Great Britain could not get its normal amount of grain imports from North America and Argentina. The problem could be solved if the Royal Navy secured the Straits for grain shipments from the Russian Empire. This would also help the Russians to service the huge wartime loans they had received from abroad.[23] The first landing at Gallipoli took place in April 1915. British, Australian and New Zealand forces were shocked by the strength of the Ottoman reaction as artillery rained down on them from on high. The expedition was an unmitigated disaster from its start to the final evacuation at the beginning of the following year.[24]

The original *casus belli* for Russia had been the defence of Serbia. This remained a war aim but was emphasized less than others once the fighting began. Not that there was much clarity for some months. The Allies, including Russia, were too much occupied with the goal of crushing Germany and Austria–Hungary to have time to agree on what kind of peace settlement was desirable. The Russians initially spoke to British Ambassador Sir George Buchanan about annexing eastern Galicia from the Habsburgs but nothing definite was put into writing.[25] When Russian forces marched into Galician territories, they anyway made them as 'Russian' as possible. Restrictions were placed on Polish and Jewish publications. Schooling in the Russian language was prioritized. The Russian Orthodox Church received privileges at the expense of other Christian denominations.

There was no need for lengthy cabinet discussion in Petrograd about the aim of annexing the territories surrounding the waterways from the Black Sea into the eastern Mediterranean. Ministers had already decided in spring 1914 that Istanbul – Constantinople or Tsargrad as the Russians called it – should be seized for Russia at the earliest opportunity.[26] Russian public opinion was exasperated by the Ottoman blockades of Russian shipping during various pre-war international emergencies. The government was determined to prevent any repetition of the problem. But no action was taken for fear of provoking a Europe-wide conflict for which Russia's preparations were inadequate – this was an attitude strongly expressed by Foreign Affairs Minister Sazonov. But he had nevertheless contended that a European war would present the Russians with an opportunity. In the winter of 1914–15 he and his ambassadors pressed the claim on British and French diplomats that the Straits of the Dardanelles, the Bosporus, the Sea of Marmara and Istanbul itself would become Russian possessions at the end of the Great War. It quickly became the war aim that preoccupied the Imperial administration.[27]

The French were chary about ceding Istanbul to Russia in a future peace settlement. But the Russians were adamant. The crucial importance of their contribution to the war effort strengthened their bargaining hand, and Sazonov obtained consent from the British and French ambassadors in early March 1915.[28] Foreign Secretary Sir Edward Grey instructed Ambassador Sir George Buchanan in Petrograd to assure Foreign Affairs Minister Sazonov that Constantinople would belong to Russia at the end of the war. The news was received with pleasure in Petrograd. Nicholas congratulated Sazonov: 'I owe you the happiest day of my life.'[29] The accord signed in Paris in April 1915 promised Constantinople to Russia. The terms were meant to remain secret. The official line was that the French, British and Russians were fighting to resist German and Austrian expansionist ambitions and military atrocities. It would not have done to admit to the world that the Allies planned land grabs of their own – the British coveted what was to become Iraq while the French wanted Syria. Nevertheless the accord quickly leaked in broad terms to the press.[30]

Nicholas still hoped for victory on the German sector of the Eastern front, but it was the southern sector where his troops had had most success. He celebrated this by making an official visit to Galicia in April 1915 which he called a 'momentous day for me'.[31] In Lvov he declared from a balcony, in a spirit of imperial aggrandizement that later generations of Russian nationalists would be able to appreciate: 'Galicia is no more but rather there is a Great Russia which stretches as far as the Carpathians!'[32]

Back in his village, Alexander Zamaraev was in high spirits. Despite the news of Russian setbacks, he thought the end of Germany and Austria was no longer distant. At night he had a dream about the Kaiser suffering punishment for his ill-doings by being burnt with hot needles.[33] Zamaraev was incensed about Germany's new methods of war: 'Letters are arriving from soldiers that the damned Germans are using gas as a weapon. This is a diabolical invention and the Kaiser is a fiend from hell.'[34] Zamaraev was reminded of the prophesy in St Matthew's Gospel that brother would fight brother and that 'nation shall rise against nation, and kingdom against kingdom'.[35] He prayed fervently for a Russian victory. So too did Petrograd metalworker and army conscript Alexei Shtukaturov while returning by rail to his regiment after recovering from a combat wound. The train conductor who was checking tickets shouted to no one in particular: 'What are we fighting for, what are we defending? Others are having a good time while we get ourselves crippled!' Shtukaturov gave him the answer that he was fighting for his nearest and dearest, their homes and the land that they cultivated. The conductor came back at him with another question: 'Do you have a big field and a good house?' In his opinion only the wealthy and powerful wanted the war.[36]

Shtukaturov and millions of the empire's soldiers proved him wrong by their personal example. They fought on when the Imperial Army had suffered defeat after defeat and the Germans seemed invincible on the Eastern front. The high command called on troops to defend the fatherland to the last. German offensives continued with Warsaw as the next objective. Huge numbers of POWs were taken and Warsaw was occupied in the last week of July 1915. The Imperial Army undertook a strategic retreat with the Germans in pursuit. Brest-Litovsk fell to them in August. Russia's defeat in Poland was complete and it was an open question whether the German steamroller could be stopped before it reached central Russia. All the gains made by the Imperial Army in Galicia could soon be forfeited and a prolonged war on three fronts against Germany, Austria–Hungary and the Ottoman Empire was the last thing that the General Staff had planned for. Its leaders also feared the growth of anti-war feelings.[37] By the winter of 1914–15 the optimists were hit by deep apprehension: even a war on a single front was of concern if it was the Germans who stood on the other side of the trenches.

4. THE IMPERIAL WAR ZONE: MILITARY GOVERNMENT, POGROMS AND DEPORTATION

Nicholas, imperious with ministers, licensed his generals to steward the war zones behind the fronts however they saw fit. The line of the war zone against the Central Powers was drawn from Petrograd in the eastern Baltic to Odessa on the Black Sea and north to Finland's border with Sweden. Everywhere to the west of that line was subjected to military authority. The area covered an entire third of the European territories of the empire.[1] The rules of governance were set out in the 'Regulations on Field Command of Forces in Time of War' which were confirmed on 16 July 1914 before the fighting began.[2] The cabinet in Petrograd could continue to govern in the zone only to the extent that it complied with the directives issued from general headquarters near the small town of Baranovichi in the southern part of Minsk province. From Baranovichi, with its two stations at the junction of three railway lines, the high command issued orders both for the front and the entire war zone.[3] Trains from Baranovichi to Petrograd, which was 700 miles to the north-east, went through Dvinsk and Vilna. A direct line ran to Moscow. The rail and telegraph networks were used for communication – and if the generals wanted an instant conversation they typed messages on a contraption known as the Hughes telegraph.

The high command's prerogatives in the war zone involved an extraordinary reordering of powers within the state – and at first no one in the cabinet objected to it. The Russian example would be followed in Germany in 1916, when Wilhelm II gave Generals Hindenburg and Ludendorff complete authority over the civil administration.

Grand Duke Nikolai Nikolaevich was the nominated driver of the engine of war. Nicholas took the precaution of banning him from bringing his protégés into the General Staff.[4] Nikolai Nikolaevich accepted this. Languid in the performance of his duties, he relied on

Chief of Staff Nikolai Yanushkevich and Quartermaster-General Yuri Danilov. The General Staff throbbed with activity. Most of its officers had passed through demanding courses at the Military Academy and were alert to the changing requirements of contemporary warfare. Although they included sons of the high aristocracy, there was a movement before the war towards social diversity: less than half of the Academy's students in 1913 came from the nobility.[5] But while privilege was diminishing, the old traditions of patriotism, Russian nationhood and the Orthodox Christian faith were upheld. Death or glory were instilled as guiding goals. Whether the entire officer corps was committed to keeping the Russian social order intact is doubtful.[6] Ex-peasants were not inclined to look upon the landowning gentry as a class of philanthropists. But there is no doubt that commanders from the top to the bottom of the armed forces were committed to the goal of victory over the empire's enemies.

A third of European Russia had been placed under martial law after the start of hostilities. The German military advance led to decisions to extend the zone to other key places including Finland, the Baltic provinces and the north and south Caucasus. Petrograd and Moscow came under the army's authority as did the port cities of Archangel in the Russian far north and Vladivostok on the Pacific seaboard. The large areas used for the training of conscripts were also subsumed under military command.[7] Throughout the length and breadth of the war zone, ministers were second-class rulers who looked on helplessly as army commanders issued decrees of governance without attention to the rule of law, public welfare or the needs of a market economy. Whenever the armed forces were short of goods or services, they requisitioned them from the local inhabitants. Free peasants felt they were being treated as serfs. The prices that they were offered for their produce were lower than what could be obtained by trade, and they were called upon to dig out and build up the army's defensive line.[8]

The relentless sequence of military drafts continued. The recruiters called up 5,210,000 men in 1915 alone. In the course of hostilities through to February 1917 about 13,855,000 men were added to the Imperial Army and Navy.[9] Towns and villages witnessed the unending sequence of recruitments. Alexander Zamaraev recorded on 15 January 1915: 'Today there was a gathering of recruits and this will not be the last of the gatherings. It seems that they are going to draft all the young men. If they were to call up us, the oldsters, I'd go with enthusiasm.'[10]

He lamented how many families were losing their menfolk and, if they perished at the front, left widows and orphans to deal with disaster. As Zamaraev recognized, life in Totma was depleted when the draft pulled in a *gimnazia* teacher by name of Shein.[11]

The Russian Empire had the largest armed forces of any combatant country. But whereas the Imperial Army had one man at the front to 2¼ men in the rear, in the French Army it was almost exactly the reverse: two Frenchmen served at the front for every one in the rear. This meant that the Russians had proportionately more than four times as many soldiers serving in rear units as the French required. Part of the reason no doubt lay in Russia's need to compensate for the inadequate rail and road networks and to surmount the difficulties of mud in the spring thaw and autumn rains.[12] But did the German forces, when they occupied Romanov territories, not require the Russian scale of human support in their rear? The basic cause of Russia's peculiarity lay in its chronic under-provision of finance to the armed forces. Two fifths of the empire's troops laboured as tailors, gardeners, cobblers, carpenters, cooks and the like. Servicemen were even deployed to earn supplementary income for the armed forces in the civilian economy by way of seasonal labour in the summer months.[13]

The demographic impact of conscription was on an unprecedented scale. Nearly half of the men between the ages of eighteen and forty-three – about 47 per cent – were drafted into the armed forces. Since most of them were from the villages, agricultural activity experienced changes that were huge and immediate. In Vologda province the call-up affected 52.3 per cent of the males classified as capable of productive labour.[14] The regulations for the Imperial draft exempted some particular religious and ethnic groups, known in official parlance as 'aliens' (*inogorodtsy*). The Imperial administration had never trusted the Muslims in central Asia and south Caucasus since their recent conquest, and it was feared that they might collaborate with the Ottomans. Finns and Mennonites, too, were spared the draft. Even Russians were excused if they were married men and the family breadwinners. This rule provoked a surge in weddings in the first year of the war.[15] Exemptions were also made for men who either were the sole sons in their families or were the only sons left working the land for them, and students were allowed to complete their courses of education.[16]

People grumbled about the unfairnesses. The rich found it easier than others to evade the draft. Zamaraev asked why a wealthy bachelor should remain undrafted while many poor fathers were being conscripted. Many young men in the countryside hid from the recruiters.

On reaching the garrisons for training, conscripts had to be fed regularly – the high command recognized the need for them to be fit and healthy. They had to receive uniforms and military equipment. They needed training in the skills of war, and the number of officers had to be increased to make all this feasible. Transport had to be commandeered for the movement of men, munitions, equipment, horses, food and hay. The larger the army, the greater the demand on supply organizations that were under-manned and underfunded. With the start of the war, moreover, the daily meat ration for troops was doubled to a pound. The diet of millions of peasants in the Russian Empire was of abysmal quality, but in the army a soldier could expect to receive two and a half pounds of bread every day. Butter and other dairy products were supplied from western Siberia. Dried vegetable products came from the horticulture of the region around Rostov-on-Don, and supplies were supplemented from territories near to the front.[17] The German press reported appreciatively on how well the Russian soldiers were fed.[18]

But the reality was not quite as impressive as the official standards laid down. When Alexei Shtukaturov reached his regiment in Poltava, he was issued with an Imperial Russian uniform but an Austrian cup and cutlery and a tatty Austrian kit bag. Shtukaturov noted that informal trading took place with residents of the localities. Some of the newest recruits were already selling the boots that they received from the army stores.[19] But the salary for soldiers was 75 kopeks a month.[20] This was not a fortune but was enough for them to buy extra food if they were near a vegetable or fruit stall. When deployed to Kherson in present-day Ukraine, Shtukaturov visited a monastery and bought a copy of the New Testament. He and his comrades could afford to have their photographs taken in the city.[21]

Russia's military censorship found that the letters sent home by soldiers were remarkably free from complaints about their conditions. Thirty per cent were categorized as buoyant and cheerful, and 67 per cent appeared calm, neither approving nor criticizing how troops were being treated.[22] They wrote knowing that others would read them before their loved ones could. This discouraged putting inflammatory thoughts to paper. Even so, it would seem that the Imperial Army was not seething with revolutionary turbulence. Deserters earned contempt.

Half a million of them went on the run in the first year of the war.[23] The average soldier expected solidarity from his fighting comrades. Whatever he thought of the reasons of state that had led to his call-up, he was committed to standing by the men in his unit – and he assumed that others would do the same.[24]

The main anxiety for troops was about how their families were coping in their absence with the demands of ploughing and harvesting. As relatives wrote from home to the front about the soaring increase in prices, the army leadership was troubled by the impact that this had inside regiments.[25]

Conscripts had been moved hundreds or thousands of miles from home, but the war, if anything, stiffened their feelings about how society should be organized. In letters, they expressed anger about police, traders (often called 'speculators') and gentry landowners.[26] One soldier wrote that putting merchants on trial was too good for them and that they ought to be hanged. The wartime lifestyle of the rich and privileged caused resentment at the front and in the garrisons. Another soldier wrote that they 'don't find a common language with us, as if they don't share the same motherland'. He added that they were 'stuffing their pockets and pray to God for the war to be dragged out for another year to let them earn near to a million'.[27] Georgi Zhukov, future Marshal of the Soviet Union and first to occupy Berlin in 1945, was to recall his acrimonious reaction to being called up as a young man in 1915: 'I experienced no special enthusiasm because at every step in Moscow I came across wretched cripples who had come back from the front, and at the same time alongside them I saw how the sons of the wealthy were living their same old high life'.[28]

Discipline was harsh in the forces of all the states at war, but especially so in the Imperial Army. Peasants of the Russian Empire, despite being used to abiding by the orders of their family elders, were shocked by their bullying drill sergeants. Recruits suffered punches and insults on a daily basis. Alexei Shtukaturov was shocked at a junior ensign who administered a heavy beating to four soldiers for falling asleep on guard duty. Shtukaturov wrote in his diary:

> Obviously the officers (*nachal'stvo*) had the aim of terrifying soldiers with the fear of punishment, imagining that this was the way to raise the fighting capacity of the Russian soldier but as I noticed from the mood and conversations of the soldiers, the result was the opposite. Every soldier saw himself in the

> one beaten in front of him, and despite trying honourably to fulfil his duty, none of us can be sure that tomorrow he too won't be subjected to the same fate for some casual failing.[29]

Soldiering in the tsar's name was extremely harsh.

The disciplinary regime in rear garrisons was no gentler. Sometimes the brutality got too much for the men, who were provoked into taking reprisals. Georgi Zhukov remembered how he and some young friends in the Imperial Army ganged up on their tormentor. They pounced on him in a dark corner, threw a blanket over his head and beat him into an unconscious heap on the floor.[30] Sometimes the retaliation happened on a wider scale. In autumn 1915 there was a riot of 30,000 troops in Moscow who rose in protest against their conditions. A city policeman was killed and the rioters showed no fear in liberating those of their comrades who were arrested. Only with difficulty did the officer corps restore calm and order.[31] There were further disturbances among the latest round of recruits in Petrograd and other cities. Internal Affairs Minister Shcherbatov ordered provincial governors to suppress the growing trouble by whatever measures appeared necessary. Garrisons, if not yet the front, were a powder keg ready to explode.[32]

Millions of Russian troops, on being conscripted, suddenly discovered that they could exercise fewer rights than they had been able to in their villages. A garrison soldier could not smoke in the street. He could not enter a tavern for a drink. He could not even walk down all the town's main streets. He could not take a tram ride, and on the gates to parks there were signs banning troops and dogs – a linkage that demeaned their human dignity.[33] The daily routine was frequently passed in boredom. Distractions in military barracks were few apart from Orthodox Church services and games of poker. Conditions on the front line involved both the dangers of combat and periods of dreary inactivity. Wherever they were, at the front or the rear, soldiers resented the rules and practices of discipline. Middle-ranking officers had gripes of their own. The writer and humanitarian activist Shloyme Rappaport-Ansky, who wrote under the pseudonym S. An-sky, was on a train near the front when he overheard an Imperial officer say: 'Russia is fighting three enemies: the Germans, lice and our generals.' Of these, the officer said, the generals were the most dangerous.[34] Every army in the war had its internal tensions and woes, and it was not unusual for a lieutenant to blame his commanders. Troops were treated badly everywhere but those in the Russian Imperial Army were exposed to indignities and severities of an extreme kind.

On the positive side, medals were awarded for acts of valour. Alexei Shtukaturov won a St George cross, fourth class, on an early tour of duty at the front. He ought later to have received a third-class cross but an administrative mix-up occurred and only another fourth-class medal arrived for him.[35] During the war over a million crosses were awarded in the Russian armed forces. The award of a medal brought little benefit apart from personal acclaim, but when Shtukaturov's company was deployed for a while near Kherson, the shopkeepers gave out free bread, sausages and chocolate to those wearing their St George cross.[36]

Troops had always had ways of their own to raise morale in the ranks. Humour and fantasy crept into some of their unsupervised chants, as in this one about a soldier and his horse:

> One poor old soldier lives on his own
> Hurrah, hurrah, hurrah!
> And grooms his horse and drinks no vodka
> Hurrah, hurrah, hurrah!
> 'Faithful black horse of mine,
> Hurrah, hurrah, hurrah!
> Shall you and I go off to battle?'
> Hurrah, hurrah, hurrah!
> The first bullet killed the horse
> Hurrah, hurrah, hurrah!
> And the second one struck me down
> Hurrah, hurrah, hurrah![37]

Melodies could be jaunty despite the themes of death and nostalgia for loved ones. Another song contained these verses:

> There's grass over all the graves,
> A cross has been placed upon mine.
> To all my comrades I call out:
> Come along and grieve, lads,
> And bow three times to the ground
> In memory of me, my brothers.[38]

Such verses expressed the stoicism for which the Russian conscript was rightly renowned.

Other forms of amusement were less innocuous. Many soldiers when off duty whored, gambled – and worse. Rapes of local women, looting and drunken brawls were commonplace. Officers had difficulty in bringing them to an end even when they wanted to – and they did not always want to. Complaints from nearby peasants were ignored.[39]

When the armed forces were forced back into the territories of the Russian Empire, the General Staff resolved to leave no one and nothing behind of potential use to the German forces. The Imperial Army came into towns and villages and gave people between twenty-four or thirty-six hours to leave their homes with whatever baggage they could carry.[40] Factories and other enterprises were closed and their equipment and workforces transferred deeper into the war zone or beyond. A scorched earth regime was implemented along a sixty-mile-wide strip along the entire front line. If the enemy breached the line, they would find nothing to sustain them. These orders caused huge distress. The Council of Ministers discussed the shutting down of sugar-beet-refining facilities for which there was no prospect of relocation and renewed operation. The economic and social damage was unmistakable to ministers, who refused to endorse the recklessness of the military commanders.[41] Only the emperor could resolve this question and he rejected the conclusions made in his cabinet. For him, if his leading generals wanted something it was for everyone to seek ways to satisfy their request.

This meant that even many Russian peasant households lost home and land. Alexei Shtukaturov's wife wrote to him on the Eastern front from Smolensk province in August 1915 – she panicked after hearing rumours that everyone was going to be deported to Siberia before the next German offensive. People even said that wounded servicemen were no longer going to be treated in hospitals in the rear. The absence of official announcements spawned wild talk. Shtukaturov wrote back telling her to ignore all the rumours.[42] Whether or not she did, is not known. But she went on living in the family home.

The high command at any rate reserved the harshest treatment for those ethnic groups which it categorized as 'suspect'. Deportations had taken place in the nineteenth century to secure Imperial authority in the newly conquered zones in central Asia and the Caucasus whenever a people was judged irreconcilable to the Imperial order. They were repeated on an increased scale in the Great War and laid the basis for the campaigns of ethnic cleansing that were to be practised by the early Soviet administration.[43] Certain national groups near the Eastern front were also targeted. At the end of 1914 all inhabitants were ordered out of Warsaw except those of Slavic parentage.[44] About 200,000 ethnic

Germans were ejected from 'Russian' Poland and their property confiscated. Many were sent under military escort to Siberia and northern Russia, far away from where they might damage the Imperial war effort. The deportations continued from other western borderlands after the retreat from all Polish territories. Emperor and government reinforced the anti-German measures. Publications in the German language were banned. Ethnic Germans were prohibited from holding meetings. Farms were confiscated that had belonged to German settlers since the time of Catherine the Great. Many Baltic German officials were fired from responsible posts.[45]

Alexander Zamaraev witnessed an influx of German families into his Totma district in August 1914. Civilians to a man, woman and child, there were 200 of them.[46] Vologda province was adjudged a territory where they – potential spies or collaborators in the eyes of the high command – could safely be kept for the duration of war.

Other groups, too, suffered. In the south Caucasus, where war intensified against Ottoman forces, the Ajarians and other Muslim groups were expelled from their towns and villages. Ethnic cleansing was introduced to the war zone behind the Caucasus front.[47] Poles, Lithuanians, Latvians and Roma near the Eastern front were expelled in a sequence of operations.[48] Although they were Romanov subjects, they were seen by army commanders as likely to provide a warm welcome to the invading Central Powers. The deportations were intended to prevent them from being used as spies by the German and Austro-Hungarian forces. There was also a strong element of vengeful spite in a time when national and religious tensions were on the rise. Anyone thought to be a potential subversive received harsh treatment.

But it was Jews who experienced the worst treatment. Army leaders explicitly described the process of deportation and expropriation of Jews as a 'cleansing'.[49] Jewish inhabitants suffered terribly in the territories occupied by Russian armed forces in Germany and Galicia in 1914.[50] The misery continued throughout towns and villages near the front line as it was pushed back deep into the western parts of the Russian Empire. The Imperial war zone itself covered a large part of the so-called Pale of Settlement, where the law had confined most Jews since Catherine the Great's acquisition of lands in eastern Poland at the end of the eighteenth century. The Romanov lands possessed the world's largest number of Jewish subjects. All but 4 per cent of the empire's Jewish population lived in the provinces of the Pale.[51] Exceptions were made only for the richest businessmen and for a few key occupations. Three hundred and forty thousand of them were driven out of the empire's Polish provinces alone before the Imperial forces themselves were forced out.[52] According to a recent estimate, as many as 600,000 Jewish residents in the entire war zone lost their homes during the Great War.[53] Unlike ethnic Germans, they were simply uprooted without any thought of allocating them places of subsequent settlement.

Nikolai Nikolaevich declined to stop the mayhem, and Yanushkevich felt no impulse to change policy because he knew that Tsar Nicholas shared the contempt and distrust of his Jewish subjects. The sovereign of all Russia and its empire was not going to reproach him for suppressing their supposedly treasonous potential in the western borderlands. The high command's anti-Semitism drew on old sources. Orthodox Church doctrine held the Jewish people responsible for the killing of Jesus Christ. Hatred and fear of Jews coexisted. Military paranoia was increased because Yiddish, the language of the shtetls, was close to German – and few officers and fewer soldiers understood either language. At the highest levels of command the standard word for Jews was 'Yids'.[54]

Shloyme Rappaport-Ansky witnessed the horrendous scene in which an eighty-two-year-old blind Jewish man was treated as a German spy.[55] Jews were disallowed from making journeys alongside a retreating Russian unit for fear that they might learn sensitive information and pass it on to the Central Powers. In February 1915 the army prohibited Jewish people from moving from town to town in Galicia. The result was a drying up of trade and supplies across the region.[56] In midsummer a total ban was placed on publications in the Yiddish and Hebrew languages, and Jewish soldiers were prevented from writing home in Yiddish.[57] For countless Jews the order to move east came too late to prevent pogroms by Cossack units which were as vicious as those conducted by Cossacks in the eighteenth century in the same region. Often, once a pogrom started, local peasants would join the looting.[58]

The violence was accompanied by humiliations which could be sadistic in the extreme. Jewish residents in the shtetl of Volkovisk in Grodno province were stripped naked by troops and then forced to dance with each other and to ride around on pigs. One in ten of those Jews taken captive by the army were executed. This was all the more shocking in light of the fact that a tenth of the entire Jewish population were serving in the Imperial Army.[59] Around 500,000 Jews joined the wartime forces and over half of them were volunteers.[60] They were fighting for tsar and motherland, and 1,957 of them were awarded the St George cross medal. Even so, they received no public thanks and the press was forbidden to mention them by name after acts of valour.[61] The political far right advocated a still more severe policy and called for the removal of all Jews from the armed forces. The General Staff rejected the advice.[62] But it maintained its ban on promoting any Jew higher than the rank of ensign (*praporshchik*).

In April 1915 the high command made a sensational claim about an incident of Jewish collaboration with the enemy. Army investigators accused Jewish residents in Kuzhi, a tiny village in Courland province, of having sheltered the advancing German units before they occupied the district. Arrests and beatings of the 'guilty' Jews followed. The General Staff endorsed the story and ordered the immediate expulsion of all the Jews from Kovno and Courland provinces. Kuzhi became a byword for the internal threat to Imperial security.[63] Such torments in the war zone were no mere regional sideshow. They disturbed the already unstable foundations of society. They marked politics at the time and the memory of the military leadership's barbaric treatment of fellow Romanov subjects never faded. Victimizers as well as victims were brutalized, and the message was spread and amplified that violence was a normal part of life. It was a message that would continue to be delivered in 1917 and subsequent years.

5. GOVERNMENT SHACKLED: THE FAILURE OF THE MINISTERS' REVOLT

The Imperial Army's savagery against the Jews in the Great War was the most barbaric episode of anti-Semitism in the twentieth century before the Nazi Holocaust. It was the crashing wave in a tide of brutalization that swept over the entire war zone. The soldiers learned through military discipline and combat experience that might was right. Many troops were involved in the outrages against innocent civilians. In both urban and rural settings the social atmosphere was increasingly explosive. Living conditions for most people severely deteriorated because of food shortages, maladministration, migratory pressure and loss of family members to the war.

Fear was expressed in confidential cabinet discussions that the situation could easily spin out of control – and the General Staff's indifference to the injustice and disorder intensified the concern. In the Duma there were several deputies who refused to still their voices. Two of them, Alexander Kerensky and Naftali Fridman, travelled to the Eastern front to examine the situation for themselves. Kerensky and Fridman easily discovered the army's claim that Jews had enabled the German seizure of Kuzhi was false.[1] On 19 July 1915 they and the Menshevik deputy Nikolai Chkheidze spoke out at the Duma against the lies of military commanders. The Kuzhi outrage scandalized a wide segment of public opinion.[2] Whatever was said at the parliament or written in the press, however, only Nicholas had the authority to step in and halt the army's anti-Semitic brutality. His own prejudice against Jews made him shrink from taking action, and he hated to impugn the behaviour of the high command, but the publicity about Kuzhi was hard for him to ignore.

Nicholas also had to take the international reaction into account. Finance Minister Bark had gone to Paris and London at the beginning of 1915 to raise loans from the Allies. He learned that the French and the British governments were chary of being seen to bail out the Russian finances while Jewish people were suffering so much at the hands of Nicholas and his armed forces. Lord Kitchener, secretary of state for war, reinforced the message. He badly wanted to sustain the Russian armed forces but could not help them if Nicholas proved intransigent.[3] Bark made overtures to senior figures in the Rothschild family. Édouard de Rothschild, who was on the Banque de France council, and his uncle Edmond stipulated the need for changes in Russia's policy towards its Jewish subjects.[4] Leopold de Rothschild in London delivered the same message: if Russia wanted the money, there had to be changes in the treatment of its Jews.[5]

On returning from western Europe Bark explained to Nicholas the dire budgetary consequences that would occur unless he altered policy.[6] He issued the same warning at the Council of Ministers, no longer using the civilized language of his talks with the Rothschilds. He told of his difficulties with 'the horde of discontented Yids'. He blamed 'world Jewry' for 'the revolutionary wave' that was sweeping across Russia.[7] Bark argued, on practical rather than moral grounds, that the high command's behaviour was a disaster. Other ministers highlighted the needless chaos caused by the refugee tide. Jews from the emptied shtetls had arrived in the eastern parts of the Pale only to be refused permission to stay. Russians and Ukrainians in Poltava and Chernigov provinces had initially welcomed them as tragic victims. But the kindliness faded when local prices increased as more and more people chased a limited amount of goods.[8] The civilian authorities panicked. Ten thousand newcomers were ordered out of Poltava province. Some of them tried to move further eastward, which would soon mean they would be 'filling up Russia' in breach of the limits of the Pale. The cabinet discussion, however, was a disappointment for Bark because a majority of ministers insisted on maintaining the Pale and its regulations intact. The decision was that Jews should stay somewhere within its boundary. Failing that, they should emigrate.[9]

Nobody clarified how any Jewish family could ever hope to travel through the lines of the Eastern front or across a North Sea patrolled by German submarines. The deliberations in government were yet another sign of the carelessness of Romanov rule. Anti-Semitism had an official imprimatur.

Three of the empire's richest Jewish businessmen – Alexander Ginzburg, Boris Kamenka and Mark Varshavski – sought out Bark for talks. Their opinions could not be ignored while ministers relied on their cooperation in matters of finance, commerce and industry. They warned, as if Bark needed to be told, that Russia would have difficulties in obtaining fresh foreign loans in the light of the army's abuses.[10] On hearing about this, Nicholas agreed on the need for a lighter policy towards Jews in the war zone. In March 1915 he asked Bark to go to general headquarters at Baranovichi and explain the need for change to Grand Duke Nikolai Nikolaevich. Justice Minister Ivan Shcheglovitov would accompany Bark – evidently Nicholas was trying to balance Bark's anti-Semitic advice with Shcheglovitov's arch-conservative views.[11] Yanushkevich was less than welcoming at general headquarters. After requesting Bark to state his business, he exited to confer with Nikolai Nikolaevich before letting Bark speak with him. Nevertheless Nikolai Nikolaevich proved open to reason. He indicated that he did not share Yanushkevich's spy mania about the Jews (despite having let it run to riot), and he agreed to release the hostages.[12]

When they talked about the military situation, Yanushkevich disclosed that the army was suffering from a severe shell shortage. The General Staff had until then kept this a secret. Even more stunning for Bark was Yanushkevich's comment that the General Staff had decided on the need for a further strategic retreat deep into Imperial territory. The implication was that Russia could be facing complete defeat. When Shcheglovitov reported back to the Council of Ministers, disquiet was voiced about the high command's entire performance. Goremykin was horrified: for him it was no business of the cabinet to interfere in military operations or even to express an opinion about them. But he was in a minority, and ministers at their next meeting insisted on being briefed by War Minister Sukhomlinov about the state of the armed forces. Sukhomlinov suggested that Nikolai Nikolaevich was emotionally volatile and no longer fit for his post. He judged that the General Staff had become dysfunctional. As an example, Sukhomlinov said that the high command frequently issued impractical orders for factory production and designated conscription quotas without considering how many recruits it was capable of training.[13]

Duma parties were discontented with the deteriorating situation and the press began to raise concerns about military competence and economic performance. A group of the less conservative ministers led by Krivoshein and Sazonov urged that the emperor had to keep the Duma on side by changing the ministerial line-up. Even the nationalist right-winger Rukhlov agreed with them. They all sought the removal of Justice Minister Shcheglovitov, Internal Affairs Minister Maklakov, Ober-Procurator Sabler and War Minister Sukhomlinov.

How to bring this about was less than obvious. The plotters decided that Goremykin had to be brought into the scheme and that Goremykin should present it to the emperor. A tense conversation took place between Goremykin and the ministers before he agreed to send a memorandum to Nicholas, who received him next day at Tsarskoe Selo. This time it was Goremykin who felt the heat. Nicholas was affronted at being told who should or should not belong to the Council of Ministers. He disapproved of the breakdown of cabinet solidarity. He could not conceive of army officers ganging up on other officers, and he expected the same behaviour from his ministers.[14]

But he thought it prudent to remove the four whom the plotters hoped to see fired. Alexei Polivanov, whom Sukhomlinov in 1912 had sacked as his deputy in the War Ministry, was brought back as his replacement.[15] Alexander Khvostov took over the Justice Ministry and Prince Nikolai Shcherbatov the Internal Affairs Ministry. Alexander Samarin was appointed ober-procurator. Nicholas was in a sour mood. He had been dragged into making changes which he felt was an affront to his monarchical dignity, and he refused to make Krivoshein chairman of the Council of Ministers as the conspirators suggested.[16] By keeping Goremykin in post, Nicholas wanted to retain his own full control. The new justice minister, Khvostov, was a notorious Judeophobe who would stem any tendency for gentleness on the Jewish question.[17] Nicholas had made the minimum of compromises in the ministerial line-up. The prospect of reconciliation between Duma and government was dimmer than many at the time assumed.

On Sunday 14 June 1915, halfway through his purge of the cabinet, he summoned the remaining ministers to a joint session with the General Staff at Baranovichi. It was an extraordinary event, being the first meeting of cabinet and high command since the start of hostilities. Until then the high command had acted as if it could run the empire alone. Krivoshein assured fellow ministers in advance that Nicholas had at last decided to take their complaints to heart. The proceedings took place next to a big birch wood by the railway siding. Archpresbyter Georgi Shavelski conducted a service in a field church at which ministers and commanders said their prayers together. It was a glorious summer day, and a marquee had been put up for lunch beside the Imperial train. The mood was buoyant and Nicholas was in the chair. Agreeing to recall the Duma, he signed a proclamation calling on his subjects to continue the fight and crush the invading enemy.[18]

Changing ministerial personnel was an important but still secondary requirement unless Yanushkevich was removed from the General Staff but Grand Duke Nikolai Nikolaevich was unbending even though, according to officers at the General Staff, Nicholas himself had tried to persuade him.[19] Nikolai Nikolaevich refused to strip himself of the Yanushkevich and Danilov pairing.[20] In another environment this might have been reason for disgruntled ministers to press for Nikolai Nikolaevich's own removal. He was in truth a languid supreme commander who had an aversion to contact with wounded officers and men and understood little about trenches for the basic reason that he never visited any of them.[21] But his openness to the idea of political reform made friends for him in the government and the Duma, where he was seen as the liberal Romanov. Ministers feared that if he left the high command, someone even less desirable might be appointed to succeed him.

While holding on to Yanushkevich and Danilov, the Grand Duke accepted the need for a different military policy. Before the Baranovichi meeting, after weeks of demands by ministers, he had already issued an order that regimental commanders of troops who carried out pogroms should themselves be brought to field courts-martial, and on 20 June 1915 he proclaimed a complete cessation of the deportations. Russian forces were told that when they had to yield ground, they should only destroy property that might be of use to the occupying enemy. Driving people from their homes was to become an exceptional occurrence, and expellees were to be allowed to carry a sufficiency of food stocks with them. Families should not be split up as they departed.[22]

These changes came too late for the hundreds of thousands of innocent Imperial inhabitants who had suffered death, torture and expulsion at the hands of Russian troops – and it by no means brought an end to the ill-treatment of Jews in the war zone. Chernigov and Poltava provinces were crowded with refugees from the rest of the Jewish Pale of Settlement, and the provincial administrations intensified their warnings about the explosive consequences for public order. The swelling population caused an increased demand for food and other necessities and there was a rise in local prices. Discontent grew and with it the potential for an outbreak of further anti-Semitic pogroms. Internal Affairs Minister Shcherbatov issued a circular that opened three provinces – Penza, Tambov and Voronezh – outside the Pale of Settlement to Jews in desperate need of housing. The Council of

Ministers gave approval despite recognizing the questionable legality of a measure that essentially shifted the bounds of the Pale. The decision predictably had the inflationary effect already observable elsewhere. As Jewish families moved eastward from the Pale, food became more expensive there and violent disturbances occurred in town markets.[23]

The model of state power and governance that prevailed in the first full year of the fighting was crumbling. On 24 July 1915 an exasperated Shcherbatov complained that he could not improve his links with the Duma because the high command acted as if it was in sole charge.[24] Goremykin no longer raised an objection. He recognized that the cabinet majority was justified in querying the General Staff's judgement of possibilities and needs.

The Duma had debated the Kuzhi scandal just days earlier, and the cabinet seized the moment to assert itself against the generals. On 30 July 1915 Bark tried to show that the Finance Ministry could conduct economic warfare on Germany. Although Russian commerce was blocked from the Mediterranean, this at least had the effect of depriving the Germans of wheat and rye from Russia and Ukraine. Bark wanted to tighten the screws. He proposed that Russia buy up the entire Bulgarian and Romanian harvest. He treated it as a serious project, working out how much it would cost and bringing it up at the Council of Ministers. But Transport Minister Rukhlov pointed out that Romania's railway network was incapable of conveying so vast a quantity of freight to the Russian Empire. The Imperial state budget, for which Bark held responsibility, was also on the brink of collapse. The idea was quietly forgotten without further discussion. Bark was on firmer ground when repeating the case for revising policy on the Jewish question. The Imperial budget was unsustainable without financial assistance from abroad. Foreign loans were vital to prevent total budgetary collapse, and Jewish bankers in France and Great Britain refused to lend money while Jews in the Russian Empire were being treated so abominably.[25]

The same cabinet session discussed the Great Retreat and there was much criticism of the General Staff's performance. The new War Minister Polivanov – no admirer of the high command – painted a shocking picture for fellow ministers. The army leadership at GHQ was hysterical. The armed forces were demoralized. Desertions were increasing. Troops were surrendering to the enemy. The General Staff found it convenient to blame the government rather than admit to its own incompetence. The high command had begun to rely on repeating the strategy followed by General Kutuzov to defeat Napoleon's invading forces by surrendering vast swathes of territory after emptying them of people and provisions. The idea was to stretch the German supply lines until they snapped. The cabinet was dismayed by the plan. It was pointed out that the French in 1812 had advanced on a narrow front and the Russian scorched-earth withdrawal had consequently affected few communities under Romanov rule. In the current war the retreat was taking place along a vast line stretching from Courland to Galicia. The General Staff's primitive grasp of Russian history had given rise to a strategy that devastated a huge number of homes and enterprises for no military benefit.[26]

Rancour persisted at the Council of Ministers on 4 August 1915. Alexander Krivoshein tore into the high command's performance. Internal Affairs Minister Nikolai Shcherbatov focused on the resistance to the widening of the age range for conscription. Shcherbatov went on to describe the appalling fate of deported Jews and complained: 'Our efforts to make the high command see sense have been futile.'

A final decision on policy was postponed to the next meeting.[27] Two days later, the 'Jewish question' was still dividing the cabinet.[28] Goremykin tried to close the discussion. After having managed to persuade Nicholas to make a previously unimaginable concession, he shuddered at the idea of asking for more. Other ministers agreed with Goremykin. This prompted Finance Minister Bark to ask how he could be expected to raise loans abroad when Jewish owners of big foreign banks complained that nothing was being done to stop Cossack troops from tormenting the Jews in the Pale of Settlement. The Council of Ministers adopted the compromise of changing the rules of the Pale without revoking the law. Apart from fearing to push Nicholas too far, ministers dreaded uproar among right-wing Duma deputies if the matter was taken to the Duma for approval.

The semi-concession to Jews was not the only momentous outcome of the meeting on 6 August. Goremykin stunned the cabinet with the news that Nicholas intended to leave Tsarskoe Selo and base himself at general headquarters, nearly 500 miles to the west, to take his cousin's place as supreme commander-in-chief. Goremykin and Polivanov had not changed the mind of an emperor who continued to regret not having stayed on campaign with his forces in 1904. Nicholas also hated anyone criticizing the high command. Polivanov resented this. The General Staff was in chaos after the defeats of 1914–15, and further defeats would bring the monarchy itself into disrepute. Ministers were frustrated about the limited scope of the government's power.

An absentee emperor would not improve the situation. But Nicholas insisted on making himself supreme commander-in-chief. There was an outcry in the cabinet and Krivoshein rallied support for an overture to be made to the emperor.[29]

Ministers were livid about the emperor's failure to consult their opinion.[30] Russia's semi-autocrat was behaving like an autocrat. But there was nothing that would divert Nicholas from his chosen path: he was the tsar and his mind was made up. The awful prospect arose of a continued split between military and civil agencies of power while their sovereign quarantined himself at the front.

The ongoing strategic crisis also agitated the Council of Ministers, which began considering secret plans for the evacuation of Petrograd.[31] Asked for his opinion, the emperor forbade the transfer to Nizhni Novgorod of treasures from his palaces or from the Hermitage art collection. But he ordered Goremykin and Nikolai Nikolaevich to hold discussions about the fate of the capital. Tongues were already wagging in Petrograd restaurants about official intentions. The cabinet met on 18 August to review the situation. Ministers agreed on the need to avert a public panic and to tighten their precautions on secrecy. Their own anxiety, however, continued to grow, especially when War Minister Polivanov informed them that if the Germans managed to take Riga, military zeppelins could soon be flying over the Russian capital. The cabinet shelved any decision when it was pointed out that the relocation of Petrograd factories would involve the loss of half of their productive capacity – and a depletion of armaments output would be disastrous.[32]

The cabinet met again on 20 August 1915 with the emperor in the chair. Nicholas was still determined to base himself at general headquarters as supreme commander-in-chief. In despair, Krivoshein asked him at least to retain Grand Duke Nikolai Nikolaevich as his deputy in the high command. Nicholas refused. But he assured the cabinet that he would not interfere in the General Staff's waging of the war. He knew he lacked the professional competence. He thought, though, that his presence near the front would raise morale at every level of the armed forces. He intended to retain Goremykin as chairman of the Council of Ministers and requested all current ministers to stay in their posts.[33] His self-confidence and sense of dynastic duty were undeniable. The ill-advised nature of his decision, however, was obvious to everyone but himself.

The cabinet majority submitted a written petition to the emperor.[34] This was as close as they could go in expressing an objection without infringing the etiquette of rulership.[35] The ministerial plotters had met on 21 August at Sazonov's home. Neither Goremykin nor his friend Khvostov was invited. Finance Minister Bark drafted the petition. War Minister Polivanov declined to sign but only because he thought it would be some kind of breach in military discipline. Bark's wording emphasized that 'we are losing confidence in the possibility of serving you and the Motherland'.[36]

On 22 August 1915 Nicholas left for general headquarters after a last consultation with ministers in the Winter Palace and a church service at Tsarskoe Selo. Whilst he recognized that he lacked the expertise needed to tell the General Staff how to fight, he had always believed in his duty and capacity to raise morale among officers and men by staying close to the front. He opted to transfer Nikolai Nikolaevich to lead Russian forces in the Caucasus sector. Yanushkevich would depart with the grand duke. The high command had already decided to move headquarters more than 200 miles eastward from Baranovichi to a railway siding on the outskirts of Mogilëv by the river Dnieper on 21 August 1915.[37] Nicholas was met there by his cousin Nikolasha in the middle of the afternoon on 23 August 1915.[38] They had always got on well and the demoted grand duke may even have been pleased about no longer having to carry the blame for military reverses. Nicholas then received General Mikhail Alexeev, who had come to Mogilëv four days earlier as the designated successor to Yanushkevich as chief of the General Staff.[39]

Until then Alexeev had commanded the north-west sector of the Eastern front. He was popular with other commanders and the entire officer corps, who looked up to him as a brother.[40] He had performed impressively during the Great Retreat: Alexeev had earned his place in the Russian high command. Broad-shouldered and moustachioed, Alexeev walked with a slight stoop, his head lowered as if deep in thought.[41] He had had a meritorious career from the Russo-Turkish war of 1877–8 through to the Russo-Japanese war of 1904–5 and beyond. He had risen from a humble social background. He was unostentatious and laconic. Not everyone welcomed his appointment. Some asked how he could attend French military manoeuvres if he spoke no foreign language. (In reality the likelihood of his visiting France before the end of the war was non-existent.) Such was Alexeev's modesty that people forgot that he was one of the outstanding graduates of Russia's military academies. He was a master of the latest technical and logistical knowledge and had a stupendous memory. Alexeev never shouted at men or officers and was a general who led by example. 'Swine' and 'scoundrels' were his worst expletives that anyone heard when he was annoyed by poor performance. A devout Christian, he crossed himself before starting a meal and regularly attended evening services.[42]

Next day Nicholas acquainted himself with the town, visiting its cathedral and the provincial administration. Before returning to general headquarters he signed the order giving himself the supreme command. He also took a walk on the far side of the river Dnieper. In the evening he played dominoes. He was starting as he meant to go on by leaving the daily staff work to Alexeev. They instantly formed a warm partnership, often playing innocuous card games like Nain Jaune in the evenings.[43]

Ministers felt abandoned and frustrated. When the cabinet met on 24 August Krivoshein and Polivanov repeated a proposal to create a War Council. If Nicholas was going to absent himself from Petrograd and work from general headquarters, the need had only increased for a body to coordinate decisions at front and rear while providing the government with the authority that it deserved. Krivoshein no longer tried to contain his anger. He foresaw catastrophe for the empire unless changes were made. Kiev province was already being ordered to evacuate its entire population. Krivoshein exclaimed: 'It took a thousand years to create and build Russia and in the space of an hour various bold military commanders, acting on an unknown order, are wiping it from the face of the earth!'[44]

There was the same presentiment of horror inside the Duma where a loose coalition was formed to press for basic reform. Known as the Progressive Block it brought together the Kadets, Progressists and the left wing of the Octobrists. While continuing to have their disagreements, all agreed that the war effort would continue to deteriorate until Nicholas agreed to allow the formation of a 'government of confidence' that would undertake a series of political changes including an amnesty for those convicted of offences on the basis of their politics or religion. Freedom of conscience should be proclaimed. The Polish territories should be granted autonomy and the curtailments on the rights of Poles abolished. A conciliatory policy should be instituted towards the Finns. Anti-Jewish legislation should be repealed. The Ukrainian-language press should be legalized and persecution of the Uniate Church should be ended. Approval should be given to the Duma's call for local administrative bodies to receive widened powers.[45]

Nicholas had departed for Mogilëv without giving instructions as to what to do about these demands which had come from the heart of the Duma. The Council of Ministers discussed the situation on 26 August 1915. Goremykin said the Block's internal divisions made it liable to rapid collapse, and he argued against taking its demands seriously.[46] But he failed to persuade the meetings and Kharitonov was deputed to hold exploratory talks on their behalf with the Block's leaders. Kharitonov reported back on the terms laid down by the parliamentarians. Most notable was Pavel Milyukov's requirement for a fresh cabinet that would include representatives of the Block.[47] Milyukov had a political profile that was unlikely to reassure the emperor. He was a notable historian of Russia whose struggle against the Romanov autocracy had twice landed him in prison in his younger days. In 1905 he had founded the Constitutional-Democratic Party. In 1906 he had called on people to refuse to pay taxes or obey calls for military service. In subsequent years he had tempered his tactics while remaining dedicated to the goal of turning the Russian Empire into a constitutional monarchy.

War Minister Polivanov wanted to continue the talks on the grounds that the purposes of the government and the Block were not fundamentally incompatible. Goremykin, the reluctant premier, disagreed. Krivoshein, who wanted to see Progressive Block leaders made ministers, lost his temper. He argued that Nicholas had to be told to appoint a new premier with the authority to choose the composition of the cabinet. This understandably annoyed Goremykin, who nevertheless consented to put the collective case in Mogilëv.[48]

On 1 September Goremykin returned empty-handed: Nicholas had turned down his request to resign and ordered ministers to stay in post. Krivoshein asked Goremykin how he could permit himself to stay on as premier.[49] This failed to inhibit Goremykin who continued to serve a monarch who was determined to defy his critics. On 3 September 1915 Nicholas prorogued the Duma.[50] The timing was not accidental. The emperor no longer felt worried about Allied opinion after Bark on his latest trip to western Europe finally secured financial credits from western Europe.[51] Nicholas, concluding that he no longer had to feel bothered about criticism by Russia's liberals, set his face against introducing Progressive Block members into the administration. Distrust between the emperor and the Duma plumbed fresh depths. Goremykin's reputation among cabinet colleagues was in tatters – Foreign Affairs Minister Sazonov thought he had gone off his head.[52] When Duma Chairman Rodzyanko cornered Goremykin, he warned him that he was making a ghastly mistake.[53]

The demoralized Goremykin pleaded with Nicholas to be relieved of the premiership. Nicholas again rejected the request, and Goremykin as usual heeded his sovereign's wishes.[54]

This was Nicholas's last good chance to build a bridge to the Duma majority. Whether such a step would have prevented revolution and the monarchy's collapse is doubtful because long-term problems were already lapping over the walls of the empire's economic capacity, military resilience and social patience. But Nicholas was foolish to discard the opportunity.[55] He was too accustomed to assuming that he could get away with ruling imperiously, and he failed to recognize that he could not control everything in high politics. The signs of this were increasingly evident. Although Nicholas had the right to nominate half of the State Council membership, the Block's leading figures could still stand for election to the other half. In September this had the result of Octobrist Party leader Alexander Guchkov and the business tycoon and liberal Pavel Ryabushinski joining the Council. The Imperial couple were appalled. Alexandra had once written to Nicholas that Guchkov ought to be hanged. She called on him to take proper control: 'You are the master.' Why, she asked him, were individuals such as Guchkov, Ryabushinski and Grigori Weinstein ('a real Jew for sure') being infiltrated into the highest bodies of state?[56]

Nicholas hardly needed any marital prodding. He summoned all his ministers to Mogilëv on 16 September 1915, signalling his annoyance as soon as they alighted their carriage. He made them have breakfast in an ill-kempt trackside buffet. In case they had not yet understood the message, he refrained from inviting them to lunch with him before talks started in the late afternoon. Alexandra would have been proud of him. Whether he was sensible in humbling sincere ministerial dissenters is another matter.[57]

The petition sent to him by ten of his ministers had infuriated him: 'What is this, a strike against me?' Goremykin explained that he had disagreed with the cabinet, and Krivoshein repeated the case for change and was supported by Sazonov. Samarin implored Nicholas: 'Your Majesty, you rebuke us for not wanting to serve you. No, we serve you according to the covenants of our forebears, not out of fear but true to our consciences. And we shan't do anything that is against our consciences.' Nicholas turned red in the face at this. The silence was excruciating. Shcherbatov hoped to ease the situation by venturing that there was a clash of generations inside the government. Goremykin, kindly mannered as ever, found some humour in it all:

'I'd rather clash with a father than a son!' Nicholas declared the session closed after indicating: 'Since we cannot agree on anything I'll return to Tsarskoe Selo and chop this whole question apart'. He shook hands coolly with each minister before they all took the Imperial train back to Petrograd. It was obvious that the cabinet's composition would soon undergo yet another change – but not one that the ministerial critics were likely to approve.[58]

6. PATRIOTIC ASSISTANCE AND PATRIOTIC SUBVERSION: THE WARTIME ACTIVITIES OF CIVIC ORGANIZATIONS

The emperor had never trusted the empire's elected civic bodies. The war hardened his suspicions. He thought there were no lessons the Russian state could learn from countries to the west. The concessions he had made after the revolution of 1905–6 continued to cause him pain. When the London *Times* reporter Stanley Washburn, an American, asked him about this, he replied: 'You are always writing and talking about public opinion but we have no public opinion in Russia.'[1]

But in the first month of the war it was already obvious that the Imperial state was in desperate need of assistance for its war effort and this could happen only at a political and financial price. One of the leading liberals, Prince Georgi Lvov, approached Goremykin with a plan to create all-empire unions of zemstvos and town administrations. Introduced in the 1860s in Alexander II's series of reforms after the Crimean War, elected zemstvos provided the rural social and welfare services which had been woefully inadequate. The city and town councils (or dumas) were elected by urban residents and had existed since the eighteenth century but it was only in 1870 that the suffrage was extended to all tax-payers. Zemstvos and dumas oversaw agencies in education, healthcare, veterinary provision, the economy, food supplies, insurance, roads and charities. They had a proud record of relief services in the years of epidemics and famine.[2] But both Nicholas and his father Alexander III feared that they might undermine monarchical rule if they were allowed to centralize their activities. The wartime emergency in mid-1914 changed Nicholas's mind and, against his instincts, he endorsed Lvov's proposal.[3]

On 9 August 1914 the cabinet agreed on the funds to be made available to the new Union of Zemstvos and the Union of Towns.[4] Anxiety grew that Lvov would exploit the change for his political advantage, and Internal Affairs Minister Maklakov insisted that Lvov's team should stick to humanitarian activity.[5] Prince Georgi Lvov was elected head of the Zemstvos Union. A liberal and a sympathizer with Tolstoy, he was hardly the likeliest organizer of a war effort, but he was also a fervent patriot. Mikhail Chelnokov, Moscow mayor and a brick-factory owner, was his counterpart as head of the Towns Union.[6] Each Union established its central offices in Petrograd and Moscow. The war-wounded and sick were their primary initial focus while the Russian Red Cross gave medical services at the front. By November 1914 the Zemstvos Union was already running 1,700 hospitals.[7] At the end of the year there were 140 cities in the Towns Union, a number that rose to 464 over the following twelve months.[8] The two Unions extended their activities to the front in response to worsening conditions. Field surgery stations, canteens, bathhouses and laundries were set up. Their presence was appreciated by the army commanders from Grand Duke Nikolai Nikolaevich downwards.[9]

The zemstvos also won friends in the rear through their efforts for food supply and welfare. Alexander Zamaraev noticed that the Totma zemstvo was selling oats brought from Siberia. Wives of serving soldiers could buy at a discount.[10] Every zemstvo in the empire was extending its activities.

State funds had always been crucial for this activity. Towards the end of August 1914 Lvov asked for a three-million-rubles subsidy for the Towns Union.[11] Forty-three million rubles had already been disbursed by the Finance Ministry before November 1914.[12] Internal Affairs Minister Nikolai Maklakov warned that the conferences held by the Unions would be used for revolutionary activity. Empress Alexandra agreed, accused Lvov and his like of helping the war effort only to win credit in public opinion and force political concessions from her husband. Liberals and liberal conservatives certainly used the zemstvos and dumas to disseminate their ideas. Their ambition increased. In mid-1915 they brought together the Zemstvos Union and Towns Union in a new organization called Zemgor.[13] Nicholas was recognizing, however grudgingly, that the two Unions performed indispensable work by relieving the pressures on the Red Cross and the pre-war hospital network. The General Staff too supported the need for Zemgor and Chelnokov praised the generals for their support.[14] But State Controller Kharitonov lamented that the high command and the empire as a whole had greater confidence in the Duma and the various elected civic bodies than in the cabinet that Nicholas had appointed.[15]

Zemgor organized public meetings. Although it had to ask permission, the cabinet could seldom refuse if it wanted to retain Zemgor's services. Or as State Controller Kharitonov put it, ministers sought to avoid aggravating the public 'nervousness'.[16] The zemstvos and dumas gained in confidence. Krivoshein even advised Nicholas to improve his image abroad as a forward-thinking monarch by talking directly with Chelnokov.[17] Nicholas seemed to see the logic but his heart was not in changing his ways and he only rarely granted an audience to members of Zemgor.[18] It was not only the monarch who shunned them. Both the Towns Union and the Zemstvos Union encountered obstruction near the front. Chelnokov was to say that the Towns Union was allowed to operate solely on the principle that 'you have the right to sit around over there but you have no right to do anything'.[19]

Internal Affairs Minister Maklakov, like other ultra-conservative ministers, resented giving up any more authority to the Union of Towns than he had to. His ministry tried to deal with cities and towns on an individual basis. According to Chelnokov, the result was financial waste that had been completely avoidable.[20]

Another administrative body was entirely new, created directly by the needs of the war. At the outbreak of war the army leadership was still commissioning all of its own supplies of manufactured goods from greatcoats to guns. Prominent figures led by Alexander Guchkov, Pavel Ryabushinski and Mikhail Tereshchenko argued that this was too staid a way of handling a wartime emergency. They proposed to establish war-industries committees that would help to uncork the bottlenecks. Guchkov, Ryabushinski and Tereshchenko had businesses of their own. They argued that shell shortages and other supply problems could only be tackled when industrialists could form organizations unshackled by governmental control. Entrepreneurs would succeed where ministers and the army leadership had been found wanting. As the military defeats continued, the emperor felt obliged to agree to the call for change, and Guchkov and Ryabushinski assembled the Central War-Industries Committee for the first time on 4 May 1915.[21]

Guchkov was a monarchist conservative who had founded the Octobrist Party in 1905 to lay a path of compromise between the monarch and the State Duma which was about to be elected. He was a restless public figure. He took risks with life and limb, having volunteered to fight on the side of the Boers against British imperialism in southern Africa. He never got on with Nicholas who resented his demands for the Duma to exercise increased influence, and Nicholas exasperated Guchkov by doing little or nothing to reduce the tension between government and Duma. When war came, Nicholas felt more than ever that Guchkov was playing at politics. In promising to redeem the shortfalls in output for military requirements, Guchkov highlighted his own capabilities and pointed to the state's underperformance. The Kadets were wary of him because he had lambasted their policies after the 1905–6 revolutionary upheaval.

The practical performance of the committees was less impressive than they claimed, although it was not entirely their fault. Ministers distrusted Guchkov and his supporters. Many industrialists were wary of joining the committees for fear of ruining their links to government. The result was that even the Central War-Industries Committee, which dwarfed the activity of war-industries committees at lower levels, received only 6.2 per cent of military orders.[22] Committees in Petrograd, Moscow and Kiev received commissions but most of those in the provinces were poorly served – and it was noticeable that small and medium-sized enterprises seldom obtained a contract.[23]

Guchkov continued to use them as a platform for his public activity. In early August 1915, he wrote to Goremykin calling for a change of political course. Goremykin the ultra-loyalist treated this as sheer cheek and did not reply. Transport Minister Rukhlov said Guchkov was turning the Central War-Industries Committee into 'some kind of second government' and putting out appeals to factory workers. Justice Minister Khvostov added that the Kadets had conquered their hostility to Guchkov because they saw him as someone to lead a battalion on Tsarskoe Selo. He warned that the Central War-Industries Committee could become 'a dangerous weapon in the political game.'[24] Guchkov was making visits to army commanders at the front and criticizing the state's performance in the rear. When Guchkov met with junior officers, he seemingly tried to undermine confidence in the government.[25]

The Okhrana, the secret police force of the Russian Empire, kept him under surveillance.[26] He openly canvassed for factory workforces to receive their own representation in the war-industries committees.[27] The cabinet felt it could not say no and risk damage to the output of military equipment. But ministers still worried that the workers' elected delegates would cause trouble.

By 1917 there were fifty-eight workers' groups across the country.[28] Bolsheviks initially dismissed the committees as a trick to get the working class to boost production for 'the imperialist war'. But they changed their stance after realizing that the committees offered an opportunity for political organization and publicity. When the election was held in September 1915, they won places for themselves despite accusations of some kind of chicanery. But it was the Mensheviks who held the majority.[29] Kuzma Gvozdev, a Menshevik working at the Ericsson Telephone Factory in Petrograd, emerged in the leading position as negotiator and spokesman.[30] Ryabushinski, while promoting the need for the war-industries committees, retained a concern that the workers' groups might exploit the opportunity to form 'some kind of soviet of workers' deputies at the top' as they had done in 1905–6.[31]

Justice Minister Khvostov had exactly the same worry.[32] The Okhrana was agitated enough to keep an informant, the Menshevik Vladimir Abrosimov, in the Workers Group.[33] But while the government tried to tighten its hold on the war-industries committees, its authority weakened in other parts of the war effort. Duma Chairman Rodzyanko had called since spring 1915 for the creation of an agency with general oversight of military supply that would combine ministers, Duma and State Council politicians, Zemgor leaders and stock-exchange dignitaries. This won approval from the General Staff and the armaments industry.[34] At a time when the war was going badly on the Eastern front, Nicholas felt compelled to agree.[35] The new agency was to be known as the Special Conference of Defence and on 22 August 1915 Nicholas himself chaired its deliberations. Although the Special Conference was too big to get into the minutiae of planning decisions, its subcommittees grew adept at preparing the ground for them.[36] The Special Conference appeared an oasis of conciliation at a moment when the emperor was rejecting the Progressive Block and intending to prorogue the Duma. When departing for Mogilëv, Nicholas entrusted War Minister Polivanov with chairing the agency – and it was laid down that the agency would operate independently of the cabinet as a whole.[37]

7. ORDERING THE REAR: AN ABSENT EMPEROR AND THE RISE OF POLITICAL OPPOSITION

The emperor's presence at the front slackened his grip on the daily business of government. Ministers had warned him this would happen, and his departure left them feeling abandoned and underappreciated. They were also angered on discovering that the police were snooping on them. When seven of them held an informal discussion at Sazonov's apartment, a policeman posted himself at the door. It seemed that Nicholas – or perhaps the Internal Affairs Ministry – saw reason to distrust them.[1]

Despite being 500 miles from Petrograd, Nicholas assumed he could keep effective touch with affairs in the capital by summoning ministers to Mogilëv for personal consultations. Goremykin, coughing and spluttering, made two trips before Christmas. Nicholas anyway received daily briefs about governmental business and Alexandra kept watch over Petrograd politics on his behalf. She stuffed her letters and telegrams with derogatory comments about Duma leaders and with advice about whom to appoint to the cabinet. She missed her husband terribly and urged him at least to move headquarters nearer to Petrograd.[2] Some people whispered that she had become the true ruler and it was true that sometimes Nicholas did follow her advice on cabinet appointments. But Nicholas ruled as he wished and the central governance of empire, always ramshackle, became more disjointed and ineffective.

Krivoshein, having spilled out his feelings to the emperor, was fired on 26 October 1915. Bark, one of Krivoshein's cabinet allies, stayed at the Finance Ministry but was not granted an audience with Nicholas until the end of December. At last on 18 January 1916 Goremykin was allowed to retire from the cabinet. Nicholas was sorry to have to let 'good old Goremykin' depart.[3]

But he wasn't minded to appoint a more dynamic Council of Ministers. His next premier was Boris Stürmer, a former provincial governor of right-wing views who belonged to the State Council.[4] Sixty-seven years old, people remarked on his tendency to doze off in the middle of conversations.[5] Few people had ever found him impressive and his way of taking tiny steps rather than a comfortable stride seemed comical.[6] But the emperor and empress thought he passed their main requirement for the post: he was endlessly obsequious and studiously avoided contradicting either of them. They overlooked his inexperience at the highest level and lack of imagination about what to do about the empire's multiple crises. Soon after occupying the premiership he added the Ministry of Internal Affairs to his duties but his personal ambitiousness could not disguise the sheer decline in the cabinet's competence. Liberals were predictably infuriated by the latest cabinet reshuffle. At the Kadet party congress in February 1916 Andrei Shingarëv declared: 'We need to take the measure of Stürmer's nature once and for all: he's a hundred times worse for us than Goremykin.'[7] Contempt for the government peaked in the Duma.

Nicholas, however, believed obstinately in the rightness of his decisions. He enjoyed his time in Mogilëv. He had had his son and heir Alexei with him there until mid-December 1915. They slept in the same room on camp beds. Alexei, one of nature's cheerful souls, raised Nicholas's spirits. It was with regret that Nicholas decided that he had to release him back to Alexandra's care. Nicholas missed his exuberance and looked morosely round a bedroom in which only one camp bed remained.[8] In Petrograd, meanwhile, Stürmer battled against the surging difficulties in the Russian war effort. War Minister Polivanov had told the Council of Ministers on 26 August 1915 that a further great round of call-ups was necessary to replace the losses at the front. Other ministers counselled caution. Nikolai Shcherbatov at the Internal Affairs Ministry reminded Polivanov about the 'sharp discontent' that had broken out in the first recruitment rounds. The riots of 1914 had been no accident: peasants resented authorities who took so much and gave so little in return. An eruption of popular fury grew likelier as the war dragged on.

The instruction from Stürmer was for provincial governors to use their powers to keep the lid on trouble. Something akin to martial law had already operated in at least half of the entire empire before the outbreak of war. In 1912, 63.3 million people – nearly half the number of subjects of the tsar – lived under 'reinforced protection', which meant that the governor in any one of these provinces could act in disregard of zemstvos, dumas and the normal rule of law.[9]

Governors in such provinces had acted like mini-tsars in peacetime. As the administrative edifice crumbled after 1914, some of them coped with their food-supply troubles by ignoring orders issued by ministers and banning the 'export' of goods beyond the provincial boundary.[10] The high command was a different matter, and many governors felt savagely treated by its decisions. Civilian administration throughout the war zone – and in many provinces beyond its limits – was reduced to chaos by the surging tide of deportees and refugees. No governor could alleviate problems in rail transport while the military authorities were piling men, horses and stores onto the trains. The high command continued to omit to give timely alerts about army shipments. Tsar-like governors were mere minions in the eyes of generals. The nearer a province was to the front line, the likelier its governor was to experience humiliating treatment. Minsk and Smolensk provinces reported severe food shortages even at a time when the army possessed a sufficiency of supplies.[11] In Pskov province army commanders were personally disrespectful towards the governor, while in Estland province (now northern Estonia) they deported all the Lutheran pastors, leaving no one who could conduct baptisms, weddings or funerals.[12]

Internal Affairs Minister Shcherbatov was infuriated. As he saw it, the only solution was to scrap the entire war-zone framework of rule with its privileges for the high command: 'Dual power in the heart of Russia. An unbearable situation for the governors: they are pushed around by the military but they are the ones who bear responsibility in the eyes of the country.'[13] But the same governors were still able to oppress the inhabitants of their provinces. The lands of the Romanovs had a reputation of being a police state but Russia's law enforcers were more thinly spread than in more industrialized countries to the west. Great Britain, home of European liberalism, had seven times the number of policemen per head of the population than the Russian Empire, where rural self-rule was the norm. The peasantry had traditions of respect, fairness, compensation and retribution that had developed over the centuries. A peasant who infringed them could be roughly handled, even beaten up or killed – and land captains usually knew better than to intervene. After the 1905–6 revolutionary upsurge, everyone from the towns was wary of disturbing peace and quiet in the countryside unless accompanied by an army detachment.

Much in fact continued to operate as normal at the lowest levels of Imperial governance. Alexander Zamaraev trudged into town on 2 December to pay his annual taxes.[14] The district (*volost*) machinery of administration and justice worked normally. Zamaraev noted that the land captain continued to have influence over who might be elected to office.[15] Peasants were still not the free agents of their fate. Zamaraev accepted his situation. He was lucky in being too old for the military draft even though he said he would have gone if called up. That day in town he conscientiously paid his fiscal dues as well as those of others who had entrusted their money to him.[16] Policing was heaviest in the bigger urban centres but control was not easily realized. The pay for gendarmes was poor and they had always taken bribes to supplement their income. At the same time they were thuggish enforcers of law and order. Their unpopularity increased in wartime as they hunted down evaders of the draft. The question was often asked as to why able-bodied gendarmes themselves were not made to fight at the front. There was a flood of men from the police ranks wanting to move into better-paid and less unpopular occupations. Many gendarmes took jobs as railway loaders.[17]

All political parties were strictly policed. The Okhrana had already penetrated their leaderships and reported in detail on their plans and considerations. There were gradations in how parties were handled. The Octobrists and Kadets were not molested by arrests because it was recognized that they at least supported the war effort. They remained dangerous critics of the Imperial authorities, however, and a watch was kept over their activities. Confidential reports were passed to the Ministry of Internal Affairs, usually within hours of a meeting, and Nicholas regularly received the summary analysis. As for the parties of the political right, the Okhrana quietly looked after the Union of the Russian People and distributed subsidies from a secret 'reptile fund' which it used to subsidize the right-wing press.[18] The rational judgement was made that there was no need to subject such parties to the same degree of surveillance because they were reactionary rather than subversive – their main displeasure with Nicholas lay in his fondness for Rasputin and his reluctance to follow his instincts and crush the politicians who argued for democratic reform.[19]

It was the socialists – Mensheviks, Socialist-Revolutionaries and Bolsheviks – who were most monitored. Although some of their groups advocated defence against the Central Powers, every socialist faction opposed the government's goal of grabbing new territory for the empire.

They were united in hostility to 'imperialism'. Among the Bolshevik groups, one went further than the rest of them. Its leader Vladimir Lenin, Bolshevism's founder, even called for Russia's military defeat as a prime objective, and he called for the same policy to be adopted by foreign Marxists towards their own governments in all the belligerent countries. Exiled in Switzerland, he was shunned by most of the fellow members of his faction as a reckless extremist. Bolsheviks in the Duma had joined with Mensheviks and Trudoviks (the parliamentary group that included Socialist-Revolutionaries) in refusing to vote for war credits. Although they were only a small number of Duma deputies, the authorities did not ignore the Bolshevik capacity to wreak serious trouble. They had led the revolutionary uprising in Moscow in 1905 and were capable of re-emerging as a mortal threat to the monarchy.

On 7 November 1914 Justice Minister Shcheglovitov informed the cabinet that all five Bolshevik deputies to the State Duma had been arrested. The Okhrana had been tipped off about a secret gathering across the Finnish border north of Petrograd from which a haul of pamphlets was confiscated calling for the defeat of the Imperial Army.[20] A week later Goremykin noted that the arrests had sparked 'disturbances' among industrial workers and students.[21] Put on trial for subversion in February 1915, the deputies were sentenced to exile in eastern Siberia.

The Okhrana had long recognized that totally eliminating the revolutionary parties was unrealistic. The strategy was to confuse, demoralize and reduce their active membership, prioritizing the arrest of troublesome leaders. It didn't always work in the way they wanted. Pëtr Sudakov, a Menshevik metal turner in Petrograd who tried to cement cooperation between Mensheviks and Bolsheviks was taken into custody in autumn 1915. But the Okhrana had failed to take into account the warmth felt toward Sudakov by the capital's workers who valued his efforts in establishing their sickness insurance scheme. Internal Affairs Minister Shcherbatov had to admit to the cabinet that the arrest was a mistake which was causing unrest in factories. There were complaints that the Okhrana had lost touch with the situation.[22] War Minister Polivanov blamed the arrests for a strike by 50,000 workers at the Putilov Works in Petrograd. He argued that the police action had needlessly exacerbated hostility to the government and depleted vital military production.[23]

Hoping to increase its funds and the number of personnel available at its disposal, the Okhrana had its own incentive to report to the authorities of the threat posed in the most alarming terms. But there was no doubt that discontent was rising. One year of fighting had been enough to seed thoughts inside governing circles that the war might have been a terrible mistake. At various soirées in the summer of 1915, seditious talk was rife. At one, Nicholas's favourite 'holy man' Rasputin was reported as saying 'the war must be stopped'. At another, Alexander Guchkov, the Octobrist Party leader, predicted a revolution which would bring Nikolai Nikolaevich to power as Russia's first constitutional monarch. Guchkov felt safe in saying all this in front of Foreign Affairs Minister Sazonov – and indeed of Anna Vyrubova.[24] Guchkov had spent years trying to bring about deeper political reform in Russia and he despaired of this coming about while his current sovereign occupied the throne.

8. ECONOMIC MANAGEMENT: INDUSTRIAL CONCENTRATION, PRICE INFLATION AND GROWING FOOD SHORTAGES

By early October 1915 even the most patriotic and confident minister had to accept that the empire was in for a long war. A cabinet discussion recorded the abandonment of the 'naïve belief' that the conflict would be a short one.[1] As the war went on the pressure on trade at home and abroad became intense. Transport, industrial supply and food security were all compromised.

The Turks had closed the Bosporus to Russian ships. Exit from the Baltic Sea was barred by the German navy. Although the empire was not fully landlocked, commerce across the North Sea from Archangel was disrupted by patrolling German submarines, and anyway the single-track railway from Petrograd to the White Sea was not complete until 1916 despite the use of German and Austro-Hungarian POWs to hasten the work.[2] Shipping was untroubled from Vladivostok to Japan, Canada and the United States, but the Pacific trade carried only a tiny proportion of Russian exports and imports, and the Trans-Siberian railway took nearly thirty days to and from Petrograd and Moscow with the government mandating a priority of goods for the military. The land route by rail remained open from Finland through to Sweden and Denmark, and Russian entrepreneurs and bankers maintained their old contacts across Scandinavia.[3] Commerce was also conducted with Romania and, until autumn 1915, with Bulgaria.[4] Although these active outlets eased the problems of international economic constriction, they could never match the pulsating arteries of transport that the empire had enjoyed when its ships could ply the Black and Baltic Seas and its rail freight had direct access via the Polish lands to central Europe.

Russia was not the only power affected by economic warfare. Even Great Britain, whose Royal Navy dominated the seas, was subjected to German submarine attacks on its merchant shipping. Germany itself was in greater jeopardy because British warships pinned the German merchant fleet in port. German cities depended heavily upon food imports and Russia was no longer one of its crucial suppliers. The American administration's hostility to Germany's cause became acute after a German submarine sank the ocean liner *Lusitania* in May 1915, and Germany's urban consumers complained about the emptying shelves in stores. With industry also running out of crucial raw materials, the German war machine was threatened with a ruinous rundown in capacity. Austria was in no better shape. By 1916 the bread ration was reduced to less than half a pound a day and the long queues, the black market and food theft became commonplace.[5]

In Russia's case, near-isolation enforced self-reliance and there were many reasons for the Imperial authorities to feel confident in the first year of the war. Their territories possessed virtually all the natural resources that were needed. Coal and iron were abundant even after the loss of the Polish minefields. Agricultural output was diverse. The only crop in serious deficit was cotton, half of which had to be imported.[6] The grain harvest in 1915 was 97.5 per cent of the annual average for 1909–13, and the year 1913 produced a record bumper harvest.[7] It looked as if agriculture would survive untroubled. The halt to cereal exports would mean that the entirety of agricultural output would become available for purchase on the domestic market.

But revenues from grain exports were a crucial component of the budget. The empire had been the world's largest cereal exporter before the war. Nearly all the wheat of southern Russia and Ukraine had left Odessa, Nikolaev or Kherson on their way to central and southern Europe. Once the Ottomans proclaimed their adhesion to the German-led coalition, Russian commercial shipping ceased. If grain stayed landlocked, the Finance Ministry faced crisis. The Imperial debt was serviced with difficulty before 1914. The closure of the Straits ratcheted up the debt problems.[8] The government's options were few, each of them being tricky. The printing presses could be speeded up to flood the economy with extra paper currency. The government could raise loans from the public, appealing to its patriotism. The finance minister could travel abroad and ask Allied governments and their bankers to grant credits. He could also try to introduce a system of income tax to increase the budgetary contribution from the better-off.

A quarter of all tax revenue had been lost when the liquor tax was abolished.[9] Finance Minister Bark thought it demeaning for a great state to depend so heavily on a tax that encouraged the Russian people to drink themselves into a stupor, and he and the emperor had agreed before the war to phase it out. They had intended to spread the process over several years.[10] They abandoned caution at the outbreak of fighting in 1914. Bark highlighted the benefits of the change in policy: that fewer houses and businesses would be destroyed in fires caused by drunken owners and that productivity would rise in industrial enterprises.[11] It proved true that fewer peasants and workers got blind-drunk on religious feast days and that people were returning punctually afterwards for work. Week-long binges became a rarity.[12] Bark's critics were unimpressed. The Kadet economist Andrei Shingarëv told the Duma that he could scarcely believe what the Finance Ministry was doing.[13] Some of Bark's fellow ministers too were taken aback by his initiative: they knew that Russia's drinking culture would never be eliminated overnight. But although the government relented a little by allowing sales of wine and beer, the ban on vodka was held in place.[14]

The empire's balance of trade had been poor in the last years before the war. One of the drains on the budget had been the costs of military modernization, and the expenditure would hugely increase as the fighting began. The Finance Ministry had barely been able in peacetime to meet the interest demands on the empire's foreign loans. In August 1915 Bark secured the assent of the State Duma and the State Council to plan for the introduction of an income tax. His basic idea, as laid out in April 1916, fixed the fiscal bar so that only people earning 850 rubles or more per annum would have to pay.[15] Such a tax had never been popular with the wealthy of other countries and Russia was no exception. It was made doubly difficult as the task of collecting the necessary information about how much people earned was almost impossible in time of war. Bark's team worked hard on the plan, which he scheduled to put into effect in 1917.[16]

The government also organized six successive war loans. The first was raised at the start of the war and paid at 5 per cent interest. Three followed in 1915, the last of which offered a return of 5.5 per cent per annum. The sixth loan, announced in 1916, brought the total loans to nearly eight billion rubles. Bark's loans came close to fulfilling his stated objectives.[17] Subscribers wanted to support the war effort and more people than ever had more ready cash because they were spending less.[18]

The war loans, however successful, were never going to be enough to fund the military effort by themselves. The ruble plunged in value abroad after news came of the Russian defeats. Russia's international credit worthiness tumbled.[19] At home, Bark became the greatest printer of banknotes in Russian history but predictably the price of goods rose steeply in the shops. Although there was more grain in the empire than in peacetime, the army took a larger share of it than usual. Agricultural producers reacted to economic uncertainty by releasing less of their harvest to the market than they normally would. Consumers felt the pinch with rye bread costing 34 per cent more in the first twelve months of war. Meat rose by 23 per cent.[20]

The Russian war effort would have juddered to a halt without economic sustenance by the Western Allies. As early as February 1915, when Pëtr Bark travelled to meet Allied finance ministers in Paris, Russia was on the brink of budgetary collapse. Great Britain and France offered loans of £25 million each, and the Bank of France opened a huge credit facility to ease Petrograd's needs. Bark had to promise the resumption of grain deliveries to Allied countries when the British were planning action against the Ottomans to force the reopening of the Straits of the Dardanelles. Grain shipments were assembled in expectation on the Odessa quays. The Ottoman defences beat back Great Britain's amphibious campaign, and the exit from the Black Sea remained blockaded.[21] Despite their concerns about Russia's treatment of its Jewish subjects, the French and British had their own urgent need to keep Russia in the war. They knew that if the Russians signed a separate peace on the Eastern front, a vast number of German divisions would be transferred for service on the Western front. Even if Russia's famed military steamroller was stalled on the Eastern front it was a crucial factor in preventing a German triumph in northern France. The Western Allies might well apply conditions to their assistance but they could not afford to withhold it entirely.

The capacity of France and Great Britain to satisfy the Russian financial needs decreased, though, as their own costs slipped out of control. The two Western Allies themselves had to apply for loans from New York banks. They simultaneously did this on Russia's behalf. Such a division of functions stemmed from the reluctance of many American financiers to help a government they saw as anti-Semitic and authoritarian. The change in the General Staff's leadership in August 1915 had initially raised hopes of further improvement in the treatment of Jews. But although there was an end to the mass deportations from the war zone, Alexeev continued with other discriminatory measures and prohibited the employment of Jewish people in Zemgor organizations anywhere near the Eastern front.[22] Britain and France struck deals with J. P. Morgan and Co. and the National City Bank to ease their own financial crisis and at the same time to help the Russians. The United States administration gave its approval despite its policy of neutrality during the European war.[23] In 1916 National City Bank set up direct operations in Russia and J. P. Morgan continued to act as an intermediary for Russia.[24] Aided by these credits, Russia could sign contracts, especially with American companies, to fill the gaps in Russian industrial production. Rifles, explosives and rail locomotives were badly needed.[25]

The Western Allies laid down conditions for assisting the Russian war effort. In summer 1916 Russia had to promise to make shipments of its gold reserves to the British in return for any more financial credits. The French opened an additional credit facility only if Russia agreed to use the money solely for military requirements and, somewhat unrealistically, to export agricultural goods to them.[26] The cool calculations among the Allies were getting cooler. The Russians were annoyed but were in no position to do more than complain.

The Ministry of Trade and Industry pressed for the big factories with governmental contracts to form industrial syndicates. The rationale was to smooth the decisions about what to make, how soon and at what price.[27] There was a cosiness between government and the very largest companies in manufacturing and mining. When a favoured enterprise hit financial trouble, as had happened to the Putilov Works before the war, ministers feared a ruinous drop in deliveries.[28] At the Special Conference of Defence there was a proposal to requisition the entire business. A threat by the management to walk out stymied this.[29] But the Putilov accounts were in such a mess that by February 1916 the government decided to take the business into state ownership. If the Putilovs could not make a profit, the enterprise's contribution to the empire's armaments capacity was too important to be allowed to disappear.[30] The Putilov family emerged with their bank assets undamaged. Socialists complained that ministers always stepped in to save the skins of the wealthy. Ministers argued that the war effort took precedence and demanded the saving of such an important armaments plant.

By 1916 there had been an increase of 10 per cent in the amount of freight carried on the railways.[31] But priority was given to transporting men, horses, armaments, uniforms, medicines, food and hay to the front, which caused havoc to the civilian sector of the economy. On the Trans-Siberian line, for example, vital dairy products received reduced wagon space and military supplies took precedence over butter.[32] When in November 1915 the cabinet met to discuss the coal shortages in factories it was recognized that some of the problem lay with excessive strains put on the rail network.[33]

The large farming estates of Ukraine and southern Russia were the worst-affected sector of agriculture, as unlike peasant smallholdings they depended on the export trade and on hired labour. The closure of the empire's access to Mediterranean waters disrupted the pattern of commerce for the big farms and cereal merchants. The mass conscription of millions of able-bodied men made the situation even worse as adequate manpower vanished. The sown area across the empire decreased to 82 per cent of its 1913 total.[34] This was not enough in itself to result in harvests too small to feed the population, but nevertheless there was a growing problem with food supplies, especially in the towns and cities of northern and central Russia. The immediate reason was that half the grain sales went to the armed forces, and the effects were adverse on civilian families.[35] Meat and ice cream were arriving from Siberia, and imported dairy products from Great Britain alleviated shortfalls in domestic deliveries, but by late 1915 there was already a butter shortage in Petrograd.[36]

Mass conscription meant the state needed to feed its new soldiers and sailors. This put the budget and the administrative machinery under huge strain. Whereas in peacetime the villages discharged that responsibility, now it was army commanders and government ministers who had to discharge it.

Despite all these difficulties, the Russian Empire experienced an immense spurt of industrial growth in wartime, with state contracts fuelling the process. The largest firms formed syndicates. Prodamet, founded in 1902, dominated metallurgy throughout the empire, while Produgol was created in 1906 to bring together the leading companies in the coal mines. The two syndicates edged out the competition in their sectors. Nearly two thirds of all coal output came from Produgol while Prodamet produced 85 per cent of metallurgical production.[37] Meanwhile the waves of conscription affected activity and so the authorities had to work out which categories of labour ought to be exempted. Suggestions were made to lower the working age as well as to bring women into the workforce.[38] Iron and coal from the Donbas became crucial after the loss of the Polish mining lands.[39] Companies that had produced for the civilian market went over to involvement in the war effort. The state sought simplicity and dependability by favouring existing syndicates and large corporations with proven records of accomplishment. As in all belligerent countries, there were bottlenecks and inefficiencies. Shell shortages became a grievous difficulty and there were incapacities in factories that made explosives, chemicals and medicines.[40]

Fresh techniques were rushed into industrial practice. Workers were given prolonged shifts and asked to accept different modes of work and organization. Holidays were reduced. At the same time owners had to keep hold of their skilled teams and wages were augmented in the competition for their labour. But the existing industrial workforce was never going to be sufficient for wartime needs. Recruitment occurred at a frantic pace. Shopfloor workers in large-scale manufacturing climbed from 1,844,000 in 1913 to 2,193,000 by 1916.[41]

Food shortages and the subsequent price inflation caused widespread discontent. A national system of rationing had to be introduced in Germany in 1915 and was applied to sugar, fat, bread and soap but the government in Petrograd hesitated to follow the German precedent. Finance Minister Bark argued for greater state control of trade by fixing prices for certain goods that were in deficit on the market. He thought this could be done for matches and refined sugar but that it was technically too difficult to organize for tobacco and oil. The Transport Ministry considered the idea of placing limits on what could be purchased by individuals to prevent an outbreak of panic-buying.[42] Nervousness remained about introducing such measures but this did not save the emperor and his cabinet from blame. In an empire where they claimed ultimate authority it was natural for them to suffer heavy reproach. Nicholas could not be criticized in public but informally his reputation was in tatters among a wide stratum of society.

9. THE EASTERN FRONT: RUSSIAN MILITARY RESILIENCE AND GERMAN OVERTURES

In September 1915 the Russian Imperial forces on the Eastern front at last showed that the advance of the Central Powers could be stopped. The Great Retreat had taken place and the front was stabilized along a line stretching 750 miles southwards from Riga's outskirts on the Baltic coast and down the river Dvina as far as Czernowitz, which lay on the river Prut to the east of the Carpathians. The defeats and the forced strategic withdrawal had involved the surrender of Russian Poland as well as great swathes of Latvia, Lithuania and Belorussia. The entire front line except for south-eastern Galicia lay deep inside the pre-war frontier of the Russian Empire. But the German high command was wrong to think that the Russians were on the point of collapse and Russian military resilience and competence were about to show their strength.

In Vologda province, a year after the war's outbreak, Alexander Zamaraev had lost what was left of his confidence in Russia's military prospects. He faced troubles of his own at home. The threshing season in north Russia was being disrupted by sudden downpours of rain.[1] Zamaraev worried that his harvest would be ruined. He continued to work hard every day, taking occasional trips as usual into Totma to buy provisions for the family. He read about what was happening in the rest of the empire and wartime Russia and regularly attended church. By New Year 1916 he could no longer see any chance of Russia beating the Central Powers. His patriotism was undimmed and he was no pacifist but the German victories appeared to him unstoppable, and he wanted an end to all the fighting. The daily press confirmed his pessimism. As he wrote in his diary, he had come to yearn for a peace that would 'dry the tears of widows and orphans'. He ached for 'people to cease destroying each other because all of us are brothers'.[2]

The mud of autumn 1915 and the snows of early winter halted the fighting and gave respite to the empire for the first time in the war. The Eastern front stabilized. The huge defensive effort was paying off but the Russian high command could see that victory was at best a distant prospect. Chief of the General Staff Alexeev recognized that whatever else happened in the war, it was the Germans he had to beat. In September 1915, he actively considered the possibility of exploring whether the Ottomans might be agreeable to a separate peace. He calculated that if he could divide the enemy powers in this way, victory over Germany could be won. But he knew that a Russo-Ottoman peace would not go down well in the State Duma opinion. The war aim of the Dardanelles had become a fetish in Russian public life and Alexeev avoided pressing his case.[3]

Russian military resilience and the Polish weather were not the main reason for the stabilization of the Eastern front. The Germans had given priority to the Western front and the Austro-Hungarian forces were caught up in their campaigns against Serbia and Italy. So the Russians dug in and resupplied. Alexeev demanded more conscripts, artillery, rifles, horses, food and clothing from the rear. The government announced a lowering of the age of liability for recruitment so that nineteen-year-olds could be impressed into the armed forces.[4] By early November 1915 the Imperial Army had 4,900,000 men on active service.[5] Six hundred and fifty thousand of them were at the front. They had 2,590 machine guns and the trenches stretched from Tallinn on the Baltic south to Czernowitz in mid-Galicia.[6] By mid-1916 the Russian had 1.75 million troops on the front line and another 750,000 in the reserves.[7] By October 1916 there were 8,269,000 men on army service, a total covering all sectors of the Eastern and Caucasian fronts. Another estimate put the number at 6,191,000. The discrepancy was later explained as the result of whether or not the employees who performed auxiliary work for the armed forces were included.[8]

The fighting on the Eastern front settled into a static pattern from autumn 1915. Trenches were dug and artillery was fixed in place. Transport links were reorganized – no easy undertaking on the Russian side. The Russians were getting the defensive war that their brightest commanders had always preferred before 1914 when they planned for conflict with Germany.[9] The line no longer moved eastward as had been happening since Tannenberg and the Masurian Lakes. Riga was untouched despite the proximity of German armed forces, and talk about evacuating Petrograd or Kiev was suspended. The advancing German armies were halted. Both sides of the front suffered immense losses. The deaths and casualties suffered by the Russians were publicized by the revolutionary parties and have become a staple of historical narrative, but in fact Germany experienced a higher proportion of military fatalities on the Eastern front than on the Western front.[10]

As the Belorussian and Lithuanian territories became a charnel house, the Russian General Staff held its nerve. Nicholas and Alexeev had a working partnership based on mutual trust. While Nicholas felt he had made the right choice of man to head the General Staff, Alexeev's appointment served to assure the other generals that Nicholas's arrival in Mogilëv would do no damage to military effectiveness.[11] A few leading commanders, however, had doubts. One was Alexei Brusilov on the south-western sector of the Eastern front. He never got on with Nicholas, thinking him 'a mere child' in military matters, and he looked down on Alexeev as a leader with 'no real personality'.[12] Alexeev, however, was effective at his job and Nicholas left him to get on with it. Nicholas's only requirement was to receive reports on the military situation each morning at eleven o'clock about the military situation at all sectors of the Eastern front. This caused some annoyance to the colonels who had to compile them, but Alexeev was grateful that Nicholas did not proceed to interfere in operational and strategic decisions.[13]

The emperor was the symbol, not the director, of military endeavour. In mid-November 1915, a few weeks after moving to Mogilëv, he went south on a tour of Imperial forces. In Kherson near the Black Sea he inspected a military parade. The NCO Alexei Shtukaturov, who was to die at the front a month later, was one of the troops who stood in line with the many regiments. He recorded the occasion in these words: 'The sovereign rode round on horseback while his heir travelled in a car. The sovereign is very thin and pale and he has sunken eyes. The heir is a very sweet, fine boy.' Shtukaturov was pleased that Nicholas brought his horse in front of every company to express his thanks to the forces about to be deployed to the front. Nicholas shook hands with all the battalion commanders and, before the day was finished, voiced the hope that the young riflemen would serve him and the motherland to the glory of their regiments.[14]

Whilst the socialist parties assumed that Nicholas's unpopularity in the 1905–6 revolution was fixed for ever in the popular mind, the mystique of the Romanov dynasty endured for millions of men on active service. Nicholas himself felt sure that the Russian people loved him. But Shtukaturov, not a political dissenter, was probably not alone in being less than inspirited by the occasion. His mood was not improved by the poor meal served to his regiment that evening. Soldiers grumbled that the cooking would have been better if officers had known that Nicholas might witness what was served to them.[15]

Nicholas kept up his trips to his forces near the Eastern front but the feeling was growing that the Romanov dynasty contributed little of value to the war effort. Vasili Kravkov, a veteran of the Japanese war and a senior doctor on the Eastern front, no longer felt optimistic about Russia's military chances and he dreaded the possibility that Nicholas would bring his favourites like Rasputin to general headquarters and worsen an already grave situation.[16] He formed a low opinion of such Romanovs as toured the front line. On one such journey, Grand Duke Andrei Mikhailovich met Kravkov and told him that the application of butter was the best treatment for internal stomach wounds. Kravkov concluded that the court was full of idiotic parasites, and he felt sure that the people would exact revenge on them.[17] There was horror amongst the General Staff when it was heard that Rasputin had expressed a wish to visit Mogilëv. On 26 November 1915 Alexeev put his foot down, telling Nicholas that no one in the high command was happy about the idea. Nicholas prudently denied Rasputin permission.

The empress, however, on her trip to Mogilëv in August 1916 took Alexeev for a garden stroll. She asked him: 'What have you got, general, against Grigori Rasputin?' 'Nothing, your Imperial Majesty,' he replied: 'I've never seen him.' Alexandra snapped back: 'But why do you oppose his visits here? Surely he would be such a support for the Tsar. We're so much in his debt. Alësha [Alexei] has twice been saved from death by his prayers.' Alexeev was tactful but firm in reply: 'Your Majesty, the voice of the people is the voice of God. I, a true servant of my Sovereign, am willing to do everything to give him respite but I cannot permit the presence here of a person about whom the army and the people are unanimously of the most negative opinion.'[18] Nicholas stood by Alexeev. But when Alexeev went further by raising the matter of Rasputin's notoriety, Nicholas cut him short: 'I know this!' It was one thing for the chief of staff to keep Rasputin out of army headquarters but quite another to proffer an opinion about his influence.[19]

Commanders on both sides on the Eastern front were baffled as to how to end the military stalemate. On 14 April 1916 Nicholas chaired a conference of his generals in Mogilëv. Only one of them, Alexei Brusilov, expressed any optimism that an offensive against the Germans could now be effective in the south-western sector where he had recently taken control. His opinion was disdainfully dismissed by the other generals, but Brusilov remained firm, telling the emperor that there was no justification for staying in the trenches.[20]

Nicholas gave approval to Brusilov on condition that his offensive would not call upon reinforcements from elsewhere on the line. It helped his case that the Russian high command was under pressure from the Western Allies to start a new offensive operation. Brusilov applied his own fresh thinking to the summer campaign, plotting a sudden advance that would fool military intelligence on the other side. In preparation, Brusilov retrained his artillery units. He assembled a vanguard of 'shock troops' who could surge across no man's land at short notice. He used the new aeroplanes to spy on the Austro-Hungarian defences, and he improved his communication network. On 22 May 1916 he ordered the start of his offensive and as he had hoped, the opening salvoes caught the Austrians napping. The Russians destroyed the enemy's defences at four places along a line that was nineteen miles long. As the Russians pushed on, Eastern Galicia and the entire Bukovina region fell back under Russian occupation. The campaign brought 370,000 Austro-Hungarian prisoners into custody, a third of Austria–Hungary's armed forces.[21]

Newspapers in Russia celebrated a great victory. The peasant Zamaraev was delighted by the Russian success. After so many defeats, at last the Russians were making a solid advance. Zamaraev called Brusilov one of his heroes.[22] Nicholas II, however, was less admiring. Perhaps still suspecting Brusilov of taking too many risks, he sent him a congratulatory note that Brusilov thought 'insipid'.[23] In fact the press was exaggerating the durability of the success. Brusilov had failed to reinforce the positions gained across the Austrian lines. The German high command reacted swiftly and withdrew some of its divisions from the Western front to halt the Russian advance and then the Russians were pushed back onto the defensive and the Eastern front reverted to static warfare.[24]

In July 1916 the Germans amassed forces to attack the Russian line along the river Stokhod. A tremendous battle ensued before the German offensive was beaten back, and the Russians claimed the benefit was not confined to their own position on the Eastern front. In eastern

France the siege of Verdun was reaching a climax. General Philippe Pétain was willing to pay any price in French troops' lives rather than surrender, but it was said that Verdun would have fallen if the German high command could have transferred divisions from the east. Nicholas was roused in August 1916 by proof that his armed forces could take on and hammer the enemy.[25]

The German government and high command remained confident about the superiority of their own forces but gave priority to achieving victory on the Western front. For this reason, and this alone, they had put out feelers to the Russians from 1915 about the possibility of a separate peace on the Eastern front. Three secret approaches were made to Nicholas II.[26] A letter from Princess M. A. Vasilchikova, based in Germany, confided that she had it on good authority that the German leadership was willing to concede the Dardanelles to Russia in a future settlement. Grand Duke Ernst of Hesse, Alexandra's brother no less, reinforced the message by writing that Gottlieb von Jagow, state secretary at the German Foreign Office favoured the same idea. Similar suggestions were relayed to Sazonov by the Russian ambassador to Sweden after being approached by Deutsche Bank officials in Stockholm.[27] The follow-up dispatch from the embassy somewhat harshened the taste of the overtures by adding that the Germans expected to take full possession of Poland.[28] Grand Duke Ernst, keen as ever, wrote directly to Empress Alexandra, his sister, with a plea for the way to be cleared to a separate peace.[29]

The Germans kept up their efforts despite Nicholas's failure to reply. They misjudged how the tsar might see the situation. Personal honour was at the core of his identity and he refused to contemplate the shame of seeking a separate peace. He knew the dynasty was on trial in the hall of public opinion. If ever he were to appear less than committed to military victory, he would put his throne in jeopardy. Rumours about pro-German inclinations at the court and in the government had grown since the start of the war. They were taken seriously by Great Britain's Ambassador Sir George Buchanan who worried that Empress Alexandra was indulging those in her circle of intimates who wanted a peace deal with Germany.[30] It did not help that Alexandra was born a German princess of Hesse and by Rhine or that premier Boris Stürmer had a German name. Most harmful to the Imperial family's reputation was the widely known fact that Grigori Rasputin, their dearest 'Friend', had advised against entering the war and favoured stopping it by making peace.

Although Duma politicians kept their eyes and ears open for the slightest evidence of treason in high places, the truth was that Nicholas and Alexandra were as committed to the goal of military victory as the General Staff. Patriotic zeal motivated all official Russia, as it had since the outbreak of hostilities. The defeat of the Central Powers remained the towering goal.

10. VILLAGES AND CITIES IN THE GREAT WAR: ANGRY PEASANTS, HUNGRY URBAN CONSUMERS

The disruptive consequences of prolonged total war grew as the fighting went into its second year, and the Russian Imperial rear – its economy, society and administration – acted as a drag anchor on the chances of victory. Every combatant state was put under unprecedented strain, but a semi-modernized Russia was especially vulnerable to the pressures of a long war, which only its resilience at the front could disguise.

Peasants constituted 85 per cent of the empire's population and were an official category in the social hierarchy. They were widely regarded by others with fear and condescension, and as an amorphous whole. The reality was very different. The peasantry was a legal, not an occupational, category. Some were day labourers with little or no land who mainly worked the huge estate farms of Ukraine and southern Russia. But there were also peasants with substantial amounts of land, livestock and machinery, who were indistinguishable from independent farmers in the other parts of Europe except that they had borne the name of peasant since birth and carried it throughout their lives. The emperor and his government remained terrified of the power the peasants could wield, so although they could vote in the Duma elections, the electoral regulations – especially the amended ones that Stolypin introduced in 1907 for the third Duma – segregated them from the rest of the electorate and denied them representation proportionate to their numbers.

At the outbreak of war it was still less than a decade since the revolutionary upsurge of 1905–6, and many in rural areas had bitter memories of the punitive detachments which had been deployed to put down the uprisings against the landowners. Violence on both sides had been intense in the central black-earth region and throughout the mid-Volga region. The Tambov district zemstvo recorded the pattern of events:

> The peasants . . . go to the owners of an estate or to his manager and propose first of all that he leave the estate. Then the destruction of all the property begins. They take away everything in the house, haul away the grain, drive away the cattle and the buildings are burned.

Over three quarters of the peasant disturbances were aimed against gentry landowners, and arson and looting occurred in a third of instances. Actions against the clergy were only 0.25 per cent of peasant disturbances – and those against 'kulaks', as the better-off peasants were called, constituted just 1.4 per cent.[1]

The authorities then punished peasants who had taken an active part in the troubles. Punishment beatings were common, sometimes carried out after the village's inhabitants had been assembled and forced to kneel on the snow-covered ground. In some districts Cossacks and other troops were dispatched to burn down homes. Entire villages were put to the flames.[2] Field courts-martial sentenced to death those found to have fomented and led the trouble. The hangman's noose was known as Stolypin's necktie after the Chairman of the Council of Ministers Pëtr Stolypin who oversaw the campaign.

Many noble families sold up and left after the violence had abated, wanting to be anywhere but in the countryside. They worried about the security of their families in areas which were only thinly policed after the punitive military units had departed. Many of them gave up agriculture and invested the profits of their land sales in banks and businesses – or simply spent it or gambled it away. The government and its Peasant Land Bank actively facilitated the process. Before the rural disturbances, peasants had bought 67,550,000 acres since the 1861 Emancipation Act. In the years from 1905 to 1915 they bought 1,391,530,000 acres.[3] But this still left much landed property in the possession of gentry landowners: they had 135 million acres in European Russia in 1905, they still had 116 million acres in 1915.[4] The Imperial family, the state, the Church and the high aristocracy too remained owners of huge tracts of land.[5] If peasants wanted to cultivate it, they had to pay the going rate to rent it. The old resentments festered among the peasants and the growing trend was for landowners to put in bailiffs to manage their rural assets.

Rents fell in real terms at the start of the Great War. This happened as a consequence of the mass conscription that took so many men from the countryside. The responsibility for feeding them no longer fell to them or their families but to the armed forces. Competition decreased among peasant households to lease land from the gentry landowners. It is true that rental prices doubled in the first two wartime years but they always stayed below the rate of inflation.[6] Even so, the peasantry still burned with resentment at the payments they had to make to landowners. Anyone who had lived through the murders, burnings and thefts in 1905–6 knew that there was the possibility that if the peasantry saw a chance to seize what it regarded as belonging to it by natural right, they would take it.

As able-bodied rural males became fewer, landowners and peasant households had to find other sources of labour. Families in thousands of villages brought mothers, wives and daughters deeper into the workforce. Hard work was not a novelty for them. Women had always laboured in the plot around the house and helped in the fields as well as doing the cooking and raising the children. They had always had a part in the ploughing, sowing and harvesting. But it had been the man who had been head of the household, and he had the final word over any matter of importance in the home or at work. His authority was weakened in wartime when women came to supply over seven tenths of the rural workforce. Widows understandably took decisions that their late husbands would normally have taken. Whilst female members of peasant households gained additional responsibilities, they also gained an unprecedented degree of control over their lives. Their influence grew in meetings of the land commune, and male peasants had no choice but to accept the infringement of ancient tradition.[7]

Meanwhile the conscription of men from the villages left private estates short of the labour they needed. Landowners successfully petitioned to employ prisoners-of-war. Over 600,000 POWs were working in the fields of the Russian Empire by the end of 1916.[8] Such prisoners were sent wherever there was a labour shortage. They cleared roads, loaded river boats and – if they had the skill – cobbled boots.[9]

Nonetheless the war led to a decline in the husbandry of the countryside in many places. Both gentry and peasant landholdings experienced problems. Vegetable plots were falling into disuse. Livestock wandered on the land untended and trampled the winter crops. Village life lost much of its pre-war vibrancy.[10] Governmental efforts to reform the system of peasant land tenure fell into disuse.[11] Ministries in time of war were preoccupied with the demands of the fighting on the fronts, and it would have made little sense to provoke the peasantry's hostility by continuing to impose the Stolypin agrarian reform in a forceful manner. By 1916 it was still the case that only one in eleven peasant households in European Russia ran its own separate farm of some kind.[12] Two of Alexander Zamaraev's fellow peasants separated from the commune under the terms of Stolypin's measures.[13] Zamaraev chose not to and continued farming as he liked according to local tradition. Even though he rejected Stolypin's reform for himself, he was in many ways the independent kind of peasant that Stolypin wanted for the countryside.

Many peasants had more money during wartime because they could no longer spend it at liquor stores. But they had to spend more on products from food to domestic equipment. One estimate suggests that their general consumption rose by 25 per cent in wartime.[14] Nevertheless the prices they received for agricultural produce did not keep pace with inflation. There was also irritation because even if a peasant took grain or vegetables to the nearest town, the shops and stalls no longer had many of the goods that peasants weren't producing for themselves. By late 1915 there was no sugar on sale anywhere in Totma. In spring 1916 the stalls had no white flour, malt, rye flour, tobacco, soap or kerosene on the market – sugar was available again but had rocketed in price along with salt, butter and millet. When Zamaraev went into town again in August even fish had disappeared from sale. He heard that granulated sugar was being sold at the zemstvo administration, only to find that availability depended on the social status of the customer: urban artisans could buy a pound and a half each month whereas peasants were allowed only three quarters of a pound.[15]

The price of draught animals had soared. Alexander Zamaraev in Vologda province complained that even old nags fetched a vast sum.[16] He loved his horses. He and his wife Nadezhda cried when he decided that their nineteen-year-old gelding Karek had come to the end of his working life. He had tried to spare him the heavier jobs but regretfully had to sell him to his neighbour Pasha Tsygan. He was irate on discovering that Tsygan sold Karek on to someone else for a higher price by pretending that the animal was only twelve years old. Zamaraev disliked such deceit.[17] Family life became tougher after his wife Nadezhda suffered a serious facial injury when the family horse fell on top of her. Zamaraev took her to the hospital in Totma. Praying for her recovery, he wrote about feeling distressed and lonely. Although their daughter

Lidia lived at home, she was young and left the house early each morning. He had nobody to talk to: 'The truth is that a woman is of great importance in the life of a family and it's absolutely impossible without them.' Some days later, as Nadezhda showed signs of recovery, Alexander hoped that things would soon return to normal.[18]

Blame was increasingly directed at the government. Zamaraev wrote of his Totma district in late March 1915: 'Baked bread is now five kopeks a pound. And it's the war that's done this. The railways are bringing nothing to us. Ministries have bought up the wheat wherever there's a lot of it.'[19] Circumstances pushed Totma district's rural households into involuntary economic self-sufficiency within a 'natural economy' of barter and exchange.[20] Zamaraev was used to performing the farming tasks for himself, passing only a few of them to others like the local carpenter and the village shepherd. He was proud of growing most of the crops that he needed. Occasionally, in a bad year, he had to buy extra hay for the livestock. He grew his own vegetables and milled his own grain at the monastery. He complained that the few items he had usually bought in town were running out, but this only served to strengthen his desire to be self-sufficient.[21]

There was plenty that peasants could do with their agricultural surplus if they thought that urban demands were being made on unfair terms. They could put more of their output on their own tables, and there is good evidence that the peasant diet improved from late 1914. The conscription of young male villagers meant at least that there were fewer mouths needing to be fed in the villages. The cereal crop could also be used for animal feed, and horses, pigs and cows ate better. When the vodka distilleries were closed, peasants revived their skills at illicit production of alcoholic spirits. Instances of spirit-induced blindness were frequent. Breakdowns in law and order occurred. In Vologda province it was reported that 'they are brewing various beers, get drunk and as a result there are murders and robberies'.[22] War disrupted living and trading conditions in every town and village. Not everyone was badly affected. The cobblers of Totma – there were several of them – thrived on commissions to make boots for the armed forces.

On 11 September 1915 Manager-in-Chief of Land Organization and Agriculture Krivoshein and Internal Affairs Minister Shcherbatov alerted the government to the decline in the food supply. Sugar and oats were running out. The railways were in chaos and Petrograd failed to obtain the scheduled freight deliveries. Moscow and other cities were inadequately provisioned. As refugees arrived from the war zones, the danger of 'hunger riots' was growing and were a bigger threat than revolutionary disorder. Restrictions on the flow of refugees were needed. War Minister Polivanov agreed, advising the cabinet to reject the General Staff's request for an expansion of the war zone to accommodate the fleeing subjects of the emperor.[23] Emergency arrangements were also made to expedite urban supplies. Transport Minister Alexander Trepov claimed that the problem was at least 'partially eliminated'. Butter had become available after Great Britain had helped with its shipments. Rye and wheat flour were coming through again to cities. More railway carriages had been ordered from the United States, which would alleviate the difficulties.[24]

Many cities were in some ways the same as they had been before the war. Whilst families had seen many of their young men lost to the war, shops and stalls opened as normal, and the trams ran on time. Factory machinery whirred with activity. School pupils continued their education. Police, caretakers and watchmen performed their usual duties. The urban populace, moreover, increased sharply in size as peasants flooded into the cities to fill the jobs in the expanding manufacturing and mining centres. Mass conscription also brought millions of young men to urban garrisons prior to their deployment to the front. Cities meanwhile teemed with refugees from the western war zone regions. Lev Tikhomirov, who gave shelter in his house near Moscow to one of them, grew concerned about the effect of the miserable stream of humanity on morale, and he felt certain that a lot of the newcomers were German spies.[25] Petrograd was another great magnet. Existing occupants of its tall tenement blocks found that landlords seized the chance to raise rents. Anton Okninski, an official at the Russo-Asiatic Bank, decided to move out of town to a winter dacha at Levashevo on the Finland railway.[26] Not everyone could afford such an option.

The need for armaments and military uniforms meant that factories in Petrograd, Moscow and Ivanovo-Voznesensk called out for novice workers. The competition for labour spurred a rise in wages. Owners complained about the drain on their funds while pocketing profits that outstripped what had come to them in time of peace. The newcomers to industrial life, at least most of them, flowed from the villages and had to get used to urban ways and factory discipline. Training courses proliferated. Housing became overcrowded. The old systems for sewage, gas and electricity as well as health and safety inspections were expected to cope without provision for expansion. Higher wages brought little consolation in such conditions, especially as they were outmatched by the rocketing rate of inflation and the growing unreliability of food supplies.

As in the rural areas, basic products cost substantially more. Between the summers of 1915 and 1916 alone consumers had to pay an additional 24 per cent for rye bread, 44 per cent for milk, 70 per cent for meat and 73 per cent for potatoes.[27] Eggs were in deficit on Moscow markets as early as the winter of 1914–15. Cheese, ham and fresh meat were getting hard to find.[28] Wages fell in real terms in the parts of industry outside the defence sector by 15 per cent between 1913 and 1916. The situation was better in the munitions factories, where the shopfloor workers secured on average a rise of 23 per cent – this was in contrast with white-collar workers across all industry who experienced a 22 per cent drop in their payments.[29]

The Imperial administration always had a strained connection with those in professional occupations. Engineers, scientists, journalists, lecturers, teachers, doctors and land surveyors were recognized as vital to the empire's pursuit of modernization. Many 'professionals', however, resented the curtailments on their freedom to carry out their work as they wished. They read the newspapers and knew that they would face less obstruction and enjoy higher status in North America or the rest of Europe. Ideas of reform, or of revolution in many cases, were widespread among them and indeed inside the administration itself. By and large, though, these professional classes caused little open trouble in wartime and patriotic feelings were widespread among them. They perhaps felt lucky not to be drafted as the death count on the Eastern front mounted, but like many as they suffered the adverse impact of financial inflation and retail shortages that the war had brought about, they shared the idea that much of the blame was attributable to mismanagement by the emperor and his ministers.

Unless they lost sons or fathers in battle itself, the gilded families of the aristocracy and big business were mainly shielded from misfortune – and there was popular ill-feeling about the ease with which rich young men evaded the call to arms.[30] Conspicuous consumption stayed the norm for civilians with wealth and status. The high life in wartime was lived at the old heights. Nicholas II may have banned vodka sales for the duration of hostilities and set an example by pledging to eschew spirits, but upper-class parties and salons where vodka was available from illegal stills flourished in Petrograd. Balls continued to be held, often being held as occasions to raise a cheer for the war effort and funds for hospital charities – some were attended by Nicholas and Alexandra before he removed himself to Mogilëv.

As privations grew across most of society, and tension and discontent with it, the government sought to allay suspicion that it was pandering to the rich. In October 1916 restrictions were applied to imports of luxury products, and in November 1916 Finance Minister Bark announced a ban on anyone transferring more than 500 rubles abroad without the permission of his ministry, but such measures did little to stem the growth of social resentment.[31]

Alexander Zamaraev read in the *Russkoe Slovo* newspaper that 'the English' had given up all luxuries from the outbreak of war. From this he concluded: 'All classes of the population, from the highest lords down to the very poor (even the ecclesiastical department buys nothing in church) content themselves with what's old and cheap, and all money goes to the war. You don't notice anything like this in our country. Over there even ministers and the highest officials have voluntarily cut their salaries.'[32] The truth was that the dining tables in gentlemen's clubs and country mansions in Great Britain and France continued to heave with their usual haute cuisine.[33] But Zamaraev was right when he added about Russia's elite: 'There aren't any drunks now because there's no wine. But they say that there's vodka in some houses in the town. It means that everything's possible for the rich.'[34]

11. CHURCH MILITANT: RUSSIAN ORTHODOXY ON CAMPAIGN

For centuries the tsars showered privileges on the Russian Orthodox Church while denying them to the other Christian denominations. Although increased toleration of other denominations was introduced at Easter 1905, the Church's exceptional status was maintained. Metropolitan bishops had served at every coronation and prayers were offered for the emperor's health and success throughout his reign. Nicholas II and his family received the sacraments every Sunday. The emperors required the Church to behave as it was told by the Imperial authorities. For two centuries the Synod had lacked permission to elect its own patriarch. This prohibition, extraordinary when Peter the Great had first applied it, continued to prevent the emergence of an ecclesiastical leader who might rival the emperor in authority.

The 40,000 parishes of the Russian Orthodox Church were a rock for their communities throughout the war. In 1914 the Church had sixty-seven dioceses with around 50,000 priests and deacons. There were a thousand monasteries and convents, containing 21,000 monks, 73,000 nuns and novices.[1] The clergy could count on almost all its registered believers, perhaps 90 per cent of them, to make confession and take communion on at least an annual basis – higher than for the leading Christian denominations in western Europe in that period.[2]

Church bells were rung for the early victories in Galicia and Anatolia. New conscripts paraded in cities and villages to swear an oath of loyalty to their emperor and of obedience to their officers administered by a bishop or priest. The Holy Synod endorsed the supply of Red Cross medical personnel and equipment to the front lines. Appeals for donations were issued. The government's appeals for war loans were supported. Parish clergy taught the virtues of patriotism in church schools and a Saturday requiem was sung in churches for those who had fallen in action. Alms were disbursed to the needy families of serving soldiers. Priests assured their parishioners that it was a

Holy War for faith, tsar and fatherland and that God was on Russia's side.[3] Alexander Zamaraev recorded a sequence of prayers and fasting between 26 and 30 August 1915 when believers sought victory over Germany.[4] At the front itself, there was compulsory attendance at services for those soldiers who were registered as Orthodox. Many of them had brought miniature icons away with them when they left to join the forces. The NCO Alexei Shtukaturov drew comfort from his replica of St Nicholas the Miracle Worker.[5]

Urban businessmen and agricultural landlords, especially those in the Moscow region who were Old Believers, were keen to maintain religious faith among their workforces while petitioning for a reduction in the days reserved for feasts. If Russian industry was to be competitive with the world's great powers, they argued, employers had to keep the factories running for a larger part of the year. The local religious festivals were a particular cause for complaint.[6] Emperor Nicholas, an enthusiastic follower of Orthodox tradition, had come some way to meeting these concerns in 1897 by laying down a maximum of sixty-six work-free days for industrial workers. In 1900, after complaints from the factory floor, the maximum was raised to sixty-nine days.[7] Workers, however, continued to press for all their old customary holidays. Sentiment in the country was with them. People across Vologda province who agreed to work on a feast day were harangued as being 'godless'. Their bishop agreed. In 1909 he had asked, sarcastically, whether 'our government has not converted to the faith of the Germans'.[8]

Priests accompanied the armed forces to the garrisons and the front as chaplains, but Orthodox clergy were not the only clerics on campaign. Since the 1905–6 revolution there had been official tolerance of religious diversity in the Russian Empire. The impact inside the forces was slow until the Great War quickened the pace, and Old Believers, Lutherans, Catholics, Armenian Orthodox clerics followed the Orthodox chaplains to the front, as did Muslim imams and Buddhist lamas. Nevertheless the Russian Orthodox Church still aimed to conduct a campaign of religious imperialism at least at the expense of other Orthodox denominations when the Imperial Army occupied large parts of Galicia in the war's first year. Among the targets were the Ruthenians, a Slavic people who for centuries had protected their spiritual autonomy by remaining in communion with the Roman Catholic Church and, like millions of Ukrainians, were known as Uniates.[9] The Holy Synod sent Archbishop Yevlogi who, according to testimony given to the playwright Shloyme Rappaport-Ansky, 'terrorized the Ruthenian population' into accepting Russian Orthodoxy.[10]

Yevlogi operated under military protection and the Uniate Metropolitan Archbishop Andrey Sheptytsky was arrested. Protests by Ruthenian congregations were dismissed. A spirited discussion of the situation took place on 10 September 1914 in the Council of Ministers, where it was appreciated that trouble could flare up in Galicia unless Sheptytsky was treated with some caution. Foreign Affairs Minister Sazonov, while denouncing Sheptytsky as a 'bandit' who was 'worse than a Jesuit', thought it prudent to send him into exile. Sazonov also condemned the practice of forcible conversion to Orthodoxy. Internal Affairs Minister Maklakov and Agriculture Minister Krivoshein agreed.[11] So did Supreme Commander-in-Chief Grand Duke Nikolai Nikolaevich, and the emperor gave assurances of his support. But nothing changed in Galicia.[12] The General Staff wanted the government to deal with Sheptytsky and sent him on to Kiev. Goremykin, usually more measured in his contributions to cabinet discussion, wanted him hanged. Maklakov proposed putting him on trial or deporting him to Constantinople. There was nervousness about keeping him in any Russian province for fear of his potential popularity. Ober-Procurator Sabler feared the impact he might have on Nizhni Novgorod's Old Believers.[13]

The discussion was the sign of a cabinet lacking in confidence about the Russian Orthodox Church's capacity to compete with the other Christian denominations. Nor was it explained why on earth the Old Believers, who cleaved to the Russian Orthodoxy that had been official until the mid-seventeenth century, would be tempted to go over to the Uniate liturgy. At any rate, the aggressive measures of evangelization in Galicia were entirely counter-productive and had the effect of turning Russophile Ruthenian peasants against Russia.[14] Ruthenians had a dreadful time of it even after the Russian Imperial Army retreated from Galicia. When the Austro-Hungarian forces reoccupied Galician territory, they treated the Ruthenian people as enemies.[15] The Ruthenian people were damned by the Russians as not being Russian enough and by the Austrians as being altogether too friendly to the Russians.

Nicholas and Alexandra had a deep commitment to Russian religious traditions. They had joined pilgrimages to places of peasant piety before the war, and in what they saw as a further example of their commitment to the peasantry, they welcomed the 'holy man' Grigori Rasputin into their midst. Rasputin had emerged from the Tobolsk countryside and never took the vows of priest or monk. But his untutored mode of expression and brisk self-confidence appealed to Nicholas and Alexandra who thought of him as their conduit to the minds of their grateful people.

The Imperial couple chose to overlook reports on the seamy side of his character. Rasputin was a sexual predator who conducted his seductions with religious mumbo-jumbo – he may even have believed in it himself. Most likely he belonged to the sect of *khlysty*, best-known in Siberia, who believed that redemption came to him or her who first had engaged in sin before practising repentance. Whereas their leaders underwent castration to staunch the stream of their evil-doing, Rasputin did not engage in self-mutilation. His individuality also expressed itself in his tolerant attitude to Jews and homosexuals, which was in contrast to the Imperial couple's attitudes.[16] Many wealthy women in the capital fell for his sexual charms when they were presented in a spiritual framework. He entranced Anna Vyrubova, Alexandra's lady-in-waiting, who made her family apartment available to him. Confident of the Imperial couple's protection, he appeared invulnerable. But the Church hierarchy, in a rare instance of self-assertion, aligned itself with press criticism of Rasputin's behaviour and in 1912 he was forced to retreat to his home village at Pokrovskoe in Tobolsk province in west Siberia. Goremykin ordered his staff to discard 'that filth' from his in-tray whenever he received a letter from Rasputin.[17] Duma Chairman Rodzyanko implored the Justice Ministry to put him under arrest.[18] Nothing, however, would ever persuade Nicholas to abandon 'Our Friend'.[19]

The Church itself was quietly in ferment about how to deal with the many challenges to its spiritual authority in a society that was in the grip of rapid change. Urbanism, industrialism and secularism were dangerous trends for a hierarchy that held tight to old traditions – and revolutionary socialists regularly castigated priests as exploiters of the Russian poor. Orthodox peasants were expected to render an annual tithe of the value of their harvest to their parish clergy. The priesthood in return was expected to maintain the ceremonies and festivals of the religious calendar, to bless the fields when the grain was sown and when the harvest was lifted, for rain in times of drought and for sun to nurture crops. Alexander Zamaraev recorded that in summer 1914, when the fields were unusually dry, the peasants of Totma district asked one of their priests to lead them on a procession of the Cross (*krestny khod*) around their fields in hope of getting the Lord to release His rain from the heavens.[20] The parish clergy conducted baptisms, marriages and funerals. The best of them offered consolation to parishioners who experienced death, serious illness or destitution in their families. The priests themselves, especially in rural areas, had a way of life not very different from that of the peasantry themselves, suffering from the same impoverishment and sometimes from the same sinful proclivities such as a passion for strong drink.

A reform movement was growing inside the Church during the pre-war years. There were many younger priests who had received a new modern education and who recognized the risk of maintaining the old ecclesiastical traditions. They argued for liturgical and doctrinal change but recognized that this could not happen unless accompanied by organizational reconstruction. They were frustrated by the conservative inclinations and disciplinary powers exercised by the Church leadership. Some reformers were equally exasperated by the blight cast upon the entire Church by Nicholas's reactionary monarchism. They wanted political transformation of one kind or another so that the Church could adapt to the shifting social and economic environment. But their voices were necessarily muted while Nicholas and the Holy Synod held sway. It was impossible for the priest-reformers to air their concerns about the ecclesiastical status quo. In wartime, their freedom of expression was further trimmed. Their fury had to be confined to conversations with like-minded fellow clerics. But they continued to hope that conditions in Russia would take a different direction and that religious reforms would become a reality. When they pondered the possibilities, many of them thought no improvement to be possible unless and until the ancient order of society underwent basic reconstruction.

12. PARTIES, THE PRESS AND WARTIME CONTROL: POLITICAL CHALLENGES AND THE OFFICIAL REACTION

The military defeats of 1914–15 left an indelible mark on Russian politics even though the Progressive Block disintegrated after its failure to extract constitutional concessions from the emperor and its parties were initially too demoralized to support the protest strikes that took place in factories.[1] Soon afterwards, however, the liberals and liberal conservatives recovered the spirit of defiance. Humiliation and frustration had fed anger against the rampant evidence of official incompetence and corruption. Oppositionists believed they were at last living through tsarism's last days. With luck, they thought, their own time in power was at hand.

Nicholas was determined to stop this happening. He disliked Alexander Guchkov, the Octobrist Party leader, even though the Octobrists were a loyalist party that had been founded to make Nicholas's parliamentary reforms of 1906–7 work in practice. Guchkov, though, was no longer a member of the State Duma, having lost his Moscow seat in the 1912 election. The Octobrist Party put up Mikhail Rodzyanko to become Duma chairman. Rodzyanko was emollient when communicating with Nicholas, which produced a modicum of monarchical forbearance. Nicholas nevertheless kept the Duma on a tight rein. It was allowed to meet only for strictly limited periods after its dispersal on 3 September 1915. It was not until 9 February 1916 that the next session was called – and these proceedings lasted a mere dozen days. That the Duma met at all was not a sign of the Imperial couple's love for it. Alexandra spat out her fury about its leaders in letters and telegrams. Nicholas was doleful more often than angry about them, but shared her contempt for the empire's parliamentarians. He was also conscious of the need to show a degree of tolerance of the

Duma if he wanted to lead the empire to military victory. When he announced he was making himself commander-in-chief, Rodzyanko was among those who warned him that further defeats would be blamed on Nicholas and that a point of political crisis might be reached and revolution could overnight become a realistic possibility.

Alexander Zamaraev recorded his sorrow at the deaths of three Duma deputies who 'nobly had laid down their heads' on active service.[2] He did not share the emperor's contempt for the Duma, and his attitude was shared across large swathes of society.

Censorship of newspapers and journals tightened, and the Imperial family and its entourage were protected from adverse commentary. Sensitive information about military operations on the Eastern and Caucasian fronts was withheld from the public domain, but there were ways of attacking the monarch and the high command without aiming directly at them. Party leaders in the Duma, including conservatives but especially liberals, regularly criticized cabinet ministers. Concerns could be raised in any parliamentary session about the economic dislocations that were already discernible early in the war. The fact that Goremykin eschewed the opportunity to appear in person to defend the government's performance spread the feeling in the empire that Duma politicians were the true patriots. The Duma was still allowed to print the verbatim record of its proceedings and the daily newspapers supplied detailed reports. Increasingly, too, the waging of the war both at the front and behind the lines came under press scrutiny as the competence of military and civilian authorities were questioned. Bolsheviks and Mensheviks as well as liberals and conservatives contributed to Petrograd's serious journals, and the Menshevik Osip Yermanski was even able to argue that Germany was likely to revert to the kind of commercial cooperation with Russia that had existed before the outbreak of war. Intellectual discussions, though hobbled, continued to be vibrant.[3]

The Western Allies threw a protective blanket over at least the Duma parties by inviting a Russian parliamentary delegation to visit London, Paris and Rome in April 1916. The Kadet Central Committee since autumn 1915 had pleaded with Ambassador Sir George Buchanan for closer contact with the British, and Buchanan facilitated their trip. Rodzyanko chose not to travel but put together an impressive list of seventeen politicians, eleven from the Duma and six from the State Council.[4] Kadet leader Milyukov was among them. The delegation was led by Alexander Protopopov, a prominent Octobrist. Whilst in London the Kadets made no effort to disguise their frustration with Nicholas while proclaiming their patriotic commitment to the Allied cause. They themselves heard, as Finance Minister Bark had heard before them, that influential circles in Britain were repelled by how the Imperial authorities persecuted Nicholas's Jewish subjects. Leopold de Rothschild said he felt deceived by Bark's assurances and demanded that Jews be given legal equality.[5]

The theme of trickery gained a tightening hold in the Russian Empire itself, where the regulatory regime of censorship only served to feed feral rumours outside the public arenas. The Imperial couple were the prime victims. The monarchist Lev Tikhomirov heard some of the extravagant ideas that were spreading like an uncontrolled blaze:

> Take, for example, what the old peasant women are gabbling when they come along with produce for sale. [One of them] loudly declares that those in power are all traitors. When told that nobody should believe such nonsense, she says, 'What sort of nonsense is it when the empress practically every day sends a train with supplies for Germany? The Germans are feeding themselves at our expense, and they're conquering us.'

Rumours about the pro-German sympathies of Nicholas and Alexandra were everywhere. Anti-Romanov sentiment flourished in clandestine cartoon art. A favourite motif was the alleged cuckolding of Nicholas II by Rasputin, and salacious postcards circulated with depictions of the holy man having sexual intercourse with the empress. The Zemgor agencies at the front became a conduit to provide troops with the same images. No officer or soldier could send one through the military mail but everyone in the trenches knew about the tales of treachery and lewdness at the Imperial court.

The censors permitted wide reporting about the battles won or lost. The loss of the Polish provinces was covered by every newspaper as early victories gave way to defeat and retreat. In mid-July 1915 Alexei Shtukaturov, while journeying back to his regiment after being wounded in Galicia, had been able to read the latest reports on the German advance on the Warsaw front.[6] There was also abundant discussion of economic developments. Perhaps the authorities understood the need to encourage society to feel involved in the war. The administration was discredited in the eyes of far too many of the emperor's subjects for the government to risk giving undue annoyance, and public co-operation was crucial for the war effort.

Ministers, however, were on edge about the growing instability in society. As early as 21 August 1915, a time of acute tensions with the Duma, Justice Minister Khvostov told the Council of Ministers that 'dark individuals' were 'fishing in muddy waters' and trying to stir up trouble amongst the working class. Although he believed that workers were ignoring much of the political propaganda, he admitted that the situation was more volatile in Petrograd than in Moscow. Indeed he could not discount the possibility of an armed uprising in the capital against the government. His advice was to hold to a hard line in policy. Concessions, he said, would only be exploited by the emperor's enemies.[7] On 24 August Internal Affairs Minister Shcherbatov reported on the political agitation being conducted by revolutionaries in rear garrisons. Whereas Goremykin doubted that it would come to very much, Shcherbatov predicted an explosion of disturbances and warned that Kadet leader Milyukov was boasting that he only had to press a button for public disorder to begin.

Nicholas still felt unruffled and continued to invoke his right to pause the Duma proceedings. When he did this on 3 September 1915, there was exactly the kind of trouble that Shcherbatov warned him about. The situation was exacerbated by War Minister Polivanov's announcement of an extension of the age range for conscription, resulting in strikes breaking out in Petrograd and Moscow. This was the first time in the war that the two greatest cities of the empire experienced serious industrial unrest and the trouble quickly spread across the empire. Draft riots took place in seventy cities and towns. Peasant families had experienced a year of difficulties working the fields after the first waves of recruitment took millions of youths from the countryside. They also suffered from the mortal losses at the front. Many of the rioters shouted for their demands to be met before they agreed to join the armed forces. In Rostov-on-Don the cry went up: 'Long live the State Duma! Give us the Duma!'[8]

The secret police, the Okhrana, took pride in its success in crushing the underground Bolshevik organizations.[9] Such 'undergrounders' of the socialist parties were dispatched to the Russian far north or to eastern Siberia. They gave little trouble and there were few successful attempts at escape. In Yeniseisk province the authorities held 1,442 men and women in exile. Conditions were grim but they were decently fed and rarely short of money, and the police had only 103 employees to keep them under observation across a vast territory.[10] The Okhrana maintained effective scrutiny of free workers and conscripted troops across the rest of the empire. Some, including Vladimir Dzhunkovski who headed the Corps of Gendarmes, were repelled by the idea of paying individual servicemen to spy on their fellows, and he stopped the practice, but it was resumed when he was removed from his post in autumn 1915. The default assumption of the Ministry of Internal Affairs was that even men fighting for the empire could not be automatically trusted.[11]

Lev Trotsky, the sharpest wit and snappiest dresser on the Marxist far left, wrote from Paris and New York for one of the main liberal newspapers in Kiev. He was born on a Jewish agricultural colony in Kherson province in 1879 to a prosperous farming family. As a youth he joined the revolutionary movement. In 1905 he was the Petersburg Soviet's most eloquent speaker. Arrested and deposited in Siberia, he escaped to write a coruscating account of his secret journey into freedom and European exile. Trotsky advocated the immediate formation of a workers' government at the point when the monarchy fell – even Lenin avoided such ultra-extremism until 1917. For many years, too, Trotsky had unsuccessfully tried to persuade the various Marxist factions to coalesce. Many in the Russian Social-Democratic Workers Party suspected him of ambitions to become party leader, a post that did not exist. When war began his influence within the Russian Empire waned. Naturally he had to avoid political commentary in the legal press. But the inter-Allied postal services remained at his disposal and he was able to earn an income from his pieces. Before being deported from France, he wrote pieces for the Russian-language *Nashe Slovo* ('Our Word') in less restrained fashion which were removed by the French censors.[12] The Okhrana worked to disrupt the Russian revolutionaries abroad, knowing that all the parties and factions were producing books, journals and newspapers to be smuggled into the empire.

Conservatives and liberals in the Russian capital had greater freedom than the socialists. They continued to hold soirées where politics were discussed. The conversations frequently crossed party allegiances. They could even involve pleasant exchanges between Nicholas's loyalists and those who desired to turn him or an alternative Romanov family member into a constitutional monarch. The Okhrana often had an informer present. Everyone knew about this danger but many were past caring about it. Individuals close to Nicholas and Alexandra such as Anna Vyrubova even held parties to which they invited politicians. Even then the debate could be surprisingly frank.

Meanwhile the artistic intelligentsia was more muted than in peacetime. Novelists had been the barometer of critical opinion since the middle of the nineteenth century. Some of their works had provided savage assaults on the entire social order even though, if they wished them to appear legally, they had to avoid direct commentary on the current Imperial family. But a novel takes time to be written and during the early war years there were no Russian novels that described the impact of the war. One of the bestsellers of the time was *The Pit* written just before the war by Alexander Kuprin. It became notorious for its depiction of a world of prostitutes, pimps and brothel madams with seedy scenes of gendarmes taking bribes to overlook city crime. It was a wartime book but not a book on the war. Also published at this time was one of the great novels of literary modernism, Andrei Bely's *Petersburg*. This novel too, however, was begun before war was declared. Swinging between ministerial circles and a group of revolutionary terrorists, the scenes provided a portrait of society in the capital that was simultaneously dazzling and grubby. The plot involved a student radical who is deputed to show his commitment to the cause by murdering a high official, none other than his own father. Novels such as *The Pit* and *Petersburg* caused no trouble for the authorities. It is true that Alexander Blok's fine 'Petrograd's Sky' was laden with foreboding about the fate awaiting troops who were on their way to the fighting in Galicia, and he was not alone among poets in his despondency. But increasingly it was patriotic poetry that gained the support of publishers.

Naturally the authorities encouraged cultural output that either supported the war effort or distracted the minds of subjects from the military setbacks. Circuses had to accept the demands by the Imperial army for their trained horses, but otherwise their performances continued as usual in front of large crowds. Lively plays were put on at the theatres and in cabarets. At night it was sometimes hard to remember that soldiers were fighting and dying on the Eastern front. But the war nevertheless entered contemporary culture. Patriotic charity concerts were organized with the Red Cross and Zemgor printing posters bidding everyone to show support for the armed forces. 'Bivouac' performances were arranged for troops near the front line.

The question increasingly arose, however, of whether the political order was capable of surviving all the wartime pressures. The Okhrana could only limit the damage to monarchical power but not eradicate it entirely. Its officers and operatives knew that they stood no chance of winning over political parties, oppositional public figures and cultural critics to the cause of conserving things as they had been before 1914. The war had increased public dissatisfaction with the Imperial order and the threat to the Romanov rule was growing. Discontent had never been absent since the revolutionary upsurge of 1905–6, but now it was suppurating in all classes of society. The grievances against the monarchy mounted, and there was a widespread feeling that Nicholas was mismanaging the empire's war effort. At the same time, particular social classes could scarcely contain their grievance about how society was ordered. Peasants, workers and soldiers sought a redressal of their complaints. Duma politicians understood the volatility of the situation. Most of them relished the prospect of revolutionary change but some already had trepidations about the possible consequences.

13. HOLDING DOWN THE EMPIRE: SUPPRESSION AND SUBVERSION

The Russian military occupation in Galicia in 1914–15 had shown off Romanov self-confidence at the start of hostilities. Habsburg insignia were torn down with one set of double-headed eagle flags replaced by another. Clocks were reset to Petrograd time. The Julian calendar was imposed and inhabitants had to accept dates thirteen days different from the Gregorian one that they had previously followed. Shops were ordered to display their names and wares in the Cyrillic alphabet. The Ukrainian-language press was prohibited and Polish was allowed in administrative offices only on a temporary basis. The very word 'Ruthenian' was prohibited.[1] Imperial aggrandizement had become a Russian war aim as soon as war was declared even though the Allies, including Russia, had yet to sign agreements on which territories each of them should be entitled to acquire. The Russification measures in Galicia signalled the intention to expand the empire.

Poland had been broken up at the end of the eighteenth century and shared between Russia, Prussia and Austria–Hungary. The 'Russian' Poles had risen in revolt against Romanov rule in 1830, 1863 and 1905. In the Great War, as the Russians fought against the Germans and Austrians, the prize of Poland's future was contested. In August 1914 Commander-in-Chief Grand Duke Nikolai Nikolaevich issued a proclamation: 'Let the Poles be re-united under the sceptre of the Russian Tsar.' Greater Poland under such a scheme would be incorporated by the Russian Empire but awarded national rebirth and freedom 'in her faith, language and self-government'.[2]

By late summer 1915, however, all Poland was entirely under occupation by the Central Powers, so Russia offered the Poles the opportunity for self-rule if they were to rise up and support Russia. This was a contentious change of policy for leaders of the Russian political right who had demanded that both the 'Russian' Polish provinces and the 'German' and 'Habsburg' ones should be brought under

Romanov rule by force of arms. Liberals and socialists by contrast canvassed for Poland's right to outright independence. Foreign Affairs Minister Sazonov believed that ministerial silence was unsustainable. On 29 June 1915 he asked Nicholas at Mogilëv to agree to sign a manifesto promising freedom for all Poles.[3] Sazonov secured approval from Chief of the General Staff Alexeev before talking to Nicholas who promised to overrule the expected opposition in the Council of Ministers.[4] When it was reported that many Poles were going off to Germany in search of employment, he recommended the dispatch of financial aid that would show that the Russian government had Polish interests at heart even though Poland was no longer under its rule. He exclaimed: 'Poland isn't Germany but Russia!' He omitted to explain how to disburse such aid in German-occupied Polish territories.[5]

On 16 July 1915 Goremykin spoke in cabinet against Sazonov's proposal, but Sazonov continued to press the case for Polish autonomy after the war. By mid-1916 Nicholas had had enough and fired him from the Foreign Affairs Ministry. Premier Stürmer took his place. Alexandra was delighted, urging her husband to make no announcement about Poland's future. Rasputin, she wrote, was of the same opinion.[6]

On 5 November 1916 [NS] the German and Austrian emperors tried to attract support from the Poles by promising to establish an independent Polish state at the war's end.[7] The Germans also funnelled money for anti-Romanov revolutions from Finland to the Caucasus. Ukraine was a prime target.[8] Alexander Parvus-Helphand, a leading social-democrat from the Russian Empire, was used as an agent for financial transfers to Ukrainian separatists. The Austrians too prioritized help for the Ukrainian movement for independence. They had traditionally treated their own Ukrainian-speakers with respect and allowed freedom of schooling and publication in the Ukrainian language whereas the Petrograd authorities had stiffened their many curtailments of Ukrainian self-expression in the Great War. The Union for the Liberation of Ukraine, which was set up in August 1914 by political exiles from the Russian Empire, received funds from Vienna.[9]

The Ottomans had made similar efforts through their contacts with friendly imams in the Muslim-inhabited regions of the south Caucasus and central Asia. But War Minister Enver Pasha as well as Ottoman consular officials in the Russian Empire doubted that the Muslim subjects of Nicholas II would rise against him. The assumption was that 'Russian' Muslims would show active loyalty to their sovereign.[10]

Enver was proved right. The news of the Russian military incursion into eastern Anatolia convinced imams in most parts of the Russian Empire of the imprudence of hearkening to jihadi appeals from Istanbul. The government in Petrograd meanwhile increased its precautions against separatist trends among Ukrainians, Georgians, Armenians and Azeris. This activity was facilitated by the recognition among leading Georgians and Armenians that if ever they got rid of the Russians, they might have to contend with an Ottoman invasion. Finland continued to be viewed with suspicion from the Russian capital because of the strategical importance of its border with Sweden in the north and its proximity in the south to Petrograd. Russia's moves to tighten control there, though, led to protests by the Finnish nationalist Pehr Evind Svinhufvud, who was exiled to Tomsk in mid-Siberia.

The conundrum for the Imperial administration, as the Svinhufvud case highlighted, was how to balance the suppression of national dissent within the empire while encouraging the nations to fight enthusiastically for the tsar. Nicholas was proclaimed as father to all of them, wanting to lead his 'sons' to fight under his banner in the Imperial cause. As recently as 1905–6 Poles, Georgians and Chechens had fought for their independence, and Finland had long been in a condition of restless discontent. In order to win the Great War, the government in Petrograd needed to do more than simply extend repression and administrative control. The peoples under Romanov rule were surrendering their young men to serve in the armed forces. A positive spirit of empire had to be cultivated, and actions such as the consignment of Svinhufvud to Siberian exile did little to help to persuade Finns to cooperate with the central authorities.

The territories in central Asia were less troublesome for the authorities in Petrograd. The empire had a term, *inorodtsy* (very roughly, 'aliens'), to categorize its non-Christian subjects. On 1 January 1916 a war tax was introduced for people who were exempted from service in the armed forces. 'Aliens' were to pay more than Russians for the fighting that was done by others. But by early 1916 the shortage of manpower on the Eastern front compelled a change of policy, and on 3 May 1916 the Council of Ministers considered a request from Alexeev to supply the Imperial Army with an additional million-strong workforce behind the lines.[11] 'I need workers,' confirmed War Minister Shuvaev, 'come hell or high water.'[12] It soon became clear that the largest source of fresh recruits that would not disrupt food supply or armaments production was to be found among those national and religious groups in central Asia and the Caucasus which had previously been spared the military draft.[13]

Muslims from Turkestan who actually volunteered for military service had caused some official nervousness. In 1915 the idea was floated in the Okhrana that the troublemakers among them could be identified by circulating fake subversive leaflets among the Turkestan sapper battalions and conducting surveillance on the reaction. The General Staff wanted nothing to do with such a scheme.[14]

But on 25 June 1916 Nicholas signed a decree revoking the military exemption of peoples in Turkestan, the steppe provinces, the north and south Caucasus and parts of Siberia. This meant that seven additional million of his subjects, mostly Muslims, were abruptly made liable to conscription.[15] It was not intended to use them directly to fight the Central Powers. They would be put into labour battalions to dig trenches, build earthworks and clear roadways. The pledge was made that those who were conscripted would never be sent into action against Turkish forces. Muslim would not be fighting Muslim. It was stressed that arrangements were in hand to provide food in accordance with Islamic requirements. The recruits would not be served pork. They would be free to observe their daily prayer times. There was little trust in these official assurances in central Asia, especially after it became known that Muslims were suffering abusive treatment in the armed forces. The conscripts also resented being deployed mainly in digging and building rather than military activity.

Anger had been stoked in Turkestan since 1906 by the arrival of Russian settlers who received land belonging to Kazakhs and Kyrgyz. Passions increased in the Great War when taxation was increased and, in common with the rest of the empire, economic inflation harmed incomes. The vast region had been conquered by Russia only half a century earlier and the brutal military campaign had not been forgotten. An uprising in Andijan in 1898 demonstrated the continuing bitterness of anti-Russian feelings.[16] Muslims in Turkestani towns and villages disliked the undermining of their traditions by Christian occupiers. The first wartime disturbance began in early July 1916 in Khujand in modern Tajikistan. A larger uprising then occurred in Jizzakh, now in Uzbekistan, and resulted in the slaughter of Russian officials and the destruction of the railway station and telegraph office. A revolt followed in Semireche in the districts that straddle modern south-east Kazakhstan and northern Kyrgyzstan. The rebels clashed with both Imperial officialdom and Russian settlers. The worst violence was in Pishpek and Przhevalsk where 3,000 Russians perished.[17]

General Alexei Kuropatkin was redeployed from the Eastern front to suppress the revolt. His Order no. 220 called for land seizures 'where Russian blood was shed'.[18] Entire villages were put to the torch on the premise of collective guilt. Russian settlers joined in the savagery. In late August 1916 Alexei Kaplin led two score of settler vigilantes and four or five soldiers to an *aul* in Chumichev district. Kaplin knew the people because he had traded with them. He and his marauders looted the homes, stealing blankets and a silver-mounted saddle and forcing a couple of Kyrgyz to write him a promissory note for 10,000 rubles. Before leaving the *aul* he slaughtered the son of a wealthy inhabitant. The gang of Russians drove off 1,500 sheep, forty horses, fifty cattle and two camels. A subsequent inquiry found that seventy-four Kyrgyz including women and children were massacred.[19] Kuropatkin overlooked all the criminality. His sole purpose was to terrify the Muslims of Turkestan into compliance. By the end of the year around 150,000 Kazakhs and Kyrgyz had died. A quarter of a million Kyrgyz, knowing the fate that awaited them at the hands of Kuropatkin's forces and the settler vigilante detachments, fled south across the border into China.[20]

Duma deputy Kerensky, who had recently undergone kidney surgery, visited Turkestan in August 1916 to collect evidence on the repressive campaign. He had spent some of his early years in Tashkent and was appalled by what he now discovered was happening. On returning to Petrograd, he denounced the 'planned and systematic terror' that Kuropatkin was inflicting.[21] It was not the first revolt in recent years that the authorities had savagely crushed but commanders treated it as a supreme act of treason at a time the empire was fighting for its very existence on the Eastern front.[22] The British had suppressed the Easter rising in Dublin that year in the same spirit. Kerensky insisted, however, that governments should show prudence in dealing with rebels. Apart from his moral revulsion, he could see no practical benefit for the empire in the indiscriminate mass butchery that Kuropatkin was inflicting in Turkestan.

14. 'IS THIS STUPIDITY OR TREASON?': THE COURT, PLOTS AND STRIKES

On 15 June 1916 Chief of the General Staff Alexeev complained to Nicholas about the state of industry. Neither the War Ministry nor the Special Conference of Defence had proved capable of making the necessary improvements. At the front there was a shocking shortage of cartridges. The Putilov Works and other factories were short of fuel and metal. Workers were going hungry. Transport was in a mess. Strikes were ruining production. Alexeev called for a total reorganization of the war effort. He argued for the creation of the post of supreme minister of state defence who would have authority over every ministry and public agency and be answerable to no one but Nicholas.[1] Alexeev had never previously told Nicholas, however respectfully, how to put the Imperial state in order. Now he was arguing that only a dictator could compel the rear to perform its duty for the needs of the front. Nicholas concurred with the proposal, adding only one detail of his own. Whereas Alexeev had proposed excusing solely industry's technical experts from the draft, Nicholas wanted to exempt agricultural specialists as well.[2]

Unlike the parties of the former Progressive Block, Alexeev did not call for a 'government of public confidence' or delineate how to reorganize the interplay between the front and the rear. On receiving a copy of Alexeev's proposals, Rodzyanko was troubled by two questions. If a military commander were to be made the dictator, how would he resolve the crisis in cities and villages? If a civilian received the post, what would he do about conditions on the front lines? Rodzyanko sped to Mogilëv to explain his concerns to Alexeev in person. On the same trip he warned Nicholas that if such a dictator were to make a success of the post, people would conclude that everything would be better if Nicholas were removed from power.

Nicholas hailed Rodzyanko's analysis but failed to think about it for long or at all seriously. Instead he decided to adopt Alexeev's advice in a reduced form by endowing Stürmer with authority over the wartime Special Conferences. He also made Stürmer minister of foreign affairs. This involved firing Sazonov, who had helpfully gone on leave to Finland. Stürmer's starry elevation can scarcely have been to the liking of Alexeev, who shared the widespread judgement that Stürmer was out of his depth as premier and was managing affairs no more dynamically than old Goremykin had done.[3] Even Stürmer, though, recognized he could not run the Internal Affairs Ministry after extending his reach into both the Foreign Affairs Ministry and the Special Conferences. He welcomed Alexander Protopopov as his replacement at Internal Affairs that September. Protopopov, an Octobrist, might earlier have been welcomed as someone who would moderate the government's repressive policies, but Protopopov developed a passionate belief in the need for harsh measures of rule. Whereas Nicholas, Alexandra and Rasputin found him endearing, the Duma liberals and liberal conservatives despised him as a 'traitor'.[4]

Protopopov met with his ex-colleagues on 19 October 1916 in an attempt to obtain conciliation between Duma and government. Milyukov rejected his request for the discussion to be off the record, which inhibited Protopopov from uttering anything of substance. He was asked why he had accepted appointment to a cabinet headed by Stürmer. Protopopov in an emotional outburst declared his love for Nicholas and his belief that Nicholas loved him too. The meeting quickly turned into a pathetic farce, leaving its participants convinced that Protopopov was mentally ill. Milyukov told him bluntly: 'You're leading Russia to ruin!'[5]

Pavel Milyukov on 1 November 1916 abandoned caution and delivered an inflammatory speech at the Duma. He chose Stürmer as his target stressing how pleased the Germans were by Stürmer's rise at Sazonov's expense. He dwelled on the malign influence of Ivan Manusevich-Manuilov, Stürmer's personal assistant, who was notorious for having worked as one of Rasputin's aides. Rehearsing the recent history of cabinet measures, Milyukov paused repeatedly to ask: 'Is this stupidity or treason?' The speech was a press sensation.

Milyukov had deliberately played upon the unfounded rumour that Stürmer was seeking out possibilities for a separate peace with Germany. Stürmer understood the danger he was facing and, as the potential for trouble grew in the capital, contacted Alexeev with a view towards replacing the troops of the Petrograd garrisons. Alexeev, however, drew the line at using his front-line men to suppress domestic disturbances.[6]

Stürmer's premiership was badly damaged in public opinion and on 8 November 1916 Nicholas tried to placate the Duma critics – or at least those who believed in his right to rule – by firing him and inviting Alexander Trepov, the transport minister and an enthusiastic advocate of the war effort, to take his place. Although Trepov lacked a high opinion in Duma circles, he was at least known to detest Rasputin, which helped to quieten some of the voices of discontent. Nicholas wrote to Alexandra: 'Only I beg you, don't get Our Friend involved in this. I'm bearing the responsibility, and I wish to be free in making my choice.'[7]

There was speculation that Minister of Internal Affairs Protopopov would be fired. The empress travelled to Mogilëv with him to plead for his retention in post, and Nicholas granted the request. The cabinet's reputation in the country fell still lower when Trepov denied permission for the Zemstvos Union and Towns Union to hold congresses in December 1916.[8] The Zemstvos Union leaders signed a protest and published the speech which Prince Georgi Lvov had planned to deliver.[9] The cabinet refused to compromise. Policies were retained without any attempt to reconsider their usefulness. Ministers were unrepentant and put it about that the employees of both Unions were draft evaders.[10]

Liberals were not the only group angered by the high-handed actions of those running the war effort. A group of friends in high society decided that only Rasputin's liquidation could save the monarchy from itself and halt the alleged moves for a separate peace with Germany. A conspiracy was formed by the wealthy young monarchist Felix Yusupov and his friends Grand Duke Dmitri Pavlovich and the politician Vladimir Purishkevich, who had helped to found the ultra-nationalist Union of the Russian People. They inveigled Rasputin to join a drinking session on 17 December 1916 in the Yusupov residence in Petrograd. There they plied him with poisoned sweets and drinks. Yet the toxins had no effect. Nor did further rounds of drinks. At that point the plotters decided simply to shoot him. A gun was fired and Rasputin slumped to the floor, apparently lifeless. But as they heaved his body outside and into the icy river Moika, Rasputin suddenly revived and let out a shriek. More shots were fired into him in the dark, icy waters. He was dead at last. The corpse was retrieved from the Moika in the morning and identified by police.

The news had a shattering effect on Nicholas and Alexandra, who had lost their psychological and spiritual prop as well as the one person who could ease the handling of their son Alexei and his haemophilia.

The police quickly discovered those responsible for the murder but Nicholas let them off lightly because of their high social status. He probably recognized, too, his own need to avoid offending public opinion. Grand Duke Dmitri Pavlovich was banished to military service in Persia and Yusupov was ordered to stay on one of his distant rural estates. Rasputin was buried on 21 December 1916 in church grounds outside the park of the Alexander Palace. Nicholas called the killers fiends. The Imperial family sat in the front row and the Romanov children wept.[11]

The murderers had been motivated by the belief that Rasputin had used the empress to exert a malign influence on the emperor and Russian politics, a belief that was shared in public life. Petrograd gossip mocked Nicholas as the echo chamber of her strident, ignorant opinions. Grand Duke Nikolai Nikolaevich wrote to Nicholas that Alexandra was damaging the monarchy and that he should appoint a 'responsible government'.[12] With or without Rasputin, she certainly pressed her opinions on her husband. The Imperial couple had always discussed matters of state and he depended on being able to exchange ideas with her in a way that he disliked doing with ministers, whom he regarded as his temporary servants. But at no great point of decision about the conduct of the war, apart from personnel appointments, did she provably change his mind. Nicholas was quite capable of making glaring misjudgements without her assistance. He was his own worst adviser.

Other plotters saw no point in getting rid of Rasputin if the emperor retained the Imperial throne. Already in summer 1916 Guchkov had written confidentially to Mikhail Alexeev about the worsening situation in the rear. He wanted to give an alert to the likelihood of a Petrograd coup while steering him away from being used to suppress it. Alexeev refrained from replying, as was his habit with such letters from oppositionists, but he didn't tell Nicholas about Guchkov's initiative.[13] Alexandra, however, discovered what had happened and informed her husband. When Nicholas asked her for proof, she produced a copy of Guchkov's offending letter.[14] Nicholas refrained from confronting Alexeev, perhaps finding it hard to believe that his highest-ranking commander, a man known for his decency, was capable of deceiving him. The emperor tried to see the positive side of the situation by assuring Alexandra that Alexeev hated Duma Chairman Rodzyanko. The implication was that Alexeev deserved the Imperial family's trust.[15] But it would not be surprising if Nicholas started to worry about the direction that events were taking.

Alexeev himself was exhausted by an excessive workload at the General Staff. His health was collapsing. On 11 November 1916, no longer able to overlook a chronic kidney problem, he left Mogilëv to convalesce in Crimea. While he was there, he received some leading representatives from the Duma who spoke about a possible coup and enquired how the military leadership might react. Apparently Alexeev replied that it could only disrupt an army that was already in poor shape.[16] Yet again he said nothing to his sovereign. While being unwilling to endorse a move against the emperor, he shared the gloomy analysis of his visitors. A few months later he wrote: 'It became obvious that not only had the current government suffered bankruptcy but that the entire state was falling apart.' Alexeev had seen Nicholas at close range for more than a year and knew him as weak-willed, indecisive, vain and distrustful even while he issued peremptory and damaging orders.[17] When the Duma group talked to other commanders, including Brusilov, they were said to have welcomed the idea of bringing the reign of Nicholas Romanov to an end.[18]

Overtures were made to Alexeev's subordinates in Mogilëv.[19] The Octobrists, Kadets and Progressists avoided saying or writing anything directly critical of the army high command even though they knew the generals had much to answer for. They praised the valour of Russian soldiery while heaping blame upon the government. (They still could not mention the emperor by name.) They understood that if and when they acted to overthrow Nicholas, it was essential to have the General Staff on their side.[20] Mikhail Chelnokov hosted a discussion in Moscow that was attended by Milyukov and Georgi Lvov. When asked why the State Duma was not organizing a coup d'état, Milyukov exclaimed, 'Just bring us two regiments at the Tauride Palace and we'll seize power.' Milyukov was understandably furious after all this was leaked to a Kadet gathering.[21] But for once the Okhrana knew nothing about the discussion and nothing reached the emperor.

The discussions continued in secret about the future nature of the political system. Guchkov, Rodzyanko and Milyukov wanted a British-style constitutional monarchy – Milyukov in particular was a well-known Anglophile. By contrast Kerensky, a Socialist-Revolutionary, hoped for a republic. There was no love between Milyukov and Kerensky, but in the winter of 1916–17 they agreed that they shared an imperative need to get rid of Nicholas. Other would-be revolutionaries included Mikhail Tereshchenko, Vladimir Lvov and Nikolai Nekrasov. They met in private homes, restaurants and their illegal masonic lodge, the Grand Orient of Russia's Peoples. They knew that any kind of coup, however peaceful, would set off public disturbances in Petrograd and elsewhere but thought this was a price that had to be paid to bring the empire back to its feet. They were confident of being able to restore order because they intended to eliminate the hated features of Nicholas's rule. They themselves expected to rise at last to the apex of power.[22] Competence and expertise would replace ignorance. Corruption would be expunged. But before any of this could happen, Nicholas had to be dislodged from the Imperial throne that the Romanov dynasty had occupied since 1613.

The emperor had other things on his mind. The empire's economy was crumbling in many sectors. Food supply had collapsed. State grain collections had risen from 5 million tons in 1914–15 to 8.9 million tons in 1916–17. This was impressive but inadequate for the empire's needs. The armed forces and the northern consumer region alone needed nine million tons, and shipments to them were already declining in 1916.[23] Transport was in disorder with locomotives and lines in disrepair. Inflation was rampant with the ruble worth only 27 per cent of its value in 1914.[24] Andrei Shingarëv and other Kadet economists argued for a more planned economic response from the government and for the establishment of a grain trade monopoly.[25] Among the socialist parties the eagerness for state intervention in the economy had always been deeply felt. The government had increased its control over industrial orders and agricultural deliveries and, unlike its critics, was conscious of the limitations on its agencies' performance. It was easier to change policies than to enforce administrative compliance and efficiency. Chronic deficiencies in comparison with the German enemy were accentuated in wartime.

Popular discontent was intense in the capital. Goods were plentiful in the stores and the upper and middle classes could afford the sharply rising prices, but the gaudy shop fronts full of groceries and luxuries angered the many who could not afford them.[26]

Alexander Rittikh took over the Ministry of Agriculture in November 1916 and his main task was to boost food supplies for the army and the cities. He announced a grain supply quota for each province, based on the government's information about past harvests. The Agriculture Ministry's land surveyors made the necessary estimates and inspections. No agency of government, however, had the necessary access to information about each and every village. Peasants had always been adept at concealing whatever they wanted to keep secret, and trouble was inevitable when the peasantry thought the authorities were behaving unfairly. Rural disturbances flared up. Rittikh felt he had no option but to use force to secure the vital deliveries. It was wartime and he was tackling a practical problem with the only resources available to him.[27] The true test of Rittikh's scheme took place in Ukraine and the Volga region where most of the empire's marketed wheat was grown, but despite the new measures Kiev province supplied only a quarter of its quota, Tambov province just two-thirds. Such results boded ill for the empire's food supplies.[28]

A ration-card system was introduced in all urban areas from Petrograd to small provincial towns. It was applied to specific products, depending on local circumstances. New measures to try and alleviate the problems often didn't work. When the government restricted the sale of meat to certain days of the week, consumers with money in their pockets simply responded by buying up extra on the allowed days. Ration cards, moreover, offered entitlement, not the surety of receipt of goods in the stores.[29] The authorities were helpless to improve the situation for the urban populace and there were concerns about malnutrition and starvation.

The focus on feeding the towns did not go down well with rural inhabitants. Alexander Zamaraev's household was nearly self-sufficient and was never going to starve but nonetheless he was aware of the wider changing conditions. White flour was one of the products that he did not make for himself. As a peasant he was ineligible for a ration card in Totma whereas the townsfolk could each purchase ten pounds every month, so if the Zamaraevs needed oats, they had to do a deal with a friendly seller out of public view.[30] Zamaraev took little comfort from newspaper reports about the difficulties being experienced in the German cities. Shortages of bread, salt and meat were widespread across Germany with people 'sitting in darkness and there's no kerosene'. It troubled Zamaraev that Russia was suffering in the same way.[31]

In late 1916, as well as facing food-supply problems, the high command requested an additional 300,000 recruits to fill the gaps left by the summer campaigns. The Special Conference of Defence advised against satisfying the request. The number of available fit and able males of military age was reaching its limit. The Special Conference and War Minister Shuvaev warned of dangers if the usual conscription process was applied. Older conscripts did not make good soldiers.[32] Opinion was growing among thoughtful officers such as Lieutenant-Colonel Alexander Verkhovski that the Imperial Army was too big to be effective and was hampering the economic output on which it depended. Verkhovski liaised with those in the Duma who agreed that a partial demobilization was needed.[33] Even Alexei Brusilov saw that his summer successes in the south-west had made no decisive strategic benefit. But he believed that the Germans could have been crushed if only the high command had agreed to repeat his offensive methods on the northern sectors.[34]

In the final months of 1916 the crisis of the Imperial state became acute with a wave of industrial strikes in Petrograd and other cities.[35] Workers were demanding higher wages and better conditions in factories. The socialist parties had long believed that a single spark could light an uncontainable conflagration and liberals likewise. Progressist Party leader and businessman Alexander Konovalov said that a 'revolutionary movement' was inevitable and that 'all the signs of anarchy were visible'. Konovalov predicted civil war. He argued for big business to protect its interests by getting on better terms with its workforces and establishing regular arbitration procedures.[36]

But most other owners were unwilling to make such a move, and strikes continued. When workers were locked out of their enterprises, they moved to the streets outside the barracks of the 181st Rear Regiment and pleaded for the troops to support their cause. When gendarmes used violence against the crowd, soldiers fired on them. Army officers intervened to restore order but the regiment was no longer trusted and the command was given for its disbandment after disciplinary action was taken.[37] But the problem was not confined to a single regiment and there was talk amongst the authorities about the unreliability of the capital's garrisons.[38] Soldiers in one of the Moscow barracks stormed their regimental kitchens in November 1916 and pelted their lieutenant-colonel with stones. They had grievances about food and clothing: 'Just look at us and how tattered we are: give us some boots and trousers!' The Central Workers' Group resolved to support the creation of a 'provisional revolutionary government'.[39] The strike movement continued, and the tiny Bolshevik groups grew confident that the final days of the monarchy were at hand despite the police raids that devastated their activity in the capital.

In this atmosphere ministers were concerned about when and even whether to call the Duma back into session. The cabinet itself was in turmoil. Nicholas belatedly recognized that he had been unwise in appointing Trepov to the premiership at a moment of industrial strikes and aggravated political tension. On 27 December 1916 he replaced Trepov with Prince Nikolai Golitsyn. The hope was that Golitsyn would be able to work with the Duma in a less confrontational way. But the strike movement continued to intensify and in January 1917 Internal Affairs Minister Protopopov ordered the arrest of the Workers' Group in its entirety. This provoked outrage in the Central War-Industries Committee, and Guchkov and Konovalov attended a meeting at which they declared that if the workers were guilty then so too were they themselves. Milyukov was present, as were the socialists Chkheidze and Kerensky.[40] A nervous cabinet decided to postpone the reopening of the Duma until 14 February 1917.[41] Golitsyn prayed that the delay would enable him to stabilize the situation in Petrograd. He had never wanted the premiership and showed little confidence in his ability to bring the raging tempers to a halt.

The Russian Empire's responsibilities to its Allies were increased by a war conference convened in November 1916 on French soil, at Chantilly, to agree the commencement of offensives on the Western and Eastern fronts in spring 1917 within three weeks of each other. The operational plan was confirmed in January 1917 at an inter-Allied conference in Petrograd. Although both the cabinet and the General Staff had their doubts about the readiness of their forces for such action, their financial dependency on the favours of Britain and France – as well as military honour – compelled acquiescence.[42]

On 3 February Georgi Lvov wrote to the emperor warning that reforms were essential to heal the split between the people and the authorities.[43] Rodzyanko, too, sent a letter that set out the problems as he saw them. He expressed unhappiness about Golitsyn's appointment and lamented how 'civic forces' were being treated like enemies whereas in western Europe they and their governments worked in cooperation. If Nicholas wanted to help the armed forces and improve food output, Rodzyanko told him, he should have appointed 'a person enjoying public confidence' as his ancestor Alexander I had done in 1812. 'The midnight hour is striking,' he stressed: 'and the time is too near when any appeal to the people's common sense [*razumu*] will be overdue and in vain.'[44] Rodzyanko received permission for an audience with Nicholas on 10 February 1917. Ignoring the official etiquette, he called for a new cabinet: 'I'm demanding, your Majesty: previously I begged but now I'm demanding.'[45]

Nicholas, however, was steadfast as he took a break at Tsarskoe Selo and read the Petrograd newspapers. When the Duma met on

14 February, its deputies were still angry. By 22 February the emperor's patience with them snapped and he signed papers to prorogue the proceedings yet again. He declined to let the continuing strikes bother him. Nicholas was used to doing things in his own way and he failed to appreciate the risk that he was running for his throne and the dynasty.

15. THE FEBRUARY REVOLUTION: PETROGRAD FACTORY WORKERS, GARRISON SOLDIERS AND THE STATE DUMA

The Imperial train with Nicholas on board left for Smolensk and pulled into Mogilëv at 3 p.m. on 23 February 1917. His reading on the journey was a French book about Julius Caesar's conquest of Gaul. After receiving a briefing from Alexeev on the latest military situation, he repaired to Governor's House. At that moment he thought fondly again of his son and the time they had spent together at GHQ. He missed his company. The day was cloudless and there was a rise in temperature after weeks of heavy snow and severe cold. A breeze was blowing. Nicholas stayed indoors at Governor's House to avoid exacerbating a cough he had picked up in Tsarskoe Selo. The General Staff continued its work as normal. Over cups of tea in the evening Nicholas wrote in English to Alexandra, who had sent a telegram with news of an outbreak of measles among their children. After jotting down some words of sympathy, he recalled her message about acting like a true tsar: 'What you write about being firm – the master – is perfectly true. I do not forget it – be sure of that, but I need not bellow at the people right & left every moment. A quiet sharp remark is enough very often to put the one or the other into his place.'[1]

On 24 February 1917 Alexandra wrote that unofficial sources told her of violent looting of bread stores on Nevski Prospect in central Petrograd and elsewhere in the city.[2] The cabinet advised eliminating the Duma as a potential trouble centre but behind the scenes Premier Golitsyn was secretly exploring with Duma Chairman Rodzyanko how to remove Nicholas from power. Nicholas' own younger brother Mikhail himself was involved in their discussions. Golitsyn's idea was for Mikhail to become regent, fire the cabinet and appoint a new one.

Mikhail, however, refused to be tempted: he could see only danger and complication in such an act of treason.[3] The crisis in government deepened and on 26 February a message went to Nicholas from ministers asking for a new premier who would have the right to select his own cabinet. They had given up on the hapless Golitsyn. They also requested the appointment of a Petrograd military commander who stood a chance of public approval. Nicholas's brother Mikhail sent Nicholas a telegram calling for Georgi Lvov to be made premier.[4]

Away in Mogilëv, Nicholas took a while to appreciate the acuteness of the crisis. Far from co-opting leading parliamentarians into a fresh cabinet, Nicholas the next day signed a decree suspending its proceedings and indicating that they were to restart no sooner than April.[5] But he was at least beginning to appreciate the seriousness of the situation, as he wrote in his diary: 'Disorders started in Petrograd several days ago; lamentably, troops have begun to take part in them. It's an awful feeling to be so far away and in receipt of the sketchy bad news!' He made preparations to leave for Tsarskoe Selo and for boarding the Imperial train at one o'clock at night.[6] He summoned General Nikolai Ivanov before departure and they held a lengthy discussion and drew up a plan for Ivanov to become military dictator. Ivanov was to hasten to the capital taking a reliable force with him. Nicholas turned in for the night at 3.15 a.m. after ordering the train's departure from Mogilëv at five o'clock that morning.[7] He knew that something drastic needed to be done in Petrograd and that he could not fully rely upon the garrisons there. But he gave no impression of being overly worried. He trusted that Ivanov's units would restore calm.

The Petrograd strike movement acquired a strong momentum. Although snow remained on the ground and the spring thaw was weeks away, the mood among factory workforces was hotly defiant. Moreover, the garrison soldiers showed their sympathy for the industrial workers they were being ordered to suppress. On 27 February the leaders of the dispersed State Duma assembled to form its own Provisional Committee. The Petrograd Soviet was created on the same day, a renaissance of one of the labour movement's sharpest challenges to governmental power in 1905: the leaders, some of whom belonged to the Central War-Industries Committee, were determined to ensure that the Duma's liberals and liberal conservatives did not form a revolutionary administration without consulting them. As the disorder continued in the capital, both the Provisional Committee and the Petrograd Soviet strove to shape the course of events. By 28 February 1917 their loosely coordinated uprising had become unstoppable. Prisons were burned down and their inmates released.[8] There were attacks on police stations in the capital and files were tossed into the street.[9] The State Duma Provisional Committee saw the time had come for decisive action to remove Nicholas from power, and a plan was discussed for Alexei to succeed him with Nicholas's brother Mikhail as regent. An act of abdication was prepared for Nicholas to sign.[10]

On 1 March 1917 Mikhail Alexeev at the General Staff sent an order to Ivanov to avoid the use of force in Petrograd, which was tantamount to saying he should do nothing to avert revolution.[11] Talks took place that morning between the Duma Provisional Committee and the Petrograd Soviet leadership about the formation of a new government and its policies. Power on the streets lay in the Soviet's hands if it wanted it. But Mensheviks, Socialist-Revolutionaries and many Bolsheviks were not keen. Their doctrines told them that a fully capitalist economy was needed before socialists ought to move on to a revolution that would install a socialist order in society. They were also loath to assume responsibility in government for the economic troubles that had bedevilled the wartime activity of Nicholas's administration. But they did have the determination to influence what a 'bourgeois government' might do. The Soviet's Executive Committee was already meeting in the final two days of February.[12] Its Menshevik and Socialist-Revolutionary leaders – as well as their allies in the Jewish Labour Bund – were people of action who had been hardened by years of persecution by the Imperial administration. They both exasperated and scared the Duma Provisional Committee. One of its members, the conservative Vasili Shulgin, exclaimed that if they were not going to take power, they should step aside and let others govern who had the necessary sense of duty.[13]

Soviet leaders stuck by their basic demands. They wanted an immediate amnesty for all those held prisoner on political and religious grounds – including anyone found guilty of terrorist offences. They called for freedoms of the press, conscience, assembly and strikes, and they desired these freedoms to be extended to those on active military service. Their Order No. 1 proclaimed the right of troops both to elect their own committees and to cease having to salute their officers. When Milyukov failed to get the Soviet leadership to temper its demands, Kerensky took over the negotiations.[14] A form of words was found that satisfied the Duma Provisional Committee's requirement for the maintenance of military discipline at the front and in the garrisons. The Soviet nonetheless persisted with its other demands. It wanted a new people's militia to conduct policing functions. It called for all the practices of discrimination based on religious, national and social status to be abolished. The Duma Provisional Committee gave way on such matters but baulked at the demand for the creation of a democratic republic. This provoked the Soviet Executive Committee to reply that it would withhold its recognition of the Provisional Government. Duma and Soviet leaderships were drifting apart and Nicholas still remained in power.[15]

Both bodies understood the urgent need to preserve cooperation. Nicholas had sent a military expedition by rail from Mogilëv. As the threat increased, the Duma Provisional Committee invited two of the Petrograd Soviet's leaders, Nikolai Chkheidze and Matvei Skobelev, to join its Military Commission. Led by Guchkov, the Military Commission had been set up to gather support from the city garrisons and prevent action by any units loyal to Nicholas. A plan was quickly made for an uprising across the whole central zone of the capital, to seize control of all ministries, police stations, food-supply agencies and post and telegraph offices.[16] No important public office was to be left in the hands of the emperor's supporters. The moment of revolution had arrived. Word was passed to foreign embassies about what was afoot. The Duma revolutionaries were cheered when words came to the Tauride Palace that the French and British ambassadors were indicating unconditional approval of the Provisional Committee.[17]

Soldiers came for Pëtr Bark at his private apartment in the afternoon of 1 March. Their leader, Nikifor by name, was well known to both Bark and his wife Sophia because he had worked for them as a servant, and Sophia had helped get his wife a job at the Finance Ministry. This did not stop Nikifor from pointing his gun at Sophia Bark and saying: 'When I asked you for bread, you gave me a stone.' Pëtr Bark's phone had been disconnected that morning. The troops walked him down the stairs not letting him take the lift. The janitor handed him a fur coat at the front door. Minister Bark was taken to the office of his own deputy minister Nikolaenko where he found a commissar of the newly created State Duma Provisional Committee, who told Nikifor that he was wrong to have arrested Bark. Nikifor was told to take Bark to the State Duma at the Tauride Palace. Commissar and troops clambered into a truck flying the red flag and containing several machine guns. The truck had to take an indirect route to avoid barricades. Arguments broke out between the soldiers and sailors of the escort. When one of the soldiers decided he needed a cup of tea, he halted the driver at the

Field of Mars. The truck remained stationary until it became clear that no beverages were available in the neighbourhood.[18]

Outside the Duma a huge crowd had gathered which held up the progress of Bark and his accompanying party. Some onlookers wanted to beat him up. On reaching the palace building, Bark was presented to two Duma deputies who expressed surprise that anyone should have arrested him. Two hours passed before the situation was clarified. Alexander Kerensky came along to explain that Bark would be in physical danger if released. The newly formed Petrograd Soviet of Workers' and Peasants' Deputies was holding a raucous session in the Catherine Hall, and some of the soldiers and sailors might take it into their heads to harm Bark. The revolution had been won and the Duma Provisional Committee wanted to prevent a violent settling of scores. Kerensky deposited Bark in a room under guard with six others who included Minister of Internal Affairs Protopopov. The occupants were strictly banned from talking to each other. A telephone call was put through to let Sophia Bark know that her husband was safe. She sent their French governess with overnight clothing and toiletries for him. He slept for half the night on a sofa before giving his place to Minister of Trade and Industry Count Shakhovskoi. Others stretched themselves out on newspapers.[19]

Shcheglovitov was less lucky than Bark and given no chance to put on an overcoat. He was marched in the freezing cold into the Tauride Palace. Red in the face and bedraggled, he was roughly handled. His reputation as a former justice minister and director of repression went before him and only Kerensky's intervention saved him from being beaten up or worse.[20] Reports from around the city told of between 1,300 and 1,600 fatalities.[21]

The Duma Provisional Committee started one of its most decisive sessions just before midnight on 1 March and stayed in session into the early hours of the next day. Those present were no longer willing to delay the formation of a new government. News of the disturbances on the streets heightened the sense of urgency. The Duma leaders were aware that unless they acted quickly, they would lose all control over events. Milyukov performed a key role in drafting a list of potential ministers. Absent from it was Duma Chairman Rodzyanko, whom his colleagues suspected to be either too ready to compromise with Nicholas or too eager to assume dictatorial power for himself. Instead a consensus grew that Georgi Lvov should be asked to head the government, but it was recognized that this could not safely happen at the

Provisional Committee's command. Consultations were hurriedly held with the Petrograd Soviet's Executive Committee – an early sign of the emerging balance of power in the capital. The socialists Kerensky and Chkheidze were included in the proposed cabinet which would hold power until a Constituent Assembly could be elected.[22]

By the morning of 2 March the celebrations had already reached Moscow. Nikita Okunev, an accounts administrator working for a Moscow river-port company, walked around Moscow's central district and observed the crowds and garrison units streaming to the city duma. They waved their hats and scarves while shouting 'hurrah!' and whistling at the tiny groups of gendarmes as they were led into the building as if under arrest. Okunev felt the twinge of an unexpected emotion:

> I even felt sorry for them from the depths of my soul: they seemed such Russian people, most of them being middle-aged men with families, and they were walking like damned pariahs. At [a time of] such joy they too should be made joyful – and one should be awaiting their free transition to a new side and give them, as they repent their sins great and small, the possibility of joining spiritually with the common movement of liberation and occupy a position of warriors, if not of citizens.

Okunev felt relief when the policemen were allowed to depart unharmed. A sense of unity prevailed across the usual social barriers. No one could any longer think of reverting to the old ways of doing things. He encountered soldiers wearing ribbons and noticed that colonels were frequently striding out with them. Army bands struck up triumphant marches. 'People's power' appeared to be everywhere.[23]

The abdication when it came on 2 March was fast and calmly executed. The State Duma Provisional Committee had sent Alexander Guchkov and Vasili Shulgin to talk to Nicholas II. By the time they reached his train at Pskov he had already made up his mind to relinquish the throne.[24] Even his generals at Mogilëv wanted this outcome. Nicholas saw the armed forces as the sanctum of faith and nationhood, and he could not imagine clinging to power without their active support. He suddenly looked older. More grey hairs had appeared. There were new lines on his brow.[25]

Nicholas knew, though, that after him there could legally be only one possible emperor, young Alexei. But Alexei had an incurable medical condition and was immature and untrained. Nicholas slackened the educational demands made upon the boy because of his haemophilia but the result was that Alexei in his thirteenth year had still not mastered the arithmetic of simple fractions.[26] Even so, Nicholas considered the idea of abdicating in his favour. The Duma politicians, however, indicated their insistence on Alexei, if made emperor, living separately from him. Nicholas could not bear the thought of handing over his beloved son to others, so he took the momentous decision to transfer power to his brother Mikhail. Such a step would infringe the Basic Law. But Nicholas, a ruler with imperious impulses, had made known his desire and expected it to be fulfilled. With that, he signed the decree of abdication and started the winding railway journey to Tsarskoe Selo and to the bosom of his family. The affairs of state which had been his responsibility since 1894 had passed for ever from his hands.

His draft decree enjoined his brother to rule 'in full and unbreakable union with the representatives of the people in the legislative institutions'.[27] In practice this would ease the advance on governmental power of those whom the Provisional Committee of the State Duma might choose as ministers. Whilst the new cabinet's make-up had yet to be determined, there was no doubt about the will to rule.

Alexander Zamaraev and his fellow Totma residents had known nothing about the situation in Petrograd until 1 March 1917 and even then they had only scanty information. Zamaraev could only guess that 'important political events' were taking place.[28] When the news came through to the town, he shared the almost universal relief that the era of the Romanovs, which had lasted since 1613, was at an end:

> Nicholas Romanov and his family have been overthrown. They are under arrest and receive groceries with their ration cards really on the same basis as everyone else. They paid no concern at all to the well-being of their people and the people's patience snapped. They have brought their state to the point of hunger and darkness. What went on at their court! It was all horror and shame. It wasn't Nicholas II who ruled over the state but the drunken Rasputin.[29]

Unfair on Rasputin, no doubt, but Zamaraev was not stating an unusual opinion: it was what nearly everyone thought. The people of the Russian Empire, aristocrats as well as workers and peasants, were relieved that Nicholas had vacated the throne.

But the semi-autocratic order and its former would-be autocrat were not Russia's sole problem. Although he made a bad situation worse, he was also the victim of the modernizing changes in the economy and society that he had endorsed. Whether a constitutional monarchy could have coped better is a moot question. Nor is it entirely clear that he would have survived in power if he had chosen the path of peace and diplomacy rather than war in mid-1914. Russian liberals and liberal conservatives had longed for an opportunity to demonstrate that they would prove more effective in asserting imperial power in the world. The empire's vulnerabilities were painfully exposed by the Great War. By early 1917 the economy, infrastructure, ethnic relations, training and administration had been strained to the point of rupture. Whoever assumed power in the lands of the Romanovs was going to inherit tremendous problems. German forces were within striking range of Petrograd. The sinews of industry and transport were stretched to breaking point. Food supplies were perilously short, and ordinary people had discovered the extraordinary strength of their potential to challenge their rulers.

16. THE PROVISIONAL GOVERNMENT: A CARETAKER CABINET IN POWER

On 3 March it was still not a settled situation in central Petrograd. The employees of Goldberg's prestigious apothecary took down the Romanov coat of arms after years of Imperial patronage. Much care was taken to avoid breakage of the double-headed eagle emblem on its descent to the pavement. An American journalist recorded: 'Goldberg evidently thought that he might need it again. The women in a bread line right below smiled as if they knew better.'[1]

The queuing customers probably knew the Petrograd Soviet would have brought thousands of its supporters onto the streets if an attempt was made to keep a Romanov on the throne. Inside the Duma Provisional Committee there was still no agreed policy on the framework of rule. Rodzyanko, Guchkov and Milyukov were pressing the others for a constitutional monarchy. When they met that afternoon in Mikhail Romanov's apartment, they begged him to comply with his brother's wish for him to succeed him. Mikhail was tempted until seeing other members of the Duma Provisional Committee did not approve. Among the dissenters was Alexander Kerensky, whose influence had grown during the uprising. Mikhail declined to allow his name to go forward in the absence of unanimity. Milyukov, Guchkov and the monarchist lobby expressed anger with Kerensky but they recognized the danger of any early split inside the Duma Provisional Committee. Perhaps they also sensed that their preferred policy would not endear them to the workers and soldiers who had brought down Nicholas. Mikhail's point-blank refusal anyway left them little choice but to accept that the Russian future would be a republican one.

Rodzyanko favoured a reopening of the Fourth State Duma to institute some kind of parliamentary rule. His Octobrist Party leader Guchkov agreed so long as the Duma's composition was replenished with representatives of public groups as yet not included.[2] The Octobrists wanted to preserve a continuity of governance by establishing a constitutional monarchy under the Duma's authority. They saw this as a way of saving ministers from being accused of replacing one form of arbitrary governance with another.

The Duma Provisional Committee by a majority rejected this as likely to provoke mass protest. If the Petrograd Soviet, already a political force, suspended cooperation, the result would be continued instability.[3] Kadets, including Milyukov, recoiled from expanding the powers of a parliament that had been formed under the old regime. The Duma's many reactionaries would make it impossible to provide the revolutionary administration with popular legitimacy. What is more, precious time would be lost if the cabinet were made beholden to the outcome of Duma debates. Action would also be delayed if there had to be an election before the next government was formed. The Duma Provisional Committee acted with dispatch to end the uncertainty. After a brief discussion it selected and announced a cabinet, to be called the Provisional Government, that would hold a plenitude of power until polls were organized for a Constituent Assembly. Some basic reforms would be decreed. The war effort would be reinforced. The Provisional Government would reach out to everyone in society who wanted to help build a democratic order and bring prosperity to all. Free Russia would show what it was made of.

There was agreement for Georgi Lvov to head the cabinet. He became both minister-chairman and minister of internal affairs, hardly a sinecure. Lvov's performance at Zemgor had enhanced his reputation among fellow liberals. The choice of him as premier was thought particularly appropriate because he had never belonged to a particular party or stood for the Duma. It was hoped that he would be able to hold the ring when policies were disputed in cabinet. His liberal credentials were also thought useful to dilute any hostility from the socialist parties who led the Petrograd Soviet. Lvov embodied the idea that Russia would be governed in a new fashion. He was a coordinator who took pains over details.[4] No minister wanted another tsar in democratic guise, and Lvov was the last person who could be accused of autocratic pretensions.

Leading figures from the Duma, Zemgor and the war-industries committee network made up most of the cabinet. They had rubbed alongside each other for many years. Several belonged to the same masonic lodge, which had made friendship and conspiracy possible. The outstanding figures were Milyukov, Guchkov and Kerensky. Milyukov became foreign affairs minister and Guchkov took over the

War Ministry. Their experience made them obvious appointments. But their ideas were bound to cause tensions with the Petrograd Soviet and indeed with their ministerial colleagues because, like the tsar whom they had deposed, they wanted an all-out military victory which would bring about territorial annexations. The only minister who matched them in energy and prominence was Alexander Kerensky. Being associated with the Socialist-Revolutionaries, he sought the Soviet's approval before entering the government. His presence in the cabinet was a counter-balance to Milyukov and Guchkov.

Guchkov, Milyukov and Kerensky played leading parts in the shaping of arrangements for the new government. Although Guchkov and Milyukov were well-known in public life, they could not have managed the revolutionary process without Kerensky's capacity to handle both the crowds and the Petrograd Soviet. The three men worked productively together even though they belonged to parties with different objectives. They conquered their personal dislike for each other. They accepted the common duty of bringing down the old order as speedily and quietly as possible.

Other cabinet members included Alexander Konovalov, who moved from the Central War-Industries Committee to the Ministry of Trade and Industry. He owned one of the country's largest textile concerns and had often advocated the need for conciliation between factory owners and their workforces. Mikhail Tereshchenko, the new finance minister, had inherited huge personal wealth in banks, beet farms and sugar processing. Young and informal, he went to every opera and play at the theatre. He was an impressive negotiator and a valued member of the Duma Provisional Committee's inner circle. He had a leading role in the Russian Red Cross, had headed the Kiev War-Industries Committee and had recently managed foreign-currency exchange at the Central War-Industries Committee.[5] Andrei Shingarëv became agriculture minister. He had started life as a zemstvo doctor but he knew economics and had expertise in questions of food supplies. Transport Minister Nikolai Nekrasov had famously rebuked the Imperial government for its responsibility for the Lena goldfields massacre in 1912. He had started his career at the Tomsk Engineering Institute. These were liberal-minded ministers who set out to steer politics by a different route.

Georgi Lvov chaired the proceedings. The pace of change was frantic and some days the cabinet met twice. The Provisional Government had to obtain popular recognition for itself as the ruling authority.

It issued a carefully worded appeal to 'Citizens of the Russian State'. The word 'empire' was avoided because of its unpleasant meaning for the millions of the former emperor's subjects who were not Russians. Emphasis fell on the many years of attempts made to effect reform by way of the State Duma. Compromise had been tried and found to be ineffective. Without naming Nicholas, the appeal recounted the rough handling experienced by the parliamentarians. People and Duma had at last risen to claim their freedom and to establish the Provisional Government. The appeal pledged war against the external enemy until victory was secured and until agreements with the Allies were realized. A Constituent Assembly was promised that would be elected as soon as possible on the basis of universal suffrage (although in fact it was not until the summer that women were formally enfranchised).[6]

Decrees were issued as fast as they could be written to revoke much Imperial legislation. Civil liberties were guaranteed for conscience, speech, organization and assembly. Press censorship was abolished.[7] Political prisoners received free railway tickets to return from Siberia and northern Russia. Only the courts would deal with offenders, and an end was put to the practice of administrative exile.[8] The industrial labour force received the right to go on strike. Workers' committees were accorded legal status.[9] The imposition of military labour duty on 'aliens' from Turkestan and elsewhere was revoked.[10] Poland was promised its independence at the war's end. All discrimination on religious or ethnic grounds was proscribed. The Orthodox Church was stripped of its age-old privileges. The Pale of Settlement was abolished. Jews could live wherever they liked and would no longer be subject to occupational restrictions.[11] Ukrainian nationalist exiles were allowed to return to Ukraine.[12] Kerensky, who quickly became the cabinet's most travelled minister, went to Helsinki to tell an enthusiastic audience that Pehr Evind Svinhufvud had been freed and would soon be back in the Finnish capital.[13]

Altogether the revolutionary decrees made Russia, according to one obscure commentator in foreign exile, 'the freest of all the combatant countries in the world'. The commentator's name was Vladimir Lenin.

Ministers recognized that their decrees would be ineffectual unless supported by a network of governance. Some degree of continuity was necessary to ensure order and welfare, and the old officials were kept in place so long as they swore fealty to the Provisional Government. Even the last cabinet's functionaries kept their jobs.[14] Sessions were held in the Marinski Palace which had been the seat of the Council of Ministers – the Winter Palace, grander by far, was reserved for the election of the Constituent Assembly.[15] Although the Duma deputies were not ejected from the Tauride Palace, they were not encouraged to resume their proceedings, and Rodzyanko made no fuss about this. The State Council fell into disuse. Definitive constitutional reform, however, was postponed until the future Constituent Assembly. In the meantime the cabinet worked through the current administrative bodies below the level of central government. Zemstvos and dumas were treated as essential to the maintenance of services and control. They were not going to be left to themselves. Lvov and his cabinet wanted them to demonstrate their revolutionary credentials by submitting themselves to the test of re-election – unlike the government itself. The hope was that local government would be refreshed by the entry of people who supported the Provisional Government and its policies.

The cabinet decreed that Petrograd factory workers should not be left out of pocket because of the strikes and demonstrations that had brought down the Romanovs.[16] This sense of gratitude was extended to everyone who had massed on the streets. In Moscow, the city authorities announced financial compensation could be claimed by owners of motor cars commandeered in the insurgency.[17] The tensions between rich and poor were somewhat relaxed, and ministers nurtured an atmosphere of unity.

The composition of the General Staff's leadership was left untouched. Mikhail Alexeev had helped to edge the emperor from power and genuinely supported the new government. Alexei Brusilov, hero of the previous year's summer offensive, declared his allegiance to the cabinet and was carried around Berdichev by his soldiers waving red flags.[18] But not all generals could automatically be thought reliable. They had sworn an oath of personal loyalty to Nicholas and many had beliefs at variance with the Provisional Government's political direction. Guchkov and Alexeev liaised in dispatching over a hundred of them into retirement. This was a disruptive step at a time of war but a necessary one if all traces of monarchism were to be expunged from the armed forces.[19]

On 4 March 1917 the cabinet abolished the provincial governorships, replacing each post-holder with the current zemstvo chairman of each province who received the title of commissar.[20] Although this was designed to eliminate the vestiges of the old system of authority, it was not to the liking of the unofficial bodies that sprang up 'in the localities' in the course of the revolution – usually they called themselves committees of public security or of public organization.[21] When such committees complained that provincial zemstvo chairmen in many places were ultra-conservative public figures, the government adjusted its stance and appointed provincial commissars of its own.[22] Certain local hotspots received urgent attention, none more so than Turkestan, where the military strongman Kuropatkin had conducted a campaign of terror against Muslim inhabitants. In mid-March the cabinet sent Illarion Vasilchikov, an hereditary count as well as a Duma deputy who aligned himself with the Octobrist Party, as commissar for the region.[23]

The old policing system was rooted out. The Okhrana and the corps of gendarmes were abolished. The policy was adopted to end the military exemption for their personnel and to call them up into the armed forces.[24] In most cases, police officers had already fled into hiding for fear of being lynched or beaten up. To the peasantry's delight, the detested post of 'land captain' was terminated.[25] In some districts the peasants got rid of them without waiting for an official ordinance.[26] Planning began to recruit and train volunteers for a new militia.[27]

Revolutionaries in foreign exile made plans to return. Bolshevik leader Vladimir Lenin and Menshevik leader Yuli Martov made their way back to Russia. Lev Trotsky, the far-left Marxist, took longer than most because he was briefly interned in Halifax, Nova Scotia before getting permission to resume his Atlantic crossing to Scandinavia. The Provisional Government meanwhile purged its administration of everything that reminded people of autocracy. The official calendar was changed by abolishing days of commemoration devoted to the achievements of the Romanovs. Ministers wanted Russia to see its history afresh. Funds were laid aside for a monument to be raised in Petrograd to celebrate those who fell as victims in the struggle for freedom.[28] Ceremonies were held in most cities. Red Square in Moscow provided an impressive scene on 4 March for a vast military parade.

Kerensky visited Nicholas at Tsarskoe Selo to confirm the terms of his custody. For a few days it was mooted that the Romanovs would leave for exile in Great Britain, but neither King George V – Nicholas's cousin – nor the Soviets on the railway to Archangel were minded to permit this. Consequently Nicholas and his family had to stay in the Alexander Palace at Tsarskoe Selo. They lived in comfort and were left alone. Rasputin's corpse was dug out of its coffin in the grounds and carted off for incineration. Nicholas stoically bore his fate. The cabinet ordered his last Internal Affairs Minister Alexander Protopopov to be investigated for 'anti-state activity'.[29] The former empress's confidante Anna Vyrubova was imprisoned in the Peter–Paul Fortress.[30]

Action was taken against the political far right. The Petrograd Soviet hurried the process along by proscribing the most strident newspapers of Russian nationalism.[31] 'Freedom of expression' in the new Russia would operate with a few important qualifications. The printing press of the Union of the Russian People was impounded and its leader Alexander Dubrovin was taken into custody.[32]

Once the brief period of bloodshed was over in Petrograd, it became the quietest of revolutionary transitions in most cities and villages. Two young men appeared at the monarchist Lev Tikhomirov's home outside Moscow on 8 March 1917, threatening to take him into custody. Tikhomirov was absent at the time. On learning what had happened, he hurried to the police station to seek an explanation but was told that higher officials needed to deal with the matter. He took his place in a long queue and signed a form expressing loyalty to the Provisional Government. Eventually a clerk confirmed that the revolutionary authorities had nothing against him and that he could move around freely, but Tikhomirov voiced concern that suspicions might linger over his head. The police assured him that he need not worry and gave him the telephone number to call in the event of any trouble. While others were giving thanks for the revolution, Tikhomirov felt sorry for himself and pondered sombrely about what lay ahead for Russia.

The Western Allies – Great Britain, France and Italy – quickly gave official recognition of the Provisional Government and affirmed, at least in public, that the end of the Romanovs would liberate the patriotic efforts of the Russians. General Mikhail Alexeev and the Imperial high command acclaimed the new cabinet. Grand Duke Nikolai Nikolaevich in the Caucasus front sent congratulations. The Holy Synod of the Russian Orthodox Church, for centuries a pillar of the Romanov state order, appealed to its believers to render support to the Provisional Government.[33]

Ministers still had to function within the constraints exerted by the Petrograd Soviet. Tense negotiations took place. The Soviet's socialist leaders threatened trouble if the government rejected their basic demands. An emergency partnership was born. Ministers insisted that while the war continued and until the Constituent Assembly gave its ruling, no resolution of the land question was possible. They continued to refuse to declare a democratic republic on the grounds that only the Constituent Assembly could decide the matter. The Petrograd Soviet

1. Emperor Nicholas II and his son Alexei near the Eastern front in the Great War.

2. Nicholas II in Muscovite garb.

3. Grigori Rasputin, the Imperial couple's 'holy man'.

4. Mikhail Alexeev, chief of the Imperial General Staff from 1915.

5. Alexander Guchkov, Central War-Industries Committee leader and, briefly in 1917, war minister.

6. Georgi Lvov, Zemstvos Union leader and the first premier of the Provisional Government.

7. Pavel Milyukov, Kadet party leader and, briefly in 1917, foreign affairs minister.

8. Alexander Kerensky, Duma critic of the Imperial government and, from July 1917, premier of the Provisional Government.

9. Lavr Kornilov, supreme commander-in-chief under Kerensky until the abortive August revolt.

10. Vladimir Lenin, Bolshevik party leader and Sovnarkom chairman.

11. Lev Trotsky, anti-Bolshevik-turned-Bolshevik, people's commissar for foreign affairs and people's commissar for military affairs.

12. Grigori Zinoviev, Bolshevik Central Committee member and chairman of the Comintern Executive Committee.

13. Lev Kamenev, Bolshevik Central Committee member and chairman of the Moscow Soviet.

14. Nikolai Bukharin, Bolshevik Central Committee member and *Pravda* editor.

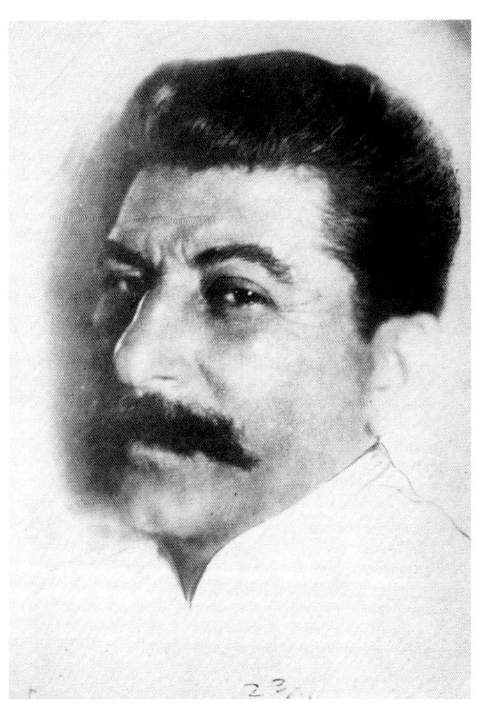

15. Joseph Stalin, Bolshevik Central Committee member and, from 1922, party general secretary.

16. Patriarch Tikhon, elected to the post in November 1917.

17. Alexander Kolchak, White army commander and Supreme Ruler.

18. Anton Denikin, leader of the Armed Forces of Southern Russia.

19. Soldiers of the Imperial Army on parade in the Great War.

20. A Jewish family forced by the Imperial high command to flee the war zone – and lucky to be allowed to make their way in a carriage.

21. Factory officials and workers during a wartime morale-raising visit by Nicholas II.

accepted such strictures at a time when its own focus was on urban, military and international policies – and here too there was much strain. While appreciating the promise of free wage bargaining, the Soviet leaders wanted the government to decree an eight-hour working day. The case was also pressed for the war to be fought with exclusively defensive objectives. Territorial expansion was anathema to the socialist leadership.

Totma's Alexander Zamaraev, who never identified himself with any particular party's policies, hoped for the best:

> And we'll be facing real disaster if we don't put our trust in the Provisional Government. The ministers are of the people. They are all of them good, honest and selfless individuals. They genuinely want only good – and good for our motherland. If they depart before the Constituent Assembly meets because of the ill-informed [*nesoznatel'nye*] masses (and there are a lot of them), Russia will suffer inevitable disaster.[34]

He obviously did not have complete confidence that a radiant future lay ahead.

17. PARTNERSHIP OF RIVALS: THE SOVIETS AND 'CONDITIONAL SUPPORT' FOR THE GOVERNMENT

Nikita Okunev witnessed the public euphoria about Nicholas's fall from power.[1] According to his diary, nobody wanted to spoil the mood by debating details of future policy. Even so, discussion could not be endlessly postponed. The questions of war, government, land, empire and social justice began to arise in day-to-day conversation.

Okunev felt pulled in many directions. From the works and personal example of late novelist and pacifist Lev Tolstoy he had learned the principle of non-resistance to evil.[2] The political parties that attracted Okunev, however, were anything but pacifist. Like most people, he sheltered a jumble of ideas in his head as he tried to make sense of events. He read the daily newspapers. He closely observed passers-by on his way to and from work. Whenever something unusual was happening he wrote down his impressions in his diary. He blocked his ears to siren calls from both the political far right and the far left but could not decide whether the Octobrists, the Kadets or one of the two main socialist parties – the Mensheviks and the Socialist-Revolutionaries – offered the best way forward.[3] None of them, of course, endorsed a Tolstoyan commitment to peace at any price, and Okunev was anyway proud of his son Leonid who had been serving in the armed forces since January.[4] Okunev, indeed, was a patriot who was horrified by the growing talk about proposals for a separate peace with Germany.

The parties in the current government and its quasi-partners in the Soviet continued to shape policy. But their disagreements exasperated Okunev, and he gave up trying to decide which party he preferred. He never joined a political party – a condition that was common to the vast majority of his fellow citizens.

Okunev's father was a peasant who left the countryside to set up as a small trader in town. Nikita was two at the time. The Okunevs returned yearly to their village, where Nikita as a boy shared in the heavy toil that uncles, aunts and cousins had to perform in the fields. Work in his father's business began early for him. He was sent on long carriage trips with money and packages. On one occasion, aged fifteen, he had to make his way in temperatures of –30°C along the snow-heaped roads from Nizhni Novgorod to distant Vyatka. It was a dangerous trip but his father refused to lend him a pistol. Young Nikita, like other boys in that period, had to grow fast into manhood, and to his lasting regret he could not complete his schooling. He witnessed the drudgery of Russian traders when lodging with a Simbirsk grocer who opened his stall at six in the morning and sold pies, cabbage soup and jams till nine at night.[5] Okunev opted for a different kind of employment for himself and found it in Moscow, where he worked for shipping companies in the river port. Able and industrious, he became an accounts administrator in the Samolët company in February 1911.[6]

Okunev married young. His wife bore two children, Leonid and Galina. But the marriage foundered and from 1909 Okunev had lived with Antonina Makri. Antonina was a fine-looking woman from a Polish noble family in Piotrków province and had previously been married to a Romanian landowner of Greek extraction. In their new life together she and Nikita shared a commitment to fairness, duty and the Christian faith. Nikita strove to fill the gaps in his education and made friends with several published authors.[7] Three years after she and Okunev began living together, his two children Leonid ('Lelya') and Galina ('Galya') joined them. The home was a happy one.[8]

After Lelya left to join the army there were three family members left in the Moscow apartment. As Nikita walked around central Moscow he lamented the breakdown in order and felt sorry for the ex-members of the corps of gendarmes. He saw them as ordinary Russians and family men who deserved the chance to join the movement of liberation.[9] He feared the violence of crowds. He read that a mob in Tver had lynched provincial governor Nikolai von Bünting and ransacked the wine cellars.[10] Nikita Okunev admired Milyukov for telling a mass meeting that unless he and fellow ministers had announced an unelected cabinet, other thoroughly unpleasant types would have grabbed power.[11] Okunev sympathized with some of the socialists' ideas but he could see no good coming from the Petrograd Soviet behaving as if it was Russia's true government.[12] He scoffed at calls for worldwide action by workers to bring the war to an end – in Okunev's opinion this showed a complete lack of realism.[13] He also dismissed as absurd the objective of proletarian mastery over public affairs.[14] Like other admirers of Tolstoy, he welcomed the abolition of capital punishment. But at the same time he admired Guchkov's efforts to maintain military discipline.[15]

Okunev was essentially a Kadet with a soft heart. The leadership of the Kadets allowed themselves no such gentleness. They and the rest of the cabinet wished to prove Russia's military worth to the Western Allies. Chief of Staff Alexeev wrote to War Affairs Minister Guchkov on the subject on 12 March 1917. Munitions were again running short as they had done in 1915. Alexeev had lost confidence in his forces' ability to fulfil the objectives agreed with the Western Allies for Russia to reopen their campaign on the south-western sector of the Eastern front three weeks after the French and British opened their big spring offensive in northern France. Alexeev asked Guchkov to seek a delay until the first days of July. Four months of 'sitting quietly' were vital for military preparations.[16] The French and British offensive in northern France began a month after the February Revolution without the simultaneous Russian offensive that had been agreed. The welcome for the revolution in Paris and London began to dissipate almost as soon as it had been made.[17]

When the cabinet discussed Russia's wartime accords with the Allies, Foreign Affairs Minister Milyukov expressed his endorsement of them.[18] On 22 March the Kadet newspaper *Rech* carried an interview with him. Milyukov was forthright. He spoke of Russia's territorial right to Constantinople and the Straits of the Dardanelles as well as to the Ukrainian provinces of Austria–Hungary. Victory in war was to lead to expansion of Russian domains. He spoke bullishly as if he did not need to worry about the Petrograd Soviet which had stipulated a non-expansionist policy in war as the price of its recognition of the Provisional Government. Dr Vasili Kravkov, who was still directing medical services at the front, could not understand why Milyukov was talking about Constantinople and the Dardanelles when the Russian Army was in no condition to achieve such a victory.[19] Kravkov was expressing an opinion which had been current in the high command since the first year of the war. Alexeev as chief of the General Staff had never believed that Russia could simultaneously beat the Germans and the Ottomans, and many others, including Kravkov, independently came to the same conclusion. But Nikita Okunev admired Milyukov for his candour: 'It's better to scratch oneself than tell a lie.' Even so, Okunev equally saw that there could be big political trouble about the matter.[20]

Okunev was right. Milyukov's interview infuriated the Petrograd Soviet Executive Committee where two Georgian Mensheviks, Irakli Tsereteli and Karlo Chkheidze, together with the Socialist-Revolutionary Avram Gots exercised a leading influence. Others prominent in the Executive Committee's work were the Menshevik Fëdor Dan and the Bundist Mark Liber – both of them being Jewish. They formed an energetic team committed to holding the government to account.

Tsereteli had a commanding voice in debate and the revolutionary aura of a returnee from Siberian exile. His friend Chkheidze could think on his feet and, as a State Duma member and a freemason, had links with several of the newly appointed ministers. Gots was also a freemason and had been prominent in the Petersburg Soviet of 1905 before escaping into foreign exile abroad. He had a knack of getting on with people from other parties. This was also true of Liber, who brought the socialists of the Jewish Bund into a prominence unimaginable in earlier years. With his jet-black beard, reminiscent of Assyrian relief sculptures, he had an unforgettable appearance.[21] Dan, a doctor by profession, looked less impressive but was a redoubtable negotiator. His political activism had started in the early 1890s and he knew everyone of importance in the revolutionary movement. Such was the influence of Dan and Liber behind the scenes that the Soviet line of the day was known to their opponents as 'Liberdanism'.

It was a crucial time in the Great War and the Soviet leadership wanted clarity about Russian war aims. The United States had joined the Allies as an Associated Power after Germany refused to halt submarine attacks on American shipping in the Atlantic and was revealed to have tried to coax Mexico into an anti-American alliance. President Woodrow Wilson successfully addressed a joint session of Congress to request approval of a declaration of war, and Soviet leaders were hoping that the Americans would share their hostility to goals of annexation and indemnity.[22]

Tsereteli and Chkheidze carried the greatest heft when working an audience in the Petrograd Soviet's General Assembly and took a delegation to complain directly to Lvov about Milyukov's interview. The delegation knew that Kerensky, who was not present, shared its annoyance about what Milyukov had said. Chkheidze reminded Lvov about the Soviet's requirement for conducting only defensive operations and attaining a 'democratic peace'. Lvov stressed his commitment to 'the democratic character of our politics' and although he declined to endorse the Soviet's peace policy, he gave his word to Tsereteli that something would be done to bridle Milyukov.[23] He also asked for time to consult the Allies before making an announcement of official policy. If there was to be any change in Russia's war aims, Petrograd had first to talk to Paris and London. The Soviet leaders, while recognizing his difficulty, warned him that a war of territorial conquest was totally unacceptable to them.[24]

Lvov did in fact issue a declaration affirming that cabinet policy was opposed to 'the forcible seizure of foreign territories'.[25] A few days later, on 2 April, the British ambassador Sir George Buchanan asked him about war aims. Lvov surprised him by saying that Constantinople and the Dardanelles remained an official objective. He made the weaselly argument that this would not involve annexation but rather 'liberation from the enemy yoke'. Buchanan was delighted to hear that the Provisional Government stood by the old war aims – and he saw that Lvov could not afford to put this on public record.[26]

Mensheviks and Socialist-Revolutionaries continued to emphasize that they would sustain the Provisional Government only to the extent that ministers facilitated progress towards peace, workers' rights and democracy. This was their policy of 'conditional support'. The Menshevik Chkheidze advocated strengthening military defence while negotiating a peace with all the other warring peoples, not one concocted with the German emperor.[27] He did not make clear how he expected that this might be achieved. About wages and working conditions in the factories there was greater precision about Menshevik proposals. The Petrograd Society of Works and Factory Owners acceded to the demands of workforces and the Soviet in return encouraged workers to end the strikes and return to the factories while the terms of agreement were finalized.[28] Mensheviks and Socialist-Revolutionaries did not cease to regard big businessmen as exploiters of the working class, but they could point to the gains being made through the partnership with Lvov's cabinet.

The policy of conditional support was endorsed by Bolshevik Lev Kamenev who led its Russian Bureau after returning from Siberia. Kamenev accepted that the Bolsheviks were currently a minority in the Petrograd Soviet. He and Iosif Stalin, a fellow former exile, aimed for the Bolsheviks to act as a ginger group on the political far left. In later years they would be depicted as having become Mensheviks in all but name. This was misleading. The aim of Kamenev and Stalin was to split the more radical Menshevik wing away from the other Mensheviks and amalgamate efforts to campaign against the priority being given for military defence. Stalin saw the Petrograd Soviet as having the potential to constitute a government. He also advocated the immediate transfer of all agricultural land to the peasantry. Both Kamenev and Stalin derided the willingness of leading Mensheviks like Tsereteli and Chkheidze to cosy up to the Lvov cabinet.[29]

The cabinet at that moment had more pressing problems than worrying about the Bolshevik minority in the Soviet. Ministers were sensitive to the widespread demand for fast action from the new authorities. The Provisional Government wanted to satisfy this expectation. The difficulty for ministers was their lack of the right to pass legislation before a Constituent Assembly was elected and formal democracy was established. The sole alternative was to rule by decree, and the government did this with enthusiasm in spite of opponents on the political far right and left who accused it of instituting a dictatorship.

Ministers rarely discussed military and foreign affairs in formal session, and Alexeev had a free hand in running the high command.[30] Deliberations on the economic crisis, too, were infrequent. Lvov ran his government on the principle that ministries should be left to get on with their work unimpeded. He did, however, ensure that channels of consultation were kept open with the unofficial leaders of those great groups in society which had decisive influence on affairs of state – workers, conscripts, peasants, big businessmen and – to some extent – army commanders. A Main Economic Council and a Main Land Committee were established to draft future legal frameworks for industrial development and land ownership.[31] Engineers, teachers, land surveyors, dentists, lawyers and sanitation inspectors joined the chorus of advice to the government, and the press gave them a platform free from censorship. The 'professionals' themselves welcomed the arrival of a government that was committed to 'science' and 'progress'.

Most ministers trembled at the thought of clashing with the Soviet. There were two exceptions, Milyukov and Guchkov, who regarded Order No. 1 as an affront to the dignity of the government and high command. Guchkov refused to accept that his ministerial duties required him even to talk to the Soviet leadership.[32] The rest of the cabinet was readier to consider compromise. Konovalov assured Guchkov: 'At the first spillage of blood, I'll hand in my resignation.' Konovalov as trade and industry minister pursued the goal of conciliation between owners and workforces. He removed all constraints on trade union activity. He introduced arbitration agencies, which he saw as 'so necessary for the relations between labour and capital'.[33]

The government worked hard to end the food-supply shortages that had helped to bring down the monarchy. One of its early discussions was about whether to cut back the daily allowance of bread in the armed forces.[34] Bread ration cards were introduced in Petrograd and Moscow on 12 March.[35] On 25 March 1917 the government proclaimed a state monopoly in the trade of grain, banning most cereal producers from selling their stocks to anyone apart from agents of official procurement bodies.[36] 'Food-supply committees' (*prodovol'stvennye komitety*) were set up to oversee the pricing and purchasing process.[37] But state finance was dangerously depleted, so Finance Minister Tereshchenko announced the intention of bringing Bark's income tax plan into effect and a plan was agreed to approach the Americans for emergency credit.[38] The cabinet also approved Tereshchenko's scheme for a '1917 Freedom Loan' to raise three billion rubles.[39] The early results were encouraging. The Pale of Settlement's abolition removed the Rothschilds' reservations about the Russian war effort and they alone contributed one million rubles to the Freedom Loan.[40]

Alexander Zamaraev was busy trying to deal with the difficulties of day-to-day life. The first ship to reach Totma from Vologda arrived on 10 April.[41] The ice on the river Sukhona had begun to crack. The snow had disappeared. But it had been a long hard winter and although the Easter festival had been celebrated as usual in the churches, Zamaraev commented that the thaw came too late for the usual decorations to be available for sale in town.[42]

Prices continued to rise when urban trade was resumed in springtime. Zamaraev kept a worried eye on the cost of living but it was his farming tasks that preoccupied him. He and some of his neighbours started their sowing.[43] Even so, politics and war affected everybody. The tremors of revolution were brought to Vologda when a contingent of demobilized troops arrived who had been released from service because they had reached their forties. Zamaraev was pleased by reports that the French and British were giving the Germans a hard time.[44] Meanwhile the little town's civic affairs began to change. A newspaper called *Totma Life* was founded.[45] Parties were setting up branches. Demonstrations and meetings were being organized.[46] Zamaraev saw people enjoying their new freedom (*volya*) and no longer needing to be careful about what they said to others.[47] But he was one of those who did not share in the widespread euphoria: 'The new government have a horrible amount of business on their plate. They keep having to go to the front, to factories and plants to drum in some sense and explain everything.'[48]

18. STANDING TALL: THE 'MASSES' AND SELF-LIBERATION

All across Russia the lower social classes, the 'masses', were standing up for themselves and securing radically better treatment. Politicians and public commentators were divided about the surge of popular assertiveness. Some thought it wonderful and were in awe of it. Others feared it could be the prelude to a collapse of civilization.

Whilst Petrograd workers and soldiers had started the revolutionary process, a whole society was soon in ferment. The demands for basic change came from house servants, cab-drivers, shopkeepers, market stallholders, tavern owners, restaurant cooks, kitchen skivvies, bartenders, waiters, barbers, nightwatchmen and seamstresses. Lev Tikhomirov experienced the new atmosphere at Sergiev Posad outside Moscow when local servants, who had been used to being at the beck and call of their masters and mistresses, organized an assembly on 7 March 1917 to discuss how to limit their working hours and improve their conditions of employment. The more militant among them denounced what they saw as the autocracy of property ownership. Ex-revolutionary Lev Tikhomirov advised his servant Masha to go along to the assembly. Masha rejected her master's kindly suggestion. Perhaps she was content with her terms of employment beneath Tikhomirov's roof or felt participation in social protest would count against her if ever there was a thinning in the revolutionary atmosphere.[1] But for several weeks it grew denser. Nikolai Okunev complained that soldiers blew cigarette smoke in the faces of their officers.[2]

Okunev disliked the impact that the revolution was having upon his lifestyle. On 12 May he wrote that waiters, kitchen staff and female servants in Moscow's restaurants, clubs, coffee shops and hotels were on the fourth day of their strike for higher wages.[3] Waiters won a pay rise to 400 rubles a month and returned to work. By the beginning of June, Okunev was recording:

> But at this moment a strike by caretakers has started, and thanks to this the streets of Moscow, not excluding those in the centre, look like rubbish dumps. Everything that is tossed out on to streets and pavements is just lying there without being collected for four days. The pavements are soft under foot: paper litter, cigarette packets, leftovers, sunflower husks, etc.: rubbish everywhere while the caretakers sit around on their stools, munch their sunflower seeds and play on their accordions.[4]

The new Moscow militia had to intervene in a strike of hospital workers to stop them throwing an elderly honorary citizen into the river Moscow.[5] A few days later the militiamen themselves went on strike. They were paid only 150 rubles a month and could not see why waiters were earning so much more than them.[6]

The capital's industrial workers continued to assert their influence. Although they had managed to negotiate higher wages in wartime, the increases even for the skilled workers had been outpaced by price inflation. There was no improvement to working conditions and foremen acted like bullies on the factory floor. It was normal for labourers to be fined for minor infringements in time-keeping. Workers saw the factory system as the embodiment of oppression and humiliation.

On 10 March 1917 the Petrograd Soviet presented the Society of Manufacturers and Plant Owners in the capital with its demand for immediate, comprehensive reforms in labour relations. The call was issued for a working day of eight hours – something that most British, French and German workers had yet to achieve – without a lowering of wages. Industrialists complained about being battered by huge wage claims. Leading Menshevik Boris Bogdanov reported that Petrograd wage levels had risen by 200 per cent and still the workers demanded more. Productivity was falling, conflicts growing.[7] In Petrograd, chronic resentment boiled over in the capital's factories against foremen who had made daily life miserable for the workers. Now the humiliators were attacked and humiliated themselves. In one instance a hated foreman was thrown into the icy river Neva. The violence was intended not just as retaliation but as insurance against anyone trying to revive the indignities of the industrial past.[8] Factory owners offered concessions but feared that they would be followed by demands for still larger ones. Soviet activists had no patience with complaints made on this basis. The labour movement was determined to attain deals that would benefit the entire working class in each sector of manufacturing and mining.

Revolutionary fervour spread to the countryside too. Some peasants sported red flags, telling priests to stop praying to Jesus Christ as their 'Heavenly Tsar' and to supplicate for the long life of the Provisional Government.[9] Scarcely had the Lvov cabinet come into being than bulletins arrived about peasant disorders (*besporyadki*) in Kazan province. Ministers worried about a potential recurrence of the disruptions of 1905–6. On 9 March the government promised to call an election for a Constituent Assembly that would resolve the land question. The peasantry was asked to show patience. The cabinet threatened court action against those who carried out acts of violence and pillage. At the same time it ordered local authorities to avoid using firearms.[10] On 17 March it approved Agriculture Minister Andrei Shingarëv's appeal to all peasants to refrain from seizures of land belonging to others. Shingarëv pledged to compile the inventories of property and insisted that all the democratic parties were committed to 'land reform'.[11]

Country people resented that factory workers were striking for higher wages while they were being asked to give up hard-won grain stocks at low fixed prices for the public good.[12] Many opted to refuse and the decline in grain supplies to cities was severe. Peasants might be patriots with sons in the army but they saw no reason to surrender their produce without decent compensation. They asserted their property claims. They had always eyed gentry land as legitimately belonging to them because it was they who worked it. They sometimes approached the district administration to validate their case. Usually this failed. The next option was to go to the new land committees.[13] But lawlessness was also spreading with peasants finding it easy to despoil the gentry's possessions. No longer were there land captains, bailiffs or troops to stop them. Most landlords prudently laid low. The clergy did noticeably little to curb the law-breakers because so many rural priests were as poor and disgruntled as the rest of the village inhabitants. The peasant movement took diverse forms. Some peasants simply refused to pay their rent to a gentry landlord or forced the payment of a lower amount.[14] Some grazed their cattle on the gentry's fields or took timber from the woods. Some seized gentry equipment for their own use or plundered grain from gentry barns, and some set fire to the gentry's manor houses. A rural revolution was under way in which the aristocrats and gentry were spectators of their own overthrow.

People belonging to the middle layers of society like accounts administrator Nikita Okunev were frightened by the way things were going. There were disorders in the countryside. The government's war loan was failing to rescue the budget, and workers everywhere were making greater and greater demands. Okunev gave a bleak assessment: 'We've all floated around in the clouds for a whole month and now we're beginning to come down to earth and we regretfully agree how premature it was to give complete freedom to the Russian individual.' He lamented the fact that his hero Tolstoy the novelist, whom he regarded as Russia's true prophet, was no longer alive to help Russians understand and improve the situation.[15]

Okunev was horrified by the indiscipline of the sailors at the Kronstadt naval garrison. Situated in the Gulf of Finland just nineteen miles from the capital, Kronstadt had been in tumult since the opening days of the revolution. Resentment at harsh conditions had existed there for many years. The Kronstadters had mutinied in 1904, giving hope to revolutionaries who were to challenge the Imperial administration in the following year. Socialist activists stirred up violent feelings throughout the Baltic fleet in the first days of the February 1917 Revolution. Admiral Robert Viren was bayoneted to death in Kronstadt on 1 March and a further fifty officers were killed. A group of mutineers seized Admiral Nepenin in the port of Helsinki on 4 March and he was shot in the back before the violence eventually abated.[16]

The Provisional Government sent out patriotic appeals for calm in all the armed forces. Troops at the front and in the garrisons were required to swear a new oath on their honour as citizens – instead of as subjects of the former emperor – to fight 'to the last drop of blood' for the Russian state (*Rossiiskoe gosudarstvo*) under the Provisional Government and the Constituent Assembly.[17] Military units were mustered on the marketplace in tiny, distant Totma to pledge their allegiance. Then local dignitaries gave speeches and a military band struck up the *Marseillaise*.[18] As the marching song of the French Revolution, it had not enjoyed official favour in the days of Romanov power, but now it was played incessantly at Tsarskoe Selo by army regiments wanting to annoy the ex-emperor.

Peasants-in-uniform at the front were aggrieved by how men just a little older than them or who had escaped the draft could continue to work the land and make money. They had scant patience with the workers' demand for an eight-hour working day when they themselves were in constant danger of being killed or wounded. Soldiers, moreover, felt bitter about those of their comrades who deserted the front line. Many troops said that as soon as peace came, they would refuse to lay aside their rifles until something was done for the country's welfare. They prickled with animosity towards the comfortable middle-class civilians, whom they dismissed as the *burzhui*, and their hatred of gentry stayed undimmed. One serviceman made his feelings clear in a letter to home: 'Please God, we'll remain alive and crush all the gentry after the war. Enough of them drinking our blood: we go on dying while all of them just think of how to keep their bellies full.'[19] Soldiers did not need Bolshevik agitators to shape their thinking. Pay and conditions were an ongoing grievance. As wheat supplies to northern Russia slackened, soldiers' diets consisted mainly of lentils. The troops in the rear had not been pacified by the gains of the revolution: they had become surly and were getting surlier.[20]

The one thing that pleased them was that the German high command had paused its plans for an offensive. Ludendorff and Hindenburg were hoping that the February Revolution would lead to Russian military dissolution, and the reports of Order No. 1 fuelled their optimism. Germany's calculation was that it was best to let the Russians themselves dissolve their military capacity. The Provisional Government acted to prevent such an outcome, continuing to appeal to troops' patriotic feelings. Civilians were urged to show their solidarity with the Russian war effort. Although the Central Powers refrained from a big offensive in spring and early summer, fighting did not cease. Nikita Okunev worried about his son who had been sent to the front in the days before the February Revolution. Every report of military operations made him pray for the safety of his 'young hero'.[21]

19. COMPLICATIONS OF COALITION: CABINET POLICIES AND THEIR CRITICS

One of the Marxist factions, the Bolsheviks, had their leader Vladimir Lenin living in Zurich when Romanov rule ended. After a winter of arrests, the small Bolshevik organization in Petrograd was headed by Alexander Shlyapnikov and Vyacheslav Molotov, who had no intention of compromising with the emergent Provisional Government. They were pushed aside by Lev Kamenev, Iosif Stalin and other Bolshevik veterans who arrived in the capital after being released from exile in Siberia. These newcomers adjusted Bolshevik strategy towards a degree of recognition of the cabinet. But both Kamenev and Stalin were harsher than the Mensheviks in the conditions they laid down for any compromise. Lenin sent them angry telegrams from Switzerland demanding an all-out political assault on 'bourgeois' ministers. For him, the moment for socialist revolution had to be grabbed. With a group of revolutionary exiles he negotiated a free travel pass from the German authorities to enable him to take a train across Germany and commence anti-war activity on Russian soil.

Lenin got off the train at Finland station in the capital Petrograd on 3 April 1917. It was Easter Monday. He angrily rebuked the Mensheviks in the band of socialists who turned up to welcome him back to Russia. They thought he would be cured of his madness once he became acquainted with the situation as it really was in Petrograd. But over the coming days Lenin stuck to his own idea of revolutionary opportunity. Socialism, he argued, was not only possible: it was the only practical alternative to a continuation of the Great War. He denounced the Provisional Government as 'imperialist' and the Mensheviks and Socialist-Revolutionaries as traitors to international socialism. Lenin campaigned for the transfer of all power to the soviets.

He spent his time giving speeches at public gatherings and writing articles for *Pravda*. Like other revolutionary leaders he wore a standard three-piece suit. When stopping in Stockholm en route to

Petrograd, he had been persuaded to buy town shoes to replace the all-purpose brogues he preferred. He also purchased a jaunty hat to replace his homburg. When speaking to crowds in the Russian capital, he pinned his thumbs in the armholes of his waistcoat like a schoolmaster. He exuded confidence as he swayed backwards and forwards. His tenor voice was squeaky, yet it conveyed a sense of urgency. He had spent his life acquiring a mastery of Marxist doctrine and was fluent with the pen. A formidable communicator was emerging on the political stage.

While Lenin led the assault on the Provisional Government, ministers were clashing with each other about cabinet policy. Lvov strove to keep internal tension out of the public gaze but the appearance of unity could not be sustained indefinitely. A wide spectrum of opinion divided the Octobrist Guchkov from the Socialist-Revolutionary Kerensky, just as it had before Nicholas abdicated. Even before Lenin appeared, Guchkov had been a reluctant minister. Nothing he learned at the War Ministry encouraged him to think differently. He energetically fulfilled his duties despite a worsening of his chronic cardiac problem, but he disliked the direction that official measures were taking. The obligation to compromise with the Lvovs and Kerenskys got both Guchkov and Milyukov down.[1] Their opinion of their fellow ministers was low and fell lower, and they frequently asked themselves whether the Provisional Government was capable of saving the country from ruin. Guchkov was to offer a sharp assessment when he wrote that the cabinet was filled with 'slush'.[2]

The first great crisis for the Provisional Government was provoked by Foreign Affairs Minister Pavel Milyukov on 18 April when he sent a telegram to Russian ambassadors in Allied countries confirming that the cabinet stood by obligations to the Allies and would fight until victory in the war was accomplished. Milyukov was responding to an Allied request for clarification of Russian foreign policy. At the end of March the cabinet had agreed on a verbal fudge after disputes among ministers. When published, it had annoyed the Petrograd Soviet which had constantly demanded exclusively defensive war aims. Kerensky, while rejecting any wish to annex foreign territory, claimed that official policy targeted only the internationalization of the Dardanelles. Milyukov was never happy about the cabinet fudge and was infuriated by challenges from both Kerensky and the Soviet. His telegram used ambiguous language but his opinions were well-known – people had taken to calling him Milyukov-Dardanelski. He had deliberately passed up the opportunity to affirm that Russia was waging only a war of territorial defence.[3]

The Mensheviks and Socialist-Revolutionaries called the telegram a betrayal of the deal they had done with the government a month earlier. A protest demonstration was organized in which all the socialist parties, including the Bolsheviks, took part. The Kadets organized a counter-demonstration. Cries of 'Long live Milyukov!' were drowned out by socialist activists who demanded his ejection from the cabinet – and Bolsheviks simply demanded the entire government's removal.[4] War Minister Alexander Guchkov alone stood by Milyukov. They were already the cabinet's odd couple – Guchkov's own ministerial team disapproved of his refusal to concede to the Soviet's request for a further extension of Order No. 1 at the expense of officers' authority.[5] Milyukov and Guchkov had been brought into the cabinet to maximize the breadth of collaboration. Now their presence was harming its capacity to govern with consent.

Lvov, whom Milyukov had not consulted about the telegram's wording, strove to regain the Petrograd Soviet's confidence. Confidential talks began to reach an acceptable compromise by way of forming a coalition cabinet. Milyukov exploded after learning what was afoot, but the Kadet party leadership was split on the matter. Knowing that some Kadets supported him, Lvov continued his efforts to bring government and soviet back together. Milyukov and Guchkov saw that they had lost the struggle and resigned.[6] The Bolsheviks, who had warned for weeks that the government was not to be trusted, felt vindicated. While taking part in the demonstrations alongside Mensheviks and Socialist-Revolutionaries, they declared the need for an exclusively socialist government. But Bolsheviks were still only a minority in the Petrograd Soviet, with other socialist parties regarding them as unrealistic zealots.

Lenin was certainly a fanatic with a scorching zeal to establish a 'dictatorship of the proletariat' but his reputation for taking no notice of what the other Bolsheviks thought is ill-founded. Under the influence of Kamenev and others, he saw that he would not win the support of workers if he told mass meetings that he aimed at dictatorship and even a European civil war. For months, though, he continued to canvass for land nationalization whereas Stalin argued for the peasants to be left to seize the land for themselves in whatever way they liked. They had disagreed on this for years and Stalin refused to give way.[7] The Bolshevik faction, which steadily turned into a fully separate party from the Mensheviks, was a hub of constant wrangling. But although Lenin did not dominate absolutely all the crucial choices over policy, his voice and pen were the most influential on the biggest question of all, the question of state power. Lenin successfully convinced fellow Bolsheviks that they should aim at the speedy removal of the Provisional Government and the installation of an all-socialist government.

Meanwhile, in the wake of the trouble over Milyukov's telegram, Lvov pressed the Petrograd Soviet leaders to join him in a governmental coalition. Mensheviks and Socialist-Revolutionaries continued to demur. They disliked taking responsibility for a war of which they had originally disapproved. Unlike the Bolsheviks, moreover, they refused to commit themselves to socialist revolution until Russia's capitalist development had been completed. Lvov answered that they were duty-bound to join the cabinet when Russia was in turmoil and that they themselves had caused the disintegration of the cabinet by bringing people on to the streets in April. With much unease they yielded to his argument that they could no longer content themselves with being political bystanders.

And so Tsereteli took over the Post and Telegraph Ministry and Skobelev became minister of labour, bringing Mensheviks into the cabinet for the first time. Kerensky, a Socialist-Revolutionary sympathizer, already belonged to it and Lvov transferred him to the War Ministry. The Socialist-Revolutionary Viktor Chernov, who had founded the party, was appointed to the Agriculture Ministry. The centre of gravity had shifted leftward. Now not only were there four socialists in post but Guchkov had gone, which meant that the Octobrist Party had lost its representation in government. Lvov recognized that his Menshevik and Socialist-Revolutionary ministers would push for more radical policies but he aimed to attain enough consensus in cabinet that would stabilize politics. He hoped that a direct experience of power would discourage impractical schemes, and he trusted Tsereteli and his minister-comrades to bring the Petrograd Soviet into line.

Germany's high command saw an opportunity in all this since the Soviet had always sought an end to the war. A radio-telegram was sent to Soviet headquarters at the Smolny Institute with a German promise to suspend offensive operations if Russia moved towards agreeing a separate peace.[8] With Milyukov and Guchkov out of the way, the Germans were probing whether the introduction of Tsereteli, Chkheidze and Chernov to the cabinet would soften Russian military policy.

The governmental coalition, however, ignored such overtures and focused on further reforms on the home front. Viktor Chernov at the Agriculture Ministry campaigned for changes in policy towards the peasantry.[9] Labour Minister Matvei Skobelev pushed for state regulation of prices as essential to prevent economic ruin and improve workers' conditions. But it was War Minister Kerensky who attracted the greatest attention as he rallied support for the war effort. He was short, slim and clean-shaven, whereas most of the ministers in the first cabinet were moustachioed and overweight.[10] When wanting to identify himself with the armed forces, he put on an army tunic. His rhetoric had a visceral patriotic appeal. He addressed troops as 'warriors' whose duty was to fight for 'the fatherland', and he assured them: 'You carry peace, right, truth and justice on the tips of your bayonets!'[11] He shook hands so often that he had to adopt a sling to prevent permanent damage to his right hand.[12] Nikolai Okunev compared his habit of hugging political enemies to the way Russians at weddings embraced the very people they had been calling 'swine': 'Passionate applause, happy faces, kisses. Kerensky, for example, kissed Tsereteli – and A. K. Kerensky is a kiss enthusiast.'[13]

Governmental regulation of industry was enlarged. Trade and Industry Minister Alexander Konovalov tried to set a maximum level for both profits and prices as a way of persuading workers to moderate their wage demands. He urged owners and shareholders in turn to give 'convincing proof' of their readiness to make 'all possible sacrifices for the common good'.[14] A man of big business himself, Konovalov had forgotten that most businessmen were motivated by a lust for money. At the same time, though, he opposed those ministers who called for heavier taxes of the wealthy elite. Fed up with the wrangles inside the cabinet, he resigned on 18 May 1917.[15]

On 12 June Shingarëv, the new finance minister, pushed forward with a business tax that had earned Konovalov's ire. Enterprises that had an annual profit of less than 1,000 rubles would be taxed at the rate of 30 per cent. Those with profits above 100,000 rubles were to pay 60 per cent of them to the government. This was in line with Tsereteli's call for a 'limitation' on the profits being made by industrialists and bankers. Shingarëv intended his measures as a great one-off levy needed to rescue the budgetary revenues from disaster. He also aimed to implement the agreed annual income tax. No one earning less than 1,000 rubles would pay a single kopek. People who cleared between 1,000 and 1,100 rubles were to pay twelve rubles. Those who earned 400,000 were required to hand over 120,000, 30 per cent of their total income. Wealthy Russians were being asked to comply with a highly progressive tax, one that was more progressive than any other government in Europe was daring to exact.[16]

Implementation was a different matter. Official appeals for fiscal compliance fell on deaf ears and the hole in the budget deepened. The prospect of total economic collapse induced Tsereteli to call for comprehensive limits on profits, prices and wages but he failed to obtain the consent of a majority of the cabinet. The economy's travails increased and Tsereteli's exasperation along with it.[17]

No such vexation affected the reform of local government that Lvov had begun on 15 April. At its heart were changes in the electoral process for urban and district dumas. Voting was to take place on a universal, direct basis. The ballot would be secret and there would be no social distinctions.[18] Lvov had endured over a month in which the soviets of nearly every town and city had acted as if their word was law, so by removing the obstacles to unrestricted local elections, he hoped to stunt the growth of 'soviet power'. Lvov envisaged providing the towns with a full administrative structure based upon class-free principles that had been lacking under the Imperial regime. The reform was a long-held liberal dream, and in current circumstances it answered an urgent practical need. On 21 May Lvov followed this up with his Internal Affairs Ministry's plan for rural administrative reform. He projected to hand over wide-reaching powers to the district (*volost*) zemstvos in which the peasants would have the vast majority of votes alongside gentry, priests and other inhabitants of the countryside. Lvov believed this would counteract the peasantry's current resort to illegal and disorderly activity.[19]

On 30 May 1917 the Provisional Government discussed the Ukrainian Central Rada's request for autonomy.[20] The Rada (or Council) had been formed after the All-Ukraine National Congress in April, and it quickly behaved as the regional organ of government throughout Ukraine. Kadet ministers looked askance at anything that might presage a diminution of central authority. Their socialist partners in the ruling coalition disagreed, arguing that only a looser structure of governance was appropriate for the new democracy. The 'national question' began to bedevil governmental deliberations.

Soaring over every discussion, though, was the problem of war and peace, and it spread to every corner of society. Alexander Zamaraev in Vologda province was not optimistic:

> We need to make an offensive and relieve our Allies but the army has no order and discipline. There are more than two million deserters. On the railways there are terrible outrages. Passengers are being turfed out of carriages and trains are being forced to change routes. Tens of thousands of ignorant soldiers are harming the common cause.[21]

Like many other patriotic civilians, he bought lottery tickets in aid of the wounded and the POWs. On 2 June he discovered that he had bought five winning tickets but otherwise it was not a lucky day. A fire broke out in the monastery bell-tower. The wind got up and spread the flames. Peasants rushed to rescue church valuables. Icons were saved and the bigger of the two bells survived the intense heat.[22] Once the disaster was over and the rains returned, Zamaraev gave thought again to conditions at the front. He felt shame about Russia's incapacity to fulfil its promises to the Western Allies. He grieved that troops were paying attention to 'a certain harmful Lenin and his henchmen'. He concluded that the Russian Army was full of parasites.[23]

The Provisional Government, however, remained intent upon reopening operations on the Eastern front in line with its promises to the Western Allies. But first, on 2 June, it briefly discussed Robert Grimm's report on Germany's latest overture for a separate peace. Grimm was a Swiss socialist who had organized multinational anti-war conferences in Switzerland in 1915 and 1916 – Lenin had attended despite ridiculing him as a soft-bellied pacifist and broke links with him afterwards. But Grimm kept up his efforts in the cause of peace and made a trip to Petrograd to explain the diplomatic possibilities. The Germans wanted the Russians to give back the territories they had conquered in Austria–Hungary in return for the Germans offering a mutually acceptable settlement in the Baltic territories that Germany now occupied – there would be no German offensive if peace talks could be started. Tsereteli and Skobelev interviewed Grimm on his arrival and formed no kindly opinion of his claim to have shunned links with the German government. Grimm was asked to leave Russia, and Kerensky could concentrate on plans for the long-delayed Russian offensive on the Eastern front.[24]

20. AT THE FRONT, IN THE REAR: MILITARY DEFEAT AND ECONOMIC BREAKDOWN

The offensive began on 18 June after a preparatory two-day barrage. By that time Alexeev, in poor health and full of gloom about Russia's military capacity, had been allowed to resign as supreme commander-in-chief. His successor was Brusilov who buoyantly believed that victory was possible for the Russian armed forces.[1] He had been pressing Alexeev for permission to recruit new shock troops on the south-western sector, and Alexeev had grudgingly agreed. Brusilov now received licence from War Minister Kerensky to demonstrate that his optimism had a basis in military reality.[2]

They were taking a large gamble because commanders had only a frail hold on the armed forces that they led. Ever since the February Revolution, Russia's fighting servicemen had thrown aside the old norms of hierarchy. Soldiers and sailors not only stopped saluting on sight but also listened to their elected committees rather than their officers. Military units reserved for themselves and realized the right to reject orders from above, and the officer corps had the memory of the naval murders in March etched on its thinking. Many officers were inexperienced and 92,500 of them had been killed or wounded before 1917.[3] Their replacements were more frequently men who had risen from lower levels in society than had been the case before the war.[4] Kerensky and other ministers, furthermore, curbed the powers of the General Staff. Civil governance stayed firmly under government control and generals could no longer treat ministers and provincial officials in a casual fashion. The army's practice of providing for its needs by means of 'autonomous requirements', which was the term used for peremptory local requisitioning, was abolished. Under the current condition, the high command had no choice but to obey and try to raise the level of battle readiness.[5]

But by midsummer 1917, the Russian Army had lost the staggering number of 5,330,000 officers and troops either killed or wounded since mid-1914, and now the government was ordering a fresh offensive.[6] War weariness had spread to all fronts and garrisons. On taking over the War Ministry, Kerensky announced a ban on requests for retirement from members of the General Staff. (When making an exception for Alexeev in late May, he insisted on keeping him on as an adviser.[7]) He introduced new punishments for deserters, including their exclusion from voting in the Constituent Assembly election. They would also lose the right to any share in the agricultural land that would be redistributed under the expected reforms of ownership. Their families too would be punished by the withdrawal of their ration cards.[8] Kerensky established political departments inside the armed forces to guarantee that discipline and patriotism were upheld. He ordered the secret surveillance of the army, putting the War Ministry's Political Directorate in charge of the process.[9]

Kerensky also rejected demands by Ukrainian officers and troops for permission to form their own national regiments. In May 1917 the Ukrainians went ahead with a congress in Kiev. The 700 delegates had experience of the high command's disregard for Ukraine's interests and traditions. Cities and villages had been despoiled. The ethnic deportations of Germans and Jews from provinces next to the front had wrought havoc. Ukrainian religious sensibilities had been offended by the incursions of the Russian Orthodox Church hierarchy. At the congress, leaders argued that nothing would change for Ukraine until Ukrainians had separate formations in the army. Fearing they wanted to break up the multinational state, Kerensky banned a second congress which was scheduled for June.[10]

Brusilov and Kerensky addressed the Russian soldiers' congress on the south-western sector of the Eastern front in early May 1917. As was by then normal practice, opponents of the Provisional Government were also allowed to attend. The Bolshevik Nikolai Krylenko denounced all cabinet ministers as warmongers. Kerensky and Brusilov carried the day, with a one-armed lieutenant snatching the George Cross medal off his own chest to give to Kerensky.[11] Even so, soldiers were increasingly sceptical of the war minister. Nikita Okunev read in the press that when Kerensky finished one of his speeches, the troops simply continued to 'chew their sunflower seeds and make various demands.'[12] By contrast when the Petrograd Soviet sent envoys to the Eastern front to explain the meaning of Order No. 1, they were welcomed with military bands before delivering speeches with slogans like 'land and freedom!', 'no annexations and indemnities' and 'self-determination of the peoples'. Cheering soldiers carried the envoys around on their shoulders.[13] Such a military environment offered little prospect of operational success. The sole positive factor was that the Germans had moved some of their best forces from the Eastern to the Western front before opening their own offensive in northern France. The Russian high command could reasonably hope that its own intended initiative in Galicia in the Austro-Hungarian sector of the Eastern front would achieve durable success before Hindenburg and Ludendorff had time and men to intervene.[14]

The Russian offensive in Galicia opened on 18 June after a two-day preparatory barrage by heavy artillery. More forces were amassed than for the previous year's summer offensive. Brusilov took the precaution of relying heavily on regiments from outside those of Russia's heartland provinces where political propaganda had sapped military morale. The objective was nothing less than to retake Lvov, one of the great Galician cities that the Russians had occupied and lost in 1914–15.[15]

The all-out attack from the trenches by shock troops was initially a great success and 18,000 enemy combatants were taken prisoner. It seemed that the Russians would carry all before them until some of their regiments ignored orders and refused to move forward from the Austro-Hungarian trenches that they had occupied. Commanders succeeded in re-energizing the campaign but little territory was gained, and General Erdeli had to report that many soldiers were 'dominated by the conviction that they have done their duty'. When General Kornilov mustered efforts for a renewal of attacking operations, the German high command proved able to release reinforcements for their Habsburg allies. The Russian offensive lost all momentum and soon the Russians had to evacuate all the territories they had seized in Galicia.[16]

The defeat led to mass desertions throughout the summer months. By the autumn about two million troops had absconded from the armed forces.[17] Many of them took their rifles with them, as being armed they could commandeer seats on trains. They brought their weapons back to their villages where peasants had customarily used mainly fists, knives, axes and sickles as their weapons in social strife.

At the front, the dangers of warfare were omnipresent and the socialist talk of 'peace without annexations and indemnities' increased the unwillingness of troops to risk their lives any longer.[18] Socialists also had the freedom to spread their idea that the war itself was part of a wider struggle between imperialistic capitalist coalitions for world domination. Socialist groups grew in Germany, Austria, Britain and France that called for peace negotiations and an end to the fighting. The Western Allies, harassed by critics inside and outside parliaments, were under pressure to permit their nations' socialists to join a peace conference in Stockholm in summer 1917. The Russian Provisional Government lacked authority to forbid Russian attendance – and the Mensheviks and Socialist-Revolutionaries sent a handful of their leading cadres. The Kadets and everyone to the right of them expressed horror that such a conference was taking place at all.[19] The Bolsheviks agreed with them, but for an entirely different reason. Scorning the conference as having no chance of bringing the fighting to an end, they claimed that only they could bring about peace. The growing support for the Bolsheviks in Russia alarmed Allied ambassadors.[20]

By then it was obvious that the Russian Army was unlikely to attempt another offensive. Even so, Russian forces, merely by continuing to stand on the Eastern front, continued to prevent the transfer of more German divisions to northern France. Germany's leaders understood that once US armed forces landed in Europe, the possibility of a German victory would be drastically reduced. With this in mind, Ludendorff and Hindenburg maintained a priority to aid the pro-peace elements in Petrograd. Direct overtures to the Provisional Government had been a failure, so the Bolsheviks seemed the next best option. Having helped Lenin and other anti-war Marxist leaders with their return to Petrograd, they secretly channelled funds to the Bolshevik Central Committee. German money was laundered before being conveyed through Finland to Petrograd where it was used to subsidize premises, printing presses and party committees.

Meanwhile, with the war at a stalemate and the economy collapsing, wild rumours spread among the Russian people. Nikita Okunev wrote in his journal:

> Talk is intensifying that we'd be glad to end the war but that the Allies won't permit it. It's said that they are already threatening to throw us over and that they are deciding to wage war on the Germans without us but that in order to render us useless as future allies of the Germans, [the Allies] are getting 500,000 Japanese ready to occupy all Siberia through to the heights of the Urals.[21]

Alexander Zamaraev too felt gravely despondent: 'Our state is almost coming to its end. Everywhere there's terrible disorder. Soldiers in their thousands are fleeing from both the front and the rear. Discipline has collapsed and orders aren't being obeyed.'[22]

The total military account rose from 8.7 in 1915 to 14.9 billion rubles in 1916 and hit 26.1 billion rubles by the end of 1917.[23] The consequence was that only one sixth of the budget was left to the Finance Ministry for 'normal' expenditure.[24] As long as Russia stayed in the war, governmental finances would remain under severe strain. The Freedom Loan raised 3.2 billion rubles. But by July 1917 the Finance Ministry was 15 billion rubles short of what was needed to cover military expenditure through to the end of the year.[25] Petrograd Soviet spokesmen welcomed the income tax reform as a means to strip back the privileges of the propertied urban and rural elites. This hardly enticed cooperation from the wealthy. The project to bring in half a billion rubles for the Finance Ministry obtained only 100 million rubles – a mere plaster cast for the wounded budget.[26] Funds had to be sought from abroad and the Russians successfully approached politicians in Washington and bankers in New York for promises of loans to buy American military equipment.[27] The US administration took over the burden of financing the Allies from J. P. Morgan and Company and other banking centres, and the Provisional Government eventually received about 365 million rubles (or 188 million dollars) in credits.[28] More had been promised than arrived and the Finance Ministry ordered the printing of more money. Bank notes in circulation grew by 70 per cent. Increased currency depreciation and price inflation were inevitable. The ruble tumbled in the summer months and by October would retain only half of its February value.[29]

The impact on daily life was drastic. Between the summers of 1916 and 1917 the price of rye bread increased by 140 per cent. Butter rose by 54 per cent, milk by 90 per cent, butcher's meat by 186 per cent and potatoes by an extraordinary 663 per cent.[30] Urban consumers suffered the worst. But they were not alone. Many peasants bought staple products in the nearest town. Alexander Zamaraev, living in the Russian far north, was among them. After his trips into Totma he regularly recorded the upward surge of prices. In early May 1917 he noted the expansion of the ration-card system to include sugar. He wanted to buy tobacco and oats but none was to be found.[31] Oats were back on sale a month later and, with much effort, Zamaraev discovered some tobacco. Leather had disappeared from the stalls. By late June there was again no sugar with or without a ration card. Tobacco and millet had entirely vanished. Bread could be bought in town only by soldiers.[32] Food aid had to be supplied to Vologda province in 1916 and continued to be needed under the Provisional Government.[33]

Retail prices across the country rose by 120 per cent in the first half of 1917 from their level in January–June 1916. In some places, especially the northern and central Russian cities, the ascent was even sharper. Moscow consumers in the same period were having to pay 276 per cent more for their products.[34] The railways were deteriorating fast and in every way. Half the engines on some lines were in such disrepair as to have become unusable. The Trans-Siberian line, one of the few arteries left for imports, was juddering to a standstill, and huge piles of goods from North America rotted or rusted in Vladivostok on the Pacific coast.[35] Coal output in the Donbas, the main mining region, dropped by a fifth between March and July 1917. Fuel for factories was running short.[36] Whereas steel foundries produced the same in 1916 as immediately before the war, in 1917 it collapsed by 28 per cent.[37]

In 1916, 7,238 artillery guns were made and only 3,538 the following year. Shell output nearly halved in the same period.[38] The 133,400 ploughs made in 1916 were a fifth of the total made in 1913. In 1917 the number had tumbled to 22,902 – metallurgical factory owners evidently did not prioritize agricultural over military needs: only scythes were boosted in output, by an extraordinary 909 per cent over the total in 1913.[39] Oil production was exceptional in registering a wartime increase and dipping only slightly after the February Revolution. Baku and Grozny thrived as centres of hydrocarbon output.[40]

As difficulties grew in the economy, the fissures widened between one important sector and another. Bankers were understandably worried about lending to industrialists whose profitability was harmed by the revolutionary disturbance. Easy credit was no longer made available. The banks themselves experienced a squeeze on their incoming funds. The soviets kept up their tirades against profiteering, pointing to the cabals that were draining state revenue. The Trade and Industry Ministry announced its determination to cleanse the economy of corruption. But the chaos of war and revolution made investigative work unrealistic. The Soviet parties nonetheless accused the cabinet, some of whose ministers were leading industrialists, of having too cosy a rapport with Russian capitalist interests. But the cabinet, however, had a duty to protect production against damaging disruption. Mining and manufacturing were experiencing a run-down of their activity, and owners were genuinely threatened by unsupportable financial losses.

Meanwhile worry about food supplies deepened. The Imperial government's attempt to increase them by fixing prices and assigning delivery quotas to provincial zemstvos had attained only a third of the intended amount by the end of February 1917.[41] The Provisional Government's grain trade monopoly initially appeared a success. Ninety-eight per cent of the month's plan for procurement was realized in March – an improvement on February when only 62 per cent had been obtained. Agriculture Minister Shingarëv was delighted but the change for the better did not last. Peasant hostility to the trade monopoly deepened and in April only 38 per cent of the target was hit. The food-supply committees reinforced their efforts and the next two months produced higher amounts. In June, indeed, the authorities were able to collect 12 per cent more than the procurement plan.[42] Even so, there was growing concern that the rise might be a fleeting phenomenon. Talk spread about the possibility of a winter of hunger. The frustrations of consumers increased, and deliveries to the armed forces and to the cities of northern and central Russia became ever more unreliable.[43]

Excessive blame has been attached to the Provisional Government for its performance. The strikes for wages were hardly its fault and undoubtedly disrupted production and harmed profitability. They were intense in March, falling away in April and surging again in May to an unprecedented pitch.[44] Productivity also fell on the days when the factories were at work. Until 1917 it had stayed at a steady level in large-scale industry – in 1914–16 it had even risen to slightly above its level in the last year of peace. All this changed with the February Revolution when the average output for each worked day slipped to 76 per cent of the figure for 1913.[45] Revolutionary activism stiffened working-class resolve to ensure that owners, not workers, should make the material sacrifices and concessions. The inherited disorder in the wheels of transport and commerce was aggravated, and entrepreneurs had second thoughts about investing new capital in their companies.

The behaviour of agricultural producers added to the disintegrative tendencies in the economy. Although vegetables were grown and picked in spring and early summer 1917, peasants remained averse to selling them to governmental purchasing agencies when they could earn more in private deals. Moreover, goods from the countryside tended to be sold locally rather than delivered to regions of known shortage. The urban food supplies situation, dire though it was in northern and central Russia, was no better in Germany and Austria where turnips had to be used as a substitute for potatoes. The German War Food Office reduced the planned intake of foodstuffs per person to a mere 1,100 calories.[46] But German metallurgy still turned out the guns for the armed forces with efficiency. Austria–Hungary maintained output in factories in its Austrian, Bohemian and Polish territories. Whereas there was a growing unwillingness in the Russian Army to continue the fight, German and Habsburg troops still obeyed orders, and civil unrest and labour strikes did not reach Russia's level of disruption. The Russian disarray was also greater than anything witnessed in France, Great Britain and Italy. The exception was the massive mutiny that occurred in the French Army in mid-1917 which its high command suppressed with brutal severity. But governments in Paris, Westminster and Rome suffered little political disturbance, and industrial production and food supplies were buoyant in their countries. War weariness existed but the determination to go on fighting remained high.

21. FAITHS AND THE ARTS: REORGANIZATION, ASSERTION AND DISORIENTATION

The Russian Orthodox Church was no more effective than the Provisional Government in binding the Russian people together. Internal ecclesiastical divisions abounded as well as rivalry with other denominations across the Russian Empire. New religious freedom had been granted and the Orthodox clergy found itself in a tumultuous situation having to examine its needs and opportunities at an unforgiving speed.

After February 1917, some dioceses went on saying prayers for 'the most Orthodox, most autocratic tsar', but in most places the Church proclaimed its recognition of the Provisional Government.[1] Church leaders aimed to keep out of high politics and focused on matters of religion. The entire clergy simultaneously saw it as their patriotic duty to sustain the war effort. On 12 March 1917 Bishop Andrei of Ufa led prayers for victory in Petrograd's Kazan Cathedral. He deplored the indiscipline in the armed forces, issuing a call to the troops: 'Esteem your officers, be submissive to them, and the enemy at the front will be broken.' Ministers, however, were suspicious of a Church that they identified as a pillar of Romanov rule. Their first instinct was to abolish its privileges and the Church underwent disestablishment in all but name. Great state occasions were no longer to be accompanied by religious blessings.

While keeping their distance from the Church, however, ministers tried to guide it in the direction that they wanted. For this purpose they preserved the office of ober-procurator. The monarchist Nikolai Raev was fired as ober-procurator and replaced by Vladimir Lvov, a Christian activist of long standing who had campaigned against Rasputin and advocated internal ecclesiastical reform.[2] Vladimir Lvov – no relative of Prince Georgi – had belonged to the State Duma

Provisional Committee. The new cabinet endorsed his plan to purge the Holy Synod of leading clerics who were closely identified with Nicholas and Rasputin. In June the government nationalized all the Church's elementary schools – a third of the country's educational network. Ministers were determined to remove the priesthood's influence over young minds.[3]

The Church itself undertook internal change. Open debate and internal elections renovated the Church hierarchy with diocesan clergy taking an active part. Fifteen bishoprics – nearly a quarter of the total number – were removed between March and October, with those associated with the coterie around Nicholas the prime targets for removal. Clerics discussed the future of Russia and the Church's role in it. They agreed on the need to call a Church Council (*Sobor*) which all succeeding emperors and empresses had prohibited since the seventeenth century. They were divided about whether the Church should ask to retain its established status. Some argued for an end to the state connection while others wanted to preserve it. The cabinet was sufficiently alarmed at the idea of a loss of governmental authority that it suggested that only the Constituent Assembly should have the final decision.[4] Elections to the Church Council were held in July with each diocese having the right to choose two clergymen and three lay members. When the results were established, the membership gave 299 out of 564 places to the laity. The laymen were mainly professors and instructors from theological colleges.[5]

Discussion then focused on whether or not to elect a patriarch. To ecclesiastical conservatives it was obvious that the Church needed a single authority to navigate it through stormy waters, and they favoured candidates from their own ranks. Many younger priests, however, wanted the Church to move with the revolutionary current, endorsing such things as the transfer of all agricultural land to the peasantry. The patriarchy would invest a single individual with the kind of monarchical authority that had been overthrown. Priests in some dioceses took matters into their own hands by removing bishops who rejected calls for reform in Church life.[6]

For both sides an urgent objective was to explore how to present the Church to the faithful in such a way as would sustain their faith.[7] Every cleric knew that there was a problem. Nikolai Okunev in Moscow recorded: 'In the churches there is a sad fall-off in congregations, and generally it is as if everything appertaining to God has been eliminated.'[8] The drift of believers away from the Orthodox

Church was noticeable that Easter when religious services in Petrograd were poorly attended. In abolishing the general restrictions on religious organization, moreover, the Provisional Government was exposing the Russian Orthodox Church to unprecedented competition for the allegiance of Christian believers. The Ukrainian Uniate Church, which combined a liturgy of Eastern Orthodoxy with allegiance to the Vatican, had suffered centuries of persecution from the Russian capital. Its leader Andrey Sheptytsky, the metropolitan archbishop of Lvov, was released from confinement in March. On 25 July, ministers confirmed the Georgian Orthodox Church's freedom from subordination to the Russian Orthodox Church.[9] Next day it accorded Roman Catholics the right to build churches and found parishes – another extraordinary expansion of official tolerance even though the government simultaneously reserved its authority to approve appointments at the highest levels of the Catholic hierarchy in its territories in consultation with the Vatican.[10]

Jews and Muslims lived more freely than at any time since before Catherine the Great's acquisition of millions of them as her subjects in the late eighteenth century. Anti-Semitic pogroms, however, were still widespread, usually carried out by ill-disciplined soldiers or hungry townspeople. The authorities intervened to stop the violence.[11] Jewish religious life was unshaken by any kind of reform movement. The awful recent experiences in the war zone had the effect of turning religious Jews away from ideas for change in Judaism's spiritual thought and practices. The same was not true of Islam. Muslims, at least those who lived outside Turkestan, had suffered less than Jews at the hands of the Imperial Army. Among them there was a rising generation of imams who saw no hope for their fellow believers unless Muslim communities recognized the requirements of cultural modernity. Islamic teachers were in constant dispute as the young argued against the old.

An oath of loyalty was prepared for all civilians to take. The wording was varied for the diverse faiths but Christians, Jews and Muslims were all expected to affirm their belief in God and swear to work for the benefit of the Russian state even at the cost of their lives. No mention was made of the Provisional Government. Ministers wanted people to show their patriotism regardless of what they thought of the government itself.[12]

The Russian Orthodox Church's Council opened on the Feast of the Dormition on 15 August in the Dormition Cathedral in the Moscow

Kremlin.[13] It quickly elected Moscow Metropolitan Tikhon to chair the proceedings. Generally the Church leadership avoided involvement in controversies of a political nature and shrank from commenting on public debate except for when the Church's own position was being discussed. The end of the monarchy nevertheless gave clerics the opportunity to focus their efforts on ecclesiastical reform. There was an exception in August when the Church Council denounced 'German spies and hirelings', by which they meant the Bolshevik party, but even then they did not mention them by name.

Novelists and poets by contrast had for decades offered their works, however surreptitiously, as commentary on politics; and many of them were popular for proposing a vision of life at variance with Church and state. Suddenly ministers had come to power who were so unconcerned by what authors wrote about them that they abolished the censorship. Alone of the countries at war, Russia under the Provisional Government allowed complete freedom of the press. When the new rules were formalized on 27 April, the only requirement was for publishers to hand over copies of books and newspapers to the authorities. But there was no accompanying restriction on what could be published or sold with the exception of the far-right political press. Plays, poems, films and pieces of music could be performed or shown without any hindrance beyond the need to hand over transcripts. No ban was yet placed even on printing material of strategic or operational sensitivity – a quite astonishing wartime dispensation.[14]

Publishing became the sole industry that expanded while the rest of the economy contracted. The shelves of bookshops were filled with works which had been banned under the Imperial administration. The late Lev Tolstoy's prohibited prose was printed in big new editions. But while this pleased millions of readers, novelists, poets and composers were losing their role as unofficial directors of public opinion. New writing seemed slow to react to political events while the revolutionary times were calling out for instant comment. Creative artists were bewildered by the same daily concerns that afflicted everyone else – and most of them were equally baffled about the meaning of events. The poets Zinaida Gippius and Marina Tsvetaeva were horrified by their experiences but they did not have the confidence to say why. Sergei Yesenin, poet and balladeer, ignored the revolution and continued to write about other themes: his love life, his mother, evening carousing and the beauty of forests. Anna Akhmatova felt near-despair about her country but decided to hope for the best. Calmest of all was Boris Pasternak, who compared the natural energy and beauty released by the onset of spring with the liberating tumult of crowds surging onto the streets.

Alexander Blok did more than most writers to immerse himself in the revolutionary current. But he was no revolutionary himself. Far from it: his political preferences lay with the Kadets. He claimed that 'Kadetism' was in his blood and that he was fearful of the idea that Finland and Ukraine might break away from 'Great Russia'.[15] Blok, though, talked to soviet leaders and to soldiers as he wanted to hear what he called 'the music of the times'.[16] Whereas other members of the artistic elite hated the disorder of revolution, Blok found a lot to admire despite his Kadet leanings. He dismissed the widespread talk about dual power at the apex of public life and thought 'powerlessness' was a more accurate description. But he added that sheer apathy prevailed at the base of society. He denied that Russians were behaving like 'revolutionary people'.[17] He was trying to make sense of the confusion of what he was witnessing, and it would take some months – after he had digested what he saw on the streets – before he wrote *The Twelve*, one of the greatest poems of the twentieth century.

Out on the political far left, the Futurist poet Vladimir Mayakovski felt no need to wait to make up his mind about what he saw. Dropping his fascination with abstract concepts and bizarre images, he adopted both Bolshevism and a more direct literary style. In 'Call to Account!' he denounced the military carnage that had raged since 1914:

> The drums of war are beating and beating.
> They are calling for iron to be shoved into the living.
> Slave after slave
> from every land
> is hurled on to the bayonet's steel tip.
> What's the point of it all?
> The earth is trembling,
> hungry,
> stripped naked,
> Humanity's been steam-bathed in blood
> just so that
> someone
> somewhere or other
> can feast
> on Albania.[18]

Enlisting as a Bolshevik political warrior, Mayakovski produced a memorable two-liner for them on class struggle:

> Eat up your pineapples, chew on your grouse,
> Your last day's at hand, you filthy bourgeois![19]

Mayakovski's artistic development was in line with an environment where songs, cartoons and posters became popular for providing fast and often irreverent reactions to the latest events. The newspapers too were filled with lively discussion. Often it seemed as if the time of the tsars and Nicholas Romanov had never existed. And it was not all about the serious concerns of the war and the collapsing economy. The theatres were packed with audiences eager to get away from such day-to-day concerns. The world-famous operatic bass Fëdor Shalyapin gave concerts to huge audiences and Tamara Karsavina thrilled enthusiasts of the ballet. The arts uplifted the mood of readers and spectators who experienced many traumas in their daily lives.

22. SOVIETS AND SOCIALISTS: THE EROSION OF MENSHEVIK AND SOCIALIST-REVOLUTIONARY INFLUENCE, SPRING TO SUMMER 1917

The Provisional Government was compelled to deal with problems that no cabinet could quickly resolve, and the Petrograd Soviet shared responsibility for their management after agreeing to supply leaders to become ministers. Wartime strains and disruptions antedated the February Revolution, and the ensuing process of political, administrative, ethnic and economic disintegration had its own momentum. Government and Soviet were like joint heirs who had looked forward to the reading of a will, only to find that they faced the probability of bankruptcy.

The cabinet's original composition and direction of policies had been agreed in consultation with the Petrograd Soviet. The Soviet itself issued public instructions. Its most influential was Order No. 1 which was proclaimed to the armed forces without prior notice to ministers. The Soviet Executive Committee had also issued an independent ban on newspapers of the political far right.[1] Governmental policies were constantly vetted and when the Soviet objected, ministers usually conceded amendments. Even when the government was following a line approved by Soviet leaders, the Soviet's General Assembly and Executive Committee remained a forum for critique of the cabinet's latest measures.

The network of soviets was spread to every city in the empire – and not just to provincial capitals. Assemblies of elected representatives took place, often on a daily basis in the early weeks of the revolution, to the newly created executive committees. Workers and soldiers were active at all levels, but the socialist intelligentsia attained a steering influence. The higher the level, the greater the proportion of intellectuals. Debates were often encrusted in the Marxist jargon that all the socialists – Mensheviks, Socialist-Revolutionaries, Bundists and Bolsheviks – liked to use. But speakers also had to be able to talk in plain language. Regional and provincial soviets were formed to coordinate efforts between towns over a wide distance. The ambition was present to build an 'all-Russia' framework. The Mensheviks and Socialist-Revolutionaries in the Petrograd Soviet leadership took the initiative in April by calling a conference from everywhere in the country. Nikolai Chkheidze presided. Kamenev spoke for the Bolsheviks and against the Provisional Government – Lenin arrived in Petrograd only on the last day of the conference. Menshevik and Socialist-Revolutionary delegates and supporters anyway constituted a large majority, and endorsed supporting the cabinet so long as ministers held to the agreement on policies already agreed with the Petrograd Soviet.

Whilst soviets were diverse in their mode of composition, they were mainly an urban phenomenon and there were few of them in most rural areas. To redress the balance the Bolshevik party sent 'agitators' into such areas. Bolsheviks also went among the groups of factory workers from particular provinces and asked them to send people back home to spread the party's message.[2]

The soviets did not confine themselves to putting pressure on the Provisional Government about its policies but began to function as an alternative fulcrum of governance. They sequestered premises for their activities and commandeered printing presses and founded newspapers – in Petrograd alone there were dozens of them. Although some of the funding came from workers and soldiers, soviets usually ran up debts to supply welfare and cultural facilities for those whom they served. They established their own militias, often known as Red Guards, to enhance public security. They liaised with local garrisons and called upon soldiers to treat the soviets' orders as paramount. In many towns and cities, it became that nothing of importance could be done that contravened the wishes of their socialist leaders.

Soviets had been formed in a spirit of socialist cooperation but as time went on the splits between the parties became intense. A sailor in the Helsinki garrison who refused to join any particular party wrote in disappointment about the 'Be-ki', 'Me-ki' and 'Es-ery' – Bolsheviks, Mensheviks and Socialist-Revolutionaries:

> A plague on your programmes
> Your -isms and -ites,
> Your Be-ki and Me-ki, Es-ery and the like!

They aren't made for us, they aren't worth a damn!
A plague on your ranting, your parties and strife,
The people won't take it, the people will strike,
They want you together! The cause is the thing![3]

The habit of keeping Bolsheviks on soviet executive committees was nevertheless maintained even though the same Bolsheviks were categorizing their Menshevik and Socialist-Revolutionary 'comrades' as traitors to socialism and collaborators with a bourgeois, imperialist administration.

The soviets were organized in such a way that there could be fresh elections whenever deputies fell out of favour with those who had voted for them. The turnover of personnel was built into the system and so no deputy could feel safe in his or her seat.

While sticking to their slogan of 'All Power to the Soviets', Bolsheviks insisted that only they would arrange a speedy Constituent Assembly election. This was unfair on the Provisional Government, which worked hard on plans for a democratic parliament. The Bolshevik party objective lay across a fault line between taking power on behalf of a class-based section of society – a very large section if the peasantry was going to be included – and making arrangements for everyone in society, regardless of class, to vote in the Assembly election. The Bolsheviks were in no rush to define the objective more exactly when campaigning began in the summer elections to the urban dumas. These were the first such elections since the Provisional Government had decreed new rules on a universal ballot, secret, direct and without distinction of social class.[4] They canvassed for victory in the district dumas in Petrograd in late May. The results were not unencouraging for the Bolsheviks even though they secured 20 per cent of the votes. The Kadets performed only marginally better with 22 per cent while the Mensheviks, Socialist-Revolutionaries and other socialists took 56 per cent.[5] This was a sign of the shifting direction of travel of political forces in towns and cities. Whereas both the Bolsheviks and Kadets obtained substantial minorities of seats, only the Bolsheviks were confident about their prospects for making further gains in local government in urban Russia.

On 16 and 21 May 1917 the Kronstadt Soviet, a few miles off the coast from Petrograd, declared its refusal to recognize the Provisional Government's authority and threw many naval officers into prison.[6] Essentially it was a declaration of independence, and it was not the first time that the Kronstadters had challenged the country's leaders. Trotsky was pleased by the news, telling Tsereteli: 'When a counter-revolutionary general tries to put a noose round the neck of the revolution, the Kadets will grease the rope but the Kronstadt sailors will come to fight and die at our side.'[7] This hardly reassured Tsereteli, who thought that the best news from Kronstadt was no news.

The Provisional Government saw no point in sending anyone but socialist ministers to bring the garrison to order. Tsereteli and Skobelev went and were shaken by their experience. At a public meeting Tsereteli asked: 'Do you want to break with the entire revolutionary democracy?' There were voices shouting: 'Yes, yes, that's what we want!' The ministers managed to carry the crowd on the day but it still took several days to secure agreement to the release of the naval officers, and then only by giving way to the demand that the cabinet should only appoint a commissar for the island who had the Soviet's prior approval. This was hardly the kind of deference that the ministers wanted, but it was the best arrangement that they could achieve.[8] And within days the Provisional Government heard that the Kronstadt Soviet had gone back on its word by reaffirming its right to rule the island.[9]

The Kronstadt example was noticed by others around the country. In June, at the height of the Russian offensive on the Eastern front, the Tsaritsyn Soviet on the banks of the river Volga voted to transfer the powers of government to the soviets. This was a step further than even the Kronstadters had taken. The men of Kronstadt had demanded self-rule whereas those in Tsaritsyn were calling for the removal of the cabinet in Petrograd.[10] How this would turn out elsewhere was not at all clear. But the Menshevik and Socialist-Revolutionary leadership of the Petrograd Soviet were deeply agitated.

They had kept their nerve in late May 1917 when the All-Russia Congress of Soviets of Peasants' Deputies met in Petrograd. Socialist-Revolutionaries had obtained nearly half of the 1,157 delegates. Five hundred and fifty-eight of the delegates came from the armed forces. The dominant mood was in favour of satisfying peasant demands for an immediate agrarian reform.[11] Lenin addressed the Congress in its closing days, emphasizing the Bolsheviks' determination to hand over all agricultural land to the peasantry. He was as much interested in winning favour from peasants-in-uniform as from delegates who came directly from the villages. If he could win support among troops, the task of organizing a socialist seizure of power would become easier. The Socialist-Revolutionaries saw the danger and called on everyone to show patience with the government's measures in a time of crisis. They promised to push for the maximum of possible concessions to the peasantry.

The first All-Russia Congress of Soviets of Workers' and Soldiers' Deputies opened in Petrograd on 3 June 1917. The Mensheviks and Socialist-Revolutionaries had 533 out of the 822 delegates and easily outnumbered the 105 Bolsheviks. Liber and Tsereteli led in the debate 'on power', praising the utility of the governing coalition. This irritated all those in the hall who hated the cabinet for approving military operations on the Eastern front. Tsereteli incautiously claimed: 'At the present moment in Russia there's no political party that would say, "Give power into our hands, go away and we'll take your place! There's no such party in Russia!"'[12] Lenin saw the chance to make his mark. Rising from his seat, he disdained to mention Tsereteli by name or recognize him as a comrade: 'The citizen Minister of Post and Telegraphs has declared that there's no political party in Russia which would agree to take power wholly upon itself. My reply is: "There is!" . . . No party can shrink from this. All parties engage in struggle and must struggle for power, and our party doesn't shrink from this. It is ready at any moment to take power in its entirety.'[13]

His intervention caused many to laugh at his self-aggrandizement. Yet the laughter was accompanied by feelings of discomfort. The Bolshevik party had adopted the slogan of 'All Power to the Soviets!' in late April, and in the minds of most this meant forming a government that would include all socialist parties. Suddenly their leader was saying that the Bolshevik party rather than the soviets should become the vehicle of revolutionary progress, with no time for Mensheviks and other Socialist-Revolutionaries.

The Congress came to an end without further disruption. But the Bolsheviks made preparations for a political demonstration in the capital. They had their slogans sewn onto their banners and painted on their posters: 'All Power to the Soviets', 'Down with the Capitalist Ministers', 'All the Land to the People' and 'Peace to the Whole World'. The Congress leadership, consisting mainly of Mensheviks and Socialist-Revolutionaries, were alert to the danger. Some suspected the demonstration, which would have the participation of soldiers of the Petrograd garrison and sailors shipped over from Kronstadt, to be a cover for a Bolshevik coup d'état. Lenin, despite his general enthusiasm for an insurrection, was probably only seeking to probe the scale of his support in the capital, but he certainly hoped to cause some serious trouble. He cannot have been surprised when Congress leaders placed a ban on the Bolshevik-led demonstration. If nothing else, it was evidence of where ultimate power lay, that the Congress of Soviets and not the Provisional Government were strong enough to do this.

The Menshevik and Socialist-Revolutionary leaders themselves, though, needed to show self-confidence on the streets of the capital. After prohibiting the Bolshevik-led demonstration they announced one of their own for 18 June. It was to be a Soviet occasion, with the Bolsheviks able to join in but only under their own controlled conditions. The Mensheviks and Socialist-Revolutionaries aimed to show the watching populace that the governmental cabinet was worth supporting. Although it was not planned this way, it was the first day of the June offensive. To that extent it was a test of official policy on the war. Lenin did not march. Nor did the rest of the Bolshevik Central Committee, but thousands of Bolshevik party activists turned out and their rallying shouts had an impact. They wanted power to pass from the cabinet of 'bourgeois ministers' to the soviets. They urged soldiers, sailors and industrial workers to support the Bolshevik cause. They preached that the Provisional Government had to be removed for the great questions of land, peace and industrial regeneration to be resolved.

The Bolsheviks were not entirely alone in rejecting the cabinet's policies and legitimacy. All political parties had internal conflicts along such lines and only old loyalties prevented the Mensheviks and Socialist-Revolutionaries from undergoing splits of their own. But the Bolsheviks were benefiting from having a clear and radical message, of being the sole big party promising unconditionally an end of the war and 'bourgeois' rule. There were some Bolsheviks who were appalled by Lenin's extreme policies. Many of them left the party ranks, and some of these joined the Mensheviks. Tsereteli hoped that such changes of allegiance were signs that Petrograd and the rest of the country would follow a sober, moderate path towards a socialist future. Lenin, however, could take heart that those Mensheviks who thought their leaders had conceded too much to the Provisional Government were switching towards Bolshevism. Some Marxists like Lev Trotsky who had stayed outside the factional fray before 1917 saw the need to choose definitively between the Bolsheviks and the Mensheviks. Trotsky in particular reckoned that Lenin, by dropping his doctrinal commitment to a bourgeois-democratic revolution being necessary before a socialist one, had come over to his standpoint. Some of the Bolshevik leaders couldn't abide Trotsky but Lenin successfully insisted that he be made welcome and elected to its Central Committee.

23. THE JULY DAYS: THE CABINET'S BREAK-UP AND THE ABORTIVE BOLSHEVIK RISING

Russian misery on the Eastern front in the last week of June 1917 was Bolshevism's opportunity. Army morale was sinking and soldiers' indiscipline increased to the exasperation of the officer corps. The Bolsheviks aimed to exploit the unrest in the capital. They had been banned from holding an armed demonstration against the Provisional Government in early June but wanted to try again. When the Bolshevik City Committee adopted this idea, however, Lenin said this would be premature and too dangerous.[1] His caution was not appreciated after so many weeks when he had been urging his party to work for the cabinet's removal. The City Committee as well as the Bolshevik Military Organization started planning another march through the streets of the capital. Lenin departed for a short break in Finland in late June while the planners of the armed demonstration contacted sympathizers in the Petrograd garrisons and among the sailors on Kronstadt. Accompanying Lenin were his sister Maria and the poet Demyan Bedny. Lenin hoped for a few days of relaxation.

The cabinet was alert to the passions stirring in the armed forces but was undergoing its own internal crisis on the question of Ukraine. Ministers Kerensky, Tereshchenko and Tsereteli were sent to Kiev to hold talks with Ukrainian politicians. Premier Lvov did not like to place divisive items on the cabinet agenda while they were away, so priority was given on 29 June to a discussion about prohibiting the production of sweets and candies at a time when sugar was in short supply. On 1 July 1917, a decision was made to allow the import of 420 million safety matches in boxes containing no more than seventy-five matches, and working conditions in the universities were also discussed.[2] Next day Kerensky, Tereshchenko and Tsereteli returned to Petrograd from Kiev. They reported that they had agreed to recognize the General

Secretariat of the Central Rada as the regional authority in the Ukrainian provinces – and the Rada laid claim to both Kharkov and the Donbas. The deal with the three ministers involved the General Secretariat in promising to drop the demand for separate Ukrainian armed forces. The Provisional Government met that evening to discuss the Kiev agreement. Kadet ministers were angry at what had been conceded and they rejected what they feared was but the first step towards Ukraine's complete independence. After acrimonious exchanges, every Kadet minister except Nikolai Nekrasov resigned his post. The Lvov-led coalition was in pieces.[3]

While all this was happening, many Bolsheviks outside their Central Committee concluded that the time had come for action on the streets. A machine-gun regiment based in Petrograd was about to be transferred to the Eastern front but few men in the regiment relished the idea of going into battle against the victorious German forces. The Bolshevik Military Organization sought authorization for an armed demonstration from the Central Committee. Soldiers were fiercely arguing for a march on the Tauride Palace and the overthrow of the Provisional Government. Bolshevik Central Committee members faced a tricky choice. They had repeatedly called for an end to 'bourgeois' and 'imperialistic' rule. When their own followers were offering to take the initiative, it was difficult for them to withhold approval. But the Central Committee appreciated that an uprising was unlikely to succeed and the Bolshevik Military Organization received orders to take no part in the projected march.[4]

On 3 July 1917 Tsereteli appeared at the joint Bureaux of Central Executive Committees of the recent Congresses of Soviets in the Tauride Palace. Although he knew of the planned marches, he kept his focus on securing a working cabinet. Tsereteli was able to assure the Central Executive Committees that governmental policy would shift in favour of democratic demands. He knew this involved the risk of Georgi Lvov's resignation. Lvov objected to Agriculture Minister Chernov's proposal to place a ban on land sales in advance of the Constituent Assembly.[5] The Main Land Committee had warned of the danger that fields and woods might change hands to the disadvantage of peasants who were waiting for the great agrarian reform that they were being promised. Lvov, a large landowner himself, wanted to let people like him do whatever they liked with their property. Autonomy for Ukraine, he could tolerate, but not a ban on rights of land ownership.[6] Tsereteli assured the Soviet leadership that the Provisional Government could continue with or without Lvov.[7]

The dangerous situation on the streets of the capital, however, could no longer be ignored when Bolshevik leader Stalin burst into the meeting and revealed that his party's Central Committee and Petrograd City Conference had just told the machine-gunners that the party was against the demonstration. Tsereteli knew that this did not mean that the demonstration would not go ahead. There was the belief that Bolshevik leaders were simply positioning themselves to take advantage of the violence when it occurred. The tension mounted in the Tauride Palace.[8] Disturbances took place in various districts around the capital into the evening. Tsereteli, though, was confident that the trouble was containable. Troops at the front had sent messages of support and asked for a propaganda campaign against the Bolsheviks to calm the roiling waters.

Next day, in answer to the original summons by the Bolshevik Military Organization, sailors arrived from Kronstadt, armed and ready to liaise with the capital's machine-gunners and workers to destabilize the Provisional Government.

This added to the concerns of some among the Bolshevik party leadership. An article by Kamenev and Zinoviev appeared in *Pravda* calling for the march to be abandoned. The piece was removed from the front page and nothing was put in its place. The blank space told of the tensions inside the leadership. Stalin tried to steer a middle way by writing an appeal for the procession to go ahead on a peaceful basis.[9] Throughout the morning the Military Organization, whose leaders had wanted an armed demonstration, liaised with the marchers. The idea was to proceed to the Tauride Palace after stopping at Bolshevik headquarters at the Kshesinskaya mansion (which the Bolsheviks had sequestered from Matilda Kshesinskaya, who had been Nicholas II's lover before his marriage to Alexandra). The Central Committee failed to quieten the mood. Many on the march carried weapons and still hoped to turn the event into an armed uprising if circumstances proved favourable. The Kronstadt Bolshevik leader Fëdor Raskolnikov mingled with the sailors. Like them, he expected to meet violent resistance on the streets. Under Central Committee pressure, Raskolnikov agreed to moderate his intentions. He remembered it all later with a smile: 'To hold the masses back from an unorganized direct action was something that we jokingly compared to the role of firemen. It must be admitted that it was not the most pleasant role but it was one that was absolutely necessary at that time.'[10]

The Soviet Central Executive Committee, in expectation of Bolshevik-led violence, rallied support from the Petrograd garrisons.

War Minister Kerensky and the capital's army commanders agreed on the necessary practical measures, including a defensive ring that was put around the Tauride Palace. Hospitals were asked to make themselves available. Institutions and commercial premises in the central area were shuttered.

An emissary from the Bolshevik Central Committee had taken an early train that day from the Finland station to tell Lenin to terminate his holiday. Lenin rushed back to the capital. Everything he saw near Bolshevik headquarters confirmed his belief that the political demonstration would be a disaster.[11] He arrived in time to see the marchers who had stopped in front of the Kshesinskaya mansion. He reportedly told the Military Organization leaders that they deserved a thrashing for creating such a situation. When he appeared on a balcony at the mansion, he was applauded by the crowd which was massed below. In his brief speech he tried to put a brake on the enthusiasm for an uprising. But the marchers either did not hear or did not like what they heard. Instead, they went on to the Nevski Prospect, where sailors broke into stores and apartment blocks, exchanging fire with soldiers who were loyal to the authorities. It became clear that the Provisional Government could call upon superior military strength and the fighting petered out with nightfall.[12]

There was a perilous moment in the middle of the afternoon when Agriculture Minister Chernov appeared outside the Tauride Palace to explain the political situation to the sailors who had gathered there. Chernov was pleased about the Kadet exodus from the cabinet: 'We don't regret their departure. The path is clear in front of us.' The crowd was unpersuaded. Sailors shouted: 'So why did you sit in the same government as them?' When Chernov turned to go back into the building, he was manhandled into a parked limousine and there was concern that he might be beaten up or killed. Word of this was swiftly communicated to the Central Executive Committee inside the building. Menshevik and Socialist-Revolutionaries sensed that it would not help to send another of their number to intervene, and Chkheidze asked Trotsky, who was present for the Executive Committee discussion, to talk to the sailors before it was too late. Trotsky rushed outside. Trusted by the sailors as an enemy of the government, he put the question: 'Let him who is in favour of using force raise his hand!' No one moved and Trotsky secured the captive minister's release. He indicated to Chernov to leave the scene after addressing him with words of friendly hostility: 'Citizen Chernov, you are free!'[13]

Inside the Tauride Palace Tsereteli spoke against giving an inch to those responsible for disorder and bloodshed in the capital but majority opinion in the Soviet leadership favoured confining policy to a mere refreshment of the coalition cabinet's composition.[14]

The Bolsheviks had fomented a muddled quasi-uprising that became known as 'the July Days' and ended before it properly began. Much as he tried, Lenin could not escape a share of the blame. In a *Pravda* article that had been published that morning he called unequivocally for power to pass to the soviets and argued that democracy would not be achieved in Russia until this came to pass.[15] Neither he nor others in the Bolshevik Central Committee ever explained their reasons for holding back. Lenin cannot have been unaware that the anti-government soviets were too few in number and Bolsheviks were still a minority political force inside them. He also knew that the cabinet and the Soviet Executive Committee could still muster loyal military units. What is more, no command centre had been formed for an uprising and there was no operational plan in place apart from surging to the Tauride Palace. Compared to the Duma Provisional Committee in the days of the February Revolution, the Bolshevik Military Organization was chaotic and lacking in clear structure and operational planning. Some Bolsheviks talked the talk but without clear leadership they ran off when the first shots were fired. They did not pass the obvious test of would-be insurrectionaries.

On 5 July some Petrograd newspapers published material supplied by Justice Minister Pavel Pereverzev on how German subsidies had funded the Bolshevik Central Committee. Pereverzev wanted to prepare public opinion for the mass of arrests he intended among the Bolshevik hierarchy.

The press reports, however, inadvertently gave an alert to those Bolsheviks likely to be taken into custody, and the Provisional Government lost the chance to catch them unawares. Karl Radek, identified as the intermediary for the reception of the German funds, fled back to Stockholm.[16] Lenin took refuge with Bolshevik friends in Petrograd before making his way back north towards the village of Razliv near the Russo-Finnish frontier. One day he buried himself in a haystack to escape a search by soldiers. He decided to seek sanctuary in Finland. Putting on a heavy disguise which included a theatrical wig and an adhesive face mask, he boarded trains for Helsinki. Grigori Zinoviev, who had accompanied him in Razliv, returned secretly to Petrograd and hid out with Bolshevik militants before being discovered and arrested. Lev Kamenev, Alexandra Kollontai, Fëdor Raskolnikov and dozens of others who had instigated the public disorder were also taken into custody. Lev Trotsky quixotically offered himself for arrest, and his proposition was accepted.

The evidence of Bolshevik complicity with the German state authorities was strong but not conclusive, not least because Lenin had covered up many of the traces. Tereshchenko and Nekrasov begged for time for the investigation to be completed. Pereverzev's premature move had weakened the chances of a successful trial even if the absconders were caught. Although leading Bolsheviks had fomented protests on Petrograd's streets, few of them had openly called for insurrection. But the government somehow had to do something and on 6 July Lvov signed a decree to bring those guilty of armed disturbances before the courts for 'treason to the Motherland and betrayal of the Revolution'.[17] It was almost his last measure as premier. For days Tsereteli and Skobelev had been pushing him to implement reforms that would enhance the interests of workers and peasants. They also called for a Russian initiative for a conference with the Western Allies on war aims. Lvov told them he would rather resign than agree.[18] He resolved to step down from the premiership.

On 7 July he announced his departure. Not long afterwards he was to confide: 'Essentially I stepped down because there was nothing left for me to do. In order to save the situation it was necessary to break up the soviets and fire on the people. I couldn't do that. But Kerensky can.'[19] Kerensky was such an obvious choice for the premiership that nobody bothered to record his appointment. He had no equal in fame and dynamism, and he had retained his vital links with the socialist parties.

He aimed to run the cabinet in a more presidential style than the modest Lvov had done. With this in mind, he expanded the premiership's administrative team.[20] On policy he did not disguise the military difficulties ahead but insisted that Russia could still fight on to victory. He promised to expand local self-rule and to halt the economic collapse. In industry he committed himself to strengthening the arbitration chambers and providing everyone in employment with social insurance. Praising the work of the land committees, he assured the peasantry that everything was being done to prepare for the 'transfer of the land into the hands of those who laboured [on it]'.[21] Tough new measures were also introduced. On 9 July he established a Special Investigative Commission to report on the recent disorders in Petrograd.[22] Two days later he got the cabinet's agreement to restore capital punishment at the front. 'Military-revolutionary courts' were created, each consisting of three officers and three soldiers.[23] A few days later the war and internal affairs ministers received powers to close down any newspapers which they thought were provoking disobedience in the armed forces.[24]

It took several days to recruit a full new cabinet. Tsereteli initially agreed to succeed Georgi Lvov in the Internal Affairs Ministry. The other socialist ministers, including Chernov at the Agriculture Ministry, also stayed in post and Kerensky was cheered by his friend Nekrasov's decision to resign from the Kadet party rather than abandon him in a time of emergency. Tereshchenko and Vladimir Lvov also stayed on. But Kerensky still hoped to retrieve leading Kadets from their self-imposed political quarantine. The broader the coalition, the better. Chernov was annoyed at discovering that his policy for land reform had disappeared from the new coalition's programme that Kerensky announced to the country. Tsereteli too expressed disquiet. But Kerensky's ebullience was undimmed. He trusted that most people in Russia and the outlying regions were relieved that the disturbances in Petrograd had been halted. Until July the well-informed peasant Alexander Zamaraev had taken no notice of the Bolsheviks. In June 1917 Zamaraev read the news and was appalled by the Petrograd violence: 'Things in Russia are not going at all well. The disgusting party of the Bolsheviks has made its appearance, aiming to destroy everything and recognizing nothing [of value].'[25]

24. THE KORNILOV REVOLT: KERENSKY AND THE CRUSHING OF THE MILITARY COUP

The cabinet's policies angered the Kadets and everyone to their political right. Milyukov in the *Rech* newspaper harangued ministers for refusing to face down the soviets and their demands. But the Kadets had lost their friends in the high command by walking out of the cabinet at a time when the armed forces were fighting a desperate campaign on the Eastern front. They were not going to be quickly forgiven. The prospects of political liberalism grew dimmer as autumn approached.[1]

The flame of monarchism hardly flickered except in the minds of a few die-hards who plotted to liberate Nicholas and his family from captivity. Later, on 14 August, Kerensky would move the Romanovs to Tobolsk in western Siberia. He did this not because of any rescue plots but out of concern that a crowd of unruly workers might storm the Alexander Palace and do them physical harm. Nikita Okunev felt pity for the former emperor and asked why he was not allowed to go into foreign exile. Okunev wrote that he was not alone in asking this.[2] The problem for the old right-wing organizations was that the government and soviets had closed down their presses and newspapers in March. Vladimir Purishkevich could not bring his Union of the Russian People onto the streets. His only hope – as it was for the Octobrists and Kadets – was that the army leadership would depose the cabinet. Purishkevich discreetly probed opinion among the generals. Brusilov's chief of staff, Anton Denikin, turned down the invitation to join any conspiracy.[3] Ex-War Minister Guchkov and the industrialist Putilov refused to give up. They gathered funds from banks and insurance companies to organize propaganda across the entire Eastern front.[4]

Kerensky was unaware of these stirrings when going with Foreign Affairs Minister Tereshchenko for a war conference in Mogilëv on 16 July 1917. Things started badly when Brusilov failed to meet

Kerensky on arrival, and Kerensky was angered enough to stay in the train carriage until Brusilov appeared.[5] A rancorous tone persisted at the conference, which was attended by most of the army's leadership. General Denikin outlined the difficulties the commanders faced at the front and with a cabinet that knew nothing of military life. He dismissed the Bolsheviks as 'mere filthy worms which have found their way into the abscesses of the army organism'. When he even showered blame on Kerensky himself, even Brusilov thought he had gone too far.[6] But Denikin knew he was speaking for the commanders in the room. His demands were shared by all of them. Soldiers' committees and commissars had to be abolished. Revolutionary orders should be put aside and capital punishment restored. Looking straight at Kerensky, Denikin exclaimed: 'But you . . . you have trampled our banners in the mud!'[7]

Kerensky amazed everyone by standing up and shaking Denikin's hand: 'Thank you, general, for your courageous, sincere words.'[8] The magnanimous gesture settled the atmosphere around the table before Kerensky explained that he had his own complaints to make. He accused the commanders of shrinking from pressing for necessary military reforms under Nicholas II, and then of giving inadequate support to the Provisional Government. A telegram from Kornilov was read aloud, making roughly the same demands as Denikin and calling for a purge of those commanders who lacked a commitment to victory over the Central Powers.[9] Brusilov looked downcast and said little – he was 'unrecognizable' as the fighting general he once had been.[10] Kerensky decided that he had to replace him with a new supreme commander-in-chief, and Kornilov seemed to fit the bill. On 19 July, after going back to Petrograd, Kerensky confirmed his promotion.[11]

Kornilov was of humble origins and once described Alexander Guchkov to his face as too much of a *burzhui* to head the War Ministry.[12] His own ethnic background was probably a mixture of Don Cossack, Polish and Altai Kalmyk. Having entered military school in Omsk in mid-Siberia, he was seen as a soldier of much potential. After further training at the Mikhailovski Artillery School in St Petersburg, Kornilov went on intelligence missions in Turkestan, Persia and Afghanistan. He learned several Asian languages. After fighting at the battle of Mukden in 1905 in the Russo-Japanese war, he was made colonel and appointed as a military attaché to China. In the Great War he became a major-general. In 1915 he was captured by Austrian forces. Feigning illness, he made a daring escape through Romania into Russia. He was welcomed back into the Imperial Army on the south-western sector under Brusilov, where he acquired a reputation for disobeying orders and for squandering the lives of his men. Kornilov welcomed the downfall of the Romanovs. He had received charge of their initial confinement in the Alexander Palace and issued an appeal to 'soldiers of the people's army and citizens of a free Russia'.[13]

Kerensky assured the Western Allies that the recent defeat on the Eastern front would not get in the way of Russia's push for victory.[14] He knew that faith in Russian military capability was in sharp decline in London, Paris and Washington, and his Finance Ministry was desperate for new credits. Cabinet members put on a show of confidence, assuring the Allied ambassadors of the fighting spirit of Russian armed forces.

It was still a struggle for Kerensky to form a full cabinet and attract the Kadets back into ministerial posts. On 20 July, when they yet again demanded that he made compromises on policy, he announced his resignation from the premiership and left for a stay in the Finnish countryside.[15] The Kadets continued to keep their distance. Kerensky's sense of duty made him come back and try to create a cabinet of the willing. Tsereteli felt the need to give up his ministry to free himself for work in the soviets where he would be able to strengthen support for the governmental coalition of which he would no longer be a member. The line-up was finalized on 23 July. Into the cabinet came members of lesser socialist parties where they joined fellow socialist ministers Chernov and Skobelev. It was a matter of relief for Kerensky that he managed to retain some key liberal members who were his confidants: Tereshchenko, Konovalov, Nekrasov and Vladimir Lvov.[16]

Kerensky dominated all governmental discussion and his ministers avoided contradicting him in meetings.[17] No one called a friend by his name: it had to be 'Mr Minister', and anyone leaving without permission received a reprimand. It was Kerensky's cabinet and he expected its members to work, like him, at full tilt. There was a churn of personnel as ministers resigned from office or lost his approval. By August even regular insiders were finding it hard to know everyone who was sitting in the room.[18] Kerensky's workload was overwhelming as he flitted between Petrograd and the front despite no longer being the war minister. Deputy premiers chaired the cabinet in his absence but they seldom took initiatives of importance.

The government kept most of its previous policies in place. The Kadet party predicted a fiasco, arguing that shifts to the right were essential, whilst the Bolsheviks charged Kerensky with betraying the revolution. One change annoyed all socialists, which was the decision to restore capital punishment at the front. Kerensky had bowed to Kornilov's pressure despite neither of them having any idea how they would get anyone to carry out the executions – and Kerensky weeks later hinted that he would always in fact refuse to sign a death warrant.[19] Kornilov could see no hope for the country until restraints were also applied to the soviets. He and Kerensky agreed on a plan to bring experienced front-line troops to the capital to keep order. The Petrograd garrisons were useless for this purpose because their soldiers were an important part of the problem.

Kornilov's stance was popular with right-wing and liberal critics of government and he was starting to see himself as Russia's saviour. He arrived late for the Moscow State Conference in mid-August, deliberately keeping Kerensky waiting. He had assured Kerensky in advance that his speech would do nothing to undermine the government. Even so, he was feted by those who yearned for rule by a strong hand and were in despair about Kerensky and his governing coterie. Big businessmen at the All-Russia Trade and Industry Congress in Moscow in the same month exhaled fury at the government's failure to protect production and commerce. Pavel Ryabushinski, the banking and textile millionaire, reviewed what he saw as the 'destructive path' taken by social reforms since February 1917. He lamented that the 'commercial and industrial class' had no capacity to exert an influence upon ministers. Catastrophe, he declared, was imminent:

> But unfortunately it will take the bony hand of hunger and the people's destitution to grab the people's false friends by the throat – those members of various committees and soviets – for them to come to their senses.[20]

Ryabushinski had come to believe that only the disappearance of food from the table would chasten the minds of the socialists in the soviets who saw the bourgeoisie as their irreconcilable enemy.

Finance Minister Nikolai Nekrasov was equally despondent. In August 1917 he made his concerns public. Although the Provisional Government had inherited a fifteen-billion-ruble deficit in the state budget, since March 1917 there had been a fall-off in revenues as a result of the widespread refusal to pay taxes. The ministry had dealt with this by printing paper rubles ever more energetically which predictably had stoked inflation. Nekrasov could see no alternative for the cabinet but to levy indirect taxes on consumer goods, which he recognized would be hugely unpopular.[21] A new set of currency notes had to be created, which quickly became known as *kerenki* after the minister-chairman, to cope with the need for a larger money supply. The Russian public reacted suspiciously. They had little confidence in the new notes and hung on to their old ones whenever possible.[22]

On 23 August Riga fell to the Germans after four days of fighting.[23] Priority was given to conducting an organized retreat followed by the drawing of new lines of defence. The fate of Petrograd hung in the military balance, as Kornilov had warned at the Moscow State Conference. The news depressed Zamaraev: 'Our glorious forces have surrendered Riga . . . Brave, honest officers are dying in the hundreds while soldiers – cowardly scoundrels who are the shame of Russia – flee in their thousands.'[24] Zamaraev felt depressed: 'Everything's getting worse and worse.'[25]

On 26 August Vladimir Lvov arrived in the capital to report on the situation at GHQ. The former ober-procurator, who was unique in being a confidant of both Kerensky and Kornilov, had recently undergone mental deterioration. Talking to Kerensky, he made the sensational claim that Kornilov was scheming to seize power.[26] Kerensky arranged for Lvov and himself to converse with Kornilov on the Hughes apparatus, a device that enabled the live exchange of typed messages. Lvov arrived late, and Kerensky was able to masquerade as Lvov for the early part of the conversation. He asked Kornilov to confirm his commitment to carrying out his plan. Kornilov assumed that Lvov was referring merely to the agreed measures to suppress political disorder in the capital, so Kornilov replied yes. To Kerensky, however, it appeared that Kornilov had confirmed his intention to overthrow the cabinet. Fellow ministers heard from Kerensky that Kornilov was plotting to establish a military dictatorship.[27]

Kerensky quickly revoked the order for Kornilov to send front-line troops to Petrograd. Kornilov concluded that if Kerensky no longer intended to restore metropolitan order, he was unfit to head the government. Thus it came about that Kornilov decided to undertake the very coup that Kerensky had accused him of plotting. On 28 August Kornilov issued an impassioned general appeal that condemned the Provisional Government for its weakness and indecision. He declared that the gates of Petrograd and Moscow were being opened to the Germans and that the very existence of the Russian people was in jeopardy, and he prepared his troops to move on the capital.[28]

On 30 August 1917 Kerensky made himself supreme commander-in-chief and reappointed Alexeev as chief of staff. Socialist 'agitators' boarded trains carrying the army units bound for Petrograd. Troops from the front proved easy to persuade to disobey Kornilov. The Russian Orthodox Church Council refused to support him, preferring to try to mediate between the two sides.[29] Kornilov halted his advance. Kerensky gave orders for Kornilov's arrest and for an official commission of inquiry.[30] Kornilov was taken into custody at Bykhov prison near Mogilëv.[31] Kerensky treated him with a degree of respect, allowing a double guard consisting of units loyal to the Provisional Government and Kornilov's personal Turkmen escort.[32]

The Mensheviks and Socialist-Revolutionaries were appalled by how the Kadets had obviously wished Kornilov well even though they did nothing actively to help him. The political disarray also had the effect of bolstering the cause of Bolshevism. Trotsky, persuaded by Lenin, joined the Bolshevik party after deciding that he agreed with it on the urgent political questions. He was elected to its Central Committee while still in custody in the Kresty prison. The Bolsheviks had supplied many of the militants who persuaded Kornilov's Special Army troops to desist from their advance on Petrograd, helping to avert the military coup. They had repeatedly warned that Kerensky's premiership ought not to be trusted, and the dangerous shambles of the 'Kornilov affair' appeared to prove them right.

Kerensky recognized that he had to make concessions and consented to the release of Bolshevik leaders from jail. On 2 September Trotsky, Zinoviev and others walked out of the Kresty prison to freedom and applause. The poet Alexander Blok tried to make sense of the movement of events. He ridiculed Kornilov for both his ineptitude and his policies. In Blok's opinion, a military coup could succeed only if its leaders put on 'hedgehog gloves', a Russian metaphor for brutal repression.[33] He was not to know that soon others would put on such gloves and bring themselves to power in pools of blood.

25. THE CLAIMS OF NATIONS: NATIONAL CHALLENGES AND THE CABINET'S EFFORTS AT ACCOMMODATION

Across Russia, political and administrative breakdown was at an advanced stage with little hope of reversal. The vertical hierarchy of authority had disappeared, and certain national and ethnic groups were beginning to take their opportunity to make demands for concessions from the government that before March 1917 would have been unthinkable.

The first Lvov cabinet had promised that Poland would have its independence at the end of the war. A Liquidation Commission was created to plan for this outcome.[1] In June 1917, the post of governor-general of the Kingdom of Poland was abolished. It had been inoperative for over two years and the cabinet wanted to show that Russian intentions were sincere. Polish prisoners-of-war were released from custody.[2] But ministers, both liberals and socialists, were of one mind about the goal of avoiding any further loss of the territories. Lithuania and much of Latvia – both of which were territories divided into provinces of the Russian Empire – had come under German occupation. Lithuanian politicians applied to Germany's military authorities for the right to elect a national assembly. Meanwhile prominent Lithuanians who were based in Russia and Ukraine drew up plans for Lithuania to be recognized as a 'sovereign state' in the event of an Allied victory – and they indicated the borders of the territory that they had in mind when independence became a reality.[3]

The Provisional Government refused to offer the Lithuanians what had been promised to the Poles. The Latvians and Estonians met with the same rebuttal. When the Riga Soviet was created it was the Bolsheviks who came to the fore with their radical policies for peace, national self-determination and land redistribution. Bolshevik militants were successful among Latvian and Russian troops, and the Bolshevik party captured a majority in the city election before the fall of Riga. Latvian liberals approached Kerensky in mid-September with a demand for official endorsement of national self-rule in the territories where Latvians were in a majority. Kerensky gave them twenty minutes to put their case before telling them bluntly that he could not make the concession without opening himself to demands from all the nationalities of the territories once ruled by the Romanovs.[4]

Early in Lvov's premiership by contrast it had been agreed in cabinet to expand the boundary of Estland province in line with Estonian national pretensions. This was another way of permitting self-rule to Estonia without using words such as 'autonomy'. The various Baltic provinces presented the government with a bundle of demands. Ministers responded patchily, hoping to shelve the final general resolution of 'the national question' until the Constituent Assembly. Even the decision on the reform of Estland province was explicitly stated to be provisional.[5] But trouble boiled over at the end of June when the Soviet Executive Committee in Tallinn announced the removal of the provincial commissar and asserted its own claim to authority over the province. The Provisional Government declared this an illegal action and demanded the reinstatement of its commissar and the bodies of local government elected on the basis of universal suffrage.[6]

Finland had been brought separately under Romanov rule in 1809 as a Grand Duchy. It had been allowed its own parliament after the 1905–6 revolution but Stolypin closed it down in 1909. The Provisional Government tried to win Finnish trust by endorsing its reopening. At the same time it appointed its own governor-general.[7] The authorities in Petrograd understood Finland's continuing potential to damage Russian security. Spies were reported as still passing across the Finnish border with Sweden.[8] When Lenin escaped to Finland in July, he evaded arrest because the Finnish police service made few efforts to detect where he was hiding. For weeks, indeed, he lodged in an apartment that belonged to the Helsinki police chief himself, Gustav Rovio.[9] The Bolshevik party and the Finnish Social-Democrats liaised closely with each other, and Rovio was among them.

In Turkestan, after the military violence of 1916, Muslim communities were assured that ministers sought internal peace. Conscripts were no longer sought from central Asia for the front. Official statements were posted up in Tashkent assuring Islamic believers that the government would never again interfere in their publications and practices. An amnesty was announced for those who had been chased out of Turkestan by Governor-General Alexei Kuropatkin's forces.[10] Kuropatkin was fired from his command in March and placed under house arrest, but the government recognized that even his continued presence in Turkestan was a threat to stability. Few additional administrative resources, however, could be spared for the region and difficulties in transport and communication grew. The government entrusted the Internal Affairs Ministry with holding elections based on universal suffrage throughout the troubled region.[11]

A poor harvest had led to food and water shortages. Tensions mounted between Russian and Muslim inhabitants. By September the popularity of Bolsheviks among urban workers and garrison troops was on the rise. The political atmosphere turned red-hot when the Tashkent Soviet under their influence declared itself the governing body in the city and arrested the military commander. This was both mutiny and revolution. The Provisional Government denounced the Soviet's action and an army contingent was dispatched to enforce order, and negotiations led to a restoration of calm. But Muslim communities were still furious about Kuropatkin's savage military expedition in the previous year. Muslims who had fled to China were streaming back to the region, expecting to take back their land and property and finding that local Russian officials were less than helpful. Turkestan was enveloped in turmoil.[12]

The Provisional Government was eager to conciliate Islamic believers wherever they lived. In Georgia, earlier in the war, the authorities had laid treason charges against the entire Ajarian minority. In mid-June 1917 the cabinet revoked the charge.[13] Reports of rising dissent in Muslim communities in central Asia, the Volga region and the north and south Caucasus made it essential to show that no one in government would allow discrimination on grounds of faith.

No region, however, was more troubling for ministers than Ukraine. The Central Rada in Kiev had never thought well of the high command at Mogilëv and the Kornilov revolt increased Kiev's distrust. Rada leaders resumed their call for the 'Ukrainization' of armed forces on Ukrainian soil. On 11 September Kerensky recognized the need to conciliate public opinion in Ukraine and told the Central Secretariat that he would no longer stand in the way of the process.[14] But although Ukraine in practice had almost total autonomy, many members and supporters of the Central Rada wanted the position to be formally confirmed. Kerensky insisted that only the Constituent Assembly would have the right to do this, but he knew the Central Rada governed Ukraine and he did not interfere. Civic administrations in Kharkov and in the Donbas recognized Kiev's authority.[15] Even so, the Rada had problems in imposing a vertical line of authority. Urban soviets in Ukraine displayed little willingness to submit to any higher body of governance, whether it was in Petrograd or Kiev. This was not the sole difficulty for the Rada. Ukrainian peasants, like the peasantry elsewhere, settled the affairs of their villages and the landed estates without reference to external bodies. The Rada was getting a taste of the meal that was being served to every would-be governing agency in the former Russian Empire.

Ukraine, moreover, contained a patchwork of national, ethnic and religious groups. Apart from the Ukrainians there were Russians, Cossacks, Jews, Poles, Greeks and Tatars – as well as POWs from Austria–Hungary. The Rada strove for harmony among them all. In mid-September Ukraine's political leaders hosted a Congress of the Peoples in Kiev. Invitations were extended to groups throughout the territories of the former empire. Estonians, Lithuanians, Latvians, Buryats, Georgians, Belorussians and Muslims of diverse branches and places of the Islamic faith attended. The debates were focused on how to secure a decentralized structure of governance. Autonomy, not secession, was the general principle that won support, and it was thought that this would be best guaranteed by some kind of federalism. The congress argued for the need to secure a cooperative relationship with the Provisional Government. It also stressed the need for friendship with the Russian people. At the same time it endorsed the Rada's assertion of its rights vis-à-vis the authorities in Petrograd. The future was said to lie in a blend of local and central interests.[16]

Ethnic and religious groups within Ukraine were wary of Ukrainian nationalism, and none were more nervous than the Jews. The Provisional Government had torn down the Pale of Settlement and proclaimed universal religious tolerance. Jewish soldiers received the pleasant surprise of being furloughed at Passover.[17] But Jews in the Ukrainian cities stayed on their guard even though almost all soviets warned against the evils of anti-Semitism. It did not take much for Ukrainians – or Russians – to start blaming 'Yids' for everything that went wrong in their lives. Many clerics of the Russian Orthodox Church and other Christian denominations still preached that Jews were Christ-killers, and the army high command and officer corps retained the personnel who had conducted violent outrages against them. As the Provisional

Government sank in popular esteem, it was not uncommon for Russians and Ukrainians to mutter that Kerensky too was Jewish, as if that explained all the troubles of the government's performance.

Violent anti-Jewish incidents occurred, usually in the course of riots and looting in Ukrainian and Belorussian cities. Nearly all soviets – Tambov was an exception – tried hard to suppress outbreaks of anti-Semitism.[18] But pogroms were on the increase and the political far right became more prominent, accusing Jews of greed and subversion.[19]

There were volatile and complex interethnic relations across the old empire. In the south Caucasus fierce rivalries persisted. Georgians resented the commercial thrall exercised by Armenian merchants in the Georgian capital, Tiflis, which itself had been the sea of the viceroys of the Romanovs. The Georgian Mensheviks, nationally proud, had dominated the political scene in the 1905 revolution and resumed their leadership in 1917. The Tiflis Soviet issued decrees to benefit the Georgian workers – and the Armenian businesses felt the impact of their socialist administration. Georgian Menshevism retained an internationalist perspective. The Mensheviks stood up for the labouring poor and for the Georgian nation while recognizing that Russian power gave Christian Georgia its only sure shelter against the Ottomans. Menshevik leaders asked for autonomy, not independence. While endorsing the legitimacy of the Provisional Government, they got on with their own revolution in Georgia. No longer being under the authority of an Imperial viceroy, they relished their chance to rule in their homeland.[20]

Armenians were still mourning the genocide perpetrated against their co-nationals in the Ottoman Empire. Like most Georgians, they were unlikely to fight for Armenia to secede from the multinational state based in Petrograd, but at the same time they demanded the freedoms of self-rule. Armenians governed themselves with enthusiasm while showing an appreciation of the conciliatory gestures that the Provisional Government had made since its creation. They knew that only with Russia's assistance could they have any hope of terminating the repressions that the Ottomans were unleashing in their empire. As for the Ottomans, they still had their eyes on Azerbaijan and the oil fields owned by the Nobel Company at Baku on the Caspian coast. Azeris had only a limited national consciousness. For the Russian parties the danger was that the Azeri inhabitants, who spoke a close variant of Turkish, would be seduced by appeals from Istanbul.

Baku was already a city of ethnic tensions, and the Armenian commercial class were hated by Azeris.

By late September 1917 the Provisional Government had decided to make a declaration on how it expected to calm the mood in many regions. Ministers endorsed the principles of national self-determination and guaranteed the rights of national and ethnic minorities within each territorial unit of administration. Linguistic freedoms would be protected. The cabinet created for itself a Council of Nationalities' Affairs.[21] In the eyes of the socialist parties in Russia this was too little, too late. The Mensheviks thought all nations should be empowered to form national organizations that would promote 'national-cultural autonomy'. The Bolsheviks campaigned to provide nations with self-rule in those regions where they formed the demographic majority – and even to let them secede if they so wished. Either of the main Marxist parties dismissed the other's plans as lacking in practicality.[22]

Whereas Mensheviks and Bolsheviks at least made public their long-term objectives on the 'national question', the Provisional Government's announcement fell short of delivering concrete solutions about future arrangements in the old empire. National and ethnic groups were losing their patience. As economic and social conditions worsened in their regions, they saw less reason to hope for rescue or improvement coming from Petrograd. The demand for autonomy was spreading. Some of the national movements sought complete secession. Territorial break-up was no longer just a gleam in the eyes of the German high command.

26. CITIES: PRESSURES AND OPPORTUNITIES OF URBAN LIFE

In the great cities of Russia much had changed over the revolutionary months of 1917. People in the middle and upper classes had hoped Kornilov would restore some semblance of traditional social discipline. After Kornilov's arrest their morale plummeted. The propertied classes, big businessmen and bankers needed no reminding about how vulnerable they were to the forceful vigour of the urban workers and their soviets, trade unions and factory-workshop committees.

They were also hurt by the economic situation. Even many better-off citizens had to trim their outgoings and adapt to the new cultural and social atmosphere where their life of comfort was no longer guaranteed. The wealthy were having to learn to treat their domestic servants with care. Writer Rachel Khin-Goldovskaya felt concern after deciding to move out of her Moscow apartment to a country dacha. Her long-time maid Feklusha, despite seeming worryingly 'touched' by propaganda, agreed to go with her. Along with them they took two younger maids, a cook and an accounts keeper called Sasha. When they left for the dacha, however, the limousine broke down and they had to wave down a horse-cab to get to the rail station. Sasha haggled about the price. There was chaos at the station and yet again Khin-Goldovskaya relied on her servants' energetic intervention to secure seats. She began to appreciate how they dealt with a level of turbulence for which her own life experience had not prepared her.[1]

As deference to social superiors faded, the only thing persuading many housemaids, cooks and gardeners to stay in domestic service was the knowledge that there were few other jobs to go to. When factories closed, it was not just the industrial workers who suffered unemployment. Managerial and administrative staff were also being cast out onto the streets and there was no scheme of welfare relief available to them.

Lev Tikhomirov's aged mother belonged to the upper classes. She too wanted to escape from the revolutionary turmoil:

> My Mama is keen to leave for Novorossiisk [on the Black Sea coast] but it's impossible to go because she can't get a ticket and the bridge has been washed away in Rostov, and above all else the soldiers who are flooding on to the railways are simply causing mayhem for the public in some places by snatching their seats and there have been instances where people have been thrown off the train.[2]

The houses of the very richest in Petrograd and Moscow were locked up and deserted by owners who expected to return after the revolutionary turmoil faded – it still seemed a temporary phase in Russian life. Yet the pessimists were growing in number and some of the rich tried to emigrate by fleeing north across Finland to Sweden.[3] The Russian currency that they carried had halved in value between the February Revolution and the Kornilov mutiny. Many wealthy travellers took jewellery and small but expensive items with them to bolster their reserves.[4]

The aristocrat Felix Yusupov had been part of the conspiracy to murder Rasputin and had been banished to the family's Rakitnoe estate in central Russia. Such were the riches of the Yusupovs that they were said to need to go on tour for two months if they wanted to visit all their estates. They also possessed a vast strip of oil-rich land beside the Caspian Sea. Yusupov was shocked by the events of the spring and summer of 1917 and three times he returned to Petrograd to retrieve at least a few of the family heirlooms. On one trip he cut two of the finest Rembrandts from their frames, *The Man in the Large Hat* and *The Woman with the Fan*, before taking them by train to Crimea. He also gathered up some of the finest Yusupov diamonds, but only got them as far as Moscow where he had to leave them in the basement of the family's palace there.[5]

Confidence in the Russian financial system was collapsing and some of the very richest families tried to transfer funds to banks abroad, either before fleeing abroad or because they calculated that Western banks were a safer place for their funds than in Russia. The Finance Ministry introduced measures to end such capital flight, which was disrupting an already chaotic economy, and make the country's taxable assets available to the fiscal authorities.[6]

The middle stratum of society didn't have the option of flight. Nikolai Okunev was aghast at the breakdown in law and order, and he treated news reports with a dose of sarcasm: 'On 11 May in Moscow there were *only* two muggings'.[7] Okunev now had to buy his own daily newspaper because his servants had to queue so long for nearly every other basic product: milk, bread, tobacco, tea, cloth and shoes. He needed to get his shoes repaired but baulked at the price now charged by his local cobbler. He could buy a new pair for seventy rubles but did not fancy standing in a line for three days before reaching the counter. Okunev reduced his visits to the barbers for a weekly shave. He went to the office by tram, which was not a pleasant experience when he could not get a seat and had to hang off the rails at the back. The mood of his team in the office had changed. Subordinates at work started to treat him as a *burzhui*. One day he decided to avoid disrespectful exchanges by sitting firmly behind his desk and toiling without taking a meal break from nine in the morning till six in the evening. All this soon depressed him, and sometimes he consoled himself by slipping out for a two-hour lunch and comforting himself with port wine and cognac – something that had been prohibited under Nicholas's wartime regime.[8]

Nearly all towns experienced the damaging effects of falling output and supplies. Alexander Zamaraev saw this for himself on a trip to Totma:

> There's no fish, no peas, no millet, no cabbages, no mushrooms – there's absolutely nothing. Tobacco now costs 12 rubles a pound. Hunger riots are inevitable. They are providing traders with 25 pounds of flour a month. Meat sells at 90 kopeks a pound . . . What makes it all still worse is the hooliganism: gardens are being robbed of onions, swedes and potatoes. To hell with the war. All the troubles are the result of it.[9]

In that obscure market town of the Russian north the problems of the economic depression, social disruption and war were just as impactful as in the capital city, and in central and northern Russia it was not just the cost of living but also the sheer unavailability of staple products that was causing such distress. The urban stalls in the regions of the Volga, the Don and Ukraine had plenty of farm produce for sale, but most residents even there were hit by the rocketing price of food.

By autumn 1917 there were reports of 'hunger riots' in cities as far apart as Astrakhan, Tambov, Minsk, Baku, Tashkent and Yekaterinburg. One outburst occurred in autumn in the Yagodkin store on Petrograd's Apraksin Lane whose owners had filled barrels of its products for dispatch elsewhere. A crowd gathered and asked what was being sent.

A store clerk replied: 'What business is it of yours?' At that moment one of the barrels slipped out of a loader's grasp and split open to reveal the baked foodstuffs inside. Up went the cry: 'Damned twisters! They're hiding groceries! Beat them!' Other barrels were broken into. Sweets and biscuits as well as manufactured goods were discovered. The gathering crowd rushed into the shop, terrifying the staff. The owner made off in fear of being lynched. The crowd grew in size and fury and targeted the nearby Apter store. Fifteen stores were ransacked that day.[10]

Ration cards had become a life-or-death necessity for most city dwellers. The dumas, which continued to provide official social services, used apartment-block committees elected by the residents to hand out the cards on a dependable basis. When Vladimir Sukhanin, a military censor, was transferred to Petrograd in August, he was grateful to obtain a card enabling him to buy bread, fats and sugar.[11]

With commercial companies and governmental agencies crippled by shortages and other difficulties, humble private traders and producers would take flour, vegetables and meat into the cities. Carrying bulky sacks onto the trains, they became known as *meshochniki* or bagmen. Some bagmen were peasants in search of a better price for the produce that they or their neighbours had grown. Others were urban inhabitants who saw the chance to make more money than they earned in a factory or office. Much of this activity was illegal because state agencies were meant to have a monopoly in the grain trade. The bagmen set up at street corners and furtively displayed their wares. Townspeople with sufficient money in their pockets eagerly bought what they could despite the prices being higher than those fixed by the government. The idea spread that a winter of famine was approaching.

More and more big companies were having to close, often with their owners making off with any remaining capital. Several key armaments factories went bankrupt and were taken into state ownership to maintain output. Lock-outs, however, also increased in frequency. This was an old move by owners to starve their labour force back into work. In summer there were coordinated efforts to apply the tactics in the Urals and the Donbas.[12] Even in Petrograd, where labour militancy was stronger than elsewhere, industrialists adopted a tough stance by cutting back output and throwing workers onto the street. The workers only became more militant, taking up the slogan of 'workers' control' in labour forces threatened by closure. Bolsheviks adopted the slogan and made it their own. If the owners could not or would not keep their businesses running, those who sweated at their machines and work benches announced their intention of taking them over.[13]

Soviets centralized their activities at their first congress in June 1917 when they elected an All-Russia Central Executive Committee of Workers' and Soldiers' Deputies (VTsIK). The soviets had a large impact even in towns without much industrial activity. No soviet depended exclusively on the industrial labour force and at least as important were the troops of the local garrison. Troops were stationed in the rear throughout the country and they dwarfed the size of the army on the Eastern front. It was common for a soviet to have a soldiers' section alongside one drawn from industrial workers. A town's authorities had traditionally turned to the garrison commander to lead their troops against local troublemakers. In 1917 the troops were often at the origin of the trouble and it was a rare commander who dared to flout their desires.

Soviets offered assistance and encouragement to workers and soldiers whose prospects in life had been stifled under the old regime. Educational facilities were established to fill the gaps in schooling. Lectures on public affairs were given in the evenings. Painting and writing classes were provided. Hardship funds were disbursed to the urban poor and distressed. 'Victims of the revolution' – those who had suffered under the Imperial administration or more recently in the March uprising – received support.[14]

Enthusiasm for the soviets among workers and soldiers rose high in spring 1917 before dipping in the following months as the revolutionary fervour diminished. But one thing that did not fade was the willingness to vote in elections. The process was a dynamic one because any soviet deputy could be recalled and replaced at any time. Parties had to stay ready to justify their policies at mass meetings. It was a system of direct democracy operating in a limited constituency of potential voters. No one could cast a ballot who belonged to the hated *burzhui* – a category that covered all the middle and upper classes together with anyone regarded as their supporters. An exception was made for the thousands of leaders and activists who came from the higher reaches of society but had identified themselves with the socialist cause. Soviet democracy mixed formal procedures with informal understandings, and its voters kept a watch on how well their elected representatives protected their interests.

Factory and workshop committees, elected on enterprise premises, also grew in number and confidence. When a soviet proved unwilling to support a particular demand by workers, they could turn to the committee in their factory or workshop. A protest or a strike might follow, putting pressure on the owner to come to terms. There were forty-six workshop committees in the Putilov Works operating under the aegis of a central body chaired by a Bolshevik. Business owners who had tried to get used to dealing with soviets and their demands were exasperated by the profusion of factory-workshop committees as any one of them at any moment had the capacity to bring all production to a halt.

Trade unions also expanded. Under Nicholas unions were restricted to being local organizations only. The All-Russia Railwaymen's Union came into existence in April 1917 and was an instant force in politics under Menshevik leadership. The threat of a rail strike that would spread to the entire transport system was a powerful bargaining card for Vikzhel, the union's central body, whenever it objected to the government's measures. The union movement as a whole met in June for a conference in Petrograd, claiming to represent nearly a million and a half members belonging to 976 unions. The membership went on increasing in late summer and autumn.[15] Manufacturing output continued to fall. Heavy-industry factory owners, even if they had a workforce, could not obtain the metals and chemicals needed to maintain activity at the level of 1916.

The future of the Russian towns was discussed in print and urbanity was often celebrated over life in the countryside. Mensheviks and Bolsheviks shared a wish for centralized institutions with authority over the entire economy. The Menshevik Vladimir Groman, who advised the Petrograd Soviet on food-supply policy, insisted that only a supreme state planning agency would be able to regenerate output, wages and distribution on fair principles. The Bolsheviks Vladimir Lenin, Yuri Larin and Nikolai Bukharin agreed but, unlike Groman, argued that none of this could happen until the yoke of capitalism was totally removed. Larin was fanatical about the shortcomings of rural life. He wrote that the goal should be the 'industrialization' and 'urbanization' of the countryside.[16] He saw no hope for the peasantry until farm settlements were managed like factories and peasants were turned into labourers.

One group of writers and painters, the Futurists, idealized factory machinery as the founding metaphor of a new and better society. They loved America's skyscrapers and France's Eiffel Tower and took delight in steamships, locomotives and limousines whilst ridiculing the virtues of the hand plough, artisanal craftsmanship and the villages. They claimed to love 'the masses', decrying individualism as bourgeois and retrogressive. For them, modern industry and modern cities with their gigantic facilities for manufacturing and construction were the only desirable path for humanity to adopt.

Average urban residents were untroubled by such intellectual goals. The task of keeping a job and getting food and healthcare involved drudgery and exhaustion. Whilst the movement for 'democracy' and 'people's power' displayed a surge of idealism there was also the feeling that there was no practical alternative available for those people who stood on the lowest rungs of society's ladder. Only a minority of inhabitants of towns and cities belonged to organizations that could offer assistance. Collective self-help became the norm and tenants of apartment blocks met to schedule who was to do the sweeping and cleaning. The British nurse Florence Farmborough had been employed by a rich doctor's family near Kiev before the Great War. As she made her way back home via the Trans-Siberian railway, food supplies grew short on her train. Her carriage's occupants rushed out with a kettle for boiling water at every station stop, and villagers were usually waiting with pies and cakes for sale. Male fellow passengers took it in turns to guard the internal corridor and keep the stove well stoked.[17]

As a supporter of the Russian war effort, Nurse Farmborough had no high opinion of Bolsheviks and was appalled by the gains they were making in the 'mass organizations'. The Kronstadt Soviet was one of their earliest bastions and soviets in big cities such as Ivanovo-Voznesensk, Yekaterinburg, Tsaritsyn, Minsk and Krasnoyarsk had been under their control before the July Days. Elsewhere they kept chipping away at the majorities held by the Menshevik and Socialist-Revolutionary alliance. In August their influence expanded across the entire Urals region and in Kharkov in eastern Ukraine. In Petrograd they began to shake off the widespread shame of the July Days and won an increased presence.[18] When Kornilov stepped onto the path of rebellion, his only success was in clearing the ground for a Bolshevik political advance. The Mensheviks and Socialist-Revolutionaries became tainted by their support for a government that was incapable of resolving problems that assailed voters in the soviets. The left wing of Menshevism under Yuli Martov made no secret of its dislike of official party policy and the Socialist-Revolutionaries were riven by noisy disputes. By September the Bolsheviks – and not just impatient would-be insurgent leaders like Lenin – were wondering how best to exploit the changed urban situation.

27. VILLAGES: PEASANTS TAKE CONTROL

In 1917, for the first time in the Great War, the area of land devoted to growing food ceased to diminish and may even have increased by a tiny amount.[1] Even so, the grain harvest dropped by about 13 per cent from pre-war years. Siberia was the only region that produced wheat and meat in increased quantities, presumably because private landholdings were the norm there and clashes between peasantry and gentry were few.[2] Elsewhere the cereal barns were not as full as in peacetime. This would usually have had a serious impact on the country's ability to feed itself, but perversely, the blockade by German, Austro-Hungarian and Ottoman forces meant that nearly all the harvested grain was going to stay in the country rather than being exported. The problem was not the size of the harvest but the strengthened reluctance of producers to release their stocks to the authorities. Ministers persisted with their efforts to impose state control and took steps to compile a detailed survey of grain holdings in every province. The government was trying to be fair about the way that it set quotas for cereal deliveries.

But such inspections annoyed the local producers and rural confidence in the Provisional Government collapsed. Peasants wanted the land that they farmed for the gentry and were increasingly willing to use force to obtain it. They also demanded freedom to trade without governmental interference. The rural order of official authority had never been so fragile.

Peasants could take some heart from some of the decrees and instructions coming from Petrograd. In mid-July 1917 Agriculture Minister Chernov issued an 'instruction' to the land committees strengthening their right of authority over those fields that had been left unworked by the gentry. At the district (*volost*) level he permitted committees to rent out such land to the local peasantry at a rate of payment to be agreed after consultation between committees and peasants. Disputes were to be referred for arbitration to higher levels of the land committee system.[3] Gentry landowners were neither consulted nor offered financial compensation. The government's objective was to expand the area under cultivation and secure the food supply but many peasants thought that Chernov had simply endorsed their right to seize fields that they had always coveted.[4] Other orders by Chernov put a partial ban on land sales so as to prevent gentry landowners from making a profit from landed property that the Constituent Assembly was expected to transfer to the peasantry. Likewise Chernov moved against the Stolypin land reform that encouraged individual peasants to separate from the commune.[5]

But peasant dissatisfaction and unrest had their own momentum and had been happening for months before Chernov's initiatives. They were intense in the richest agricultural regions where 'land hunger' had always been acute, such as in the central black-earth provinces immediately to the south of Moscow, the mid-Volga region and the provinces of Ukraine to the west of the river Dnieper, where wheat and beet were cultivated on the large modern farming estates.[6] Disturbances, or the threat of them, were commonplace where the peasantry faced resistance, but they were not ubiquitous. In the Russian north and west Siberia there were few gentry landowners, and only seven peasant disturbances were reported in Vologda province between the February Revolution and late October 1917. Farming people like Zamaraev were getting on with their lives without the conflict that broke out in the regions of severe land hunger or resentment.[7]

Many of the most violent disturbances were fomented by soldiers who had deserted from the front.[8] In Tambov province in August 1917 Prince Boris Vyazemski's late brother Dmitri had earned the hatred of peasants on the family estate at Lotarevo for his harsh punishment of rebels in the 1905–6 revolution. The Vyazemski lands and properties had already been attacked in spring 1917. Boris, a political liberal, appealed to the Petrograd authorities for help in calming the trouble. His call was not answered. In July a committee of peasants presented a demand for him to give up all but twenty-seven acres of his land holdings and a small number of livestock. Boris's wife Lili and his personal servant pleaded with him to take the family away from Lotarevo, which was not the only estate that they owned. In late August the peasants returned to the mansion, goaded by a political agitator. They took hold of Boris and Lili and locked them up for the night. Only then did Boris understand the danger in which they found themselves: 'My friends, just let me go unharmed and whatever you like, you may take – be it money, land or the estate, only leave me in peace.'

Vyazemski had left it too late. Next day the peasantry on his estate – most of whom were the offspring of serfs who had belonged to the Vyazemski family for centuries until the Emancipation Edict of 1861 – carted him off to the railway station intending to get him sent to service on the Eastern front. A group of army deserters were milling about the station and in a furious mood they clubbed Vyazemski to death with metal rods. The mutilated corpse was dumped in a freight car on the sidings.[9]

His brutal fate was unusual only because other families with huge landholdings, remembering the peasant violence of 1905–6, stayed away from their estates or proffered no active resistance. Rachel Khin-Goldovskaya was horrified to hear of rampages that occurred in the absence of landowners. The Sheremetev estate in Mtsensk district in Orël province was pillaged by 'soldiers and peasants headed by two ensigns':

> They wrecked it like real barbarians. The road for [five miles] to the estate was strewn with pages from French books, shattered pieces of glass and shreds of carpets. Inside the residence the furniture and doors were reduced to smithereens, the gallery of paintings was destroyed along with the walls, valuables, crockery, five grand pianos and so on. I can't bear to talk of the agricultural implements, machinery, grain, seed-stock, working livestock, pedigree cattle and stud farm. Everything's been carried or led off or hurled into oblivion.[10]

Owners of estates complained to the Union of Landowners, which made representations to the Provisional Government. The Kadets, while continuing to say that they wanted the Constituent Assembly to transfer the agricultural land to the peasantry, supported tough measures against illegal seizures. But state power had been replaced by peasant power. The best that landowners could do was to renegotiate the rents for the land cultivated by local peasants while hoping that those same peasants would abide by any deal that was agreed. Similar agreements were struck about the proceeds of the harvest, but as the news spread about successful seizures of land and property elsewhere, the temptation was for peasants to take matters into their own hands.

The vast majority of disturbances or attacks, 84 per cent, were directed against the gentry. But the peasants also had other targets. Wherever they felt done down by landholding neighbours, they felt emboldened to settle scores. Three per cent of disturbances were aimed against clergy and 6 per cent also against other peasants, especially those who had left their communes and profited from the Stolypin agrarian reforms.[11] Raids and assaults took place. The peasant Stepan Chevekov owned an enclosed farm near the village of Tilikovka in Samara province. Having taken the opportunity of Stolypin's agrarian reforms to leave the village land commune, he had grown rich enough to buy a large stretch of fields in the district. He paid for his son Mikhail's education at one of the best secondary schools in neighbouring Saratov province. Stepan built a mill and vast barns. He bought a powered threshing machine. He lent money to peasants who were less successful in dealing with the market economy – several had declared themselves bankrupt in wartime, leaving the loans unpaid. When revolution came to Tilikovka local peasants banded together and dispossessed Chevekov of 3,000 acres. His mill was expropriated. Three barns and their grain were seized. Livestock including a stallion worth 10,000 rubles was driven off his farm.[12]

Chevekov was more successful than most 'separators' and therefore lost more land. He was a very rich man. But peasants who had stayed in communes made no distinction according to wealth. Moves were made in Russia and Ukraine to pull back land into communal ownership. The process gathered in pace in summer and early autumn. District land committees in Simbirsk province in the mid-Volga region ordered a total reversion of independent peasant farms to their original communes. In half of Saratov province all the Stolypin peasant-separators were forced to rejoin the communes.[13] Or else they simply decided it was in their interest to do this in order to forestall reprisals from other peasants or to benefit from the transfer of gentry land. Peasants in any case got together even in regions such as west Siberia, the Russian north and Ukraine's zones of large-scale estate farming where land communes did not exist. They were breathing the spirit of collectivism that was everywhere in the air.

Land seizures increased throughout the summer and into September and October of 1917. Despite this the Provisional Government continued to insist that only the Constituent Assembly could decide on the ultimate questions of land ownership. The Kadets made this policy a condition of their remaining in their ministries. The worry for the cabinet was that talk of a coming great redistribution of land was going to damage work on the harvest. Peasants were in fact usually eager to reap and store the crops that landowners had planted. State procurement agencies, however, had difficulty in persuading them to release their stocks. On 20 August 1917 Food-Supply Minister Alexei Peshekhonov gave an order to all provincial food-supply committees that 'in instances of a refusal to hand over grain, coercive measures including armed force must be applied'. One district commissar interpreted this as a command to wage war on the peasantry. Officials elsewhere suggested that supplies would fall until troops fired on the resisters. Peshekhonov had to draft specific instructions as to when and how to use weapons of violence to meet the quotas.[14]

Peasants with marketable surpluses vented their anger against the grain monopoly and the delivery quotas being imposed on them. The commissars had to call on help from the army and from the local administration but reliable troops were hard to find. District committees were under an obligation to assist the commissars but this was by no means universally realized, especially when no army units were made available. Peasants in one of Kazan province's districts held a village assembly and decided to take vengeance on S. M. Zapolski, the head of their district land committee. They grabbed hold of him and carted him off to the riverbank where they made a pile of books and papers and set him on fire. The peasants then went back into town and wrecked the offices of the administration.[15]

A contingent of 2,800 soldiers was dispatched to suppress trouble in Kazan province alone. Men, women and children obstructed them from seizing their produce. Army detachments could usually disperse a crowd by firing into the air but fatal shootings also occurred.[16] Peasants had spent months asserting their rights as they conceived them and they were not minded to back down, and ministers recognized that improved terms of payment for produce were essential.

The Provisional Government considered the food-supply emergency at a lengthy session on 26 August. They proposed to double the fixed prices for grain as a way to secure provisions for urban inhabitants in the months ahead. It was agreed to give extraordinary powers to the Food-Supply Ministry, including the right to set a schedule for the delivery of produce to collection points. Wherever peasants would not cooperate, official agencies were to impound cereal stocks. If such a step proved necessary, the price paid was automatically to be reduced by 30 per cent. Although force was not directly mentioned in the decree, it was heavily implied. The Provisional Government braced itself to get tougher with the peasantry.[17] Commissars were appointees of the Provisional Government and directly subject to the Internal Affairs Ministry. Each of them had the duty to enforce official policies throughout the province. They were instructed to use whatever methods of coercion that appeared necessary. Force returned to civil governance.[18] It was a reversion to the administrative principles of tsarist times when the provincial governor ruled a province like a mini-tsar. The difference was that Nicholas's governors had plenty of reliable troops at their command and knew how to deploy them. Like so many of Kerensky's decrees, this one was a dead letter in most provinces as soon as it reached its destination. Serving soldiers who resented the deterioration in their daily rations were persuadable to march into villages which were withholding grain. But army discipline and morale had fallen to their lowest point, and peasant resistance grew stronger. The countryside had become a maelstrom of violence whenever the army units arrived.

Work on land reform went too slowly for the provincial commissar in Nizhni Novgorod, the Socialist-Revolutionary Mikhail Sumgin. He had complied with orders to send armed units to the countryside to halt the land seizures and secure the grain supply but many soldiers refused to obey orders. Sumgin could see no solution by early October other than to pass authority to the land committees. He wrote to Petrograd to report on what he had done. He knew it was against governmental policy but he argued that this was the only way to have any hope of restraining the peasantry. The message came back from the capital that only the Constituent Assembly would have the right to rule on land reform. By then it was too late for Sumgin to reverse his decision.[19]

Kerensky too felt frustrated by the slow pace of reform, and he vented his anger on Pavel Malyantovich, who had only been justice minister since late September 1917.[20] But truly it was Kerensky himself who, however understandably, had always said that fundamental agrarian changes would aggravate the problem of desertions from the front. But while his cabinet concentrated on forcing peasants to release their stocks from the summer harvest, the Socialist-Revolutionaries – the party with which he had once been associated – tried to show that they took the peasantry's side. This gave rise to a discussion as to whether to withdraw support for Kerensky and his ministers. Party policy was ultimately to transfer all agricultural land to the peasants with a priority being given to communal tradition and usage, at least in those places where the village land commune existed. Through the summer and early autumn of 1917 the party held a debate on timing, and many Socialist-Revolutionaries thought that any further delay would harm their political position in the country. The Mensheviks, their partners in the soviets, had once believed in allowing the elected urban authorities to control the transfer of agricultural land but now proposed to hand such matters to the land committees that had been created after the February Revolution. The Kadets remained committed to transferring agricultural land to the peasantry but were angry with socialist schemes that trod upon the interests of existing landowners who were going to forfeit their possessions.[21]

Peasants were little minded to take notice of politicians and their disagreements. They were solving 'the agrarian question' by direct action. Only one party, the Bolsheviks, were unconditionally endorsing immediate land seizures by the peasantry. But peasants in most provinces were on the move without need for instigation from the towns.

28. BOLSHEVIKS: THE PARTY THAT WORKED FOR A SECOND REVOLUTION

All Bolsheviks were committed to getting rid of the Provisional Government and creating a socialist administration through a second revolution. They promised to end the war if they came to power and said they were the sole party that could accomplish this. Despite the party's subsequent reputation for iron-willed central control administered by Lenin alone, it was no more tightly organized than the other socialist parties. Hierarchy and discipline gave way in practice to a looseness that allowed committees in the provinces to ignore the official policies of which they disapproved.[1] On the questions of both land and nationalities they were sharply divided. On the future pace of ending private ownership of factories and workshops, they also lacked agreement. Lively disputes took place at every level of the party. Only when facing their Menshevik and Socialist-Revolutionary enemies in the soviets did the Bolsheviks show the degree of unity that they would need if power was ever to come into their hands. Their leaders felt confident that Bolshevism alone could resolve the crisis of state and society in the old empire. They were sure that Europe, too, was on the brink of socialist revolutions.

The party's driving slogan was 'All Power to the Soviets'. Lenin, though, had reservations about it. Immediately after the July Days, when most soviets were still under Menshevik and Socialist-Revolutionary authority and continued to support the Provisional Government, he demanded the slogan's withdrawal since he objected to calling for a socialist administration if it was to be led by rival parties. Instead he called for immediate revolution through an armed uprising and rebuked the rest of the Central Committee when, in his absence in Finland, it rejected his heated counsel. Iosif Stalin and Yakov Sverdlov were leading the Bolsheviks in the weeks after the July Days, and Stalin supplied a standpoint for the party that better fitted current conditions: 'We are unambiguously in favour of those soviets in which we are a majority, and we shall try to establish such soviets.'[2] The Central Committee wanted to retain 'All Power to the Soviets' on Bolshevik banners while the work of winning soviet majorities proceeded.

Lenin kept up his tirades against Kerensky's 'dictatorship' whilst the Central Committee of the Bolsheviks continued to ignore his calls for immediate armed uprising. But as the government went on with its arrests of prominent Bolsheviks and shut down Bolshevik publications in Petrograd, the Central Committee reconsidered its rejection of his demand for a change of slogan.

A Bolshevik party congress started secretly in the capital in late July. The delegates prided themselves on successfully avoiding being penetrated by government spies and were unaware that the authorities in this instance knew the congress was taking place. Yekaterina Breshkovskaya, one of the founders of the Party of Socialist-Revolutionaries and a woman often referred to as the Grandmother of the Revolution, sought out Kerensky and pleaded with him to arrest the Bolshevik conferees. Kerensky agreed but did nothing about it. Whereas he still aimed to take Lenin and other leaders of the July Days into custody, he shrank from putting the entire Bolshevik leading cadre into custody.[3]

The Bolshevik congress went ahead and adopted Stalin's proposed new slogan. It was one that lacked the punchiness that was needed at mass meetings: 'the complete liquidation of the dictatorship of the counter-revolutionary bourgeoisie'.[4] Soon, however, the Kornilov mutiny and the leftward political shift inside the labour movement changed the political atmosphere once again, and the Central Committee restored 'All Power to the Soviets' to its sloganeering. By early September the Petrograd Soviet had started to vote by a majority for the Bolsheviks. Petrograd was followed by Moscow and other large cities in northern and central Russia, and confidence within the party rose. The Bolsheviks were shaming the rival socialist parties with their commitment to the soviets, unions and factory-workshop committees. They were not going to endorse or negotiate with a 'bourgeois' government. Their eyes were fixed unflinchingly on installing a socialist administration that would brook no compromise in implementing socialism.

Whilst Kerensky's so-called dictatorship did not involve the return of comprehensive censorship, *Pravda*'s name was changed as a precaution against trouble from the Internal Affairs Ministry. The party leadership functioned on its old 'conspiratorial basis' and the Central Committee communicated with Lenin in Helsinki through secret couriers.

Lenin insisted that Bolshevism's message had to reach out beyond the working class to the peasantry. In August, after years of advocating land nationalization, he welcomed 242 'peasant instructions' compiled by the Socialist-Revolutionaries from many regions. It had at last become clear to him that peasants would never be satisfied by any government that stopped them doing as they liked about the gentry's fields and property. From then onwards he adopted the Socialist-Revolutionary land programme in most essentials.[5] Without acknowledgement, he was accepting Stalin's policy proposal. Lenin's change of stance was not to the liking of leftist Bolsheviks like Nikolai Bukharin who wanted to prioritize the creation of collective farms regardless of the peasantry's wishes. Bukharin was a brilliant, charming, flaxen-haired young Bolshevik based in Moscow who often challenged Lenin's ideas. But Lenin and Bukharin agreed that even if the peasants took over every field currently in the possession of others, there would still not be enough land for most of them in their millions to earn enough to do better than subsist. Ultimately, they thought, units of agriculture in Russia had to be raised to a higher scale and removed from the small-scale peasant style of production. Big was considered beautiful for economic modernization, and Lenin shared Bukharin's belief that this could only be achieved through the collectivization of agriculture. But whereas Bukharin wanted instant action, Lenin wanted to delay in the interest of winning power for the party.[6]

On industrial policy too there was tension between Lenin and Bukharin. Lenin urged a certain caution about the pace of nationalizing factories and mines. Although he mapped out an agenda of immediate state ownership of all banks and all foreign trade, he proposed to take only the biggest factories and mining enterprises into the state's possession in the first stage of the socialist revolution. Bukharin rejected the case for patience and wrote in favour of total nationalization regardless of size.[7]

Another difficult question for the party was about workers' control. Until 1917 this had not been a Bolshevik aim. Bolshevism had stressed the need for state ownership and said little about the rights of workforces. Lenin slowly came to appreciate that how the factory was organized was an important matter for revolutionaries. He admired the powerful activity of workers seeking to avert factory closures and unemployment. Predictably he proposed limits on their authority to run their enterprises. Other Bolsheviks were less restrained, wanting to encourage workers to kick out their managers and run factories and mines without them. The party at its lower levels supplied activists to the factory-workshop committees. The Bolsheviks, unlike the Mensheviks, were encouraging strikes and other disruptive action in industry. They fanned the flames of the anti-governmental campaigns being waged by factory-workshop committees and trade unions.[8] The party left undiscussed the future relations of the party, the unions, the factory-workshop committees and the soviets.

Lenin called for a 'dictatorship of the proletariat and the poorest peasantry' – usually Marxists spoke only of 'a dictatorship of the proletariat' if ever they mentioned dictatorial rule at all.[9] Over summer 1917 he further clarified his aims. While hiding in Helsinki, he drafted a summary of his thoughts on political strategy. Although he was distracted from finalizing the draft by events in autumn, he was to be content enough with it to publish it in the following year as *The State and Revolution*.

In this booklet and in many of his other articles he advocated violent revolution as the prerequisite for achieving socialism. He scoffed at the German Marxist luminaries who had no stomach for dictatorship. He expressed admiration for the Jacobins and their reign of terror in 1793–4 in the French Revolution. But whereas Maximilien Robespierre had sent the king and aristocrats to the guillotine, Lenin argued in *Pravda* that it would be enough to arrest between fifty and a hundred business tycoons and hold them for a few weeks '*so as to uncover their dirty deals*'.[10] Trotsky went further. In a speech in Kronstadt he had said: 'I tell you, heads must roll, blood must flow, there must be no mercy if we want to win! The strength of the French Revolution was in the machine that made the enemies of the people shorter by a head.'[11] Lenin and Trotsky made a case for mass terror as a weapon of socialist governance. They were also optimists who believed that 'the people' would win by superior numbers, organization and confidence. Lenin told his followers that the 'bourgeoisie' would swiftly be defeated in any civil war, and that a socialist seizure of power in Russia would trigger revolutions abroad. The war would be over with socialism triumphing in all the warring countries. If the need arose, the Bolsheviks would carry a 'revolutionary war' of their own into Europe. However it happened, they believed a socialist triumph was unstoppable.

Lenin brushed aside all opponents who pointed to the impracticability and contradictions of Bolshevik policies. He utterly refused to appreciate the dangers of what he was proposing, intent on carrying out the great experiment regardless of risks. Once the new socialist state had consolidated itself, it would move on to a higher stage of development: communism. The ultimate objective was to remove the need for statehood. There would be no armies, no prisons, no bureaucracies, no religion or social discrimination. People would administer themselves.[12]

But such ideas would have impact only if the Bolsheviks succeeded in overturning the Provisional Government, and there could be no certainty of this. Although Lenin's articles were carried in *Pravda*, not every Bolshevik read them. Around 90,000 daily copies of *Pravda* were printed by August, but they were patchily distributed across the country, and half of them were kept for sale in the capital.[13] Local party committees asked for Lenin or Zinoviev personally to travel to them and offer their leadership but this never happened – and, of course, could not happen when one of them was in hiding and the other was in prison.[14] The complaint was anyway that the Central Committee operated as if it was only servicing the Bolsheviks of the capital and offered little detailed guidance to local committees. Veteran Bolsheviks in the provinces wanted help but in any case insisted on choosing their policies for themselves. Stepan Shaumyan in the Baku Committee and many other leaders like him elsewhere worked on whatever concerns were being expressed by workers and soldiers in their cities. Abuses of power were seized upon as evidence that the Provisional Government was as oppressive and untrustworthy as the Romanov cabinets had been.[15]

The party became a catch-all – or catch-nearly-all – organization for those on the political left who were impatient for an end to the war and to Kerensky's rule. The ideological training that had been traditional before 1917 fell into the background and now all who wanted to join were welcomed, especially if they paid the membership fee. No knowledge of Marxism or the party's policies was required. Sverdlov claimed that by late July there were 240,000 members. From a handful of thousands in the February Revolution they rose to being a mass party.[16] Three fifths of the membership, according to a later official estimate, were of the working class.[17] When Moscow Committee man Timofei Sapronov was taken aback by the crudity of members' political knowledge, he was told not to bother and just to keep a basic slogan in mind: 'Our programme is the struggle with the bourgeoisie.'[18] The new Bolsheviks were attracted by a vision of giving welfare, dignity and power to the poor and powerless. The rival socialist parties shared the vision but continued, however reluctantly, to support the failing

Provisional Government. Bolsheviks, old and new, believed that they alone had the policies and the resolve to make a break with the past.

'Political agitation' among 'the masses' was one of their primary immediate tasks. Since the Bolsheviks were not yet in government, they could easily blame every misfortune in the country on 'bourgeois' malevolence. They claimed without a shred of evidence that Kerensky was plotting to surrender Petrograd to the Germans as a way of holding back the far-left revolutionary surge. Bolsheviks at the same time described Kerensky as a puppet manipulated by the Western Allies. The contradictions in their stories did not embarrass thc Bolsheviks. They told whoever would listen that reactionary, imperialistic forces were ranged against the people's interests and that only a government by socialists and for socialism could change the situation for the better.

As Bolsheviks won more places in the soviets, they gained access to increased resources – funds, premises and printing presses – for the task of ousting the Provisional Government. The party's message about peace, food supply and employment appeared increasingly convincing to workers. Soldiers both at the front and in the rear were attracted by the promise of an end to the Great War. The Mensheviks and Socialist-Revolutionaries had difficulty in defending their own policies as well as their support for the Provisional Government. No Bolshevik said explicitly that the Bolsheviks would rule alone after getting rid of Kerensky. But the Bolshevik leaders did continually accuse the Mensheviks and Socialist-Revolutionaries of betraying socialism. The requirement for Bolshevik dominance in a new revolutionary government was taken for granted without being expressed. But most Bolsheviks believed that the result would be a grand socialist coalition of some sort as yet to be specified.[19]

Bolshevik leaders looked on factory labourers and army conscripts with a mixture of admiration and condescension, whilst not being able to see or accept that their own ideas were full of incoherence and danger. The Kadets quickly recognized the party's menacing potential, never looking upon the Bolsheviks as a joke party even when it had little support in the soviets. They saw Lenin's party as the purest evil that had to be stamped out. Mensheviks and Socialist-Revolutionaries shared soviet platforms with the Bolsheviks and, hoping to persuade them and their supporters that their way was better, criticized the programme for government that the Bolshevik party put forward. Mensheviks warned that a class dictatorship would inevitably lead to civil war, a war that would be intense and barbarous. They declared that it was far from clear that the 'European proletariat' would rise in alliance with the workers of Russia. While the Menshevik party too sought peace without annexations, its official leadership – the Organizational Committee – continued to fear German military occupation as a serious possibility. Meanwhile the Socialist-Revolutionaries saw Lenin's adoption of the core of their agrarian policy as theft by an unprincipled opportunist.

These rival parties, however, were unable to puncture the Bolsheviks' growing appeal to the social groups on which they concentrated their efforts. As summer turned to autumn the fortunes of the Kerensky cabinet were sinking. Bolshevik committees and militants readied themselves to take power, and no one could doubt that they might now realize their ambition. The Bolshevik leaders prized their vision of a glorious triumph that was at hand. They had a religious way of thinking except that it was atheist in content – and the Orthodox Church clergy were hateful to them and, when in government, they intended to expropriate the Church's wealth and end its influence in society. Priests were not the sole cause for Bolshevik displeasure. Bankers, industrialists, gentry landlords, army officers and gendarmes as well as aristocrats and members of the Romanov family were hateful to Bolsheviks. It was no secret that their promise of welfare and prosperity for workers, peasants and soldiers would involve conflict. Bolshevism was an unapologetic doctrine of uncompromising class struggle.

29. IF NOT NOW, WHEN?: THE BOLSHEVIK DECISION ON INSURRECTION

Kerensky still believed that Russia had to continue fighting the war. He knew Allied financial support would disappear if Russia unilaterally withdrew from the Eastern front. He also feared the consequences of millions of demobbed soldiers being sent home from the front. Putting in place any sort of land reform would be chaotic and law and order would break down.

He was getting anxious, however, because he knew Russia and its armed forces were at breaking point. On 25 September 1917, hoping to raise morale, he issued a Declaration about the kind of society he wanted to build after the war. Victory for the Allies remained his refrain but he recognized that people were living through a time of 'troubles' – the word had associations for Russians with the anarchic decades of the mid-seventeenth century when the people of Muscovy were dragged down into destitution and despair. Peace alone, he recognized, could bring about the conditions that might enable prosperity. He looked forward to 'the gradual and painless demobilization' of the economy. He aimed to avert the ills of mass unemployment by commissioning a vast scheme of public works. Taxes would be set on a fairer basis by raising the levy on inheritance and luxury goods. A property tax would be introduced. He also argued for the need for an increase in indirect taxes, which he admitted would hurt the interests of the lower social classes, but he promised to reform the fiscal system by stamping out tax evasion. Local self-government would be enhanced. The rights of national minorities would be protected.[1]

He had always stressed the role of the state in the recuperation and renewal of society but now official agencies exercised a collapsing authority. Organizations such as the soviets were obstructing ministerial wishes. Peasant gatherings were exercising rural self-rule. Soldiers had reversed the old rules of military hierarchy. Disobedience of higher authority had become normal. The Provisional Government also functioned in a constitutional void of its own making. Polls were held for city dumas and provincial dumas as well as for the lower levels of governance, but at the centre, in Petrograd, the cabinet was self-formed and self-appointed. It had got rid of irksome pieces of Imperial law and introduced some of its own legislation.[2] But while it issued many decrees and regulations many had no impact once promulgated. The Provisional Government was not truly governing. Its power was increasingly confined to the Winter Palace's corridors.

On 1 September Kerensky, in an attempt to prove his abiding radical commitment, proclaimed Russia as a republic despite knowing such a step could have no constitutional or legal force.[3] He also created a Directory of five persons including himself as an inner body of the cabinet which could take rapid decisions in an emergency. The Directory's other members were his friend and Foreign Affairs Minister Tereshchenko as well as Army Minister Alexander Verkhovski, Navy Minister Dmitri Verderevski and Post and Telegraph Minister Alexei Nikitin.[4] This drew criticism as being another move towards dictatorship, especially since no one in the Directory except Kerensky and perhaps Tereshchenko had much public prominence. Lenin said this was proof that Kerensky had the ambition to be the Napoleon Bonaparte of the revolution.

The military crisis deepened at the end of September when German forces, which had been resting since Riga's capture in late August, attacked three islands including Saaremaa off the Estonian coast to the north of the Gulf of Riga. This completed the Russian Baltic Fleet's enclosure in the Gulf of Finland.[5] Meanwhile the Bolsheviks spread the rumour that the Provisional Government was preparing to surrender Petrograd itself as a way of cauterizing the party's attempts to overthrow it.

As Kerensky knew, one of the government's abiding shortcomings was the lack of a sense of popular legitimacy. He tried to resolve the problem by announcing the creation of a Provisional Council of the Republic, a quasi-parliamentary body that he envisaged as operating until the Constituent Assembly took place. The membership would be drawn from parties, public bodies and pressure groups. He opened the Council, which was to become known as the Pre-Parliament, at the Marinski Palace on 7 October. In the same week he was spurring his ministers to prepare drafts for the institutional framework and basic laws that might be created by the Constituent Assembly.[6] But it was the immediate crisis that grasped his attention, as he admitted to the Pre-Parliament: 'We are threatened in the very near future of remaining without fuel and food. All measures that were at all possible to supply the army at the front as a priority were taken but these measures were shattered in contact with the passivity, apathy and absence among the broad masses of conscious responsibility to the government and to freedom.'[7]

Trotsky delivered a speech to the Pre-Parliament on the Bolshevik party's behalf as the recently elected chairman of the Petrograd Soviet's Executive Committee. Tsereteli's months of dominance were over.[8] Bolshevik leaders were divided about whether to stay at or walk out of the Pre-Parliament. Trotsky was for walking out, Kamenev for staying on to criticize. Lenin said the Pre-Parliament was a sham to be shunned altogether. Trotsky won approval for a walk-out. He filled the Palace hall with a tirade of splenetic eloquence warning of the deadly danger facing the country after forty months of war. He blamed governmental policies on industry, land reform and food supplies for deepening the ruin of the economy. He denounced ministers for using hunger to quieten people's discontent. Trotsky was interrupted by shouts about German financial support for the Bolsheviks, but he pushed on regardless, announcing the party was going to abandon the Pre-Parliament. He declared: 'We are appealing to the people: Long live an immediate, honourable, democratic peace! All power to the soviets! All land to the people! And long live the Constituent Assembly!'[9]

Trotsky left the Marinski Palace to concentrate on plotting for a Bolshevik-led uprising, but although his new party comrades recognized him as a master of oratory and prose, they had not forgotten about his past polemics against Bolshevism. The one Bolshevik leader who had the influence to force the insurrectionary question onto the Central Committee agenda was Lenin, who had secretly returned to Petrograd from Helsinki. A clandestine meeting of the Central Committee was arranged for 10 October at the home of Galina Flaxerman, who worked for the Secretariat. Living in the Petersburg Side district, she was married to the Menshevik Internationalist Nikolai Sukhanov who discreetly agreed to stay in his office overnight to leave the Bolsheviks to hold their discussions. Twelve members attended. For Lenin, it was the first time he had been present since early July.

Lenin spoke at length and with rancour, rebuking the Central Committee for showing indifference to the uprising question:

'Nevertheless the question now stands very sharply and the decisive moment is at hand.' He alleged that the authorities were giving active consideration to surrendering Narva in eastern Estonia, which was supposedly a prelude to giving up Petrograd. He argued that the Bolsheviks had failed to overturn the government in the July Days because they lacked a majority. He claimed that the current situation was different: 'Now the majority is with us. Politically the situation has completely matured for a transition of power.' Quite how he measured the majority, he did not say, but it could not have been a majority of the entire electorate because he admitted that the party would fall short of victory at the forthcoming Constituent Assembly election. He also acknowledged that 'the masses' displayed a growing apathy about politics. But he insisted that people were fed up with mere words and wanted action, and he pointed out that the peasant movement was now unstoppable.[10]

His arguments persuaded the Central Committee by ten votes to two. Awkwardly for him, the two who voted against him were Kamenev and Zinoviev. Although Kamenev had often disagreed with him, they had worked together closely. Kamenev and Zinoviev denied that the mood of the working class was dependably pro-Bolshevik and that the rest of Europe was on the brink of socialist revolutions. They warned that a seizure of power would lead to a war that would only alienate most soldiers from Bolshevism. They argued it was better by far to wait for the Constituent Assembly in which the socialist parties would dominate. Even though the Bolsheviks would probably get no more than one third of the seats, this would be enough to form a governing coalition of socialist parties and to be an influential force inside it. Kamenev and Zinoviev concluded that Lenin had lost his head and that his demands for an instant insurrection were irresponsible. They wrote to the leading party committees in Petrograd and Moscow and to the party faction in the All-Russia Central Executive Committee of the Congress of Soviets to explain their analysis. They desperately wanted to stop Lenin from taking the catastrophic step of seizing power in the name of a single party.[11]

The Central Committee met again on 16 October to review its decision, and this time there was an expanded attendance. Bolshevik leaders were invited from the Petersburg Committee and the Military Organization as well as from the Petrograd Soviet and the trade unions and factory-workshop committees. Central Committee members from outside the capital had arrived for the session, including several who had been less than enthusiastic about the direction Lenin was arguing for. Lenin was prepared and took account of the letter that Zinoviev and Kamenev had distributed. He made the case that the Bolsheviks had already suffered snubs when offering compromise to the Mensheviks and the Socialist-Revolutionaries. He asked everyone to recognize the nature of the current situation: 'Either a Kornilovite dictatorship or a dictatorship of the proletariat and the poorest layers of the peasantry.' He dismissed the objection that the popular mood was not in favour. Lenin said that moods were always changeable and that it was necessary to take an objective measure of the situation. He denied that revolutions were unlikely in Europe. He said that events in Germany showed that it was on the verge of political explosion. Armed uprising in Russia, he said, was the only serious option for Bolsheviks.[12]

An abrasive debate followed. Several of those who took Lenin's side admitted that many workers and soldiers were apathetic about getting rid of the Provisional Government. Vladimir Milyutin, who was based in Petrograd, denied that the party had the capacity to head an uprising. Zinoviev and Kamenev repeated their earlier arguments, and urged the party to avoid isolating itself from the other socialist parties. Stalin, usually a cautious contributor, supported the policy of insurrection. Lenin wrangled with Zinoviev and Kamenev. At the end of it Lenin proposed a policy of 'an omnilateral and strengthened preparation of an armed uprising' at a moment to be designated by the Central Committee and 'the Soviet'.[13] His motion was accepted by nineteen votes to two. Four Central Committee members abstained.[14]

Kamenev resigned from the Central Committee. He released a letter to the writer Maxim Gorki's independent Marxist newspaper *Novaya zhizn* ('New Life') revealing and denouncing the decision for an armed uprising.[15] Lenin wrote furiously to the Central Committee calling, unsuccessfully, for Kamenev's expulsion from the party's ranks. He accused Kamenev and Zinoviev of 'strike-breaking'.[16]

On 9 October the Petrograd Soviet, which the party had dominated since early September, had established an agency to oversee military requirements in the capital.[17] Three days later this became the Military-Revolutionary Committee. The Bolshevik Central Committee wanted the agency to coordinate the uprising. Trotsky was already a member of the Military-Revolutionary Committee and the Central Committee appointed a further five of its leading members to join him.[18] The Military-Revolutionary Committee's chairman was the Left Socialist-Revolutionary Pavel Lazimir but Bolsheviks controlled its activity and established links with the Red Guards, the factory-workshop committees and the army committees in the garrisons. Fiery anti-Kerensky pamphlets were printed and measures were planned against preventive measures being taken by the Provisional Government. A coup by stealth was under way. Lenin would have loved to join the organizing team but he was the main personal quarry of Kerensky's armed units and could not afford to break cover. Instead he stayed in hiding, intensely frustrated, in the Bolshevik Margarita Fofanova's apartment on the city outskirts while others got on with the Military-Revolutionary Committee's preparations.

Kerensky publicly dismissed his enemies' potential to put their words into action but behind the scenes he knew all too well that power was slipping away from him.[19] Others in the cabinet were also becoming demoralized. Tereshchenko said he wanted to step down. Kerensky pleaded, tears in his eyes: 'If you leave who can I find to replace you? I personally, as you must know, cannot possibly take the Ministry of Foreign Affairs under my charge.'[20] Konovalov felt the same as Tereshchenko. He stayed on, like Tereshchenko, out of a duty of patriotism and friendship.[21] With the military prospects for Russia worsening, Kerensky's replacement for army minister after the Kornilov mutiny, the young Lieutenant-General Alexander Verkhovski, wrote to Alexeev on 4 September that the capital's garrison had unilaterally declared itself exempt from deployment to combat duties. Currently, he estimated, the Russian forces were 674,000 troops short.[22] But he simultaneously assured Allied military attachés that Russia's fighting troops at the front would be kept at adequate strength. He recognized that any loss of support from the US, France and Britain would lead to a military debacle.[23]

The Allied embassies in Petrograd pressed Kerensky to re-establish order in the armed forces. He insisted: 'Russia is still a great power.'[24] On 1 October he called in British intelligence agent Somerset Maugham to the Winter Palace to carry a message directly to Prime Minister David Lloyd George in Westminster stressing the need for the Allies to augment their supplies of money and military and industrial equipment. He proposed that Lloyd George should offer Germany a peace without annexations or compensations. The Germans would refuse but when this became known, Kerensky would be able to tell his troops to continue the war. Otherwise, he wrote to Lloyd George, he would not be able to keep the Russian Army in the trenches.[25]

His secret communication was a symptom of the despair of the situation he was facing. The next military conference of the Allies was scheduled to take place in Paris in November, and Army Minister Verkhovski asked Alexeev to lead Russia's delegation. Alexeev refused, wanting no part of any pretence that the forces on the Eastern front were battle-ready. Russians could no longer honestly promise to undertake an offensive or even an effective defence. Verkhovski kept up his spirits by imagining that, if it came to it, government and army could make a stand on the banks of the Volga.[26] Russia's military prospects fell from poor to desperate.

Kerensky persisted with efforts to strengthen the framework of governance. The cabinet finalized the rules and preparations for the Constituent Assembly election in November.[27] In mid-October, in a bid to increase the Provisional Government's impact, Kerensky approved a plan to strengthen the powers of the provincial commissars.[28] He was whistling in the wind. Ukraine, the richest of agricultural regions, experienced urban disorders in Kiev and the Donbas as price inflation bit into people's incomes – and on 14 September the cabinet approved severe measures to prevent the spread of trouble.[29] At the front, the northern sector had only enough flour on 10 October for the next fifteen days and meat for less than four days. Commanders thought that 'hunger riots' were likely among the troops. The situation was no better in the cities of northern and central Russia. By 20 October, Food-Supply Minister Sergei Prokopovich could only guarantee food stocks for half the people for whom he was responsible. Alexander Liverovski, the minister of communications, warned that the railway network would fall apart if the number of railwaymen eligible to receive rations was reduced. But a halving of the size of the armed forces at the front and in the rear would ease Prokopovich's dilemma.[30] Kerensky shrank from any such suggestion, which would have required a drastic change in his war policy – and mass demobilization would bring dangers of its own.

All this time the fighting continued sporadically at the Eastern front. Zamaraev's views had changed totally and he could no longer see the point of the war, only its pity. On 23 October he wrote in his diary: 'We've received the sad news that Nikolai Gavrilov [sic] has died in Romania. [I feel] sorrow for the poor fellow who's left a heap of children behind. Totally innocent children are suffering because of the whims of mad autocrats.'[31]

The cabinet still refused to abandon its struggle to stabilize the situation. On its agenda on 21 October was a discussion about how to bring together employers and the workforces in the Moscow leather factories.[32]

But the objective of industrial conciliation had long been unfulfillable. Ministers had been unable, despite acting together with Menshevik Soviet leaders, to prevent strikes on the railway network in late September. Wage rises that strained the state budget were necessary before the railwaymen went back to their duties. Post and Telegraph Minister Alexei Nikitin, a Menshevik, had denounced the strike. Fellow Mensheviks reacted by calling on him to resign from the party.[33] Trouble flared up in the Donbas, where miners withdrew their labour. As fuel shortages mounted, the oil-workers in Baku joined the strike movement. In every sector of the economy there was labour unrest. Office clerks also struck for higher pay. Hunger riots occurred in dozens of towns and cities in Russia and Ukraine.[34] The peasantry continued to seize gentry land and property, and conditions in the countryside fell completely out of official control.[35] The former Russian Empire was governed no longer. The door to the next revolution was already ajar.

30. OCTOBER REVOLUTION: THE BOLSHEVIKS SEIZE POWER IN PETROGRAD

On 24 October a strange semblance of normality still covered Petrograd. The post was still being delivered and work continued in offices and factories. Most newspapers appeared as usual. But it was common knowledge that the Bolsheviks were planning an uprising, and Kerensky had ordered emergency measures to be put in place. Raids were made on Bolshevik printing presses. Parts of the tram network were suspended. Some bridges across the Neva river were raised.[1] Kerensky felt he could call upon sufficient armed units to deal with any trouble. Trotsky was determined to prove him wrong. The All-Russia Congress of Soviets of Workers' and Soldiers' Deputies was scheduled to begin next day and its delegates were piling off trains from the provinces and heading for the Smolny Institute where the proceedings would begin. When Trotsky heard of the government's preparations he alerted his Military-Revolutionary Committee comrades: 'Kerensky is on the offensive . . . We need everyone at Smolny.'[2]

Vladimir Stankevich, the Provisional Government's commissar at the General Staff in Mogilëv, arrived in Petrograd to report to Kerensky. He expected him to be in a state of agitation but instead he found the premier in a calm and cheerful mood. Kerensky's first question was: 'Well, how do you like Petrograd?' Seeing that this flummoxed Stankevich, he joked: 'How come you don't know there's an armed uprising going on here?' They both laughed.[3] Cabinet Secretary Vladimir Nabokov witnessed a similar chirpiness when he asked Kerensky how he was coping with the threat of a Bolshevik revolt. Kerensky retorted: 'I'd be willing to hold a prayer service for such an uprising to take place.' Nabokov, who knew him better than most others did, tried a further question: 'But are you sure you can deal with it?' Kerensky replied that the Bolsheviks were facing defeat:

'I've got more strength than I need. They are going to be definitively crushed.'[4] Tereshchenko, his friend and foreign affairs minister, felt the same, or at least tried to give that impression. Meeting US Ambassador David Francis on the same day, he spoke about the coup attempt that was universally expected: 'I think we can suppress it. I hope it will take place whether we can or not – I am tired of this uncertainty and suspense.'[5]

Kerensky and Tereshchenko were putting on brave faces. The government had been shaken by an internal crisis on 20 October when Army Minister Verkhovski spoke to a closed session of the Pre-Parliament's international commission. Verkhovski stated that the Russian Army was no longer in a fit condition to defend the front lines – it could neither be equipped nor even fed properly. Tereshchenko was angry at the breach of cabinet solidarity: ministers were meant to keep the military truth unspoken.[6] Kerensky placed Verkhovski on sick leave. This was really a way of firing him and Kerensky took over Verkhovski's ministry. But the Pre-Parliament's discussions added to the confusion at Mogilëv where Commander-in-Chief Dukhonin was trying to coordinate the Russian defence preparations.[7] News of Verkhovski's departure was meanwhile leaked to the Petrograd press and distorted versions of the event were published. Subsequent corrections only increased the atmosphere of chaos.[8]

The Pre-Parliament met again on 24 October for an emergency debate. Boris Kamkov, speaking for the Left Socialist-Revolutionaries, denounced the Provisional Government and called for the formation of 'a revolutionary democratic authority' (*vlast*). But the Menshevik Fëdor Dan spoke angrily about the 'criminal initiative' that the Bolsheviks were planning. Although he despaired of Kerensky, he predicted that even if the uprising succeeded, it would not be long before the Bolshevik party – and all democracy – was swept aside. The only way to prevent catastrophe, Dan declared, was to create a Committee of Salvation.[9] He called for the date of the Constituent Assembly election to be brought forward to enable a resolution of the crisis of power. Dan had also changed his stance on other policies and advocated both immediate peace on the Eastern front and the handing over of the agrarian question to the land committees.[10]

Whilst the many conflicting opinions on this occasion suggested the unlikelihood of a socialist governing coalition, the tide of opinion in the Pre-Parliament had definitely turned against Kerensky. Kamkov and Dan had made a deep impact and the motion was accepted by

123 votes against 102 with 26 abstentions. All socialist parties and factions were in favour. An urgent challenge was being thrown down to the Provisional Government.[11] Vladimir Stankevich phoned the news through to Kerensky in the Winter Palace before going over to join him. Kerensky for the first time appeared deeply shaken. As he talked about resigning the premiership, there was suddenly the prospect of a headless government having to confront a Bolshevik-led insurgency. Fellow ministers implored him to remain in post. It was nearly dawn on 25 October before he agreed to stay on as minister-chairman.[12]

Lenin had spent the previous day trying to stiffen the Military-Revolutionary Committee's resolve and bring forward the moment for action. Trotsky was no democrat but, unlike Lenin, he wished to make the seizure of power look as 'democratic' as possible by waiting for the start of the All-Russia Congress of Soviets of Workers' and Soldiers' Deputies. This Congress, however, could not reflect the opinion of society as a whole because the delegates were elected predominantly by urban soviets, and most people even in the towns had no vote in soviet elections. But if the Congress was not going to embody universal democracy, at least it was not the plaything of a single party. Trotsky stuck to his tactical approach and Lenin, who remained miles away on the city's outskirts, could not interfere. The Military-Revolutionary Committee's plans were anyway at an advanced stage and its first practical moves were being made.

Lenin's mood was volcanic. He sent Fofanova on a mission to the Smolny Institute, demanding action. He raged that the Bolshevik leaders should show themselves adequate to their revolutionary duty. The whole situation gnawed away at him. That evening he threw aside Central Committee orders for him to stay in the apartment and took the tram to the city centre. For disguise he wore a wig and a face bandage and had shaved off his beard. The tram was carrying only a few passengers, so when Lenin discovered that the conductor sympathized with the political left, Lenin abandoned caution and expounded why he wanted an uprising. Alighting from the tram, he walked in the dark to the Smolny Institute, reaching there around midnight of 24–25 October after picking his way through the ring of machine guns. The building had become a fortress. He met his party comrades and told them all to speed up the action. Then he worked on the texts of decrees on land, peace, the press and the transfer of power. He cajoled anyone whose nerve was cracking. This was the time to which Lenin had devoted his entire life.

At ten in the morning on 25 October he completed an appeal, 'To the Citizens of Russia', that declared: 'The Provisional Government has been overthrown. State power has passed into the hands of the organ of the Petrograd Soviet of Workers' and Soldiers' Deputies, the Military-Revolutionary Committee, which stands at the head of the Petrograd proletariat and garrison'. He foresaw 'a democratic peace', the abolition of gentry estates, workers' control of enterprises and the creation of a Soviet government.[13]

The Military-Revolutionary Committee secured places of strategic importance. Accounts were later written about the brilliance of Bolshevik methods, but they were really doing little that differed from what the Duma Provisional Committee had done in early March. Trotsky and his comrades were seizing all points in Petrograd from which their enemies could issue information, make protests or organize counteractivity. The insurgents were already in command of the Smolny Institute. Their next priority was to obtain authority over the army barracks across the city. Trouble was expected from the officer corps and precautions were taken against resistance wherever it occurred. Clashes occurred between troops obedient to the Military-Revolutionary Committee and those who were either still loyal to the Provisional Government or simply horrified by the prospect of a Bolshevik administration, but with vastly superior numbers the Military-Revolutionary Committee quickly squashed any military opposition. The Provisional Government in vain issued a radio-telegram to the Russian people appealing for support, whilst the Military-Revolutionary Committee gave orders to enforce the surrender of the Winter Palace and the Marinski Palace where the Provisional Government and the Pre-Parliament were holding out.[14] The Bolsheviks made preparations for a final assault while completing the capture of Petrograd's rail and tram stations, its post and telegraph offices, and setting up road blocks on the main thoroughfares throughout the city.

Kerensky walked out of the Winter Palace late morning, leaving Konovalov to chair the cabinet. A story was later invented by the Bolsheviks that he was dressed in a nurse's uniform, but the truth was that Kerensky strode across Palace Square to his military headquarters to discuss the situation and assemble forces loyal to him and the government. The insurrectionaries, however, had impounded all the official limousines, so he sent out aides to borrow a US diplomatic vehicle. Embassy Secretary Sheldon Whitehouse was not best pleased but he relented when the circumstances were explained. A friend of

Kerensky's also lent another car. The two vehicles sped off, the American one sporting the Stars and Stripes on its bonnet despite Whitehouse having made its removal a condition for the loan.[15] Kerensky travelled onwards to safety nearly 200 miles away in Pskov. There he enlisted support from Lieutenant-Colonel Pëtr Krasnov, the Don Cossack who commanded the Third Cavalry Corps. Various officer cadets also joined the enterprise. The counter-coup was under way.[16]

The Bolshevik uprising, however, had already tipped the political scales in the capital. The Pre-Parliament was ordered out of the Marinski Palace, which was surrounded by military units. As soldiers and sailors raced into the corridors, Chairman Avksentev saw there would be pointless bloodshed unless he complied. He organized the departure of his colleagues with the intention of reconvening the Pre-Parliament as soon as circumstances allowed.[17] Only the Winter Palace, where the Provisional Government kept itself in session, was left holding out. Artillery at the Peter–Paul Fortress on the other side of the river Neva as well as on the cruiser *Aurora* was readied to shell the Winter Palace.

That afternoon at 2.35 p.m. Trotsky left his duties in the Military-Revolutionary Committee and opened the Petrograd Soviet's scheduled session in the Smolny Institute. The session hall was packed with both its own deputies and with delegates who had arrived from the provinces for the Second Congress of Soviets. Until then Trotsky had publicly denied planning to organize a revolt. Now he celebrated what had happened: 'On behalf of the Military-Revolutionary Committee I declare that the Provisional Government no longer exists!' He listed the institutions and facilities around the city held by the insurgents, assuring everybody that the Winter Palace too would soon fall. Then Lenin entered the hall and was greeted by noisy applause. He told the hall that a government was about to be formed with no bourgeois members. A proletarian socialist state would be constructed. The cause of 'the world socialist revolution' would be advanced. Someone shouted that all this pre-empted the will of the Congress of Soviets. Trotsky dismissed the intervention, claiming that the uprising of workers and peasants had already taken place and that the urgent task lay in consolidating the victory. He expressed confidence that the Congress would give its approval.[18]

The news throughout the same afternoon and early evening indicated that the uprising had become unstoppable. Fëdor Dan was infuriated with the Bolsheviks but saw no point in delaying the opening of the Congress. At nearly eleven o'clock that night he took the platform to speak on behalf of the outgoing All-Russia Central Executive Committee. The credentials committee counted the delegates and found that 300 out of 670 belonged to the Bolshevik party. Though this fell short of an absolute majority, it was enough for the Bolsheviks to obtain fourteen of the twenty-five seats in the new Central Executive Committee.[19] Kamenev, who a few days earlier had resigned from the Bolshevik Central Committee, returned to the Bolshevik fold and chaired the rest of the Congress session. He announced an agenda which would include discussion about the transfer of power, the war and the Constituent Assembly. This was all too much for Martov, who demanded an end to the bloodshed on the streets of the capital. Even many Bolsheviks applauded him and the motion was passed without a single vote against.[20]

Martov's intervention did not placate most of the Mensheviks and Socialist-Revolutionaries present in the hall. But when they called out for talks to be held with the Provisional Government, they could not make themselves heard above the noise of hostile shouts. It was obvious that they were not going to win a vote even if one was held. They demonstratively swept out of the proceedings, leaving only the left wings of both of their parties behind them in the hall.[21] Martov, who was one of those who stayed in the hall, tried to salvage the situation by calling for negotiations with all the socialist parties to form a coalition government. Trotsky dismissed the idea: 'An uprising of the popular masses does not require justification. What has happened is an uprising and not a plot.' He rejected the plea for conciliatory moves: 'To those who walked out and to those who come forward with these proposals, we have to say: "You are pathetic isolated individuals, you are bankrupts: your role has been played out. Depart for where you belong from now onwards: into the waste bin of history!"' This snapped even Martov's patience: 'In that case we're leaving!' Trotsky calmly read out a motion denouncing the 'collaborationists' who had opposed the will of the Congress.[22]

The Bolsheviks, without lifting a finger, thereby acquired an absolute majority at the Congress. Their delight overshadowed any concern about forming a new administration. But the other socialist parties, far from terminating their own activity, were meeting separately to formulate tactics for the new situation – only Left Socialist-Revolutionaries, apart from the Bolsheviks, had stayed in the hall, and it was far from clear that the two leaderships would be able to form a governing coalition. For the moment, though, Trotsky and Lenin savoured their Congress victory.

At the Winter Palace, the Military-Revolutionary Committee now had the building under siege. Konovalov persisted with the cabinet discussions after Kerensky's departure despite the depletion of the military contingent that protected the ministers around the table. Stankevich contacted Mogilëv, from where Supreme Commander-in-Chief Dukhonin promised to render speedy armed assistance. The Provisional Government appointed Kishkin to be the new governor-general of Petrograd.[23] It was a sign of resolve but it came all too late. At 7 p.m. a frantic Tereshchenko sent a message to Dukhonin informing him that the Winter Palace was under threat of bombardment from the Peter–Paul Fortress and the cruiser *Aurora* unless ministers agreed to hand over power to the soviets. Tereshchenko continued to insist that only the Constituent Assembly would have such a right. He pleaded with Dukhonin: 'Speed up the dispatch of forces.'[24] Dukhonin explained that he was making the necessary preparations but he also asked Tereshchenko to recognize that railway travel to Petrograd from Mogilëv was disrupted by hold-ups. The cabinet could not expect the speedy arrival of salvation from the Eastern front.[25]

Ministers stoically refused to enquire about terms for a potential surrender. Konovalov and Kishkin spoke out against surrendering the Provisional Government's last citadel, and they had Justice Minister Malyantovich's support even though his face betrayed his low morale – like all his colleagues, he knew the cabinet's time was up. Military cadets loyal to the government improvised wooden barricades on Palace Square.[26]

Alexander Liverovski, the communications minister, kept a personal record of the last hours of the Provisional Government in the Winter Palace. At 11.50 p.m. he heard shots, followed by a grenade thrown by sailors, in the unlit corridors. A military cadet was wounded in the head. Minister of Welfare Kishkin made a bandage and Finance Minister Bernatski supplied a handkerchief. A fire in the corridor was put out. At 12.30 a.m. a general phoned from the Petrograd Military District headquarters to say that units were being assembled to break the siege. One of Kishkin's assistants asked whether anyone had a revolver that could be used to repel attackers. Only Liverovski could hand over a weapon.[27] Konovalov and Tereshchenko stayed on despite the physical danger and thanked the officer cadets who helped to defend them. But they were helpless to resist the Soviet forces who swiftly rushed the corridors.[28]

Shortly after 1 a.m. on 26 October the head of the Palace defences reported that fifty people had been arrested. Then a 300-strong 'delegation' arrived from the besiegers. At 2.10 a.m. those left holding out, including ministers, were escorted from the premises in convoy and taken as prisoners.[29] The seizure of power in Petrograd was complete. The Provisional Government had been overthrown and the Bolsheviks could set about forming a new administration and announcing its policies. A more extraordinary outcome was hardly imaginable. A party that had been a poorly coordinated faction with unclear policies, a divided leadership and only a few thousand members had risen to authority in the world's biggest land empire. The names of Lenin, Trotsky and Zinoviev had been obscure before March 1917 and were now on everyone's lips. As the exhausted ministers of the Provisional Government were led to their cells in the nearby Peter–Paul Fortress, the equally tired but ebullient Bolsheviks looked forward to days when they would raise their banners for socialist revolution throughout Russia and the world.

31. SOVNARKOM: PROMISES AND INSECURITIES

The Congress of Soviets' first session finished at 5 a.m. on 26 October after proclaiming its assumption of power. Before it met again later that day, Kamenev had talks with the Left Socialist-Revolutionaries but failed to entice them into a coalition. The Bolsheviks had to form a government on their own. They had claimed that they could solve the country's problems. Now they had to prove it.

Kamenev announced the new revolutionary government to the noisy, smoke-filled hall in the Smolny Institute. The word 'minister' had too bourgeois a sound for the Bolsheviks, who wanted to mark themselves off as different from what had gone before, so the government would call itself the Council of People's Commissars (or Sovnarkom in its Russian abbreviation). Lenin was to become the Sovnarkom's chairman. He had proposed that Trotsky should head the government but Trotsky refused to budge even when Lenin asked: 'But why not? You headed the Petrograd Soviet which conducted the seizure of power?' Nor would he accept Lenin's other idea, which was for him to occupy the People's Commissariat for Internal Affairs.

He reasoned that it would be asking for trouble for the government if a Jew was put in charge of its policing. Finally, Trotsky agreed to become people's commissar for foreign affairs. Trotsky accepted but could not help quipping: 'What kind of diplomatic work are we going to have? I'll issue a few revolutionary proclamations to the peoples [of the world] and then shut up shop.'[1]

It happened to be Trotsky's birthday on 26 October, a birthday which he had no time to celebrate.[2] Sovnarkom was born in a frantic environment. Decisions and announcements came thick and fast. The Bolshevik party was on its own in facing up to political as well as armed resistance.

Alexander Shlyapnikov, who had been a metalworker in London earlier in the war, became people's commissar of labour. Stalin was to create the People's Commissariat for Nationalities' Affairs. Whereas Stalin had previously expressed concerns about the revolt, others like Alexei Rykov and Viktor Nogin had unequivocally objected to it. This was not thought a ground to exclude them from the cabinet, and Rykov took over the People's Commissariat for Internal Affairs. Nogin received the portfolio for trade and industry and Milyutin the one for agriculture. The People's Commissariat for Military Affairs was to be led jointly by Vladimir Antonov-Ovseenko, Nikolai Krylenko and Pavel Dybenko, who had close connections with the armed forces. All of them in Sovnarkom were men – it was another four days before the sole woman, Alexandra Kollontai, was made people's commissar of state welfare. The message anyway went forth that Sovnarkom would be a government like none in history. The socialist era was inaugurated. The Bolshevik leadership contended that what was happening in Petrograd would soon be spread to the rest of Russia and central and western Europe.

Even so, it was not the government that the Bolshevik Central Committee wanted. The Left Socialist-Revolutionaries had stayed for the duration of the Congress of Soviets. Although they had not yet formally broken away from the Party of Socialist-Revolutionaries, the split already existed in everything but name. Bolsheviks still hoped to form a coalition with them but the Left Socialist-Revolutionaries had abiding concerns about the Bolshevik fascination with dictatorship and violence, and judged it best to wait to see how things unfolded over the coming days.

The Bolshevik leadership could not afford the luxury of time. Stalin was said to have had no rest for five whole days. When Lunacharski saw him fast asleep, he tip-toed over and kissed him on the head. Stalin took the gesture in the humorous spirit intended. Lenin was persuaded to go to fellow Bolshevik Vladimir Bonch-Bruevich's nearby apartment. When he put on his wig before leaving the Smolny Institute he was reminded that this was no longer necessary. He was drowsy in the car. Bonch-Bruevich gave him the bedroom while he himself dozed on a sofa. Lenin was soon itching to get back to work and he crept into the living room to complete his drafts of the decrees that he wanted to present to the Congress.[3] Meanwhile Trotsky could hardly stand on his feet any longer. He laid himself out in the Smolny Institute and called across the room to Kamenev for a cigarette. Seconds later he fell asleep. Kamenev was alarmed enough to ask him when he awoke: 'Perhaps we ought to get some medicine?' At that moment Trotsky remembered that he had not eaten for twenty-four hours. He commented: 'It would be a lot better to find some food.'[4]

Wearied but ecstatic, Bolshevik leaders set to work. Physical exhaustion was not going to stop them playing their part in a drama of global importance. The first twenty-four hours were crammed with activity. The Decree on Peace demanded an immediate end to the Great War. Soldiers of all countries were urged to lay down their arms. But Lenin, the decree's author, adopted a pragmatic tone in one important respect. After months of denouncing all the belligerent governments as 'imperialist' he merely urged them to bring about peace. He made no reference to a 'European socialist revolution' or 'revolutionary war'. He did not even state that Sovnarkom was committed to building socialism in Russia. A 'just or democratic peace' was his overarching purpose. Sovnarkom called on every warring country, government and people, to agree to a truce and then negotiate a peace that would involve no annexations. The settlements ought to be ratified by 'authoritative assemblies of the people's representatives'. At this point Lenin began to bare his revolutionary aims, committing the Russian government to disclosing the secret agreements made by the Provisional Government. Heralding an unprecedented era in diplomacy, he pinpointed the importance of 'the class-conscious workers of the three most advanced nations of humanity and the biggest states taking part in the current war: England, France and Germany'.[5]

The Decree on Land was issued on the same day. Vladimir Milyutin and Yuri Larin had made a draft after the Bolshevik Central Committee grew impatient at Lenin's failure to produce one. Lenin finalized the text, adding a preamble which was a direct appeal to every peasant household. The decree declared all agricultural land to be an 'all-people's possession'. Estates belonging to the Imperial family, the gentry and the Orthodox Church were to be expropriated. The benefits for peasants were confirmed. They got free use of the land and no longer owed rent or debts to the previous owners. The peasantry received the right – even the encouragement – to dispose of the forfeited property in whatever way they wished. The Bolshevik party still hoped to keep the big commercial grain and beet farms of Ukraine and southern Russia intact once the owners had been dispossessed, recognizing that these big farms supplied an essential part of the harvest that was brought to the cities. The immediate intention was to bring about an alliance between Sovnarkom and the peasantry by telling peasants that they could divide landed property in whatever way they desired and that the government would not interfere.

The Decree on the Press came exclusively from Lenin's pen. Sovnarkom intended to close hostile newspapers and eliminate the freedom of conservative and liberal political organizations to affect public opinion. The net was spread wide. The revolutionary administration indicated that it would shut down any publishing enterprise found to have 'sown confusion by means of an obviously defamatory distortion of the facts'. It was a vague enough formulation to allow the Bolsheviks to break into the premises of all their political opponents. No censorship agency was proclaimed but a clear intent was implied.

Whereas the entire Bolshevik leadership was disappointed by the Left Socialist-Revolutionaries, it had deep internal divisions about how to regard the other socialist parties. The Central Committee had decided to seize power without having the slightest discussion about the composition of the government that would be put in place. Lenin and Trotsky had never wanted to share power with Mensheviks and Socialist-Revolutionaries, whom they accused of a complete betrayal of socialism. The walk-out from the Congress hall had only confirmed Lenin and Trotsky in their opinion. But others in the Central Committee felt differently. Kamenev headed a group which expressed horror at the idea of the Bolshevik party engaging in political self-isolation. The Central Committee was inclined to forgive the behaviour of Mensheviks and Socialist-Revolutionaries at the Congress if they affirmed the position they had taken at the Pre-Parliament on 24 October 1917 when voting for an all-socialist administration. Kamenev was now being backed by Bolshevik leaders who had gone along with the policy of seizing power but had never dreamed that this might mean that the Bolsheviks alone would wield it. He devoted his efforts to arranging inter-party talks while Lenin focused on composing and issuing decrees and Trotsky guided the Military-Revolutionary Committee's operations to put down the expeditionary force assembled by Kerensky and Krasnov on the Pulkovo Heights outside Petrograd. The Bolshevik-led forces quickly achieved victory.

The Bolshevik Central Committee, in the absence of Lenin and Trotsky who were both elsewhere, met on 29 October to discuss its tactics for talks with the Mensheviks and Socialist-Revolutionaries. A majority of the eleven participants at the Central Committee meeting were unequivocal supporters of the seizure of power who wanted to widen 'the base of the government'. The expectation was that 'Soviet parties' would receive posts and that the cabinet would be subject to confirmation by the All-Russia Central Executive Committee of the Congress of Soviets. There was concurrence on insisting on the preservation of the Decree on Land and the Decree on Peace. By a vote of five to three it was decided that the talks would happen on the basis of 'the right of mutual withdrawal of candidatures'. This clumsy phrase signified an openness to each side being able to object to the inclusion of particular individuals in the government. It was a point of importance because the Mensheviks and Socialist-Revolutionaries had no intention of letting Lenin and Trotsky hold on to their posts. Kamenev and Sokolnikov were delegated to negotiate on behalf of the Central Committee.[6]

The All-Russia Executive Committee of the Railways Union went on strike at midnight on 30 October 1917. Still under Menshevik leadership, it pushed for an end to the violence and the creation of a governing coalition drawing together the main socialist parties. Pressure was also applied in the same direction by the Central Council of Factory-Workshop Committees – a Council in which the Bolsheviks held a majority.[7]

From being the Central Committee pariah, Kamenev had risen to leading its negotiating team. His opinions on power were widely shared in the Bolshevik party. When rank-and-file Bolsheviks had called for a government based on the soviets, they assumed that all the 'soviet parties' – including Mensheviks and Socialist-Revolutionaries – would be involved. A questionnaire was issued about current events to the Congress of Soviets delegates. This was something that Bolsheviks and other socialists liked to do at their larger gatherings. They were ahead of their time in conducting surveys of opinion among their followers, and the October questionnaire showed that delegates voted for power to the soviets because they hoped for a democratic socialist coalition.[8] They saw this as the necessary step towards terminating the war on the Eastern front. There was also a wish among them to save the economy from the utter ruin into which it was falling. It is clear that workers, threatened by the wave of enterprise closures, wanted to remove the factories and mines from the hands of their owners. Soldiers on the front line and in the garrisons strongly supported the moves towards peace that would deliver them from the dangers of war.

Anatoli Lunacharski, people's commissar of enlightenment, tried to be optimistic. He had supported the Bolshevik uprising in hope of the creation of a grand coalition of Lenin, Martov, Chernov, Dan and

Verkhovski, and he still advocated this outcome. But he admitted that good will and political wisdom were in short supply.[9] He was right to have doubts because the Mensheviks along with the Socialist-Revolutionaries, emboldened by the strike called by the Railways Union, specified stern terms for any compromise. They had agreed at the Pre-Parliament on 24 October on the need for peace, land reform and reorganized state power. Now they told Kamenev that they would join a Soviet government but only if Lenin and Trotsky were excluded from it. They blamed the two for generating armed strife and bringing the country to the edge of civil war. Kamenev had some sympathy with their demands because he had warned the Central Committee weeks earlier about the recklessness of Lenin's insurrectionary schemes, and he returned to the Central Committee with the terms for final resolution.

Tempers unravelled at the Central Committee meeting on 1 November 1917. Trotsky said there had been no point in seizing power if the Bolsheviks could not receive a majority of places in Sovnarkom and he argued that Lenin should hold on to the chairmanship.[10] Kamenev insisted that he had stuck to the previous meeting's instructions. Dzierżyński retorted that Kamenev had thrown them over. Lenin called for a complete end to the bargaining with the Mensheviks and Socialist-Revolutionaries and for Vikzhel to be faced down. The Bolsheviks were militarily supreme in Petrograd and Lenin wanted troops to be sent to Moscow where Sovnarkom's supremacy had yet to be secured.[11] At this point Kamenev drew some support from Rykov but it was not enough to win a majority at the meeting. Even Zinoviev wished to demand that any coalition should both accept Sovnarkom's October decrees and recognize the soviets as the legitimate governing power.[12] David Ryazanov, a member of the Bolshevik negotiating team, warned that the party was in danger of becoming totally isolated, and he noted that Sovnarkom was already going to have to reduce the daily bread ration in Petrograd to half a pound.[13] Lenin's motion to end the talks with the other socialist parties was defeated. But the final resolution was confined to a desire to negotiate with the Left Socialist-Revolutionaries.[14]

Further governing proclamations were produced. The Decree on the Eight-Hour Day was issued on 29 October 1917, affecting the employees of all factories, mines and other enterprises. It fell short of being a comprehensive project for the economy's urban sector, with nothing said about nationalization in industry and banking or about central state planning. The intent was to persuade all workers and employees that their working conditions would soon improve. Sovnarkom's priority was to attract increased support. People's commissars could not enforce the decree even in Petrograd unless workforces too were to flex their muscles. Revolutionary action from below was meant to strengthen the revolution from above. Sovnarkom showed its ambition in the Decree on Popular Education, which was published on the same day and which promised universal, free, secular schooling for children. As with other such announcements, the government lacked the administrative and financial capacity to implement its scheme – and the scheme was anyway phrased in general terms, but an undertaking had been given that was designed to win popularity across society.

On 2 November 1917 it made the Declaration of the Rights of the Peoples of Russia, guaranteeing an end to national and religious privilege. It was signed by Lenin and Stalin, the people's commissar for nationalities' affairs. The Provisional Government had offered the same guarantee. But whereas Lvov and Kerensky had tried to maintain the borders of the multinational state, Lenin and Stalin coupled this with a commitment to national self-determination – and the principle was extended even to the right of secession. If a nation wished to leave the old empire, Lenin and Stalin declared a willingness to accept such an outcome. The Declaration was made at a time when Sovnarkom's authority was limited to the capital, but it was sent by telegraph and railway to every town and city.

The breakdown of talks with the Mensheviks and Socialist-Revolutionaries, however, horrified several Bolshevik leaders even if they supported Sovnarkom's initial cycle of decrees. On 4 November 1917 Kamenev, Rykov, Milyutin, Zinoviev and Nogin resigned from the Central Committee, calling yet again for the creation of a broad coalition of the 'Soviet parties'. Sovnarkom had not yet lasted a fortnight and was already losing several of its most talented figures, but by vacating the Central Committee and Sovnarkom, they were giving more room for Lenin and Trotsky to end the talks with Mensheviks and Socialist-Revolutionaries. Reprimands were issued to Kamenev, Zinoviev and their fellow departers from the government and party leadership. Sovnarkom went on operating at pace, not least because its members knew the days of Bolshevism in power might soon be cut short. Lunacharski, while confiding his gloom about the political prospect, still insisted to his wife: 'But we've nevertheless taken a big step forward. Even if we're blown apart, the people are not going to forget the decrees on peace and land and control over production.'[15] Veteran Bolsheviks were used to a life on the run and Bolshevik leaders and their families kept their suitcases packed in case they suddenly needed to escape the capital.

Sovnarkom's legislative messages were mainly meant to have a 'demonstrative' impact which would attract workers, conscripts and peasants – as well as diverse national groups – to support the Soviet cause and encourage them to find their own ways to make a socialist revolution. It would take time to write a constitution and even longer to establish a new administrative order. Bolshevik Central Committee Secretary Sverdlov received frequent appeals for detailed guidance. He encouraged local committees to exercise their judgement and initiative. Lenin specially urged the Moscow Soviet to hurry its measures to overturn the existing authorities.[16]

Apart from the Decree on the Press the emphasis of announcements fell upon freedom and opportunity for the working 'masses'. The implication for the middle and upper classes was dire, and the armed operation against Kerensky's expeditionary contingent signalled fierce intent. In public, little was said about broader plans to enforce authority but behind closed doors it was a different matter. Trotsky spoke with characteristic frankness to the Bolshevik Petersburg Committee:

> There is no going back. We're introducing the dictatorship of the proletariat. We'll force people to work. Why did sabotage exist in the past? Well, here we don't merely have terror but rather the organized violence of the workers as applied to the bourgeoisie . . . The workers have to be told clearly and sincerely that we're not in favour of coalition with the Mensheviks and others; that's not the nub of the matter. What counts is the programme. We have a coalition with the peasants, the workers and the soldiers who are fighting right now . . . [We'll] get nowhere if we merely keep a few Bolsheviks [in the government]. We seized power and now we must also bear responsibility.[17]

32. SPREADING 'SOVIET POWER': CITY SOVIETS AND THE SOVNARKOM COALITION

Across most of Russia on 25 October 1917 life carried on much as usual. It was a dry day in the Totma countryside and Alexander Zamaraev was working at home. The recent snow had melted and he needed to tackle some domestic tasks. His newspaper told him that Kerensky's government was introducing a state sugar monopoly. Usually sceptical about ministerial announcements, Zamaraev hoped to be able to buy a bag of sugar in town in the near future. Next day he went into the woods and chopped some timber. On 27 October he took his horse into Totma and stocked up on salt and kerosene. There Zamaraev learned that the Bolsheviks had put Provisional Government ministers and other personnel under arrest but that Kerensky was sustaining his effort to suppress the insurrection. Zamaraev was doubtful about his chances: 'There's no exercise of strong power. No one is listening to anyone else and nobody is showing compliance.'[1]

While Vologda province waited mostly undisturbed, Moscow was in tumult. Nikolai Okunev wrote on 27 October: 'Utter disorder has broken out. Moscow's streets are decorated with proclamations from two governments: Kerensky's and Lenin's. Each talks of the illegality of the other. So this is the situation of your humble son of the fatherland! Who is to have his obedience?' The Moscow Soviet, led by Bolsheviks, had set up a Military-Revolutionary Committee that included Georgi Lomov who was a Bolshevik Central Committee deputy member. Okunev was no better informed about Bolshevism's leadership than most people: 'God only knows who these people are but they're taking supreme power in Moscow.' Against the Military-Revolutionary Committee stood an anti-Bolshevik coalition that emerged from the City Duma and formed a Committee of Public Safety that drew some support from the soldiers' section of the Moscow Soviet.[2]

Violent clashes took place in the city's central districts. Several in the Moscow Bolshevik leadership, including Nogin who had resigned from the Central Committee, wished for a grand socialist coalition. But the party's militant wing rejected any compromise and continued the fight. Their will was stiffened when many Socialist-Revolutionaries rallied to the Committee of Public Safety.

After ten days of hard conflict the Bolsheviks ground out a victory for Sovnarkom's cause in Russia's second city.[3] In the rest of central and northern Russia, Soviet administrations were also taking control. The great textile centre of Ivanovo-Voznesensk, 200 miles to the north-east of Moscow, already had a duma where the Bolsheviks held a majority. By 4 November the Mensheviks and Socialist-Revolutionaries had been edged out of the leadership. Novgorod, 150 miles to the south of Petrograd, was declared a Soviet domain by mid-November. In the Urals, a region where the Bolshevik party had risen in strength over late summer, the transition to Bolshevik rule was almost as quick in Yekaterinburg as it had been in the capital.[4]

Alexander Zamaraev observed the process in Totma. A soviet of workers' and soldiers' deputies was created which held its sessions in the crafts school. It made a poor impression on Zamaraev, who opined that 'there'll hardly be anything sensible coming out of this soviet.'[5] As a peasant he had no say in the hustings or proceedings, and the entire rural electorate was excluded from voting for a soviet whose central government in Petrograd claimed to rule on the peasantry's behalf. Zamaraev's experience was reproduced in many other towns and cities even though the Bolsheviks claimed to be promoting the peasant cause.

Their urban successes were crucially enabled by their ability to rely on army garrisons to apply the force that was necessary. The soldiers' sections of the soviets helped to coordinate the process in the conflicts of the Volga region and Ukraine. Kazan fell to insurgents at the end of October. Nizhni Novgorod, a huge commercial and industrial hub, followed in November. In other cities there was prolonged armed strife. It took until January 1918 before the Tambov Soviet could declare a completed transfer of power, and conflict was particularly intense in Ukrainian cities where there were national suspicions of 'Russian' Bolshevism and of any government based in Petrograd. The Bolsheviks of Kiev were themselves divided about whether to try to overturn the Central Rada, which had frequently caused trouble for the Provisional Government and demanded freedom for Ukraine. Clashes between the

Rada and the City Soviet took place. Sovnarkom dispatched an armed expedition to support the Bolshevik cause.

But elsewhere Russian nationality was not the sole key to the speed of revolutionary success. Baku, which sat over the great oil-producing resources of the Caspian Sea and had supplied 95 per cent of Imperial hydrocarbon output, had a mainly Azeri workforce. But by spring 1918 its city soviet, led by the Armenian Bolshevik Stepan Shaumyan, would proclaim its allegiance to Sovnarkom. Meanwhile the Mensheviks under Noe Zhordania headed the administration in Georgia and denounced the seizure of power in Petrograd. Across most of the south Caucasus there were preparations to form an agency, based in the Georgian capital Tiflis, which would govern the entire region until such time as Sovnarkom collapsed – the timing could not be predicted but Mensheviks felt certain that this would be the end of the Bolshevik 'adventure'. In central Asia, several rival local executives emerged and none of them was beholden to Sovnarkom. The same was true for nearly all Siberia. The Bolshevik government could only leave the outer regions to be dealt with at a later date while the regional administrations themselves waited to see who would emerge victorious from the conflicts between Bolsheviks and their enemies.

Sovnarkom was also exercised by the situation on the Eastern front. Lenin had hoped Russia's pursuit of peace would produce a chain reaction of revolutions in Berlin and Vienna, bringing about an end to the Great War, with the first necessary step being a truce at the front. When General Dukhonin at Mogilëv refused to obey orders to parley with the German high command, he was set upon by a mob of soldiers who ripped off his epaulettes before he was shot and killed. His corpse was subjected to disgusting mutilation.[6]

While People's Commissar for Military Affairs Nikolai Krylenko took over Dukhonin's post, Trotsky issued a call for a general armistice. His words cut no ice with the Western Allies, and talks began on 14 November for a separate cessation of hostilities with Germany and Austria–Hungary. They were held in Brest-Litovsk in Grodno province which had been under German military occupation since August 1915. The premises were the old, three-storey Officers' Assembly building. The German generals and diplomats, led by Prince Leopold of Bavaria, were on their best behaviour. They believed they were witnessing the first step towards Russian capitulation to their demands. They hoped to produce a separate peace on the Eastern front which would enable them to transfer army divisions westward to crush the French and British forces in northern France. Adolf Ioffe, a new Bolshevik like his friend Trotsky, headed the Soviet delegation. After securing consent to make the proceedings public, he read out the entire Decree on Peace.[7] The Germans and Austrians surprised Ioffe by approving terms for the talks that precluded annexations. They wanted to use the principle of national self-determination as a cover for turning the territories they occupied into German protectorates.

Patriotic opinion was affronted. The Bolsheviks were the only political party ready to talk to the Central Powers, and Rachel Khin-Goldovskaya consoled herself with the thought that the revolutionaries were wasting their time:

> There's no dancing to celebrate the peace that has been promised with such 'pomp'. The 'delegates' of Lenin and Trotsky travelled out to pay homage to the Germans. General Hoffman received them but obviously the Bolsheviks' 'proposals' were insufficiently attractive and the German general sent them away with nothing.[8]

Her prediction proved incorrect. Both sides at Brest-Litovsk for different reasons wanted the fighting to cease and on 2 December an armistice was signed.

The flood of decrees and ordinances from the capital continued. 'Workers' control' was declared mandatory on 14 November 1917. The Ordinance on Workers' Control did not require nationalization (or 'statization') of enterprises but instead provided workers with the right to supervise decisions by employers or managers and to inspect the account books. Owners were required to open their accounts to their employees.

The decree was a contradictory jumble. Some features pointed towards centralization, others in the direction of local powers. The Bolsheviks had always been nationalizers. The sole question for them was whether they should immediately proclaim the state's total ownership of industry or proceed in stages. Individual factories were taken into state ownership soon after the October uprising. Perhaps as many as twenty-seven enterprises in Petrograd province alone experienced this between November 1917 and March 1918. In other places under Bolshevik rule, city soviets conducted their own expropriations. It was a patchy process, often instigated in companies abandoned by their owners. Sovnarkom tried to inject some order into the process on 2 December 1917 by announcing the creation of the Supreme Council of the People's Economy. Led by Valerian Osinski, its primary function was to undertake the 'organization' of every aspect of manufacturing, mining, farming, food supply, transport and finance. The Supreme Council received the right to nationalize and requisition whatever it desired.[9]

The foundations were being laid for state economic planning but Osinski quickly discovered that the task was beyond his Supreme Council's capacity. He lacked the personnel and administrative infrastructure. He and Lenin had to be satisfied with the thought that the government had indicated its preferred destination and would travel towards it later. The banking sector was more easily nationalized than other important economic sectors. Sovnarkom made it an early target. It was part of Bolshevik doctrine that financiers were the masters of the whole economy. A decree was issued on 14 December for the nationalization of all banks, big or small. While the 'interests of small investors' were to be protected, the other assets would immediately pass into state property under the supervision of the State Bank.[10] Access to personal wealth held in banks was curtailed. Limits were placed on how much anyone could withdraw from a personal account. When Sergei Obolensky returned to Moscow in 1918 he was allowed to receive only 10,000 rubles from all his holdings.[11] Unlike many rich Russians, he had kept the family jewellery in his residences but if he had not done this, all the precious stones would have become Soviet state property.[12]

Bank nationalization transferred huge resources to the government. But banking assets alone were insufficient to stave off economic ruin, and Acting People's Commissar of Finance Vyacheslav Menzhinski knew better than to appeal to financiers abroad. It would also have been a waste of energy to tender for a voluntary Freedom Loan as Mikhail Tereshchenko had done. No man or woman of wealth was going to invest funds in Sovnarkom. The Bolsheviks also increased their budgetary difficulty through their own commitment to eliminating indirect taxes, which they saw as the bane of the poorer sectors of society. The alternative option was to bring into effect the progressive income tax that the Provisional Government had promised but failed to implement, and to tilt it severely against the interests of people of wealth. The People's Commissariat for Internal Affairs ordered soviets in the provinces to conduct 'the merciless taxation of the propertied classes'.[13]

The new revolutionary government had yet to cope with the Constituent Assembly election which would be conducted across the entirety of the former empire between 12 and 26 November 1917.

Lenin wanted a total suspension.[14] His fellow leaders rebuffed his proposal even though they knew the party's electoral chances to be slim. It was too early in their time in office for them to agree on breaking a political promise, and Lenin had to accept the decision. The Provisional Government had established the rules and arrangements. The election would be the first in the country's history based on universal suffrage, stripped of social or gender privilege. The Bolsheviks now had the advantage of free access to the press and telegraph, and they also had disrupted the party life of Mensheviks, Social-Revolutionaries and particularly the Kadets. Whilst the Bolsheviks knew that they would not win a majority of seats, they set out to obtain as big a minority as they could. The electoral process lasted a fortnight and the counting of votes from thousands of villages was inevitably a slow process. But in the end, as Bolshevik leaders anticipated, the party suffered defeat and obtained merely 168 of the 703 seats. The Socialist-Revolutionaries gained 324 seats – and were able to add 110 seats to this if their Ukrainian counterparts were included.[15]

The general result involved a popular endorsement for socialist policies to the left of the Provisional Government's programme. The sole consolation for Bolsheviks was the paltry showing by both Kadets and Mensheviks. The Kadet leaders had never expected an electoral triumph. Many were disinclined to ally themselves again with Socialist-Revolutionaries and Mensheviks as they had done in the early months of the February Revolution. But Kadets were determined one way or another to organize practical resistance. On 28 November 1917 Lenin persuaded Sovnarkom to proscribe them as 'enemies of the people'.[16] This measure put them outside the framework of the law, and made them automatically subject to arrest.

Lenin had already moved to persuade Sovnarkom on the need for a policing agency that could eradicate all troublemakers. On 21 November 1917 it approved the creation of an All-Russia Extraordinary Commission for Combating Counter-Revolution, Speculation and Sabotage (which was soon known under its acronym Cheka). This was to become the revolutionary security police. Feliks Dzierżyński, a veteran Polish Marxist who had joined the Bolsheviks in mid-1917, was Lenin's choice to head the organization. Dzierżyński had belonged to the Central Committee since August. He was a man of ascetic, hard-working temperament. Lenin felt confident he had the resolve to carry out the acts of revolutionary surgery that lay ahead even though he had spent his years before 1917 criticizing the Bolshevik faction. Under

Dzierżyński's leadership it recruited likely personnel, taking some of them from the Military-Revolutionary Committee to which he had belonged. Techniques of search, infiltration, arrest and interrogation had to be learned on the job, but Dzierżyński – a former exile in Siberia – had the advantage of knowing and being able to use the methodology that the Okhrana had applied against him.

In the chaotic conditions after October 1917, moreover, he and his Cheka could make mistakes and conduct 'excesses' in the knowledge that Lenin would convince most of Sovnarkom's membership that severe policing was essential to protect the so-called proletarian dictatorship. The Chekists, as they liked to be known, began to be feared for their arbitrary rule. They continued the activity of the Military-Revolutionary Committee in imprisoning prominent individuals from parties to the right of the Mensheviks and the Socialist-Revolutionaries. They cleared the streets of illicit traders. They recruited informers to discover where the plots against Sovnarkom were being organized. The Cheka aimed to hunt down any individual or organization that refused to accept the legitimacy of the October Revolution.

The Bolshevik central leadership, though, was uncomfortable about its political isolation. The Constituent Assembly poll results were vivid proof that poorly as the Bolsheviks fared in the towns, they did worse in the countryside. This spurred the Central Committee to renew the coalition talks with the Left Socialist-Revolutionaries, who might have done better in the election if they had broken earlier from the Party of Socialist-Revolutionaries and been able to enter separate candidates. The Bolshevik leaders tempted them again with offers of people's commissariats. The Left Socialist-Revolutionaries were impressed by the Decree on Land as providing foundations for the kind of agrarian transformation that they had always wanted for the peasantry. Lenin had done what Chernov had not managed to achieve. They were equally moved by the Decree on Peace. Whereas Menshevik and Socialist-Revolutionaries had talked about ending the war, the Bolsheviks had made overtures to the Central Powers and issued appeals to the Western Allies. Sovnarkom appeared to have taken serious practical steps to bringing a halt to the carnage on the Eastern front.

The Left Socialist-Revolutionaries already took an active part in the All-Russia Central Executive Committee of the Congress of Soviets and steadily their resistance to the idea of coalition crumbled. On 10 December an official concordat was finalized. The Left Socialist-Revolutionaries would hold seven of the people's commissariats. Andrei

Kolegaev became people's commissar of agriculture, a vital posting for a pro-peasant party, and Vladimir Karelin occupied the People's Commissariat of Justice expecting to act as a brake on Bolshevik fondness for terror. The Left Socialist-Revolutionaries were also given leading posts in the Cheka.[17] But Bolshevik dominance would continue in Sovnarkom, and the Bolsheviks gained from the coalition's existence an improved capacity to present themselves as friends of the peasantry. Whether the reformed government could manage the inevitable tensions between the parties remained to be tested in the rest of the long winter.

33. SOCIALISM, SCARCITY AND DICTATORSHIP: SOVIET LEGISLATION AND DEEPENING DISORDER

The basic question of who would govern the country had yet to be settled despite the coming together of Bolsheviks and Left Socialist-Revolutionaries. The uncertainty and danger touched every aspect of life. On New Year's Day 1918 Lenin was attacked in central Petrograd by a pair of armed men. They fired on the limousine that was taking him back from a public meeting to the Smolny Institute. The would-be assassins were later revealed as monarchists but blame at the time was deceitfully heaped on the rival socialist parties in advance of the forthcoming first session of the Constituent Assembly. Although Lenin escaped unharmed, the atmosphere in the capital was tense, a situation made worse by the crime wave that surged in most cities. Central Committee member Yevgeni Preobrazhenski was robbed later in the same month when thieves masquerading as Moscow Soviet officials conducted a personal search and ran off with his overcoat, wallet and revolver. Urban life had become disorderly and dangerous as administrative control and social self-restraints broke down in an environment where weapons were plentiful and the criminally inclined were using them.[1]

Sovnarkom discussions were nonetheless directed at what to do about the Constituent Assembly, the election of which had put the Socialist-Revolutionaries in the leading position. Nikolai Bukharin, *Pravda*'s editor, suggested withdrawing the mandates from those Kadets who had been elected. Although the Bolshevik Central Committee rejected his idea, it acted to thicken the air of menace. On 3 January the All-Russia Central Executive Committee of the Congress of Soviets published a Declaration of the Rights of the Labouring and Exploited People, which it accompanied with a commitment to treat as counter-revolutionary any organizations which rejected it.[2] Russia was proclaimed a Republic of Soviets of Workers', Soldiers' and Peasants' Deputies, and the soviets were confirmed as the supreme power 'at the centre and in the localities'. The announcement was made regardless of whatever the Constituent Assembly might decide. Sovnarkom decrees were presented as having an authority that no one had the right to challenge.[3]

Troops loyal to Sovnarkom surrounded the Tauride Palace in bitter cold as Constituent Assembly deputies gathered there to begin their proceedings on 5 January 1918. The atmosphere in the capital's snowy central zone was charged with danger. Near the building a peaceful demonstration took place in favour of the Assembly. Orders were given to fire on the crowd. It was a bloody start to the day of the opening of Russia's first freely elected parliament.

Viktor Chernov, leader of the Socialist-Revolutionary caucus, was made Assembly chairman after an initial attempt by Sverdlov, chairman of the Soviet Central Executive Committee, to preside over the session. Sovnarkom had supplied the building with guards who intimidated speakers but the shouts from Bolsheviks and Left Socialist-Revolutionaries failed to discourage Chernov from expounding the policies that a future – and different – government should follow. Bolsheviks took the platform to demand a ratification of the Sovnarkom decrees. Chernov rejected the sovereignty demanded by Sovnarkom. In the early hours of the following morning, the anarchist leader of the guard unit, a sailor called Anatoli Zheleznyakov, approached Chernov to say that he and his comrades were tired and intended to close the building. With that, the Constituent Assembly's doors were firmly closed for the last time. Protests against Sovnarkom took place on the streets. Political tensions led to a horrific incident in a Petrograd hospital when Baltic fleet sailors loyal to the government burst into the premises and murdered two Assembly deputies, ex-minister Andrei Shingarëv and prominent Kadet Fëdor Kokoshkin, in their beds. A horrified Zamaraev sarcastically wrote when he read of the news: 'Bolshevik power is so good!'[4]

The Bolsheviks and Left Socialist-Revolutionaries had the weaponry of power and intended to keep it. Lenin pressed forward with the arrangements for the third Congress of Soviets, which met on 10 January in the same Tauride Palace from which the Constituent Assembly had been driven. A merger was proposed with the network of rural soviets to show that Sovnarkom represented not just workers and soldiers but peasants too. Although Socialist-Revolutionaries and Mensheviks were permitted to speak at the Congress, the Sovnarkom coalition was dominant. A new statehood was announced with the birth of the Russian Soviet Federative Socialist Republic (or RSFSR). Lenin described the Congress as having 'opened a new epoch in world history'.

Sovnarkom sustained a cannonade of legislative activity. A commission was established to draft a Constitution for the RSFSR.[5] Sverdlov and Stalin did the chairing, which was a sign of the importance attached to the task. The All-Russia Central Executive Committee also issued decrees on foreign policy. Among them was the unilateral annulment of the debts incurred by the administrations of Nicholas II and the Provisional Government. The RSFSR absolved itself of all the financial obligations to foreign as well as domestic lenders. An exception was made for citizens of the RSFSR who held bonds of less than 10,000 rubles in value. Such bonds were to be translated into ones that the People's Commissariat of Finance was about to create.[6]

The land question gave rise to an enthusiastic discussion between Bolsheviks and Left Socialist-Revolutionaries, and on 27 January 1918 the Central Executive Committee of the Congress of Soviets issued a Decree on the Socialization of Land. Peasants received the right of usage but not of possession. The amount of land to which each was entitled would vary according to region as assessed by the local soviet hierarchy. The calculation would be made on the basis of a 'consumption–labour norm' that took into account the number of family members who could work, and allowance would be made for those who were not of working age. No one was to transfer land to anyone else in a private deal. It was specified that the poor of the village were to receive favoured treatment. The state would maintain a monopoly on trade in grain, seeds and agricultural equipment. The principle of collective farming was to be encouraged over individual enterprise, pointing the peasantry towards a socialist economy, which was touted as the most effective use of labour.[7]

There were 47,550 'agitators' dispatched to the villages to explain the government's purposes.[8] The official preference for collective farms and for the rights of the landless was not necessarily in line with the traditions of the village and of universal peasant opinion. Nor were several other Sovnarkom ordinances. As committed modernizers the people's commissars officially switched everywhere under their rule to the Gregorian calendar that was in use in the rest of Europe. The disquiet of the Orthodox priesthood and its congregations was ignored.

With seven days' notice the new dating system was to be introduced at the end of the month.[9]

While Sovnarkom celebrated its political successes, it failed to halt the degradation of living standards for millions of people. Alexander Zamaraev in Totma recounted that the mind of every inhabitant was focused on the bread supply. He and his brother Nikolai made donations for the relief of the destitute.[10] The ration had been reduced as supplies underwent further depletion. Tensions rose between peasants and the many urban residents who held them responsible for the shortages. In the town marketplace, barter was replacing the usual monetary exchange as rural households bargained their cereal stock for salt or tar. The price of wheat flour rose. Rye flour was no longer available despite rye being a local crop. There had been no sugar for months. Small traders became desperate after hearing that they would have to wait another two weeks before they got any bread. The peasantry's own plight worsened despite the acquisition of a little additional land from the Church. The average peasant householder had to decide what to do in the forthcoming spring, whether to work as a day labourer for better-off neighbours or to stick to ploughing and sowing his own land.[11]

Even in places like Vologda province, where Bolsheviks were few, the impact of Bolshevik governance was growing. Alexander Zamaraev lamented: 'All private trade has ceased.' He also complained that the communists had closed down the newspapers that he liked to read.[12] The few Vologda communists were a hardy group. Although they could keep contact with the capital by telegram, transport links remained patchy. By the end of the year it was not unusual for five days to pass between the arrivals of trains from Petrograd. Bolsheviks had to make their revolution largely without external assistance.[13]

A survey of Totma district, where Zamaraev lived, found that 57 per cent of peasant households were cultivating expropriated land.[14] Already in April 1918, after the spring thaw, the peasants were dividing up the vegetable garden areas among themselves. But disputes over fairness lasted many stressful days. Zamaraev was exasperated by the lengthy discussions on land redistribution and other issues which were held in the building of the town administration. All his neighbours expressed an urgent interest in securing access to supplies of food that they could not produce for themselves in a northern climate where the soil was poor. Wheat flour was in dire shortage and so agreement was reached for each household to contribute five rubles for the attempt to make a joint purchase. The snag was that no merchant was willing to sell. The peasants saw this as the fault of 'our hateful authorities and their policies'.[15] If Lenin and the Bolsheviks had thought that the Decree on Land would win them unconditional gratitude, they were learning from thousands of places like Totma that the peasantry guarded its interests without sentimentality.

Mikhail Chevekov, a *gimnazia* pupil in Khvalynsk in Saratov province, recorded in February 1918 that Bolsheviks in his native Samara province were already levying compulsory loans from all but the very poorest of the peasantry. Non-compliance was violently punished. An emergency was declared in Khvalynsk to fill the budgetary requirements. The town's merchants were ordered to present themselves at the soviet's premises. They were held there under arrest while money was extorted from them or their families. One of the detainees went off his head. He was only released in return for his wife taking his place.[16]

Another woman told Chevekov's school headmaster: 'I was in the soviet and was told that if your husband doesn't hand over 500,000 rubles we're going to kill him like a dog and throw him on to the street, and we won't let you give him a burial.' The Bolshevik leader in the district issued a decree that anyone resisting his administration would be shot on the spot. Chevekov's father was a prime target since he was a well-known landowning peasant. Having suffered at the hands of fellow peasants who seized possession of his land and livestock in 1917, he had no intention of allowing himself to be arrested by Bolsheviks. When in March 1918 the Red Guard appeared in the village, he and his wife fled to the river Don. The Red Guard aimed to take his twenty-year-old son Mikhail hostage until such time as the family paid a 'contribution' of 25,000 rubles. Mikhail disguised himself in woman's clothing and escaped at five in the morning.[17]

Villages with a tradition of communal repartitioning fell back on past practices, the difference being that they were taking decisions not about their own fields, meadows and woods but about those which had been the property of monarchy, Church and gentry. Villages abounded with returning family members, many of whom were demobbed soldiers. Others had been at work in the towns but had lost their jobs or hoped to get food and a share of the redistributed land. Household elders had previously dominated such discussions but wartime had changed the rural mood. Women had shouldered much responsibility whilst their men were conscripted, and they had an unprecedented opportunity to influence deliberations. Young ex-conscripts, having breathed the air of freedom in 1917, were now reluctant to give automatic assent to what their fathers and uncles demanded.[18]

In the grain-rich Volga provinces like Tambov and Saratov the peasantry had opposed the Provisional Government's restrictions on private trade and were not minded to tolerate their reinforcement by Sovnarkom. The shackles of governmental fixed prices were struck off and peasants sold their produce freely at whatever price they could obtain.[19] This did nothing to improve supplies to those distant provinces of the former empire where supplies were in deficit and whose inhabitants received inadequate rations. The so-called consumer regions received only a fifth of the number of rail freight wagons planned by central authorities, and the depletion continued in ensuing months.[20]

Throughout the long winter of 1917–18 the Soviet authorities imposed their new revolutionary order. Nikita Okunev learned in late November that a ban had been introduced on house ownership. The home that his own father had worked hard to buy no longer belonged to the Okunev family. As the co-heir, Nikita Okunev could have sold it for a large sum before the decree was announced. The dacha was his sole material asset: he and his wife had no other precious possessions.[21] He recalled an old saying that the place of one's birth was where honesty and justice could be counted upon. He reeled from the impact of recent events: 'We don't have justice, so we've lost our native land!'[22] He lamented that the Bolsheviks had abolished the courts that had existed since the time of Emperor Alexander II and had replaced them with 'revolutionary tribunals'. Okunev wrote that Soviet officials were immune from arrest and that countless crimes were no longer investigated. Russia in his personal experience had become a place of lawlessness. He mourned the murder in Sochi of old Goremykin and his family. Although Okunev had no affection for the pre-revolutionary government, he was revolted by such butchery.[23]

Okunev's own career was in turmoil. In December 1917 he registered the renting of the Samolët steamship dock in Moscow under the latest rules. Usually quickly accomplished at the city administrative offices, it was a simple task no longer under the Moscow Soviet. A strike of public officials was taking place against Sovnarkom. Several administrative departments of the City Duma were closed and the strike-breakers had no idea how to run things in the absence of their colleagues. It was a similar story in the banks that had been nationalized. No one was depositing money in them and nobody could draw upon their accounts. Financial chaos grew daily. People did not know 'what to pay for, how much to pay or whom to pay it to', whilst the decrees continued to be issued from Soviet agencies threatening arrest or confiscation of property for disobedience. Okunev agreed with an article in *Utro Rossii* that the government was guilty of 'daylight robbery'.[24] At the personal level he was shaken by a Sovnarkom decree to nationalize all commercial shipping enterprises, including ships, bank deposits and dividends. He could only expect to be demoted to clerk in an office where he had always been the boss.[25]

In late January 1918 Alexander Lukashev, the new commissar for Moscow's commercial ships and quays, turned up at the company and told the eleven members of staff to elect a representative to serve on the new agency that he headed. They elected Okunev. Lukashev found him unacceptable as a *burzhui* and demanded that they made a choice from among Okunev's subordinates. Okunev was told that he would not even be allowed to work as an ordinary clerk.[26] In fact he managed to stay on because his fellow workmates did not like the idea of seeing him fired. All of them, at all levels, were suffering from the same worsening conditions in the office and at home. Okunev also had another piece of good fortune. His son Lelya had lost his post as an army officer in December 1917. For a while he was unemployed but then inveigled his way into a lowly job in Trotsky's People's Commissariat for Military Affairs and could share some of his modest salary with his father. Lelya Okunev was carrying out office work. Collaboration with the Bolsheviks became a necessity as even people who disliked their politics sought out ways to put food on the family table.[27]

People in many parts of Moscow sawed up their interior doors and parquet floors to burn for fuel.[28] When horses collapsed and died on the street, passers-by quickly stripped them clean of all the meat. Abandoned automobiles were used as toilets. While Sovnarkom promised a radiant future for Russia and the world, conditions in Russian towns reached rock bottom.[29]

The middle classes had begun to suffer hardship, as inflation soared and their money became worthless and they no longer had access to investments and savings. British nurse Florence Farmborough noted in her diary in January 1918: 'Domestic servants have ceased to exist.'[30] Friends in Moscow told her that her clothes were dangerously smart if she wanted to avoid trouble.[31] Anton Okninski, a former official at the Russo-Asiatic Bank, dressed down for his family's train journey from Petrograd to Tambov province. He bought third-class tickets to avoid being taken for bourgeois oppressors. This did not save his daughter from cries of 'Kill the damned *burzhuyka*' when alighting at a station en route to sort out permission for onward travel. Conmen dressed as railway guards stopped the train and ordered everyone to leave the carriage while they pretended to carry out a search for 'speculators' and robbed the suitcases. The crowd at Moscow's Kazan station overflowed onto the platforms, and Okninski needed to hire help to buy tickets and board a carriage with his family. A tall, muscular porter agreed to do the job for 300 rubles – he pointed out that he too would have to employ assistants to bundle the Okninski family onto the train. People on the platform shouted: 'Don't give seats in the carriage to the *burzhui*!' Some grabbed the leg of one of his daughters before the exhausted family reached their seats.[32]

It was both a help and a hindrance to be a middle-class traveller. One needed to hide any money in case of theft, but porters still wanted tips in cash. Bribes to staff at the station baggage department were best paid in cigarettes, preferably those manufactured before 1917 – the quality of output had fallen in the revolutionary year.[33] Lieutenant Semën Tolstoi, a landowner's son from Simbirsk province witnessed soldiers robbing stalls and shops on their journey and showing that 'nothing was sacred' for them.[34] He himself left the front in January 1918 on a train that was packed with troops. Those who could not get a seat piled themselves and their belongings onto the carriage roofs, although when the train moved off, many of them were abandoned by the side of the track.[35]

Travel in automobiles was dominated by soviet officials, party bosses and Red Army personnel.[36] Although many wore uniforms, Nikita Okunev said they could really be anyone from a commander-in-chief to a simple 'conman-as-expropriator'. Cab drivers grew fewer and pricier. In Moscow it was difficult even to board a tram because soldiers took up all the room.[37]

People's commissars reserved many comforts for themselves and their families. Even so, they and their comrades on lower steps of the ladder of authority were aware that decrees and regulations were widely disobeyed. Nikita Okunev recorded that the nightwatchman in his apartment block asked for a six days' furlough to operate as an illegal bagman because he could not live on his wages. But he did not want to lose his modest living quarters and needed to find a way of coping with life in a deep economic crisis. Thousands were doing the same. Okunev exclaimed: 'The bagmen are now in vogue.'[38] Whereas the Provisional Government's militias had tended to overlook infringements of the grain trade monopoly, Bolshevik commissars looked askance at all private commerce. As food shortages grew still more severe, the bagmen became indispensable in making goods available. The black market was a life-saver. Townspeople, especially those living on a paltry ration allowance or none at all, bought flour, vegetables and meat from them. The Cheka hunted for bagmen and for all those who flouted the orders of Sovnarkom and the All-Russia Central Executive Committee (VTsIK). Some former company owners searched out corrupt officials in the Soviet financial bodies and bribed them to make credit transfers of funds in return for sharing the proceeds.[39]

This was how Prince Pëtr Obolenski regained the valuables from the family's Crédit Lyonnais deposit box. He then made the error of describing in his journal what he had done which dangerously complicated his case after the Cheka got hold of it.[40] It is not known how Obolenski managed to achieve his release from confinement. Others who fell foul of the Chekists, especially if they had an illustrious name like Obolenski, could expect a grimmer outcome.

34. TARGETING THE CHURCH: THE OFFENSIVE AGAINST ORTHODOXY

The Soviet authorities wanted to change mentalities as well as social and economic policies. A crucial objective was to erode the popularity of religion, which the Bolsheviks, like all Marxists, regarded as 'the opium of the people'. They appreciated the difficulties of waging their campaign. In many regions of the former Russian Empire, religious belief and national and ethnic loyalty were intertwined, and the party was hoping to win support by promising rights of national self-determination. People's Commissar for Nationalities' Affairs Stalin announced total tolerance in matters of religion. He wanted to assure Jews, Muslims and the followers of diverse Christian sects that Sovnarkom would respect their freedom of belief and practice.

Removing the hold of religious beliefs on the minds of millions of citizens, however, was inevitably going to be a long-term project. Sovnarkom feared that the biggest Christian denomination, the Russian Orthodox Church, could meanwhile do it much damage. The Church leadership had favoured Kornilov, denounced peasant assaults on ecclesiastical land ownership and predicted the coming of the Antichrist – which unambiguously referred to a government of Bolsheviks and the Left Socialist-Revolutionaries who were spreading doctrines of atheism.[1] Sovnarkom kept up its aggressive measures. Its Decree on Land had already deprived the Church of its landed property. The stream of income from its lands, bank accounts and governmental subsidy was blocked, which meant that the priesthood was reduced to complete dependence on voluntary financial contributions. Communication with parishes was obstructed when the Bolsheviks confiscated the ecclesiastical printing presses.[2] In mid-December 1917 the government annulled its role in the registration of birth, marriages and deaths.[3] Legislation was prepared for a formal separation of Church and state. Whilst universal freedom of faith was proclaimed, there were some caveats. Religious societies lost all property rights and their buildings passed into the possession of the state. The teaching of religion was forbidden in schools. Soviets were empowered to intervene whenever religious ceremonies disrupted public order and security. This dispensation gave obvious scope for persecution of clergy and their congregations.[4]

The Church leadership weathered the storm. Only its Council had the right to elect a patriarch, something that had not happened since the late seventeenth century. On 28 October 1917 the Council, sitting at the Diocesan House a few hundred yards north of the Kremlin, announced an election. The last round in choosing the patriarch was made by drawing lots from the names of the three leading candidates that had the Council's approval. The winner was announced on 5 November: Tikhon the metropolitan archbishop of Moscow.[5]

Born Vasili Bellavin in 1865, Tikhon had taken monastic vows as a young man and was immediately identified as a cleric of outstanding talent. In his mid-twenties he was made bishop of the Church's North American diocese. Returning to Russia in 1907, he became bishop of Yaroslavl and then of Vilna. He fled to Moscow in 1915 when German forces occupied the Lithuanian territories. His standing among fellow clerics continued to rise and in July 1917 he was elected metropolitan. Tikhon accepted the new political reality: he never spoke about the former emperor or called for the dynasty to be restored. The priority for the Church, as he saw it, had been to find ways of attracting believers back into its embrace in a Russia where the Provisional Government was stripping it of many old privileges. Tikhon impressed fellow clergy with his sincere faith and modesty of manner. Stoical and courageous, he seemed the man to lead the Church through the storms ahead under Bolshevik rule.

By the time of the enthronement ceremony later in November 1917, the Bolsheviks were in control of Moscow and made difficulties for admittance to the ceremony in the Kremlin's Dormition Cathedral. Armed guards were kept on patrol. The building's cupola had been damaged in the recent fighting, and Tikhon lamented 'the blasphemous hole' that remained.[6] Afterwards on Red Square, he sprinkled holy water on the crowd of people who had been stopped from attending the service. The Bolsheviks were at the same time holding an event that commemorated the militants who had perished in the struggle for power in the city. An orchestra was playing the *Marseillaise*, but even soldiers on guard for the Bolsheviks doffed their caps at Tikhon and sought his blessings.[7] The Soviet press ignored the enthronement but this failed to muzzle the news about the new patriarch. Every Moscow parish church tolled its bells throughout the day.[8]

On 3 January 1918 Alexandra Kollontai, people's commissar of state welfare, wrote to Lenin asking for approval to turn one of Russia's largest and most prestigious monasteries, the Alexander Nevski Lavra in Petrograd, into a care home for the elderly. Sovnarkom turned her down for fear of provoking civil unrest.[9] Kollontai repeated her request in the middle of the month and this time secured governmental endorsement. Holy vestments were ordered to be removed from church icons. She also oversaw the expulsion of all the monks from the Lavra.[10] On 19 January 1918 a Red Guard detachment pushed its way into the monastery and demanded the handover of all valuables. When Bishop Prokopi refused, he was manhandled into a cell. Prokopi's people sounded an alarm from the bell tower. A crowd of the faithful succeeded in disarming the Red Guards. The authorities dispatched reinforcements armed with two machine guns. Shots were fired, one of which hit a priest in the forehead and killed him.[11]

Patriarch Tikhon issued an Epistle on the same day calling upon 'the madmen' to come to their senses and abandon their 'truly Satanic cause' for which they would perish in the fires of Gehenna. He made no direct summons to violence and offered no advice on practical measures, and he did not mention the Bolsheviks and Left Socialist-Revolutionaries by name. He focused instead on the physical destruction suffered since the October Revolution: the damage to cathedrals during the fighting in central Moscow and the pillage of Petrograd's Christ the Saviour Chapel and Alexander Nevski Monastery. He denounced the seizure of property belonging to churches and monasteries 'by the godless rulers of darkness'. The Epistle ended with an appeal to the 'the true-believing children of the Church' to stand up in its defence.[12]

On 28 January 1918 Okunev, though not a regular churchgoer, joined a procession of the Cross on Red Square in protest against the persecution of Christianity. He saw the latest proclamations of the Moscow Soviet which promised non-interference but explained to 'conscious soldiers, workers and peasants' that the Revolution intended to 'destroy all forms of slavery' and to seize all Church lands. While Okunev knew the clergy had propped up the tsarist order, he objected to the way that the communists were treating religion. He pointed out that most people gathering on Red Square were neither capitalists nor gentry landowners but citizens like himself who were their employees – or their lackeys, as the communist authorities liked to call them. Looking around, Okunev recognized craftsmen and kitchen staff in the throng. He felt inspired when Patriarch Tikhon uttered prayers in the freezing cold outside St Basil's Cathedral.[13]

In Vologda province, Alexander Zamaraev was horrified by the persecution of the Orthodox Church. In February 1918 the Totma parishes joined a procession of the Cross to the marketplace where prayers were said about the direction being taken by 'our life'. Priests were unpopular with local supporters of the October Revolution and some shots were fired but the crowd of believers refused to be intimidated. Calm was restored and the procession was resumed.[14] A peaceful town had experienced a new level of violence and the 'Church question' continued to disturb public life as a consequence of the Totma Soviet's endorsement of Sovnarkom's rulings on landed property. The abolition of ecclesiastical ownership threatened the local clergy with destitution. Totma's peasants decided that men of the cloth should have the right to a share of the fields but Church possessions had been quickly redistributed after the Decree on Land, and the recent beneficiaries did not warm to the idea of losing what they had obtained.[15] The peasantry met again in June 1918 in one of the town's schools and confirmed the decision to compel a peasant named Izvoilov to return property to the clergy.[16]

The Soviet authorities kept up the pressure on the Totma churches. In July 1918 they refused permission for the procession of the Cross on the feast day of St Panteleimon.[17] In September 1918 orders were issued for the removal of all icons and religious decorations from official buildings and schools in Totma.[18] Bolsheviks were quartered in the monastery and ate and slept in one of the buildings. The rest of the premises were abandoned except for twelve monks who were allowed to huddle in a poky corner. There was no fuel for heating. To Zamaraev it was as if the words of St Luke's Gospel had been fulfilled: 'Behold, your house is left unto you desolate.'[19] The Totma Bolsheviks practised their Bolshevism lightly that year at Christmas, which they celebrated on the date in the old Julian calendar. Orthodox believers noted that they caroused as heartily as everyone else in the district.[20] These Bolsheviks evidently still felt the seasonal tug of tradition. They changed their minds a few weeks later when they brought in the New Year according to the new Gregorian version, which was only mid-December by the Julian calculation.[21]

As the party and government pondered its next moves against the Church, the Cheka recruited an informant at the highest level of the Russian Orthodox Church to spy on the patriarch.[22]

In 1919 the Soviet authorities stepped up their harrying of the Orthodox Church. In Totma, where Zamaraev lived, there was a procession of the Cross round the town on the feast of the Assumption but the relics of the Venerable Feodosi at the monastery had been stripped of their vestments on governmental orders. A crowd of the faithful gathered at the monastery and a reclothing took place before the procession began. Prayers were offered for rain. The Soviet authorities were infuriated. Abbot Kirill and seven of his clerical staff were put under arrest. The monastery was closed. The bishop in Vologda had to plead for their release on the grounds that Kirill had been acting under pressure from believers.

The Soviet authorities found difficulty in getting the peasantry to hate their priests. Peasants were more likely to owe money to a 'kulak' than to a man of the cloth. Inhabitants of Podgornoe district of Tambov province were served by Father Gleb, by origin a peasant from the Voronezh countryside. Okninski remembered him fondly:

> As a peasant himself, he had a good knowledge of the life of the peasants, their customs, needs and prejudices. He himself lived like a working peasant [*muzhik*]: he ate the same food as them; he tended his own livestock; his family – he had a wife and five children – dressed simply, in the peasant manner, and in their general way of life were indistinguishable from the peasants he lived among.

The peasantry loved their priest and saw him as an improvement on his grumpy predecessor who had not even allowed his parishioners to choose names for their children at baptism. Father Gleb drove his cart, wearing old boots and a cassock, to visit sick parishioners. A typhus epidemic afflicted the province, and he made many such trips. But the money he received was barely enough to feed his family or buy oil to light the church.[23]

The Bolsheviks accused Father Gleb of omitting both to register ownership of a pig and deliver the seven hundredweights of grain that was demanded of him. He pleaded that they had already seized possession of his bullock, sheep, two geese and some hens. When he said he never produced anywhere near the amount of required grain, they replied that he should go out and buy it. The men at his door were stony-faced and took his hog away with them.[24]

Preparations for May Day 1918 became a tussle between secular and religious authorities. It was both International Workers' Day and, in the Orthodox calendar, Passion Wednesday. The 'Marseillaise' competed with the sad peals of church bells. Trotsky appeared at a parade of Red forces on Khodynka field. A great red drape was stretched across the Kremlin's Nikolski Gates to cover the destruction that had occurred in the October Revolution, including the damaged icon of St Nicholas the Miracle Worker.[25] Patriarch Tikhon competed by appealing to Moscow's believers to join in a procession of the Cross to the Nikolski Gates. The Cheka predicted disturbances. In fact the occasion was peaceful, just as Tikhon had wanted. A newspaper report claimed that people from every generation and all walks of life, including soldiers, joined the throng.[26]

There were signs that the religious calendar was winning a renewed popularity. Whether this was a lasting phenomenon was unclear but Tikhon was determined to expand his activities and rally the faithful. In June 1918 he took a party of the clergy by train to Petrograd. It was his first trip to the city since his enthronement as patriarch. The Bolsheviks put no obstacle in the way of the eight-day trip and huge crowds turned out for his every appearance. The warm reception surprised even Tikhon. His support staff drank heartily on the return journey not knowing that the Cheka had decided to arrest the patriarch en route on a charge of giving a subversive speech on the course of his visit. But the Chekists stopped the wrong train, and Tikhon slept undisturbed all the way to Moscow.[27]

Sovnarkom put Tikhon under temporary house arrest in autumn 1918.[28] Tikhon struck back in the only way he could. On 26 October, a year after the Bolshevik seizure of power, he issued an appeal to Sovnarkom, writing that 'all they that take the sword shall perish by the sword'. He accused people's commissars of unlocking rivers of blood while refusing to fulfil the undertakings that they had made:

> You promised freedom . . . Is it freedom when nobody can obtain food for himself or rent an apartment and when families and sometimes all the residents of entire housing blocks are expelled and their property is flung on to the street – and when citizens are artificially separated into categories, some of which are delivered into the grip of hunger and robbery?

Tikhon accused them of having surrendered the country to Germany. He listed the baleful results of their rule: armed strife, robberies, executions of the innocent, hostage-taking, expropriations, excessive taxation and persecution of the well-off and the so-called *burzhui* and kulaks. And all this while pursuing 'the spectre of world revolution'.[29]

In November 1918 Tikhon was taken back under house arrest, where he remained until 6 January 1919 – twenty-four hours before the Orthodox Christmas Day.[30] His denunciation of the Soviet state inevitably seemed to the Bolsheviks like a Church which was siding with their enemies. If Tikhon was not for Sovnarkom, he was going to be treated as acting against it. In fact Tikhon refused to support any of the forces in the many armed conflicts that had broken out since the October Revolution. He would constantly oppose any violence of Russian upon Russian. Tikhon wanted peace in Russia. He did not endorse communism, far from it: he was steeped in conservative social values, but he aimed to defend the Church from further harm and saw the need to avoid embroilment in politics.

One way or another, the Church had managed to survive but it was in a desperate condition. Attendances dropped and churches in Moscow became a sorry sight, even at the religious festivals. Nikita Okunev recorded in October 1919:

> There's an absence of archpriests to take services or a celebrated choir of singers. Instead there is half a dozen people at prayer (old women in the majority of instances), meagre lighting (well, who is going to buy ten candles where just a small one now costs 5–10 rubles) and an atmosphere during services that depresses the soul. In many places of worship there are no deacons. They've either been taken into the Red Army or have run off to work for Soviet institutions or for speculators' enterprises as the result of their inability to survive on their church pay. There are no priest's assistant or singers and the service is conducted by a solitary, sad-looking priest and the choir consists of some faithful parishioner who can recite what's laid down and sing what's required.[31]

Okunev blamed the impact of communist propaganda, which he felt was eroding the faith of millions. He reckoned that congregations would get scantier in the winter months when the clergy were no longer able to obtain logs to heat their churches.[32]

The Bolsheviks were internally divided. Since summer 1918 Martyn Latsis, the Cheka's deputy chairman, gave orders for any priest or monk who opposed the Reds in word or deed to be shot. Although he had support among Chekists, he was opposed by those in the People's

Commissariat of Justice who wanted to debilitate the Church by fostering and strengthening the internal divisions that already troubled it. Both factions sought to catch Lenin's approval. The fate of the Russian Orthodox Church in Bolshevik hands had yet to be determined.[33]

35. CULTURE AND THE MEDIA: STATE SYMBOLISM, ENTERTAINMENT AND OFFICIAL CONTROL

Soviet Russia as yet had no formal censorship agency, but the central party leadership, Cheka and the People's Commissariat of Enlightenment functioned in a semi-official fashion as watchdogs of what was printed and displayed. Officials sequestered presses wherever they detected active hostility to Sovnarkom. Kadet publications disappeared in November 1917. The Menshevik and Socialist-Revolutionary ones were frequently closed down in ensuing months.

Sovnarkom, however, had grander aims than mere suppression, and was trying to secure change across the whole of society. A primary objective in the long term was education. Literacy and numeracy were priorities for Lenin, who continued the process of academic secularization that had begun under the Provisional Government – not everything that Bolsheviks claimed as their innovation was without precedent. But the schools were in chaos. Although many teachers were glad to see the back of the priesthood in their classrooms, they were unhappy about an authoritarian government interfering in their work. Their salaries also fell below what they needed for a comfortable existence. The People's Commissariat of Enlightenment demanded a shift in the country's pedagogical policy towards a uniform system that included some industrial training. Lunacharski, with Lenin's wife Nadezhda Krupskaya as his deputy, believed in the reform of all young working-class criminals. When Lunacharski visited an agricultural colony school at Volosovo in Petrograd province, he made the error of hugging one of the pupils who was a notorious young thief. At lunch Lunacharski discovered that his watch had disappeared. The offender owned up: 'I was only joking. I wanted to show him how nifty I am.'[1]

On the margins of approved institutions stood the Proletarian Culture movement headed by ex-Bolshevik Alexander Bogdanov.

Once he had been a Bolshevik and one of Lenin's leading comrades. They fell out when Lenin wanted the faction to compete in the Duma elections of 1906. They also disputed questions of epistemology – a storm in a teacup, as Stalin put it. Bogdanov detested Lenin's authoritarian style in handling dissent amongst comrades, and he did not change his opinion after October 1917. He had always believed the working class had to take control of its own cultural development without domination by intellectuals. He saw this as the prerequisite for a decent socialist revolution. With the acquiescence of the Bolshevik leadership he set up clubs and schools where workers could develop their skills and ideas. His ambition was to de-Leninize Bolshevism from within the zone of Soviet rule. Bogdanov had always been an optimist, and Lenin was not minded to ban an opponent who challenged his variant of socialism but at least did not try to challenge Sovnarkom's right to rule.

Tsarist statues, flags and insignia had been attacked and ripped down since March 1917, and the pace of destruction quickened from October. Bolsheviks employed willing painters and sculptors to fashion replacements to explain their priorities and purpose to society, with an emphasis on vivid simplicity. Soviet leaders gave priority to winning and keeping the support of 'the masses'. Posters and cartoons were produced in fast order. Banners were raised proclaiming the birth of a new era with the establishment of 'Soviet power'. The colour red was used in every public space to disseminate the message, even more so than had been the case in the early days of the February Revolution. Women who looked up at the huge revolutionary drapes complained about the waste of valuable cloth at a time when they themselves could not buy any of it to clothe their families.[2]

The government commissioned new statuary to suit its political purposes and monuments were erected to commemorate Karl Marx and Friedrich Engels. The Soviet administration also subsidized production of a statue of Spartacus, the leader of the slave rebellion against the Romans in 73–71 BCE. Nikolai Chernyshevski, an early socialist critic of the tsarist order in the mid-nineteenth century was reimagined in bronze form. A plan was announced to demolish the obelisk in the Alexander Gardens, next to the Kremlin, which had been erected to celebrate the Romanov dynasty's tercentenary in 1913. Lenin raised an objection and ordered the retention of the obelisk while replacing the names of tsars with those of historical figures venerated by Russian revolutionaries: Thomas More, Tommaso Campanella, Gerrard

Winstanley, Charles Fourier and Nikolai Chernyshevski.[3] Sovnarkom adopted the hammer and sickle as a joint symbol of its revolution.[4]

Few writers, artists and musicians were in a position to militate against communism. If the novelist Lev Tolstoy had been alive, he would have denounced Lenin and Trotsky, but the cultural intelligentsia no longer contained willing martyrs. Most of them detested Bolshevism but like most inhabitants of the former Russian Empire, they chiefly wanted an end to the chaos and violence all around them. They continued to seek meaning from their experience. But at the time they added little to the public debate – and Sovnarkom and the Cheka anyway did not tolerate criticism.[5]

Many of them had to turn to the Soviet authorities for food and income. Konstantin Rozov, the renowned Orthodox Church singer, found a niche with the First State Choir. He spent most of his earnings in horse-cab rides from engagement to engagement. He would have preferred to receive groceries rather than rubles, and complained that when he sang for the Church he was fined for missing performances with the State Choir. At the personal level he was grateful for not having to sing the *Internationale*. At most he would be asked to sing the solo part of the Song of the Volga Boatmen (*Dubinushka*).[6] Nikita Okunev wrote in his journal at the start of August 1918 that he was back in work but on a reduced salary which meant he could no longer afford a servant, entertain guests or go to hear Shalyapin at the Bolshoi Theatre. His earnings no longer stretched to being able to buy a bottle of wine.[7] One day he spotted Shalyapin himself in a horse-cab on Myasnitskaya Street. This astonished Okunev. Where was Shalyapin's limousine and why had he grown so thin? He earned a colossal fee for his performances, so what explained all this?[8] The simple answer which did not occur to Okunev was that the Soviet state had impounded all the limousines.

Entertainment was not required to be political but if satire was involved, it had to be gentle about Bolshevism. The popular circus clowns Bim and Bom developed an act in which they competed to hang pictures of Bolshevik leaders on the wall. Bim wanted Lenin while Bom chose Trotsky. Behind them was a throne decked out with tsarist insignia. Bim 'Lenin' and Bom 'Trotsky' cavorted in a struggle to sit on it, and Okunev wondered whether they might suffer for their impertinence.[9] He was proved right when the pro-Bolshevik Latvian Riflemen let off their weapons after objecting to their satire.[10]

In distant Vitebsk the Jewish artist Marc Chagall received funding for an art school which would teach the poor. Chagall continued to produce his wonderful pictures of life in the shtetls. Like many contemporary artists, he distorted perspective and physical shapes, sometimes portraying people levitating from the floorboards in an exultant mood. His pictures of Jewish life beatified communal happiness amidst the poverty and drunkenness. He celebrated fiddlers, weddings, donkeys and haycarts. Chagall took Soviet money without adopting communist ideology. Other intellectuals were open to aligning their creative impulses with Marxism. A network of Higher Artistic and Technical Studios was set up to recruit and train workers to paint, sculpt and design furniture. The People's Commissariat of Enlightenment found some of the exhibitions too abstruse and veteran Bolsheviks asked for a more 'realistic' approach to pictures and pottery. Lenin was among those who preferred traditional ideas of cultural excellence, but he huffed and puffed without seriously interfering.

Some artists did very well out of official patronage. The poet Vladimir Mayakovski turned his hand to painting posters and put in a bill for thirty-two million rubles.[11] His visual art also appeared in his writings. The illustration for the poem 'Man' (*Chelovek*), published in February 1918, has the image of a man wearing pinstriped trousers and with a huge gold chain gazing down from the height of skyscrapers onto lines of tanks streaming along the streets below – and squadrons of warplanes flying above him. Mayakovski was drawing attention to the global carnage caused by capitalist greed, a popular Bolshevik message. Other cartoonists in communist newspapers concentrated on Russia. Pictures of bloated businessmen, bloodthirsty generals and decadent bishops purveyed the idea that the well-being of 'the people' depended on the October Revolution's survival. Communists also used art for educational purposes, depicting communism as the golden dawn for humanity. Sobriety, horticulture and bodily fitness were encouraged and art was devoted to appeals for working people to join the party and its armed forces. Workers were depicted as muscular and flint-faced, usually waving a hammer or a rifle, wearing simple factory attire or stripped to the waist. The key themes were commitment, physical strength and determination.

Propaganda of this sort was not a Bolshevik invention; for the enemies of Sovnarkom used the same artistic conventions without the 'proletarian' preoccupation. But the Soviet authorities had the advantage of easier access to the means of production and dissemination. They also explored using the latest technology. Lenin was badgered into appearing on film in late 1918. Bashful in front of the cameras, he was less shy in 1919 about recording some short speeches. Trotsky, who had never been shy with the photographers, employed a cinematic team to follow him as he sailed along the river Volga in late summer 1918. He also brought a printing press along with him on railway trips. Newspapers were published in a carriage of the Trotsky train as it moved from place to place.

Blok's essay 'The Intelligentsia and Revolution' appeared in January 1918. It provocatively displayed his contempt for what he saw as the incapacity of most intellectuals to adapt to the changed times.[12] He criticized those who disapproved of the Bolshevik seizure of power. In his diary on 26 January 1918 he wrote: 'The October coup [*perevorot*] is anyway better than the February one which somewhat smells of the autocracy.' He began to work for Soviet agencies, not least because he had to generate some income if he wanted to eat. He attended an official meeting about ideas to simplify the old Russian alphabet. People's Commissar of Enlightenment Anatoli Lunacharski took part and at the close of the proceedings he walked over and said: 'Permit me to shake your hand, comrade Blok.' The poet warmed to Lunacharski because he appeared so 'non-intellectual'.[13]

This was not a judgement shared by many Bolsheviks, to whom Lunacharski seemed so bourgeois in his manner and tastes. But everything that Blok witnessed in 1917 convinced him that Russians – poor, downtrodden, ordinary Russians – could transform the affairs of humanity. He wallowed in the prospect of violence, hoping that 'old', 'sophisticated' Europe was about to be overturned. He knew that he himself was a bourgeois sophisticate, but he insisted that the coming transformation would have a cleansing effect despite all the chaos and unpleasantness. Blok thought the October Revolution would spread the values and behaviour of 'the East' to the rest of the world. Russians in his opinion had proved themselves to be true 'Asiatics'. He wrote in his journal: 'Are we barbarians? Well, that's good.'[14]

He brought together his thoughts and artistry in a lengthy poem, *The Twelve*, to eulogize the animal vivacity on Petrograd streets. Along with W. B. Yeats' *The Second Coming* and T. S. Eliot's *The Wasteland*, it stands as one of literature's most powerful reflections on the cultural and social tumult at the end of the Great War. *The Twelve* was a hymn to the spirit of October but not at all to Bolshevism. He wrote of a dozen Red Guards striding through the Petrograd tumult and adding to it as they pass along. They talk in street slang. They curse, smoke and attract the company of prostitutes. They swagger while singing songs of no obvious political content. Blok drew inspiration not from any revolutionary party and certainly not from Lenin but from the content and imagery of Revelation in the New Testament – his twelve Red Guards correspond to Christ's twelve apostles.[15] The following stanzas give a flavour of the poet's feelings:[16]

> The city's noise cannot be heard,
> No sound above the Neva's tower,
> There are no policemen any longer –
> So have your fun, lads, without wine to drink!
> A bourgeois stands at the crossroads
> And shoves his nose into his collar.
> Beside him huddles with bristling hair
> A mangy dog, tail between its legs.
> The bourgeois stands like a hungry dog,
> He stands just like a wordless question mark.
> And the old world like a mongrel dog,
> Stands behind him, its tail between its legs.

The Bolsheviks were left wondering whether the poem was for or against them. The same concern existed in the mind of Blok himself. When an official from the Petrograd Soviet offered to publish it, Blok could not help asking, 'Don't you find that there is a somewhat regressive [*zapozdalaya*] note in *The Twelve*?' The official said that this had been a matter for discussion but that the decision had been in favour of publication, and Maxim Gorki assured Blok that Lenin and Lunacharski had given their blessing. The artist Yuri Annenkov was commissioned to supply the illustrations.[17]

But Blok's health, both physical and mental, was breaking down. In summer 1921 he pleaded for permission to go and convalesce at a Finnish sanatorium, but by then the Soviet authorities barred foreign travel to all but officially approved officials – or intelligence agents. A concession came too late for the poet, who died at the early age of forty. A writer who had welcomed the October Revolution had lost the desire to endorse the furies that it had released.

36. THE TREATY OF BREST-LITOVSK: CAPITULATION TO THE CENTRAL POWERS

Trotsky arrived at the peace talks with the Central Powers at Brest-Litovsk on 27 December. He immediately imposed his authority on the Russian negotiators by stamping out the informality that he felt had crept into proceedings and he ordered his team to eat their meals separately from the Germans and Austrians.[1]

Like Ioffe, he dazzled the Germans and Austrians with his command of the German language and its dialects and he enjoyed confusing them. When the Central Powers described their demands, he also mocked their jumbled usage of terms like state, nation and people. German diplomats thought they had an ace card in their hands with their proposal to give the territories under discussion the right of self-determination. This was their way of plotting to obtain sovereignty over the western borderlands of the former Russian Empire. Trotsky stayed calm and replied that he too supported the idea of plebiscites. The Germans' more effective initiative was to invite the Ukrainian Rada to take an independent part in the talks. But yet again Trotsky raised no objection. He remarked that some of the territories that Kiev claimed to be Ukrainian, especially those along the Black Sea coast, should be governed only by whoever won most votes in a referendum in the region – he was aware that several provinces contained Russians, Jews, Poles and Greeks who might be uneasy about the prospect of rule from Kiev. Trotsky, disregarding the Russo-Ukrainian boundary that Kerensky had accepted, exploited the fact that tsarist maps had not demarcated Ukraine as such. His purpose was to drag out the talks and gain time for revolutions to occur in Berlin, Vienna and Budapest.[2]

Sovnarkom aimed for world revolution and if it could not be accomplished in Europe, the Bolsheviks and their Socialist-Revolutionary allies would proclaim a 'revolutionary war' to bring about the desired result. Quite how long they would wait for Germany, Britain or France to experience a revolution like their own was unclear, but they were encouraged by the course of events in central Europe. Strikes broke out in Vienna after a cut was made in the flour ration. There was severe industrial unrest in German cities and in Budapest.[3]

By the turn of the year, though, the Central Powers presented an ultimatum at Brest-Litovsk, threatening to push on with their armed conquest unless Sovnarkom agreed to a separate peace on their terms. Trotsky thought a revolutionary war should now be conducted and saw the need for renewed military cooperation with the Western Allies – he would expect to turn on them as soon as revolution broke out in Berlin and Vienna. He returned to the Bolshevik Central Committee in Petrograd on 11 January 1918 to deliver his report on the Brest-Litovsk stalemate and outline his plans. In Petrograd, however, he suffered an unexpected collision: his comrade Lenin, famous for his advocacy of revolutionary war, had changed his mind about the Bolshevik war policy.

Lenin worried how willing the Russian troops might be to resume military operations. The answer was obvious to anyone who witnessed the emptying of Russia's trenches in summer and autumn – a phenomenon that Lenin's propaganda had played a part in instigating. Now Lenin saw no alternative to signing a peace with the Central Powers.

An angry dispute broke out at the Central Committee. Trotsky wanted to be authorized to return to Brest-Litovsk and drag out the talks further so as to give time for a German socialist revolution to take place. Bukharin countered that Sovnarkom should simply proclaim its promised revolutionary war. Lenin, who argued that such ideas were mere 'revolutionary posturing' after the Russian armed forces had already been demobilized, found himself in a minority. He was somewhat embarrassed by having Stalin as his strongest ally because Stalin denied that revolution was brewing in Europe. For Lenin, this was tantamount to a disavowal of the entire Bolshevik project, which was premised on the imminence of 'European socialist revolution'. But the Central Committee majority was against Lenin who had to accept help from whomever he could. The vote went in Trotsky's favour by twelve votes to one. Only two out of thirteen members, though, supported a declaration of war and Trotsky got ready to slow down the talks at Brest-Litovsk.[4]

Alexander Zamaraev of Vologda province was angry about Germany's territorial demands. On 3 January 1918 he wrote in his journal:

> At midday another snowstorm started, and it raged until morning [next day]. The kind of world that the Germans are agreed upon has astounded even our Bolsheviks. They are set to take from us Poland, Lithuania and Courland and a monetary contribution in return for the upkeep of prisoners, and our men must purge Galicia and part of Turkey. We are going to have to bear this German yoke for a long time. The war has left us a difficult legacy. Food alone is all that now occupies everyone's minds.[5]

Zamaraev was so sickened by Soviet rule that he cheered the rumours that the Germans had already conquered Petrograd: 'Everyone's almost pleased [. . .] if at least they'll bring about order instead of the detestable Bolshevik government that nobody needs.'[6] Like a vast number of other Russians, however, his deep desire was for the war to end with an honourable peace. Few could imagine Russia resuming the military struggle with Germany. Nikita Okunev in his journal on the same day asked where the Bolsheviks could possibly imagine getting anywhere near enough soldiers to fight for them. He scoffed at the idea that Sovnarkom would gain suitable men for combat from among the many army deserters or unemployed industrial workers.[7]

In January 1918 President Woodrow Wilson announced his Fourteen Points, which outlined what he wanted in the peace settlement to be made after military victory was achieved. Blame was heaped on Germany, which was to be required to leave the territories it had occupied in Belgium, France and Russia. Autonomous development was demanded for the diverse peoples of Austria–Hungary and the Ottoman Empire. Poland was to be set free. Wilson denounced 'the imperialists' and proclaimed the right of every nation to determine its future. His words overlapped the intentions of Sovnarkom's Decree on Peace in some respects but there was one crucial difference: the US president was aiming to bring the war to an end through the military defeat of the Central Powers, and he wanted global capitalism to survive and flourish. American diplomats distributed thousands of copies of translations of the Fourteen Points on the streets of Petrograd. Five and a half million copies were printed for shipment to the former Russian Empire.[8]

The Central Powers scythed through Trotsky's diplomatic ambitions at Brest-Litovsk by pursuing a separate peace settlement with the Ukrainian Rada. State Secretary Richard von Kühlmann signed the treaty with the Ukrainians on 27 January 1918.[9] The Central Powers also formally accepted the principles enunciated by President Wilson in his Fourteen Points. They were putting on a show of democratic, peace-loving intent while intending to subject the Central Rada to their control. Hindenburg and Ludendorff planned for Ukraine's military occupation and economic exploitation. They were silently marking down Ukrainian wheat, coal and iron for use by the Central Powers.

On 24 January, ever ready to tease, Trotsky sent a telegram asking for a visa to visit Vienna 'for the conduct of negotiations with representatives of the Austrian proletariat'. But he also had a serious move in mind which was without precedent in international diplomacy, and on 28 January unilaterally announced at the talks that the state of war with Germany, Austria–Hungary, Turkey and Bulgaria was 'terminated'. The Russians would not sign the German peace terms but at the same time were ceasing to fight. For von Kühlmann this was intolerable. If Trotsky was refusing to endorse a treaty, what was to be done about borders, trade and other matters of importance for the region under consideration? Trotsky replied that he had done all the talking that the powers entrusted to him permitted. As far as he was concerned, the negotiations – and the war – were at an end.[10]

Back in Russia itself, ideas of military counter-revolution had not disappeared with the suppression of Kornilov's revolt in August 1917. While most officers of the old army were content to be demobilized, a sizeable minority was determined to take up arms again. In the safety of the Don region of southern Russia, Kornilov and Mikhail Alexeev began to assemble their Volunteer Army. The Cossack settlements were a prime zone for military recruitment.[11] Alexeev had long thought Kornilov to have been over-promoted and to be lacking in operational judgement, but he overcame these reservations and the two of them worked to attract recruits, with initially most of their troops being ex-Imperial Army officers.

To prepare for the possibility of war at both home and abroad, Sovnarkom issued a call for volunteers to join a Workers' and Peasants' Red Army that would replace the now-demobilized Russian Army. Pay was offered at fifty dollars a month. A guarantee was given to look after their families.[12] A promise was also made to give recruits their old jobs back at decent wages when victory was won.[13] The Red Army also sought out military veterans with technical expertise and encouraged suitable former generals in the army of the tsar to join up.

Whereas the Left Socialist-Revolutionary Central Committee

maintained its total opposition to Lenin's advocacy of a separate peace, within the Bolshevik Central Committee he was making progress. He was encouraged that not all Bolsheviks who opposed him were reckless enough to call for a resumption of military operations. Trotsky espoused his own option of 'neither war nor peace' – Stalin scoffed that this was no policy at all from a practical standpoint. Yet still in the lower reaches of the party there was a large following, at least among committee members and militants, for resuming hostilities. But the war party quickly found that demobbed soldiers and Red Guards were usually unwilling to take the fight back to the Germans. The tide of opinion among Bolsheviks began to turn in favour of signing a peace with the Central Powers.

On 18 February Trotsky presented a report on the military situation to the Bolshevik Central Committee. Dvinsk had fallen to the Germans, and Soviet intelligence assessments suggested that they might be about to invade Ukraine. Lenin insisted: 'We mustn't play around with war.' Trotsky claimed that his delaying tactics had allowed the strikes to break out in Berlin and Vienna. Bukharin argued that even if the Germans were to take Petrograd, Sovnarkom could still mobilize Russia's workers and peasants against them. Lenin jabbed back: 'The peasant doesn't want war and won't go to war.' Zinoviev commented that it would have been better if a separate peace had been signed in November, but Trotsky's slogan of 'neither war nor peace' retained favour and he and Lenin composed a note of enquiry to be dispatched to the Central Powers.[14]

As Lenin and Zinoviev had predicted, the German terms had hardened further as the impatience and confidence of Germany's leadership grew about Russia's vulnerability. Sovnarkom was required to relinquish its claims to sovereignty over huge territories in the western territories of the former empire. Failure to sign the draft treaty would lead to a renewal of military operations that Soviet forces were bound to lose. The Central Committee met on 23 February in sombre mood. Its members were conscious that Germany had given them an ultimatum that would expire in twenty-four hours. Another deep military advance by the Germans was frighteningly close at hand. Petrograd was under threat. After Bukharin put forward his case for revolutionary war, Lenin barked at him: 'If you don't sign [these terms], you'll be signing the death warrant of Soviet power within three weeks.'[15] The point of decision between war and peace was reached and the voting went seven to four in Lenin's favour with Trotsky, Ioffe,

Dzierżyński and Krestinski abstaining. It was a stunning political victory for Lenin: the Bolshevik leadership had at last agreed that there was no practical alternative to signing a separate peace on the conditions that Germany required.[16]

Ukraine, Belorussia, Lithuania, Latvia and Estonia were assured their freedom from Russian pretensions. The Ottoman Empire would receive Kars and the port of Batumi. These 'lost' territories of the former Russian Empire amounted altogether to 1.2 million square miles and a combined population of around sixty million people. Although Lenin was Russia's prime mover of the case for a separate peace, he himself had no intention of signing the 'obscene' treaty and Trotsky had no intention of returning to Brest-Litovsk either. It therefore fell to another senior member of the negotiating team, Grigori Sokolnikov, to put his signature to the treaty on 3 March 1918.

A party congress was hurriedly convoked on 6 March. Lenin made no attempt to disguise the humiliation that the treaty brought upon Soviet Russia, but he declared that peace with the Central Powers provided a 'breathing space' to consolidate the revolution at home and get ready to promote it abroad.[17] He also secured a change of name for the party, that stressed the party's commitment to building communism, which was now to be called the Russian Communist Party (Bolsheviks). Trotsky had resigned from Sovnarkom in protest at the treaty, but Lenin coaxed him back by offering him the People's Commissariat for Military Affairs. The new Red Army would come under his control. Bukharin, who had campaigned for a policy of revolutionary war, stayed loyally at his desk at the *Pravda* editorial offices. But whereas the Bolshevik central leadership stayed largely intact, the Left Socialist-Revolutionaries denounced the treaty as a total betrayal of the revolution and all their people's commissars resigned from Sovnarkom.

The Bolsheviks did not trust the Germans and decided to move the capital from Petrograd to Moscow. Anger at the Brest-Litovsk treaty was widespread in Russia, despite the Bolsheviks clamping down further on the remaining newspapers in Moscow and Petrograd. Kadets and every political organization to the political right of them denounced the Brest-Litovsk terms as treason against the Russian people, and the Bolsheviks as the hirelings of German power. The Left Socialist-Revolutionaries remained in parts of the Soviet administration below the top level and maintained contact with Bolshevik leftists who had opposed the separate peace. The Western Allies, infuriated by the treaty, were equally active in seeking out anti-treaty Bolsheviks. Fearful of assassination, the precaution was taken for the Soviet leading cadre and their staff to live either inside the Kremlin precinct or at nearby grand hotels, and a heavy guard was mounted in Moscow's central zone.

The loss of Ukraine wrecked Sovnarkom's hopes of an early end to the food-supply crisis. Ukrainian farms had stopped trading with Russia in recent months, and the treaty terminated the possibility of a resumption. Most of the other Russian provinces, except for those in the southern Volga region, consumed more grain than they produced – and the Volga provinces were not yet under Soviet control. With the treaty signed, the Bolshevik leadership realized that the German and Austro-Hungarian forces might soon occupy all the Ukrainian provinces, including those in the Donbas. The Central Committee put in place plans to flood the mines and remove the coal stocks in the region. Workers too were to be evacuated.[18] As predicted, the German high command meanwhile maximized its advantage by transferring forty-eight divisions to the Western front in pursuit of decisive victory over the Anglo-French armies before the Americans could fully reinforce them.[19]

The Great War was entering its terminal phase. Morale in Germany's armed forces was high and its economic planners looked forward to getting food supplies from Ukraine.[20] The Ukrainian Central Rada kept secret the provision in its own treaty for Ukraine's grain to be shipped to the Central Powers.[21] In April, when the Rada failed to meet requirements, the Germans replaced it with an administration headed by Pavel Skoropadskyi.[22] Skoropadskyi, an aristocrat and monarchist, agreed to his elevation because he thought a Bolshevik plague had been seeded in Petrograd and he hoped to protect Ukraine against contagion. Twenty-nine German infantry divisions and four and a half cavalry divisions were shipped to occupy the Ukrainian provinces with Skoropadskyi as marionette ruler.[23]

The occupation forces in Ukraine itself were 300,000-strong.[24] The Germans, acting behind the screen of their puppet Ukrainian government, demanded the surrender of all weapons on the territory of Ukraine.[25] Soviet armed units had only 3,000 fighters in the Kiev area and about the same number elsewhere in Ukrainian territories. The last of them evacuated Ukraine in early May 1918.[26] Partisan actions were subsequently organized by Bolsheviks. This mainly involved sabotage of industrial installations and caused greater irritation than harm to the Skoropadskyi administration. For every German or Habsburg soldier killed the Central Powers shot the first ten 'Russian soldiers' or civilians they encountered.[27] There was consternation in the Bolshevik leadership in early May when German armed forces advanced from south-eastern Ukraine and occupied Rostov-on-Don, which was a Russian city by any definition except Berlin's. Many Bolsheviks suspected that the Brest-Litovsk treaty had been a trick to gain territory without a fight and then to take neighbouring parts of Russia itself by force. Grigori Sokolnikov and Stalin, who in early 1918 had backed the moves for a separate peace, demanded a change of plan. Lenin again ultimately held on to a majority in favour of abiding by the treaty but only by a small margin.[28]

Soviet politics and diplomacy needed to break out of its international isolation. Trotsky continued to cultivate ties with Allied representatives and to stress that Sovnarkom had not totally abandoned the idea of war with Germany. Kamenev was sent to France to re-establish links with its government but was banned from entering French territory. Adolf Ioffe set himself up in Berlin. As someone who had refused to endorse the peace treaty, Ioffe dedicated his efforts to fomenting revolutionary enthusiasm among his contacts within Germany's political far left.[29] The Western Allies, however, took a jaundiced view of Sovnarkom and secretly supplied encouragement and finance to those Russian political and military organizations that wanted to bring 'Soviet power' to an end and bring Russia back into the war.

37. A BREATHING SPACE FOR DICTATORSHIP?: CONFRONTING THE THREATS TO SOVNARKOM

Lenin had promised that the Brest-Litovsk treaty would give his party a breathing space to consolidate the revolution in Russia. Sovnarkom's security, if anything, became more precarious. As opposition to the Bolsheviks grew at home, an all-out civil war seemed inevitable.

Armed conflicts already proliferated throughout the former empire. Sovnarkom reinforced its reform agenda in April by proclaiming a state monopoly of foreign trade, on both imports and exports. But military preparedness took a fast-growing priority. The intention of forming a Red Army had already been announced in January but the People's Commissariat for Military Affairs was better at composing projects than in realizing them. Recruitment was difficult after so much effort had been put into demobilizing the old army. Meanwhile peasant challenges to 'Soviet power' gathered strength and violence broke out in the Urals region when Red Guards were sent out both to quell the trouble and obtain produce for the cities. Clashes occurred with ex-soldiers rallying to the cause of their villages. When the Perm Soviet dispatched artillery against revolts, the local peasantry dug earthworks to defend their positions and more than a hundred Red Guards were killed or wounded.[1] Workers across the Urals region joined in protests against Sovnarkom. There was also a concern among Bolsheviks that the Cossack force that Ataman Alexander Dutov had raised in Orenburg might move against Yekaterinburg, the Urals' capital.[2]

Political disruption became more frequent in April and May 1918 when a series of soviet elections were held. In city after city Mensheviks won majorities, almost surprising themselves by their success. The Bolsheviks were overturned in Tula and other important industrial centres. An alliance of Socialist-Revolutionaries and Mensheviks also triumphed in the cities of the Volga and the Russian north. Nizhni

Novgorod, Saratov and Archangel joined in the trend of disputing Sovnarkom's sovereignty. Even sleepy Vologda did.[3] There was also growing trouble for the Bolshevik party in its citadel, Petrograd, where workers bypassed the Bolshevik-dominated City Soviet and created the Assembly of Petrograd Factory Delegates.[4]

But the working class no longer had the organized potency it had been able to deploy in spring 1917. Many industrial workers had left industrial employment and returned to their villages, and there was widespread apathy about politics and the socialist movement was deeply divided. Sovnarkom, the sponsor of 'Soviet power' and 'proletarian democracy', had armed might at its disposal and the will to use it by closing down the Assembly and other such organizations. Force was also intensified in rural areas in a bid to deal with the crisis over food shortages. Requisitioning squads were strengthened even in regions that had scanty grain surpluses. The hope was to form 'committees of the village poor' to help in targeting the better-off peasantry.[5] In May 1918 Lenin proclaimed a Food Supply Dictatorship. He told Trotsky that the People's Commissariat for Military Affairs should direct nine tenths of the Red Army's efforts in getting grain from the villages. Peasants who hoarded their stocks should be treated as 'enemies of the people'. Lenin urged Sovnarkom to carry out 'a merciless and terroristic defence and war against the peasant bourgeoisie and any other bourgeoisie holding on to grain surpluses'.[6] He and Trotsky insisted that sufficient grain existed in the country if only it could be extracted from the grasp of 'the kulaks'. Trotsky called for the 'hand of force' to be used and for hoarders to be imprisoned for up to ten years.[7]

The Left Socialist-Revolutionaries, still irate about the Brest-Litovsk treaty, were appalled by Lenin's violence against peasants. In vain he explained that it was still his objective to promote a socialist transformation of the countryside. His former coalition partner saw the new committees of the village poor as an intolerable attempt to drive a wedge down the middle of the peasantry. In their eyes, Lenin was betraying his own Decree on Land.

When the Fifth Congress of Soviets met at the Bolshoi Theatre in Moscow on 4 July 1918 the scene was set for confrontation between the former coalition partners. Sverdlov, the diminutive chairman, made it clear that he would keep order in what everyone knew would be angry proceedings. German ambassador Count Wilhelm von Mirbach looked down from his box. Alongside Mirbach sat the Austrian, Hungarian, Bulgarian and Turkish ministers. Rudolph Bauer, head of the German intelligence service, was also in attendance. Across the auditorium sat the Allied diplomatic corps, who seethed with fury about the respect shown to the Central Powers. Many Bolsheviks felt the same, particularly those who had campaigned against the separate peace. Lenin spoke for the treaty, prowling the platform as he argued in favour of the opportunities provided by peace. The Left Socialist-Revolutionary leader Maria Spiridonova shouted out her party's fiery intransigence. She finished by shaking a fist at the box that held Mirbach, declaring that Russia would never submit to being one of Germany's colonies.[8]

Lenin already knew the Bolsheviks had a substantial voting majority at the Congress.[9] The Left Socialist-Revolutionaries were also aware of this, and so secretly they were plotting to get their way by a single spectacular act of terrorism. They planned to murder Ambassador von Mirbach at the German embassy on Denezhny Pereulok, a 'provocation' that would induce the Germans to rip up their agreement with the Bolsheviks, and put Sovnarkom back onto the path of revolutionary war with the Central Powers. A wild young Left Socialist-Revolutionary called Yakov Blyumkin was chosen to lead the action. Blyumkin worked for the Cheka and had the necessary warrants to enable him to enter the embassy building, where he carried out his task with efficiency. After securing an audience with the ambassador, Blyumkin shot and killed him at close range, then fled the scene amidst the noise and confusion.

The Left Socialist-Revolutionaries' action backfired though, as suddenly there was an opportunity for the Bolsheviks to clamp down on them. Lenin and Radek sped to the German embassy to offer their condolences and guarantee that severe reprisals would take place. Cheka Chairman Dzierżyński imprudently rushed to the Left Socialist-Revolutionary headquarters where he was placed under arrest until units of the Latvian Riflemen arrived to free him. Dzierżyński's deputy chairman, the Left Socialist-Revolutionary V. A. Alexandrovich, was among those executed. The last vestiges of the government coalition had disappeared and the territories under Soviet authority became a one-party state.

Resistance was on the rise even in central Russia. British agent Robert Bruce Lockhart surreptitiously passed funds to Boris Savinkov – the Socialist-Revolutionary who had served as one of Kerensky's military aides – for an armed uprising in Yaroslavl, 155 miles north-east of Moscow. Lockhart had told the War Cabinet in Westminster that success would depend on assistance from the British expeditionary force that had landed in Archangel. Savinkov had links to both the Volunteer Army in the Russian south and the Czechoslovak Legion. The French ambassador gave him exaggerated indications of the Allies' plans, even suggesting that a full-scale invasion was imminent. In Yaroslavl, Savinkov proclaimed the end of the Bolshevik dictatorship and restored freedom of trade. As a Socialist-Revolutionary he felt sure that this would spark a vast peasant rebellion in many provinces. Over-confidence had always been his prominent feature. No bigger risk did he take, however, when he occupied Yaroslavl. Within days his force was isolated and defeated – and Savinkov belatedly saw the foolishness of his *démarche*.[10]

Foreign military intervention, however, continued. The French landed a naval squadron at Odessa on the Black Sea coast. The Japanese conducted a strategic incursion into eastern Siberia, and the Americans, being both wary of Japan's imperial ambition and determined to overturn Sovnarkom, sent forces to occupy the eastern section of the Trans-Siberian railway. When the British expeditionary contingent helped to establish a northern government in Archangel under the Socialist-Revolutionary Nikolai Chaikovski, the Bolsheviks had to organize a military operation to protect Petrograd. They also took ruthless measures against the 'bourgeoisie' to ensure security in Soviet-occupied territories. Hostages were seized to deter actions by enemy forces or their local supporters. Alexander Zamaraev witnessed that several better-off inhabitants in Totma, which lies nearly 500 miles south of Archangel, were taken into custody. Not everyone put under arrest was rich by any standard. Teachers were included as teaching was treated as a suspect occupation.[11]

A still sharper threat to Sovnarkom came from the Volga region where the Socialist-Revolutionary deputies of the dispersed Constituent Assembly established an alternative government in Samara, calling itself the Committee of Members of the Constituent Assembly, to challenge Sovnarkom. Known by its acronym Komuch, it raised the red flag over their buildings, determined not to let the Bolsheviks have a monopoly of that colour in public symbolism. Komuch assembled its own People's Army and readied itself for a military offensive that would crush the Red Army and reinstate the Constituent Assembly as the fount of political power. But the Socialist-Revolutionaries had constant difficulty in gaining peasant support. Peasants wanted to keep the land they had acquired since the fall of the Romanovs. They also resented the conscription campaign imposed upon them, and the demands for supplying grain. Komuch reacted by ordering beatings and executions.[12] The Socialist-Revolutionaries' reputation amidst the peasantry collapsed.[13]

They were no more sympathetic to Bolshevik commissars who treated the rural population simply as a resource for grain and conscripts. Trotsky had soon recognized that workers alone would not supply a sufficient number of recruits and that mass conscription in the countryside was essential. Red Army squads went into the countryside and ordered peasant elders to supply young men of the age cohort that was required. Non-compliance meant severe punishments.

Trotsky coordinated the Red Army's operational response while Lenin steadied nerves in Sovnarkom. By July 1918 the Czechs were approaching Yekaterinburg where the former emperor Nicholas II and his family were now being held captive. There was concern among Bolsheviks in the Urals that, if liberated, the Romanovs would become figureheads of an offensive against Sovnarkom. Such a fear was ill-founded in the short term because the Czechs had no fondness for Nicholas, but Bolsheviks were in no mood to take risks with their security. Lenin gave secret instructions for Nicholas, Alexandra and their four children to be killed. At dead of night on 17–18 July 1918 the family were roused from their sleep in Ipatev House in Yekaterinburg. The order was suddenly given for the detainees to assemble in the cellar. The family thought they were about to be transported to another place of confinement. They were ordered to stand in a line along with some of their servants and the family's pet dog. Alexandra was allowed to sit in a chair by reason of her ill-health. But then suddenly the armed men facing them in the cellar were commanded to level their weapons. Nicholas despairingly asked what was happening, but the firing started and was soon over. The entire Romanov group was riddled with bullets. Their corpses were loaded onto lorries and ferried beyond the city outskirts to a disused mining area, where they were dumped into old mineshafts. Acid was poured over them to disguise their identities.

Pravda announced Nicholas's execution but was silent about the others who were murdered. Responsibility for the killing was attributed exclusively to the Yekaterinburg communist leadership. No hint was given of Moscow's part in the decision.[14] In the weeks that followed, the Soviet administration also executed other captured Romanovs in Petrograd and elsewhere in the Urals. Anyone with a genetic tie to the deposed dynasty was liable to be killed. News about the murders was severely restricted but Metropolitan Antoni in Kiev conducted a funeral mass for Nicholas which was well attended.[15]

The Cheka throughout the year had been extending its policing efforts and hardening the way it treated alleged 'enemies of the people'. In mid-March 1918 the Moscow Soviet ordered people not carrying out 'publicly necessary work' to leave the city by the end of the month. They were told they would no longer be receiving ration cards. How they were meant to find refuge or food was not made clear.[16] Rules on inheritance were changed in April so that a deceased person's property automatically passed to the state, which received discretionary power over whether or not to hand it on to the family.[17] In July 1918 the fifth Congress of Soviets approved the draft for a new Constitution. The dictatorship advocated by Lenin throughout the previous year was tightened, and civic rights were withdrawn from the aristocracy, gentry, industrialists, bankers, clergy and ex-gendarmes. In chilling language they were all described as 'former people'. They could not vote and had no access to state welfare. On 26 July it was proclaimed that young men of 'bourgeois' origin were not welcome as Red Army recruits. Instead they were required to offer themselves to carry out manual labour. If they shirked their assigned tasks they would face a revolutionary tribunal and forfeit their property.[18]

The earliest recruits to the Red Army by design were volunteers from the working class. Bolshevik leaders believed that a proletarian vanguard was the best way to guarantee victory. Some workers were genuinely eager to further the revolutionary cause. Others, having lost their factory jobs, saw military deployment as the best way to obtain better rations and pay for themselves and their families. Trotsky's organizational dynamism had an immediate impact. Officers from the Imperial Army were offered command roles as they prepared for action against Komuch. This caused consternation among veteran Bolsheviks like Stalin. The tsarist officer corps had crushed the 1905–6 Revolution and had promoted Russian chauvinism and anti-Semitic behaviour of the ugliest form in the Great War. Many of its members had assisted or sympathized with Kornilov when he attempted his coup d'état and they could not be trusted. This seemed to be borne out, when in July, Mikhail Muravëv, who led the Red Army on the Eastern front, mutinied. He planned to expand his revolt over the whole Volga region. He was shot in Simbirsk after being surrounded by troops loyal to Sovnarkom. Trotsky was more careful about his subsequent military appointments.

Even so, an order was put out in mid-August 1918 for all previous Imperial Army officers under the age of sixty to report for duty. Many feared it was a cover for their arrest and execution, but Trotsky was definite about the need to recruit them. By 1920 an impressive number of around 75,000 of them were enlisted. The Red Army also recruited 12,000 from those who had fought against it in the series of conflicts that raged throughout the former Russian Empire after 1917 – many such officers, having fallen into Red captivity, took up service with the Reds as the alternative to being shot.[19] There were grumblings among Bolsheviks that Lenin was foolish to trust Trotsky, but when reports came through that Komuch's People's Army had taken Simbirsk Trotsky's presence and the skills of the Latvian Riflemen turned things around, and the People's Army was prevented from moving onwards to Nizhni Novgorod. The Reds, destroyers of the old Imperial Army, were proving that they themselves had military potential. Trotsky sent a telegram to Lenin on 17 August 1918 advising against allowing the Red Cross to sail ships down the Volga at a time when he had ordered his artillerymen and aviators to fire into 'the bourgeois districts' of Kazan, Simbirsk and Samara. He wanted there to be no illusions about the possibility of avoiding civil war.[20]

Lenin set a murderous agenda throughout summer 1918 in order to clamp down on any enemies, real or imagined. On 11 August he ordered the party in Penza:

> Comrades! The rising of the five kulak districts should be pitilessly suppressed. The interests of the whole revolution require this because 'the last decisive battle' with the kulaks is now under way everywhere.
>
> An example must be demonstrated.
>
> 1. Hang (and make sure that the hanging takes place in full view of the people) no fewer than one hundred known kulaks, rich men, bloodsuckers.
> 2. Publish their names.
> 3. Seize all their grain from them.
> 4. Designate hostages in accordance with yesterday's telegram. Do it in such a fashion that for hundreds of kilometres around the people might see, tremble, know, shout: they are strangling and will strangle to death the bloodsucking kulaks.

Lenin finished his orders with the command: 'Find some truly hard people.'[21]

He evidently believed that 'the people' had to be brought into line by both brutality and the spectacle of it. Despite his many appeals to the mass of the peasantry in 1917, he told V. P. Antonov-Saratovski, the leader of the Saratov Bolsheviks, that the peasants were 'an evil people'.[22] When the Soviet-held city of Baku on the Caspian coast was reported as likely to be attacked, Lenin ordered the Cheka leadership there to threaten to raze it to the ground. His rationale was that a public proclamation to this effect would deter potential collaborationists from entering the fray against Soviet rule.[23]

An attempt had been made on Lenin's life in January but he had escaped unharmed. On 31 August, he gave an open-air speech to the Mikhelson Factory workforce. Afterwards as he made his way to the waiting limousine, shots were fired at him. Lenin slumped to the ground and blood poured from him. His chauffeur Stepan Gil sped him back to the Kremlin rather than to the nearest hospital in case doctors or nurses made a further attack on him. No surgeon was on duty at the Kremlin curtilage. One bullet had hit Lenin's shoulder blade and punctured his lung, and another was later found at the base of his neck. Two wives of leading Bolsheviks who had some clinical training carried out some rudimentary care, whilst Lenin's wife Nadezhda and sister Maria sought out medicines. Fanny Kaplan, a Socialist-Revolutionary, was accused of firing the shots. Her extremely poor eyesight made it unlikely that her party comrades would have selected her to be the assassin, but the Chekists, wanting to announce a quick outcome, took her from her cell and executed her. Elsewhere hundreds of captives were executed in the prisons with aristocrats and any wealthy citizens the prime victims.

Lenin survived and was back at meetings in mid-September, his power and reputation as leader consolidated.[24] He and Sverdlov created an informal duumvirate. Lenin chaired Sovnarkom and the Bolshevik Central Committee while Sverdlov served as Central Committee secretary and as chairman of the All-Russia Central Executive Committee of the Congress of Soviets. Severe hostility grew between Trotsky and Stalin, and it was Lenin who had to manage it. Trotsky complained that Stalin was conducting a terror campaign on the Southern front near Tsaritsyn on the river Volga and continually flouting the orders of the high command. Stalin was unrepentant. He could expect Lenin's approval about this. But Trotsky persuaded Lenin that Stalin was disrupting military effectiveness by firing and abusing experienced officers from the Imperial Army. Lenin had become the arbiter of all disputes.

In August the Brest-Litovsk treaty was called into question yet again after Ludendorff and Hindenburg demanded a revision of the original terms. Germany's March Offensive had failed to crack the spine of the British and French forces on the Western front. American troops were being shipped and readied for service on the continent. Panic gripped the German military planners. Russian money and material resources were urgently needed for victory. A supplementary treaty was signed on 27 August. Soviet Russia had to transfer gold reserves to the value of six billion German marks to Berlin. It was also compelled to disclaim sovereignty over northern Latvia and Estonia. The Germans would be allowed to purchase a quarter of Baku's oil output, and Sovnarkom undertook to make an effort to eject Great Britain's expeditionary force from Archangel and Murmansk and to aid whatever operation that Germany might mount against the British in northern Russia.[25]

But while Imperial Germany aimed to gouge one last offensive out of its exhausted armies, Ioffe's reports from the German capital boosted Sovnarkom's confidence. The Central Powers were falling apart militarily and financially. Chancellor Max von Baden resigned in early November. Kaiser Wilhelm abdicated after seeing that his own position was untenable. On 11 November 1918 an armistice was signed in the Compiègne forest between Germany and the Western Allies. Bolshevik leaders experienced a renewal of the confidence that had carried them into the seizure of power in Petrograd in October 1917. Events were appearing to confirm their case for revolutionary optimism. Sverdlov took the initiative in September in making plans for an international communist congress in Moscow.[26] Lenin halted shipments of Russian gold bullion to Berlin.[27]

In early October 1918 he had ordered grain to be laid aside in Soviet warehouses for transfer to Germany when the expected revolutionary upsurge took place there. His priority was for the Bolshevik party to supply Red Germany with whatever assistance it might need. The requisitioning squads, helped by committees of the village poor, were to build up food supplies not only for the hungry cities of Russia but also for dispatch to the 'German workers'. Lenin simultaneously demanded a further expansion of military conscription to build a Red Army of three million troops by spring 1919. His intention was to afford help for 'the international workers' revolution'.[28]

His Soviet administration had survived the summer months by the slimmest of margins. If Germany had triumphed on the Western front, neither the Brest-Litovsk treaty nor its August supplementary provisions would have saved Sovnarkom from a German invasion. Now, however, the Red Army could concentrate on the internal uprisings. The Red Army showed surprising resilience by retaking Kazan on 8 September. Komuch ordered the evacuation of Samara eleven days later. The Volga region was coming under Soviet rule.[29]

But just when the Bolshevik Reds were triumphing over the Komuch Reds in their armed struggle, civil war spread to other regions and brought other forces into contention. Counter-revolutionary forces calling themselves the Whites emerged from outlying parts of the former empire to challenge Sovnarkom. Starting from late 1918, White offensives spread throughout Russia, including Siberia and Ukraine. The Whites chose their colour as a symbol of purity to distinguish themselves from the Bolsheviks. Their contingents were led by ex-commanders from the armed forces of Nicholas II and the Provisional Government. They felt stung by the humiliations endured by the officer corps in 1917. Their propaganda emphasized a commitment to 'Russia One and Indivisible' and to 'Holy Russia'. National minorities, the Jews above all others, were excluded from the vision of the desired state that White commanders were fighting for. Stress was placed on the need to restore the Russian Orthodox Church to the forefront of public life. They condemned the communists as 'Jew-Bolsheviks' who had taken pieces of silver from the Germans and committed treason against the fatherland. The need to reconstitute and restore 'order' to the lands of the Russian Empire was an article of faith for Whites. When the Finnish commander Mannerheim offered military assistance in return for approval of Finland's independence he was turned down. Similar overtures from the Poles in 1920 were ignored in the same spirit.

But each of the White contingents had to surmount severe difficulties before being ready to confront the Red forces. The Volunteer Army formed by Alexeev and Kornilov in the winter of 1917–18 met resistance in southern Russia and had to retreat to the Don region. Kornilov himself had been killed in action in April 1918 and Alexeev died of chronic cardiac disease in September. Anton Denikin, who had spoken his mind to Kerensky in July 1917, had taken over the army's leadership and prepared for a spring 1919 campaign. On 18 November 1918, as the Volunteer Army reorganized itself in the south of Russia, Admiral Alexander Kolchak overthrew the Socialist-Revolutionaries who still held power in Omsk in western Siberia. He then proclaimed himself Supreme Ruler. Kolchak had commanded the Black Sea fleet until midsummer 1917, when he resigned his post under pressure from both Kerensky and the revolutionary parties in Sevastopol. He had yet to define his ties to Denikin and the Volunteer Army but with encouragement from the Western Allies he massed his Russian Army to move through to the Urals in the direction of Moscow. It seemed at last that the White movement would present an effective threat to Sovnarkom.

The Red Army dug trenches and erected barricades to halt Kolchak's advance at Perm on the western slopes of the mountain range. But the Urals regional party and governmental leadership in the city had crumbled and the Red Army units fled the defence of Perm both into the provincial hinterland and along the railway towards the capital. Kolchak seemed invincible. Having spent most of the year concerned about containing the German military might, Lenin finished it near to despair about the Red Army's capacity to defend the October Revolution against its Russian foes.

38. STATE-BUILDING IN REVOLUTION: THE ONE-PARTY STATE AND THE RED ARMY

The Perm disaster terrified the communist leaders – even Trotsky and Stalin stopped quarrelling for a while. In January 1919 Stalin and Dzierżyński were sent to investigate what had happened in the Urals fighting. Trotsky argued that there had been too much 'softness' and he urged Stalin to purge the guilty commissars: as long as Stalin was kept out of military strategy, Trotsky could find a use for him.[1] Stalin and Dzierżyński reported back to Moscow on an alarming situation that involved the complete collapse of the Soviet administration in the region. The Red Army was in chaos, demoralized and ill-disciplined. The local communist party bodies were ineffectual, and their leadership had failed to show the necessary resolve. Stalin and Dzierżyński called for a complete reorganization to avoid further catastrophes. The vertical hierarchy had to be strengthened. Functions in party, government and army had to be clearly demarcated. The entire Soviet state required immediate radical reform if victory was to be achieved in the civil war between Reds and Whites.[2]

For the commanders of the White armies, by contrast, military operations were the preoccupation. They themselves spared little thought for the tasks of state-building. All of them had had long careers in the Imperial armed forces. They had been scarred by their experiences in 1917 when, in their opinion, Russia had been betrayed by Kerensky's poor statesmanship and delivered into the hands of Bolshevik devils. While Kolchak rampaged westward along the Trans-Siberian railway through the Urals in December 1918, Denikin was finishing preparations for a campaign that he would launch from southern Russia in the springtime. An anti-Bolshevik army under Nikolai Yudenich, too, was forming in newly independent Estonia within striking range of Petrograd. Stung by the humiliations endured by the officer corps in 1917, Kolchak, Denikin and Yudenich aimed to recover the lands of the old empire and reintroduce the orderly traditions in which their forces would enjoy respect and authority.

The early White volunteers were themselves ex-officers but soon the Whites were conscripting peasant recruits from the countryside. Kolchak and Denikin attracted Kadets and other politicians who formed local governments in the territories they occupied and tried to attract popular support. Administration was based on the foundations of the pre-revolutionary dumas and zemstvos. Finance was initially hard to come by. Kolchak benefited from the rescue of a huge part of the Imperial administration's gold reserve from Kazan in summer 1918, which allowed him to pay for foreign military supplies.[3] Overtures were made to the Western Allies, who appointed representatives to the White general headquarters. Money, rifles and, more plentifully, advice were made available in Omsk and Novocherkassk. The British remained in Archangel, the French in Odessa. Into eastern Siberia flooded forces from Japan and the United States. The Whites controlled the provincial presses and their armies hunted down not just Bolsheviks but everyone who had been active in the socialist movement before the October Revolution. Torture and savage executions were commonplace and the White terror became just as barbaric as the Red terror.

Military aims took precedence over civil governance. The dominant goal was to occupy Moscow and the physical destruction of 'Soviet power'. Kolchak fought under the slogan of 'Russia One and Indivisible'. He aimed to reconstitute the Imperial lands and made no concessions to ideas of national autonomy for the non-Russians. On land reform he wanted to win peasant support, but he did nothing to stop the former landowners from reclaiming their estates as his army advanced westward, and all the White armies were ruthless in the requisitioning of grain to feed their forces. There were also many anti-Semites among White officers. Jews were few in the Urals but there were large communities in southern Russia and Ukraine where Denikin was on the move, and many pogroms took place in the areas under occupation by the Volunteer Army.

The Western Allies wrote to Kolchak from Paris on 26 May 1919 to spell out their policy towards Russia. Their support would depend on the anti-Bolshevik forces agreeing to hold a free election to a Constituent Assembly in the event of a White victory. A requirement was laid down for land reform. There was to be recognition of the independence of both Poland and Finland. Governments in the Baltic region, the Caucasus and the territories east of the Caspian Sea were to exercise autonomy until such time as a settlement could be reached in consultation with the League of Nations. Kolchak was also asked to reconfirm the recognition of Russia's foreign debts.[4] His reply on 4 June 1919 was less than positive on certain matters. A new Constituent Assembly would be elected when victory and peace was realized. Poland would keep its independence, but Kolchak declined to offer the same guarantees about Finland and the other territories of the former Russian Empire mentioned in the dispatch from Paris – he insisted that this was for the Constituent Assembly to decide.[5] The Western Allies expressed satisfaction at Kolchak's attitude. While he was showing at least some degree of flexibility they declined to press him further.[6]

Although Kolchak and Denikin kept contact with each other, they did not coordinate their campaigns. The unspoken assumption was that whoever got to Moscow first would be doing Russia a favour. Military operations were their consuming passion. Leading Bolsheviks were equally determined to prosecute the war but they also gave priority to achieving unity of purpose between the front and the rear. With this in mind, they ensured that the big decisions stayed in the hands of the central party leadership. The war was going to be fought on terms that were set by the civilian leadership. The Bolshevik civilian leadership showed remarkable facility in studying the arts of war. Even Lenin, Bukharin and Kamenev, who never went near any of the fronts, regularly sought advice from experienced army commanders. The fate of the October Revolution depended on this willingness to learn.

About politics, though, they thought for themselves. In 1917 the party leadership had welcomed as many new members as wanted to join the ranks. Within months of the October Revolution, some of these recruits were discovered to be abusing their authority, and in May 1918 a purge of the ranks – or 'cleansing' – was ordered to get rid of 'idlers, hooligans, adventurers, drunkards and thieves'.[7] Others left the party voluntarily, disappointed about the lack of implementation of much of what had been promised in 1917. With the outbreak of the Civil War, the Red Army sought new recruits and Bolshevik leaders called upon party members to enlist. Soon a majority of members were on active military service. If they refused the call-up, they had to leave the party. Commitment to the Soviet cause now meant risking your life for the Reds.

Many party members, moreover, stayed true in their daily habits to the precepts that had drawn them to Bolshevism. In late summer

1918 Anton Okninski met a communist railway official called Ochnev, a former fitter at the Nikolaev Railway Main Works, who told him that although he had the formal right to a first-class coupé all to himself, he wanted communism to mean something in practice.[8] At the other end of the party membership range was the unfortunate postman who talked to Okninski a few weeks later in Tambov province. He was a Lithuanian who had come south, like Okninski, in search of food and shelter, and had married locally. Disaster struck when his wife succumbed to typhus. A postman's wages were not enough to look after their children. His mother-in-law, a woman of foul temper, physically assaulted him until he agreed to join the Bolshevik party. She had told him that this was the best way to improve conditions for the family. The Lithuanian did as she demanded and enrolled. But as things turned out, party membership was not always a ticket to prosperity and the family continued to live in poverty.[9]

Chaos and insubordination, moreover, were rampant in the making of policies and their practical implementation. The Civil War accentuated the need for drastic measures to make the process more effective. Soviets and trade unions were in the habit of doing as they pleased and the further they were from Moscow, the likelier it was they would ignore official policies. The government and other public agencies were full of internal tensions. Alexander Shlyapnikov's People's Commissariat of Transport clashed with the All-Russia Railwaymen's Union even though Shlyapnikov was a passionate believer in the rights of unionists. Institutional rivalry intensified with the onset of civil war. The Red Army and Trotsky's People's Commissariat for Military Affairs wanted to maximize the number of peasant conscripts whereas the People's Commissariat of Agriculture wanted calm in the villages for its officials to spread modern farming techniques amidst the peasantry. Meanwhile the Cheka acted as a law unto itself and overrode every civilian public body. At Central Committee and Sovnarkom meetings there were frequent altercations before policies could be settled.

Lenin was a stern arbiter of discussion and introduced a ten-ruble fine for late attendance at Sovnarkom.[10] He set time limits on contributions to discussions. When Cheka Chairman Feliks Dzierżyński lit up a cigarette at the green-baize table, he received a reprimand and had to repair to the chimney breast where his smoke would not annoy Lenin. Most of the other people's commissars were also smokers but everyone acknowledged that the word of Lenin, who hated the use of tobacco, was final in matters of procedure.

The leadership also realized that every public institution had officials in place who disapproved of the October Revolution. Many had stayed in post only because they needed to earn a living, and hatred of Bolshevism was rife. From Menshevik economists to former Imperial Army officers there was plenty of reason for Bolsheviks to feel distrustful. They came to the practical judgement that the party should be turned into the primary agency of Soviet statehood. There had always been a fundamental tension in Bolshevik thinking between the beliefs in strong control from above and strong control from below. The Bolsheviks were centralists and localists before they took power. The experience of government increasingly convinced them that the urgent current need was to prioritize the building of a centralized state order with the party at its core.

Lenin functioned as a kind of state coordinator-general. It was ironic that he took on such a role. He had given his party a lifelong model of personal disobedience. His wrangles with the Left Communists, who were a majority in the central and provincial leaderships, had very nearly caused an irrevocable split. Except for occasional country breaks he stayed constantly in the capital. He seldom even left the Kremlin apart from when he was scheduled to deliver a public speech. Until March 1918 he and Sverdlov governed in tandem but there was never a doubt as to which of the two was in charge. When Sverdlov died of the Spanish influenza in mid-March 1919, only Lenin remained. But the other members of the core of the central party leadership were willing to confront him on the principles of Bolshevism, and party congresses continued to have stormy debates. It took all Lenin's tactical acumen to preserve party unity. The Central Committee could not meet frequently with so many of its members absent at the front or elsewhere. The solution was to create a couple of inner subcommittees, the Political Bureau (Politburo) and Organizational Bureau (Orgburo).

The foundations had been laid for a singular invention: a one-party state in which the party was the dominant institution. At every level of governance it was a party committee that directed policy and selected personnel. The hierarchy that stretched from the Central Committee and Politburo down to the district party committees was strictly enforced.

The result was the emergence of the committee chairman as the real power. By autumn 1920 this process was to be given formal endorsement from Moscow with a small change in nomenclature: instead of chairmen, the bosses of party committees were to be called secretaries.[11]

This reflected a lingering wish to avoid the impression of one-person rule even while imposing it. The 'centre' was the exception to this trend. Lenin went on chairing the Central Committee and its Politburo but never received the permanent title of chairman. The Politburo and, in its infrequent meetings, the Central Committee continued to hold spirited debates. When the Politburo could not arrive at agreement, the Central Committee acted as arbiter. If ever the Central Committee could not settle its internal dispute, the yearly party congress imposed a settlement. To that extent, central party management retained its flexibility. But it sat over a growth of quasi-military inflexibility down through the provincial levels to the lowliest party cell.

Party 'patriotism' grew at every level of the hierarchy. Bolshevik veterans began to form their own caste – Trotsky was to denounce this in later years but not at the time of its early development. The party's officials were thinly spread in the Soviet state they were building. They compensated by toughening their rhetoric. Some of them took their cue from Sverdlov by commissioning leather apparel. Black boots, jackets and trousers were widely worn. When Bolshevik political commissars returned on furlough from one of the fronts of the Civil War, they reinforced the military ethic in party life. Increasingly the party looked on the state as the instrument it needed to transform society whether workers or peasants liked it or not. The 'people' became seen as a huge pile of wax to be moulded as the Politburo and party committees in the localities demanded.

The precise nature of the mould was yet to be decided, and workers were encouraged to play an active role in the Soviet administration and to offer themselves for public office. It was to be a dictatorship of the proletariat with as many proletarians as possible. Institutions were flooded with entrants. It was the soviets that constituted the supreme bodies of power and as their agencies increased in number, the appeals intensified for the working class to volunteer for administrative service. Promotions from the factory bench were plentiful. Jobs with managerial responsibility were attractive as a respite from heavy manual labour. But many workers were at the same time siphoned off into the Red Army and still the civilian agencies of the revolutionary state were crying out for staff. Literacy and numeracy were essential qualifications. Posts were increasingly filled by people who pretended to be of working-class origin. Alexander Zamaraev saw this for himself in Totma. As normal business ceased, artisans and tradesmen faced penury. They gained pay and ration cards by taking up employment in official agencies. Eleven of them gained jobs at the Totma fever station as a typhus epidemic spread.[12] Applicants for administrative posts had an advantage if they had an education, but it was also a drawback because others in the office could accuse them of hiding a 'bourgeois' background. Ex-bank official Anton Okninski had this kind of trouble on arrival in Tambov province from Petrograd. With his cover blown, he bribed an official with some of his precious cigars to keep quiet.[13]

Only a few of the leading Bolsheviks had experience in occupations outside journalism and publishing. People's Commissar of Trade and Industry Leonid Krasin was a qualified engineer. Generally, though, engineers, land surveyors, schoolteachers, medical doctors, statisticians and even professional economic planners were rare in the party. If Soviet Russia was to make progress in science, order, social discipline, coordination and outreach of governance, the Bolsheviks had to fish in the pool of available talent outside the party's membership.

Sovnarkom, like the Provisional Government before it, recognized the need for help from people with specialist expertise. Although the Bolsheviks regarded them with suspicion, they could not govern without them. The professionals for their part shared in the zeal to 'modernize' society. Some famous left-wing economists eagerly produced prospectuses for a comprehensive economic plan. The Menshevik Vladimir Groman and Kerensky's former Deputy Agriculture Minister Alexander Chayanov drew up schemes for the modernization of town and countryside, and their works were widely published. Many teachers were only too happy to drop God from the curriculum and experiment with new methods of education. The land surveyors and agronomists working for the People's Commissariats of Agriculture and Food Supply were pleased about official encouragement to nudge the peasantry into innovative ways of tending the soil.

The Bolsheviks abolished the dumas, the zemstvos, the old courts and other existing organs of governance, which they regarded as bastions of 'bourgeois' privilege. Soviets and party committees were empowered to supplant the old official networks of administration. This was harder to accomplish in the countryside than in the towns. The villages had few soviet and party cells, and so Sovnarkom controlled the rural areas mainly by the practices of occasional visitation, always armed to the teeth. From mid-1918 the nascent Soviet network was supplemented by committees of the village poor. But rather than securing state rule in the countryside, the committees divided peasant against peasant and disrupted Soviet administrative progress.[14] They also became notorious for injustice and corruption.[15] It was said that the new rural courts merely gave the local horse thief a chance to become a judge and take bribes. Honest peasants lamented the loss of the old district system of justice.[16]

Almost without planning, Bolshevism's inner tension between centralist authoritarianism and mass democratism was resolving itself by extremes of authoritarianism that no Bolshevik leader had predicted before seizing power. Authoritarian tendencies had always been part of Bolshevik thinking, but it had been accompanied by assurances about a revolution from below. Very quickly these assurances had been smashed on the anvil of the harsh reality of civil war.

39. THE PIVOT OF CIVIL WAR: REDS VERSUS WHITES

At the start of 1919 it had looked perfectly possible that Kolchak's Russian Army would advance westward and occupy Moscow. His intelligence units reported on the panic in the Soviet leadership. Kolchak ordered the main part of his forces to fight its way along the southern branch of the Trans-Siberian railway from Perm towards Ufa, some 250 miles away. Ufa quickly fell to the Whites as Perm had done. But by late April the Red Army had found the resilience to counterattack and halt the White advance. Ufa was reoccupied by the Reds on 9 June.[1]

Trotsky was ecstatic but continued to face criticism both for disrespecting veteran Bolsheviks and for employing former Imperial Army officers. A so-called Military Opposition in the party had formed to reverse his policies. His Bolshevik enemies had not forgiven him for sanctioning the execution of the communist Nikolai Panteleev, a political commissar who served in the Volga region in the previous summer. Panteleev had joined a Red retreat which he had been ordered to prevent. Trotsky approved his execution as a cowardly deserter.[2] Moreover, he insisted on continuing to recruit experienced 'specialists' from the Imperial Army. Trotsky told Lenin of the thousands of such officers who were performing necessary military functions, and Lenin spoke on Trotsky's side of the dispute at the party congress in March 1919.[3] He also recounted the irresponsibility of communist leaders on the Southern front in the previous year – a sparsely disguised jibe at Stalin.[4]

In July 1919 Trotsky replaced Jukums Vācietis as main commander-in-chief with Sergei Kamenev. The Reds had a total strength of 788,000 troops at the beginning of 1919. Of these, most had non-combat roles. The People's Commissariat for Military Affairs could muster 102,000 troops for fighting on the fronts. Nearly all of them were kept in the east against Kolchak, who had assembled 110,000 front-line fighters.

The Reds had a slight edge in artillery and machine guns at their disposal.[5] Kolchak's Russian Army was remorselessly driven back eastwards along the Trans-Siberian railway. The retreat provided no opportunity to strengthen his frail administration, and his gaze stayed on purely military concerns. He became reliant on the material and diplomatic support from the Western Allies, which he knew would become elusive if his combat readiness appeared to be flagging. The British supplied munitions via Vladivostok as Siberian stores and output were wholly inadequate. London, however, could not solve the problem of the thinness of Siberia's population. The conscription squads had their work cut out. Young peasant men ran off to evade enlistment in the White cause. Anti-White uprisings grew frequent. The quality of officers also left much to be desired. Few of them had gained training at a high level before the Great War.[6]

Denikin broke out of southern Russia and by late June 1919 reached Tsaritsyn on the Volga and Kharkov near the Donbas. Unlike Kolchak, he had the advantage of being able to count on Cossack cavalry. Denikin also received Allied aid of 200,000 rifles, 1,000 artillery and 6,200 machine guns with tanks and aircraft also supplied.[7]

His combined contingents called themselves the Armed Forces of Southern Russia and in their initial northward surge they trounced everything that the Reds threw against them. Trotsky appreciated the professionalism of the enemy but he castigated Alexander Shlyapnikov, the leading political commissar in the region, for his failure to stem their advance. Shlyapnikov in turn blamed Moscow for refusing him the reinforcements he had demanded.[8] But as Denikin's army moved north, supplies from his base dwindled. Supplies of equipment from the British slowed, and the French in April 1919 were already starting their withdrawal from Odessa.[9] Local Ukrainian peasants suspected that a White victory would put land reform in jeopardy, and feared losing grain stores and conscripts to the Whites. They formed armed bodies, which became known as the Greens, and their attacks on Denikin's forces held up his progress northward. The Reds too were strengthening their forces. After evacuating Kharkov, they formed a defensive line to save further large cities from the White advance.

On 3 July 1919, from his temporary base at Tsaritsyn, Denikin issued his secret Moscow Directive to the Armed Forces of Southern Russia which set out his priority to move on to the capital and overthrow Sovnarkom. The plan was to make the advance along the railway lines, splitting the offensive into three sectors under Generals Pëtr Vrangel, Vladimir Mai-Maevski and Vladimir Sidorin. Coordination among them was loose, though, and some of Denikin's contingents took initiatives to occupy cities en route rather than sustain the focus on a lightning strike in the direction of Moscow. His 'Armed Forces of the Southern Front' became too thinly spread for the decisive clashes ahead.[10] Mai-Maevski's attempt to shift north from Kharkov stalled in July and August. Vrangel and Sidorin were met by strong Red counter-attacks. Denikin's offensive was halted.

Fighting was vicious and intense. The Reds regularly shot captured White officers and the Whites killed Bolsheviks and labour activists who fell into their hands. Torture of enemy POWs was frequent on both sides. Baron Roman von Ungern-Sternberg, a White commander who operated deep in Siberia, became infamous for devising vicious treatment of Red prisoners. Béla Kun, who returned from Hungary to become a political commissar on the Red side, would help to execute thousands of White prisoners in Crimea who had surrendered on the explicit promise of their lives being spared.

Lenin, inflamed by the dangers of military emergency, called for the Soviet republic to be turned into a 'single armed camp'. The Reds could now put 80,000 combat troops into action against Denikin's forces, which included between 45,000 and 50,000 troops for their operations in the north. Red strategy was directed at conducting a counteroffensive in the Volga region which started in mid-August 1919. City after city along the great river fell to the Red Army and by early September it had moved towards Tsaritsyn. Trotsky had originally wanted to make a thrust through the Donbas and when the advance down the Volga started to slow down, he returned to the idea. The Politburo decided against him, preferring to reinforce the campaign on the Volga. The White defences could not hold back the Reds for long and they had to retreat. Denikin's eastern flank had been smashed and his forces in Ukraine were cut off from supplies.[11]

But he redoubled his Ukrainian effort with a view towards breaking through to Russia while Tsaritsyn still held out against the Reds. Kursk succumbed to Denikin's forces on 20 September 1919. Orël was next in mid-October. It appeared likely that Tula, a place of armaments production 120 miles to the north, would soon be seized from the Reds. Sovnarkom placed Moscow under martial law in preparation of the expected White attack.[12] But the Red Army struck back and retook Orël. Its strategic planners had planned a many-sided, simultaneous offensive. Its success took even Bolshevik leaders by surprise. From November 1919 to January 1920 Denikin was pushed into a sprawling retreat back beyond the river Don to Crimea. Denikin was defeated and exhausted – and in April 1920 he resigned his command. He had made his fullest effort and it had not been enough.

Hardly had Denikin started his long retreat to the Crimean peninsula than a third White general, Nikolai Yudenich, emerged with his North-Western Army from independent Estonia. Yudenich had worked underground in Petrograd till autumn 1918. As chief of staff of the Caucasus Army he had defeated the Ottomans at the battle of Sarykamysh (Sarıkamış) in Kars province in the winter of 1914–15.[13] He had joined a move against Petrograd in summer 1919 but was repulsed. In mid-October he returned to the offensive. Tsarskoe Selo fell to him within a few days and Petrograd appeared at his mercy.[14]

Yudenich had assembled and trained an army that benefited from British arms and equipment and Winston Churchill's relentless encouragement. The Nobel family, which had lost a fortune when the Baku oil industry was nationalized, provided financial credits on condition that it would retrieve its assets in the event of a White triumph in the Civil War. Zinoviev, the Bolshevik party's ruler in Petrograd, telegraphed frantic pleas for military assistance from Moscow. His Politburo comrades Stalin and Trotsky were sent to his aid and the Soviet defences were rapidly assembled. Stalin with characteristic hard-heartedness proposed to put a line of arrested bourgeois residents in front of the Red forces as a way of deterring the White artillery fire. Trotsky wanted more orthodox methods to be used. The Reds anyway had massive superiority in numbers and plenty of armaments. Petrograd's defences were shored up in preparation. In the fierce fighting that followed Yudenich was unable to break through the cordon. Defeated, he withdrew across the Estonian border, where the national government ordered his forces to disarm and remove the uniforms of the North-Western Army.[15] Yudenich put his last hope in a plan to transfer his forces to the south of Russia where he hoped to join Denikin's army.[16]

The Whites under Kolchak, Denikin and Yudenich would have confronted severe difficulties even if their military campaigns had culminated in victory. No White army ever consolidated its authority over the territories that it conquered. Whenever the Whites moved forward or retreated, they left behind cities and villages where hostility to the White cause festered.

Lelya Okunev's experience illustrates the swirling torrent of the warfare. In May 1920 he wrote to his father Nikita that he had been captured by the Whites, but had escaped under the alias of railwayman Antoni Krolyuk. His life was saved by a kindly nurse who destroyed his compromising documents. His lover Maria Gamalei had been told he had been killed – indeed she had arranged a requiem to be held for him. Then suddenly he came back to her in Poltava. Her father, an Orthodox priest, aided the next stage of his flight. From Poltava he made his way to Nikolaev, from where he sailed to Odessa. Still in disguise, he obtained manual jobs. With Maria's help he had acquired the identity of her brother, but this subterfuge failed when he was recognized by a former Imperial Army officer. With difficulty he eluded capture and assumed yet another identity, pretending to be a sailor called Ivanov. His ship skirted the Black Sea coast to the Kerch peninsula, where he resumed contact with fellow Bolsheviks. From Novorossiisk he finally made his way to Moscow, gaunt, dishevelled and looking twice his age.

Lelya Okunev was now, as his father put it, an 'incorrigible communist' and was on his way to fight the Poles. In his Red Army service he had started as a political commissar and, having proved himself, had been appointed as a brigade commander in the Civil War in Ukraine.[17] Lelya had several times come within an inch of losing his life. Military victory over the Whites was as sweet for him as it was bitter for the White commanders as they contemplated a life in foreign exile. Like other Red veterans, Lelya looked forward to helping to rebuild peacetime Russia on communist principles.

40. PLANNED ECONOMICS AND ECONOMIC PILLAGE: CENTRALIZATION, NATIONALIZATION AND REQUISITIONING

The Russian economy was in free fall in the Civil War. Gross output across all sectors in 1919 was only 43 per cent of the pre-war total. Large-scale industry was the worst affected, tumbling to a sixth of the level recorded for 1913. In smaller enterprises it was half the value it had recorded immediately before the Great War.[1] Iron and steel output crashed and by 1920 it was a mere 3.6 per cent of the total in the last year of peace.[2] Agricultural production too was halved.[3] The Bolsheviks had inherited a disaster in industry, commerce, transport and fiscal revenues and peace alone would open the gates to recovery. The party's leaders knew all this but most of them assumed that the wartime measures had already proved themselves as a permanent panacea for the regeneration of industry and agriculture. They could not imagine reducing the scope of state ownership and control. Thus they were lurching towards economic disaster and putting the existence of communist power in severe jeopardy.

The Food Supply Dictatorship never worked as effectively as Lenin had projected. His kind of Marxist economic analysis had blinded him to the likelihood that most rural inhabitants, whether they were well-off or destitute, would detest the committees for pitting peasant household against household. Agricultural supplies to the Red Army and the cities reached a critical low. In December 1918 moves were made to phase out the committees and to revert to the system of territorial quotas for food procurement – the so-called *razvërstka* – that had been devised under Nicholas II and practised by the Provisional Government.[4] Statisticians were ordered to update the harvest data left behind by the former Ministries of Agriculture and Food Supply. The quotas were assigned to officials in provinces and districts. Provincial authorities increased the number of armed squads to carry out the requisitioning duties.

The intention was still to come down hard on the peasant rich but Lenin overrode resistance at the eighth party congress in March 1919 to implementing a lighter policy on the country's 'middle peasants' whilst offering no guidance on how to identify one category from another, and he gave no consideration to regional differences. Totma's Alexander Zamaraev was the kind of 'middle peasant' whom he aimed to win over to the Soviet cause. As food supplies to the towns dipped, Sovnarkom quickened the schedule for cereal deliveries. Seventy per cent of the annual target was set to be obtained by 1 March 1919 and the remainder by mid-July that year. Soviets in the provinces were allowed to increase the amount that was requisitioned if local needs were found to require it. Throughout the territories under Red rule there was talk of impending famine in the towns, and Sovnarkom moved to prohibit private trade over the entire range of agricultural products.[5] Peasants were unwilling to surrender their grain for what they saw as inadequate compensation. Anton Okninski witnessed his landlord Akim Nesterov – a peasant horse-dealer whom other peasants regarded as a *burzhui* – secreting his stock beneath the ground floor where he had already deposited his wife's best clothes.[6]

Alexander Shlikhter, formerly the people's commissar of agriculture, was sent as food-supply plenipotentiary to Vyatka province in the southern Urals to implement the policies. He argued that the Provisional Government's policy of compiling inventories of agricultural produce was unworkable. This was tantamount to a call for arbitrary seizures. Shlikhter's priority was to break into grain barns regardless of rural anger but by the time he left the province a number of peasant revolts had broken out.[7] Requisitioning squads were not forgiven if they returned to their urban bases without sackfuls of the produce they had been assigned to collect. Arbitrary confiscations were inevitable, and the cycle of seizure and revolt was in motion.

The countryside had changed in many ways since the October Revolution. In dividing up the land among themselves, peasants were fulfilling the dream they had for centuries but it was an uneven process. Only half of those who streamed back to the villages were lucky enough to receive an allotment of land.[8] There was a notable desire among younger peasants to set up their own households.[9] By doing this, if they happened to belong to a better-off family, they obviated the threat of heavy fiscal obligations. They also escaped the heavy tutelage of their fathers. Rural youth wanted its freedom and social deference was on the wane. As landholdings were broken up, the trend was towards fewer poor peasants and fewer rich ones too. 'Middle-peasantization' was the dominant process even though no one then or later knew how to define what middle peasants were.[10]

Agricultural output was also threatened by Soviet officials' zeal for imposing collective farms on the peasant population, disregarding their long-held hopes for more autonomy. Party leaders in northern and central Russia tried to force this type of farming on the peasantry, whether it liked it or not – and few peasants, unless they were already destitute, welcomed the change.[11]

Urban residents who could not obtain paid employment, or had simply run out of food, went back to the countryside if they still had families in their native villages. Many inhabitants of the hungry north and centre of Russia sought relief by heading south to the provinces where food was cheaper – Anton Okninski was delighted to find that the price of grain in Tambov was only 4 per cent of what he had paid in Petrograd.[12] This brought temporary advantage for incomers like himself and his family. As soon as the Soviet administrative order was consolidated and mass requisitioning commenced, the standard of living even in grain-rich provinces like Tambov displayed a downward slide.

Industrial and mining production meanwhile collapsed in every region of the old Russian Empire. Nearly all large-sized enterprises had been brought into state ownership by January 1919, and the same was true of almost every medium-sized one before the end of the year.[13] Planning agencies were created with the idea that nationalization was the only way to regenerate the economy. Bolsheviks had learned lessons from the German wartime system of orders, quotas and rations and intended to apply them to their own improvements. But managers and administrators were initially wary of being authoritarian in a workers' revolution that was meant to make life easier for the working class. But the main reason for the fall in output lay elsewhere. Fuel and raw materials were even harder to obtain than in 1917. Parts for broken machinery were difficult to find. Wages failed to keep pace with the rising prices on the black market for food and other consumer goods, and the official ration books provided little better than subsistence. Proletarian revolution had given status to the proletariat but this didn't improve living conditions or even halt the decline in them.

The Bolshevik party responded to the growing unrest and poor output by introducing the principle of 'one-person authority' (*edinonachalie*) rather than the whole workforce running a factory or mine, something that discomforted many committed Bolsheviks. But the Politburo stuck to its decision. If Red Army soldiers had to obey a commander, why should the workers not pay heed to their industrial commissar? Many commissars, however, lacked knowledge of the technology and work routines for which they had become responsible and industrial relations worsened as large enterprises experienced difficulty in restoring discipline at work. The situation in the factories also underwent change in other ways. Industry's labour force shrank in size as many urban families moved back to the countryside in search of food. Another factor in the diminution was the state's demand for conscripts for the Red Army and for workers to join the staffs of the Soviet administration.

In Moscow the smaller manufacturing enterprises and workshops were either nationalized or municipalized by the end of 1918, and the process was repeated across the entirety of the Soviet republic in the following year. Nikita Okunev recorded that shops and stalls selling gloves, watches, books, stationery and footwear were seized from their owners.[14] By mid-1919 every barber's shop in the capital was state-owned.[15] The fall-off in general economic output continued. Sovnarkom and the planning agencies were aware of this but maintained the nationalizing campaign. The ghost of capitalism, it was said by Soviet spokesmen, had been exorcized from the house of Soviet communism, but it was not just ideological enthusiasm that motivated them. Whilst there was recognition in government that the Bolsheviks could not immediately regenerate production, they could at least requisition goods in warehouses and distribute them for the benefit of social welfare and military effectiveness.

The fiscal system was still a shambles. Local soviets found infinite ways to avoid delivering their share of taxation.[16] Stern measures were announced in Moscow. An extraordinary ten-billion-ruble loan was imposed on 30 October 1918.[17] Sovnarkom intended to exact the money from citizens according to which social category they belonged. But the Soviet state was no better informed about who earned how much than the Russian Imperial state had been, and fiscal agents turned inevitably to old techniques of gathering data. Arriving in June 1919 in a rural district like Totma where Alexander Zamaraev lived, a commissar issued forms for everyone to complete about their earnings. Not a single local peasant complied even after the village elders were told there were no exemptions for anyone making more than 3,000 rubles per annum – a moderate sum in that inflationary period.[18] Zamaraev, serving at the time as a judge in his community, did not mention this in his diary, probably because formal procedures of tax collection were not followed in the locality.[19] He did, though, record plenty of arbitrary seizures of property from external urban squads pillaging the villages around Totma.

Inflation rocketed and paper currency lost value at an even faster rate than in 1917. Barter became the norm when rations ran out. Zamaraev recorded: 'No one's accepting money in exchange because everyone's got so much of it.'[20] Many in the Bolshevik leadership were delighted. They had always looked forward eagerly to the development of a moneyless economy, and the devastating pressures of the Great War and the Civil War appeared to be doing the job for them. Ordinary people did not share the joy of communist theory. It has been calculated that the volume of Soviet paper currency prices rose by twelve times between July 1918 and July 1920 whereas prices were ninety times greater.[21]

The White intelligence networks had some hope of benefiting from the discontent of workers in the big cities. In Petrograd, as they reported to Yudenich, there were endless food shortages. By the beginning of 1920 the Moscow sewage system had broken down. Inhabitants of the six-storey apartment block where the Okunev family lived were ordered to desist from using the toilet. This came after a year when the water supply had been switched off, the block's central heating been terminated, electricity been limited to a few hours each day and tram transport been suspended.[22] The postal system was also crippled. It took eighty-three days for a parcel to reach Okunev from his cousin in Simbirsk.[23]

The Bolsheviks managed to sustain their war effort in part by ransacking the storehouses of military equipment. They fought the Whites with rifles, bullets, greatcoats and boots that the empire's factories had produced for the Imperial armed forces.

Lenin was later to dub the difficulties of the economy as 'war communism' as if the party's policies were merely a way to cope with the demands of the Civil War. This was an excuse for failure. State economic management in 1918–20 was really an extension of the decrees of the October Revolution. Lenin, the initiator of committees of the village poor, quickly recognized his blunder – but not quickly enough to prevent the chaos that they wreaked. He had also regretted the agricultural and social disruption caused by the unapproved imposition of collective farms. But neither he nor any other Bolsheviks explained what they had expected to gain by nationalizing cobblers' workshops, barbers' shops and other small businesses. The party's enemies suggested that ideology had driven the hyper-interventionist state policies which had made the economic ruin much worse than it need have been.

41. THE ANTI-IMPERIALIST EMPIRE: BOLSHEVIK PROMISES, RED CONQUESTS

The Bolsheviks always wanted to wrench every region of the former Russian Empire back under their authority, which they initially expected to achieve by persuasion and through an aligning of far-left socialists who they believed would naturally come to power in other territories and seek realignment with Soviet Russia.

The principle of national self-determination was honoured for Finland as soon as Sovnarkom came to power. Finnish nationalists were surprised when the new revolutionary government in Petrograd invited a delegation to discuss the terms of separation. Arriving by train from Helsinki, they learned that the Bolsheviks intended to abide by the undertakings they had made before the October Revolution, when they themselves had enjoyed assistance from many Finns. The Great War had not yet ended and the Finnish delegation was nervous about accepting favours from the communists. But Pehr Evind Svinhufvud, whom Kerensky had freed from Siberian exile, saw no point in delay. Lenin was averse to negotiating face to face with him but did not stand in the way of Finland's becoming independent. He was not being as generous as he seemed. Bolshevik leadership thought that a Finnish civil war was imminent between the far-left socialists and the reactionary right and that the Finnish Reds would win it and seek reassociation with Russia.

Although communist leaders cynically continued to affirm the right of secession for the other ex-Imperial peoples, in reality they aimed to bring them under Soviet authority. Developments in Finland had quickly disabused them of their optimism. The Finnish Reds were beaten in their civil war, and by 1919 General Carl Gustaf Mannerheim, a former general of Nicholas II, was able to put a conservative government in power in Helsinki. The prospects for Bolshevism were no better

22. The Tauride Palace, seat of the State Duma – and later, in 1917, used by the Provisional Government, the Central Executive Committees of the Congresses of Soviets and the Constituent Assembly.

23. Peasant men and women at harvest time.

24. The February Revolution: a street demonstration with smiling people confident that things were only going to get better.

25. The Smolny Institute, the girls' school that became a base for the Petrograd Soviet.

26. Mass meeting at the Putilov Works in Petrograd, 1917: industrial production gave way to political debate and dispute.

27. A formal photograph of the two sides in the Brest-Litovsk negotiations on war and peace in late 1917.

28. A Ukrainian-language poster of a Soviet appeal to Ukraine's workers and peasants to enlist in the Red Cavalry and fight the Whites and the Ukrainian nationalists.

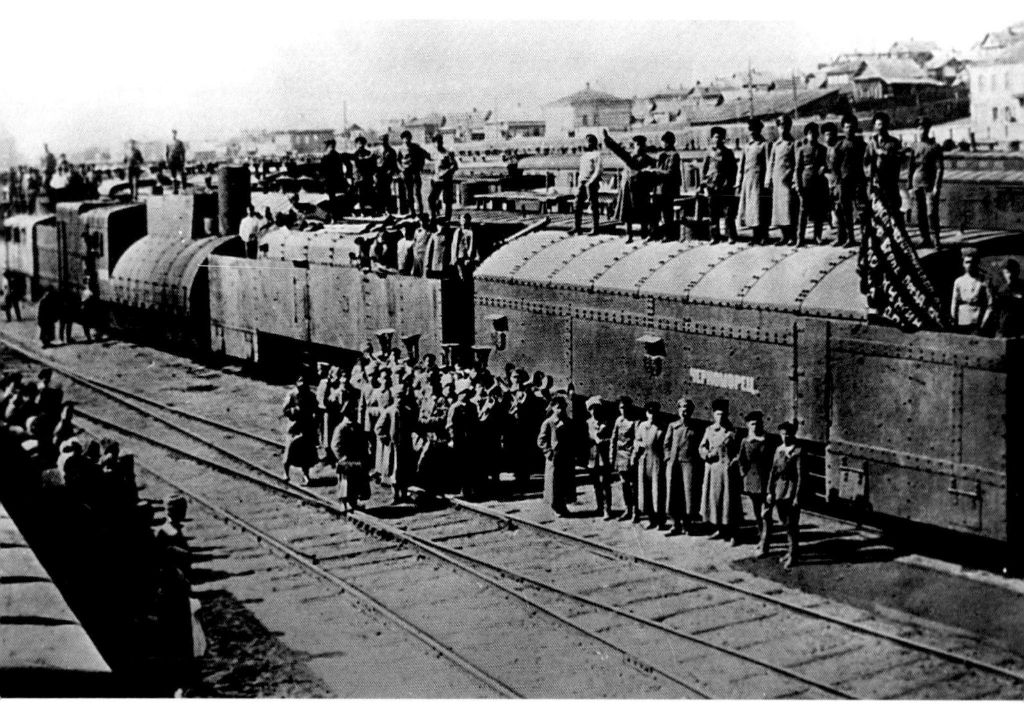

29. Red Army troops celebrate a recent success at a railway junction in the Civil War.

30. Trotsky walking at the head of a group of Red Army personnel on a trip to Red Square, 1919.

31. A Soviet team distributes food supplies from a train to hungry civilians at the end of the Civil War.

32. A White armed contingent still operating in Siberia in 1920 in the face of the relentless advance of the Reds.

33. Leading delegates to the Comintern Congress (summer 1921) gather under the Marx and Engels monument.

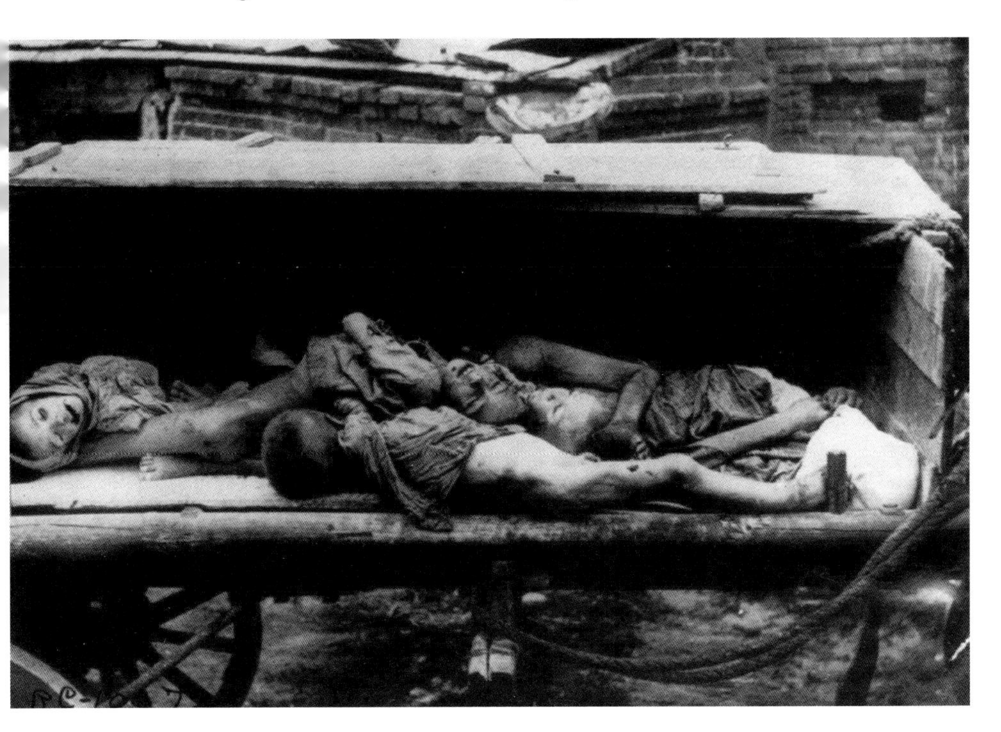

34. The corpses of some of those who died in the famine that scourged the Volga region, 1922.

35. The Lenin mausoleum in one of its early manifestations.

in Estonia, Latvia and Lithuania, which had experienced the formal status of independence under German military occupation. When Germany surrendered to the Western Allies in November, they ceased to be puppet states. Red forces were sent across the Estonian frontier to seize the city of Narva. Advancing into the country, they reached the approaches to Tallinn before being defeated by Estonian forces under Chief of Staff Johan Laidoner. The British Royal Navy's arrival discouraged the Soviet communist leaders from resuming the invasion.[1]

In Lithuania, a Soviet Socialist Republic was established in December 1918 which had the trappings of independence but was closely monitored by Russia. It was led by Vincas Mickevičius-Kapsukas, who had coordinated the Lithuanian Bolsheviks in Petrograd in 1917 and enjoyed Sovnarkom's confidence. Similarly in Belorussia in January 1919 a Belorussian Soviet Socialist Republic was proclaimed in Smolensk which would challenge the Belorussian People's Republic in Minsk. Nearly the entire Baltic region of the former Russian Empire was in political and military turmoil as diverse political groups vied for control. In February 1919 the Bolsheviks decided to amalgamate them into a state that was commonly known as Litbel, but at no point did its leadership succeed in controlling all the cities in the territories that they claimed to govern. The Lithuanian government sent its forces to crush Litbel and drive the Reds entirely from the Baltic region in August 1919. This temporarily put Bolshevik expansionist ambitions in reverse as the Red Army was drawn away to cope with the simultaneous incursions into Soviet Russia by Denikin and Yudenich.

Meanwhile at the People's Commissariat for Nationalities' Affairs Stalin continued to confirm the promises made to non-Russians about freedoms of language, religion, schooling and local self-rule. He recruited Bolsheviks who were sympathetic to this perspective, but it didn't always go to plan. The young Tatar, Mirza Sultan-Galiev, was passionate about aligning Bolshevik theories of revolution with a concern for the rights of Muslim communities and prioritized the need to unite all Muslims. In early 1919 he would receive an official reprimand for this.[2] Leading Bolsheviks were fervent internationalists and many of them were not Russians and did not want to be seen as spokespersons for their national groups. Trotsky, Kamenev, Zinoviev and Sverdlov were Jewish – and there were several other Jews in official posts in the Central Committee and Sovnarkom. Dzierżyński was a Pole. Stalin, a Georgian, was unusual in agreeing with Lenin on the urgent need to appeal to the many peoples in the old empire's outlying regions. They jointly pressed the case for this orientation in policy on the central party leadership.

Nevertheless the so-called national question was bound to be a fractious affair in the years ahead. Stalin, the party's spokesperson on matters of the nationalities, wanted Bolshevik 'liberalism' to come to an end when victory had been achieved in the Civil War and the various Soviet republics to be pulled under the sovereignty of the Russian Soviet Federative Socialist Republic. Lenin by contrast wanted to allow the Soviet republics to keep their formal independent status while staying subject to a centralized political system through the hierarchy of Bolshevik party committees. The Politburo also sought to create a 'military–economic union' between Soviet Russia and Ukraine, Latvia and Belorussia. Orders were given for people's commissariats in Moscow to have direct authority over those in the other republics.[3] This was constitutional centralization – or imperial expansion – by another name. In any case, the communist party in all these countries was already centralized with its base in Moscow. For the moment, though, the formal façade of a plurality of Soviet republics was maintained as a useful way of winning popular support in the regions of the old empire.

All Bolsheviks, including Lenin and Stalin, saw Ukraine as the great prize. Its grain output, metallurgical resources and people were coveted. Its geographical position offered a crucial pathway to carry revolution into central Europe – and the communist leadership was determined to prevent any others, including the Ukrainians, from turning Kiev into an assembly station for a crusade against Soviet Russia.

The first attempt at forming a Ukrainian Soviet republic had occurred in December 1917 when Sovnarkom dispatched an armed contingent to aid an uprising in Kiev. The Ukrainian Central Rada fought back and drove out the Red invaders. After late 1918, when the German military occupation ended, Ukraine became a focus for the fighting between Reds and Whites as well as between different Ukrainian forces. One of the strongest local armies was put together by the anarchist leader Nestor Makhno, who was briefly allied to the Red Army against Denikin's Whites. The Reds proclaimed a Ukrainian Soviet Socialist Republic in Kharkov in February 1919 in expectation of a rapid conquest of Kiev. Denikin's offensive disrupted their hopes. But the Bolsheviks had already done much to alienate Ukrainian peasant communities before they retreated. They had requisitioned grain and conscripts and had – against Moscow's explicit instructions – forcibly imposed collective farms on the peasantry.[4]

Lenin highlighted the need for warm overtures to the Ukrainian-speaking rural population if the Bolsheviks were to consolidate their hold on Ukraine. With this in mind he proposed incorporating the entire Borotbist party, the Ukrainian equivalent of the Left Socialist-Revolutionaries, into the Bolshevik party in order to build stronger links with Ukraine's peasantry.[5] Trotsky countered that the Borotbists were intolerably sympathetic to the interests of wealthy peasants, who were always hated and feared by Bolsheviks. But Lenin won the discussion among fellow Bolshevik leaders.[6] The integration of willing Borotbists was a pill that had to be swallowed if Ukraine was to be governed by men and women who could talk to peasants in their own language. But Lenin's project was never going to have an immediate success. Armed conflict between the Reds and the rebellious peasant groups known as the Greens intensified after Denikin was defeated, and the Greens attracted a growing number of insurgents who fought on to bring the Soviet occupation of their lands to an end.

While the military conflict continued, the Bolshevik leaders attended to administrative arrangements. The frontier between Soviet Ukraine and Soviet Russia was not settled until early 1920. Old tsarist maps were of no help because they had not demarcated Ukrainian territories as Ukrainian. Sovietization required the Bolshevik leadership to designate a definitive border even while the fighting continued.

Russian and other communist leaders based in Kharkov and the Donbas, where there were many Russian-speaking inhabitants, sought to have the two regions incorporated into Soviet Russia. Lenin agreed with this until he had to face the fierce objections of Soviet Ukraine's leadership. In previous years, under the Central Rada in 1917 and later under independent Ukrainian governments, Kiev had claimed authority over both Kharkov and the Donbas. Away from the public gaze, there was controversy in the party about what the Russo-Ukrainian frontier should be, and Lenin came under pressure to reverse his pro-Russia preference. The difficulty was resolved after he accepted the Ukrainian communist case and opted to incorporate the regions in Soviet Ukraine.[7] The party decided the matter without public consultation. This was predictable since the Politburo never allowed plebiscites anywhere despite its avowed commitment to national self-determination. Moreover, the truth was that there was a mixed population throughout the contested area and any line drawn between the two Soviet republics would have inevitably displeased one side or the other in the dispute. The ultimate decision anyhow made little difference for most of the people living there, whether they were Russians or Ukrainians, because the communist supreme leadership in Moscow was determined to maintain its dominion over all the Soviet republics (and several decades would pass before Russian nationalists could voice resentment about the frontier with Ukraine and, in 2022, possessed a leader willing to go to war about it).

The Ukrainian provinces came through the years of civil war drenched in the blood and tears of peaceful Jews. Denikin's campaign in mid-1919 had been accompanied by an eruption of horrendous pogroms. The mayhem makes calculations difficult but it has been estimated that an entire tenth of the Jewish population of Ukraine perished during the Civil War.[8] The White anti-Semitic rampages deepened, if anything, the barbarism inflicted by the Imperial armed forces in the Great War. Jews also experienced a hell of murder, torture, robbery and rape at the hands of anti-Bolshevik Ukrainian forces. It was a barbarism that would return to the region in an industrialized form under Nazi rule.

Communist policy denounced anti-Semitism in all its manifestations, and Lenin recorded a powerful speech about the subject on a gramophone record. Political commissars in the Red Army held meetings to explain to troops the need to do away with all national and ethnic prejudice. But old attitudes did not wholly disappear from the Red side during the fighting. One of the reasons was that the Reds employed many former Imperial officers in posts of command and drew peasant conscripts from the same demographic pool as the Whites did.[9] Sporadic pogroms took place in areas of conflict in Ukraine that were far away from the gaze of the Politburo or Trotsky's Revolutionary-Military Council of the Republic. Such atrocities were not the regular occurrence that they were on the White side but the inhabitants of shtetls understandably continued to doubt that Soviet rule would put a final end to their sufferings. Jewish communities had come to regard Whites and Reds with equal suspicion and simply wanted to practise their faith in peace and earn their living unimpeded.

The central communist leadership welcomed Jews as members of the new society that was being created. But another facet of the 'Jewish question' in Soviet-occupied territories of Russia and Ukraine was the widespread unrest that grew there out of rumours that Jews were evading military service by taking posts in the civilian administration. On 18 April 1919 Trotsky wrote to the Politburo to insist on conscription among Jewish communities. As a Jew himself, albeit a militant atheist, he perhaps wanted to demonstrate his refusal to show favouritism towards those of his ethnicity. One of the problems, however, was that Jewish families were aware of the hostility that Jews often experienced in the ranks of the Red Army despite all the promises of tolerance. They also had a well-founded dread of the appalling fate of Jewish soldiers who fell into the hands of the Whites. But the Politburo decided that it could not ignore the grumbles that Jews were evading conscription, and on 28 April 1919 it was decided to create Jewish units in the Red Army.[10]

The Bolsheviks were at any rate not without ambition to settle scores with those ethnic groups that they regarded as enemies. When the Reds reached the Don region in 1919 they dealt brutally with the Cossacks regardless of wealth or social status. Cossack communities were turned out of their settlements and robbed of their land.[11] In the following year, on Stalin's urging, Cossacks were turned out of their settlements in the north Caucasus which they had inhabited since the end of the Russian military conquest in the nineteenth century – and the Chechens were allowed to return to their ancestral homes.[12]

There was much violence in the southern Urals where the Bashkir and Russian inhabitants turned on each other. Bashkirs, a Turkic and mainly Muslim people, had formed armed units for self-defence. Initially some of them aligned themselves with Kolchak's forces in Siberia. The Reds made overtures to Bashkir troops to cross the lines and join them. The promises that had been made in November 1917 in the Declaration of the Rights of the Peoples of Russia were presented as validation that Sovnarkom offered them more than anything that Kolchak would deliver. The persuasion was successful and a mass desertion of Bashkirs from the White side of the Eastern front took place in February 1919. Their reward was the creation in Ufa of the first autonomous national administration within the frontiers of the Russian Soviet Federative Socialist Republic. The Bashkir Soviet Socialist Republic was paraded as a model of what the other non-Russian national and ethnic groups could expect from the Soviet authorities. Bashkirs were guaranteed freedom of religion, schooling and the press under Bolshevik rule.[13]

But this only enraged the Tatars. The two ethnic groups had an ancestral rivalry and now took to arms against each other. The Red Army intervened to impose a peaceful settlement. In 1920 a Tatar Autonomous Soviet Socialist Republic was founded in Kazan and Bashkirs and Tatars lived intermingled across the whole region.

Central Asia too was a patchwork of ethnicities. The Turkestan Soviet Federative Republic had been established by the Tashkent Soviet in April 1918. The Soviet's voters were mainly Russians and their attitude to Muslim communities was hostile. The new republic's forces ruthlessly imposed allegiance to Sovnarkom and whilst tribal enmities also contributed to civil war, the greatest violence occurred between the Russians and the Muslims. The Bolshevik central leadership was shocked by their fellow Bolsheviks' total disregard of Islamic sensitivities but the bigger priority in both Moscow and Tashkent was to incorporate Turkestan into the Russian Soviet republic. The Reds successfully made inroads into the mountains and deserts bordering Persia and Afghanistan. By mid-1919 Turkestan could be declared part of the Russian Soviet Socialist Republic.[14] Work began on recruiting young radical Muslims to the communist cause by persuading them that progress for the peoples of the Islamic faith would be secured only by entering the party and the soviets and allying in the struggle against the conservative Muslim clergy. Such recruits were offered educational facilities and rapid promotion.[15]

The south Caucasus region was even higher on Moscow's agenda. Georgian, Armenian and Azeri administrations, which had collaborated since the fall of the Romanov monarchy, were combining fiercely against Sovnarkom and moving towards complete independence. International powers were also active in the area with ambitions to control access to the rich natural resources, especially the Baku oil fields. The Bolsheviks had little influence except in Baku on the Caspian coast, where in April 1918 they succeeded under Stepan Shaumyan's leadership in crushing their enemies in violent clashes and forming their own coalition city government with a handful of Left Socialist-Revolutionaries.[16] The Azeri Muslims, who constituted the majority of the city's population and supplied the bulk of the labour force in the oil fields, were angry at their exclusion from power. Street protests took place and the government, with active assistance from the Armenian Dashnaktsutyun party, massacred thousands of Azeris in response. The Turks sent in their Army of Islam to protect them as fellow Muslims and a fellow Turkic people. The Baku governing coalition could not hope to repel the attack. In August 1918 the Dashnaktsutyun appealed for armed assistance from the British.[17]

The Baku Bolsheviks abandoned their own coalition. The Bolshevik Central Committee in Moscow still adhered to the Brest-Litovsk treaty and could not safely condone the pursuit of military assistance from

Germany's enemies. In any case, British help was unavailable quickly enough. The Army of Islam forced its way into the city in mid-September and a massacre of Armenians followed. As chaos spread around the eastern Caspian coast, twenty-six of the leading Bolshevik commissars including Shaumyan were captured and executed by the new Transcaspian government in Ashkhabad.[18] Bolshevik influence would not return to the south Caucasus for a whole year. Baku again became the objective of the Red Army's strategy as soon as Denikin's forces were defeated in Crimea. The Soviet economy needed its oil, and the railway from Rostov-on-Don south to the Caspian coast eased the operational tasks for Commander-in-Chief Sergei Kamenev. The Azeri administration could field only a small army against the Reds. Many of its troops were already engaged in war against Armenia. The Red Army entered Baku on 28 April 1920 and the Azerbaijani Socialist Soviet Republic was proclaimed. The Armenians were enveloped in a war with Turkey and the Reds were able to exploit the mayhem. By 4 December 1920 they entered the Armenian capital Yerevan and set about inaugurating a Soviet Socialist Republic.[19]

The Red Army immediately made preparations to complete the subjugation of the south Caucasus, where only the Georgian Democratic Republic and its Menshevik government remained independent and defiant. Indeed, by late 1920, most of the national and ethnic territories had been pulled back under the authority of the Russian capital. The exceptions were on the fringes of the old empire. Finland, Estonia, Latvia and Lithuania cherished the independence they had won while the Russians fought among themselves. The 'Russian' Polish territories had become part of an independent Poland. The Turks hung on to the provinces that they had obtained at Brest-Litovsk in 1918. In Siberia's sparsely populated far east the Japanese continued to occupy the Pacific seaboard – the Reds were not to seize Vladivostok until 1922. But even many Russian conservatives and liberals nevertheless gave credit to the Bolshevik party for 'gathering the lands' that the tsars had once ruled. The Bolsheviks themselves, however, did not want to be seen as imperialists. They put the Azeri Nariman Narimanov and the Armenian Alexander Myasnikyan in power in Azerbaijan and Armenia. Young Muslims were recruited to the Soviet administration in Bashkiria and Tatarstan. Ukrainian language schools were opened in Ukraine. Christian denominations, aside from the Russian Orthodox Church, received assurances that the authorities would not interfere with them as long as their priests kept out of politics. Imams of a progressive social inclination were invited to join the party.[20]

Lenin and Stalin in the Bolshevik Politburo held on to the idea that the concessions to different communities of nationhood and faith would take the sting out of anti-Bolshevik and anti-Russian feelings. They assumed that this would help them to entrench Marxism in the minds of millions. Their dream was that nationalism and religious fervour would die away and that a communist union of peoples would develop.

42. ABROAD: RED REVOLUTIONS AND SOVIET TRADE: UPRISINGS, COMINTERN AND COMMERCIAL OVERTURES

Governments across Europe were horrified by the rise of Bolshevism in Russia and the threat of similar uprisings in their own countries, but had to consider that their peoples were war-weary and unreceptive to any talk of mounting military expeditions to free Russia from Bolshevik tyranny. Most socialists and labour activists argued among themselves about whether the Bolshevik revolutionary model was one to be followed at home. Karl Kautsky, one of the leading German Marxist writers, thought that Marx and Engels would have disapproved of the Bolshevik obsession with dictatorship and terror.

Lenin and all his comrades remained committed internationalists. Revolution throughout Europe had been integral to the October Revolution, and Lenin's campaign for the Brest-Litovsk treaty had nearly broken the Bolshevik party into pieces. Sovnarkom knew that Red Russia needed assistance for its economic regeneration and technological development and hoped that revolution across Europe would enable them to share resources with their new political brothers. They anyway believed that Europe, especially Germany, was on the brink of a definitive clash between capitalism and socialism. The German far left led by Karl Liebknecht and Rosa Luxemburg shared in the revolutionary passion. Recently released from prison after Germany's military surrender, they aimed to take advantage of the political volatility in Berlin. They and their followers in the Spartakusbund met in December 1918 and formed the Communist Party of Germany. Although they had no intention of deferring to the Bolsheviks, they were determined to emulate their seizure of power. Plans were laid to occupy garrisons, post and telegraph offices and governmental buildings. The uprising in the capital was fixed for 5 January 1919. But the social-democratic cabinet that had governed since the end of the Great War acted swiftly to crush the insurrectionaries. Regular troops were mobilized from their barracks and reinforced by groups of demobbed servicemen known as Freikorps. The German communists had underestimated the organized force assembled against them. The Freikorps hunted down the leaders of the uprising and their defeat was symbolized when Rosa Luxemburg's battered corpse was dumped outside the railings of the Zoological Gardens.

The news from Germany caused grave disappointment in Moscow. The reasons for the debacle seemed plain. Germany lacked an equivalent of the strong network of soviets and factory committees that had covered Russia in 1917, and the Scheidemann cabinet was nothing like as unpopular as the Provisional Government in Russia had become.

Lenin, Trotsky and Bukharin had already seen the need to call a conference of socialist internationalists as soon as possible. Invitations were sent out to proceedings that were scheduled to start in Moscow on 2 March 1919. The original intention had been to hold the conference in Berlin or, failing that, somewhere in the Netherlands, but the violent disturbances in central Europe made Moscow a more suitable venue. Even Moscow was not the easiest place to reach at the time. The logistics were fiendishly complex and arriving foreign communists were few. Hugo Eberlein came on behalf of the German Spartacists and was under orders to show no deference to the Russian leadership.[1] Out of the conference came the Communist International, abbreviated as the Comintern and also known as the Third International. Lenin and Trotsky, who were treated as heroes by many of the conference attendees, made sure that all the decisions were drafted or supervised by them, and the election of the Comintern Executive Committee left power in their hands. Zinoviev became its first chairman. The objective was world revolution and priority was given to spreading the Soviet system to Germany. Funds were disbursed from Moscow through emissaries to far-left organizations around the globe to create fraternal communist parties. When the Executive Committee met for the first time on 26 March 1919, Zinoviev announced a budget of one million rubles (which was raised to three million in May).[2] Rubles were next-to useless in most countries after Sovnarkom had absolved itself of the obligation to recognize the Russian state debt. Foreign currency was required for use by Comintern agents abroad, so deposits in the nationalized bank were raided and Lenin asked Yelena Stasova,

Sverdlov's successor as Central Committee secretary, to take a case of a million pounds sterling to Zinoviev in Petrograd.[3]

Bolshevik optimism seemed to receive validation on 21 March 1919 when the newly formed Hungarian communists took power in a governing coalition in Budapest. They were led by Béla Kun, who had been a POW in Russia before returning to Hungary after Austria–Hungary's military surrender. By opposing the peace settlement being negotiated in Paris, he had gained support from patriotic Hungarians. Kun was no nationalist but he acted like one in repulsing the Romanian and Czech invading armies in April 1919.

The Hungarian communists exercised considerable zeal in implementing their policies. Banks, mines and textile factories were taken over by the state. A new security police patrolled the towns. 'Class enemies' were arrested. Kun's close comrade Tibor Szamuely recruited urban youths to seize the harvest from the countryside. Known as 'the Lenin Boys', they terrorized the peasantry and herded them forcibly into collective farms. Churches were burned down or desecrated. Grain was seized in the villages. Kun acted on the assumption that the food-supply emergency left the communists with no time to conciliate the peasants as Lenin had initially done with his Decree on Land. The result was civil war. On 4 August 1919, while mayhem enveloped Hungary, the Romanian armed forces poured over the border and overthrew communism in Budapest. White terror replaced Red terror, and vengeance was wreaked on known communists and their supporters. Jews were beaten up or murdered. With the country in chaos, the food supply collapsed and famine spread. Having originally been supportive of Romania's cross-border initiative against the communists, the Allies were disconcerted by the reckless savagery.[4] Kun himself, who was both communist and Jewish, fled abroad, eventually making his way to Moscow where he was welcomed into the Red Army as a political commissar. The experiment in Hungarian communism was over.

The same fate attended the Munich Workers' Council, which had proclaimed a Bavarian Council Republic on 7 April 1919. Led by Max Levien and Eugen Leviné, the Council replaced the cabinet led by the anti-war socialist Kurt Eisner, who had been assassinated by a German nationalist. The crisis in food supplies and mass unemployment deepened in the city. Levien and Leviné had Russian passports and were admirers of the October Revolution in Petrograd. They gave impetus to taking factories and large-scale commerce into the hands of the Council Republic, which systematically threatened the propertied elite in Munich and its environs. The Catholic Church was put on notice to stay strictly out of politics. A security police was established and telegrams were dispatched to Moscow announcing communist victory in Bavaria. Such euphoria was quickly shown to be misplaced because the national government in Berlin was able to mobilize the fierce kind of military reaction that had crushed the Spartacists in January 1919. In Munich the popularity of Levien and Leviné waned. Businesses had failed, unemployment grew, crime soared spectacularly after the Council released common offenders from prison. The government ordered its troops into the city. Levien had escaped to Vienna at the last moment. He found refuge in Moscow two years later. Leviné refused this option and was arrested, tried and executed. He was resigned to his fate: 'We communists are all dead men on leave.'[5]

Nevertheless the Politburo, except perhaps for Stalin, held on to the idea that 'Europe' was on the brink of revolution. Every time Lenin saw political stirrings abroad he told Bolsheviks that their revolutionary predictions were coming to fulfilment. In early March 1919 he announced that Birmingham in Great Britain had acquired its Soviet of Workers' Deputies and that the Lloyd George cabinet had been compelled to recognize such soviets as 'economic organizations'.[6] Lenin was either ill-informed by foreign newspapers or the victim of his own hyper-optimism. He was not wrong, however, about the volatility of politics in Europe. The end of the war had led to food shortages and rises in the cost of living. Strikes and factory occupations took place and Europe was gaining a carpet of communist parties. The People's Commissariat of Foreign Affairs needed to avoid too overt an association with the new parties to avoid the suspicion that its officials were working in alliance with them.

The usual technique of influence, through Comintern's instructions from Moscow, was to split off the left wings of socialist or labour parties. This was on display in the United States in August 1919 after the Communist Labor Party was created through a rupture inside the Socialist Party. Factional rivalries persisted in the new organization, and within days a rival Communist Party of America also emerged. Both claimed allegiance to Comintern and expressed admiration for the October Revolution. Lenin and Trotsky were their common heroes. Comintern in Moscow was annoyed at having to adjudicate between the two.[7] Zinoviev's task at Comintern became to heal divisions in the new foreign communist parties and to enforce obedience to the

Comintern Executive Committee. Parties were called up to march forward to the global achievement of communism.

At the same time Soviet Russia looked for a brisk return to trade with western states. They approached independent Estonia with proposals to restore commercial links. Sovnarkom's interest lay in using Tallinn, the Estonian capital and chief port, as an entrepôt on the Baltic for Russian imports and exports. A Russo-Estonian treaty was signed. A breach had been made in the international wall of capitalism. Now that Estonia had proved amenable to an agreement, the hope was that Sweden, Germany and even the USA or Great Britain might be next.[8] Overtures were also made to the United States through Sovnarkom's Bureau of Information on Soviet Russia, which was run by Ludwig Martens and Santeri Nuorteva. The idea was to tempt the Americans into resuming commerce with Russia by various offers. One of them involved turning over immense territories to America's control in return for America taking over responsibility for the pre-October Russian state debt, a debt that was a sticking point for the betterment of Russo-American relations. Henry Ford and J. P. Morgan Jr were among those they approached. Russian mining and agricultural resources were promised in ready abundance.[9]

The US authorities were fearful of the spread of communist influence in American cities. In November 1919, 200 suspected 'Russian Bolsheviki' were arrested. Those taken into custody included the anarchist leaders Emma Goldman and Alexander Berkman. Charles Ruthenberg, secretary of the Communist Party of America, was put in prison. Many had their activities heavily restricted and were kept under surveillance. Two hundred and forty-nine communists and anarchists held on Ellis Island were deported to Russia in December 1919 in the *Buford* transport ship, which became known in the press as the Red Ark.[10] The deportees, who had been fed a saccharine depiction of Russia under Bolshevism by American reporters such as John Reed and Louise Bryant, would discover on arrival that the oppression of the Cheka and the state machinery were basic features of life of the Soviet order. The Bolsheviks had by then grown accustomed to assuming that they had no alternative to using merciless force to cement the foundations of the one-party state.

But they had not abandoned their vision of a world communist order where everyone would live a free life and fulfil his or her potential – and their propaganda regularly emphasized this. They felt sure that communism was about to supplant capitalism in Europe and North America and to liberate the colonies of all empires. Even oppressors could still dream.

43. EXPERIMENTALISM IN ADVERSITY: ENFORCING AND COPING WITH THE SOVIET WAY OF LIFE

Sovnarkom told the world that Russia was preparing the ground for a new way of life for humanity. For a while, little notice was taken of such claims, but as the communists sank their foundations deep into Russian soil, they began to be taken more seriously.

The international image of Soviet communism among its foreign critics drew upon a storehouse of conservative and liberal political invective. Winston Churchill described the Bolsheviks as 'baboons' and Bolshevism as a 'bacillus' imported into Russia with Lenin on the sealed train ride across Germany. Western newspapers regularly reported on Soviet deceit, misanthropy and slaughter. Sermons were delivered to Christian congregations about communism as a portent of the Apocalypse. Kremlin leaders were depicted as the destroyers of civilization itself who flailed at standards of decency, tradition and peacefulness. Cartoonists depicted communists as hooded, becloaked, menacing aliens. Jews had been depicted in this fashion for centuries, and anti-Bolsheviks spread the belief that the October Revolution was part of a Jewish global conspiracy to dominate people everywhere. Communism was said to stand for human degradation, involving the crushing of religion, family ties and private property.

Communists aimed to puncture these negative images. Workers and peasants in Russia were told that the October Revolution had secured them their freedom, a freedom that had been denied them for centuries. There were acute worries about food and employment but Bolshevik pamphlets continued to herald new revolutionary modes of existence. In 1918 the letter post was made free to everyone. In the following year it was decreed that all children up to the age of sixteen should be fed at the state's expense.[1] The virtues of sharing goods and services were proclaimed. Hygiene campaigns were frequent – not the easiest lesson to give when soap was often in deficit. Drunkenness was censured and the vodka prohibition was prolonged. The Cheka sent out squads to shut down the flourishing illicit stills.[2] Bolsheviks continued to insist that a radiant future lay in wait once the civil wars were over and economic recovery was in full flow.

Students experimented with different ways of living. Some formed urban communes. Often this took place in institute dormitories or in rented apartments. Usually they pooled whatever income they received. Sexual partnerships were fluid and 'bourgeois' conventions about marriage were despised.[3]

Such experimentalism held no attraction for Nikita Okunev. Before the year was out, he decided that the new freedoms were 'really the most terrible slavery':

> All adults are now twisted round, bound tight and stretched out by political discipline, trade unions, soviets, committees, mandates, identity cards, decrees, work norms [*normirovki*], taxes, searches, self-protection, expropriations, pressures and aggravations. They've definitely assigned grey pouches to everyone, numbered everyone, restricted everyone and dished out punishments to everyone: 'Dig, spit, sleep and don't do any talking!'[4]

He added:

> And now it's only mindless youths who have such freedom as none of us ever had and didn't feel the need for. There are desperate lads hanging around on Moscow pavements and boulevards and going out skating with *papirosy* dangling from their lips, and near the bathhouses stroll girls of the same age to sell their feeble pleasures, shorn of shame or supervision, because there is no longer any prostitution or church marriages. Everything is free, everything is fenced off – but not fenced off from crimes or from awful diseases.[5]

Okunev had never expected good to come from the October Revolution but the worst aspects that came about in the following years surprised him.[6]

Rationing continued in the cities. Peasants were expected to feed themselves. Lenin and other Bolsheviks saw ration cards as a wonderful means of expunging traditional social privilege and looking after the workers and soldiers who had helped them to power. People had to register their place of habitation with the authorities. In the case of apartment buildings, the house committee had to testify to a resident's right to a ration card. Caretakers were frequently used by the Cheka as informants.[7] Identity cards with personal photos were issued by public institutions and were often needed for access to buildings or to obtain food, and losing them might mean starvation. Forgers quickly produced passable imitations of official documents.

The rationing rules gave precedence to Red Army soldiers. The British secret agent Paul Dukes solved his difficulties in getting fed by enlisting in the Red forces, which also enabled him to pick up intelligence about communist military preparations:

> Apart from greater freedom of movement and preference over civilians in applications for lodging, amusement, or travelling tickets, the Red soldier received rations greatly superior both in quantity and quality to those of the civilian population. Previous to this time I had received only half a pound of bread daily and had had to take my scanty dinner at a filthy communal eating house, but as a Red soldier I received, besides a dinner and other odds and ends not worth mentioning, a pound and sometimes a pound and a half of tolerably good black bread, which alone was sufficient, accustomed as I am to a crude diet, to subsist on with relative comfort.[8]

Next in line for rations after the troops came industrial workers, as Sovnarkom was keen to fulfil the promises it had made to the 'proletariat'.

Fëdor Stepun had several family members and friends who succumbed to the Spanish influenza epidemic. He wrote that 'it was more difficult to get buried than to be executed' in Soviet Russia. A confirmation of death certificate was required from the apartment block chairman before a grave could be secured for the deceased. The Orthodox Church no longer possessed an official function. The apartment block chairman where Stepun lived, however, had disappeared without trace. The next option was to apply to the district soviet. This involved hours of standing in a queue for the necessary permit. Then one needed a janitor to dig out a grave. Bribery across society was rife, and usually this required handing over half a bottle of vodka or five pounds of bread: the communist authorities had found it impossible to eradicate private deals of this kind. Stepun was driven to approaching an acquaintance working at a bacteriological laboratory to get the bottles of 'spirit' that he needed.[9]

Official privilege spread, and few Bolsheviks resisted its comforts. Before the October Revolution there had been no more fashionable barber's shop in Moscow than the one on Kuznetski Most. By 1920 it was closed to the general customer. Only officials of the central and Moscow Cheka could have their hair cut there. A sign was pinned at the entrance: 'Outsiders prohibited'.[10] Trotsky kept use of Nicholas II's Delaunay Belleville limousine while Lenin travelled around Moscow in the emperor's Rolls Royce. Trade union leader Mikhail Tomski got himself a smart, black Pierce Arrow.[11] Central Committee members and people's commissars had chauffeurs, house servants, nannies and access to doctors and went off at the weekends to mansions and dachas that had been expropriated from the propertied elite. Karl Radek obtained a Grand Ducal suite in the Kremlin for his family and damaged the fine furniture and paintings. This annoyed Natalya Sedova, Trotsky's wife, who was officially in charge of conserving the cultural heritage. But Trotsky and Sedova also required good food and reliable servants.

The Sukharevka market in central Moscow became one of the few public spaces where people could buy and sell. It was popular among those – the majority of the city's residents – who could not survive on their ration book. The market spread to adjacent streets. Street kids sold cigarettes, sugar and sweets. Nikita Okunev sold his ten-year-old frock coat for 1,600 rubles.[12] The authorities blew hot and cold about 'the Sukharevka', allowing it to function and then closing it down. Even when the market had permission to operate, the Cheka and the militia frequently raided its stalls and impounded goods. Permanent closure would have increased the hardship for tens of thousands of families.[13] The former upper classes and their 'hangers-on' had to look out for themselves in dire circumstances. They had been kicked out of their palatial city residences to have them divided among the poor. Those members of the old propertied elites who stayed in the cities under Soviet rule had to sell off valuable items in order to survive. You could find many fur coats and fine crockery for sale at the markets, as well as grand pianos, tapestries and candelabras. The propertied elites could no longer ship goods abroad, and to travel themselves required exceptional permission.

Bolsheviks called on workers to perform extra labour on a voluntary basis. Usually there was no work at the weekends. In 1919 they announced a regular *subbotnik*, named after the Russian word for

Saturday, when people would shovel litter, mud and snow from public places.[14] Lenin was filmed taking part as an example to everyone else.

The bourgeoisie – which the Sovnarkom decree of 10 October 1918 defined as people who lived on 'non-labour income' – were regularly ordered to clear snow from the streets and railways.[15] Under the Soviet Constitution they were no longer citizens. Whilst the very wealthy had fled south across the Black Sea to exile in central or western Europe, many continued to wait on events. Even Dowager Empress Maria Fëdorovna refused to leave, saying to the Canadian colonel who came to spirit her from Yalta onto a Royal Navy vessel: 'I am an old woman now. My life is nearly over. Here I am able to help in organizing some resistance to the Bolsheviki.' She had grudgingly complied with the local soviet's demand for her to obtain identity papers before she received her sugar ration. In January 1919, she heard of the summary execution of four Romanov grand dukes in the Peter–Paul Fortress in Petrograd. This changed her mind, and she departed for the Mediterranean under British protection.[16]

The changes in society also reached Alexander Zamaraev in Totma in late 1918:

> The monastery superintendent and treasurer have been arrested and thrown in jail. Why? Practically every merchant is in prison and compulsory contributions have been levied upon all householders – one, two, five, twenty thousand [rubles] or more. Absolute devastation. Our administration has to find 200,000 rubles. Everyone's discontented and the situation is intensifying.[17]

The pressure was unremitting upon the wealthy, who sought ways to relieve it by whatever means they could. When a demand of 50,000 rubles was presented to the Polyakov and Sarafanov families in the village of Mamontovka in Moscow province, they took the committee official aside and bribed him. As a result they had to pay up only 5,000 rubles each. The deal was celebrated with vodka.[18] Even Nikita Okunev, who worked for the Moscow river transport administration, was treated as a bourgeois resident who might be hiding possessions from the authorities. His family apartment was subjected to a compulsory search in September 1919. The two visiting commissars opened half a dozen cupboards but left him undisturbed, except that the militiaman accompanying them used the toilet and made a foul mess which they left for Okunev to clean up.[19]

The categories of wealth that the Bolsheviks applied were menacingly fluid, and it was not only the highest social classes who were targeted. Peasants like Totma's Zamaraev himself were also forced to make expensive contributions.[20] When money was not forthcoming, the authorities took produce instead. Zamaraev recorded: 'The Bolsheviks have seized horses, carriages, potatoes and onions in the name of contributions [*kontributsii*].'[21] At the same time he found himself required to perform compulsory labour tasks. In February 1919 he had to carry twenty-three pieces of timber to the Totma brickworks. It was snowing and the wind blew hard.[22]

The better-off were sought out by criminal gangs in the big cities. Muggings and burglaries were commonplace in affluent residential districts. Nikita Okunev lamented that thieves stole furs, clothes and shoes from the house where his mother, brother and niece lived.[23] Even Lenin became a victim. On a snowy Sunday in January 1919 he was being driven to a school in Sokolniki in the Moscow outskirts where his wife Nadezhda had arranged a children's fir-tree party. With him in the limousine were his sister Maria, his chauffeur Stepan Gil and a bodyguard called Chebanov. They reached the Sokolniki Chaussée in the snow and dark when three armed men sprang into the road whistling and shouting. Gil assumed they were militiamen and halted. He had got into trouble on a previous occasion when he was fired on after speeding off. Lenin produced his identity documents but was ordered out of the limousine with everyone else. When a gun was pointed at his head he shouted: 'My name is Lenin!' Maria asked to see their documents but they replied: 'Criminals don't need documents!' Lenin was relieved of his Browning revolver before the three thieves drove off in the limousine. The Cheka organized a hunt for the robbers. When arrested, they admitted to the crime and complained that they had heard Lenin identify himself as 'Levin'. Presumably they expected indulgence for robbing a wealthy Jew. One of them, Yuri Koshelnikov, said that after racing off and re-examining the stolen documents they realized that their victim was the leader of the Soviet state. The ultimate fate of the robbers is unrecorded.

Communist propaganda claimed that the entire working class was united in solidarity with Sovnarkom but this was untrue. Throughout the Civil War there were industrial strikes and rallies by disgruntled industrial workers. Protests about the food supply and the Red military draft were widespread. This came as a shock for Bolshevik leaders who in 1917 had been treated as revolutionary heroes in the same places.

After the Ericsson workers ejected Politburo member Zinoviev from their premises in March 1919, he went to the Bolshevik party congress and declared: 'Truly we cannot hide from ourselves the fact that in some places the word commissar has become a swear word. The man in a leather jacket has become hateful, as they are saying now in Perm. It would be laughable to hide this. We must face the truth.' Blame was heaped on residual groups of Mensheviks, Socialist-Revolutionaries and Left Socialist-Revolutionaries who kept up their agitation against the Bolsheviks. At the Putilov Works the Cheka took several Left Socialist-Revolutionaries captive before executing them.[24]

In the countryside the Soviet agencies' attempts to requisition grain and conscript young men met with fierce resistance. The violence was strongest in the Volga region and Ukraine where grain surpluses were usually abundant. The Bolsheviks had always planned to establish collective farms there. As soon as the Red Army moved south, they forcibly put their ambition into effect. Resistance was treated as 'banditry'. *Pravda* reported openly about the military operations of the food-supply squads in Nizhni Novgorod province: 'They shoot in the air, point rifles in people's chests and set up a machine gun in a prominent position for maximum effect.'[25] When the Reds suspected peasants of withholding produce, they whipped, beat and sometimes shot them. Peasant resisters fled to the woods and formed groups that became known as the Greens.[26]

But life and its choices were never less than complicated in Soviet Russia, as Nikita Okunev supremely exemplified:

> Look what tragedies have been brought on us by revolution. I, a passive resister and one who grieves over the ruin of the old, difficult but beautiful life and who has a son who is an undeniable and already convinced Marxist. It's sickening to think what's ahead on this basis.[27]

A few weeks later he added the explanation that his beloved son Lelya was a Chekist:

> To my deep regret, my own son is serving in it in his post as an inspector in the struggle with crime.[28]

Okunev senior had to hope his family would get through all this unscathed.

Each Okunev family member was resourceful. Nikita obtained a post as acting assistant at the Moskvoretski port administration –

it was the best that he could get as someone classified as a 'bourgeois'.[29] The pay, at 915 rubles, meant he could afford only one 'half-rotten Astrakhan herring' a day.[30] Nikita walked to work to save money.[31] He had no money for a doctor when he suffered a severe lung inflammation. He managed by selling off valuables on Sukharevka market and with some funds from his brother.[32] The family ran out of logs for fuel. His daughter Galya gave up school because she had to do the family's shopping.[33] By late 1919 Nikita was fit enough again to go out cutting down trees by the river Moskva – his work administration gave time off for staff to obtain the timber they needed. Coal and wood were no longer available to buy. Nikita and his brother sold their late father's dacha rather than lose everything inside it to vandals. It was the end of Nikita's dream of a well-heeled, comfortable existence. With half the proceeds he was only able to buy fifteen pounds of tea.[34]

Nikita and his wife Antonina started up a business by doing deals from their apartment block. As her confidence increased, she began to stand outside, often in freezing temperatures, to conduct business. The constant bargaining wore her down. Customers could be very tough. Many swore at her and on one occasion she was robbed of seven or eight pairs of galoshes. Every trader also had to contend with the Cheka. In 1919 Antonina was arrested and spent a night in prison, but this did not stop her trying to earn a living for the family.[35] Antonina was in frail health herself and Nikita hated 'sponging' on her, but he reasoned that by staying on in state employment he was protecting them against commissars who might choose to expel 'bourgeois' tenants from the apartment block.[36] Nikita had a wry turn of phrase for his condition: 'Well, if I'm a "specialist" and my wife's almost a "speculator", it's all just stuff and nonsense. It's better to go and chop logs on my days off. That's the specific method that springs from bourgeois habits.'[37]

But he fretted about his family. One of his children was rising in the Cheka while the youngster Galya started working on the black market. Galya at the age of fifteen in 1919 had initially insisted on taking a job at the Moscow port administration and became an office clerk of the third rank.[38] Soon, however, she was buying and selling in private deals in Moscow.[39] Her older brother Lelya was convalescing at the time from a wound suffered on campaign with the Red Army. On his way south to Odessa he had passed a message home. Having come close to death in action, he implored Galya 'not to marry a *burzhui*'.[40] Lelya identified himself with the objectives of 'Soviet power'.

Demobbed from the Russian Army in December 1917, he had re-enlisted with the Reds and obtained a staff work post in the People's Commissariat for Military Affairs.[41] At that time he had astonished his father by seeing communism as the path to a better future for humanity. Nikita and Lelya were fond of each other. Like many Russian families, the Okunevs found ways to agree to disagree. Whatever divided them, they all wanted the fighting to end and for peace to reign.

44. INVASION AND REBELLION: FROM THE POLISH–SOVIET WAR TO THE PEASANTS' REVOLT

By spring 1920 the civil war in Russia was nearly over and the Reds were winning. But the tide of popular discontent with communism did not abate. Nikita Okunev shared the anger of fellow members of staff at the Moscow river administration who suffered severe shortages in food, fuel, linen, clothing and footwear. Life had become unbearable and communists were held responsible.

Okunev's patience broke when his management imposed an increase in the work rate. Though he had never involved himself in politics, he was the first at his workplace to put his name to a collective protest. A hundred others added their signatures. Comrade Fantalov, who oversaw the distribution of food to employees, charged Okunev with being a troublemaker and madman and he was accused of talking like a Menshevik. There was a danger that he might be arrested but Okunev was applauded by his colleagues at their next meeting and unanimously elected to speak on their behalf. The management panicked and made him an offer of promotion. Okunev rejected it. They tried again and offered him an even higher post at Glavvod, the newly created agency in charge of Russia's entire river network. He again refused but after a while agreed to lead the Glavvod sub-department in charge of steamboat-towing business. He felt guilty because he had failed to achieve the original objectives of his protest.[1]

In March 1920 strikes broke out across Moscow over the food-supply emergency.[2] Industrial workers had listened for years to socialists telling them they were poor because of the capitalist system. Although the economy no longer had bankers, stockbrokers and factory owners, the working class remained as poor as ever. It was also under-provisioned and oppressed. As the threat from the Whites receded, Trotsky wanted to tighten the screws of state control. He proposed in particular to create 'labour armies' rather than send soldiers home to their families. Workers in factories and mines and on the railways were angered by the communist party's desire to run their lives on militarist lines. Mensheviks and Socialist-Revolutionaries saw their chance and reinforced their agitation in Moscow, Tula, Kharkov and Kiev. Still more worrisome to the party leadership was the sympathy shown to the strikers by local communists who became known as the Workers' Opposition and called for workforces to be restored to decisive influence over the management of factories.[3]

Trotsky saw that nothing could be settled unless the policy was changed on food supplies. After touring the Urals in February 1920, he reported that peasants had no incentive to produce more than they needed for themselves at a time when the authorities were requisitioning any surplus. He suggested introducing a progressive tax on output and leaving rural households with a greater amount of grain to sell to the state. He explained that, for this to have a desirable effect, the state would need to increase the supply of industrial products to the countryside. Trotsky accepted that his project had to be limited to those regions where the land was fertile and agricultural surpluses were possible. In other parts of the country he recommended creating collective farms.[4] But the Central Committee, focusing on his fiscal reform ideas, turned him down after Lenin accused him of one of the greatest crimes against the Bolshevik belief system, nothing less than 'free trade-ism'.[5]

But Lenin also still thought it perilous for the party to campaign for agricultural collectivization. In the provinces there were sporadic attempts to compel peasants to join collective farms that would be made from the amalgamation of their landholdings. One such effort was made in spring 1920 by the communist leadership in Tambov province. Hardly anyone in the locality thought this a good idea. One peasant told Anton Okninski:

> That *kommuna* just ain't the right thing for us. What really does it mean? It surely means that everybody's belongings go into a common pot: horses, cattle, rams, carts and yokes and everything else. For instance, I've got a horse that used to be worth 150 rubles and someone else had one worth seventy-five. I've got three cows, all of them good ones, while someone else has only one and it's a poor one. I've got two carts with iron-rimmed wheels and someone else has a single cart which doesn't have

> iron-rimmed wheels. I'm a clever, hard-working fellow and he's a ne'er-do-well. And it's like this all down the line. And what then happens is that no one can disentangle all this mess.[6]

But the collectivization process went ahead in parts of the province despite any such objections.

All this time the international situation was turning dark for Sovnarkom, and nowhere was this more obvious than in the western parts of the former Russian Empire. Poland's armed forces under Józef Piłsudski began a campaign to conquer territories that had been part of the old Polish-Lithuanian Commonwealth which had been dismembered in the late eighteenth century. Piłsudski signed an alliance with Symon Petliura who had proclaimed the creation of a Ukrainian People's Republic and aimed at the destruction of Soviet power in Ukraine. The Polish Army independently rolled forward without meeting serious resistance before seizing Kiev from the Bolsheviks on 7 May 1920 and overwhelming the Ukrainian Soviet Republic. But the Reds, after being caught by surprise, regathered their forces and equipment. The war was quickly resumed. On 10 June the Polish Army was driven out of Kiev and forced onto a long retreat out of Ukraine.[7]

Lenin's instinct was to pursue the Poles across the river Vistula and deep into Poland itself. On 5 May 1920 Trotsky had spoken publicly of his doubts 'that we'll emerge as the victors after utterly crushing the enemy'.[8] Lenin rejected this prognosis and stressed the opportunity, predicted by the Bolshevik leadership since 1917, to trigger the 'European socialist revolution'. Lenin carried the day in the Politburo. As the Red high command planned the Polish stage of its advance, he ordered the Reds to carry out a brutal social purge in the areas through which they passed. He advised Trotsky's deputy in the People's Commissariat for Military Affairs:

> A beautiful plan. Finish it off *together* with Dzierżyński. Disguised as 'Greens' (whom we'll afterwards heap the blame on to), we'll advance 10–15 versts and hang the kulaks, priests, landed gentry. 100,000 rubles for every one of them who is hanged.[9]

His words opened the gates to brutality and as the Red Army moved forward, repressive measures were taken in the newly occupied territory. The violence against civilians that had ravaged the Imperial war zone in 1914–17 was to be repeated in many of the same localities: only the social and ethnic targets were different.

In mid-July the Reds, freshly allied with the Lithuanian government, recaptured Minsk, Vilnius and Grodno from the Poles – it was a campaign of extreme international complexity in the east of Europe. On the Politburo's orders, a Polish Revolutionary Committee was created to form a new government in Warsaw in the near future. The Western Allies felt horror that communism might envelop Poland and they hurriedly proposed a peace settlement that would leave the eastern border of Polish territories where they had been since the eighteenth century. The mood in the Bolshevik leadership by then was optimistic and the dream of communizing central and western Europe appeared within range. Poland was to undergo 'Sovietization'. Support, not just political but also military support, would be supplied for a communist takeover in Germany. The Allied peace proposal was rejected at a moment when Poland's military collapse appeared imminent.[10]

This optimism quickly proved misplaced. The Red Army was divided into two fronts – Stalin was political commissar on the southern front in Galicia and refused requests to send reinforcements to the northern front, which was taking the fight to Polish forces around Warsaw. The Reds were stalled in the north and Warsaw was saved from occupation.[11] The Red Army fled in chaos back to central Russia. On 1 September 1920, after a sobering report from Trotsky, the Politburo agreed to parley with Poland for a peace settlement.[12]

From June 1920 there were also bilateral discussions in London about resuming trade between Great Britain and Russia. Leonid Krasin, recently appointed as people's commissar of foreign trade, headed the Soviet side and was joined by Politburo member Lev Kamenev – a sign of the urgency among Soviet rulers. Kamenev took to the high life. The sticking points were matters of finance and property. Sovnarkom had unilaterally written off the debts contracted by Nicholas II and Alexander Kerensky. It had nationalized several sectors of the economy in which British investors had been prominent. The British cabinet sought from Moscow a recognition of obligations in respect of Russian state loans contracted before the October Revolution.[13] After the defeat against the Poles the Soviet negotiating team in London was told to intensify its efforts for a deal. Lloyd George was keen to agree a compromise, but not at any price. The summer negotiations lasted through autumn and into the winter of 1920–21.

Meanwhile violence against the authorities was spreading across the Russian countryside as many peasants realized they would be unable to feed their families in the coming winter. The communist authorities described the rebels as 'kulaks' and 'bandits'. Clashes came to the boil in Tambov province where the Socialist-Revolutionary Alexander Antonov led rebel forces against Soviet rural strongholds. Antonov was the son of a locksmith and a seamstress in Kirsanov district. He had joined the Socialist-Revolutionaries as a young man and had been arrested in 1909 and condemned to death, a sentence which was commuted to hard labour. Freed by the February Revolution, he enlisted in the militia of his native province but turned against the communist dictatorship. From 1918 he rallied armed units to challenge for power in the surrounding territories.[14]

Lenin had to face a discontented Bolshevik party conference in September 1920. In a speech that wasn't made public until after the fall of communism in the late 1980s, he acknowledged that the Soviet order had experienced 'a deep defeat, a catastrophic situation'. He recognized that the Red Army had suffered 'a gigantic, unprecedented defeat' against the Poles by saying, 'It undoubtedly means that a mistake was made'.[15] He accepted that the Politburo ought to have accepted the peace terms previously offered.[16]

Some within the party justifiably believed Lenin himself to be responsible for the disaster against the Poles. The party as a whole was in crisis. The Politburo was chastened by the hostility on display at the conference and promised organizational reforms but otherwise it went its own way, such as by making overtures to German industrial corporations. Bolshevik leaders knew that German capitalism desperately needed foreign orders, and Russia was short of new locomotives to replace those which had become unusable after the years of fighting. An order was placed with Krupp's to produce 1,000 railway engines. Russian financial creditworthiness was abysmal and so German entrepreneurs would accept payment only in gold ingots. As the Western Allies would immediately impound such payment as part of their post-war reparations requirement, a Swedish bank was used as an intermediary. Further orders for railway equipment were signed in Germany.[17]

The broad economic picture across Soviet Russia was one of utter devastation. Alexander Zamaraev could see no end in sight:

> Yet another requisitioning [*mobilizatsiya*] of the horses. The republic is undeviatingly bringing the population to destitution. They levy everything in vast numbers: grain, hay, livestock from every settlement.[18]

In his Totma district, destitution was widespread:

> Meals on the farms are now very bad, just hot water and bread. Many people don't even have potatoes. Kvass and pies are a rarity. Previously peasants used to buy fish, millet, white flour, oil, tea and sugar. Now there's nothing of that kind and our surpluses, such as they were, have been seized.[19]

By September 1920 the Bolshevik party and soviet provincial leadership in Tambov, despairing of both suppressing the Green rebellion and achieving the grain levy quota, asked Moscow for military reinforcements. Lenin was firm with Dzierżyński about the supreme priority of crushing the revolt: 'The fastest (and exemplary) liquidation is absolutely necessary. I ask to be informed about what measures are undertaken. It's urgent to show greater energy and provide more forces.' By November 1920 the Cheka reported the complete defeat of Antonov's men.[20] But it was quickly recognized that the rebellion was anything but at an end and Lenin at last saw the urgent need for compromise. At the Congress of Soviets in December 1920, he outlined a scheme to reward peasant households that produced and handed over surplus grain to the state, an idea not unlike Trotsky's earlier in the year.[21] Like Trotsky he was fiercely denounced by fellow leading Bolsheviks. By New Year 1921 Bolshevism had no clear perspective on how to moderate the seething discontent in cities and villages except by force. The Mensheviks and Socialist-Revolutionaries at the Congress argued in vain that even Lenin's scheme for reform was anyway much too flimsy. They wanted grain requisitioning to be halted and replaced by a graduated tax-in-kind that would be set at a low enough level to leave the peasantry with enough to trade on the reopened market. Their suggestions were treated by Bolsheviks as a betrayal of socialist principles.[22]

Mensheviks and Socialist-Revolutionaries countered that Bolsheviks were ignoring the reality of imminent famine. But rather than debating the fundamental food-supply question, the Bolshevik party enveloped itself, from top to bottom, in a discussion instigated by Trotsky who wanted to eliminate the flimsy autonomy of trade unions and put them under direct state control. Most of the party veterans agreed that the working class should be subjected to an increased degree of discipline. Where the various Bolshevik factions disagreed was about whether or not to accept Trotsky's extreme solution. Inside the party, only the Workers' Opposition pointed out that the October Revolution had been made in order to liberate, rather than enslave, the working class.

45. THE NEW ECONOMIC POLICY: MARKET REFORM AND INTERNAL PARTY DISCONTENT

At New Year 1921, Alexander Zamaraev was dispirited by what he saw on a visit to Totma. The few surviving market stalls in town had nothing but some clay pots, two wooden tubs, some hay, firewood and a few logs for sale. Two days later an armed squad turned up to requisition the district's remaining supplies of wheat, flax, seed and wool. Zamaraev felt bitter: 'The year 1920 has ended without bringing anything good with it. The people are groaning under Bolshevism because they've seized everything from the people and given nothing in return. Squads upon squads are everywhere, bringing agents along with them.'[1]

Lenin appreciated the need to change agrarian policy even more extensively than he had suggested in December 1920. Like most other leading Bolsheviks, he had assumed that the state had the right to requisition whatever it wanted from the peasantry. Party officials and peasants visiting from areas of unrest persuaded him otherwise. His fellow leader Bukharin returned from Tambov, where trouble was intense for governmental authority, in a mood of utter alarm about the 'peasant uprising'.[2] Lenin feared that the entire Soviet state could disintegrate unless there was a basic reform. On 8 February 1921 he drafted a proposal to scrap requisitioning, replacing it with a tax-in-kind and leaving the peasants with grain that they could sell on local markets.[3] A working party was set up under Kamenev to present practical plans inside a fortnight and a cautious discussion was opened in the press. Lenin evidently foresaw that his proposal would annoy party veterans, and he managed the process with care. On 24 February the Central Committee met to rule on the matter. The decision went in Lenin's favour.[4]

Lenin knew he could expect to be accused of betraying communist economic principles. But he was determined to face down any resistance in the party. The party was also embroiled in a dispute about trade unions and the state's role in regulating demands by organized workers. Trotsky wanted unions to be put under military-style discipline. Lenin viewed this as dangerous extremism while Bukharin tried to build a bridge between Lenin and Trotsky. Factional strife was tearing the party apart.

Meanwhile, the emergency in Russia continued to deepen. Trotsky was appointed to lead a defence committee to quell the strike movement in Moscow.[5] But Petrograd factories too were ceasing production and arrests were made of Mensheviks and Socialist-Revolutionaries, including working-class ones, who were accused of counter-revolutionary agitation. Dzierżyński, who had recently stepped down from the Cheka, was recalled to guarantee firm leadership.[6] Mutiny was even brewing in the naval garrison on Kronstadt island near to Petrograd. Famine had spread across the Volga region. The central party leadership worried that the spring sowings would be jeopardized. On the eve of the party congress, as panic mounted, the Central Committee deputed Lenin, Kamenev, Alexander Tsyurupa and Grigori Petrovski to finalize the agrarian reform project. Meanwhile it decided that all communists should be armed.[7] All this was kept confidential but Nikita Okunev, despite the censorship and official propaganda, was able to read between the lines of the Soviet newspapers that 'something unpleasant for Soviet power' was happening.[8]

When Lenin opened the congress on 8 March he warned that the Revolution was at risk unless an agrarian reform was introduced. He gave some icy advice: 'The peasantry must do a bit of starving so as to relieve the factories and towns from utter starvation.' Force would be necessary to ensure compliance.[9] [10]

No progress was achievable, Lenin argued, as long as the party's disunity persisted. His speech lasted two hours: he was determined to get the congress to appreciate the sheer urgency of the situation.[11] The 'trade union discussion' also cropped up in the debate that followed. Lenin's arguments about the unions secured support from a thumping majority.[12] His position at the congress was paradoxically enhanced by the news that the Kronstadt sailors had moved to outright mutiny. Lenin, Trotsky and Dzierżyński conferred on measures to suppress them.[13] Trotsky oversaw the military operation from Petrograd, ordering Red forces to attack with all means including bomber aircraft. Mutineers who refused to lay down their arms were to be arrested. In public Trotsky alleged that inveterate counter-revolutionaries were guiding the mutiny from abroad and that sponsorship was being supplied by hostile foreign governments, but in reality the Cheka's confidential report told that trouble had grown in February 1921 not just in the naval garrison but also among Petrograd workers aggrieved about the food shortages and industrial rundown.[14]

Lenin bluntly admitted that, with his proposal for agrarian reform, 'freedom of trade means a return to capitalism'.[15] He insisted, though, that the authorities could balance the interests of the entire working class and peasantry.[16] A few governmental officials spoke against him but even Trotsky's sympathizers such as Preobrazhenski supported Lenin.[17] The new policy was endorsed.[18] Lenin reinforced this with a motion on party unity that introduced a ban on factional activity. Radek quipped: 'I have the feeling that there was perhaps being established here a rule which can be turned against anyone as yet unknown.' The condemnation of the Workers' Opposition as a 'deviation' from Bolshevism was also endorsed. Lenin had triumphed.[19]

The trade talks in London were also coming to a conclusion. On 16 March 1921, which was the last day of the party congress in Moscow, Leonid Krasin brought the policy to success in London with the signing of the Anglo-Soviet Trade Agreement. The communists had to agree to avoiding political interference in the countries of the British Empire. The benefit for communism in Russia would be a resumption of import-export commerce with one of the world's greatest economic powers. A breach in the Allied embargo was being effected despite disapproval in France and the US. Sovnarkom also protected its interests by agreeing to peace terms with the Poles in the treaty of Riga, which was signed two days later on 18 March 1921. Finland, Estonia, Latvia and Lithuania retained their independence and no effort was made to claw back territories recently ceded to Turkey. These exceptions apart, the lands of the tsars at their most extensive had been brought under Soviet authority. The Red Army's last operations after the Polish debacle of 1920 were in the south Caucasus, where Georgia was conquered by mid-March and the Menshevik government deposed. Russia was emerging from years of fighting and the Bolsheviks were looking forward to bringing communism to every corner of the life of society.

The New Economic Policy, as the agrarian reform became known, did not receive instant public acceptance. Governmental agencies sent out functionaries to explain the basis of the new policy as well as to collect the tax-in-kind. Village elders had to be contacted about the size of each household's harvest. The authorities knew that elders seldom gave honest information even while seeming to cooperate. Mutual distrust was systemic and consultations on the spot were the only way to make the policy work, and at least it lowered the degree of peasant obstructiveness.[20]

The Bolsheviks watched warily. Mensheviks and Socialist-Revolutionaries said that the peasantry ought to receive greater licence to sell their produce privately on urban markets.[21] They agitated amidst the working classes of the towns and the Cheka pursued them. Soviet officials feared the regrowth of a rival socialist movement and clamped down. By the end of the year Moscow was the only city where the Menshevik Party was able, however feebly, to operate openly.[22] Being conscious that the New Economic Policy was a strategic retreat, Bolsheviks showed their enemies an iron fist. This reinforced Lenin's determination to enforce internal party unity and discipline. The Bolsheviks worried that the Russian Orthodox Church too could become a rallying point for Russians who hated Bolshevism. The Soviet press wrote that the Christian faith was on the wane and that too few believers were available for the bells to be rung. Nikolai Okunev scoffed at such claims. At Easter 1921 the places of worship were packed with congregations. The bell peals were as loud as they ever had been, drowning out the noise made at the May Day celebrations hosted by Bolshevik leaders.[23]

A party conference was held in May 1921 to try and settle some of the disputes among communists. Lenin badly needed somehow or other to win over a sceptical audience. He condemned those in the highest echelon of the Bolshevik leadership like Central Committee member Mikhail Tomski who declined to stick to official policy on the trade unions. Lenin revealed that he had called for Tomski to lose both his seat in the Central Committee and even his party card. Unity and compliance was essential in moments of crisis.[24]

This did not deflect criticism of the New Economic Policy. Iosif Vareikis asked where Lenin intended to stop in his concessions to 'the market'. He told of how workers in Tambov province objected to the growth of private commerce. He warned that the better-off segment of the peasantry would soon throw up leaders of its own and challenge the Bolshevik party's monopoly.[25]

Nikita Okunev looked upon the situation with a wry pair of eyes:

> They are making rent offers for factories, plants and permitting artisanal production and all kinds of small concerns but you don't hear of anyone being keen to take back his former enterprise into his hands. And it's only small stalls that are springing up like mushrooms across Moscow, especially those selling prepared food or fresh vegetables. If you walk down a street you cannot help but be struck when you see 'long forgotten dreams and the charm of the distant past: salted fish fillet, salmon, caviar, ham, lemons, berries, nuts and sweets . . .'

Coffee shops and dairy bars had opened whose new operators were not shy about paying millions of rubles to hire premises: they obviously thought that high profits were in the offing.[26]

Mikhail Tukhachevski, fresh from crushing the Kronstadt mutineers, was sent south to crush the rebellious peasants known as the Tambov Greens. He appeared to relish the need for 'brutality'. If 'bandits' refused to surrender, their families were to be taken hostage and held in concentration camps before being deported to distant parts of Soviet Russia. The property they left behind would be distributed among pro-Soviet peasants.[27] Field courts-martial were held in front of peasant assemblies. Anyone who had attacked Soviet officials or Red Army personnel was shot. When a whole village rose against 'Soviet power' it could be put to the torch.[28] In June 1921 Tukhachevski issued Order no. 171 to shoot hostages from those places which refused to hand over their hidden weapons.[29] He also aimed to use aeroplanes to drop poison-gas canisters to flush out rebels from the forests.[30] His methods disturbed those Bolshevik leaders like Alexei Rykov who hoped to make a success of the New Economic Policy and feared a total breakdown of relations with the peasantry. Although Tukhachevski had to suspend Order 171, the fighting continued to torment Tambov province.[31] But by midsummer it was nearly over. In June 1922 Alexander Antonov was traced to the village of Uvarovo, where he died in a shoot-out.[32] A month later Tukhachevski could report on total victory while warning that troops would have to be stationed in the province to prevent a resurgence.

A new scheme was introduced to make income tax a universal reality in 1921. Workers had no exemption but were assigned a low flat rate along with white-collar state employees. While party rhetoric continued to place the working class on a pedestal, measures were introduced to phase out its automatic eligibility to receive food rations.[33]

The New Economic Policy's internal logic was steadily being realized. The principal intention was to lay the greatest burden on the newly legalized private traders (who until recently had been categorized as 'speculators'). By the mid-1920s direct taxation was still providing only 15 per cent of state revenues. The income tax project never raised more than 2.5 per cent.[34] Some urban markets were reopened in Moscow.[35] In mid-August 1921 even the vast Sukharevka received permission to function again. Communist misgivings about the New Economic Policy resurfaced a fortnight later, and Sukharevka was closed down.[36] Not until the May Day holiday in 1922 was it reopened.[37]

Okunev's wife Antonina died on 9 January 1922. The years of cooking, ironing, cleaning and filling the stove as well as street trading had worn her out. She had stood at her stall in all weathers. She had faced down thieving customers and oppressive Chekists. Her nerves were wrecked on that fateful day and she took out a revolver and shot herself.[38] Nikita was inconsolable. He had lost the love of his life. They had come through war, revolution and civil war together and survived. He kept on working at the Moscow port administration as he badly needed the money. But price inflation continued under the New Economic Policy. His monthly salary of forty-three million rubles was barely enough for him to live on. Nikita needed a small kerosene cooker but calculated that this by itself would swallow half his salary.[39] When someone offered him the chance to buy 500 sewing needles at 150 rubles, Nikita bought them up with the aim of selling them on to fellow traders. He too became a part-time trader.[40]

His beloved son Lelya had survived the Civil War. By May 1921 Lelya, having returned from the Polish campaign, was serving as assistant to the commander of Red forces in Ukraine with special political responsibilities.[41] His father embarrassed him by writing of a common acquaintance that he was 'a decent person even though he belonged to the party'. The military censors intercepted the letter and a report was made to Lelya's superiors. Nikita Okunev was unrepentant, quoting a line from the nineteenth-century novelist Nikolai Gogol's *Dead Souls*: 'There's only one decent person there and that's the procurator, but the truth is that the procurator is a total swine.'[42]

Distrust of Bolshevik official policy remained still sharper among peasants, and Alexander Zamaraev in Vologda province did not even bother to mention the New Economic policy in his daily jottings. Spring came early to Totma in 1921 and Zamaraev was ready to plough and sow as soon as the snow melted. The fact that he had been robbed of his harvest by a Soviet requisitioning agency in the previous year made no dent in his plans for the farming calendar as he joined together with his neighbour Vaska Parakhodёnok to carry out the early work of the season.[43] Totma district's peasantry got on with their tasks despite the traumas of recent years. But in many other villages of Soviet Russia and Ukraine, the latest rampages of the Red Army and Cheka left a residue of deep suffering and bitterness. Exhaustion was near universal after the military conflicts. Even so, it was by no means certain that the violent suppression of rural resistance would prove durably effective. In Moscow the Bolshevik leadership watched nervously to see whether more grain, meat and vegetables would reach the towns than in the years of civil war.

46. THE UNSETTLED SETTLEMENT: REINFORCED REPRESSION AND THE POLITICAL SUCCESSION QUESTION

Alexander Zamaraev's health took a sharp downturn in early 1922. His daughter Lidia took on more of the farm work and went to town for the family's needs. The entries in his diary, which Lidia had to write down for him, became briefer and briefer. The spring sowing took place as usual. Alexander, convalescing in his home, scrutinized his accounts and paid off what he owed to neighbours. He continued to do the occasional deal with them. He hated the idea of losing touch with the fields and animals in his care but he knew he could no longer do the heavy work that was the peasantry's lot in Vologda province and the rest of Russia. Lidia knew that her father's days were numbered. When he died in September that year, he was mourned by his family and the people of Totma. As cultivator, parishioner and village elder he had been one of the district's most remarkable personalities.[1]

This decent 'ordinary' man had coped as best he could under old tsarism and youthful communism. Contemptuous of Nicholas II, he nevertheless reserved his sharpest barbs for Lenin's Soviet order: 'These are the torments suffered by both people and animals. But the authorities are little bothered about the people being so tormented: they keep all the good things for themselves.'[2] A few days later he had added: 'And the people are in torment: it's just voluntary penal labour.'[3]

Simultaneously in Moscow a more powerful and conspicuous citizen, Vladimir Lenin, was also suffering a steep physical decline. Throughout the revolution and civil war his cardiac condition had worsened. Older than the other Politburo members and exhausted by his burden of duties, he suffered a stroke in May 1922 and was bedridden for the rest of his days in the Gorki sanatorium, an old gentry estate sequestered by the Bolsheviks to the south of the capital. His wife Nadezhda stayed with him. His brain remained alert and he continued to dictate letters to the Politburo and to those Bolsheviks who might influence its decisions. Nadezhda understood his need to feel involved in discussions at the highest level, and she ignored the Politburo's orders to bar him from contentious discussions of public policy. As long as he lived, Lenin was the party's patriarch whose opinions could not be ignored. In the communist elite he had his critics but few of them could imagine the party without him at its helm.

Lenin taxed his remaining strength by working to complete the agenda of policies he thought his party needed. The agricultural tax reform and associated economic changes did not constitute a full programme for governing the country. 'Tsar Lenin' did not want to leave his throne without having developed the Bolshevik prospectus and got the party's consent to do it. He devoted himself to elaborating the measures he thought would enable the eventual triumph of socialism.

A decision had been taken in December 1921, at Dzierżyński's prompting, to come down hard on the Mensheviks and Socialist-Revolutionaries, who were feared as threatening the Bolshevik supremacy.[4] In February 1922 Lenin urged Dmitri Kurski, people's commissar of justice, to put on 'a series of *model* trials' of Mensheviks and Socialist-Revolutionaries in the big cities and to compel the judges to follow the party line.[5] He then was angered on learning that the planned trial of Socialist-Revolutionaries would not end with sentences of capital punishment.[6] The Socialist-Revolutionary trial started in June. When it ended in August, after weeks of vilification even by so-called Bolshevik moderates like Bukharin and Lunacharski, several defendants were sentenced to be shot. The verdicts were commuted to long periods of imprisonment. Trotsky, like Lenin, was exasperated by what he saw as unseemly indulgence but the line had firmly been drawn showing that all resistance would be answered with repression.

The Russian Orthodox Church was another target. In March 1922 Trotsky proposed seizing its treasures for sale abroad and using the revenues to relieve the Volga famine. If the clergy were provoked into objecting then they could be depicted as indifferent to the plight of starving Russians. The policy was tested in the central Russia town of Shuya. A wave of violence against priests and their congregations took place, and a number were shot and killed. The predicted resistance they had shown, however, led Lenin from his sickbed to call for the campaign to be spread and for the Church to be hit so hard that the impact would endure for decades.[7] A show trial of priests started in Moscow in late April, accompanied by press attacks on the Church hierarchy. The seventeen defendants included Patriarch Tikhon who was charged with obstructing the confiscation of the Church's silver. Tall, white-bearded and unbowed, a large number of the watching public rose from their seats when he raised his right hand to bless them. Then he turned towards the judges who insisted on calling him by his original name, Vasili Ivanovich Bellavin.[8] The party leadership had already determined the verdict, and it was a severe one. Eleven defendants were condemned to death. Only six had their sentences commuted. Tikhon too was found guilty but instead of being shot or sent to prison, he was to be confined to the curtilage of the Donskoi Monastery.[9]

Altogether there were 250 court cases against the clergy across the country in connection with the operation to impound Church treasures. Violent clashes took place when the Soviet detachments arrived to seize silver crosses, altar pieces and gold-embroidered vestments. In the process, it is estimated around 8,100 clerics perished either in physical resistance or by judicial execution.[10]

At the same time the Politburo worked to cause an internal split in the Orthodox Church by funding the Living Church faction in the clergy, led by Alexander Vvedenski, who was willing to collaborate with 'Soviet power'. But in Vologda, the capital of Alexander Zamaraev's province, a congregation in the cathedral hissed and stamped their feet when Living Church priests conducted services. Another congregation threatened to stop donating food unless the traditional form of religion was restored. Deputy People's Commissar of Justice Pëtr Krasikov moaned that 'it is impossible to make the old women cease believing' in the miraculous powers of a relic. Even so, Tikhon's morale wilted under the pressure of persecution and in 1923 he agreed to step aside from the patriarchate.[11]

Writers and others in the arts also came under reinforced scrutiny and attack. On 6 June 1922 a comprehensive censorship organization was founded generally known as Glavlit. Its task was to review all novels, poems and journal articles before authorizing publication. Paintings, symphonies, ballets and plays were also subject to the same scrutiny.[12] Soviet rulers had regularly closed down presses but now they were restoring a system of pre-emptive censorship that had not existed in Russia since 1905 under Nicholas II.

Lenin also sought to cast the net wider. He knew that Bolshevism still only had a minority of believers amongst the Russian intelligentsia, and so he urged severe measures to be taken against anyone whom he thought might harm the revolutionary cause. He saw social and political theorists as posing an acute threat, but now anyone from civil engineers to zoologists and music academicians could become a target.[13] Lenin himself attacked the philosophers Nikolai Berdyaev and Semën Frank for their book on the anti-liberal German writer Oswald Spengler. Although they had made no criticism of the Soviet order, Lenin passed a message to the Cheka leadership: 'In my opinion this is like a "literary front" for a White Guard Organization.'[14] In May he flew into a bed-ridden rage about what he saw as laxity in prohibiting harmful publications. He helped Dzierżyński to make plans for putting all the Soviet lands into cultural quarantine, safe from any influences that ran counter to Bolshevik ideals and objectives. Communism was to be the sole school of thought that had state protection.

Dozens of 'writers and professors who aid the counter-revolution' were deported in August 1922 on a German steamship from Petrograd to Stettin in north Germany.[15] But deportation abroad was one of the lighter fates that the Soviet state meted out to its opponents. A new Criminal Code was being drafted. Lenin called for a section to be added to the Code on 'the essence and *justification* of terror'. Elimination of such a method of punishment, he complained, would be 'self-deception and deception'. Lenin had seen how terror had proved itself as a mode of rule in the Civil War. Without it, the Tambov revolt could not have been suppressed. For him it needed to remain – and to be seen to remain – in the armoury of his government. In later decades Lenin's admirers were to depict a leader who fundamentally revised his policies but the evidence suggests otherwise.

Most of his policy recommendations were passed without dissent in the Politburo, where Stalin, Trotsky, Zinoviev and Kamenev agreed with his ruthless stance in dealing with perceived opposition to Bolshevik rule. But he did not get everything his own way. Trotsky had nagged him about industrial policy since the start of the New Economic Policy. Whereas Lenin put the emphasis on rural improvements, Trotsky argued that manufacturing and technological development were being dangerously overlooked and called for an expansion of the powers of the economic planning agencies. They argued with each other throughout 1922 and neither was minded to give way.

As Lenin's condition deteriorated he dictated his ideas and guidelines for the following years of governance to a series of female assistants with him at the Gorki convalescent home. He developed a choleric obsession with Stalin, and his illness and isolation from central Moscow no doubt added to his cantankerousness. He was infuriated by the joint attempt of Stalin and Kamenev to introduce a partial repeal of the state monopoly of foreign trade which had been in place since 1918. Stalin and Kamenev argued that the policy had led to a growth of smuggling, which deprived the government of taxes. To Lenin, however, any repeal, even a partial one, seemed to him a betrayal of the October Revolution.

Lenin also clashed with Stalin over the drawing up of a new constitution. Lenin wanted to unite all the existing Soviet republics in a federation, with Russia on equal terms with the others, thereby showing to non-Russians that the era of Russian imperialism was dead. Stalin thought this unrealistic. He warned that far too many infringements of central party policy were occurring in the various republics. Instead, he wanted to incorporate all of them in the Russian Soviet Federative Socialist Republic.[16] Lenin still planned to retain a highly centralized communist party which would give orders to party bodies and therefore to governments in every republic in his proposed federation. But Lenin refused to accept Stalin's viewpoint, and Stalin decided that further wrangling was pointless and backed down.[17]

After reports reached Lenin about the abuse of the Georgian communist leadership by Sergo Ordzhonikidze, Lenin decided that drastic remedial action was necessary. Ordzhonikidze was himself a Georgian but acted like a Moscow bully. At the end of the year he began to dictate an article on the project to establish a permanent solution to the troubling question of the constitutional future of the various Soviet republics. His opening words signalled the depths of his unease: 'Evidently I am deeply guilty before the workers of Russia inasmuch as I failed to intervene with sufficient vigour and sufficient sharpness in the notorious question of "autonomization", officially designated it would seem as the question of the union of soviet socialist republics.'[18]

Such arguments, though, raised in Lenin's mind the problem of the political succession. On 23 December he also started to compose a letter to the next party congress that was to become known as his testament. In it he described the individuals whom he thought to be probable contenders to take over his role. Some were obvious like Bukharin, Zinoviev and Kamenev, others less so such as Pyatakov. In Lenin's opinion, however, there were only two genuine contenders for the leadership, Trotsky and Stalin. He saw both of them, however, as being overconfident and authoritarian (which were traits he failed to see in himself). He also expressed a fear that their rivalry might cause a disastrous split in the entire party. Lenin concluded that only a collective leadership could save the communist party from a destructive contest between them.[19] Most prominent Bolsheviks at the time did not consider Stalin a realistic candidate for leadership. Lenin undoubtedly had a better sense of the probabilities.

The question of the succession continued to bother him even after he had dictated his six summaries of the likely candidates on 24–25 December. Stalin continued to infuriate him, so much so that Lenin asked one of his faithful secretaries to record an addendum to his analysis: 'Stalin is too crude and this defect, wholly bearable in our circle and in our dealings amongst ourselves, becomes unbearable in the post of general secretary.'[20] Lenin, optimistic as ever, wished his legacy to include his vision of how the transition to full communism could be achieved. He still believed in the inevitability of that final communist stage of human history and felt a responsibility to sketch the desirable next steps towards such a paradise.

As 1923 began the other preoccupation for Lenin was to further the development of the New Economic Policy. In January 1923 he dictated an article on rural cooperatives. While in the long term he was committed to establishing a network of collective farms, he aimed to smooth the path to it by encouraging peasants to pool their commercial activities. The party's towering goal in the village ought therefore to be 'an order of civilized co-op members'. He dreamed that when this was attained in an economy where the means of production were in public ownership, the Bolsheviks would reach their goal of a socialist order.[21] Lenin also objected to the way that the Workers' and Peasants' Inspectorate operated, which had been created to supervise the accounts of the other state institutions, only to become itself a byword for bureaucratic obfuscation – and Stalin was its chairman. In Lenin's opinion there was an urgent need to renovate its personnel by recruiting from the working class. Not surprisingly, Stalin saw this as a personal attack on his leadership.

Stalin phoned Lenin's wife Nadezhda Krupskaya at the Gorki sanatorium and scolded her for breaking the Politburo's instructions that Lenin should attend to his recovery and avoid political engagement. Krupskaya apparently kept the conversation to herself for some weeks. But on 5 March 1923, on learning what had happened, Lenin dictated a personal letter to Stalin. He told him that he regarded what had been done against his wife had been done against him: 'Therefore I ask you to decide whether you agree to take back what you said and apologize or you prefer to break relations between the two of us.' Krupskaya delayed the dispatch of the letter without telling Lenin: she was anxious about the consequences. Lenin, though, felt pumped up for action. He asked Trotsky to take up the Georgian cause at the forthcoming party congress. He sent a note to the Georgian communist leaders expressing his support for them and his fury about 'the crudity of Ordzhonikidze and the connivances of Stalin and Dzierżyński'.[22]

Stalin was shocked by the receipt of the delayed personal letter: 'This isn't Lenin who's talking, it's his illness.' His instinct was to reply that if his own wife had misbehaved, as he thought was true of Krupskaya, he would not have tried to stop Lenin from punishing her. He was willing to say sorry only because Lenin was insisting. He worked on a new draft while continuing to deny his personal guilt. However, over the nights of 6–7 March 1923 the ailing Bolshevik leader, stressed by the traumas of the previous few days, suffered a drastic worsening of his condition. On 10 March he had a massive stroke. The whole right side of his body was paralyzed, and he had all but lost the faculty of speech.

Pravda and *Izvestiya* tersely reported to the public that Lenin was seriously ill and had severe difficulties with talking and moving. Nikita Okunev read about Lenin's prostration but did not comment on the possible implications. His attention was drawn to more everyday matters. He complained that the authorities avoided mention of the price inflation that affected everyday life. A rail ticket to Tula cost 53.5 million rubles by the start of 1923. If he wanted to take a tram in Moscow he had to pay 1.5 million rubles. A daily newspaper cost a million rubles. He wryly noted that the Soviet trade unions planned to send a vast quantity of grain to the workers of the Rhineland which had been occupied by French forces, at a time when people were dying of famine in southern Russia. On politics, Okunev was dependent on the Moscow press and was unaware of the repressions that were continuing in Tambov province. At Easter he noted that the churches were packed despite all the persecution and Bolshevik propaganda. He scoffed at the government's ineffectual effort to stamp out illicit vodka production. He lamented the Living Church leadership's declaration that the convalescing Lenin would 'once again stand in the front rank of fighters for great social justice'.[23]

AUDIT OF REVOLUTION: LENIN'S LEGACY AND THE END OF THE BEGINNING, 1924

Lenin was never to rise to his feet again and was dying tormented by thoughts about the Soviet future. He still yearned to introduce and safeguard his proposed changes in bureaucracy, inter-republican affairs and internal party organization. He fretted about the possibility of a split in the party that he had founded. In his winter of misery in 1922–3 he raged against Stalin's behaviour as general secretary.

This provided Stalin's critics, both at the time and in subsequent decades, with an encouragement to claim that his basic direction in politics diverged from the path that Lenin had mapped out. That Lenin and Stalin were in dispute about several policies and trends is unquestionable. But the critics failed to recognize that there were points of axiomatic accord between the two Bolshevik leaders. Both Lenin and Stalin were committed to maintaining the Soviet one-party monolith and to preventing rival parties from resurfacing. The communist party was to operate with a centralized chain of command. Strict party discipline was to be enforced. Lenin and Stalin also concurred about the party's need to preserve the instruments and practice of state terror. They were strongly in favour of persecuting the Orthodox Church and spreading atheist ideas. They sought total communist control of schooling, the press and censorship – and Marxism would maintain its public dominance. They shared a zeal to subject all the Soviet republics and autonomies to Moscow's authority while allowing them a degree of national self-expression and self-rule. They expected to be able to solve many of the country's problems only when, eventually, the European socialist revolution occurred.

Trotsky and the other communist leaders held these commitments in common, and the foundations had thus been laid for a communist state that would survive for nearly seven decades. Lenin in his own estimation had not yet completed his life's work but he had reason to feel pleased with his five years of power. He and the other Bolshevik architects of one-party communist statehood had improvised when drafting and redrafting his design sketches after 1917. Even so, they had followed a consistent line of choice and their preferences were in one direction only. They opted for force over persuasion; for central authority over democratic accountability; for the state's rights over social wishes; for collectivism over individual freedom; for ideological imposition over consultation and the loose interplay of ideas. They had turned themselves, almost without knowing it, into a Leninist vanguard ready to fight every section of society which engaged in active or even passive resistance.

Lenin believed there was work still to be done and wanted Trotsky to ensure the publication of his final articles. He wanted the next party congress in May 1923 to be acquainted with his thoughts on the political succession. Although some of Lenin's dictated pieces of the winter had already been published, his devastating critique of the six leading Bolsheviks whom he predicted as likely to contest the political succession awaited congress delegates when they arrived in Moscow. But Trotsky's nerve failed. Apprehensive about plunging the political dagger in the breast of his enemy Stalin, he accepted the decision to keep Lenin's damning letter about fellow party leaders a secret from the Soviet public. He had already failed to get the Politburo to condemn Stalin's handling of the Georgian communists. This gave Stalin the space to posture at the congress as a consistent warrior against 'Great Russian chauvinism' and as Lenin's devoted follower. Stalin came through the proceedings with his career prospects battered but intact.[1]

Zinoviev, however, had become concerned about the imperiousness in Stalin that Lenin had highlighted. Vacationing that summer in the spa town of Kislovodsk in the north Caucasus, he consulted Bukharin and other leading figures who saw the need to put a corset on Stalin's bulging powers. Zinoviev wrote to complain to Kamenev in Moscow that he was 'simply letting Stalin make a mockery of us'. The agreed plan was to appoint Zinoviev, Trotsky and Bukharin to the Orgburo where Stalin had been issuing important decisions without submitting them to the rest of the leadership. The initiative had no impact on the course of events. One reason was that the new Orgburo members simply failed to attend to Orgburo business. The other was that Zinoviev and Bukharin themselves were soon to require Stalin's bullish assistance in quelling the political ambitions of Trotsky and his factional supporters.[2]

Meanwhile Trotsky in the south Caucasus realized that Stalin, whom he regarded as an uncultured mediocrity, had run rings round him. Trotsky was also in poor health and doctors advised him to keep clear of political controversy. He recovered his poise by writing booklets on contemporary Russian literature and on Soviet everyday life.[3] Writing had always been his salve in times of stress and he used his time to think about how to extricate the party from the morass in which he thought it was becoming submerged. He returned to his case for an increase in the state industrial investment budget and in state economic planning. Trotsky and his friends on the left of the party pointed to poor decisions being made by the ascendant group in the Politburo which in mid-1923 failed to anticipate a massive dislocation in the economy. A crisis in food supply had arisen when the peasantry ceased to sell their surplus produce to Soviet agencies at prices which in real terms had tumbled to a third of their 1913 level in relation to the prices for industrial goods. Trotsky demanded an emergency adjustment of the pricing mechanisms in favour of rural commerce and a renewed focus on industry.

In the last weeks of summer 1923, nevertheless, the central party leadership surprised itself by coming together about an entirely different policy. Optimistic reports from communists in Berlin suggested that a German uprising had become a realistic possibility. Secret Politburo discussions were held in August. Trotsky, salivating at the objective of a communist United States of Europe, eagerly endorsed supporting the insurrection. Stalin was the only one who counselled caution; he justifiably pointed out that the Red Army was in no condition to supply military assistance to German communists who anyway had yet to win most of the German working class over to their side. But Stalin's standing in the Politburo was weak after the party congress and a commission was set up consisting of Trotsky, Zinoviev, Bukharin and Radek whose task was to liaise with the German communist leadership. Ignoring Stalin's doubts, they planned to send the Red Army to put all Europe into the fires of revolution – and Stalin went along with the 'plan'.[4]

In the autumn, though, the split in the party that Lenin had predicted opened up. On 8 October Trotsky wrote an open letter to the Politburo criticizing its other members for excluding him from meetings at which they fixed the leadership's decisions in advance. A week later forty-six of his leading supporters signed a declaration in the same spirit. Preobrazhenski was among them. Trotsky denied he was acting in pursuit of personal power and said he was doing his party duty in the face of recent incompetence and the underlying bureaucratic trends. As the factional struggle intensified, Kamenev and Zinoviev, who had conspired against Stalin in the summer, chose him as their attack dog against Trotsky. It soon became clear that Kamenev, Zinoviev and Stalin had won. At the thirteenth party conference in mid-January 1924 Stalin denounced Trotsky's behaviour and recommendations. Trotsky and the other Bolshevik leftists were trounced.[5]

The news of the split in the party was initially kept from Lenin. When the weather was clement he was pushed in his wheelchair around the sanatorium grounds. Krupskaya had been secretly defying the Politburo by talking to him about politics. Dreading to upset his mood, she lied that the conference had finished in a spirit of unity. He felt 'wonderful' on 18 January and was taken for a horse-drawn sleigh ride. Bukharin was staying at Gorki for a stint of personal recuperation and to do some writing. Krupskaya had sat with Lenin daily, frequently reading aloud to him. On 21 January he awoke at 10.30 a.m. and got up but returned to bed saying he felt unwell. He then slept through to the middle of the afternoon. At 5.40 p.m., propped up with pillows, he had a severe bout of nausea and fell into a coma. His temperature soared. Bukharin rushed to his bedside. The end came at 6.50 p.m. The founder of Bolshevism and embodiment of the October Revolution was dead.[6]

The Politburo met to discuss the funeral arrangements. Trotsky was at the time on his way to Sukhum on the Black Sea coast and it was Stalin who compiled the list of those to deliver eulogies on 26 January. It was decided not to cremate him as was the usual Bolshevik practice but to preserve his body. The funeral took place next day and Zinoviev and Stalin were prominent among the speakers. It was so cold that the trumpeters wiped their mouthpieces with vodka to prevent their lips from freezing to them. Restaurants and places of entertainment were closed for a week. Business stopped throughout the country. Buses, trams and trains were halted. Boats were pulled up alongside the riverbanks. Factory whistles and hooters were sounded for five minutes at four in the afternoon. The cold earth received the coffin under a darkening afternoon sky on Red Square.[7]

A joke spread around Moscow that people had applauded Lenin in his lifetime and whistled at him in death.[8] The party leadership countered such derision by creating a political cult around Lenin that would endure throughout the Soviet era in Russia and in every communist country.

His corpse was removed from its grave and mummified and displayed in a mausoleum built below the Kremlin Wall. The Marxism of Bolshevism was re-designated as Marxism-Leninism. Every contender for the Bolshevik party leadership, especially Stalin, presented himself as the mere pupil of Lenin. Even the haughty Trotsky joined in the growing tradition of cultic obeisance.

The factional fights continued throughout the decades, resulting in Stalin's emergence in 1928–9 as the paramount leader. Trotsky, Kamenev and Zinoviev on the party's left and Bukharin on its right were crushed. Stalin coiled the ropes of the party-state tighter and tighter round the body of society. Mass deportations, arrests and executions became the normal pattern of rule in the 1930s and 1940s for which Stalin must bear personal responsibility. He killed party leaders at every level as well as better-off peasants, ex-policemen, priests, former aristocrats, Mensheviks, Socialist-Revolutionaries and anyone who had belonged to a Bolshevik oppositionist group. He murdered Kamenev and Zinoviev, then Bukharin and subsequently, at last, Trotsky in his Mexican exile.

Some of Stalin's critics both at the time and in ensuing decades suggested that the Soviet one-party state would have fashioned a 'humane' and 'civilized' realization of communist ideals if only Trotsky or Bukharin had triumphed instead. But neither Trotsky nor Bukharin deviated from the Bolshevik credo of party discipline, state centralism, cultural quarantine, terror, suppression of rival parties, militant atheism and an agriculture based on a collective-farm system. They did not advocate the speed at which these objectives were sought by Stalin, and they were appalled by the horrors and excesses of his methods, but they too rejected the rule of law as necessary for the good life, believing that their variant of Marx's doctrines gave them alone the key to understanding the present and making the future.

Stalin and his several rivals saw some kind of 'European socialist revolution' not just as the fulfilment of an old communist goal but as the way to prevent a crusade against them by the world's capitalist powers. They believed in industrialism, urbanism and technological advance; they were conscious that advanced capitalism had the advantage over them in this respect. They worried that their revolutionary administration had yet to root itself at the most basic level in countryside and town. Although they had bullied workers, soldiers and sailors into acquiescence, they still faced a peasantry that rejected the vision for collective farming that the Bolsheviks had in mind for them.

The Bolshevik party campaigned to eradicate religious faith, political nationalism and alternative socialisms. An ever-tighter regime of informational quarantine was imposed. The October Revolution and the subsequent sequence of military conflict had quelled resistance but communist rule in Lenin's time had not acquired a popular sense of the legitimacy of 'Soviet power'.

Trotsky attracted a notable following in the party in the mid-1920s, which showed that thousands of Bolshevik veterans shared his impatience with current official measures. This was not just a matter of temperament and personal ambition but of ideology too. There was a feeling among many party militants that the New Economic Policy had bought them a little time but was not a durable solution to the USSR's problems. Stalin's brutal programme of measures from 1928 was the most extreme of the available options within a Bolshevik framework but none of the alternative plans suggested by others such as Trotsky could have been implemented without brutality. The October Revolution had endured by driving the former Russian Empire into a tunnel of oppression that could only come to a dead end. Over the coming years the Soviet Union would have important achievements in science, military technology, mass literacy and cultural facilities, and it played the crucial part in the defeat of Nazism. But its claim to have found a way to a superior form of modernity was disproved by the conditions which millions of its citizens endured, and the birth of the malaise occurred not with Stalin's despotism but much earlier, in the first years after October 1917.

How this came to pass has been a question of constant debate but few would deny that individual leaders made a difference to events and situations. The autocratic Nicholas II stoked up the fires of revolution. He had inherited an empire in radical need of basic reforms if stability and security were to be attained but he fatally rejected much of what could have usefully been done. Russia had not been alone in entering the Great War in being encumbered by old problems that sooner or later would need resolving, but at the core of the Russian Empire's malaise before the Great War were the peasantry's burning resentments about land shortage, high rents and social discrimination. Workers too had the potential to disrupt law and order. Also important was the alienation of the many professional groups whose activity was crucial for economic and cultural advance and military security. The empire lacked administrative integration and had little immediate prospect of attaining it. Ethnic and religious tensions piled the problems higher.

The Imperial authorities were widely despised, distrusted or simply hated and their positive efforts were constrained by straitened financial resources. Nicholas took an immense risk in declaring war on the Central Powers unless he could have produced a quick victory. A half-modernized economy along with the empire's frail infrastructure displayed unavoidable inadequacies in the face of the demands made by the Great War. As soon as the Imperial Army was forced on its Great Retreat in 1914–15, the Duma leadership enhanced its status at the expense of the emperor and his government. The monarchy's collapse in the February Revolution was not entirely the work of the emperor's hands.

The Provisional Government inherited a swollen portfolio of economic and military predicaments. The pressures proved uncontainable by the new ministers and predictably worsened as the months passed by. The cabinet set out to contrast itself with the Imperial administration and high command by using force solely in moments of extreme emergency. But its early popularity quickly faded. Ministers also operated under the severe constraint of having to cooperate with the soviets. There was agreement between the two sides on the need to defend the country against conquest by Germany. But this in itself limited the options for effective governance. Above all, the cabinet could not transfer the agricultural land to the peasantry while war continued. The Provisional Government had ceased to function outside Petrograd's central districts before the Bolsheviks overthrew it.

The October Revolution and the establishment of 'Soviet power' were a period of experimentation in the midst of international and civil war. Lenin benefited from what might be called history's law of uncertainty and chance. When politics and the economic environment are in turmoil and conventional understandings in public affairs are broken, the situation is primed for an individual to push events one way rather than another. From a small political faction at the start of 1917, the Bolsheviks became the party in power. Most of them did not want or expect the kind of revolution that Lenin engineered for them, but they got used to it as the new normality, and they stuck together for self-protection. The communist leaders were confident of regenerating society, its economy and culture but they themselves were more influenced by Russian history than they realized. The harsh traditions of the Russian Empire permeated their temperaments and opinions, and the brutalities of the Great War shaped their vision of effective and acceptable rule. The economic dislocation, which had begun soon after the start of the military hostilities, confirmed communist orientation towards state-based solutions. As they looked abroad, they concluded that capitalism had nothing good to be said about it. They felt sure that the treaties imposed by the Paris peace conferences were bound to lead to terrible wars and glorious revolutions. They were utterly convinced that the global future would be realized in victory for Soviet-style communism.

Abroad, Bolshevik rule was seen as responsible for dragging the Russian people into unimaginable horrors belonging to a long-past world. Whilst there was much truth in this, Bolshevism also drew on twentieth-century modernity. The Bolshevik leaders boasted that only they had inaugurated the ultimate great stage in human progress. In fact communism introduced a new form of what it is to be called 'modern'. The Soviet one-party, one-ideology terror state begat totalitarianism. Benito Mussolini and the Italian fascists were the first to use the term about themselves but by the time they came to power in Rome in 1922 the basic totalitarian architecture was already in place in Russia. Soviet communism held the patent to a form of rule that would be adopted in politics by both the extreme left and right, supplying a basic template for power that the Nazis would use in Germany.

The USSR gave priority to developing the Soviet communist model. It was later to be imitated by other countries and by the middle of the twentieth century had been copied across a third of the planet's earth surface. Communists everywhere espoused global ambitions of urbanism and industrialism. They admired the gigantic, the mechanical, metallurgical and electrical. They prioritized standard products for the many rather than luxury ones for the few. They trampled any localism that obstructed instantaneous obedience to central authority and its leaders. They despised the liberal political principle of a division of powers. They wanted swift and ruthless action. Millions of Soviet citizens lived through this with trepidation or resignation. They had experienced war, revolution and civil war and had to cope with a post-war settlement that none had imagined and few would have chosen.

Nikita Okunev was one of the few diarists in these chapters who survived beyond the early 1920s. Patriotic metalworker Alexei Shtukaturov was killed at the Eastern front in 1915, disappointed in his sovereign emperor. Shloyme Rappaport-Ansky, chronicler of the traumas of Jewry in the Imperial war zone, fled Soviet Russia but passed away in Warsaw in 1920. Emperor Nicholas II abdicated in

March 1917, only to be butchered along with his family in a Yekaterinburg cellar in the following year. The poet Alexander Blok wrote incomparable verses on war and revolution, hymning what he saw as a horde-like assault on 'bourgeois' civilization of which he was himself a part. He collaborated with the Provisional Government and then, in a lesser way, with Sovnarkom but his preference was for the Kadets. His health shattered, he perished in 1921. Lev Tikhomirov, a monarchist who had once been a socialist terrorist, lived quietly in the precinct of the Sergiev Posad until his death in 1923. This was also the year when Rachel Khin-Goldovskaya secured her last publication. She died in 1928. Florence Farmborough could count herself fortunate to escape Soviet Russia in 1918 and live to old age in Marple, Greater Manchester sixty years later.

These and other diarists each offered a personal, often idiosyncratic, view upon what had happened to the country. Suffering came to many of them. They recorded the dreams and dreads of their generation, usually from viewpoints that counteracted the contemporary official narrative. Nikita Okunev's account broke off in 1924. Despite living a dozen more years, he had lost the impulse to record his daily observations. The last words on the final page of his diary summarize a common experience:

> Everyone is groaning and complaining but goes on living. And it must be true, as someone said, that life must be lived so that the unhappy attain a sense of resignation and the happy begin to learn about things. Pray God will let us continue living if only to reach the point of feeling 'resigned'.[9]

Resignation was an attitude among their subjects that had long enabled Russian rulers to maintain themselves in power. Bolsheviks had undertaken a revolution in the expectation of creating a society of enthusiasm and activism. Thousands of Bolshevik veterans and new party recruits remained eager to press further and more quickly forward in the party's cause. But the effort made in the 1930s to realize it would only magnify the nightmare of killing, imprisonment, national oppression, social deprivation and economic mismanagement. Okunev's pessimism proved to be too optimistic.

Communist rule endured till the end of the Soviet Union in 1991. Democracy and market economics were proclaimed as guiding principles for the new Russia that was about to be built. But many older attitudes and practices persisted under Boris Yeltsin in the 1990s and were reinforced with severity in the twenty-first century. Vladimir Putin emasculated democratic processes and curtailed freedom of expression. Oppositionist leaders were killed, imprisoned or driven into exile. The rule of law was curtailed and the mass media neutered. The state seized back control of the commanding heights of the economy. The West was treated as a hostile concert of powers. In 2014 Russian armed forces annexed Crimea from Ukraine and military conflict was started with other Ukrainian territories including the Donbas, whose attachment to Ukraine had been controversial among Bolshevik leaders after the Civil War. In 2022 Putin ordered an all-out invasion of Ukraine. It is resoundingly clear that Russian politics are still freighted with heavy baggage from the early twentieth century. It is equally true that much has changed over the decades. Tsarism is defunct and communism has died off except in a moribund political party – and Lenin is widely and routinely denounced. Capitalism is once again dominant in Russia. But the oppressive conditions that held back the country in the years between 1914 and 1924 have yet to be consigned to the ash heap of history. Nikita Okunev and his generation were robbed of the freedoms they were promised in 1917. Their descendants in Russia today are still waiting to receive them.

THE DIARISTS

Alexander Blok

Poet of the Symbolist school who in wartime took account in his poetry of what he observed in the streets and in the ruling elite. His creativity peaked in 1914–18 when he wrote verses of unsurpassed brilliance.

Florence Farmborough

British nurse employed by a doctor's family in the Russian Empire. After years of service she opted to leave for home, travelling arduous journeys on the railways out to the far east.

Rachel Khin-Goldovskaya

Story writer and playwright. Moscow-based.

Vasili Kravkov

Senior military doctor on the Eastern front till summer 1917, when he was pleased to be relieved of his duties.

Alexei Kuropatkin

Veteran Imperial general who conducted the suppression of the 1916 revolt in central Asia.

Nikita Okunev

Moscow accounts administrator for a riverside port company who came from a peasant background and adapted readily to town life with its theatres and newspapers.

Shloyme Rappaport-Ansky

Publicly known by the pseudonym S. An-sky. Playwright and social commentator who diligently alerted society to the wartime plight of the Jews.

Nikolai Romanov

Emperor from the death of his father in 1894. Abdicated in March 1917. Murdered with his family in Yekaterinburg in July 1918.

Alexei Shtukaturov

St Petersburg metalworker who enlisted in a riflemen's regiment at the start of the Great War. He twice won the George cross and was promoted to NCO before being killed at the front in December 1915.

Lev Tikhomirov

A terrorist as a young man, he became a monarchist and worked for premier Pëtr Stolypin.

Alexander Verkhovski

A graduate of the Military Academy who served on the General Staff and was made army minister by Alexander Kerensky after the Kornilov revolt.

Alexander Zamaraev

Peasant from Totma district, Vologda province in northern Russia. No known political orientation.

BIBLIOGRAPHY

Abbreviations

DTKAAZ	[A. A. Zamaraev], *Dnevnik totemskogo krest'yanina A. A. Zamaraeva, 1906–1922* (eds V. V. Morozov and N. I. Reshetnikov: RAN: Moscow, 1995)
GARF	Gosudarstvennyi Arkhiv Rossiiskoi Federatsii
NPODM	N. P. Okunev, *Dnevnik moskvicha, 1917–1924* (YMCA-Press: Paris, 1990)
PSS	*Polnoe sobranie sochinenii* (Gosudarstvennoe Izdatel'stvo Politicheskoi Literatury: Moscow, 1958–65)
PTsK	*Protokoly Tsentral'nogo Komiteta RSDRP(b), avgust 1917–fevral' 1918* (Gosizdat politicheskoi literatury: Moscow, 1958)
RGASPI	Rossiiskii Arkhiv Sotsial'no-Politicheskoi Istorii
RGVA	Rossiiskii Gosudarstvennyi Voennyi Arkhiv
SMRI	*Sovet Ministrov Rossiiskoi imperii v gody Pervoi mirovoi voiny: bumagi A. N. Yakhontova: zapisi zasedanii i perepiska* (Dmitrii Bulanin: St Petersburg, 1999)
VOVIL	*Vospominaniya o Vladimire Il'iche*, vols 1–8 (Moscow, 1989–91)
ZZVP	*Zhurnaly zasedanii Vremennogo Pravitel'stva*, vols 1–4 (eds B. F. Dodonov, E. D. Grinko and O. V. Lavinskaya: Rosspen: Moscow, 2001–4)

Archives

HIA
- M. V. Alekseev Papers
- George Halonen Papers
- N. A. Ioffe Papers
- Aleksandr Vasil'evich Kolchak Papers
- M. J. Larsons Papers
- Gibbes Lykes Papers
- N. V. Nekrasov Papers
- Nikolai Yudenich Papers

Trotsky Collection
Ukrainian Subject Collection
US Consulate – Petrograd Papers
RGASPI
RGVA
D. A. Volkogonov Papers

Periodicals

Izvestiya (Petrograd, Moscow)
Komsomol'skaya pravda (Moscow)
Pravda (Petrograd, then Moscow)

Secondary Sources

1917: chastnye svidetel'stva o revolyutsii v pis'makh Lunacharskogo i Martova (eds G. A. Bordyugov and E. A. Kotelenets: RUDN: Moscow, 2005)

R. Abraham, *Alexander Kerensky: The First Love of the Revolution* (Sidgwick and Jackson: London, 1987)

E. Acton, V. Iu. Cherniaev and W. G. Rosenberg (eds), *Critical Companion to the Russian Revolution* (Arnold: London, 1997)

Ł. Adamski and B. Gajos, *Circles of the Russian Revolution: Internal and International Consequences of the Year 1917 in Russia* (Routledge: London, 2019)

O. R. Airapetov, *Generaly, liberaly i predprinimateli: rabota na front i na revolyutsiyu (1907–1917)* (Modest Kolerov and 'Tri kvadrata': Moscow, 2003)

O. R. Airapetov, *Uchastie Rossiiskoi imperii v Pervoi mirovoi voine* (1914–17) (Knizhny dom Universitet: Moscow, 2014)

N. Andreyev, *A Moth on the Fence: Memoirs of Russia, Estonia, Czechoslovakia and Western Europe* (Hodgson: Kingston upon Thames, 2009)

A. M. Anfimov, *Rossiiskaya derevnya v gody pervoi mirovoi voiny, 1914–fevral' 1917* (Sotsekgiz: Moscow, 1962)

A. M. Anfimov, *P. A. Stolypin i rossiiskoe krest'yanstvo* (IRI: Moscow, 2002)

S. An-sky, *1915 Diary of S. An-sky: A Russian-Jewish Writer at the Eastern Front* (translated by P. Zavadivker: Indiana University Press: Bloomington, IN, 2016)

S. Ansky, *The Enemy at His Pleasure: A Journey Through the Jewish Pale of Settlement During World War One* (Metropolitan Books: New York, 2002)

A. B. Astashov, 'Dezertirstvo i bor'ba s nim v tsarskoi armii v gody Pervoi mirovoi voiny', *Rossiiskaya istoriya*, no. 4 (2011)

A. B. Astashov, 'Russkii krest'yanin na fronte pervoi mirovoi voiny', *Otechestvennaya istoriya*, no. 2 (2003)

J. Aves, *Workers Against Lenin: Labour Protest and the Bolshevik Dictatorship* (I. B. Tauris: London, 1996)

J. Baberowski, *Der Feind ist überall: Stalinism im Kaukasus* (Deutsche Verlags-Anstalt: Munich, 2003)

S. Badcock, '1917 in the Provinces' in D. Orlovsky (ed.), *A Companion to the Russian Revolution* (Wiley Blackwell: Hoboken, NJ, 2020)

S. Badcock, *A Prison Without Walls?: Eastern Siberian Exile in the Last Years of Tsarism* (Oxford University Press: Oxford, 2016)

A. Yu. Bakhturina, *Okrainy rossiiskoi imperii: gosudarstvennoe upravlenie i natsional'naya politika v gody Pervoi mirovoi voiny (1914–1917 gg.)* (Rosspen: Moscow, 2004)

A. Yu. Bakhturina, *Politika Rossiiskoi Imperii v Vostochnoi Galitsii v gody Pervoi mirovoi voiny* (AIRO-XX: Moscow, 2000)

P. L. Bark, 'Vospominaniya', *Vozrozhdenie* (Paris), nos. 157–84 (1965–7)

Z. Bauman, *Modernity and Ambivalence* (Polity Press: Cambridge, 1991)

A. Becker, *Oubliés de la Grande Guerre: humanitaire et culture de guerre, 1914–1918: populations occupies, déportés civil, prisonniers de guerre* (Noësis: Paris, 1998)

D. Beer, *Renovating Russia: The Human Sciences and the Fate of Liberal Modernity, 1880–1930* (Cornell University Press: London, 2008)

A. B. Berkevich, 'Krest'yanstvo i vseobshchaya mobilizatsiya v iyule 1914 g.', *Istoricheskie zapiski*, no. 23 (1947)

M. Bernstam, *Nezavisimoe rabochee dvizhenie v 1918 godu: dokumenty i materialy* (YMC-Press: Paris, 1981)

M. Bernstam, *Ural i Prikam'e, noyabr' 1917 – yanvar' 1919: dokumenty i materialy* (YMCA-Press: Paris, 1982)

S. Blank, 'The Struggle for Soviet Bashkiria, 1917–1923', *Nationalities Papers*, no. 1 (1983)

R. E. Blobaum, *A Minor Apocalypse: Warsaw during the First World War* (Cornell University Press: Ithaca, NY, 2017)

A. Blok, *Dnevnik* (ed. A. L. Grishunin: Sovetskaya Rossiya: Moscow, 1989)

A. Blok, *Poslednie Dni Imperatorskoi Vlasti* (Vysheishaya shkola: Moscow, 1991)

A. Blok, *Sochineniya v odnom tome* (Gosizdat Khudozhestvennoi Literatury: Moscow–Leningrad, 1946)

A. Blyum, *Za kulisami 'Ministerstva Pravdy': tainaya istoriya sovetskoi tsentsury, 1917–1929* (Gumanitarnoe Agenstvo: St Petersburg, 1994)

R. P. Bobroff, 'Squabbling over the Spoils' in L. J. Frary and M. Kozelsky (eds), *Russian-Ottoman Borderlands: The Eastern Question Reconsidered*

R. P. Bobroff, *Roads to Glory: Late Imperial Russia and the Turkish Straits* (I. B. Tauris: London, 2006)

S. Broadberry and M. Harrison (eds), *The Economics of World War I* (Cambridge University Press: Cambridge, 2005)

V. Brovkin, 'Workers' Unrest and the Bolsheviks' Response in 1919', *Slavic Review*, no. 3 (1990)

V. Brovkin, *Behind the Front Lines of the Civil War: Political Parties and Social Movements in Russia, 1918–1922* (Princeton University Press: Princeton, NJ, 1994)

V. Brovkin, *The Mensheviks after October: Socialist Opposition and the Rise of the Bolshevik Dictatorship* (Cornell University Press: Ithaca, NY, 1987)

R. P. Browder and A. Kerensky (eds), *The Russian Provisional Government: Documents*, vols 1–3 (Hoover University Press: Stanford, 1961)

A. A. Brussilov [A. A. Brusilov], *A Soldier's Notebook* (Macmillan: London, 1930)

G. Buchanan, *My Mission to Russia and Other Diplomatic Memories* (Cassell: London, 1923)

O. V. Budnitskii, '"Evreiskie batal'ony" v Krasnoi Armii' in O. V. Budnitskii (ed.), *Mirovoi krizis 1914–1920 godov i sud'ba vostochnoevropeiskogo evreistva*

O. V. Budnitskii (ed.), *Mirovoi krizis 1914–1920 godov i sud'ba vostochnoevropeiskogo evreistva* (Rosspen: Moscow, 2005)

N. Bukharin, *Ekonomika perekhodnogo perioda: obshchaya teoriya transformatsionnogo protsessa* (Gosizdat: Moscow, 1920)

V. P. Buldakov, 'Freedom, Shortages, Violence: The Origins of the "Revolutionary Anti-Jewish Pogrom" in Russia, 1917–1918' in J. Dekel-Chen, D. Gaunt, N. M. Meir and I. Bartal (eds), *Anti-Jewish Violence: Rethinking the Pogrom in East European History*

V. P. Buldakov, *Khaos i etnos: etnicheskie konflikty v Rossii, 1917–1918: usloviya voznikoveniya, khronika, kommentarii, analiz* (Novyi khronograf: Moscow, 2010)

V. P. Buldakov, *Krasnaya smuta: priroda i posledstviya revolyutsionnogo nasiliya* (Rosspen: Moscow, 2010)

V. P. Buldakov and T. G. Leonteva, *Voina, porodivshaya revolyutsiyu: Rossiya, 1914–1917 gg.* (Novyi khronograf: Moscow, 2015)

J. Bushnell, *Mutiny Amid Repression: Russian Soldiers in the Revolution of 1905–1906* (Indiana University Press: Bloomington, IN, 1985)

L. Chamberlain, *The Philosophy Steamer: Lenin and the Exile of the Intelligentsia* (Atlantic: London, 2006)

A. Chayanov, *Osnovnye idei i formy organizatsii krest'yanskoi kooperatsii* (T. Dortman: Moscow, 1919)

B. Chernev, *Twilight of Empire: The Brest-Litovsk Conference and the Remaking of East-Central Europe, 1917–1918* (University of Toronto Press: Toronto, 2017)

M. Cherniavsky, *Prologue to Revolution: Notes of A. N. Iakhontov on the Secret Meetings of the Council of Ministers, 1915* (Prentice Hall: Englewood Cliffs, NJ, 1967)

V. M. Chernov, *Pered burei* (Mezhdunarodnye otnosheniya: Moscow, 1993)

G. V. Chicherin, *Vneshnyaya politika Sovetskoi Rossii za dva goda* (Gosizdat: Moscow, 1920)

P. Sh. Chkhartishvili, 'Chernosotentsy v 1917 g.', *Voprosy istorii*, no. 8 (1997)

C. M. Clark, *The Sleepwalkers: How Europe Went to War in 1914* (Allen Lane: London, 2012)

The Complete Wartime Correspondence of Tsar Nicholas II and the Empress Alexandra, April 1914–March 1917 (ed. J. T. Fuhrmann: Greenwood Press: Westport, CN: 1999)

Congress of the Peoples of the East. Baku, September 1920: Stenographic Report, (tr. and ed. B. Pearce: New Park: London, 1978)

Constantinople et les Détroits: Documents Secrets de l'Ancien Ministère des Affaires Étrangères de Russie vols 1–2 (ed. E. A. Adamov: Éditions Internationales: Paris, 1930–2)
W. Conze, *Polnische Nation under Deutsche Politik im Ersten Weltkrieg* (Böhlau Verlag: Cologne, 1958)
M. Cornwall (ed.), *Sarajevo 1914: Sparking the First World War* (Bloomsbury: London, 2020)
R. Crummey (ed.), *Reform in Russia and the USSR: Past and Prospects* (University of Illinois Press: Urbana, IL, 1989)
J. S. Curtiss, *The Russian Church and the Soviet State, 1917–1953* (Little, Brown: Boston, MA, 1953)
F. Dan, 'K istorii poslednikh dnei Vremennogo Pravitel'stva', *Letopis' revolyutsii*, vol. 1 (1923)
V. P. Danilov and T. Shanin (eds), *Krest'yanskoe vosstanie v Tambovskoi gubernii v 1919–1921: 'Antonovshchina': Dokumenty i materialy* (Redaktsionno-izdatel'skii otdel: Tambov, 1994)
V. Danilov, S. Yesikov, V. Kanishchev and L. Protasov, Introduction to V. P. Danilov and T. Shanin (eds), *Krest'yanskoe vosstanie v Tambovskoi gubernii v 1919–1921: 'Antonovshchina': Dokumenty i materialy*
Yu. N. Danilov, *Na puti k krusheniyu: ocherki iz poslednego perioda russkoi monarkhii* (Voennoe izdatel'stvo: Moscow, 1992)
Yu. N. Danilov, *Rossiya v mirovoi voine 1914–1915 gg.* (Slovo: Berlin, 1924)
Yu. N. Danilov, *Velikii Knyaz' Nikolai Nikolaevich* (Navarre: Paris, 1930)
M. David-Fox, *Crossing Borders: Modernity, Ideology, and Culture in Russia and the Soviet Union* (Pittsburgh University Press: Pittsburgh, PA, 2015)
M. David-Fox, *Revolution of the Mind: Higher Learning among the Bolsheviks, 1918–1929* (Cornell University Press: Ithaca, NY, 1997)
N. Davies, *Vanished Kingdoms: The History of Half-Forgotten Europe* (Allen Lane: London, 2011)
N. Davies, *White Eagle, Red Star: The Polish–Soviet War of 1919–1920* (Macdonald: London, 1972)
R. W. Davies, *The Development of the Soviet Budgetary System* (Cambridge University Press: Cambridge, 1958)
R. W. Davies, M. Harrison and S. G. Wheatcroft (eds), *The Economic Transformation of the Soviet Union, 1913–1945* (Cambridge University Press: Cambridge, 1994)
R. W. Davies, 'Industry' in R. W. Davies, M. Harrison and S. G. Wheatcroft (eds), *The Economic Transformation of the Soviet Union, 1913–1945*
R. W. Davies (ed.), *From Tsarism to the New Economic Policy: Continuity and Change in the Economy of the USSR* (Macmillan: Basingstoke, 1990)
The Debate on Soviet Power: Minutes of the All-Russian Central Executive Committee of Soviets, Second Convocation, October 1917–January 1918 (ed. J. L. H. Keep: Clarendon Press: Oxford, 1979)
J. Dekel-Chen, D. Gaunt, N. M. Meir and I. Bartal (eds), *Anti-Jewish Violence: Rethinking the Pogrom in East European History* (Indiana University Press: Bloomington, IN, 2011)

Dekrety Sovetskoi Vlasti, vol. 1 (Gosizdat politicheskoi literatury: Moscow, 1957)
A. Dem'yanov, 'Moya sluzhba pri Vremennom Pravitel'stve', *Arkhiv Russkoi Revolyutsii*, vol. 4 (1922)
A. I. Denikin, *Ocherki russkoi smuty*, vol. 1, parts 1–2: *Krushenie vlasti i armii, fevral'-sentyabr' 1917 g.* (J. Povolozky: Paris, 1921)
Desyatyi s"ezd RKP(b): Mart 1921 g: Stenograficheskii otchëty (Gosizdat: Moscow, 1963)
S. Dixon, 'How Holy Was Holy Russia?' in G. Hosking and R. Service (eds), *Reinterpreting Russia*
S. Dixon, 'Orthodoxy and Revolution: The Restoration of the Russian Patriarchate in 1917', *Transactions of the Royal Historical Society*, vol. 28 (2018)
S. Dixon, 'Superstition in Imperial Russia', *Past and Present*, vol. 199 (2008)
Dnevniki imperatora Nikolaya II, 1894–1918, vol. 2 (ed. S. V. Mironenko: Rosspen: Moscow, 2013)
T. C. Dowling, *The Brusilov Offensive* (Indiana State University: Bloomington, IN, 2008)
S. M. Dubrovskii, *Krest'yanskoe dvizhenie v revolyutsii 1905–1907 gg.* (AN SSSR: Moscow, 1956)
S. M. Dubrovskii, *Sel'skoe khozyaistvo i krest'yanstvo Rossii v period imperializma* (Nauka: Moscow, 1975)
P. Dukes, *Red Dusk and the Morrow* (Doubleday, Page: New York, 1922)
V. S. Dyakin, *Russkaya burzhuaziya i tsarizm v gody pervoi mirovoi voiny* (AN SSSR: Leningrad, 1967)
R. Edelman, *Gentry Politics on the Eve of the Russian Revolution: The Nationalist Party, 1907–1917* (Rutgers University Press: New Brunswick, NJ, 1980)
L. Edmondson and P. Waldron (eds), *Economy and Society in Russia and the Soviet Union, 1860–1930: Essays for Olga Crisp* (Macmillan: Basingstoke:, 1992)
Ekonomicheskoe polozhenie Rossii nakanune Velikoi Oktyabr'skoi Sotsialisticheskoi Revolyutsii: materialy i dokumenty, vols 1–3 (ed. A. L. Sidorov *et al.*: AN SSSR: Moscow–Leningrad, 1957–67)
L. Engelstein, *Russia in Flames: War, Revolution, Civil War, 1914–1921* (Oxford University Press: Oxford, 2018)
S. Ettinger, 'The Jews in Russia at the Outbreak of the Revolution' in L. Kochan (ed.), *The Jews in Soviet Russia since 1917*
C. Evtuhov, *The Cross and the Sickle: Sergei Bulgakov and the Fate of Russian Religious Philosophy, 1890–1920* (Cornell University Press: Ithaca, NY, 1997)
A. Ezergailis, *The 1917 Revolution in Latvia* (*Eastern European Quarterly*: Boulder, CO, 1974)
T. Fallows, 'Politics and the War Effort in Russia: The Union of Zemstvos and the Organization of the Food Supply, 1914–1916', *Slavic Review*, no. 1 (1978)
F. Farmborough, *Nurse at the Russian Front: A Diary* (Constable: London, 1974)
S. Fedorchenko, *Narod na voine* (Zemlya i fabrika: Moscow–Leningrad, 1925)
N. Ferguson, *The House of Rothschild: The World's Banker*, vol. 2 (Viking: New York, 1999)

Fevral'skaya revolyutsiya, 1917: sbornik dokumentov i materialov (ed. O. A. Shashkova: Rossiiskii Gosudarstvennyyi Gumanitarnyi Universitet: Moscow, 1996)

V. M. Fic, *Revolutionary War for Independence and the Russian Question* (Abhinav: New Delhi, 1977)

O. Figes, *Peasant Russia, Civil War: The Volga Countryside in Revolution* (Clarendon Press: Oxford, 1989)

F. Fischer, *Germany's Aims in the First World War* (W. W. Norton: New York, 1972)

D. R. Francis, *Russia from the Russian Embassy*, April 1916–November 1918 (C. Scribner Sons: New York, 1921)

J. Frankel, *Crisis, Revolution and Russian Jews* (Cambridge University Press: Cambridge, 2009)

J. Frankel (ed.), *The Jews and the European Crisis, 1914–1921* (ICJ Hebrew University of Jerusalem: Oxford, 1988)

L. J. Frary and M. Kozelsky (eds), *Russian–Ottoman Borderlands: The Eastern Question Reconsidered* (University of Wisconsin Press: Madison, WI, 2014)

G. L. Freeze, 'Counter-Reformation in Russian Orthodoxy: Popular Response to Religious Renovation', *Slavic Review*, no. 2 (1995)

G. L. Freeze, 'Critical Dynamic of the Russian Revolution: Irreligion or Religion?' in D. Schönpflug and M. Schulze Wessel (eds), *Redefining the Sacred: Religion in the French and Russian Revolutions*

G. L. Freeze, 'The Russian Orthodox Church: Handmaiden of the State?', *Journal of Ecclesiastical History*, no. 1 (1985)

M. S. Frenkin, *Russkaya Armiya i revolyutsiya: 1917–1918* (Logos: Munich, 1978)

J. A. Frieden, *Banking on the World: The Politics of American International Finance* (Harper and Row: New York, 1987)

W. C. Fuller, *Civil-Military Conflict in Imperial Russia, 1881–1914* (Princeton University Press: Princeton, NJ, 1985)

W. C. Fuller, *The Foe Within: Fantasies of Treason and the End of Imperial Russia* (Cornell University Press: Ithaca, NY, 2018)

M. Futrell, *The Northern Underground: Episodes of Russian Revolutionary Transport and Communications through Scandinavia and Finland, 1863–1917* (Faber and Faber: London, 1963)

M. I. Gaiduk, *Utyug: materialy i fakty o zagotovitel'noi deyatel'nosti russkikh voennykh komissiei v Amerike* (M. Gaiduk: New York, 1918)

Z. Galili, *The Menshevik Leaders in the Russian Revolution: Social Realities and Political Strategies* (Princeton University Press: Princeton, NJ, 1989)

J. Garrard, '*The Twelve:* Blok's Apocalypse', *Religion and Literature*, no. 1 (2003)

P. Gatrell, 'Poor Russia, Poor Show: Mobilising a Backward Economy for War, 1914–1917' in S. Broadberry and M. Harrison (eds), *The Economics of World War I*

P. Gatrell, *Russia's First World War: A Social and Economic History* (Routledge: London, 2005)

P. Gatrell, *A Whole Empire Walking: Refugees in Russia During World War I* (Indiana University Press: Bloomington, IN, 1999)

J. von Geldern, *Bolshevik Festivals, 1917–1920* (University of California Press: Berkeley, CA, 1933)
I. Getzler, *Kronstadt 1917–1921: The Fate of a Soviet Democracy* (Cambridge University Press: Cambridge, 1983)
I. Getzler, *Martov: A Political Biography of a Russian Social Democrat* (Cambridge University Press: Cambridge, 1967)
I. Getzler, *Nikolai Sukhanov: Chronicler of the Russian Revolution* (Palgrave: Basingstoke, 2002)
G. Gill, *Peasants and Government in the Russian Revolution* (Macmillan: London, 1979)
E. V. Gimpel'son, *'Voennyi kommunizm': politika, praktika, ideologiya* (Mysl: Moscow, 1973)
I. F. Gindin, *Banki i ekonomicheskaya politika v Rossii: XIX – nachalo XX v.* (Nauka: Moscow, 1997)
A. Gleason, P. Kenez and R. Stites (eds), *Bolshevik Culture: Experimentation and Order in the Russian Revolution* (Indiana University Press: Bloomington, IN, 1985)
K. I. Globachev, 'Pravda o russkoi revolyutsii: Vospominaniya byvshevo nachal'nika Petrogradskogo okhrannogo otdeleniya', *Voprosy Istorii*, no. 7 (2002)
K. I. Globachev and S. N. Globacheva, *The Truth of the Russian Revolution: The Memoirs of the Tsar's Chief of Security and his Wife* (SUNY Press: Albany, NY, 2017)
F. A. Golder (ed.), *Documents of Russian History, 1914–1917* (Peter Smith: Gloucester, MA., 1964)
N. N. Golovin, *Voennye usiliya Rossii v mirovoi voine*, vols 1–2 (T-vo Ob"edinënnykh izdatelei: Paris, 1939)
B. Gourko [V. Gurko], *War and Revolution in Russia, 1914–1917* (Macmillan: New York, 1919)
D. W. Graf, 'Military Rule Behind the Russian Front', *Jahrbücher für Geschichte Europas*, no. 3 (1974)
M. Graf, *Estonia i Rossiya: anatomiya rasstavaniya* (Argo: Tallinn, 2007)
B. B. Grave (ed.), *Burzhuaziya nakanune Fevral'skoi revolyutsii* (Gosizdat: Moscow–Leningrad, 1927)
A. Graziosi, *The Great Peasant War: Bolsheviks and Peasants, 1917–1933* (Harvard University Press: Harvard, MA., 1996)
I. N. Grebënkin, 'General L. G. Kornilov: A Rough Sketch for a Character Portrait', *Russian Studies in History*, no. 3 (2017)
P. Gregory, *Russian National Income, 1885–1913* (Cambridge University Press: Cambridge, 1983)
P. Gross (ed.), *Die vergessene Front: der Osten 1914/1915: Ereignis, Wirkung, Nachwirkung* (F. Schöningh: Paderborn, 2006)
A. S. Gruzinov, 'Rossiiskaya industriya v 1917 g.: dinamika i struktura proizvodstva' in Yu. A. Petrov (ed.), *Rossiiskaya revolyutsiya 1917 goda: vlast', obshchestvo, kul'tura*, vol. 1
[A. I. Guchkov], *Alexander Ivanovich Guchkov rasskazyvaet . . . Vospominaniya*

Gosudarstvennoi Dumy i voennogo ministra Vremennogo pravitel'stva (eds A. V. Smolin and S. M. Lyandres: Voprosy istorii: Moscow, 1993)
M. von Hagen, *War in a European Borderland: Occupations and Occupation Plans in Galicia and Ukraine, 1914–1918* (University of Washington Press: Seattle, WA, 2007)
J. Happel, 'Fears, Rumours, Violence: The Tsarist Regime and the Revolt of the Nomads in Central Asia, 1916' in A. Morrison, C. Drieu and A. Chokobaeva (eds), *The Central Asian Revolt of 1916: A Collapsing Empire in the Age of War and Revolution* (Manchester University Press: Manchester, 2020)
M. Harrison and A. Markevich, 'Russia's Home Front, 1914–1922: The Economy', SSRN Papers
T. Hasegawa, *The February Revolution, Petrograd, 1917: The End of the Tsarist Regime and the Birth of Dual Power* (2nd edn: Brill: Leiden, 1997)
A. Heywood, *Modernising Lenin's Russia: Economic Reconstruction, Foreign Trade and the Railways* (Cambridge University Press: Cambridge, 1999)
G. A. Hill, *Dreaded Hour* (Cassell: London, 1936)
G. A. Hill, *Go Spy the Land: Being the Adventures of I.K.8 of the British Secret Service* (Cassell: London, 1933)
P. Holquist, '"Information is the Alpha and Omega of Our Work": Bolshevik Surveillance in its Pan-European Context', *Journal of Modern History*, no. 3 (1997)
P. Holquist, *Making War, Forging Revolution: Russia's Continuum of Crisis, 1914–1921* (Harvard University Press: Cambridge, MA., 2002)
P. Holquist, 'The Role of Personality in the First (1914–1915) Russian Occupation of Galicia and Bukovina' in J. Dekel-Chen, D. Gaunt, N. M. Meir and I. Bartal (eds), *Anti-Jewish Violence: Rethinking the Pogrom in East European History*
G. Hosking and R. Service (eds), *Reinterpreting Russia* (Arnold: London, 1999)
J. L. Houghteling, *A Diary of the Russian Revolution* (Dodd, Mead: New York, 1918)
A. A. Il'yukhov, *Kak platili bol'sheviki: Politika sovetskoi vlasti v sfere oplaty truda v 1917–1941 gg.* (Rosspen: Moscow, 2010)
A. A. Ioffe (V. Krymskii), *Mirnoe nastuplenie* (Gosizdat: Petersburg [*sic*], 1921)
G. Z. Ioffe, 'Vyselenie evreev iz prifrontovoi polosy v 1915 godu', *Voprosy istorii*, no. 9 (2001)
H. Jahn, *Patriotic Culture in Russia during World War I* (Cornell University Press: Ithaca, NY, 1995)
S. Johnson, 'Breaking or Making the Silence? British Jews and East European Jewish Relief, 1914–1917', *Modern Judaism*, no. 1 (2010)
S. F. Jones, *Socialism in Georgian Colors: The European Road to Social-Democracy, 1883–1917* (Harvard University Press: Cambridge, MA., 2005)
V. V. Kabanov, *Krest'yanskoe khozyaistvo v usloviyakh 'voennogo kommunizma'*, (Nauka: Moscow, 1988)
N. E. Kakurin, *Kak srazhalas' revolyutsiya*, vols 1–2 (Gosizdat: Moscow–Leningrad, 1925–6)
N. E. Kakurin (ed.), *Razlozhenie armii v 1917 godu* (Gosizdat: Moscow–Leningrad, 1925)

V. V. Kanishchev, *Russkii bunt, bessmyslennyi i besposhchadnyi: pogromnoe dvizhenie v gorodakh Rossii v 1917–1918 gg.* (Tambov State University: Tambov, 1995)

A. N. Kashevarov, *Pravoslavnaya Rossiiskaya Tserkov' i Sovetskoe gosudarstvo (1917–1922)* (KP OLTsI: Moscow, 2005)

G. Katkov, *The Kornilov Affair: Kerensky and the Breakup of the Russian Army* (Longman: London, 1980)

A. G. Kavtaradze, *Voennye spetsialisty na sluzhbe Respubliki Sovetov, 1917–1920 gg.* (Nauka: Moscow, 1988)

J. L. H. Keep, *The Russian Revolution: A Study in Mass Mobilization* (Weidenfeld and Nicolson: London, 1976)

A. F. Kerenskii, *Delo Kornilova* (Zadruga, Moscow, 1918 edn)

A. Khaesh, 'Navet 1915 goda na yevreev mestechka Kuzhy', *Yevreiskaya Starina*, no. 1, 7 April 2019: http://litbook.ru/article/12906/

N. E. Khitrina, *Agrarnaya politika Vremennogo pravitel'stva v 1917 g.: monografiya* (Nizhegorodskii gumanitarnyi tsentr: Nizhni Novgorod, 2003)

H. Kirimli, 'The Activities of the Union for the Liberation of Ukraine in the Ottoman Empire during the First World War', *Middle Eastern Studies*, no. 4 (1998)

T. M. Kitanina, *Voina, khleb i revolyutsiya: prodovol'stvennyi vopros v Rossii, 1914 – oktyabr' 1917 g.* (Nauka: Leningrad, 1985)

J. D. Klier and S. Lambroza (eds), *Pogroms: Anti-Jewish Violence in Modern Russian History* (Cambridge University Press: Cambridge, 1992)

A. W. F. Knox, *With the Russian Army, 1914–1917* (Hutchinson and Co.: London, 1921), vols 1–2

L. Kochan (ed.), *The Jews in Soviet Russia since 1917* (Oxford University Press: Oxford, 1978)

D. Koenker, *Moscow Workers and the 1917 Revolution* (Princeton University Press: Princeton, NJ, 1981)

D. Koenker and W. G. Rosenberg, *Strikes and Revolution in Russia* (Princeton University Press: Princeton, NJ, 1989)

V. V. Kondrashin, 'Sel'skoe khozyaistvo i krest'yanstvo v 1917 g.' in Yu. A. Petrov (ed.), *Rossiiskaya revolyutsiya 1917 goda: vlast', obshchestvo, kul'tura*, vol. 1

V. V. Kondrashin, *Krest'yanskoe dvizhenie v Povol'zhe v 1918–1922 gg.* (Yanus – K: Moscow, 2001)

N. D. Kondrat'ev, *Rynok khlebov i ego regulirovanie vo vremya voiny i revolyutsii* (ed. L. Abalkin: Nauka: Moscow, 1991)

Konstantinopol' i prolivy po sekretnym dokumentam b. Ministerstva Inostrannykh Del, vols. 1–2 (ed. E. A. Adamov: Litizdat NKID: Moscow, 1925–6)

A. P. Korelin, 'Popytki reformirovaniya sistemy kontrol'no-reguliruyushchikh organov' in Yu. A. Petrov (ed.), *Rossiiskaya revolyutsiya 1917 goda: vlast', obshchestvo, kul'tura*, vol. 1

I. Korukhin, 'Politsiya staroi Rossii: budochniki, zhandarmy, 'faraony', *Otechestvennye zapiski*, no. 2 (2013)

S. Kotkin, *Stalin*, vol. 1: *Paradoxes of Power* (Allen Lane: London, 2015)

Y. Kotsonis, *States of Obligation: Taxes and Citizenship in the Russian Empire and Early Soviet Republic* (Toronto University Press: Toronto, 2014)
A. N. Koss, 'World War I and the Remaking of Jewish Vilna, 1914–1918' (Ph.D. dissertation, Stanford University, 2010)
V. I. Kostrikin, 'Krest'yanskoe dvizhenie nakanune Oktyabrya' in I. M. Volkov *et al.* (eds), *Oktyabr' i sovetskoe krest'yanstvo, 1917–1927 gg.*
V. Kozlovskii, *Nepodtsentsurnaya russkaya chastushka* (Russica: New York, 1978)
N. A. Kravchuk, *Massovoe krest'yanskoe dvizhenie v Rossii nakanune Oktyabrya, mart-oktyabr' 1917 g.: po materialam velikorusskikh gubernii Evropeiskoi Rossii* (Mysl: Moscow, 1971)
V. P. Kravkov, *Velikaya voina bez retushi: zapiski korpusnogo vracha* (Veche: Moscow, 2014)
Krest'yanskoe vosstanie v Tambovskoi gubernii v 1919–1921: 'Antonovshchina': Dokumenty i materialy (eds V. Danilov and T. Shanin: Redaktsionno-izdatel'skii otdel: Tambov, 1994)
[A. N. Kuropatkin], *Dnevnik A. N. Kuropatkina* (Gos. Publichnaya Istoricheskaya Biblioteka Rossii: Moscow, 2010)
É. Laloy, *Les documents secrets des archives du Ministère des Affaires Étrangères de Russie publiés par les Bolcheviks* (Brossard: Paris, 1919)
N. A. Lambert, *Planning Armageddon: British Economic Warfare and the First World War* (Harvard University Press: Cambridge, MA., 2012)
N. A. Lambert, *The War Lords and the Gallipoli Disaster: How Globalized Trade Led Britain to Its Worst Defeat of the First World War* (Oxford University Press: Oxford, 2021)
E. Landis, *Bandits and Partisans: The Antonov Movement in the Russian Civil War* (University of Pittsburgh Press: Pittsburgh, PA, 2008)
Yu. Larin, *Voina i zemel'naya programma* (Kniga: Petrograd, 1917)
A. Latyshev, *Rassekrёchennyi Lenin* (Mart: Moscow, 1996)
V. Ya. Laverychev, *Monopolisticheskii kapitalizm v tekstil'noi promyshlennosti Rossii (1900–1917)* (Moscow University Press: Moscow, 1963)
M. K. Lemke, *250 dnei v tsarskoi stavke (25 sent. 1915 – 2 iyulya 1916)* (Gosizdat: St Petersburg, 1920)
V. I. Lenin, *Polnoe sobranie sochinenii* (Izdatel'stvo politicheskoi literatury: Moscow, 1958–65)
Lenin i VChK: sbornik dokumentov, 1917–1922 (ed. S. Tsvigun: Institut Marksizma-Leninizma: Moscow, 1987)
Leninskii sbornik, vols 1–50 (Gosizdat: Moscow, 1924–85)
M. Levene, *Wars, Jews and the New Europe: The Diplomacy of Lucien Wolf* (Oxford University Press: Oxford, 1992)
R. Leviné-Meyer, *Leviné the Spartacist: The Life and Times of the Socialist Revolutionary Leader of the German Spartacists and Head of the Ill-Starred Munich Republic of 1919* (Gordon and Cremonesi: London, 1978)
D. Lieven, *Towards the Flame: Empire, War and the End of Tsarist Russia* (Allen Lane: London, 2015)

L. Lih, *Bread and Authority in Russia, 1917–1921* (University of California: Berkeley, CA, 1990)

W. B. Lincoln, *Passage Through Armageddon: The Russians in War and Revolution, 1914–1918* (Simon and Schuster: New York, 1986)

A. Lindenmeyr, C. Read and P. Waldron (eds), *Russia's Home Front in War and Revolution, 1914–1922*, vols 2 and 4 (Slavica: Bloomington, IN, 2015–18)

I. Linder and S. Churkin (eds), *Krasnaya pautina: tainy razvedki Kominterna, 1919–1943* (Ripol klassik: Moscow, 2005)

E. Lohr, *Nationalizing the Russian Empire: The Campaign against Enemies during World War I* (Harvard University Press: Cambridge, MA., 2003)

Yu. Lomonosov, *Vospominaniya o martovskoi revolyutsii* (Stockholm/Berlin, 1921)

D. A. Longley, 'Factional Strife and Policy-Making in the Bolshevik Party, 1912–April 1917' (University of Birmingham Ph.D., 1978)

D. A. Longley, 'The February Revolution in the Baltic Fleet at Helsingfors: *Vosstanie* or *Bunt*?', *Canadian Slavonic Papers*, no. 1 (1978)

D. A. Longley, 'The Russian Social-Democrats' Statement to the Duma on 26 July (8 August) 1914: a New Look at the Evidence', *English Historical Review*, July 1987

H. D. Lowe, *The Tsars and the Jews: Reform, Reaction and Anti-Semitism in Imperial Russia, 1772–1917* (Harwood: Chur, Switzerland, 1993)

[A. S. Lukomskii], *Vospominaniya Generala A. S. Lukomskogo: period Evropeiskoi voiny, nachalo razrukhi v Rossii, bor'ba s bol'shevikami*, vol. 1 (O. Kirchner: Berlin, 1922)

A. Luukkanen, *The Party of Unbelief: The Religious Policy of the Bolshevik Party, 1917–1929* (SHS: Helsinki, 1994)

G. E. Lvov and T. I. Polner, *Nashe Zemstvo i 50 let ego raboty* (P. P. Ryabushinskii: Moscow, 1914)

D. I. Lyukshin, *Vtoraya Russkaya smuta: krest'yanskoe izmerenie* (AIRO-XXI: Moscow, 2006)

B. McGreever, *Antisemitism and the Russian Revolution* (Cambridge University Press: Cambridge, 2019)

R. McKean, 'The Bureaucracy and the Labour Problem, June 1907–February 1917' in R. McKean (ed.), *New Perspectives in Modern Russian History* (Macmillan: Basingstoke, 1990)

R. B. McKean, *St Petersburg between the Revolutions: Workers and Revolutionaries, June 1907–February 1917* (Yale University Press: New Haven, CN, 1990)

S. McMeekin, *The Russian Origins of the First World War* (Harvard University Press: Cambridge, MA., 2011)

N. P. Makarov, *Krest'yanskoe khozyaistvo i ego evolyutsiya*, vol. 1 (N. Zheludkovskaya: Moscow, 1920)

N. P. Makarov, *Krest'yanskoe khozyaistvo i ego interesy* (Universal'naya Biblioteka: Moscow, 1917)

S. L. Makarova, 'K voprosu o vremeni likvidatsii pomeshchich'ego zemlevladeniya' in I. M. Volkov *et al.* (eds), *Oktyabr' i sovetskoe krest'yanstvo, 1917–1927 gg.*

A. D. Malyavskii, *Krest'yanskoe dvizhenie v Rossii v 1917 g., mart-oktyabr'* (Nauka: Moscow, 1981)

R. T. Manning, *The Crisis of the Old Order in Russia: Gentry and Government* (Princeton University Press: Princeton, NJ, 1982)

A. Markevich and Mark Harrison, 'Great War, Civil War, and Recovery: Russia's National Income, 1913 to 1928', *Journal of Economic History*, no. 3 (2011)

T. Martin, *The Affirmative Action Empire: Nations and Nationalism in the Soviet Union, 1923–1939* (Cornell University Press: Ithaca, NY, 2001)

A. P. Martynov, *Moya sluzhba v otdel'nom korpuse zhandarmov* (Hoover Institution Press: Stanford, CA, 1972)

P. Maslov, 'Ekonomicheskoe znachenie voiny dlya Rossii', *Samozashchita* (Petrograd), no. 1 (1916)

E. Mawdsley, *The Russian Civil War* (Allen and Unwin: Hemel Hempstead, 1987)

V. Mayakovskii, *Sochineniya*, vol. 1 (Khudozhestvennaya literatura: Moscow, 1978)

M. Mayzel, *Generals and Revolutionaries: The Russian General Staff During the Revolution: A Study in the Transformation of Military Elite* (Biblio Verlag: Osnabrück, 1979)

T. A. Medvedeva and S. V. Bushueva, 'Sotsial'no-ekonomicheskii krizis v Nizhegorodskoi gubernii i ego rol' v utrate legitimnosti novoi demokratii v period fevralya–oktyabrya 1917 g. (po materialam nizhegorodskoi pechati)', *Istoricheskii zhurnal: nauchnye issledovaniya*, no. 2 (2018): https://nbpublish.com/library_read_article.php?id=24635

A. M. Michelson, P. N. Apostol and M. W. Bernatzky, *Russian Public Finance During the War: Revenue and Expenditure* (Yale University Press: New Haven, CT, 1928)

P. N. Milyukov, *Vospominaniya, 1859–1917*, vols 1–2 (Izd. im. Chekhova: New York, 1955)

A. Morrison, C. Drieu and A. Chokobaeva (eds), *The Central Asian Revolt of 1916: A Collapsing Empire in the Age of War and Revolution* (Manchester University Press: Manchester, 2020)

A. Morrison, 'Refugees, Resettlement and Revolutionary Violence in Semirech'e after the 1916 Revolt' in A. Morrison, C. Drieu and A. Chokobaeva (eds), *The Central Asian Revolt of 1916: A Collapsing Empire in the Age of War and Revolution*

V. D. Nabokov, 'Vremennoe Pravitel'stvo', *Arkhiv russkoi revolyutsii*, no. 1 (1921)

R. Nachtigal, *Die Murmanbahn: die Verkehrsanbindung eines kriegswichtigen Hafens und das Arbeitspotential der Kriegsgefangenen (1915 bis 1918)* (Greiner: Remshalden-Grunbach, 2001)

I. V. Narskii, *Zhizn' v katastrophe: budni naseleniya Urala v 1917–1922 gg.* (Rosspen: Moscow, 2001)

M. S. Neiberg and D. Jordan, *The Eastern Front, 1914–1920: From Tannenberg to the Russo–Polish War* (Amber: London, 2008)

K. Neilson, *Strategy and Supply: The Anglo-Russian Alliance, 1914–17* (Allen and Unwin: London, 1984)

A. B. Nikolaev, *Dumskaya revolyutsiya: 27 fevralya–3 marta 1917 goda*, vols 1–2 (RGPU: St Petersburg, 2017)

A. B. Nikolaev, *Gosudarstvennaya duma v Fevral'skoi revolyutsii : ocherki istorii* (Nauch. Izd: Ryazan, 2002)

A. B. Nikolaev (ed.), *Revolyutsiya 1917 goda v Rossii: novye podkhody i vzglyady* (RGPU: St Petersburg, 2019)

A. Nove, *An Economic History of the USSR* (Penguin: London, 1969)

P. A. Obolenskii, 'Starye gody: semeinye zapiski', *Novyi zhurnal* (New York), no. 175

S. Obolensky, *One Man in His Time: The Memoirs of Serge Obolensky* (McDowell: New York, 1958)

Odinnadtsatyi s"ezd RKP(b): mart – aprel' 1922 g.: stenograficheskii otchët (Gosizdat: Moscow, 1961)

A. Offer, *The First World War: An Agrarian Interpretation* (Oxford University Press: Oxford, 1989)

A. Okninskii, *Dva goda sredi krest'yan: videnноe, slyshannoe, perezhitoe v Tambovskoi gubernii s noyabrya 1918 goda do noyabrya 1920 goda* (M. Didkovska: Riga, 1936)

N. P. Okunev, *Dnevnik moskvicha, 1917–1924* (YMCA-Press: Paris, 1990)

[F. S. Olferev], *Russia in War and Revolution: The Memoirs of Fyodor Olferieff* (ed. G. M. Hamburg, tr. T. A. Cameron: Hoover Institution Press: Stanford, CA, 2021)

D. Orlovsky (ed.), *A Companion to the Russian Revolution* (Wiley Blackwell: Hoboken, NJ, 2020)

D. Orlovsky, 'Democracy or Corporatism: The Russian Provisional Government of 1917' in A. Weiner (ed.), *Landscaping the Human Garden: Twentieth-Century Population Management in a Comparative Framework* (Stanford University Press: Stanford, CA, 2003)

D. Orlovsky, 'The Provisional Government and its Cultural Work' in A. Gleason, P. Kenez and R. Stites (eds), *Bolshevik Culture: Experimentation and Order in the Russian Revolution*

D. Orlovsky. 'Reform during Revolution: Governing the Provinces in 1917' in R. Crummey (ed.), *Reform in Russia and the USSR: Past and Prospects*

D. Orlovsky, 'What Was Power in 1917?' in C. Read, P. Waldron and A. Lindenmeyr (eds), *Russia's Home Front in War and Revolution, 1914–22*, vol. 4

T. V. Osipova, *Rossiiskoe krest'yanstvo v revolyutsii o grazhdanskoi voine* (Strelets: Moscow, 2001)

Osobye zhurnaly Soveta Ministrov, 1909–1917 gg., vols 6–8 (eds B. D. Gal'perina, A. D. Stepanskii and V. V. Shelokhaev: Rosspen: Moscow, 2006–8)

Padenie tsarskogo rezhima: stenograficheskie otchëty doprosov i pokazanii, dannykh v 1917 g. v Chrezvychainoi sledstvennoi komissiei Vremennogo pravitel'stva, vols 1–7 (P. E. Shchegolev: Gosizdat: Leningrad–Moscow, 1924–7)

M. Paléologue, *An Ambassador's Memoirs*, vols 1–3 (Hutchinson: London, 1924)

J. Pallot, *Land Reform in Russia, 1906–1917: Peasant Responses to Stolypin's Project of Rural Transformation* (Clarendon Press: Oxford, 1999)

B. Pearce, *How Haig Saved Lenin* (Macmillan: Basingstoke, 1987)

R. Pearson, *The Russian Moderates and the Crisis of Tsarism, 1914–1917* (Macmillan: London, 1977)

Perepiska Nikolaya i Aleksandry Romanovykh, vols 1–5 (ed. M. N. Pokrovskii: Gosizdat: Moscow, 1923–7)

Perepiska Sekretariata TsK RSDRP(b) s mestnymi partiinymi organizatsiyami: sbornik dokumentov, vols 1–8 (Gosizdat Politicheskoi Literatury: Moscow, 1957–74)

M. Perrie, 'The Peasants' in R. Service, *Society and Politics in the Russian Revolution*

Pervaya vseobshchaya perepis' naselenie Rossiisskoi imperii 1897 g. Okonchatel'no ustanovlennoe pri razrabotke perepisi nalichnoe naselenie gorodov (Ministerstvo Vnutrennikh Del: St Petersburg, 1905)

Pervyi Kongress Kominterna: mart 1919 goda (Partiinoe izdatelstvo: Moscow, 1919)

S. Pestkovskii, 'Vospominaniya o rabote v Narkomnatse (1917–1919 gg.)', *Proletarskaya Revolyutsiya*, no. 6 (1930)

Peterburgskii komitet RSDRP(b) v 1917 godu: protokoly i materialy zasedanii (eds T. A. Abrosimova *et al.*: Belveder: St Petersburg, 2003)

Petrogradskii Sovet Rabochikh i Soldatskikh Deputatov v 1917 godu: materialy i dokumenty, vol. 1 (gen. ed. P. V. Volobuev: Biblioteka 'Zvezdy': St Petersburg, 1993)

Yu. A. Petrov (ed.), *Rossiiskaya revolyutsiya 1917 goda: vlast', obshchestvo, kul'tura*, vols 1–2 (Rosspen: Moscow, 2017)

I. Petrovskii-Shtern, *Jews in the Russian Army, 1827–1917: Drafted into Modernity* (Cambridge University Press: Cambridge, 2009)

Y. Petrovsky-Shtern, 'The "Jewish Policy" of the Late Imperial War Ministry: The Impact of the Russian Right', *Kritika*, no. 2 (2002)

R. Pipes, *The Russian Revolution* (Vintage: New York, 1991)

A. Poliakoff, *The Silver Samovar: Reminiscences of the Russian Revolution* (Atlantida Press: Nottingham, 1996)

A. A. Polivanov, *Iz dnevnikov i vospominanii po dolzhnosti voennogo ministra i ego pomoshchnika, 1906–1916 g.* (Vysshii voennyi redaktsionnyi soviet: Moscow, 1924)

Politbyuro TsK RKP(b) – VKP(b) i Komintern, 1919–1943 (Rosspen: Moscow, 2004)

T. I. Polner, *Zhiznennyi put' Georgiya Evgen'evicha L'vova: lichnost', vzglyady, usloviya deyatel'nosti* (n.p.: Paris, 1932)

W. Pomeranz, 'The Provisional Government and the Law Based State' in C. Read, P. Waldron and A. Lindenmeyr (eds), *Russia's Home Front in War and Revolution, 1914–1922*, vol. 4

O. S. Porshneva, *Krest'yane, rabochie i soldaty Rossii nakanune i v gody Pervoi mirovoi voiny* (Rosspen: Moscow, 2004)

D. Pospielovsky, *Russkaya pravoslavnaya tserkov' v XX veke* (Respublika: Moscow, 1995)

S. N. Prokopovich, *Voina i narodnoe khozyaistvo* (2nd edn: Sovet Vserossiiskikh Kooperativnykh S"ezdov: Moscow, 1918)

Protokoly Tsentral'nogo Komiteta RSDRP(b), avgust 1918–fevral' 1918 (Gosizdat politicheskoi literatury: Moscow, 1958)

A. V. Prusin, *Nationalizing a Borderland: War, Ethnicity, and anti-Jewish Violence in East Galicia* (University of Alabama Press: Tuscaloosa, AL, 2005)

A. Pyman, *The Life of Alexander Blok*, vol. 2: *The Release of Harmony* (Oxford University Press: Oxford, 1980)

A. Rabinowitch, *The Bolsheviks Come to Power* (NLB: London, 1986)

A. Rabinowitch, *The Bolsheviks in Power: The First Year of Soviet Rule in Petrograd* (Indiana University Press: Bloomington, IN, 2007)

A. Rabinowitch, *Prelude to Revolution: The Petrograd Bolsheviks and the July 1917 Uprising* (Indiana University Press: Bloomington, IN, 1968)

K. Radek, 'Noyabr'. (Stranichka iz vospominanii)', *Krasnaya nov'*, no. 10 (1926)

O. H. Radkey, *The Election to the Russian Constituent Assembly* (Harvard University Press: Cambridge, MA., 1950)

O. H. Radkey, *The Unknown Civil War in Soviet Russia: A Study of the Green Movement in the Tambov Region, 1920–1921* (Hoover Institution Press: Stanford, 1976)

M. Rady, *The Habsburgs: The Rise and Fall of a World Power* (Allen Lane: London, 2020)

M. Rady, *The Middle Kingdoms: A New History of Central Europe* (Allen Lane: London, 2023)

D. J. Raleigh, 'Revolutionary Politics in Provincial Russia: The Tsaritsyn "Republic" in 1917', *Slavic Review*, no. 2 (1981)

D. Rayfield, 'The Soldier's Lament: World War One Folk Poetry in the Russian Empire', *Slavonic and East European Review*, no. 1 (1988)

C. Read, *Culture and Power in Revolutionary Russia: The Intelligentsia and the Transition from Tsarism to Communism* (Macmillan: London, 1990)

C. Read, *War and Revolution in Russia, 1914–1922: The Collapse of Tsarism and the Establishment of Soviet Power* (Palgrave Macmillan: Basingstoke, 2013)

C. Read, P. Waldron and A. Lindenmeyr (eds), *Russia's Home Front in War and Revolution, 1914–1922*, vol. 4 (Slavica: Baltimore, MD, 2018)

M. Rendle, *Defenders of the Motherland: The Tsarist Elite in Revolutionary Russia* (Oxford University Press: Oxford, 2009)

W. A. Renzi, 'Great Britain, Russia, and the Straits', *Journal of Modern History*, no. 1 (1970)

W. A. Renzi, 'Who Composed "Sazonov's Thirteen Points": A Re-Examination of Russia's War Aims of 1914', *American Historical Review*, no. 2 (1983)

Resheniya partii i pravitel'stva po khozyaistvennym voprosam (1917–1967), vol. 1 (eds K. U. Chernenko and M. S. Smirtyukov: Izdatelstvo Politicheskoi Literatury: Moscow, 1967)

A. Retish, *Russia's Peasants in Revolution and Civil War: Citizenship, Identity, and the Creation of the Soviet State, 1914–1922* (Cambridge University Press: Cambridge, 2008)

M. A. Reynolds, *Shattering Empires: The Clash and Collapse of the Ottoman and Russian Empires, 1908–1918* (Cambridge University Press: Cambridge, 2011)

T. H. Rigby, *Lenin's Government: Sovnarkom, 1917–1922* (Cambridge University Press: Cambridge, 1979)

P. Robinson, 'A Study of Grand Duke Nikolai Nikolaevich as Supreme Commander of the Russian Army, 1914–1915', *The Historian*, no. 3 (2013)

P. Robinson, *Grand Duke Nikolai Nikolaevich* (Northern Illinois University Press: DeKalb, IL, 2014)

E. Rogan, *The Fall of the Ottomans: The Great War in the Middle East, 1914–1920* (Allen Lane: London, 2015)

P. G. Rogoznyi, *Tserkovnaya revolyutsiya 1917: vysshee dukhovenstvo Rossiiskoi Tserkvi v bor'be za vlast' v eparkhiyakh posle Fevral'skoi revolyutsii* (Liki Rossii: St Petersburg, 2008)

W. G. Rosenberg, 'The Russian Municipal Duma Elections of 1917: A Preliminary Computation of Returns', *Slavic Review*, no. 2 (1969)

W. G. Rosenberg, *The Liberals in the Russian Revolution: The Constitutional Democratic Party, 1917–1920* (Princeton University Press: Princeton, NJ, 1974)

Rossiya 1917 goda v ego-dokumentakh: Dnevniki (eds N. V. Surzhikova *et al.*: Politicheskaya entsiklopediya: Moscow, 2017)

S. E. Rudneva, *Demokraticheskoe Soveshchanie, sentyabr' 1917 g.: istoriya foruma* (Nauka, 2000)

S. E. Rudneva, *Predparlament: Oktyabr' 1917 goda: opyt istoricheskii rekonstruktsii* (Nauka: Moscow, 2006)

A. G. Rumyantsev, 'Dokumenty TsGIA po delu o "razgrome"', in A. B. Nikolaev (ed.), *Revolyutsiya 1917 goda v Rossii: novye podkhody i vzglyady* (RGPU: St Petersburg, 2019)

The Russian Union of Zemstvos: A Brief Report of the Union's Activities (introduced by G. E. Lvov; P. S. King: London, 1917)

Russkaya pravoslavnaya tserkov' i kommunisticheskoi gosudarstvo, 1917–1941: dokumenty i materialy (ed. A. N. Shchapov: Bibleisko-bogoslovskii institute svyatogo Apostola Andreya: Moscow, 1996)

R. Goldberg Ruthchild, 'Going to the Ballot Box is a Moral Duty for Every Woman: The Great War and Women's Rights in Russia' in C. Read, P. Waldron and A. Lindenmeyr (eds), *Russia's Home Front in War and Revolution, 1914–1922*, vol. 4

C. A. Ruud and S. A. Stepanov, *Fontanka 16: The Tsars' Secret Police* (McGill-Queen's University Press: London, 1999)

K. Ryabinskii (ed.), *Revolyutsiya 1917 goda: Khronika sobytii* (Gosizdat: Leningrad, 1926)

K. V. Samokhin, 'The Tambov Peasantry during the First World War', *Russian Studies in History*, no. 2 (2017)

J. A. Sanborn, *Drafting the Russian Nation: Military Conscription, Total War, and Mass Politics, 1905–1925* (Northern Illinois Press: DeKalb, IL, 2003)

J. A. Sanborn, *Imperial Apocalypse: The Great War and the Destruction of the Russian Empire* (Oxford University Press: Oxford, 2014)

T. Sapronov, *Iz istorii rabochego dvizheniya: po lichnym vospominaniyam* (Gosizdat: Moscow, 1925)

N. E. Saul, 'Lenin's Decision to Seize Power: The Influence of Events in Finland', *Soviet Studies*, no. 4 (1973)

S. Sazonov, *Fateful Years, 1909–1916: The Reminiscences of Serge Sazonov* (J. Cape: London, 1928)

S. D. Sazonov, *Vospominaniya* (E. de Sialsky: Paris, 1927)

D. Schönpflug and M. Schulze Wessel (eds), *Redefining the Sacred: Religion in the French and Russian Revolutions* (Peter Lang: Frankfurt am Main, 2012)

Sed'moi (ekstrennii) s"ezd RKP(b): mart 1918 g.: stenograficheskii otchët (Gosizdat Politicheskoi Literatury: Moscow, 1962)

V. P. Semënov Tyan-Shanskii, 'Glavnyi Zemelnyi Komitet', *Arkhiv Russkoi Revolyutsii*, vol. 12 (1923)

A. S. Senin, *Russkaya Armiya v 1917 godu: iz istorii Voennogo ministerstva i Vremennogo pravitel'stva* (Veche: Moscow, 2017)

B. V. Sennikov, *Tambovskoe vosstanie 1918–1921 gg. i raskrest'yanivanie Rossii 1929–1933* (Posev: Moscow, 2004)

E. Senyavskaya, *Psikhologiya voiny v XX veke: istoricheskii opyt Rossii* (Rosspen: Moscow, 1999)

R. Service, *The Bolshevik Party in Revolution: A Study in Organisational Change* (Macmillan: London, 1979)

R. Service, *Last of the Tsars: Nicholas II and the Russian Revolution* (Macmillan: London, 2017)

R. Service, *Lenin: A Biography* (Macmillan: London, 2000)

R. Service, *Lenin: A Political Life*, vols 1–3 (Macmillan: London, 1985–95)

R. Service, *Society and Politics in the Russian Revolution* (Macmillan: Basingstoke, 1992)

R. Service. *Spies and Commissars: Bolshevik Russia and the West* (Macmillan: London, 2011)

R. Service, *Stalin: A Biography* (Macmillan: London, 2004)

R. Service, *Trotsky: A Biography* (Macmillan: London, 2009)

G. N. Sevast'yanov, J. Haslam *et al.* (eds), *Sovetsko-amerikanskie otnosheniya: gody nepriznaniya, 1918–1926* (Mezhdunarodnyi fond Demokratiya: Moscow, 2002)

T. Shanin, *The Awkward Class: Political Sociology of Peasantry in a Developing Society: Russia, 1910–1925* (Clarendon Press: Oxford, 1972)

G. I. Shavelskii, *Vospominaniya poslednego protopresvitera russkoi armii i flota*, vols 1–2 (Izd. im. Chekhova: New York, 1954)

A. Shestakov, *Krest'yanstvo revolyutsii 1905–1907* (Gosizdat: Moscow, 1926)

Shestoi s"ezd RSDRP (bol'shevikov). Avgust 1917 goda. Protokoly (Gosizdat: Moscow, 1958)

V. Shevzov, *Russian Orthodoxy on the Eve of Revolution* (Oxford University Press: Oxford, 2004)

[A. A. Shtukaturov], 'Dnevnik Shtukaturova' (ed. A. Svechin), *Voenno-istoricheskii zhurnal*, nos. 1–2 (I. D. Sytin: Moscow, 1919)

A. L. Sidorov, *Finansovoe polozhenie Rossii v gody Pervoi Mirovoi voiny (1914–1917)* (Akademiya nauk SSSR: Moscow, 1960)

J. Siegel, *For Peace and Money: French and British Money in the Service of Tsars and Commissars* (Oxford University Press: Oxford, 2014)
L. Siegelbaum, *The Politics of Industrial Mobilization: A Study of the War-Industries Committees, 1914–1917* (Macmillan: London, 1983)
F. Silano, '"In the Language of the Patriarch": Patriarch Tikhon, the Russian Orthodox Church, and the Soviet State (1865–1925)' (Ph.D., University of Toronto, 2017)
F. Silano, '(Reconstructing) an Orthodox "Scenario of Power": The Restoration of the Russian Orthodox Patriarchate in Revolutionary Russia (1917–1918)', *Revolutionary Russia*, no. 1 (2019)
J. D. Smele, *The 'Russian' Civil Wars, 1916–1926: Ten Years That Shook the World* (Hurst: London, 2015)
N. N. Smirnov, 'The Soviets' in E. Acton, V. Iu. Cherniaev and W. G. Rosenberg (eds), *Critical Companion to the Russian Revolution*
D. Smith, *Former People: The Final Days of the Russian Aristocracy* (Farrar, Straus and Giroux: New York, 2012)
D. Smith, *Rasputin* (Macmillan: London, 2015)
S. A. Smith, 'The First Soviet Generation: Children and Religious Belief in Soviet Russia, 1917–41' in Stephen Lovell (ed.), *Generations in Twentieth-Century Europe* (Palgrave: Basingstoke, 2007)
S. A. Smith, 'Introduction' to S. A. Smith and Alan Knight (eds), *The Religion of Fools? Superstition Past and Present, Past and Present Supplement 3*, (Oxford University Press: Oxford, 2008)
S. A. Smith, *Red Petrograd: Revolution in the Factories, 1917–1918* (Cambridge University Press: Cambridge, 1983)
S. A. Smith, *Russia in Revolution: An Empire in Crisis, 1890–1928* (Oxford University Press: Oxford, 2017)
S. C. Smith, *Captives of Revolution: The Socialist Revolutionaries and the Bolshevik Dictatorship, 1918–1923* (University of Pittsburgh: Pittsburgh, PA, 2011)
A. I. Solzhenitsyn, *Dvesti let vmeste (1795–1995)*, vols 1–2 (Russkii put: Moscow, 2001–2)
G. H. Soutou, 'Diplomacy' in *Cambridge History of the First World War*, vol. 2 (Cambridge University Press: Cambridge, 2014)
Sovet Ministrov Rossiiskoi imperii v gody Pervoi mirovoi voiny: bumagi A. N. Yakhontova: zapisi zasedanii i perepiska (Dmitrii Bulanin: St Petersburg, 1999)
A. I. Spiridovich, *Velikaya voina i Fevral'skaya Revolyutsiya, 1914–1917 g.g.*, vols 1–3 (Vseslavyanskoe izdatel'stvo: New York, 1960–2)
L. M. Spirin, *Rossiya 1917 god: iz istorii bor'by politicheskikh partii* (Mysl: Moscow, 1987) SSEES Depository; R-20585
Spravochnik tsen: tseny utverzhdëny Gubernskoi komissiei tsen 14-go 1921 g. (Gosizdat: Petrograd, 1921)
D. W. Spring, 'Russian Foreign Policy, Economic Interests and the Straits Questions, 1905–14' in R. McKean (ed.), *New Perspectives in Modern Russian History*
V. B. Stankevich, *Vospominaniya, 1914–1919 g.* (I. P. Ladyzhnikov: Berlin, 1920)
V. I. Startsev, 'Begstvo Kerenskogo', *Voprosy Istorii*, no. 11 (1966)

'Stavka i Ministerstvo Inostrannykh Del' (ed. M. Pokrovskii), *Krasnyi Arkhiv*, nos. 1–3 (1928)

F. Stepun, *Byvshee i nesbyvsheesya* (Progress-Litera: Moscow, 1995)

D. Stevenson, *1914–1918: The History of the First World War* (Allen Lane: London, 2004)

D. Stevenson, *1917: War, Peace and Revolution* (Oxford University Press: Oxford, 2017)

F. Stevenson, *Lloyd George: A Diary* (ed. A. J. P. Taylor: Hutchinson: London, 1971)

R. Stites, 'Iconoclastic Currents in the Russian Revolution' in A. Gleason, P. Kenez and R. Stites (eds), *Bolshevik Culture: Experimentation and Order in the Russian Revolution*

R. Stites, *Revolutionary Dreams: Utopian Vision and Experimental Life* (Oxford University Press: Oxford, 1989)

M. K. Stockdale, *Mobilizing the Russian Nation: Patriotism and Citizenship in the First World War* (Cambridge University Press: Cambridge, 2016)

M. K. Stockdale, 'News from the War: Print Culture and the Nation in World War I Russia' in Y. Tatsumi and T. Tsurumi (eds), *Publishing in Tsarist Russia: A History of Print Media from Enlightenment to Revolution*

M. K. Stockdale, *Paul Milyukov and the Quest for a Liberal Russia, 1880–1918* (Cornell University Press: Ithaca, NY, 1996)

D. R. Stone, *The Russian Army in the Great War: The Eastern Front, 1914–1917* (University of Kansas Press: Lawrence, KS, 2015)

N. Stone, *The Eastern Front, 1914–1917* (Hodder and Stoughton: London, 1975)

H. Strachan, *The First World War*, vol. 1: *To Arms* (Oxford University Press: Oxford, 2001)

N. Sukhanov, *Zapiski o revolyutsii* (Respublika: Moscow, 1992)

V. Sukhomlinoff, *La mobilisation russe à la lumière des documents officiels et des révélations du procès* (F. Wyss: Berne, 1917)

V. A. Sukhomlinov, *Vospominaniya* (Russkoe universal'noe izdatel'stvo: Berlin, 1924)

R. G. Suny, *The Baku Commune, 1917–1918: Class and Nationality in the Russian Revolution* (Princeton University Press: Princeton, NJ, 1972)

N. V. Surzhikova *et al.* (eds), Rossiia 1917 goda v ego-dokumentakh: dokumenty (Rosspen: Moscow, 2017)

G. Swain, *The Origins of the Russian Civil War* (Longman: London, 1996)

G. Swain, C. Alston, M. Hickey, B. Kolonitskii and F. Schedewie (eds), *The Bloomsbury Handbook of the Russian Revolution* (Bloomsbury Academic: London, 2023)

P. Szlanta, 'Der Erste Weltkrieg von 1914 bis 1915 als identitätstiftender Faktor für die moderne polnische Nation' in P. Gross (ed.), *Die vergessene Front: der Osten 1914/1915* (F. Schöningh: Paderborn, 2006)

Y. Tatsumi and T. Tsurumi (eds), *Publishing in Tsarist Russia: A History of Print Media from Enlightenment to Revolution* (Bloomsbury: London, 2020)

N. Taylor, *Estonia: A Modern History* (Hurst: London, 2018)

I. D. Thatcher, 'The 'Broad Centrist' Political Parties and the First Provisional Government, 3 March – 5 May 1917', *Revolutionary Russia*, no. 2 (2020)
I. D. Thatcher, *Leon Trotsky and World War One: August 1914–February 1917* (Macmillan: London, 2000)
I. D. Thatcher, 'Liberalism and the Rule of Law' in G. Swain *et al.* (eds), *The Bloomsbury Handbook of the Russian Revolution* (Bloomsbury: London, 2023)
I. D. Thatcher, 'Memoirs of the Russian Provisional Government 1917', *Revolutionary Russia*, no. 1 (2014)
I. D. Thatcher, 'Post-Soviet Russian Historians and the Russian Provisional Government of 1917', *Slavonic and East European Review*, no. 2 (2015)
[L. A. Tikhomirov], *Dnevnik L. A. Tikhomirova: 1915–1917 gg.* (ed. A. V. Repnikov: Rosspen: Moscow, 2008)
L. Trotskii, *K istorii oktyabr'skoi revolyutsii* (Russkaya Sotsialisticheskaya Federatsiya: New York, 1919)
L. Trotskii, *Moya zhizn': opyt avtobiografii*, vols 1–2 (Granit: Berlin, 1930)
L. Trotskii, *Na bor'bu s golodom!* (Kommunist: Moscow, 1918: speech to public meeting, Sokolniki, 9 June 1918)
L. Trotskii, *O Lenine: Materialy dlya biografii* (Gosizdat: Moscow, 1924)
L. Trotskii, *Voina s Pol'shei* (Literaturno-izdatel'skii Otdel PU RVSR: Moscow, 1920: speech to All-Russia Central Executive Committee of the Congress of Soviets, 5 May 1920)
The Trotsky Papers, 1917–1922 (ed. J. M. Meijer: Mouton: The Hague, 1964, 1971), vols 1–2
I. G. Tsereteli, *Krizis vlasti* (Luch: Moscow, 1992)
I. G. Tsereteli, *Vospominania o Fevral'skoi Revolyutsii*, vols 1–2 (Mouton: Paris, 1963)
'Tyazhëlye dni (Sekretnye zasedaniya Soveta Ministrov, 16 iyulya–2 sentyabrya 1915 goda)', *Arkhiv Russkoi Revolyutsii*, vol. 18 (1926)
S. V. Tyutyukin, *Istoricheskie siluety* (Nauka: Moscow, 1991)
M. I. Ul'yanova, *O V. I. Lenine i sem'e Ul'yanovykh* (2nd revised edition: Izdatel'stvo politicheskoi literatury: Moscow, 1989)
J. Veidlinger, *In the Midst of Civilized Europe: The Pogroms of 1918–1921 and the Onset of the Holocaust* (Picador: London, 2021)
S. Velychenko, *State Building in Revolutionary Ukraine: A Comparative Study of Governments and Bureaucrats, 1917–22* (Toronto University Press: Toronto, 2011)
A. Venturi, *Rivoluzionari russi in Italia, 1917–1921* (Feltrinelli: Milan, 1979)
A. I. Verkhovskii, *Rossiya na Golgofe: iz pokhodnogo dnevnika 1914–1918 gg.* (Pyataya gosudarstvennaya tipografiya: Moscow, 1921)
Vladimir Il'ich Lenin: Biograficheskaya khronika, 1870–1924, vols 1–12 (Izdatelstvo politicheskoi literatury: Moscow, 1970–82)
V. Voitinskii, *Padenie Rigi* (Litagit Otdel VTsIK: Petrograd, 1917)
I. M. Volkov *et al.* (eds), *Oktyabr' i sovetskoe krest'yanstvo, 1917–1927 gg.* (Nauka: Moscow, 1977)
P. V. Volobuev, *Ekonomicheskaya politika Vremennogo Pravitel'stva* (AN SSSR: Moscow, 1962)

P. V. Volobuev, *Proletariat i burzhuaziya Rossiya v 1917 g.* (Mysl: Moscow, 1964)

Vospominaniya o Vladimire Il'iche Lenine, vols 1–8 (eds M. P. Mchedlov *et al.*: Izdatel'stvo politicheskoi literatury: Moscow, 1989–91)

Vos'moi s"ezd RKP(b): Mart 1919 g.: Protokoly (Gosizdat Politicheskoi Literatury: Moscow, 1959)

Vtoraya i tret'ya petrogradskie obshchegorodskie konferentsii bol'shevikov v iyule i oktyabre 1917 goda: protokoly (Moscow–Leningrad, 1927)

Vtoroi vserossiiskii s"ezd sovetov rabochikh i soldatskikh deputatov: sbornik dokumentov (eds A. F. Butenko and D. A. Chugaev: Moscow, 1957)

[A. A. Vyrubova], *Freilina eë Velichestva* (ed. A. V. Kochetov: Orbita: Moscow, 1993)

R. A. Wade, *The Russian Search for Peace, February to October 1917* (Stanford University Press: Stanford, CA, 1969)

P. Waldron, 'A Sad and Heart-rending Landscape: Summer 1914 and the Politics of Russia's Wounded', *Slavonic and Eastern European Review*, no. 4 (2016)

P. Waldron, 'States of Emergency: Autocracy and Extraordinary Legislation, 1881–1917', *Revolutionary Russia*, no. 1 (1995)

S. Washburn, *The Russian Campaign, April to August 1915* (Charles Scribner's Sons: New York, 1915)

A. Watson, *Ring of Steel: Germany and Austria–Hungary at War, 1914–1918* (Allen Lane: Penguin, 2014)

A. Weiner (ed.), *Landscaping the Human Garden: Twentieth-Century Population Management* (Stanford University Press: Stanford, CA, 2003)

N. Weissman, 'Regular Police', *Russian Review*, no. 1 (1985)

S. Wheatcroft, 'Agriculture' in R. W. Davies (ed.), *From Tsarism to the New Economic Policy: Continuity and Change in the Economy of the USSR* (Macmillan: Basingstoke, 1990)

J. M. White, 'Battling for Legitimacy: Russian Old Believer Priests on the Frontlines of the First World War, 1914–1917', *First World War Studies*, nos. 2–3 (2017)

A. Wildman, *The End of the Russian Imperial Army*, vol. 1: *The Old Army and the Soldiers' Revolt, March–April 1917* (Princeton University Press: Princeton, NJ, 1980); vol. 2: *The Road to Soviet Power and Peace* (1987)

A. Willimott, *Living the Revolution: Urban Communism and Soviet Communism, 1917–1932* (Oxford University Press: Oxford, 2016)

W. S. Woytinsky, *Stormy Passage: A Personal History Through Two Russian Revolutions to Democracy* (Vanguard Press: New York, 1961)

A. Yakhontov (ed.), 'Tyazhëlye dni (Sekretnye zasedaniya Soveta Ministrov, 16 iyulya–2 sentyabrya 1915 goda)', *Arkhiv Russkoi Revolyutsii*, vol. 18 (1926)

G. L. Yaney, *The Urge to Mobilize: Agrarian Reform in Russia, 1861–1930* (University of Illinois: Urbana, IL)

[O.] A. Yermanskii, *Marksisty na rasput'i: o sbornike 'Samozashchita'* (Petrograd–Moscow, 1916)

[A. A. Zamaraev], *Dnevnik totemskogo krest'yanina A. A. Zamaraeva, 1906–1922* (eds V. V. Morozov and N. I. Reshetnikov: RAN: Moscow, 1995)

Z. A. B. Zeman, *Germany and the Revolution in Russia, 1915–1918: Documents from the Archives of the German Foreign Ministry* (Oxford University Press: Oxford, 1958)

G. K. Zhukov, *Vospominaniya i razmyshleniya*, vol. 1 (2nd edn: Novosti: Moscow, 1990)

Zhurnaly zasedanii Vremennogo Pravitel'stva, vols 1–4 (eds B. F. Dodonov, E. D. Grinko and O. V. Lavinskaya: Rosspen: Moscow, 2001–4)

S. J. Zipperstein, 'The Politics of Relief: The Transformation of Russian Jewish Communal Life during the First World War' in J. Frankel (ed.), *The Jews and the European Crisis, 1914–1921* (ICJ Hebrew University of Jerusalem: Oxford, 1988)

O. N. Znamenskii, *Vserossiiskoe uchreditel'noe sobranie: istoriya sozyva i politicheskogo krusheniya* (Nauka: Leningrad, 1976)

NOTES

Chapter 1
No Return Ticket: The Russian Declaration of War

1 C. Clark, *The Sleepwalkers: How Europe Went to War in 1914*, pp. 449–50.
2 *Dnevniki imperatora Nikolaya II, 1894–1918*, vol. 2, p. 35 (12 July 1914).
3 S. Sebag Montefiore, *The Romanovs, 1613–1918*, pp. 496–7.
4 *Dnevniki imperatora Nikolaya II*, vol. 2, p. 35 (2 June 1914).
5 R. Service, *Last of the Tsars: Nicholas II and the Russian Revolution*, p. 9.
6 D. Lieven, *Towards the Flame: Empire, War and the End of Tsarist Russia*, pp. 303–7.
7 D. W. Spring, 'Russian Foreign Policy, Economic Interests and the Straits Questions, 1905–14' in R. McKean (ed.), *New Perspectives in Modern Russian History* (Macmillan: Basingstoke, 1990), pp. 208–9 and 216–17.
8 S. Sazonov, *Fateful Years, 1909–1916: The Reminiscences of Serge Sazonov*, p. 242.
9 *Dnevniki imperatora Nikolaya II*, vol. 2, p. 9 (2 February 1914).
10 D. Lieven, *Towards the Flame*, p. 294.
11 D. Stevenson, *1914–1918: The History of the First World War*, pp. 27–8.
12 N. A. Romanov, 16 July 1914: *Dnevniki imperatora Nikolaya II*, vol. 2, pp. 46–7.
13 D. W. Graf, 'Military Rule Behind the Russian Front', *Jahrbücher für Geschichte Europas*, no. 3 (1974), pp. 390–1.
14 S. Sazonov, *Fateful Years, 1909–1916*, p. 202.
15 P. L. Bark, 'Vospominaniya', *Vozrozhdenie*, no. 160 (1965), p. 87.
16 A. N. Yakhontov to S. E. Kryzhanovskii, 31 May 1924: *Sovet Ministrov Rossiiskoi imperii v gody Pervoi mirovoi voiny: bumagi A. N. Yakhontova: zapisi zasedanii i perepiska*, pp. 472–4. This source will henceforth be abbreviated as *SMRI*.
17 P. L. Bark, 'Vospominaniya', *Vozrozhdenie*, no. 160 (1965), p. 88; P. L. Bark to A. A. Rittikh, 9 September 1922: *SMRI*, p. 437.
18 G. I. Shavelskii, *Vospominaniya poslednego protopresvitera*, vol. 1, pp. 112 and 121.
19 Yu. N. Danilov, *Na puti k krusheniyu: ocherki iz poslednego perioda russkoi monarkhii*, p. 7.
20 P. L. Bark, 'Vospominaniya', *Vozrozhdenie*, no. 160 (1965), p. 89.
21 P. Waldron, 'A Sad and Heart-Rending Landscape: Summer 1914 and the Politics of Russia's Wounded', *Slavonic and Eastern European Review*, no. 4 (2016), p. 636.

22 P. L. Bark, 'Vospominaniya', *Vozrozhdenie*, no. 160 (1965), pp. 89–90 and 93.
23 D. A. Longley, 'The Russian Social-Democrats' Statement to the Duma on 26 July (8 August) 1914: a New Look at the Evidence', *English Historical Review*, July 1987, p. 599.
24 P. L. Bark, 'Vospominaniya', *Vozrozhdenie*, no. 158 (1965), p. 81.
25 A. M. Michelson, 'Revenue and Expenditure', p. 41 in A. M. Michelson, P. N. Apostol and M. W. Bernatzky, *Russian Public Finance during the War: Revenue and Expenditure*.

Chapter 2
Russia Goes to War: Conscription, Riots and Deployment

1 *Dnevnik totemskogo krest'yanina A. A. Zamaraeva*, p. 85 (26 June 1914). This source will henceforth be abbreviated as DTKAAZ.
2 *DTKAAZ*, p. 86 (18 July 1914).
3 *DTKAAZ*, p. 87 (25 July 1914).
4 *DTKAAZ*, p. 115 (9 September 1915).
5 *DTKAAZ*, p. 79 (9 March 1914).
6 *DTKAAZ*, p. 59 (22 January 1913), p. 80 (23 March 1914), and p. 86 (29 June 1914).
7 *DTKAAZ*, pp. 39 (2 April 1912) and p. 81 (13 April 1914).
8 *DTKAAZ*, p. 27 (1 and 5 May 1908).
9 *DTKAAZ*, p. 90 (late August 1914).
10 N. P. Makarov, *Krest'yanskoe khozyaistvo i ego evolyutsiya*, vol. 1, p. 310.
11 *Pervaya vseobshchaya perepis' naselenie Rossiisskoi imperii 1897 g.: Okonchatel'no ustanovlennoe pri razrabotke perepisi nalichnoe naselenie gorodov* (Ministerstvo Vnutrennikh Del: St Petersburg, 1905).
12 N. P. Makarov, *Krest'yanskoe khozyaistvo i ego evolyutsiya*, vol. 1, p. 307.
13 *DTKAAZ*, p. 108 (23 May 1915).
14 N. P. Makarov, *Krest'yanskoe khozyaistvo i ego evolyutsiya*, vol. 1, p. 308.
15 S. M. Dubrovskii, *Sel'skoe khozyaistvo i krest'yanstvo Rossii v period imperializma*, p. 82.
16 *DTKAAZ*, p. 87 (20 July 1914).
17 *DTKAAZ*, p. 95 (24 November 1914).
18 *DTKAAZ*, p. 93 (29 October 1914).
19 N. N. Golovin, *Voennye usiliya Rossii v mirovoi voine*, vol. 1, pp. 75 and 81; there are varying estimates of recruitment figures, as Golovin noted, but they concur roughly with what he produced.
20 S. N. Prokopovich, *Voina i narodnoe khozyaistvo*, pp. 151, 155 and 231.
21 *DTKAAZ*, p. 87 (21 and 25 July 1914).
22 V. P. Buldakov and T. G. Leonteva, *Voina, porodivshaya revolyutsiyu: Rossiya, 1914–1917 gg.*, p. 281.
23 Ibid., pp. 280–1.
24 *DTKAAZ*, p. 87 (21–25 July 1914).

25 V. P. Buldakov and T. G. Leonteva, *Voina, porodivshaya revolyutsiyu*, p. 281.
26 Ibid., p. 304.
27 A. I. Verkhovskii (diary), 7 and 14 August 1914: A. I. Verkhovskii, *Rossiya na Golgofe: iz pokhodnogo dnevnika 1914–1918 gg.*, pp. 9 and 16.
28 J. L. Houghteling, *A Diary of the Russian Revolution*, pp. 6 and 10–11.
29 A. P. Martynov, *Moya sluzhba v otdel'nom korpuse zhandarmov*, p. 272; J. A. Sanborn, *Imperial Apocalypse*, p. 94. For Krivoshein see Council of Ministers, 9 June 1915: *SMRI*, p. 178.
30 *DTKAAZ*, p. 89 (19 August 1914).
31 *DTKAAZ*, p. 90 (1 September 1914).
32 Translation Robert Service, from A. Blok, *Sochineniya v ognom tome*, p. 232.

Chapter 3
Advance, Defeat, Objectives: From Victory to the Great Retreat

1 [F. S. Olferev], *Russia in War and Revolution*, p. 219.
2 W. C. Fuller, *The Foe Within: Fantasies of Treason and the End of Imperial Russia*, p. 126.
3 D. R. Stone, *The Russian Army in the Great War: The Eastern Front, 1914–1917*, pp. 76–80 and 85.
4 J. A. Sanborn, *Imperial Apocalypse*, p. 32.
5 H. Strachan, *The First World War*, vol. 1: *To Arms*, p. 291.
6 N. Stone, *The Eastern Front, 1914–1917*, pp. 70–1, 76–7, 82 and 85–91.
7 A. Watson, *Ring of Steel: Germany and Austria-Hungary at War, 1914–1918*, p. 342.
8 *DTKAAZ*, p. 91 (15 September 1914).
9 *DTKAAZ*, p. 91 (24 September 1914).
10 *DTKAAZ*, p. 92 (5 October 1914).
11 *DTKAAZ*, p. 92 (5 and 6 October 1914).
12 *DTKAAZ*, p. 92 (10 October 1914).
13 M. A. Reynolds, *Shattering Empires: The Clash and Collapse of the Ottoman and Russian Empires, 1908–1918*, pp. 110, 112 and 116–17.
14 M. S. Neiberg and D. Jordan, *The Eastern Front, 1914–1920: From Tannenberg to the Russo-Polish War*, p. 73.
15 *DTKAAZ*, p. 99 (19 January 1915).
16 *DTKAAZ*, p. 97 (31 December 1915).
17 'Dnevnik Shtukaturova', *Voenno-istoricheskii zhurnal*, no. 1, pp. 134–5: 27–8 June 1915.
18 Ibid., p. 170: 13 September 1915.
19 L. Siegelbaum, *The Politics of Industrial Mobilization: A Study of the War-Industries Committees, 1914–1917*, p. 30.
20 J. A. Sanborn, *Imperial Apocalypse*, p. 36.
21 E. Lohr, *Nationalizing the Russian Empire: The Campaign against Enemies during World War I*, pp. 78–81.

22 S. Sazonov, *Fateful Years, 1909–1916*, p. 247.
23 N. A. Lambert, *The War Lords and the Gallipoli Disaster: How Globalized Trade Led Britain to Its Worst Defeat of the First World War*, pp. 16, 94 and 133.
24 E. Rogan, *The Fall of the Ottomans: The Great War in the Middle East, 1914–1920*, p. 214.
25 W. A. Renzi, 'Who Composed "Sazonov's Thirteen Points": A Re-Examination of Russia's War Aims of 1914', *American Historical Review*, no. 2 (1983), pp. 348–50.
26 E. Rogan, *The Fall of the Ottomans*, p. 133; M. A. Reynolds, *Shattering Empires*, pp. 37–41.
27 S. Sazonov, *Fateful Years, 1909–1916*, p. 201; see also W. A. Renzi, 'Who Composed "Sazonov's Thirteen Points": A Re-Examination of Russia's War Aims of 1914', *American Historical Review*, no. 2 (1983), p. 355; R. Bobroff, *Roads to Glory: Late Imperial Russia and the Turkish Straits*, p. 131; R. P. Bobroff, 'Squabbling over the Spoils', in L. J. Frary and M. Kozelsky (eds), *Russian–Ottoman Borderlands: The Eastern Question Reconsidered*, p. 290.
28 R. Bobroff, *Roads to Glory*, p. 131.
29 S. Sazonov, *Fateful Years, 1909–1916*, p. 250.
30 *Dnevnik L. A. Tikhomirova: 1915–1917 gg.*: 2 June 1915, p. 70.
31 *Dnevniki imperatora Nikolaya II, 1894–1918*, vol. 2, p. 160 (9 April 1915).
32 P. Szlanta, 'Der Erste Weltkrieg von 1914 bis 1915 als identitätstiftender Faktor für die modern polnische Nation' in P. Gross (ed.), *Die vergessene Front: der Osten 1914/1915*, p. 160.
33 *DTKAAZ*, p. 105 (19 May 1915).
34 *DTKAAZ*, p. 109 (6 June 1915).
35 *DTKAAZ*, p. 116 (3 October 1915).
36 'Dnevnik Shtukaturova', *Voenno-istoricheskii zhurnal*, no. 1 (1 July 1915), p. 137.
37 N. A. Kudashev to S. D. Sazonov (report on Danilov's views on the Dardanelles), 8 January 1915: 'Stavka i Ministerstvo Inostrannykh Del' (ed. M. Pokrovskii), *Krasnyi Arkhiv*, no. 1 (1928), pp. 41–3.

Chapter 4
The Imperial War Zone: Military Government, Pogroms and Deportation

1 A. I. Solzhenitsyn, *Dvesti let vmeste (1795–1995)*, vol. 1, p. 479.
2 G. Z. Ioffe, 'Vyselenie evreev iz prifrontovoi polosy v 1915 godu', *Voprosy istorii*, no. 9 (2001), p. 86.
3 G. I. Shavelskii, *Vospominaniya poslednego protopresvitera*, vol. 1, pp. 109–10.
4 O. R. Airapetov, *Generaly, liberaly i predprinimateli: rabota na front i na revolyutsiyu (1907–1917)*, pp. 38–9.
5 M. Mayzel, *Generals and Revolutionaries: The Russian General Staff During the Revolution: A Study in the Transformation of Military Elite*, p. 37.

6 Ibid., p. 72.
7 P. L. Bark, 'Vospominaniya', *Vozrozhdenie*, no. 172 (1966), pp. 88–9.
8 V. P. Buldakov and T. G. Leonteva, *Voina, porodivshaya revolyutsiyu*, p. 211; J. A. Sanborn, *Imperial Apocalypse*, pp. 58–9 and 77.
9 N. N. Golovin, *Voennye usiliya Rossii v mirovoi voine*, vol. 1, p. 81. S. N. Prokopovich, *Voina i narodnoe khozyaistvo*, p. 151 has figures that are slightly different.
10 *DTKAAZ*, p. 99 (15 January 1915).
11 *DTKAAZ*, p. 105 (14 April 1915).
12 N. N. Golovin, *Voennye usiliya Rossii v mirovoi voine*, vol. 1, pp. 185–6.
13 J. Bushnell, *Mutiny Amid Repression: Russian Soldiers in the Revolution of 1905–1906*, pp. 12–13; W. C. Fuller, *Civil–Military Conflict in Imperial Russia, 1881–1914*, p. 220.
14 N. N. Golovin, *Voennye usiliya Rossii v mirovoi voine*, vol. 1, p. 120.
15 N. Stone, *The Eastern Front, 1914–1917*, p. 213.
16 N. N. Golovin, *Voennye usiliya Rossii v mirovoi voine*, vol. 1, pp. 32 and 41–4.
17 Ibid., vol. 2, pp. 74–5.
18 E. S. Senyavskaya, *Psikhologiya voiny v XX veke: istoricheskii opyt*, p. 261.
19 'Dnevnik Shtukaturova', *Voenno-istoricheskii zhurnal*, no. 1, pp. 141–2 (8 July 1915).
20 A. B. Astashov, 'Russkii krest'yanin na fronte pervoi mirovoi voiny', *Otechestvennaya istoriya* , no. 2 (2003), p. 73.
21 'Dnevnik Shtukaturova', *Voenno-istoricheskii zhurnal*, no. 1, pp. 181–2 (27 and 29 October 1915).
22 N. N. Golovin, *Voennye usiliya Rossii v mirovoi voine*, vol. 2, p. 157.
23 J. A. Sanborn, *Drafting the Russian Nation: Military Conscription, Total War, and Mass Politics, 1905–1925*, p. 33.
24 A. B. Astashov, 'Russkii krest'yanin na fronte pervoi mirovoi voiny', *Otechestvennaya istoriya*, no. 2 (2003), p. 79.
25 Ibid.
26 Ibid., p. 81.
27 Ibid., pp. 81 and 83.
28 G. K. Zhukov, *Vospominaniya I razmyshleniya*, vol. 1, p. 63.
29 'Dnevnik Shtukaturova', *Voenno-istoricheskii zhurnal*, no. 1, p. 154 (16 August 1915).
30 G. K. Zhukov, *Vospominaniya i razmyshleniya*, vol. 1, p. 69.
31 Council of Ministers, 2 September 1915: *SMRI*, p. 261.
32 N. B. Shcherbatov, Council of Ministers, 13 September 1915: *SMRI*, p. 271.
33 J. Bushnell, *Mutiny Amid Repression: Russian Soldiers in the Revolution of 1905–1906*, p. 10.
34 S. Ansky, *The Enemy at His Pleasure: A Journey Through the Jewish Pale of Settlement During World War One*, p. 83.
35 'Dnevnik Shtukaturova', *Voenno-istoricheskii zhurnal*, no. 2, pp. 174 and 187 (14 September 1915 and 25 November 1915).
36 Ibid., pp. 187–8 (25–26 November 1915).

37 D. Rayfield, 'The Soldier's Lament: World War One Folk Poetry in the Russian Empire', *Slavonic and East European Review*, no. 1 (1988), p. 71. I have slightly adjusted the excellent translation.
38 Ibid., pp. 70–1.
39 J. A. Sanborn, *Imperial Apocalypse*, pp. 37–8 and 50–1; S. An-sky, *1915 Diary of S. An-sky: A Russian-Jewish Writer at the Eastern Front*, p. 42 (4 January 1915).
40 H. D. Lowe, *The Tsars and the Jews: Reform, Reaction and Anti-Semitism in Imperial Russia, 1772–1917*, p. 325.
41 Council of Ministers, 5 September 1915: *SMRI*, p. 264.
42 'Dnevnik Shtukaturova', *Voenno-istoricheskii zhurnal*, no. 1, p. 159 (27 August 1915).
43 See the argument made by P. Holquist, 'Violent Russia, Deadly Marxism? Russia in the Epoch of Violence, 1905–21', *Kritika: Explorations in Russian and Eurasian History*, no. 3 (2003), pp. 627–52.
44 R. E. Blobaum, *A Minor Apocalypse: Warsaw during the First World War*, p. 40.
45 P. Gatrell, *A Whole Empire Walking: Refugees in Russia During World War I*, pp. 23–4; R. E. Blobaum, *A Minor Apocalypse: Warsaw during the First World War*, pp. 23–4.
46 *DTKAAZ*, pp. 88–9 (11 August 1914).
47 E. Lohr, *Nationalizing the Russian Empire*, pp. 150–1.
48 W. Conze, *Polnische Nation under Deutsche Politik im Ersten Weltkrieg*, p. 90.
49 E. Lohr, *Nationalizing the Russian Empire*, pp. 123 and 125.
50 A. Watson, *Ring of Steel*, p. 154.
51 I. Petrovskii-Shtern, *Jews in the Russian Army, 1827–1917: Drafted into Modernity*, p. 5.
52 R. E. Blobaum, *A Minor Apocalypse*, p. 151.
53 P. Kenez, 'Pogroms and White Ideology in the Russian Civil War' in J. D. Klier and S. Lambroza, *Pogroms: Anti-Jewish Violence in Modern Russian History*, p. 291.
54 P. Holquist, 'The Role of Personality in the First (1914–1915) Russian Occupation of Galicia and Bukovina' in J. Dekel-Chen, D. Gaunt, N. M. Meir and I. Bartal (eds), *Anti-Jewish Violence: Rethinking the Pogrom in East European History*, p. 56.
55 S. An-sky, *1915 Diary of S. An-sky*, pp. 53–4 (18 January 1915).
56 Ibid., p. 112 (26 February 1915).
57 H. D. Lowe, *The Tsars and the Jews*, p. 324; I. Petrovskii-Shtern, *Jews in the Russian Army, 1827–1917: Drafted into Modernity*, p. 249.
58 S. An-sky, *1915 Diary of S. An-sky*, p. 48 (16 January 1915).
59 H. D. Lowe, *The Tsars and the Jews*, p. 323.
60 O. V. Budnitskii, '"Evreiskie batal'ony" v Krasnoi Armii' in O. V. Budnitskii (ed.), *Mirovoi krizis 1914–1920 godov i sud'ba vostochnoevropeiskogo evreistva*, p. 243; A. Koss, 'World War I and the Remaking of Jewish Vilna, 1914–1918' (Ph.D. dissertation, Stanford University, 2010), pp. 1–2.

61 I. Petrovskii-Shtern, *Jews in the Russian Army, 1827–1917: Drafted into Modernity*, pp. 260 and 262.
62 Y. Petrovsky-Shtern, 'The "Jewish Policy" of the Late Imperial War Ministry: The Impact of the Russian Right', *Kritika*, no. 2 (2002), p. 253.
63 W. C. Fuller, *The Foe Within*, p. 177; A. Khaesh, 'Navet 1915 goda na yevreev mestechka Kuzhy', *Yevreiskaya Starina*, no. 1, 7 April 2019: http://litbook.ru/article/12906/.

Chapter 5
Government Shackled: The Failure of the Ministers' Revolt

1 H. D. Lowe, *The Tsars and the Jews*, p. 326.
2 P. L. Bark, 'Vospominaniya', *Vozrozhdenie*, no. 170 (1966), p. 97.
3 P. L. Bark, report to Council of Ministers, 10 March 1915: *SMRI*, p. 147; P. L. Bark, Council of Ministers, 6 August 1915: *SMRI*, p. 212.
4 P. L. Bark, 'Vospominaniya', *Vozrozhdenie*, no. 165 (1965), p. 98. See also N. Ferguson, *The House of Rothschild: The World's Banker*, vol. 2, p. 448.
5 S. D. Sazonov, Council of Ministers, 6 August 1915: *SMRI*, p. 212.
6 P. L. Bark, 'Vospominaniya', *Vozrozhdenie*, no. 166 (1965), p. 96.
7 Council of Ministers, 10 March 1915: *SMRI*, p. 147.
8 N. B. Shcherbatov (inquiry testimony), *Padenie tsarskogo rezhima*, vol. 7, pp. 228–9.
9 Council of Ministers, 10 March 1915: *SMRI*, p. 147.
10 P. L. Bark, 'Vospominaniya', *Vozrozhdenie*, no. 172 (1966), p. 93.
11 P. L. Bark to A. A. Rittikh, 9 September 1922: *SMRI*, pp. 434 and 440.
12 P. L. Bark, 'Vospominaniya', *Vozrozhdenie*, no. 172 (1966), pp. 94–5.
13 P. L. Bark, 'Vospominaniya', *Vozrozhdenie*, no. 167 (1965), pp. 92–3; P. L. Bark to A. A. Rittikh, 9 September 1922: *SMRI*, p. 434.
14 P. L. Bark, 'Vospominaniya', *Vozrozhdenie*, no. 169 (1966), pp. 76–81.
15 A. A. Polivanov (inquiry testimony), *Padenie tsarskogo rezhima*, vol. 7, p. 63.
16 P. L. Bark to A. A. Rittikh, 9 September 1922: *SMRI*, pp. 435–6.
17 S. An-sky, *1915 Diary of S. An-sky*, p. 145 (27 September 1915).
18 P. L. Bark, 'Vospominaniya', *Vozrozhdenie*, no. 169 (1966), pp. 82–3; Yu. N. Danilov, *Rossiya v mirovoi voine 1914–1915 gg.*, p. 356; Yu. N. Danilov, *Na puti k krusheniyu*, p. 101; Yu. N. Danilov, *Velikii Knyaz' Nikolai Nikolaevich*, pp. 207–8.
19 G. I. Shavelskii, *Vospominaniya poslednego protopresvitera*, vol. 1, p. 270.
20 A. A. Polivanov (inquiry testimony), *Padenie tsarskogo rezhima*, vol. 7, p. 203.
21 G. I. Shavelskii, *Vospominaniya poslednego protopresvitera*, vol. 1, p. 232.
22 Yu. N. Danilov, *Velikii Knyaz' Nikolai Nikolaevich*, pp. 202–3.
23 N. B. Shcherbatov (inquiry testimony), *Padenie tsarskogo rezhima*, vol. 7, p. 228.
24 Council of Ministers, 24 July 1915: *SMRI*, p. 205.
25 Council of Ministers, 30 July 1915: 'Tyazhëlye dni', *Arkhiv Russkoi Revolyutsii*, vol. 18 (1926), pp. 33–4.

26 Ibid., pp. 30 and 32.
27 Council of Ministers, 4 August 1915: Ibid., pp. 44–5.
28 Council of Ministers, 6 August 1915: Ibid., p. 47.
29 Ibid., pp. 52–6.
30 Ibid., p. 56.
31 Council of Ministers, 12 August 1915: *SMRI*, p. 220.
32 Council of Ministers, 18 August 1915: *SMRI*, pp. 226–7.
33 P. L. Bark, 'Vospominaniya', *Vozrozhdenie*, no. 173 (1966), pp. 101–2.
34 P. L. Bark to A. A. Rittikh, 9 September 1922: *SMRI*, p. 438.
35 P. Holquist, *Making War, Forging Revolution: Russia's Continuum of Crisis, 1914–1921*, p. 27.
36 P. L. Bark, 'Vospominaniya', *Vozrozhdenie*, no. 173 (1966), p. 102.
37 Council of Ministers, 18 August 1915: *SMRI*, p. 225; Yu. N. Danilov, *Rossiya v mirovoi voine 1914–1915 gg.*, p. 382.
38 A. N. Yakhontov to S. Ye. Kryzhanovskii, 31 May 1924: *SMRI*, p. 469.
39 *Dnevniki imperatora Nikolaya II*, vol. 2, p. 149 (22–24 August 1915); Yu. N. Danilov, *Rossiya v mirovoi voine 1914–1915 gg.*, p. 384.
40 N. N. Golovin, *Voennye usiliya Rossii v mirovoi voine*, vol. 2, p. 156.
41 [F. S. Olferev], *Russia in War and Revolution*, pp. 312 and 315.
42 M. K. Lemke, *250 dnei v tsarskoi stavke (25 sent. 1915 – 2 iyulya 1916)*, pp. 141, 143 and 148–9.
43 *Dnevniki imperatora Nikolaya II*, vol. 2, p. 149 (22–24 August 1915) and 166 (9 November 1915); Yu. N. Danilov, *Rossiya v mirovoi voine 1914–1915 gg.*, p. 384.
44 Council of Ministers, 24 August 1915: *SMRI*, pp. 239–40.
45 P. L. Bark, 'Vospominaniya', *Vozrozhdenie*, no. 172 (1966), pp. 84–5.
46 Council of Ministers, 26 August 1915: *SMRI*, pp. 245 and 249.
47 P. L. Bark, 'Vospominaniya', *Vozrozhdenie*, no. 172 (1966), pp. 85–6.
48 Council of Ministers, 28 August 1915: *SMRI*, pp. 254–5.
49 P. L. Bark, 'Vospominaniya', *Vozrozhdenie*, no. 173 (1966), pp. 103–5.
50 J. A. Sanborn, *Imperial Apocalypse*, p. 103.
51 L. Siegelbaum, *The Politics of Industrial Mobilization*, p. 83.
52 Council of Ministers, 2 September 1915: *SMRI*, p. 263.
53 M. V. Rodzyanko (inquiry testimony), *Padenie tsarskogo rezhima*, vol. 7, p. 131.
54 Council of Ministers, 2 September 1915: *SMRI*, p. 261.
55 See the discussion in R. Pipes, *The Russian Revolution*, p. 228.
56 Empress Alexandra to N. A. Romanov, 2, 16 and 17 September: *The Complete Wartime Correspondence of Tsar Nicholas II and the Empress Alexandra*, pp. 200, 239 and 243.
57 A. A. Polivanov (inquiry testimony), *Padenie tsarskogo rezhima*, vol. 7, p. 70.
58 A. I. Spiridovich, *Velikaya voina i Fevral'skaya Revolyutsiya, 1914–1917 g.g.*, vol. 1, pp. 209–10; A. A. Polivanov (inquiry testimony), *Padenie tsarskogo rezhima*, vol. 7, p. 70.

Chapter 6
Patriotic Assistance and Patriotic Subversion: The Wartime Activities of Civic Organizations

1 J. A. Sanborn, *Imperial Apocalypse*, p. 101.
2 G. E. Lvov and T. I. Polner, *Nashe Zemstvo i 50 let ego raboty*, pp. 37–59.
3 Council of Ministers, 3 August 1914: *SMRI*, p. 33.
4 Council of Ministers, 9 August 1914: *SMRI*, p. 40.
5 Council of Ministers, 19 August 1914: *SMRI*, p. 51.
6 O. R. Airapetov, *Generaly, liberaly i predprinimateli*, p. 155.
7 P. Gatrell, *Russia's First World War: A Social and Economic History*, pp. 40–1.
8 O. R. Airapetov, *Generaly, liberaly i predprinimateli*, p. 155.
9 *The Russian Union of Zemstvos: A Brief Report of the Union's Activities*, pp. 5–7 and 14.
10 *DTKAAZ*, p. 106 (23 April 1915).
11 Council of Ministers, 19 August 1914: *SMRI*, p. 58.
12 O. R. Airapetov, *Generaly, liberaly i predprinimateli*, p. 156.
13 P. Gatrell, *Russia's First World War*, pp. 41–2; T. Fallows, 'Politics and the War Effort in Russia: The Union of Zemstvos and the Organization of the Food Supply, 1914–1916', *Slavic Review*, no. 1 (1978), p. 71.
14 M. V. Chelnokov (inquiry testimony), *Padenie tsarskogo rezhima*, vol. 5, p. 308; *Vospominaniya Generala A. S. Lukomskogo*, vol. 1, p. 62.
15 Council of Ministers, 9 August 1915: *SMRI*, p. 215.
16 Council of Ministers, 28 August 1915: *SMRI*, p. 256.
17 Council of Ministers, 18 August 1915: *SMRI*, p. 229.
18 *Dnevniki imperatora Nikolaya II*, vol. 2, pp. 119, 204 and 238.
19 M. V. Chelnokov (inquiry testimony), *Padenie tsarskogo rezhima*, vol. 5, p. 307.
20 Ibid., pp. 306–7.
21 L. Siegelbaum, *The Politics of Industrial Mobilization*, pp. 45, 48 and 56.
22 Ibid., pp. 90 and 118.
23 Okhrana report, 16 December 1915: B. B. Grave (ed.), *Burzhuaziya nakanune Fevral'skoi revolyutsii*, pp. 16–18; L. Siegelbaum, *The Politics of Industrial Mobilization*, pp. 65–6 and 91–2.
24 Council of Ministers, 9 August 1915: 'Tyazhëlye dni', *Arkhiv Russkoi Revolyutsii*, vol. 18 (1926), pp. 58–9.
25 K. I. Globachev in K. I. Globachev and S. N. Globacheva, *The Truth of the Russian Revolution*, p. 49.
26 Ibid., pp. 47–8.
27 L. Siegelbaum, *The Politics of Industrial Mobilization*, p. 160.
28 Ibid., p. 170.
29 R. B. McKean, *St Petersburg between the Revolutions: Workers and Revolutionaries, June 1907–February 1917*, pp. 381–3.
30 K. I. Globachev in K. I. Globachev and S. N. Globacheva, *The Truth of the Russian Revolution*, p. 50.
31 L. Siegelbaum, *The Politics of Industrial Mobilization*, pp. 68 and 172.

32 Council of Ministers, 25 September 1915: *SMRI*, p. 281.
33 K. I. Globachev, 'Pravda o russkoi revolyutsii: Vospominaniya byvshevo nachal'nika Petrogradskogo okhrannogo otdeleniya', *Voprosy Istorii*, no. 7, pp. 104 and 108; A. Blok, *Poslednie Dni Imperatorskoi Vlasti*, p. 23.
34 Council of Ministers, 29 May 1915: *SMRI*, p. 395; *Vospominaniya Generala A. S. Lukomskogo*, vol. 1, pp. 62 and 64–5.
35 L. Siegelbaum, *The Politics of Industrial Mobilization*, pp. 37–8.
36 *Vospominaniya Generala A. S. Lukomskogo*, vol. 1, p. 65.
37 P. L. Bark, 'Vospominaniya', *Vozrozhdenie*, no. 170 (1966), p. 105.

Chapter 7
Ordering the Rear: An Absent Emperor and the Rise of Political Opposition

1 S. D. Sazonov, *Vospominaniya*, p. 365.
2 Empress Alexandra to N. A. Romanov, 28 August 1915: *The Complete Wartime Correspondence of Tsar Nicholas II and the Empress Alexandra*, p. 188.
3 *Dnevniki imperatora Nikolaya II*, vol. 2, p. 205 (18 January 1916).
4 Ibid.
5 A. I. Spiridovich, *Velikaya voina i Fevral'skaya Revolyutsiya, 1914–1917 g.g.*, vol. 2, p. 90.
6 G. I. Shavelskii, *Vospominaniya poslednego protopresvitera*, vol. 2, pp. 208–9.
7 A. I. Shingarëv, Kadet party congress, June 1916: B. B. Grave (ed.), *Burzhuaziya nakanune Fevral'skoi revolyutsii*, p. 74.
8 *Dnevniki imperatora Nikolaya II*, vol. 2, p. 173 (17 December 1915).
9 P. Waldron, 'States of Emergency: Autocracy and Extraordinary Legislation, 1881–1917', *Revolutionary Russia*, no. 1 (1995), p. 4.
10 *Dnevnik L. A. Tikhomirova: 1915–1917 gg.*: 19 March 1915, p. 48.
11 Council of Ministers, 2 September 1915: *SMRI*, p. 260.
12 N. B. Shcherbatov, Council of Ministers, 13 September 1915: *SMRI*, p. 270.
13 N. B. Shcherbatov, Council of Ministers, 8 September 1915: *SMRI*, p. 266.
14 *DTKAAZ*, p. 120 (2 December 1915).
15 *DTKAAZ*, p. 100 (28 January 1915).
16 *DTKAAZ*, p. 120 (2 December 1915).
17 Council of Ministers, 17 November 1915: *SMRI*, p. 297.
18 V. F. Dzhunkovskii (inquiry testimony), *Padenie tsarskogo rezhima*, vol. 5, pp. 109–12.
19 K. I. Globachev, 'Pravda o russkoi revolyutsii: Vospominaniya byvshevo nachal'nika Petrogradskogo okhrannogo otdeleniya', *Voprosy Istorii*, no. 7, p. 105.
20 Council of Ministers, 7 November 1914: *SMRI*, p. 95.
21 Council of Ministers, 14 November 1914: *SMRI*, p. 97.
22 Council of Ministers, 2 September 1915: *SMRI*, p. 260.
23 A. A. Polivanov, Council of Ministers, 5 September 1915: *SMRI*, p. 264.
24 [A. A. Vyrubova], *Freilina eë Velichestva*, (diary: 22 August 1915), p. 120.

Chapter 8
Economic Management: Industrial Concentration, Price Inflation and Growing Food Shortages

1 Council of Ministers, 2 October 1915: *SMRI*, p. 283.
2 A. Heywood, *Modernising Lenin's Russia: Economic Reconstruction, Foreign Trade and the Railways*, p. 24; R. Nachtigal, *Die Murmanbahn: die Verkehrsanbindung eines kriegswichtigen Hafens und das Arbeitspotential der Kriegsgefangenen (1915 bis 1918)*, pp. 41–5.
3 M. Futrell, *The Northern Underground: Episodes of Russian Revolutionary Transport and Communications through Scandinavia and Finland, 1863–1917*, pp. 180–5.
4 S. N. Prokopovich, *Voina i narodnoe khozyaistvo*, p. 33.
5 A. Watson, *Ring of Steel*, pp. 360–1; M. Rady, *The Middle Kingdoms: A New History of Central Europe*, chapter 29.
6 V. Ya. Laverychev, *Monopolisticheskii kapitalizm v tekstil'noi promyshlennosti Rossii (1900–1917)*, p. 247.
7 S. N. Prokopovich, *Voina i narodnoe khozyaistvo*, p. 160; P. Gregory, *Russian National Income, 1885–1913*, pp. 232–3.
8 N. A. Lambert, *The War Lords and the Gallipoli Disaster*, pp. 89–90.
9 A. M. Michelson, 'Revenue and Expenditure', p. 62.
10 P. L. Bark, 'Vospominaniya', *Vozrozhdenie*, no. 157 (1965), p. 61 and no. 158 (1965), pp. 77–9.
11 P. L. Bark, 'Vospominaniya', *Vozrozhdenie*, no. 158 (1965), p. 87.
12 S. N. Prokopovich, *Voina i narodnoe khozyaistvo*, p. 154.
13 A. M. Michelson, 'Revenue and Expenditure', p. 87.
14 Council of Ministers, 9 August 1914 (decree): *Osobye zhurnaly Soveta Ministrov, 1914–1916*, vol. 6, p. 271; Council of Ministers, 25 September 1914: *SMRI*, p. 76.
15 A. M. Michelson, 'Revenue and Expenditure', pp. 171 and 196.
16 P. L. Bark, 'Vospominaniya', *Vozrozhdenie*, no. 162 (1965), pp. 91 and 93.
17 P. N. Apostol, 'Credit Operations', pp. 252 and 271 in A. M. Michelson, P. N. Apostol and M. W. Bernatzky, *Russian Public Finance During the War: Revenue and Expenditure*.
18 P. N. Apostol, 'Credit Operations', p. 267.
19 S. N. Prokopovich, *Voina i narodnoe khozyaistvo*, p. 57.
20 M. W. Bernatzky, 'Monetary Policy', p. 392 in A. M. Michelson, P. N. Apostol and M. W. Bernatzky, *Russian Public Finance During the War*.
21 P. N. Apostol, 'Credit Operations', pp. 293–5 and 298–9.
22 M. K. Lemke, *250 dnei v tsarskoi stavke (25 sent. 1915 – 2 iyulya 1916)*, pp. 792–3.
23 P. N. Apostol, 'Credit Operations', p. 312; J. A. Frieden, *Banking on the World: The Politics of American International Finance*, p. 26.
24 P. N. Apostol, 'Credit Operations', pp. 314–15; M. I. Gaiduk, *Utyug: materialy i fakty o zagotovitel'noi deyatel'nost' russkikh voennykh komissiei v Amerike*, pp. 25–6.

25 Council of Ministers, 2 October 1915: *SMRI*, p. 283.
26 Council of Ministers, 12 August 1916: *SMRI*, p. 350.
27 V. Ya. Laverychev, *Monopolisticheskii kapitalizm v tekstil'noi promyshlennosti Rossii (1900–1917)*, pp. 281–2.
28 L. Siegelbaum, *The Politics of Industrial Mobilization*, p. 71.
29 Council of Ministers, 17 November 1915: *SMRI*, pp. 299–301.
30 A. P. Korelin, 'Popytki reformirovaniya sistemy kontrol'no-reguliruyushchikh organov' in Yu. A. Petrov (ed.), *Rossiiskaya revolyutsiya 1917 goda: vlast', obshchestvo, kul'tura*, vol. 1, p. 269.
31 A. S. Senin, *Ministerstvo putei soobshcheniya v 1917 godu: kratkii istoricheskii ocherk*, p. 138.
32 S. N. Prokopovich, *Voina i narodnoe khozyaistvo*, pp. 35–6 and 48.
33 Council of Ministers, 17 November 1915: *SMRI*, pp. 299–301.
34 S. N. Prokopovich, *Voina i narodnoe khozyaistvo*, p. 159.
35 T. M. Kitanina, *Voina, khleb i revolyutsiya: prodovol'stvennyi vopros v Rossii, 1914 – oktyabr' 1917 g.*, p. 71.
36 A. F. Trepov, Council of Ministers, 22 December 1915: *SMRI*, p. 307.
37 L. Siegelbaum, *The Politics of Industrial Mobilization*, pp. 4–5.
38 Council of Ministers, 17 February 1915: *SMRI*, p. 134.
39 L. Siegelbaum, *The Politics of Industrial Mobilization*, p. 22.
40 P. Gatrell, *Russia's First World War*, pp. 121–2.
41 Ibid., p. 68.
42 A. F. Trepov, Council of Ministers, 22 December 1915: *SMRI*, p. 307.

Chapter 9
The Eastern Front: Russian Military Resilience and German Overtures

1 *DTKAAZ*, p. 114 (27 August 1915).
2 *DTKAAZ*, p. 123 (31 December 1915).
3 N. A. Kudashev to S. D. Sazonov (reports on M. A. Alexeev), 10 September and 8 October 1915: 'Stavka i Ministerstvo Inostrannykh Del' (ed. M. Pokrovskii), *Krasnyi Arkhiv*, no. 3 (1928), pp. 5 and 10.
4 K. V. Samokhin, 'The Tambov Peasantry during the First World War', *Russian Studies in History*, no. 2 (2017), pp. 115–24; G. K. Zhukov, *Vospominaniya i razmyshleniya*, vol. 1, p. 63.
5 N. N. Golovin, *Voennye usiliya Rossii v mirovoi voine*, vol. 1, p. 183.
6 A. Knox, *With the Russian Army*, vol. 1, p. 348.
7 W. B. Lincoln, *Passage Through Armageddon: The Russians in War and Revolution, 1914–1918*, p. 242.
8 N. N. Golovin, *Voennye usiliya Rossii v mirovoi voine*, vol. 1, p. 179.
9 Yu. N. Danilov, *Rossiya v mirovoi voine 1914–1915 gg.*, p. 393.
10 N. Stone, *The Eastern Front, 1914–1917*, p. 12.

11 A. I. Denikin, *Ocherki russkoi smuty*, vol. 1, part 1: *Krushenie vlasti i armii, fevral'-sentyabr' 1917 g.*, p. 34.
12 A. A. Brussilov, *A Soldier's Notebook*, pp. 245 and 267.
13 [F. S. Olferev], *Russia in War and Revolution*, pp. 334–5; A. I. Denikin, *Ocherki russkoi smuty*, vol. 1, part 1: *Krushenie vlasti i armii, fevral'-sentyabr' 1917 g.*, p. 35; A. A. Polivanov (inquiry testimony), *Padenie tsarskogo rezhima*, vol. 7, p. 194.
14 'Dnevnik Shtukaturova', *Voenno-istoricheskii zhurnal*, no. 2, p. 184 (11 November 1915).
15 Ibid.
16 V. P. Kravkov, *Velikaya voina bez retushi: zapiski korpusnogo vracha*: diary, 27 August 1915: p. 171.
17 Ibid.: diary, 8 February 1915, pp. 104 and 124.
18 M. K. Lemke, *250 dnei v tsarskoi stavke (25 sent. 1915 – 2 iyulya 1916)*, pp. 261–2. See also A. I. Denikin, *Ocherki russkoi smuty*, vol. 1, part 1: *Krushenie vlasti i armii, fevral'-sentyabr' 1917 g.*, p. 34.
19 A. I. Denikin, *Ocherki russkoi smuty*, vol. 1, part 1: *Krushenie vlasti i armii, fevral'-sentyabr' 1917 g.*, p. 35.
20 A. A. Brussilov, *A Soldier's Notebook*, pp. 213–7; N. Stone, *The Eastern Front, 1914–1917*, p. 235.
21 A. A. Brussilov, *A Soldier's Notebook*, pp. 236, 241–2 and 256; N. Stone, *The Eastern Front, 1914–1917*, pp. 249 and 254.
22 *DTKAAZ*, p. 138 (18 July 1916).
23 A. A. Brussilov, *A Soldier's Notebook*, p. 236 and 241; N. Stone, *The Eastern Front, 1914–1917*, p. 249.
24 Ibid., pp. 258 and 270.
25 P. L. Bark, 'Vospominaniya', *Vozrozhdenie*, no. 178 (1966), pp. 98 and 108.
26 G. H. Soutou, 'Diplomacy' in *Cambridge History of the First World War*, vol. 2 (Cambridge University Press: Cambridge, 2014), p. 497.
27 *Constantinople et les Détroits: Documents Secrets de l'Ancien Ministère de Affaires Étrangères de Russie*, vol. 1, pp. 357–66.
28 Ibid., vol. 1, p. 367.
29 V. S. Dyakin, *Russkaya burzhuaziya i tsarizm v gody pervoi mirovoi voiny*, p. 279.
30 G. Buchanan, *My Mission to Russia and Other Diplomatic Memories*, pp. 19–20.

Chapter 10
Villages and Cities in the Great War: Angry Peasants, Hungry Urban Consumers

1 S. M. Dubrovskii, *Krest'yanskoe dvizhenie v revolyutsii 1905–1907 gg.*, pp. 65 and 67.
2 R. T. Manning, *The Crisis of the Old Order in Russia: Gentry and Government*, pp. 170–3.

3 N. P. Makarov, *Krest'yanskoe khozyaistvo i ego interesy* (Universal'naya Biblioteka: Moscow, 1917), pp. 29–30.
4 A. M. Anfimov, *P. A. Stolypin i rossiiskoe krest'yanstvo*, p. 250.
5 Ibid., pp. 237–50.
6 S. M. Dubrovskii, *Sel'skoe khozyaistvo i krest'yanstvo Rossii v period imperializma* (Nauka: Moscow, 1975), p. 158.
7 T. Shanin, *The Awkward Class: Political Sociology of Peasantry in a Developing Society: Russia, 1910–1925*, pp. 175–6; A. Retish, *Russia's Peasants in Revolution and Civil War: Citizenship, Identity, and the Creation of the Soviet State, 1914–1922*, p. 48.
8 A. M. Anfimov, *Rossiiskaya derevnya v gody pervoi mirovoi voiny, 1914-fevral' 1917*, p. 95.
9 A. Retish, *Russia's Peasants in Revolution and Civil War*, p. 42.
10 *DTKAAZ*, p. 106 (29 April 1915).
11 A. Retish, *Russia's Peasants in Revolution and Civil War*, p. 56.
12 A. M. Anfimov, *P. A. Stolypin i rossiiskoe krest'yanstvo*, p. 263.
13 *DTKAAZ*, p. 82 (1 May 1914).
14 P. Holquist, *Making War, Forging Revolution: Russia's Continuum of Crisis, 1914–1921*, pp. 32–3.
15 *DTKAAZ*, p. 122 (24 December 1915), p. 126 (15 February 1916), p. 131 (31 March 1916), p. 140 (1 August 1916), p. 141 (15 August 1916).
16 *DTKAAZ*, p. 127 (16 February 1916).
17 *DTKAAZ*, p. 117 (16 October 1915).
18 *DTKAAZ*, pp. 118–9 (5–14 November 1915).
19 *DTKAAZ*, p. 104 (31 March 1915).
20 N. P. Makarov, *Krest'yanskoe khozyaistvo i ego evolyutsiya* (N. Zheludkovskaya: Moscow, 1920), vol. 1, p. 315.
21 *DTKAAZ*, pp. 75–98 (the year 1914).
22 V. P. Buldakov and T. G. Leonteva, *Voina, porodivshaya revolyutsiyu*, pp. 301–2.
23 Council of Ministers, 11 September 1915: *SMRI*, pp. 267–9.
24 Council of Ministers, 22 December 1915: *SMRI*, pp. 307–8.
25 *Dnevnik L. A. Tikhomirova: 1915–1917 gg.*: 13 August 1915, p. 99.
26 A. L. Okninskii, *Dva goda sredi krest'yan: vidennoe, slyshannoe, perezhitoe v Tambovskoi gubernii s noyabrya 1918 goda do noyabrya 1920 goda*, p. 3.
27 M. W. Bernatzky, 'Monetary Policy', p. 395.
28 *Dnevnik L. A. Tikhomirova: 1915–1917 gg.*: 19 March 1915, p. 48.
29 P. Gatrell, *Russia's First World War*, p. 69.
30 K. V. Samokhin, 'The Tambov Peasantry during the First World War', *Russian Studies in History*, no. 2 (2017), p. 119.
31 M. W. Bernatzky, 'Monetary Policy', pp. 397 and 417.
32 *DTKAAZ*, p. 125 (28 January 1916).
33 Ibid.
34 *DTKAAZ*, p. 103 (22 March 1915).

Chapter 11
Church Militant: Russian Orthodoxy on Campaign

1 J. S. Curtiss, *The Russian Church and the Soviet State*, pp. 10–11.
2 S. Dixon, 'How Holy Was Holy Russia?', pp. 29–31 in G. Hosking and R. Service, *Reinterpreting Russia*; G. L. Freeze, 'Critical Dynamic of the Russian Revolution: Irreligion or Religion?', p. 56.
3 M. K. Stockdale, *Mobilizing the Russian Nation: Patriotism and Citizenship in the First World War*, pp. 75, 78–82 and 86.
4 *DTKAAZ*, p. 114 (27 August 1915).
5 'Dnevnik Shtukaturova', *Voenno-istoricheskii zhurnal*, no. 1, p. 163 (3 September 1915).
6 V. Shevzov, *Russian Orthodoxy on the Eve of Revolution*, pp. 151–5.
7 Ibid., pp. 160–1.
8 Ibid., pp. 158 and 169.
9 N. Davies, *Vanished Kingdoms: The History of Half-Forgotten Europe*, pp. 349–50.
10 S. An-sky, *1915 Diary of S. An-sky*, p. 68 (25 January 1915).
11 Council of Ministers, 10 September 1914: *SMRI*, p. 62.
12 P. Robinson, 'A Study of Grand Duke Nikolai Nikolaevich as Supreme Commander of the Russian Army, 1914–1915', *The Historian*, no. 3 (2013), pp. 496–7.
13 Council of Ministers, 13 September 1914: *SMRI*, p. 65.
14 M. von Hagen, *War in a European Borderland: Occupations and Occupation Plans in Galicia and Ukraine, 1914–1918*, p. 37.
15 A. Watson, *Ring of Steel*, p. 154.
16 D. Smith, *Rasputin*, pp. 400, 517, 535–7 and 546.
17 A. N. Yakhontov to V. I. Gurko, 19 December 1925: *SMRI*, p. 489.
18 Council of Ministers, 24 August 1915: *SMRI*, p. 240.
19 D. Smith, *Rasputin*, pp. 261–2, 265–6 and 279–80.
20 *DTKAAZ*, p. 85 (19 June 1914).

Chapter 12
Parties, the Press and Wartime Control: Political Challenges and the Official Reaction

1 R. Pearson, *The Russian Moderates and the Crisis of Tsarism, 1914–1917*, pp. 58–63.
2 *DTKAAZ*, p. 120 (26 November 1915).
3 [O.] A. Yermanskii, *Marksisty na rasput'i: o sbornike 'Samozashchita'* (Petrograd-Moscow, 1916).
4 P. N. Milyukov, *Vospominaniya, 1859-1917*, vol. 2, p. 232.
5 P. L. Bark, 'Vospominaniya', *Vozrozhdenie*, no. 177 (1966), p. 106; H. D. Lowe,

The Tsars and the Jews: Reform, Reaction and Anti-Semitism in Imperial Russia, 1772–1917, p. 366.

6 'Dnevnik Shtukaturova', *Voenno-istoricheskii zhurnal*, no. 1, p. 139 (5 July 1915).
7 Council of Ministers, 21 August 1915: *SMRI*, pp. 237–8.
8 J. A. Sanborn, *Imperial Apocalypse*, p. 104.
9 K. I. Globachev, 'Pravda o russkoi revolyutsii: Vospominaniya byvshevo nachal'nika Petrogradskogo okhrannogo otdeleniya', *Voprosy Istorii*, no. 7, p. 120.
10 S. Badcock, *A Prison Without Walls?: Eastern Siberian Exile in the Last Years of Tsarism*, p. 72.
11 V. F. Dzhunkovskii (inquiry testimony), *Padenie tsarskogo rezhima*, vol. 5, p. 71.
12 I. D. Thatcher, *Leon Trotsky and World War One: August 1914–February 1917*, pp. 25–37.

Chapter 13
Holding Down the Empire: Suppression and Subversion

1 A. Watson, *Ring of Steel*, pp. 190–1.
2 F. A. Golder (ed.), *Documents of Russian History, 1914–1917*, p. 37.
3 *Dnevniki imperatora Nikolaya II*, vol. 2, p. 239 (29 June 1916).
4 S. Sazonov, *Fateful Years, 1909–1916*, p. 304.
5 Council of Ministers, 29 April 1916: *SMRI*, p. 332.
6 Empress Alexandra to N. A. Romanov, 19 July and 7 September 1916: *The Complete Wartime Correspondence of Tsar Nicholas II and the Empress Alexandra*, pp. 539 and 575.
7 F. Fischer, *Germany's Aims in the First World War*, p. 272.
8 M. von Hagen, *War in a European Borderland*, pp. 54–5.
9 Z. A. B. Zeman, *Germany and the Revolution in Russia, 1915–1918: Documents from the Archives of the German Foreign Ministry*, pp. 1 and 10.
10 M. A. Reynolds, *Shattering Empires: The Clash and Collapse of the Ottoman and Russian Empires, 1908–1918*, p. 123.
11 Council of Ministers, 3 May 1916: *SMRI*, p. 333.
12 T. Totiukova, 'The Exemption of Peoples of Turkestan from Universal Military Service as an Antecedent to the 1916 Revolt', pp. 46, 51 and 53 in A. Morrison, C. Drieu and A. Chokobaeva (eds), *The Central Asian Revolt of 1916: A Collapsing Empire in the Age of War and Revolution*.
13 Council of Ministers, 3 May 1916: *SMRI*, pp. 333–4.
14 V. F. Dzhunkovskii (inquiry testimony), *Padenie tsarskogo rezhima*, vol. 5, p. 70.
15 T. Totiukova, 'The Exemption of Peoples of Turkestan from Universal Military Service as an Antecedent to the 1916 Revolt', p. 61.
16 J. Happel, 'Fears, Rumours, Violence: The Tsarist Regime and the Revolt of the Nomads in Central Asia, 1916' in A. Morrison, C. Drieu and A. Chokobaeva (eds), *The Central Asian Revolt of 1916: A Collapsing Empire in the Age of War and Revolution*, pp. 129–30; I. W. Campbell, 'Violent

Acculturation: Alexei Kuropatkin, the Central Asian Revolt, and the Long Shadow of Conquest' in *idem*, p. 200.
17 A. Chokobaeva, C. Drieu and A. Morrison, 'Introduction', in *idem*, p. 2.
18 A. Morrison, 'Refugees, Resettlement and Revolutionary Violence in Semirech'e after the 1916 Revolt' in *idem*, p. 215.
19 Ibid., p. 213.
20 A. Chokobaeva, C. Drieu and A. Morrison, 'Introduction' in *idem*, p. 2.
21 A. Bazabaev, 'The 1916 Uprisings in Jizzakh: economic background and political rationales' in *idem*, p. 89.
22 The case is put by Jon Smele in *The 'Russian' Civil Wars, 1916–1926: Ten Years That Shook the World* that the 1916 central Asian revolt was the beginning of civil wars in the Russian Empire, thus rejecting the more conventional date of 1918. He is surely right to emphasize that internal military conflict preceded the February Revolution. I prefer on balance to see the defeat of the rebels as a colonial policing campaign.

Chapter 14
'Is This Stupidity or Treason?': The Court, Plots and Strikes

1 M. V. Alexeev to Nicholas II (memo), 15 June 1916, pp. 1–5: M. V. Alekseev Papers (HIA), folder 1, file 6.
2 Ibid., p. 5.
3 V. S. Dyakin, *Russkaya burzhuaziya i tsarizm v gody pervoi mirovoi voiny*, p. 227.
4 P. L. Bark, 'Vospominaniya', *Vozrozhdenie*, no. 179 (1966), pp. 102–3.
5 A. Blok, *Poslednie Dni Imperatorskoi Vlasti*, pp. 96–105.
6 G. I. Shavelskii, *Vospominaniya poslednego protopresvitera*, vol. 2, p. 228.
7 *Perepiska Nikolaya I Aleksandry Romanovykh*, vol. 5, p. 146.
8 O. R. Airapetov, *Generaly, liberaly i predprinimateli*, p. 191.
9 *Dnevnik L. A. Tikhomirova: 1915–1917 gg.*: 11 December 1916, p. 315.
10 M. V. Chelnokov (inquiry testimony), *Padenie tsarskogo rezhima*, vol. 5, pp. 308–9.
11 *Dnevniki imperatora Nikolaya II*, vol. 2, p. 271 (21 December 1916). See D. Smith, *Rasputin*, pp. 611–12.
12 P. L. Bark, 'Vospominaniya', *Vozrozhdenie*, no. 175 (1966), p. 78.
13 *Alexander Ivanovich Guchkov rasskazyvaet . . .*, p. 9.
14 Exchange between the Imperial couple, 19 and 22 September 1916: *The Complete Wartime Correspondence of Tsar Nicholas II and the Empress Alexandra*, pp. 591 and 597.
15 N. A. Romanov to Empress Alexandra, 22 September 1916: Ibid., p. 601.
16 A. I. Denikin, *Ocherki russkoi smuty*, vol. 1, part 1: *Krushenie vlasti i armii, fevral'-sentyabr' 1917 g.*, p. 37.
17 O. R. Airapetov, *Generaly, liberaly i predprinimateli*, pp. 201–3: this contains the text of Alexeev's memorandum on Nicholas II, written at some time in the months after the February Revolution.

18 A. I. Denikin, *Ocherki russkoi smuty*, vol. 1, part 1, p. 38.
19 *Alexander Ivanovich Guchkov rasskazyvaet . . .*, pp. 18 and 20.
20 H. D. Lowe, *The Tsars and the Jews: Reform, Reaction and Anti-Semitism in Imperial Russia, 1772–1917*, p. 327.
21 P. N. Milyukov, *Vospominaniya, 1859–1917*, vol. 2, pp. 281–2.
22 *Alexander Ivanovich Guchkov rasskazyvaet . . .*, pp. 14–15.
23 S. Wheatcroft, 'Agriculture' in R. W. Davies (ed.), *From Tsarism to the New Economic Policy: Continuity and Change in the Economy of the USSR*, pp. 93–4.
24 T. M. Kitanina, *Voina, khleb i revolyutsiya*, pp. 16–17.
25 P. Holquist, *Making War, Forging Revolution: Russia's Continuum of Crisis, 1914–1921*, p. 40.
26 V. P. Kravkov, *Velikaya voina bez retushi*: diary, 2–6 January 1917, p. 263.
27 G. L. Yaney, *The Urge to Mobilize: Agrarian Reform in Russia, 1861–1930*, p. 455; L. Lih, *Bread and Authority in Russia, 1917–1921*, pp. 49–50.
28 T. M. Kitanina, *Voina, khleb i revolyutsiya*, pp. 257–9 and 263.
29 P. Gatrell, *Russia's First World War*, p. 168.
30 *DTKAAZ*, pp. 153–5 (10 February and 1 March 1917).
31 *DTKAAZ*, p. 150 (25 January 1917).
32 N. N. Golovin, *Voennye usiliya Rossii v mirovoi voine*, vol. 1, pp. 99–104 and 106–8.
33 A. I. Verkhovskii (diary), 29 December 1916: A. I. Verkhovskii, *Rossiya na Golgofe: iz pokhodnogo dnevnika 1914–1918 gg.*, p. 62.
34 A. A. Brussilov, *A Soldier's Notebook*, pp. 251 and 268–9.
35 Council of Ministers, 22 July 1916: *Osobye zhurnaly Soveta Ministrov, 1914–1916*, vol. 8, p. 354.
36 Moscow Okhrana report to the Director of the Police Department, 20 September 1916: B. B. Grave (ed.), *Burzhuaziya nakanune Fevral'skoi revolyutsii*, pp. 139–40.
37 T. Hasegawa, *The February Revolution, Petrograd, 1917: The End of the Tsarist Regime and the Birth of Dual Power*, p. 97; V. V. Kanishchev, *Russkii bunt, bessmyslennyi i besposhchadnyi: pogromnoe dvizhenie v gorodakh Rossii v 1917–1918 gg.*, p. 49.
38 A. I. Verkhovskii (diary), 29 December 1917: A. I. Verkhovskii, *Rossiya na Golgofe: iz pokhodnogo dnevnika 1914–1918 gg.*, p. 64.
39 L. Siegelbaum, *The Politics of Industrial Mobilization*, p. 181.
40 *Dnevnik L. A. Tikhomirova: 1915–1917 gg.*: 30 January 1917, p. 332.
41 A. Blok, *Poslednie Dni Imperatorskoi Vlasti*, p. 10.
42 M. V. Alexeev to A. I. Guchkov, 8 March 1917: Browder and Kerensky (eds), *The Russian Provisional Government*, vol. 2, p. 922; D. R. Stone. *The Russian Army in the Great War*, pp. 273–4.
43 B. B. Grave (ed.), *Burzhuaziya nakanune Fevral'skoi revolyutsii*, pp. 59–60.
44 *Ekonomicheskoe polozhenie Rossii nakanune Velikoi Oktyabr'skoi Sotsialisticheskoi Revolyutsii: materialy i dokumenty*, part 2 (ed. A. L. Sidorov *et al.*: AN SSSR: Moscow-Leningrad, 1957), pp. 18–32.
45 A. Blok, *Poslednie Dni Imperatorskoi Vlasti*, pp. 29–30.

Chapter 15
The February Revolution: Petrograd Factory Workers, Garrison Soldiers and the State Duma

1 *Dnevniki imperatora Nikolaya II*, vol. 2, p. 294 (23 February 1917); N. A. Romanov to Empress Alexandra, 23 February 1917: *The Complete Wartime Correspondence of Tsar Nicholas II and the Empress Alexandra*, p. 689.
2 Empress Alexandra to N. A. Romanov, 24 February 1917: Ibid., p. 690.
3 N. D. Golitsyn (inquiry testimony), *Padenie tsarskogo rezhima*, vol. 2, pp. 266–7.
4 P. L. Bark, 'Vospominaniya', *Vozrozhdenie*, no. 182 (1967), pp. 99–100.
5 R. P. Browder and A. Kerensky (eds), *The Russian Provisional Government: Documents*, vol. 1, pp. 41–2.
6 *Dnevniki imperatora Nikolaya II*, vol. 2, p. 295 (27 February 1917).
7 Ibid., p. 295 (28 February 1917).
8 P. L. Bark, 'Vospominaniya', *Vozrozhdenie*, no. 183 (1967), p. 94.
9 J. L. Houghteling, *A Diary of the Russian Revolution*, p. 113.
10 'Protokol sobytii', *Fevral'skaya revolyutsiya, 1917: sbornik dokumentov i materialov*, p. 124.
11 A. B. Nikolaev, *Dumskaya revolyutsiya: 27 fevralya–3 marta 1917 goda*, vol. 1, p. 347.
12 *Petrogradskii Sovet Rabochikh i Soldatskikh Deputatov v 1917 godu: materialy i dokumenty*, vol. 1, pp. 19–42.
13 'Protokol sobytii', *Fevral'skaya revolyutsiya, 1917*, p. 130.
14 Ibid., p. 131.
15 Ibid., pp. 131–2.
16 Duma Provisional Committee (decree), 1 March 1917: *Fevral'skaya revolyutsiya, 1917: sbornik dokumentov i materialov*, p. 151.
17 *Fevral'skaya revolyutsiya, 1917: sbornik dokumentov i materialov*, p. 153.
18 P. L. Bark, 'Vospominaniya', *Vozrozhdenie*, no. 181 (1967), pp. 95–7.
19 Ibid., pp. 97–100.
20 A. Dem'yanov, 'Moya sluzhba pri Vremennom Pravitel'stve', *Arkhiv Russkoi Revolyutsii*, vol. 4 (1922), p. 58.
21 A. G. Rumyantsev, 'Dokumenty TsGIA po delu o "razgrome"', in A. B. Nikolaev (ed.), *Revolyutsiya 1917 goda v Rossii: novye podkhody i vzglyady* (RGPU: St Petersburg, 2019), p. 40.
22 Duma Provisional Committee session, 1–2 March 1917: *Fevral'skaya revolyutsiya, 1917: sbornik dokumentov i materialov*, p. 154; T. Hasegawa, *The February Revolution, Petrograd, 1917*, pp. 567–70.
23 *NPODM*, pp. 17–18 (2 March 1917).
24 N. A. Romanov (discussion with Guchkov and Shulgin), 1 March 1917: *Fevral'skaya revolyutsiya, 1917: sbornik dokumentov i materialov*, p. 225.
25 G. I. Shavelskii, *Vospominaniya poslednego protopresvitera*, vol. 2, p. 284.
26 Ibid., vol. 1, p. 361.

27 T. Hasegawa, *The February Revolution, Petrograd, 1917*, p. 559.
28 *DTKAAZ*, p. 155 (1 March 1917).
29 *DTKAAZ*, pp. 155–6 (7 March 1917).

Chapter 16
The Provisional Government: A Caretaker Cabinet in Power

1 J. L. Houghteling, *A Diary of the Russian Revolution*, p. 137.
2 *Alexander Ivanovich Guchkov rasskazyvaet . . .*, *Voprosy istorii*, no. 12 (1993), p. 172.
3 W. G. Rosenberg, *The Liberals in the Russian Revolution: The Constitutional Democratic Party, 1917–1920*, p. 55.
4 V. D. Nabokov, 'Vremennoe Pravitel'stvo', *Arkhiv russkoi revolyutsii*, no. 1 (1921), pp. 40 and 47–8.
5 J. L. Houghteling, *A Diary of the Russian Revolution*, p. 157; V. D. Nabokov, 'Vremennoe Pravitel'stvo', *Arkhiv russkoi revolyutsii*, no. 1 (1921), pp. 42 and 57 and 59; D. R. Francis, *Russia from the American Embassy, April 1916–November 1918*, p. 118.
6 Appeal to Citizens of the Russian State (Provisional Government), 6 March 1917: *Fevral'skaya revolyutsiya, 1917: sbornik dokumentov i materialov*, pp. 176–7. On votes for women see R. Goldberg Ruthchild, 'Going to the Ballot Box is a Moral Duty for Every Woman: The Great War and Women's Rights in Russia' in C. Read, P. Waldron and A. Lindenmeyr (eds), *Russia's Home Front in War and Revolution, 1914–1922*, vol. 4, pp. 139–76.
7 Provisional Government, 8 March 1917: *ZZVP*, vol. 1, p. 56.
8 Provisional Government, 26 April 1917: *ZZVP*, vol. 1, p. 350.
9 Provisional Government, 23 April 1917: *ZZVP*, vol. 1, p. 338.
10 Provisional Government, 14 March 1917: *ZZVP*, vol. 1, p. 91.
11 Provisional Government, 20 March 1917: *ZZVP*, vol. 1, pp. 142–3.
12 M. von Hagen, *War in a European Borderland: Occupations and Occupation Plans in Galicia and Ukraine, 1914–1918*, p. 83.
13 V. P. Buldakov, *Khaos i etnos: etnicheskie konflikty v Rossii, 1917–1918: usloviya voznikoveniya, khronika, kommentarii, analiz*, p. 181.
14 A. Dem'yanov, 'Moya sluzhba pri Vremennom Pravitel'stve', *Arkhiv Russkoi Revolyutsii*, vol. 4 (1922), p. 73.
15 Provisional Government, 4 March 1917, second session: *ZZVP*, vol. 1, p. 23.
16 Provisional Government first session, 5 March 1917: *ZZVP*, vol. 1, p. 36.
17 J. L. Houghteling, *A Diary of the Russian Revolution*, p. 155.
18 *Alexander Ivanovich Guchkov rasskazyvaet . . .*, p. 190.
19 *Vospominaniya Generala A. S. Lukomskogo*, vol. 1, p. 149.
20 Provisional Government, 4 March 1917 (first session): *ZZVP*, vol. 1, p. 24 and vol. 4, p. 266; V. D. Nabokov, 'Vremennoe Pravitel'stvo', *Arkhiv russkoi revolyutsii*, no. 1 (1921), pp. 32–3.

21 W. G. Rosenberg, *The Liberals in the Russian Revolution: The Constitutional Democratic Party, 1917–1920*, pp. 60–1.
22 Provisional Government, 8 March 1917: *ZZVP*, vol. 1, p. 56.
23 A. N. Kuropatkin, diary, 12 March 1917: *Dnevnik A. N. Kuropatkina*, p. 415.
24 Provisional Government, 4 March 1917, second session: *ZZVP*, vol. 1, p. 24.
25 Provisional Government, 19 March 1917: *ZZVP*, vol. 1, p. 134.
26 A. Retish, *Russia's Peasants in Revolution and Civil War*, p. 70.
27 Provisional Government, 15 April 1917: *ZZVP*, vol. 1, p. 302.
28 Provisional Government, 16 March 1917, second session: *ZZVP*, vol. 1, p. 103.
29 Provisional Government, 7 March 1917, second session: *ZZVP*, vol. 1, p. 50.
30 Provisional Government, 5 March 1917, second session: *ZZVP*, vol. 1, p. 34.
31 *Petrogradskii Sovet Rabochikh i Soldatskikh Deputatov v 1917 godu: materialy i dokumenty*, vol. 1, p. 132.
32 A. A. Ivanov, '"My fakticheski razgromleny": ob arestakh liderov pravykh i pogromakh chernosotennogo imushchestva', in A. B. Nikolaev (ed.), *Revolyutsiya 1917 goda v Rossii: novye podkhody i vzglyady* (RGPU: St Petersburg, 2019), pp. 65–70.
33 V. P. Buldakov and T. G. Leonteva, *Voina, porodivshaya revolyutsiyu*, p. 498; M. K. Stockdale, *Mobilizing the Russian Nation: Patriotism and Citizenship in the First World War*, pp. 215–16.
34 *DTKAAZ*, p. 159 (28 April 1917).

Chapter 17
Partnership of Rivals: The Soviets and 'Conditional Support' for the Government

1 *NPODM*, p. 20 (4 March 1917).
2 *NPODM*, p. 32 (8 April 1917) and p. 38 (27 April 1917).
3 *NPODM*, p. 38 (27 April 1917).
4 *NPODM*, p. 11 (19 February 1917).
5 *NPODM*, pp. 124–5 (29 December 1917).
6 *NPODM*, p. 141 (27 January 1918).
7 *NPODM*, p. 123 (29 December 1917).
8 *NPODM*, p. 508 (13 January 1922).
9 *NPODM*, p. 17 (2 March 1917).
10 *NPODM*, p. 19 (3 March 1917).
11 *NPODM*, p. 18 (3 March 1917).
12 *NPODM*, p. 23 (8 March 1917).
13 *NPODM*, p. 26 (15 March 1917).
14 *NPODM*, p. 23 (8 March 1917).
15 *NPODM*, p. 24 (10 March 1917).
16 M. V. Alexeev to A. I. Guchkov, 8 March 1917: Browder and Kerensky (eds), *The Russian Provisional Government*, vol. 2, p. 922 from N. E. Kakurin (ed.), *Razlozhenie armii v 1917 godu*, pp. 28–9.

17 K. Neilson, *Strategy and Supply: The Anglo-Russian Alliance, 1914–17*, p. 259.
18 V. D. Nabokov, 'Vremennoe Pravitel'stvo', *Arkhiv russkoi revolyutsii*, no. 1 (1921), p. 57.
19 V. P. Kravkov, Velikaya voina bez retushi: diary, 31 March 1917, p. 313.
20 *NPODM*, p. 28 (23 March 1917).
21 A. I. Verkhovskii, *Rossiya na Golgofe: iz pokhodnogo dnevnika 1914–1918 gg.*, p. 381.
22 R. A. Wade, *The Russian Search for Peace, February to October 1917*, pp. 78–9.
23 I. G. Tsereteli at Petrograd Soviet Executive Committee, 25 March 1917: *Petrogradskii Sovet Rabochikh i Soldatskikh Deputatov v 1917 godu: materialy i dokumenty*, vol. 1, p. 549; I. G. Tsereteli, *Vospominania o Fevral'skoi Revolyutsii*, vol. 1, p. 63.
24 I. G. Tsereteli at Petrograd Soviet Executive Committee, 25 March 1917: *Petrogradskii Sovet Rabochikh i Soldatskikh Deputatov v 1917 godu: materialy i dokumenty*, vol. 1, p. 549.
25 *Konstantinopol' i prolivy po sekretnym dokumentam b. Ministerstva Inostrannykh Del*, vol. 1, p. 477.
26 K. Neilson, *Strategy and Supply: The Anglo-Russian Alliance, 1914–17*, p. 269.
27 N. S. Chkheidze in debate (March 1917): *Petrogradskii Sovet Rabochikh i Soldatskikh Deputatov v 1917 godu: materialy i dokumenty*, vol. 1, p. 328.
28 Ibid., pp. 222, 224, 236 and 254; P. V. Volobuev, *Proletariat i burzhuaziya Rossiya v 1917 g.*, pp. 105–6.
29 R. Service, *Stalin: A Biography*, pp. 120–2 and 128.
30 Provisional Government, 1 April 1917: *ZZVP*, vol. 1, p. 218; A. A. Brussilov, *A Soldier's Notebook*, pp. 308–9.
31 P. V. Volobuev, *Ekonomicheskaya politika Vremennogo Pravitel'stva*, pp. 135–7.
32 *Petrogradskii Sovet Rabochikh i Soldatskikh Deputatov v 1917 godu: materialy i dokumenty*, vol. 1, p. 153.
33 P. V. Volobuev, *Proletariat i burzhuaziya Rossiya v 1917 g.*, p. 111; *ZZVP*, 6 March 1917, vol. 1, p. 39.
34 Provisional Government, 9 March 1917: *ZZVP*, vol. 1, p. 285.
35 T. M. Kitanina, *Voina, khleb i revolyutsiya*, p. 309.
36 Provisional Government, 25 March 1917: *ZZVP*, vol. 1, p. 169. The best discussion of the introduction of the state grain monopoly is I. D. Thatcher, 'The "Broad Centrist" Political Parties and the First Provisional Government, 3 March – 5 May 1917', pp. 199–206.
37 Provisional Government, 25 March 1917: *ZZVP*, vol. 1, p. 169.
38 Provisional Government, 4 and 16 March 1917: *ZZVP*, vol. 1, pp. 26 and 104.
39 Provisional Government, 26 March 1917: *ZZVP*, vol. 1, pp. 170–2.
40 N. Ferguson, *The House of Rothschild: The World's Banker*, vol. 2, p. 448.
41 *DTKAAZ*, p. 157 (10 April 1917).
42 *DTKAAZ*, p. 157 (1 April 1917).
43 *DTKAAZ*, p. 157 (11 April 1917).
44 *DTKAAZ*, p. 157 (11 April 1917).
45 *DTKAAZ*, p. 157 (1 April 1917).

46 *DTKAAZ*, p. 158 (16 and 18 April 1917).
47 *DTKAAZ*, p. 158 (23 April 1917).
48 *DTKAAZ*, p. 158 (19 April 1917).

Chapter 18
Standing Tall: The 'Masses' and Self-Liberation

1 *Dnevnik L. A. Tikhomirova: 1915–1917 gg.*: 7 March 1917, p. 352.
2 *NPODM*, p. 26 (17 March 1917).
3 *NPODM*, p. 41 (12 May 1917).
4 *NPODM*, p. 47 (1 June 1917).
5 *NPODM*, p. 47 (3 June 1917).
6 *NPODM*, p. 47 (7 June 1917).
7 Workers' Section of Petrograd Soviet. 18 March 1917: Petrogradskii Sovet Rabochikh i Soldatskikh Deputatov v 1917 godu: materialy i dokumenty, vol. 1, p. 354.
8 S. A. Smith, Red Petrograd: Revolution in the Factories, 1917–1918, pp. 54–5.
9 V. P. Buldakov and T. G. Leonteva, Voina, porodivshaya revolyutsiyu, p. 533.
10 Provisional Government, 9 March 1917: *ZZVP*, vol. 1, p. 59.
11 Provisional Government, 17 March 1917, second session: *ZZVP*, vol. 1, p. 125.
12 L. Lih, Bread and Authority in Russia, 1917–1921, p. 72.
13 A. Retish, Russia's Peasants in Revolution and Civil War, p. 98.
14 A. D. Malyavskii, Krest'yanskoe dvizhenie v Rossii v 1917 g., mart-oktyabr', pp. 392–4.
15 *NPODM*, p. 32 (8 April 1917).
16 I. Getzler, Kronstadt 1917–1921: The Fate of a Soviet Democracy, pp. 23–4.
17 Provisional Government, 7 March 1917, second session: *ZZVP*, vol. 1, p. 50.
18 *DTKAAZ*, p. 157 (3 April 1917).
19 A. B. Astashov, 'Russkii krest'yanin na fronte pervoi mirovoi voiny', *Otechestvennaya istoriya*, no. 2 (2003), pp. 82–3.
20 L. S. Tugan-Baranovskii (oral testimony from the Polievktov collection): S. Lyandres (ed.), *The Fall of Tsarism: Untold Stories of the February 1917 Revolution*, p. 131.
21 *NPODM*, p. 36 (21 April 1917).

Chapter 19
Complications of Coalition: Cabinet Policies and Their Critics

1 V. D. Nabokov, 'Vremennoe Pravitel'stvo', *Arkhiv russkoi revolyutsii*, no. 1 (1921), pp. 53–4 and 80–2.
2 A. N. Kuropatkin, diary, 14 May 1917: *Dnevnik A. N. Kuropatkina*, p. 434.
3 R. A. Wade, *The Russian Search for Peace, February to October 1917*, pp. 38–9.

4 W. G. Rosenberg, *The Liberals in the Russian Revolution: The Constitutional Democratic Party, 1917–1920*, p. 108.
5 *Alexander Ivanovich Guchkov rasskazyvaet . . .*, pp. 190–1.
6 W. G. Rosenberg, *The Liberals in the Russian Revolution: The Constitutional Democratic Party, 1917–1920*, pp. 113–14.
7 R. Service, *Stalin: A Biography*, pp. 51 and 63.
8 I. G. Tsereteli, *Vospominaniya o Fevral'skoi Revolyutsii*, vol. 2, p. 33.
9 V. M. Chernov, *Pered burei*, pp. 321–2.
10 A. Dem'yanov, 'Moya sluzhba pri Vremennom Pravitel'stve', *Arkhiv Russkoi Revolyutsii*, vol. 4 (1922), pp. 58 and 71.
11 A. F. Kerenskii, order to Army and Navy, 12 May 1917: Browder and Kerensky (eds), *The Russian Provisional Government*, vol. 2, p. 935; *NPODM*, p. 42 (15 May 1917).
12 Yu. N. Danilov, *Na puti k krusheniyu*, p. 216.
13 *NPODM*, pp. 38–9 (28 April 1917).
14 V. P. Buldakov and T. G. Leonteva, *Voina, porodivshaya revolyutsiyu*, p. 522.
15 W. G. Rosenberg, *The Liberals in the Russian Revolution: The Constitutional Democratic Party, 1917–1920*, p. 140.
16 Provisional Government, 12 June 1917: *ZZVP*, vol. 2, pp. 239–42 and 244.
17 *NPODM*, p. 44 (17 May 1917).
18 Provisional Government, 15 April 1917: *ZZVP*, vol. 2, pp. 294–302.
19 V. P. Buldakov, 'Krest'yanstvo i agrarnoe dvizhenie' in Yu. A. Petrov (ed.), *Rossiiskaya revolyutsiya 1917 goda: vlast', obshchestvo, kul'tura*, vol. 2, p. 185.
20 Provisional Government, 30 May 1917: *ZZVP*, vol. 2, p. 192.
21 *DTKAAZ*, pp. 160–1 (20 May 1917).
22 *DTKAAZ*, p. 162 (3 June 1917).
23 *DTKAAZ*, p. 163 (8 June 1917).
24 Provisional Government, 2 June 1917: *ZZVP*, vol. 2, pp. 201–2.

Chapter 20
At the Front, in the Rear: Military Defeat and Economic Breakdown

1 A. A. Brusilov *et al.* to A. I. Guchkov, 18 March 1917: Browder and Kerensky (eds), *The Russian Provisional Government*, vol. 2, p. 925 from N. E. Kakurin (ed.), *Razlozhenie armii v 1917 godu*, p. 30.
2 M. V. Alexeev to A. A. Brusilov, 18 May 1917: Browder and Kerensky (eds), *The Russian Provisional Government*, vol. 2, p. 931 from N. E. Kakurin (ed.), *Razlozhenie armii v 1917 godu*, p. 66.
3 N. N. Golovin, *Voennye usiliya Rossii v mirovoi voine*, vol. 1, p. 160.
4 Yu. N. Danilov, *Na puti k krusheniyu*, p. 217.
5 N. N. Golovin, *Voennye usiliya Rossii v mirovoi voine*, vol. 2, pp. 96–7.
6 Ibid., vol. 1, p. 158.
7 Provisional Government, 22 May 1917: *ZZVP*, vol. 2, p. 124.

8 Provisional Government, 26 May 1917: *ZZVP*, vol. 2, p. 139.
9 F. Stepun, *Byvshee i nesbyvsheesya*, p. 377; P. Holquist, *Making War, Forging Revolution: Russia's Continuum of Crisis, 1914–1921*, pp. 216–19.
10 'The All-Ukrainian Council of Military Deputies', *Internet Encyclopedia of Ukraine*: http://www.encyclopediaofukraine.com/display.asp?linkpath=pages%5CA%5CL%5CAll6UkrainianCouncilofMilitaryDeputies.htm
11 F. Stepun, *Byvshee i nesbyvsheesya*, p. 364.
12 *NPODM*, p. 44 (22 May 1917).
13 F. Stepun, *Byvshee i nesbyvsheesya*, pp. 316 and 318.
14 *Russkie Vedomosti*, 16 May 1917: Browder and Kerensky (eds), *The Russian Provisional Government: Documents*, vol. 2, pp. 937–8.
15 D. R. Stone, *The Russian Army in the Great War: The Eastern Front, 1914–1917*, p. 288.
16 Ibid., pp. 288–91.
17 N. N. Golovin, *Voennye usiliya Rossii v mirovoi voine*, vol. 2, p. 192.
18 V. P. Buldakov and T. G. Leonteva, *Voina, porodivshaya revolyutsiyu*, p. 539.
19 R. A. Wade, The Russian Search for Peace, February to October 1917, pp. 54–68.
20 Ibid., pp. 96–100.
21 *NPODM*, p. 38 (28 April 1917).
22 *DTKAAZ*, pp. 159–60 (1 May 1917).
23 R. W. Davies, *The Development of the Soviet Budgetary System*, p. 8.
24 Ibid.
25 P. V. Volobuev, *Ekonomicheskaya politika Vremennogo Pravitel'stva*, pp. 311–12.
26 Ibid., p. 337.
27 M. I. Gaiduk, *Utyug: materialy i fakty o zagotovitel'noi deyatel'nosti russkikh voennykh komissiei v Amerike*, pp. 83–4.
28 P. V. Volobuev, *Ekonomicheskaya politika Vremennogo Pravitel'stva*, p. 377; J. A. Frieden, *Banking on the World: The Politics of American International Finance*, p. 28.
29 S. N. Prokopovich, *Voina i narodnoe khozyaistvo*, pp. 58–9; M. W. Bernatzky, 'Monetary Policy', p. 400.
30 M. W. Bernatzky, 'Monetary Policy', p. 395.
31 *DTKAAZ*, p. 159 (1 May 1917).
32 *DTKAAZ*, p. 161–2 and 163 (1 and 21 June 1917).
33 T. M. Kitanina, *Voina, khleb i revolyutsiya*, p. 239.
34 P. Gatrell, 'Poor Russia, Poor Show: Mobilising a Backward Economy for War, 1914–1917' in S. Broadberry and M. Harrison (eds), *The Economics of World War I* (Cambridge University Press: Cambridge, 2005), p. 279.
35 A. S. Senin, *Ministerstvo putei soobshcheniya v 1917 godu: kratkii istoricheskii ocherk*, pp. 99 and 164–5.
36 P. V. Volobuev, *Ekonomicheskaya politika Vremennogo Pravitel'stva*, p. 289.
37 P. Gatrell, 'Poor Russia, Poor Show', p. 242.
38 Ibid.

39 V. V. Kondrashin, 'Sel'skoe khozyaistvo i krest'yanstvo v 1917 g.' in Yu. A. Petrov (ed.), *Rossiiskaya revolyutsiya 1917 goda: vlast', obshchestvo, kul'tura*, vol. 1, p. 337.
40 A. S. Gruzinov, 'Rossiiskaya industriya v 1917 g.: dinamika i struktura proizvodstva' in Yu. A. Petrov (ed.), *Rossiiskaya revolyutsiya 1917 goda: vlast', obshchestvo, kul'tura*, vol. 1, p. 242.
41 P. V. Volobuev, *Ekonomicheskaya politika Vremennogo Pravitel'stva*, pp. 22–3.
42 N. D. Kondrat'ev, *Rynok khlebov i ego regulirovanie vo vremya voiny i revolyutsii*, p. 231 in V. V. Kondrashin, 'Sel'skoe khozyaistvo i krest'yanstvo v 1917 g.' in Yu. A. Petrov (ed.), *Rossiiskaya revolyutsiya 1917 goda: vlast', obshchestvo, kul'tura*, vol. 1, p. 354.
43 P. V. Volobuev, *Ekonomicheskaya politika Vremennogo Pravitel'stva*, p. 451.
44 D. Koenker and W. G. Rosenberg, *Strikes and Revolution in Russia*, p. 90.
45 P. Gatrell, 'Poor Russia, Poor Show', p. 254.
46 A. Offer, *The First World War: An Agrarian Interpretation*, p. 29.

Chapter 21
Faiths and the Arts: Reorganization, Assertion and Disorientation

1 J. S. Curtiss, *The Russian Church and the Soviet State*, p. 11.
2 V. P. Buldakov and T. G. Leonteva, *Voina, porodivshaya revolyutsiyu*, p. 498.
3 J. S. Curtiss, *The Russian Church and the Soviet State*, pp. 18–19.
4 D. Pospielovsky, *Russkaya pravoslavnaya tserkov' v XX veke*, p. 36.
5 J. S. Curtiss, *The Russian Church and the Soviet State*, p. 27.
6 Ibid., pp. 14–17; P. G. Rogoznyi, *Tserkovnaya revolyutsiya 1917: vysshee dukhovenstvo Rossiiskoi Tserkvi v bor'be za vlast' v eparkhiyakh posle Fevral'skoi revolyutsii*, pp. 93 and 139.
7 J. S. Curtiss, *The Russian Church and the Soviet State*, pp. 36–7.
8 *NPODM*, p. 61 (18 July 1917).
9 Provisional Government, 25 July 1917: *ZZVP*, vol. 3, p. 140.
10 Provisional Government, 27 July 1917: *ZZVP*, vol. 3, p. 162.
11 V. P. Buldakov, 'Freedom, Shortages, Violence: The Origins of the "Revolutionary Anti-Jewish Pogrom" in Russia, 1917–1918' in J. Dekel-Chen, D. Gaunt, N. M. Meir and I. Bartal (eds), *Anti-Jewish Violence: Rethinking the Pogrom in East European History*, pp. 79 and 82.
12 Provisional Government, 9 June 1917: *ZZVP*, vol. 2, p. 233.
13 D. Pospielovsky, *Russkaya pravoslavnaya tserkov' v XX veke*, p. 38.
14 Provisional Government, 27 April 1917: *ZZVP*, vol. 1, pp. 358–62.
15 A. Blok, *Dnevnik*, p. 230 (10 July 1917).
16 Ibid., p. 217 (16 June 1917).
17 Ibid., p. 210 (25 May 1917).
18 V. Mayakovski, *Sochineniya*, vol. 1, p. 136.
19 Ibid., p. 139.

Chapter 22
Socialists and Soviets: The Erosion of Menshevik and Socialist-Revolutionary Influence, Spring to Summer 1917

1 *Petrogradskii Sovet Rabochikh i Soldatskikh Deputatov v 1917 godu: materialy i dokumenty*, vol. 1, p. 132.
2 J. L. H. Keep, *The Russian Revolution: A Study in Mass Mobilization*, pp. 240–1.
3 I. Getzler, 'Soviets as Agents of Democratisation' in E. R. Frankel, J. Frankel and B. Knei-Paz (eds), *Revolution in Russia: Reassessments of 1917*, p. 22. The poem was written by E. Andring for *Izvestiya Gel'sinforskogo Soveta*, 18 June 1917. I have slightly adjusted the translation.
4 See above, pp. 123–4.
5 W. G. Rosenberg, 'The Russian Municipal Duma Elections of 1917: A Preliminary Computation of Returns, *Slavic Review*, no. 2 (1969), p. 160.
6 Provisional Government, 22 May 1917: *ZZVP*, vol. 2, p. 124.
7 L. Trotskii, *K istorii oktyabr'skoi revolyutsii*, p. 25.
8 I. G. Tsereteli, *Vospominaniya o Fevral'skoi Revolyutsii*, vol. 1, p. 413.
9 Provisional Government, 26 May 1917: *ZZVP*, vol. 2, p. 137. For a full account see I. Getzler, *Kronstadt 1917–1921: The Fate of a Soviet Democracy*, pp. 92–6.
10 D. J. Raleigh, 'Revolutionary Politics in Provincial Russia: The Tsaritsyn "Republic" in 1917', *Slavic Review*, no. 2 (1981), p. 203.
11 I. G. Tsereteli, *Vospominaniya o Fevral'skoi Revolyutsii*, vol. 1, p. 462.
12 Ibid., vol. 2, pp. 165 and 171.
13 N. Sukhanov, *Zapiski o revolyutsii*, part 2 (vol. 4), p. 260.

Chapter 23
The July Days: The Cabinet's Break-Up and the Abortive Bolshevik Rising

1 N. I. Podvoiskii, 'V. I. Lenin v 1917 godu', *VoVIL*, vol. 4, p. 186.
2 Provisional Government, 29 June and 1 July 1917: *ZZVP*, vol. 3, pp. 32, 41 and 47–8.
3 A. Rabinowitch, *Prelude to Revolution: The Petrograd Bolsheviks and the July 1917 Uprising*, pp. 142–3; S. Velychenko, *State Building in Revolutionary Ukraine: A Comparative Study of Governments and Bureaucrats, 1917–22*, pp. 74–6.
4 Ibid., pp. 135–7.
5 I. G. Tsereteli, *Vospominaniya o Fevral'skoi Revolyutsii*, vol. 2, pp. 165–6.
6 Ibid., pp. 353–4.
7 Ibid., pp. 265–6.
8 Ibid., pp. 266–7.
9 Ibid., p. 33; A. Rabinowitch, *Prelude to Revolution*, pp. 174–5.
10 F. F. Raskol'nikov, 'Vooruzhënnoe vosstanie ili vooruzhënnaya demonstratsiya?', *Pravda*, 17 July 1927, p. 3.

11 A. Rabinowitch, *Prelude to Revolution*, p. 181.
12 A. Rabinowitch, *The Bolsheviks Come to Power*, pp. 9–10.
13 I. G. Tsereteli, *Vospominaniya o Fevral'skoi Revolyutsii*, vol. 2, pp. 307–8.
14 Ibid., pp. 323–5; I. Getzler, *Martov: A Political Biography of a Russian Social Democrat*, p. 155.
15 V. I. Lenin, 'Vsya vlast' sovetam!' (*Pravda*, 5 July 1917), *PSS*, vol. 32, pp. 408–9.
16 A. Dem'yanov, 'Moya sluzhba pri Vremennom Pravitel'stve', *Arkhiv Russkoi Revolyutsii*, vol. 4 (1922), p. 95.
17 Provisional Government, 6 July 1917: *ZZVP*, vol. 3, p. 60.
18 I. G. Tsereteli, *Vospominaniya o Fevral'skoi Revolyutsii*, vol. 2, pp. 261–5 and 350–1.
19 T. I. Polner, *Zhiznennyi put' Georgiya Evgen'evicha L'vova: lichnost', vzglyady, usloviya deyatel'nosti*, p. 258.
20 Provisional Government, 8 July 1917: *ZZVP*, vol. 3, pp. 64–6.
21 Ibid.
22 Provisional Government, 9 July 1917: *ZZVP*, vol. 3, p. 68.
23 Provisional Government, 11 July 1917: *ZZVP*, vol. 3, p. 77; A. F. Kerenskii (order), 12 July 1917: N. E. Kakurin (ed.), *Razlozhenie armii v 1917 godu*, pp. 96–8.
24 Provisional Government, 12 July 1917: *ZZVP*, vol. 3, p. 85.
25 *DTKAAZ*, p. 164 (8 July 1917).

Chapter 24
The Kornilov Revolt: Kerensky and the Crushing of the Military Coup

1 W. G. Rosenberg, *The Liberals in the Russian Revolution: The Constitutional Democratic Party, 1917–1920*, pp. 213–14.
2 *NPODM*, p. 64 (2 August 1917).
3 A. I. Denikin, *Ocherki russkoi smuty*, vol. 1, part 1: *Krushenie vlasti i armii, fevral'-sentyabr' 1917 g.*, p. 410.
4 *Alexander Ivanovich Guchkov rasskazyvaet . . .*, p. 209.
5 A. A. Brussilov, *A Soldier's Notebook*, pp. 316–17; A. I. Denikin, *Ocherki russkoi smuty*, vol. 1, part 2: *Krushenie vlasti i armii, fevral'-sentyabr' 1917 g.*, p. 174.
6 A. I. Denikin, *Ocherki russkoi smuty*, vol. 1, part 2., pp. 175–84.
7 Ibid., pp. 185–6; A. F. Kerenskii (testimony to Kornilov inquiry, 8 October 1917): A. F. Kerenskii, *Delo Kornilova*, p. 14; *Vospominaniya Generala A. S. Lukomskogo*, vol. 1, p. 167.
8 A. I. Denikin, *Ocherki russkoi smuty*, vol. 1, part 2, pp. 185–6; A. F. Kerenskii (testimony to Kornilov inquiry, 8 October 1917): A. F. Kerenskii, *Delo Kornilova*, p. 14; *Vospominaniya Generala A. S. Lukomskogo*, vol. 1, p. 167.
9 A. I. Denikin, *Ocherki russkoi smuty*, vol. 1, part 2, pp. 187–8.
10 A. N. Kuropatkin, diary, 1 May 1917: *Dnevnik A. N. Kuropatkina*, p. 423.

11 A. F. Kerenskii (testimony to Kornilov inquiry, 8 October 1917): A. F. Kerenskii, *Delo Kornilova*, pp. 15–16.
12 *Alexander Ivanovich Guchkov rasskazyvaet . . .* , p. 174.
13 A. A. Brussilov, *A Soldier's Notebook*, pp. 316 and 321; B. Gourko [V. Gurko], *War and Revolution in Russia, 1914–1917*, pp. 198–9; L. G. Kornilov, 5 March 1917 (proclamation): Ukrainian Subject Collection (HIA), box 5.
14 Provisional Government, 18 July 1917: *ZZVP*, vol. 3, pp. 117–18.
15 Browder and Kerensky (eds), *The Russian Provisional Government*, vol. 3, pp. 1405–6.
16 Z. Galili, *The Menshevik Leaders in the Russian Revolution: Social Realities and Political Strategies*, pp. 346–8.
17 A. Dem'yanov, 'Moya sluzhba pri Vremennom Pravitel'stve', *Arkhiv Russkoi Revolyutsii*, vol. 4 (1922), p. 110.
18 See *ZZVP*, vol. 3, pp. 206–316.
19 A. A. Brussilov, *A Soldier's Notebook*, pp. 312–13; Boris Savinkov's recollection as reported by Claude Anet to A.W. F. Knox, *With the Russian Army*, p. 690.
20 *Ekonomicheskoe polozhenie Rossii nakanune Velikoi Oktyabr'skoi Sotsialisticheskoi Revolyutsii: materialy i dokumenty*, part 1, p. 201. Full speech is pp. 196–201.
21 N. V. Nekrasov, 12 August 1917 [OS] (speech): N. V. Nekrasov Papers (HIA).
22 M. W. Bernatzky, 'Monetary Policy', pp. 387–8.
23 V. B. Stankevich, *Vospominaniya, 1914–1919 g.*, pp. 204–5.
24 *DTKAAZ*, p. 167 (22 August 1917).
25 *DTKAAZ*, pp. 167–8 (19 to 30 August 1917).
26 F. Stepun, *Byvshee i nesbyvsheesya*, p. 436.
27 G. Katkov, *The Kornilov Affair: Kerensky and the Breakup of the Russian Army*, pp. 89–91.
28 L. G. Kornilov, 28 August (appeal): V. P. Dmitrenko, *Armiya i obshchestvo, 1900–1941: stat'i i dokumenty* (RAN: Moscow, 1999).
29 S. Dixon, 'Orthodoxy and Revolution: The Restoration of the Russian Patriarchate in 1917', *Transactions of the Royal Historical Society*, vol. 28 (2018), p. 167.
30 Provisional Government, 30 August 1917: *ZZVP*, vol. 4, p. 42.
31 *Vospominaniya Generala A. S. Lukomskogo*, vol. 1, pp. 253 and 255–6.
32 A. F. Kerenskii (note), *Delo Kornilova*, p. 178.
33 A. Blok, *Dnevnik*, pp. 251–2 (28–29 August 1917).

Chapter 25
The Claims of Nations: National Challenges and the Cabinet's Efforts at Accommodation

1 Provisional Government, 15 March 1917: *ZZVP*, vol. 1, pp. 98–9.
2 Provisional Government, 13 March 1917: *ZZVP*, vol. 1, pp. 292–3.

3 M. Graf, *Estoniya i Rossiya: anatomiya rasstavaniya*, pp. 37–8.
4 A. Ezergailis, *The 1917 Revolution in Latvia*, pp. 16–17 and 195–7.
5 Provisional Government, 31 March 1917: *ZZVP*, vol. 1, pp. 199–200.
6 Provisional Government, 28 May 1917: *ZZVP*, vol. 2, p. 183.
7 Provisional Government, 7 March 1917: *ZZVP*, vol. 1, pp. 43 and 45.
8 Provisional Government, 9 March 1917: *ZZVP*, vol. 1, p. 59.
9 N. E. Saul, 'Lenin's Decision to Seize Power: The Influence of Events in Finland', *Soviet Studies*, no. 4 (1973), pp. 496–7.
10 A. Morrison, 'Refugees, Resettlement and Revolutionary Violence in Semirech'e after the 1916 Revolt', p. 220 in A. Morrison, C. Drieu and A. Chokobaeva (eds), *The Central Asian Revolt of 1916*.
11 Provisional Government, 14 June 1917: *ZZVP*, vol. 2, p. 259.
12 V. P. Buldakov, *Krasnaya smuta: priroda i posledstviya revolyutsionnogo nasiliya*, pp. 292–4.
13 Provisional Government, 17 June 1917: *ZZVP*, vol. 2, p. 409.
14 V. P. Buldakov, *Krasnaya smuta*, pp. 277 and 324–6.
15 S. Velychenko, *State Building in Revolutionary Ukraine: A Comparative Study of Governments and Bureaucrats, 1917–22*, p. 75.
16 V. P. Buldakov, *Krasnaya smuta*, p. 323.
17 S. Ansky, *The Enemy at His Pleasure*, pp. 285–6.
18 B. McGreever, *Antisemitism and the Russian Revolution*, pp. 27–9.
19 Ibid., pp. 31–2.
20 S. F. Jones, *Socialism in Georgian Colors: The European Road to Social-Democracy, 1883–1917*, pp. 264–9.
21 A. Ezergailis, *The 1917 Revolution in Latvia*, p. 195.
22 R. Service, *Lenin: A Political Life*, vol. 2, pp. 229–32.

Chapter 26
Cities: Pressures and Opportunities of Urban Life

1 R. Khin-Gol'dovskaya (diary), 1 June 1917: *Rossiya 1917 goda v ego-dokumentakh: Dnevniki*, pp. 296–7.
2 *Dnevnik L. A. Tikhomirova: 1915–1917 gg.*: 5 May 1917, p. 355.
3 Ibid.: 8 May 1917, p. 357.
4 S. N. Prokopovich, *Voina i narodnoe khozyaistvo*, pp. 58–9.
5 S. Obolensky, *One Man in His Time: The Memoirs of Serge Obolensky*, pp. 48, 156 and 175.
6 Provisional Government, 5 June 1917: *ZZVP*, vol. 2, p. 208.
7 *NPODM*, p. 41 (12 May 1917).
8 *NPODM*, p. 60 (18 July 1917).
9 *DTKAAZ*, p. 168 (13 August 1917).
10 V. V. Kanishchev, *Russkii bunt, bessmyslennyi i besposhchadnyi*, pp. 69–70 and 71–8.

11 V. V. Sukhanin, diary, 14 August 1917: *Rossiya 1917 goda v ego-dokumentakh: Dnevniki*, p. 100.
12 P. V. Volobuev, *Proletariat i burzhuaziya Rossiya v 1917 g.*, pp. 302–6.
13 S. A. Smith, *Red Petrograd: Revolution in the Factories, 1917–1918*, pp. 163–7, 169–70 and 177–82.
14 J. L. H. Keep, *The Russian Revolution: A Study in Mass Mobilization*, p. 138.
15 Ibid., pp. 97–8.
16 Yu. Larin, *Voina i zemel'naya programma*, pp. 8–9 and 13.
17 F. Farmborough, *Nurse at the Russian Front: A Diary*, pp. 392–3 and 396.
18 J. L. H. Keep, *The Russian Revolution: A Study in Mass Mobilization*, pp. 145–7 and 149–50.

Chapter 27
Villages: Peasants Take Control

1 V. V. Kondrashin, 'Sel'skoe khozyaistvo i krest'yanstvo v 1917 g.' in Yu. A. Petrov (ed.), *Rossiiskaya revolyutsiya 1917 goda: vlast', obshchestvo, kul'tura*, vol. 1, p. 326.
2 V. P. Buldakov and T. G. Leonteva, *Voina, porodivshaya revolyutsiyu*, p. 536.
3 *Ekonomicheskoe polozhenie Rossii nakanune Velikoi Oktyabr'skoi Sotsialisticheskoi Revolyutsii: materialy i dokumenty*, vol. 3, p. 239.
4 M. Perrie, 'The Peasants' in R. Service, *Society and Politics in the Russian Revolution* (Macmillan: Basingstoke, 1992), p. 23; G. Gill, *Peasants and Government in the Russian Revolution*, pp. 101–2.
5 Provisional Government, 19 July 1917: *ZZVP*, vol. 3, pp. 124–7.
6 V. I. Kostrikin, 'Krest'yanskoe dvizhenie nakanune Oktyabrya' in I. M. Volkov *et al.* (eds), *Oktyabr' i sovetskoe krest'yanstvo, 1917–1927 gg.* (Nauka: Moscow, 1977), pp. 39–41.
7 A. D. Malyavskii, *Krest'yanskoe dvizhenie v Rossii v 1917 g., mart-oktyabr'*, p. 374.
8 D. I. Lyukshin, *Vtoraya Russkaya smuta: krest'yanskoe izmerenie*, p. 100.
9 D. Smith, *Former People: The Final Days of the Russian Aristocracy*, pp. 105–6.
10 R. Khin-Gol'dovskaya (diary), 29 April 1917: *Rossiya 1917 goda v ego-dokumentakh: Dnevniki*, p. 290.
11 M. Perrie, 'The Peasants' in R. Service, *Society and Politics in the Russian Revolution*, p. 28.
12 M. S. Chevekov, diary (family chronicle): *Rossiya 1917 goda v ego-dokumentakh: Dnevniki*, p. 127.
13 A. D. Malyavskii, *Krest'yanskoe dvizhenie v Rossii v 1917 g., mart-oktyabr'*, pp. 316–17.
14 P. V. Volobuev, *Ekonomicheskaya politika Vremennogo Pravitel'stva*, p. 453.
15 D. I. Lyukshin, *Vtoraya Russkaya smuta: krest'yanskoe izmerenie*, pp. 103–4.
16 P. V. Volobuev, *Ekonomicheskaya politika Vremennogo Pravitel'stva*, pp. 454–5.
17 Provisional Government, 26 August 1917: *ZZVP*, vol. 4, pp. 29–30.

18 Provisional Government, 19 September 1917: *ZZVP*, vol. 4, pp. 171–3.
19 T. A. Medvedeva and S. V. Bushueva, 'Sotsial'no-ekonomicheskii krizis v Nizhegorodskoi gubernii i ego rol' v utrate legitimnosti novoi demokratii v period fevralya–oktyabrya 1917 g. (po materialam nizhegorodskoi pechati)', *Istoricheskii zhurnal: nauchnye issledovaniya*, no. 2 (2018), pp. 89–103: https://nbpublish.com/library_read_article.php?id=24635
20 V. P. Semënov Tyan-Shanskii, 'Glavnyi Zemel'nyi Komitet', *Arkhiv Russkoi Revolyutsii*, vol. 12 (1923), p. 293.
21 W. G. Rosenberg, *The Liberals in the Russian Revolution: The Constitutional Democratic Party, 1917–1927*, pp. 149–51; R. Service, *Lenin: A Political Life*, vol. 2, p. 237.

Chapter 28
Bolsheviks: The Party That Worked for a Second Revolution

1 R. Service, *Lenin: A Biography*, pp. 303–5.
2 *Vtoraya i tret'ya petrogradskie obshchegorodskie konferentsii bol'shevikov v iyule i oktyabre 1917 goda: protokoly* (Moscow-Leningrad, 1927), p. 165.
3 R. Abraham, *Alexander Kerensky*, p. 252.
4 *Shestoi s"ezd RSDRP (bol'shevikov). Avgust 1917 goda. Protokoly*, p. 248.
5 R. Service, *Lenin: A Political Life*, vol. 2, pp. 236–7.
6 Ibid., vol. 2, pp. 237 and 299.
7 Ibid., vol. 2, pp. 234–5.
8 S. A. Smith, *Red Petrograd: Revolution in the Factories, 1917–1918*, pp. 153–6.
9 R. Service, *Lenin: A Political Life*, vol. 2, pp. 225–8.
10 *Pravda*, 7 June 1917.
11 W. S. Woytinsky, *Stormy Passage: A Personal History through Two Russian Revolutions to Democracy, and Freedom, 1905–1960*, p. 286.
12 V. I. Lenin, *PSS*, vol. 33, pp. 44–9.
13 I. T. Smilga, *Shestoi s"ezd RSDRP (bol'shevikov)*, p. 41.
14 Ya. M. Sverdlov, *Shestoi s"ezd RSDRP (bol'shevikov)*, p. 37.
15 R. Service, *The Bolshevik Party in Revolution: A Study in Organisational Change*, pp. 49–62.
16 Ya. M. Sverdlov, *Shestoi s"ezd RSDRP (bol'shevikov)*, p. 36.
17 R. Service, *The Bolshevik Party in Revolution: A Study in Organisational Change*, pp. 43–4.
18 T. Sapronov, *Iz istorii rabochego dvizheniya: po lichnym vospominaniyam*, p. 126.
19 R. Service, 'The Industrial Workers', pp. 154–9 in R. Service (ed.), *Society and Politics in the Russian Revolution*.

Chapter 29
If Not Now, When?
The Bolshevik Decision on Insurrection

1 Governmental declaration, 25 September 1917: *ZZVP*, vol. 4, pp. 209–12.
2 I am grateful to Ian Thatcher for advice on legal process under the Provisional Government: see his I. D. Thatcher, 'Liberalism and the Rule of Law' in G. Swain *et al.* (eds), *The Bloomsbury Handbook of the Russian Revolution.*
3 W. Pomeranz, 'The Provisional Government and the Law Based State' in C. Read, P. Waldron and A. Lindenmeyr (eds), *Russia's Home Front in War and Revolution*, vol. 4, pp. 129–35.
4 Provisional Government, 1 September 1917: *ZZVP*, vol. 4, p. 266.
5 D. Stevenson, *1917: War, Peace and Revolution*, p. 370.
6 A. Dem'yanov, 'Moya sluzhba pri Vremennom Pravitel'stve', *Arkhiv Russkoi Revolyutsii*, vol. 4 (1922), pp. 107 and 119.
7 A. S. Senin, *Ministerstvo putei soobshcheniya v 1917 godu: kratkii istoricheskii ocherk*, p. 131.
8 N. Sukhanov, *Zapiski o revolyutsii*, part 3 (vol. 6), pp. 212–13.
9 Ibid., part 2 (vol. 6), p. 236.
10 Central Committee, 10 October 1917: *PTsK*, pp. 82–3.
11 G. Ye. Zinoviev and L. B. Kamenev (letter to leading Bolshevik committees and factions), 11 October 1917: *PTsK*, pp. 87–92.
12 Central Committee, 16 October 1917: *PTsK*, pp. 93–4.
13 Ibid., pp. 94–104.
14 Ibid., p. 104.
15 L. B. Kamenev, letter to *Novaya zhizn'*, 18 October 1917 in *PTsK*, pp. 115–16.
16 V. I. Lenin to the Central Committee, 19 October 1917: *PTsK*, pp. 111–14.
17 *Izvestiya*, 10 October 1917.
18 Central Committee, 16 October 1917: *PTsK*, p. 104.
19 A. I. Verkhovskii (diary), 5 September 1917: A. I. Verkhovskii, *Rossiya na Golgofe: iz pokhodnogo dnevnika 1914–1918 gg.*, p. 117.
20 A. Dem'yanov, 'Moya sluzhba pri Vremennom Pravitel'stve', *Arkhiv Russkoi Revolyutsii*, vol. 4 (1922), p. 110.
21 V. D. Nabokov, 'Vremennoe Pravitel'stvo', *Arkhiv russkoi revolyutsii*, no. 1 (1921), pp. 60–1.
22 N. N. Golovin, *Voennye usiliya Rossii v mirovoi voine*, vol. 1, p. 110.
23 D. Stevenson, *1917: War, Peace and Revolution*, p. 370.
24 R. Abraham, *Alexander Kerensky*, p. 297.
25 Ibid., p. 298.
26 A. I. Verkhovskii (diary), 27 and 28 September 1917 and 19 October 1917: A. I. Verkhovskii, *Rossiya na Golgofe: iz pokhodnogo dnevnika 1914–1918 gg.*, pp. 124 and 133.
27 Provisional Government, 2 October 1917: *ZZVP*, vol. 4, pp. 237–8.
28 D. Orlovsky. 'Reform during Revolution: Governing the Provinces in 1917', in R. Crummey (ed.), *Reform in Russia and the USSR: Past and Prospects*, p. 122.

29 V. P. Buldakov, *Khaos i etnos*, p. 423.
30 N. N. Golovin, *Voennye usiliya Rossii v mirovoi voine*, vol. 2, p. 86.
31 *DTKAAZ*, p. 171 (23 October 1917).
32 Provisional Government, 21 October 1917: *ZZVP*, vol. 4, p. 274.
33 N. Sukhanov, *Zapiski o revolyutsii*, part 3 (vol. 6), p. 219.
34 Ibid., p. 221.
35 A. D. Malyavskii, *Krest'yanskoe dvizhenie v Rossii v 1917 g., mart-oktyabr'*, pp. 374–8.

Chapter 30
October Revolution: The Bolsheviks Seize Power in Petrograd

1 R. Abraham, *Alexander Kerensky*, p. 316.
2 A. Rabinowitch, *The Bolsheviks Come to Power*, p. 249.
3 V. B. Stankevich, *Vospominaniya, 1914–1919 g.*, p. 258.
4 V. D. Nabokov, 'Vremennoe Pravitel'stvo', *Arkhiv russkoi revolyutsii*, no. 1 (1921), p. 45.
5 D. R. Francis, *Russia from the American Embassy*, April 1916–November 1918, p. 178.
6 A. I. Verkhovskii (diary), 20 October 1917: A. I. Verkhovskii, *Rossiya na Golgofe: iz pokhodnogo dnevnika 1914–1918 gg.*, pp. 134–5; V. D. Nabokov, 'Vremennoe Pravitel'stvo', *Arkhiv russkoi revolyutsii*, no. 1 (1921), p. 59.
7 N. N. Dukhonin to A. F. Kerenskii, 21–2 October 1917: *Arkhiv russkoi revolyutsii*, no. 7 (1922), p. 281.
8 Correction by M. I. Skobelev and F. Znamenskii, *Delo naroda*, 22 October 1917: Browder and Kerensky (eds), *The Russian Provisional Government*, vol. 3, p. 1743.
9 S. E. Rudneva, *Predparlament: Oktyabr' 1917 goda: opyt istoricheskii rekonstruktsii*, pp. 215 and 217.
10 V. B. Stankevich, *Vospominaniya, 1914–1919 g.*, p. 259; D. Orlovsky, 'Democracy or Corporatism: The Russian Provisional Government of 1917', p. 72 in A. Weiner (ed.), *Landscaping the Human Garden: Twentieth-Century Population Management in a Comparative Framework*; S. E. Rudneva, *Predparlament: Oktyabr' 1917 goda: opyt istoricheskii rekonstruktsii*, pp. 218 and 220.
11 Ibid.
12 V. B. Stankevich, *Vospominaniya, 1914–1919 g.*, pp. 259–60.
13 V. I. Lenin, 'K grazhdanam Rossii', 25 October 1917: *PSS*, vol. 35, p. 1.
14 A. Rabinowitch, *The Bolsheviks Come to Power*, p. 288.
15 D. R. Francis, *Russia from the American Embassy*, April 1916–November 1918, pp. 179–80; see also V. I. Startsev, 'Begstvo Kerenskogo', *Voprosy Istorii*, no. 11 (1966), p. 203; R. Abraham, *Alexander Kerensky*, p. 317.
16 R. Abraham, *Alexander Kerensky*, p. 317.
17 A. Rabinowitch, *The Bolsheviks Come to Power*, pp. 276–7.
18 Ibid., pp. 278–9.

19 R. Abraham, *Alexander Kerensky*, p. 320; A. Rabinowitch, *The Bolsheviks Come to Power*, pp. 291–2.
20 N. Sukhanov, *Zapiski o revolyutsii*, part 3 (vol. 7), p. 335.
21 Ibid., pp. 335–6.
22 Ibid., pp. 336–7.
23 V. B. Stankevich, *Vospominaniya, 1914–1919 g.*, p. 261.
24 M. I. Tereshchenko to N. N. Dukhonin, 25 October 1917: 'Stavka 25–26 oktyabrya 1917 g.', *Arkhiv russkoi revolyutsii*, vol. 7 (1922), p. 294.
25 N. N. Dukhonin to M. I. Tereshchenko, 25 October 1917: Ibid., p. 296.
26 V. B. Stankevich, *Vospominaniya, 1914–1919 g.*, pp. 264–5.
27 A. S. Senin, *Ministerstvo putei soobshcheniya v 1917 godu: kratkii istoricheskii ocherk*, pp. 168–9.
28 A. Sinegub, 'Zashchita Zimnego dvortsa', *Arkhiv russkoi revolyutsii*, vol. 4 (1922), pp. 172 and 187.
29 A. S. Senin, *Ministerstvo putei soobshcheniya v 1917 godu: kratkii istoricheskii ocherk*, pp. 168–9.

Chapter 31
Sovnarkom: Promises and Insecurities

1 L. Trotskii, *Moya zhizn': opyt avtobiografii*, vol. 2, pp. 61–4.
2 N. Ioffe, 'Ob ottse' (typescript), part 2, p. 5: N. A. Ioffe Papers (HIA).
3 V. D. Bonch-Bruevich, 'Vospominaniya o Vladimire Il'iche', *Vospominaniya o Vladimire Il'iche Lenine*, vol. 4, p. 329.
4 N. A. Ioffe, 'Ob ottse' (typescript) in N. A. Ioffe Papers (HIA), part 2, p. 5; L. Trotskii, *Moya zhizn': opyt avtobiografii*, vol. 2, p. 46.
5 V. I. Lenin, *PSS*, vol. 35, pp. 13–17.
6 Central Committee, 29 October 1917: *PTsK*, pp. 122–3.
7 A. Rabinowitch, *The Bolsheviks in Power: The First Year of Soviet Rule in Petrograd*, p. 26.
8 *Vtoroi vserossiiskii s"ezd sovetov rabochikh i soldatskikh deputatov: sbornik dokumentov*, pp. 386–97.
9 A. V. Lunacharskii to A. A. Lunacharskaya, 25 October 1917: *1917: chastnye svidetel'stva o revolyutsii v pis'makh Lunacharskogo i Martova*, p. 283.
10 Central Committee, 1 November 1917: *PTsK*, p. 125.
11 Ibid., pp. 125–6.
12 Ibid., p. 127.
13 Ibid., p. 128.
14 Ibid., pp. 128–30.
15 A. V. Lunacharskii to A. A. Lunacharskaya, 29 October 1917: *1917: chastnye svidetel'stva o revolyutsii v pis'makh Lunacharskogo i Martova*, p. 287.
16 V. I. Lenin, *PSS*, vol. 50 (telegram, 19 November 1917), p. 8.
17 *Peterburgskii komitet RSDRP(b) v 1917 godu: protokoly i materialy zasedanii*, pp. 542–3.

Chapter 32
Spreading 'Soviet Power': City Soviets and the Sovnarkom Coalition

1 *DTKAAZ*, p. 171 (25 and 27 October 1917).
2 *NPODM*, pp. 98–9 (26–7 October 1917).
3 D. Koenker, *Moscow Workers and the 1917 Revolution*, p. 335.
4 J. L. H. Keep, *The Russian Revolution*, pp. 362 and 365.
5 *DTKAAZ*, pp. 179–80 (21 January 1918).
6 G. A. Hill, *Go Spy the Land: Being the Adventures of I.K.8 of the British Secret Service*, pp. 109–10.
7 A. A. Ioffe (V. Krymskii), *Mirnye peregovory v Brest-Litovske*, vol. 1, pp. 6–7 and 144.
8 R. Khin-Gol'dovskaya (diary), 23 November 1917: *Rossiya 1917 goda v ego-dokumentakh: Dnevniki*, p. 350.
9 *Resheniya partii i pravitel'stva po khozyaistvennym voprosam (1917–1967)*, vol. 1, p. 27.
10 Ibid., p. 28.
11 S. Obolensky, *One Man in His Time: The Memoirs of Serge Obolensky*, pp. 197–8.
12 A. L. Okninskii, *Dva goda sredi krest'yan*, p. 4.
13 R. W. Davies, *The Development of the Soviet Budgetary System*, p. 17.
14 L. Trotskii, *O Lenine: Materialy dlya biografii*, pp. 91–2.
15 O. H. Radkey, *The Election to the Russian Constituent Assembly*, p. 23.
16 Central Committee, 29 November 1917: *PTsK*, p. 149 and n. 185.
17 T. H. Rigby, *Lenin's Government: Sovnarkom, 1917–1922*, pp. 27–8.

Chapter 33
Socialism, Scarcity and Dictatorship: Soviet Legislation and Deepening Disorder

1 V. V. Kanishchev, *Russkii bunt, bessmyslennyi i besposhchadnyi*, pp. 116–17.
2 G. Swain, *The Origins of the Russian Civil War*, p. 91.
3 *Resheniya partii i pravitel'stva po khozyaistvennym voprosam (1917–1967)*, vol. 1, pp. 29–31.
4 *DTKAAZ*, p. 179 (22 January 1918).
5 Central Committee, 30 March 1918: RGASPI, fond 17, op. 2, d. 1, item 3.
6 VTsIK decree, 21 January 1918: *Dekrety Sovetskoi Vlasti*, vol. 1, pp. 31–2.
7 *Dekrety Sovetskoi Vlasti*, vol. 1, pp. 407–19.
8 J. L. H. Keep, *The Russian Revolution: A Study in Mass Mobilization*, p. 450.
9 Sovnarkom decree, 24 January 1918: RGASPI, fond R-130, op. 2, d. 1, item 1.
10 *DTKAAZ*, p. 181 (10 February 1918 O.S.).
11 *DTKAAZ*, pp. 178–80 (5 and 22 January 1918).
12 *DTKAAZ*, p. 178 (1–2 January 1918).

13 G. A. Hill, *Dreaded Hour*, pp. 47–9.
14 N. P. Makarov, *Krest'yanskoe khozyaistvo I ego evolyutsiya* (N. Zheludkovskaya: Moscow, 1920), vol. 1, p. 384.
15 *DTKAAZ*, p. 186 (25, 29 and 30 April 1918).
16 M. S. Chevekov, diary, 5 and 27 February 1918: *Rossiya 1917 goda v ego-dokumentakh: Dnevniki*, pp. 124 and 125.
17 Ibid., 5 and 27 February, 2 and 15 March, 5 and 31 May 1918: pp. 124–6, 128 and 130.
18 T. Shanin, *The Awkward Class: Political Sociology of Peasantry in a Developing Society, 1910–1925*, pp. 175–7.
19 T. V. Osipova, 'Razvitie sotsialisticheskoi revolyutsii v derevne v pervyi god diktatury proletariata' in I. M. Volkov *et al.* (eds), *Oktyabr' i sovetskoe krest'yanstvo, 1917–1927 gg.* (Nauka: Moscow, 1977), p. 56.
20 Ibid.
21 *NPODM*, p. 114 (27 November 1917).
22 *NPODM*, p. 114 (27 November 1917).
23 *NPODM*, p. 120 (23 December 1917).
24 *NPODM*, p. 122 (29 December 1917).
25 *NPODM*, p. 141 (27 January 1918).
26 *NPODM*, pp. 145–6 (30 January 1918).
27 *NPODM*, p. 141 (27 January 1918) and p. 179 (15 May 1918).
28 *NPODM*, p. 330 (19 March 1920).
29 F. Farmborough, *Nurse at the Russian Front: A Diary*, p. 380.
30 Ibid., p. 382.
31 Ibid., p. 374.
32 A. L. Okninskii, *Dva goda sredi krest'yan*, pp. 7 and 12–16.
33 Ibid., p. 14.
34 S. V. Tolstoi, diary, 16 December 1917 [NS]: *Rossiya 1917 goda v ego-dokumentakh: Dnevniki*, p. 157.
35 Ibid., 11 January 1918 [NS], p. 163.
36 G. A. Hill, *Go Spy the Land: Being the Adventures of I.K.8 of the British Secret Service*, p. 254.
37 *NPODM*, p. 137 (16 January 1918).
38 *NPODM*, p. 150 (21 February 1918).
39 S. Obolensky, *One Man in His Time: The Memoirs of Serge Obolensky*, pp. 197–8.
40 P. A. Obolenskii, 'Starye gody: semeinye zapiski', *Novyi zhurnal* (New York), no. 175, p. 195.

Chapter 34
Targeting the Church: The Offensive Against Orthodoxy

1 J. S. Curtiss, *The Russian Church and the Soviet State*, pp. 31 and 33.
2 G. L. Freeze, 'Counter-Reformation in Russian Orthodoxy: Popular Response to Religious Renovation', *Slavic Review*, no. 2 (1995), pp. 331 and 334–5.

3 A. N. Kashevarov, *Pravoslavnaya Rossiiskaya Tserkov' i Sovetskoe gosudarstvo (1917–1922)*, p. 94.
4 Sovnarkom decree, 20 January 1918: RGASPI, fond R-130, op. 2, d. 1, item 2; *Russkaya pravoslavnaya tserkov' i kommunisticheskoi gosudarstvo, 1917–1941: dokumenty i materialy*, pp. 29–30.
5 S. Dixon, 'Orthodoxy and Revolution: The Restoration of the Russian Patriarchate in 1917', *Transactions of the Royal Historical Society*, vol. 28 (2018), pp. 149–50.
6 F. Silano, '(Reconstructing) an Orthodox "Scenario of Power": The Restoration of the Russian Orthodox Patriarchate in Revolutionary Russia (1917–1918)', *Revolutionary Russia*, no. 1 (2019), pp. 13–14.
7 S. Dixon, 'Orthodoxy and Revolution: The Restoration of the Russian Patriarchate in 1917', pp. 151; F. Silano, '(Reconstructing) an Orthodox "Scenario of Power": The Restoration of the Russian Orthodox Patriarchate in Revolutionary Russia (1917–1918)', pp. 13–14.
8 Ibid., p. 15.
9 *Russkaya pravoslavnaya tserkov' i kommunisticheskoi gosudarstvo, 1917–1941: dokumenty i materialy*, pp. 22–3.
10 *NPODM*, p. 137 (16 January 1918).
11 A. N. Kashevarov, *Pravoslavnaya Rossiiskaya Tserkov' i Sovetskoe gosudarstvo (1917–1922)*, pp. 105–6.
12 Patriarch Tikhon (Address), 19 January 1918: https://azbyka.ru/otechnik/Tihon_Belavin/poslanie-patriarha-tihona-s-anafemoj-bezbozhnikam/
13 *NPODM*, pp. 142–3 (28 January 1918).
14 *DTKAAZ*, pp. 180–1 (17 February 1918).
15 *DTKAAZ*, p. 184 (18 March 1918).
16 *DTKAAZ*, p. 189 (10 June 1918).
17 *DTKAAZ*, p. 192 (27 July 1918).
18 *DTKAAZ*, p. 194 (8 September 1918).
19 *DTKAAZ*, p. 200 (30 December 1918).
20 *DTKAAZ*, p. 200 (25 December 1918).
21 *DTKAAZ*, p. 215 (19 December 1918).
22 A. N. Kashevarov, *Pravoslavnaya Rossiiskaya Tserkov' i Sovetskoe gosudarstvo (1917–1922)*, p. 224.
23 A. L. Okninskii, *Dva goda sredi krest'yan*, pp. 219–20 and 231.
24 Ibid., pp. 224–9.
25 *NPODM*, p. 175 (3 May 1918).
26 R. Stites, *Revolutionary Dreams: Utopian Vision and Experimental Life*, p. 83; F. Silano, '(Reconstructing) an Orthodox "Scenario of Power": The Restoration of the Russian Orthodox Patriarchate in Revolutionary Russia (1917–1918)', *Revolutionary Russia*, no. 1 (2019), p. 19.
27 *NPODM*, p. 445 (21 April 1921). For the month of the visit see F. Silano, '"In the Language of the Patriarch": Patriarch Tikhon, the Russian Orthodox Church, and the Soviet State (1865–1925)', p. 206.

28 A. N. Kashevarov, *Pravoslavnaya Rossiiskaya Tserkov' i Sovetskoe gosudarstvo (1917–1922)*, p 31.
29 Patriarch Tikhon (Appeal), 26 October 1918: https://www.sedmitza.ru/lib/text/440025/
30 A. N. Kashevarov, *Pravoslavnaya Rossiiskaya Tserkov' i Sovetskoe gosudarstvo (1917–1922)*, p. 31.
31 *NPODM*, p. 295 (14 October 1919).
32 Ibid.
33 A. N. Kashevarov, *Pravoslavnaya Rossiiskaya Tserkov' i Sovetskoe gosudarstvo (1917–1922)*, pp. 227–8.

Chapter 35
Culture and the Media: State Symbolism, Entertainment and Official Control

1 N. Andreyev, *A Moth on the Fence: Memoirs of Russia, Estonia, Czechoslovakia and Western Europe*, pp. 32–3.
2 A. L. Okninskii, *Dva goda sredi krest'yan*, pp. 8 and 10.
3 R. Stites, 'Iconoclastic Currents in the Russian Revolution' in A. Gleason, P. Kenez and R. Stites (eds) *Bolshevik Culture: Culture and Order in the Russian Revolution*, p. 23.
4 J. von Geldern, *Bolshevik Festivals, 1917–1920*, p. 46.
5 For an outstanding account of the impact on the creative intelligentsia see C. Read, *Culture and Power in Revolutionary Russia: The Intelligentsia and the Transition from Tsarism to Communism*.
6 *NPODM*, p. 444 (21 April 1921).
7 *NPODM*, p. 207 (1 August 1918).
8 *NPODM*, p. 208 (10 August 1918).
9 *NPODM*, pp. 416–17 (17 January 1920).
10 J. von Geldern, *Bolshevik Festivals, 1917–1920*, p. 114.
11 *NPODM*, p. 482 (14 September 1921).
12 A. Blok, 'Intelligentsia i revolyutsiya', reprinted in A. Blok, *Sochineniya v odnom tome*, pp. 452–7.
13 A. Blok, *Dnevnik*, pp. 263–4 (26 January 1918).
14 Ibid., p. 260 (11 January 1918).
15 J. Garrard, '*The Twelve*: Blok's Apocalypse', *Religion and Literature*, no. 1 (2003), pp. 45–65.
16 A. Blok, '*Dvenadtsat'*': *Sochineniya v odnom tome*, p. 260.
17 A. Blok, *Dnevnik*, p. 288 (6 January 1919).

Chapter 36
The Treaty of Brest-Litovsk: Capitulation to the Central Powers

1 L. Trotskii, *Moya zhizn': opyt avtobiografii*, vol. 2, p. 90.
2 A. A. Ioffe (V. Krymskii), *Mirnye peregovory v Brest-Litovske*, vol. 1, pp. 32, 52–3, 67–8 and 124.
3 B. Chernev, *Twilight of Empire: The Brest-Litovsk Conference and the Remaking of East-Central Europe, 1917–1918*, pp. 110 and 119.
4 Central Committee, 11 January 1918: *PTsK*, pp. 167–73.
5 *DTKAAZ*, p. 178 (3 January 1918).
6 *DTKAAZ*, p. 182 (15 February 1918 O.S.).
7 *NPODM*, p. 129 (3 January 1918).
8 R. Service, *Spies and Commissars: Bolshevik Russia and the West*, p. 73.
9 Peace treaty between Ukraine and Germany, Austria–Hungary, Turkey and Bulgaria, 9 February 1918: Ukrainian Subject Collection (HIA), box 5.
10 A. A. Ioffe (V. Krymskii), *Mirnye peregovory v Brest-Litovske*, vol. 1, pp. 208–10.
11 P. Holquist, *Making War, Forging Revolution: Russia's Continuum of Crisis, 1914–1921*, p. 119.
12 Sovnarkom, 3 August 1918: GARF, fond R-130, op. 2, d. 1, item 9.
13 *NPODM*, p. 140 (25 January 1918).
14 Central Committee, 22 February 1918: *PTsK*, pp. 200–4.
15 Ibid., pp. 211–13.
16 Ibid., p. 215.
17 *Sed'moi (ekstrennii) s"ezd RKP(b): mart 1918 g.: stenograficheskii otchët*, pp. 21–3.
18 Central Committee, 15 March 1918: RGASPI, fond 17, op. 2, d. 1.
19 A. Watson, *Ring of Steel*, p. 517.
20 B. Pearce, *How Haig Saved Lenin*, pp. 8–10.
21 M. von Hagen, *War in a European Borderland*, p. 91.
22 Ibid., p. 93.
23 N. E. Kakurin, *Kak srazhalas' revolyutsiya*, vol. 1, p. 193.
24 M. von Hagen, *War in a European Borderland, 1914–1918*, p. 91.
25 General Hans von Gronau (order), 17 April 1918: HIA.
26 N. E. Kakurin, *Kak srazhalas' revolyutsiya*, vol. 1, pp. 193 and 197.
27 M. von Hagen, *War in a European Borderland*, p. 90.
28 Central Committee, 10 May 1918: *Izvestiya Tsentral'nogo Komiteta KPSS*, no. 4 (1989), pp. 143–4. See also R. Service, *Lenin: A Political Life*, vol. 2, pp. 17–18.
29 Sovnarkom, 4 April 1918: GARF, fond R-130, op. 2, d. 1, items 1–2; Central Committee, 7 April 1918: RGASPI, fond 17, op. 2, d. 1, item 2.

Chapter 37
A Breathing Space for Dictatorship? Confronting the Threats to Sovnarkom

1 *Den'* (Petrograd), 27 March 1918, cited by M. Bernstam, *Ural i Prikam'e, noyabr' 1917 – yanvar' 1919: dokumenty i materialy*, p. 106.
2 R. Service, *The Last of the Tsars*, pp. 194–7.
3 V. Brovkin, *The Mensheviks After October*, p. 159.
4 M. Bernstam, *Nezavisimoe rabochee dvizhenie v 1918 godu: dokumenty i materialy*, pp. 97–105.
5 Sovnarkom, 8 May 1918: GARF, fond R-130, op. 2, d. 1, item 2.
6 Sovnarkom, 8 and 9 May 1918: GARF, fond 130, op. 2, ed.khr.1 (3/4).
7 L. Trotskii, *Na bor'bu s golodom!*: speech to public meeting, Sokolniki, 9 June 1918, pp. 9–11, 14–16, 26 and 29.
8 G. A. Hill, *Go Spy the Land: Being the Adventures of I.K.8 of the British Secret Service*, pp. 207–9.
9 T. V. Osipova, *Rossiiskoe krest'yanstvo v revolyutsii o grazhdanskoi voine*, p. 144.
10 R. Service, *Spies and Commissars: Bolshevik Russia and the West*, p. 123.
11 *DTKAAZ*, p. 192 (26 July 1918).
12 V. V. Kondrashin, *Krest'yanskoe dvizhenie v Povol'zhe v 1918–1922 gg.*, pp. 77–8, 113, 152–7 and 163.
13 Ibid., pp. 158–61 and 249. For an account emphasizing Komuch's popularity with peasants because of its commitment to free trade see G. Swain, *The Origins of the Russian Civil War*, p. 189.
14 R. Service, *The Last of the Tsars*, pp. 262–4 and 288.
15 *Pravda*, no. 153, 24 July 1918.
16 *NPODM*, p. 159 (12 March 1918).
17 Sovnarkom, 24 April 1918: GARF, fond R-130, op. 2, d. 1, item 2.
18 *Pravda*, 26 July 1918; *NPODM*, p. 205 (26 July 1918).
19 A. G. Kavtaradze, *Voennye spetsialisty na sluzhbe Respubliki Sovetov, 1917–1920 gg.*, p. 222.
20 L. D. Trotskii to V. I. Lenin, 17 August 1918: RGVA, f. 33987, op. 1, d. 23.
21 *Komsomol'skaya pravda*, 12 February 1992.
22 V. P. Antonov-Saratovskii, 'Otbleski besed s Il'ichem', *Proletarskaya revolyutsiya*, no. 4 (1924), pp. 183–4.
23 A. Latyshev, *Rassekrëchennyi Lenin* (Mart: Moscow 1996), p. 20.
24 Sovnarkom, 17 September 1918: GARF, fond R-130, op. 2, d. 1.
25 G. V. Chicherin, *Vneshnyaya politika Sovetskoi Rossii za dva goda* (Gosizdat: Moscow, 1920), p. 5; B. Pearce, *How Haig Saved Lenin*, p. 71.
26 Kh. Rakovski, 'Avtobiografiya' (HIA), p. 9; RGASPI, f. 17, op. 84, d. 1, p. 1, reproduced in I. Linder and S. Churkin (eds), *Krasnaya pautina: tainy razvedki Kominterna, 1919–1943*, p. 24.
27 K. Radek, 'Noyabr'. (Stranichka iz vospominanii)', *Krasnaya nov'*, no. 10 (1926), p. 140.

28 V. I. Lenin, *PSS*, vol. 50, pp. 185–6: note to Trotskii and Sverdlov, 1 October 1918.
29 G. Swain, *The Origins of the Russian Civil War*, p. 221.

Chapter 38
State-Building in Revolution: The One-Party State and the Red Army

1 L. D. Trotsky to V. I. Lenin, 1 January 1919: RGASPI, f. 17, op. 109, d. 42, p. 42.
2 I. V. Stalin, *Sochineniya*, vol. 4, pp. 197–224.
3 I owe this point to a discussion with Jon Smele. See also J. D. Smele, *The 'Russian' Civil Wars*, p. 76.
4 Allied and Associated Powers to A. V. Kolchak, 26 May 1919: Aleksandr Vasil'evich Kolchak Papers (HIA).
5 A. V. Kolchak to Allied and Associated Powers, 4 June 1919: Aleksandr Vasil'evich Kolchak Papers (HIA).
6 Allied and Associated Powers to A. V. Kolchak, 12 June 1919: Aleksandr Vasil'evich Kolchak Papers (HIA).
7 *Pravda*, 22 May 1918.
8 A. L. Okninskii, *Dva goda sredi krest'yan*, pp. 18–19.
9 Ibid., p. 55.
10 Sovnarkom, 25 January 1918: GARF, fond R-130, op. 2, d. 1, item 6.
11 R. Service, *The Bolshevik Party in Revolution: A Study in Organisational Change*, p. 147.
12 *DTKAAZ*, p. 236 (31 March 1921).
13 A. L. Okninskii, *Dva goda sredi krest'yan*, p. 35.
14 T. V. Osipova, *Rossiiskoe krest'yanstvo v revolyutsii o grazhdanskoi voine*, p. 187.
15 A. L. Okninskii, *Dva goda sredi krest'yan*, p. 154.
16 Ibid., p. 292.

Chapter 39
The Pivot of Civil War: Reds Versus Whites

1 E. Mawdsley, *The Russian Civil War*, pp. 133–4.
2 L. D. Trotskii, speech to joint Central Committee and Central Control Commission, 5 August 1927: RGASPI, fond 17, op. 2, d. 317 (V-iii), p. 69.
3 L. Trotskii, *Moya zhizn': opyt avtobiografii*, vol. 2, pp. 180–1.
4 *Vos'moi s"ezd RKP(b): Mart 1919 g.: Protokoly*, pp. 167–9.
5 E. Mawdsley, *The Russian Civil War*, p. 146.
6 Ibid., p. 145.
7 J. D. Smele, *The 'Russian' Civil Wars*, p. 121.

8 E. Mawdsley, *The Russian Civil War*, p. 162.
9 Ibid., p. 167.
10 Ibid., pp. 172–3.
11 Ibid., pp. 175–6.
12 Ibid., pp. 195–6.
13 J. D. Smele, *The 'Russian' Civil Wars*, p. 127.
14 Ibid., p. 129.
15 City Commandant (Revel), 28 November 1919: Nikolai Yudenich Papers (HIA), box 4, folder 2.
16 N. I. Yudenich to S. D. Sazonov, A. V. Kolchak, A. I. Denikin and Ye. K. Miller: Nikolai Yudenich Papers (HIA), box 4, folder 6.
17 *NPODM*, pp. 347–50 (17 and 21 May 1920).

Chapter 40
Planned Economics and Economic Pillage: Centralization, Nationalization and Requisitioning

1 A. Markevich and M. Harrison, 'Great War, Civil War, and Recovery: Russia's National Income, 1913 to 1928', *Journal of Economic History*, no. 3 (2011), p. 680.
2 R. W. Davies, 'Industry' in R. W. Davies, M. Harrison and S. G. Wheatcroft (eds), *The Economic Transformation of the Soviet Union, 1913–1945*, p. 135.
3 A. Markevich and M. Harrison, 'Great War, Civil War, and Recovery', p. 680.
4 V. V. Kabanov, *Krest'yanskoe khozyaistvo v usloviyakh 'voennogo kommunizma'*, p. 175; L. Lih, *Bread and Authority in Russia, 1917–1921*, p. 168.
5 T. V. Osipova, *Rossiiskoe krest'yanstvo*, p. 298.
6 A. L. Okninskii, *Dva goda sredi krest'yan*, pp. 96 and 102.
7 A. Retish, *Russia's Peasants in Revolution and Civil War*, pp. 174–5.
8 V. V. Kabanov, *Krest'yanskoe khozyaistvo v usloviyakh 'voennogo kommunizma'*, p. 219.
9 Ibid., p. 228.
10 Ibid., pp. 228 and 236.
11 Ibid., p. 25.
12 A. L. Okninskii, *Dva goda sredi krest'yan*, p. 33.
13 E. V. Gimpel'son, *'Voennyi kommunizm': politika, praktika, ideologiya*, p. 46.
14 *NPODM*, p. 237 (21 November 1918).
15 *NPODM*, p. 267 (15 June 1919).
16 R. W. Davies, *The Development of the Soviet Budgetary System*, p. 17.
17 T. V. Osipova, *Rossiiskoe krest'yanstvo*, p. 247.
18 Y. Kotsonis, *States of Obligation: Taxes and Citizenship in the Russian Empire and Early Soviet Republic*, p. 320.
19 *DTKAAZ*, pp. 206–10 (May to July 1919).
20 *DTKAAZ*, p. 97 (31 December 1914) and p. 215 (23 December 1919).

21 R. W. Davies, *The Development of the Soviet Budgetary System*, p. 29.
22 *NPODM*, p. 319 (3 February 1920).
23 *NPODM*, p. 331 (25 March 1920).

Chapter 41
The Anti-Imperialist Empire: Bolshevik Promises, Red Conquests

1 N. Taylor, *Estonia: A Modern History*, pp. 36–7.
2 People's Commissariat of Nationalities' Affairs, 8 March 1919: GARF, fond 1318, op. 1, d. 2.
3 Politburo session, 28 May (item 1) and 1 June 1919 (item 1): RGASPI, fond 17, op. 3, dd. 9 and 10.
4 R. Service, *Lenin: A Political Life*, vol. 2, pp. 82–3.
5 R. Service, *Lenin: A Biography*, p. 403.
6 L. D. Trotskii, 'Nashe otnoshenie k borotbistam', unpublished paper, December 1919: Trotsky Collection (HIA), box 9, folder 35.
7 V. I. Lenin to L. D. Trotskii, written 28–9 March 1920: V. I. Lenin, *PSS*, vol. 52, p. 116; V. P. Antonov-Saratovskii, 'Otbleski besed s Il'ichem', *Proletarskaya Revolyutsiya*, no. 3 (1924), pp. 189–90.
8 P. Kenez, 'Pogroms and White Ideology' in J. D. Klier and S. Lambroza, *Pogroms: Anti-Jewish Violence in Modern Russian History*, p. 302.
9 J. Veidlinger, *In the Midst of Civilized Europe: The Pogroms of 1918–1921 and the Onset of the Holocaust*, pp. 163–5 and 296–9.
10 O. V. Budnitskii, '"Evreiskie batal'ony" v Krasnoi Armii' in O. V. Budnitskii (ed.), *Mirovoi krizis 1914–1920 godov i sud'ba vostochnoevropeiskogo evreistva*, pp. 243 and 255.
11 P. Holquist, *Making War, Forging Revolution: Russia's Continuum of Crisis, 1914–1921*, pp. 178–9.
12 Politburo session, 14 September 1920: RGASPI, fond 17, op. 3, d. 108, item 1.
13 S. Blank, 'The Struggle for Soviet Bashkiria, 1917–1923', *Nationalities Papers*, no. 1 (1983), pp. 12–16.
14 J. D. Smele, *The 'Russian' Civil* Wars, pp. 228–9.
15 J. Baberowski, *Der Feind ist überall: Stalinismus im Kaukasus*, pp. 320–34.
16 R. G. Suny, *The Baku Commune, 1917–1918: Class and Nationality in the Russian Revolution*, pp. 225–33.
17 J. D. Smele, *The 'Russian' Civil Wars*, pp. 63–4.
18 Ibid., pp. 230–1.
19 Ibid., pp. 142–3.
20 J. Baberowski, *Der Feind ist überall: Stalinismus im Kaukasus*, pp. 320–34.

Chapter 42
Abroad: Red Revolutions and Soviet Trade: Uprisings, Comintern and Commercial Overtures

1 *Pervyi Kongress Kominterna: mart 1919 goda*, p. 131.
2 *Politbyuro TsK RKP(b) – VKP(b) i Komintern, 1918–1943: Dokumenty*, pp. 26 and 28.
3 J. Berzin to G. E. Zinoviev, 28 August 1919: Ibid., p. 28.
4 Reports, August 1919: Gibbes Lykes Papers (HIA), box 1.
5 R. Leviné-Meyer, *Leviné the Spartacist: The Life and Times of the Socialist Revolutionary Leader of the German Spartacists and Head of the Ill-Starred Munich Republic of 1919*, p. 153.
6 V. I. Lenin, *PSS*, vol. 37, p. 490.
7 R. Service, *Spies and Commissars: Bolshevik Russia and the West*, p. 230.
8 Ibid., pp. 249–50.
9 *New York Times*, 27 June 1919; L. K. Martens and S. Nuorteva (memorandum), n.d. but probably March or April 1919: George Halonen Papers (HIA).
10 R. Service, *Spies and Commissars: Bolshevik Russia and the West*, pp. 234–5.

Chapter 43
Experimentalism in Adversity: Enforcing and Coping with the Soviet Way of Life

1 R. W. Davies, *The Development of the Soviet Budgetary System*, p. 39.
2 A. L. Okninskii, *Dva goda sredi krest'yan*, p. 195.
3 A. Willimott, *Living the Revolution: Urban Communism and Soviet Communism, 1917–1932*, pp. 51–2, 68 and 102.
4 *NPODM*, p. 123 (29 December 1917).
5 Ibid.
6 Ibid.
7 G. A. Hill, *Go Spy the Land: Being the Adventures of I.K.8 of the British Secret Service*, pp. 222–3.
8 P. Dukes, *Red Dusk and the Morrow*, pp. 222–3.
9 F. Stepun, *Byvshee i nesbyvsheesya*, pp. 489–90.
10 *NPODM*, p. 325 (9 March 1920).
11 A. Poliakoff, *The Silver Samovar: Reminiscences of the Russian Revolution*, p. 73.
12 *NPODM*, p. 264 (30 May 1919).
13 *NPODM*, p. 295 (14 October 1919).
14 *NPODM*, p. 148 (17 February 1918).
15 V. V. Kabanov, *Krest'yanskoe khozyaistvo*, pp. 190–1.
16 R. Service, *The Last of the Tsars*, pp. 276–8.
17 *DTKAAZ*, p. 198 (19 November 1918).
18 A. Poliakoff, *The Silver Samovar: Reminiscences of the Russian Revolution*, p. 49.

19 *NPODM*, p. 290 (19 September 1919).
20 *DTKAAZ*, p. 198 (19 November 1918).
21 *DTKAAZ*, p. 195 (16 September 1918).
22 *DTKAAZ*, pp. 202–3 (13 February 1919).
23 *NPODM*, p. 148 (17 February 1918).
24 V. Brovkin, 'Workers' Unrest and the Bolsheviks' Response in 1919', *Slavic Review*, no. 3 (1990), pp. 353–67.
25 *Pravda*, 27 March 1919.
26 V. Brovkin, *Behind the Front Lines of the Civil War: Political Parties and Social Movements in Russia, 1918–1922*, especially pp. 98–9, 106–7 and 137.
27 *NPODM*, p. 213 (3 September 1918).
28 *NPODM*, p. 240 (10 December 1918).
29 *NPODM*, p. 243 (16 December 1918).
30 *NPODM*, p. 258 (6 February 1919).
31 *NPODM*, p. 289 (13 September 1919).
32 *NPODM*, p. 259 (6 May 1919).
33 *NPODM*, p. 260 (6 May 1919).
34 *NPODM*, p. 302 (9 November 1919) and p. 311 (26 December 1919).
35 *NPODM*, p. 508 (13 January 1922).
36 *NPODM*, p. 508 (13 January 1922).
37 *NPODM*, p. 365 (20 July 1920).
38 *NPODM*, p. 298 (24 October 1919).
39 *NPODM*, p. 361 (25 June 1920).
40 *NPODM*, p. 324 (7 March 1920).
41 *NPODM*, p. 141 (27 January 1918) and p. 179 (15 May 1918).

Chapter 44
Invasion and Rebellion: From the Polish–Soviet War to the Peasants' Revolt

1 *NPODM*, pp. 350–2 (20 May 1920).
2 *NPODM*, p. 332 (28 March 1920).
3 *Kommunar* (Tula), 20 November and 3 December 1920.
4 D. A. Volkogonov Papers (HIA), reel 13: L. D. Trotskii, 'Osnovnye voprosy prodovol'stvennoi i zemel'noi politike', pp. 1–2.
5 *Desyatyi s"ezd RKP(b): Mart 1921 g: Stenograficheskii otchët*, pp. 349–50.
6 A. L. Okninskii, *Dva goda sredi krest'yan*, p. 217.
7 N. Davies, *White Eagle, Red Star: The Polish–Soviet War of 1919–1920*, pp. 125–7.
8 L. Trotskii, *Voina s Pol'shei* (speech to All-Russia Central Executive Committee of the Congress of Soviets, 5 May 1920), p. 14.
9 V. I. Lenin to E. M. Sklyanskii (note), August 1920: *The Trotsky Papers, 1917–1922*, vol. 2, p. 278.
10 Politburo session, 10 August 1920: RGASPI, fond 17, op. 3, d. 101, items 3–4.

11 N. Davies, *White Eagle, Red Star: The Polish–Soviet War of 1919–1920*, pp. 200–6.
12 Politburo session, 1 September 1920: RGASPI, fond 17, op. 3, d. 106, item 10.
13 R. Service, *Spies and Commissars: Bolshevik Russia and the West*, p. 307.
14 V. Danilov, S. Yesikov, V. Kanishchev and L. Protasov, introduction to *Krest'yanskoe vosstanie v Tambovskoi gubernii v 1919–1921: 'Antonovshchina': Dokumenty i materialy*, p. 17.
15 V. I. Lenin, Ninth Party Conference, 22 September 1920: RGASPI, f. 44, op. 1, d. 5, p. 26.
16 Ibid., pp. 27–8.
17 Locomotive deals between Soviet Russia and German companies, 15 October 1920; M. J. Laserson to Dr Freund, 1 December 1947 (explanation of the Soviet–German negotiations): M. J. Larsons Papers (HIA), box 1.
18 *DTKAAZ*, p. 229 (14–15 October 1920).
19 *DTKAAZ*, pp. 230–1 (1 December 1920).
20 *Krest'yanskoe vosstanie v Tambovskoi gubernii v 1919–1921: 'Antonovshchina': Dokumenty i materialy*, p. 72.
21 V. I. Lenin, *PSS*, vol. 42, pp. 176 and 179.
22 *Vos'moi s"ezd Sovetov rabochikh, krest'yanskikh, krasnoarmeiskikh i kazach'ikh deputatov: stenograficheskii otchët* (22–29 dekabrya 1920 goda), pp. 42, 49, 122 and 201.

Chapter 45
The New Economic Policy: Market Reform and Internal Party Discontent

1 *DTKAAZ*, p. 232 (31 December 1920, 6 January 1921 and 8 January 1921).
2 Politburo session, 2 February 1921: RGASPI, fond 17, op. 3, d. 128, item 1.
3 V. I. Lenin, *PSS*, vol. 42, p. 333.
4 Central Committee, 24 February 1921: RGASPI, fond 17, op. 2, d. 58, item 2; *Leninskii sbornik*, vol. 20, p. 59.
5 Politburo session, 28 February 1921, item 2a: RGASPI, fond 17, op. 3, d. 136.
6 Ibid., items 2d, 2e and 2f.
7 Central Committee, 7 March 1921, item 4a and 13: RGASPI, fond 17, op. 2, d. 61.
8 *NPODM*, p. 428 (1 March 1921).
9 *Desyatyi s"ezd RKP(b): Mart 1921 g: Stenograficheskii otchët*, p. 37.
10 Ibid., pp. 24–8.
11 Ibid., pp. 28–37.
12 Ibid., p. 137.
13 Ibid., pp. 167 and 310; *Vladimir Il'ich Lenin: Biograficheskaya khronika*, vol. 10, pp. 203 and 204.
14 D. A. Volkogonov Papers (HIA), box 3, reel 2: Ya. S. Agranov to the Presidium

of the Cheka, report 'on the results of investigation of the mutiny in the town of Kronstadt'.

15 *Desyatyi s"ezd RKP(b)*, p. 406.
16 Ibid., p. 404.
17 Ibid., p. 425.
18 Ibid., p. 445.
19 Ibid., pp. 533, 539 and 542.
20 Y. Kotsonis, *States of Obligation: Taxes and Citizenship in the Russian Empire and Early Soviet Republic*, pp. 340–1.
21 L. Lih, *Bread and Authority in Russia, 1917–1921*, pp. 163–5.
22 J. Aves, *Workers Against Lenin: Labour Protest and the Bolshevik Dictatorship*, pp. 176–7.
23 *NPODM*, p. 448 (7 May 1921).
24 V. I. Lenin, Tenth Party Conference, 27 May 1921: RGASPI, f. 44, op. 1, d. 3, pp. 18–19.
25 I. M. Vareikis, Tenth Party Conference, 27 May 1921: RGASPI, f. 44, op. 1, d. 2, pp. 114–19.
26 *NPODM*, p. 470 (12 July 1921).
27 M. N. Tukhachevskii (orders), 12 and 15 May 1921: *Krest'yanskoe vosstanie v Tambovskoi gubernii v 1919–1921: 'Antonovshchina': Dokumenty i materialy*, pp. 164–5.
28 V. V. Kondrashin, *Krest'yanskoe dvizhenie v Povol'zhe v 1918–1922 gg.*, pp. 287–9.
29 M. N. Tukhachevskii (order), 11 June 1921: *Krest'yanskoe vosstanie v Tambovskoi gubernii v 1919–1921*, p. 179.
30 M. N. Tukhachevskii (order), 12 June 1921: B. V. Sennikov, *Tambovskoe vosstanie 1918–1921 gg. i raskrest'yanivanie Rossii 1929–1933*, p. 83.
31 E. Landis, *Bandits and Partisans: The Antonov Movement in the Russian Civil War*, pp. 239–41.
32 M. I. Pokalyukhin (memoir, 1923), *Krest'yanskoe vosstanie v Tambovskoi gubernii v 1919–1921: 'Antonovshchina': Dokumenty i materialy*, pp. 300–1.
33 J. Aves, *Workers Against Lenin: Labour Protest and the Bolshevik Dictatorship*, pp. 163–5.
34 Y. Kotsonis, *States of Obligation: Taxes and Citizenship in the Russian Empire and Early Soviet Republic*, pp. 335–7.
35 *NPODM*, pp. 350–2 (21 May 1920).
36 *NPODM*, pp. 478 and 481 (17 August and 1 September 1921).
37 *NPODM*, p. 535 (1 May 1922).
38 *NPODM*, p. 508 (13 January 1922).
39 *NPODM*, p. 532 (27 April 1922).
40 *NPODM*, p. 451 (19 May 1921).
41 *NPODM*, pp. 458–9 (30 May 1921).
42 *NPODM*, p. 459 (30 May 1921).
43 *DTKAAZ*, p. 446 (2 May 1921).

Chapter 46
The Unsettled Settlement: Reinforced Repression and the Political Succession Question

1 *DTKAAZ*, pp. 236–42.
2 *DTKAAZ*, (1 February 1921) p. 233.
3 *DTKAAZ*, (9 March 1921) p. 235.
4 Central Committee plenum, 28 December 1921, item 14: RGASPI, fond 17, op. 2, d. 76.
5 V. I. Lenin to D. I. Kurskii, 22 February 1922: *PSS*, vol. 44, pp. 396–7.
6 *Pravda*, 11 April 1922.
7 V. I. Lenin to Politburo, 22 March 1922: *Izvestiya Tsentral'nogo Komiteta KPSS*, no. 4 (1990), pp. 191–3; A. N. Kashevarov, *Pravoslavnaya Rossiiskaya Tserkov' i Sovetskoe gosudarstvo (1917–1922)*, p. 237.
8 *NPODM*, pp. 536–7 and 541 (11 May and 6 June 1922).
9 Ibid.
10 A. N. Kashevarov, *Pravoslavnaya Rossiiskaya Tserkov' i Sovetskoe gosudarstvo (1917–1922)*, pp. 238–9.
11 G. L. Freeze, 'Counter-Reformation in Russian Orthodoxy: Popular Response to Religious Renovation', *Slavic Review*, no. 2 (1995), pp. 305 and 310–15; E. E. Roslof, 'The Heresy of "Bolshevik" Christianity: Orthodox Rejection of Religious Reform during NEP', *Slavic Review*, no. 3 (1996), pp. 625 and 629.
12 A Blyum, *Za kulisami 'Ministerstva Pravdy': tainaya istoriya sovetskoi tsentsury, 1917–1929* (Gumanitarnoe Agenstvo: St Petersburg, 1994), p. 79.
13 *Lenin i VChK: sbornik dokumentov, 1917–1922*, p. 465.
14 V. I. Lenin to N. P. Gorbunov, 3 March 1922: *PSS*, vol. 54, p. 198.
15 V. I. Lenin to N. P. Gorbunov, 19 May 1922: Ibid., p. 265.
16 I. V. Stalin to V. I. Stalin, 22 September 1922: RGASPI, fond 5, op. 2, d. 28, p. 19.
17 I. V. Stalin to V. I. Stalin, 22 September 1922: Ibid., p. 23.
18 V. I. Lenin, dictated notes, 30 December 1922: *PSS*, vol. 45, p. 356.
19 This part of Lenin's notes was dictated on 24–5 December 1922: Ibid., pp. 344–6.
20 This part of Lenin's notes was dictated on 4 January 1923: Ibid., p. 346. Not everyone accepts that Lenin's so-called testament was certainly dictated by him: see S. Kotkin, *Stalin*, vol. 1: *Paradoxes of Power*, pp. 498–501.
21 V. I. Lenin, 'O kooperatsii' (dictated notes), 4–6 January 1923: *PSS*, vol. 45, p. 373.
22 V. I. Lenin to I. V. Stalin, dictated 5 March 1923: *PSS*, vol. 54, p. 330.
23 *NPODM*, pp. 566–70 (22 January to 3 June 1923).

Audit of Revolution: Lenin's Legacy and The End of the Beginning, 1924

1 R. Service, *Stalin: A Biography*, pp. 212–13.
2 Ibid., pp. 214–17.
3 R. Service, *Trotsky: A Biography*, pp. 314–19.
4 Ibid., pp. 305–7.
5 R. Service, *Stalin: A Biography*, pp. 216–17.
6 Ibid., pp. 478–9.
7 *NPODM*, p. 597 (diary: 3–18 March 1924), p. 588.
8 Ibid.
9 *NPODM*, p. 597 (diary: undated, 1924).

INDEX